国家林业和草原局普通高等教育"十三五"规划教材

International Documents on the Conservation of Natural and Cultural Heritage

自然与文化遗产保护

相关国际文件选编

Chinese & English Edition（汉英对照）

曹 新 ◎ 编译

中国林业出版社
China Forestry Publishing House

内 容 简 介

　　本书是关于自然与文化遗产保护的国际文件选编，其中包含国际法规，如公约等，亦有宪章、宣言、建议、指南、准则、重要决议等相关国际文件，择其重要的文件进行介绍，以汉英对照版本进行展示，以期加深和扩展遗产保护相关专业人员和大众对遗产、遗产保护的概念及其成型理论的全面了解。这些文件以遗产保护相关全球性国际组织的正式文件为依据。编译者对其中缺乏正式中文版本的文件补充了中文翻译。所有文件按照其相关性进行排列，主要分为以下几类：世界遗产公约及相关、文化遗产（包括建筑遗产、景观和园林遗产、历史地区、考古遗产、水下文化遗产、工业遗产、文化线路等）、农业遗产、自然遗产、无形文化遗产、文献遗产等。

　　本书适合高等院校的建筑学、风景园林、城乡规划、考古学、文物与博物馆学、文物保护技术、文化遗产、旅游管理、生态学、艺术学类、地理科学类、地质学类、林学类、自然保护与环境生态类等遗产保护相关专业及领域的本科生、研究生等作为教材或教辅书，亦适合广大相关专业人员参考。

图书在版编目（CIP）数据

自然与文化遗产保护相关国际文件选编：汉英对照 /曹新编译. —北京：中国林业出版社，2021.4

国家林业和草原局普通高等教育"十三五"规划教材

ISBN 978-7-5219-0858-9

Ⅰ.①自… Ⅱ.①曹… Ⅲ.①自然遗产—保护—法律—汇编—世界—高等学校—教材—汉、英 ②文化遗产—保护—法律—汇编—世界—高等学校—教材—汉、英 Ⅳ.①D912.109

中国版本图书馆CIP数据核字（2020）第202734号

中国林业出版社·教育分社

策划、责任编辑：康红梅　　　责任校对：苏　梅
电话：83143551　　　　　　　传真：83143516

出版发行	中国林业出版社 (100009 北京市西城区刘海胡同7号) E-mail：jiaocaipublic@163.com　电话：(010)83143500 http://www.forestry.gov.cn/lycb.html
经　销	新华书店
印　刷	北京中科印刷有限公司
版　次	2021年4月第1版
印　次	2021年4月第1次印刷
开　本	889mm×1194mm 1/16
印　张	39
字　数	1179千字
定　价	98.00元

未经许可，不得以任何方式复制或抄袭本书之部分或全部内容。

版权所有　侵权必究

前　言

"世界遗产"这一理念是联合国教科文组织在1972年通过的《保护世界文化和自然遗产公约》中正式提出的。它强调的是不论是哪个国家或哪个地区的文化和自然遗产，都应作为全人类共同的遗产来进行保护。而公约重点保护的就是具有突出普遍价值的遗产，由此建立了《世界遗产名录》这个保护体系。除了"世界遗产"这一全球性的保护体系之外，还有另外一些全球性的保护体系，如国际重要湿地、世界生物圈保护区、世界地质公园、全球重要农业遗产系统、非物质文化遗产、世界记忆遗产等，从不同的层面对各类自然和文化遗产的保护提出了重要的原则、方法和措施。

此书是关于自然与文化遗产保护的国际文件选编，其中包含国际法规，如公约等，亦有宪章、宣言、建议、指南、准则、重要决议等相关国际文件，择其比较重要的文件进行介绍，以汉英对照版本进行展示，以期加深和扩展遗产保护相关专业人员和大众对遗产、遗产保护的概念及其成型理论的全面了解。这些文件以联合国（UN）、联合国教科文组织（UNESCO）、国际古迹遗址理事会（ICOMOS）、世界自然保护联盟（IUCN）、湿地公约组织（RAMSAR）、人与生物圈计划（MAB）、世界地质公园网络（GGN）、联合国粮农组织（FAO）等全球性国际组织的正式文件为依据，其中如有多个版本的经过版本比较和选择。如正式文件有英文版本而无中文版本的，选择已公开的正式翻译版本，其中文化遗产相关文件主要采用国家文物局和中国古迹遗址保护协会（ICOMOS CHINA）的翻译版本；如无合适的翻译版本，或缺乏翻译版本，编译者则补充中文翻译。所有文件按照其相关性进行排列，主要分为这样几类：世界遗产公约及相关、文化遗产（包括建筑遗产、景观和园林遗产、历史地区、考古遗产、水下文化遗产、工业遗产、文化线路等）、农业遗产、自然遗产、无形文化遗产、文献遗产等。由于篇幅所限，本书选择了部分更为重要的文件，其中有些内容选择了后期较新的文件，因此还有一些相关的文件或较早的文件其原文在此书中未出现，但那些文件仍具有重要意义。本书绪论对遗产保护相关国际文件进行了概述、简介和讨论，读者可参阅。

本书适合高等院校的建筑学、风景园林、城乡规划、考古学、文物与博物馆学、文物保护技术、文化遗产、旅游管理、生态学、艺术学类、地理科学类、地质学类、林学类、自然保护与环境生态类等遗产保护相关专业及领域的本科生、研究生等作为教材或教辅书，亦适合广大相关专业人员参考。

本书得到中国古迹遗址保护协会（ICOMOS CHINA）的大力支持，并提供了几份较新的文件，此次翻译的ICOMOS文件也经过协会的审校，在此表达衷心的感谢！感谢协会秘书处燕海鸣主任、王珏女士在此书编撰过程中提出建议和给予协助！感谢世界地质公园网络办公室以及其他遗产相关部门对本书的支持！感谢中国林业出版社教育分社康红梅副社长的支持和不懈努力,以及诸位编辑的辛勤工作!感谢叶明勇先生以及诸多朋友对本书编撰的帮助!研究生Olivier Clement Gatwaza、王界贤协助了大量校对工作,Adeeb Asham、孟宇飞、Aline Umutoni、朱翊伦、袁紫琪等也协助了部分工作,在此一并致谢!

本书出版受北京林业大学"十三五"规划教材项目资助(资助编号:BJFU2017JC016)和研究生课程建设项目资助(资助编号:YWKC18003,JCCB2030),在此特别致谢!

曹　新

2021年4月

缩略语

FAO	联合国粮食及农业组织（联合国粮农组织）
GGN	世界地质公园网络
GIAHS	全球重要农业遗产系统
ICCROM	国际文物保护与修复研究中心
ICOMOS	国际古迹遗址理事会
IFLA	国际风景园林师联合会
IUCN	世界自然保护联盟
MAB	教科文组织人与生物圈计划
MoW	教科文组织世界记忆计划
RAMSAR	湿地公约
TICCIH	国际工业遗产保护委员会
UGG	教科文组织世界地质公园
UNESCO	联合国教育、科学及文化组织（联合国教科文组织）
UN	联合国
WHC	世界遗产公约 / 世界遗产委员会 / 世界遗产中心

Acronyms and Abbreviations

FAO	Food and Agriculture Organization of the United Nations
GGN	Global Geoparks Network
GIAHS	Globally Important Agricultural Heritage Systems
ICCROM	International Centre for the Study of the Preservation and Restoration of Cultural Property
ICOMOS	International Council on Monuments and Sites
IFLA	International Federation of Landscape Architects
IUCN	International Union for Conservation of Nature
MAB	Man and the Biosphere Programme of UNESCO
MoW	Memory of the World Programme of UNESCO
RAMSAR	Ramsar Convention (Convention on Wetlands)
TICCIH	International Committee for the Conservation of the Industrial Heritage
UGG	UNESCO Global Geoparks
UNESCO	United Nations Educational, Scientific and Cultural Organization
UN	United Nations
WHC	World Heritage Convention/World Heritage Committee/ World Heritage Center

本书图片来源

除以下图片外,其他图片均为曹新拍摄。

水下文化遗产:由重庆白鹤梁水下博物馆提供。

工业遗产:由徐苏斌拍摄。

文献遗产:引自:国家图书馆编.《国家图书馆藏样式雷图档:圆明园卷初编》1–10. 国家图书馆出版社,2016.

目 录

前言

缩略语
Acronyms and Abbreviations

绪论 ··· 1

世界遗产 ··· 15
 保护世界文化和自然遗产公约 ··· 16
 Convention concerning the Protection of the World Cultural and Natural Heritage ·············· 23
 实施《世界遗产公约》操作指南（节选） ··· 34
 Operational Guidelines for the Implementation of the World Heritage Convention(excerpts) ······ 38
 关于在国家一级保护文化和自然遗产的建议 ··· 44
 Recommendation concerning the Protection, at National Level, of the Cultural and Natural Heritage ············ 50

文化遗产 ··· 59
 关于历史性纪念物修复的雅典宪章 ·· 60
 The Athens Charter for the Restoration of Historic Monuments ······································ 63
 关于在武装冲突的情况下保护文化财产的公约 ····································· 67
 Convention for the Protection of Cultural Property in the Event of Armed Conflict ················· 74
 关于古迹遗址保护与修复的国际宪章（威尼斯宪章） ··························· 84
 International Charter for the Conservation and Restoration of Monuments and Sites
  （The Venice Charter） ··· 86
 关于保护受公共或私人工程危害的文化财产的建议 ····························· 89
 Recommendation concerning the Preservation of Cultural Property Endangered by Public or Private
  Works ·· 94
 关于禁止和防止非法进出口文化财产和非法转让其所有权的方法的公约 ········ 101
 Convention on the Means of Prohibiting and Preventing the Illicit Import, Export and Transfer of
  Ownership of Cultural Property ··· 106
 奈良真实性文件 ·· 113
 The Nara Document on Authenticity ··· 115

教科文组织关于蓄意破坏文化遗产问题的宣言 ········· 118
　　　UNESCO Declaration concerning the Intentional Destruction of Cultural Heritage ········· 121

建筑遗产 ········· 125
　　关于乡土建筑遗产的宪章 ········· 125
　　　Charter on the Built Vernacular Heritage ········· 127
　　建筑遗产分析、保护和结构修复原则 ········· 130
　　　Principles for the Analysis, Conservation and Structural Restoration of Architectural Heritage ········· 133
　　木质建成遗产保护准则 ········· 136
　　　Principles for the Conservation of Wooden Built Heritage ········· 141

景观和园林遗产 ········· 147
　　关于保护景观和遗址的风貌与特性的建议 ········· 147
　　　Recommendation concerning the Safeguarding of the Beauty and Character of Landscapes and Sites ········· 151
　　佛罗伦萨宪章 ········· 157
　　　Historic Gardens (The Florence Charter) ········· 160
　　ICOMOS-IFLA 历史城市公园文件 ········· 164
　　　ICOMOS-IFLA Document on Historic Urban Public Parks ········· 168
　　ICOMOS-IFLA 关于乡村景观遗产的准则 ········· 173
　　　ICOMOS-IFLA Principles concerning Rural Landscapes as Heritage ········· 178

历史地区 ········· 185
　　关于历史地区的保护及其当代作用的建议（内罗毕建议） ········· 185
　　　Recommendation concerning the Safeguarding and Contemporary Role of Historic Areas ········· 192
　　保护历史城镇与城区宪章（华盛顿宪章） ········· 202
　　　Charter for the Conservation of Historic Towns and Urban Areas（The Washington Charter） ········· 204
　　关于城市历史景观的建议书，包括定义汇编 ········· 207
　　　Recommendation on the Historic Urban Landscape, Including a Glossary of Definitions ········· 213
　　关于维护与管理历史城镇与城区的瓦莱塔原则 ········· 221
　　　The Valletta Principles for the Safeguarding and Management of Historic Cities, Towns and Urban Areas ········· 229

考古遗产 ········· 239
　　考古遗产保护与管理宪章 ········· 239
　　　Charter for the Protection and Management of the Archaeological Heritage ········· 242
　　公共考古遗址管理的塞拉莱指南 ········· 247
　　　Salalah Guidelines for the Management of Public Archaeological Sites ········· 253

水下文化遗产 ········· 261
　　水下文化遗产保护与管理宪章 ········· 261
　　　Charter on the Protection and Management of Underwater Cultural Heritage ········· 265
　　保护水下文化遗产公约 ········· 270
　　　Convention on the Protection of the Underwater Cultural Heritage ········· 282

工业遗产 ... 298

关于工业遗产的下塔吉尔宪章 ... 298
The Nizhny Tagil Charter for the Industrial Heritage ... 302

ICOMOS-TICCIH 保护工业遗产遗址、构筑物、区域和景观的原则（都柏林原则）... 307
Joint ICOMOS-TICCIH Principles for the Conservation of Industrial Heritage Sites, Structures, Areas and Landscapes（The Dublin Principles）... 310

文化线路 ... 314

文化线路宪章 ... 314
The ICOMOS Charter on Cultural Routes ... 321

文化遗产其他文件 ... 329

国际文化旅游宪章——遗产地旅游管理原则 ... 329
International Cultural Tourism Charter: Managing Tourism at Places of Heritage Significance ... 333

壁画保护、修复和保存原则 ... 338
ICOMOS Principles for the Preservation and Conservation-Restoration of Wall Paintings ... 341

文化遗产阐释与展示宪章 ... 346
The ICOMOS Charter for the Interpretation and Presentation of Cultural Heritage Sites ... 351

中国文物古迹保护准则 ... 357
Principles for the Conservation of Heritage Sites in China ... 363

农业遗产 ... 371

全球重要农业遗产系统（GIAHS）（节选）... 372
Globally Important Agricultural Heritage Systems (GIAHS)(excerpts) ... 374

自然遗产 ... 377

关于特别是作为水禽栖息地的国际重要湿地公约（湿地公约）... 378
Convention on Wetlands of International Importance especially as Waterfowl Habitat ... 382

国际重要湿地标准 ... 387
The Ramsar Sites Criteria（The Nine Criteria for Identifying Wetlands of International Importance）... 388

联合国人类环境会议宣言 ... 389
Declaration of the United Nations Conference on the Human Environment ... 393

世界自然宪章 ... 398
World Charter for Nature ... 401

关于环境与发展的里约热内卢宣言 ... 405
Rio Declaration on Environment and Development ... 408

生物多样性公约 ... 412
Convention on Biological Diversity ... 423

联合国气候变化框架公约 ... 439
United Nations Framework Convention on Climate Change ... 450

联合国关于在发生严重干旱和/或荒漠化的国家特别是在非洲防治荒漠化的公约（防治荒漠化公约）... 466

United Nations Convention to Combat Desertification in those Countries Experiencing Serious Drought and/or Desertification, Particularly in Africa ……… 480

世界生物圈保护区网络章程框架 ……… 501

The Statutory Framework of the World Network of Biosphere Reserves ……… 504

可持续发展问题世界首脑会议执行计划（节选）……… 508

Plan of Implementation of the World Summit on Sustainable Development (excerpts) ……… 518

教科文组织世界地质公园操作指南（节选）……… 533

Operational Guidelines for UNESCO Global Geoparks(excerpts) ……… 537

保护地管理分类应用指南（节选）……… 542

Guidelines for Applying Protected Area Management Categories(excerpts) ……… 546

无形文化遗产 ……… 551

保护非物质文化遗产公约 ……… 552

Convention for the Safeguarding of the Intangible Cultural Heritage ……… 560

保护和促进文化表现形式多样性公约 ……… 571

Convention on the Protection and Promotion of the Diversity of Cultural Expressions ……… 581

文献遗产 ……… 595

关于保存和获取包括数字遗产在内的文献遗产的建议书 ……… 596

Recommendation concerning the Preservation of, and Access to, Documentary Heritage Including in Digital Form ……… 600

联合国教科文组织世界记忆计划：通用指南（节选）……… 606

UNESCO Memory of the World Programme: General Guidelines (excerpts) ……… 609

绪 论

1. 遗产保护的相关国际组织

国际上与世界遗产公约相关的重要组织和机构有：联合国教科文组织（United Nations Educational, Scientific and Cultural Organization，UNESCO）；世界遗产委员会（The World Heritage Committee，WHC）；世界遗产中心（World Heritage Centre，WHC）；国际文化遗产保护与修复研究中心（International Centre for the Study of the Preservation and Restoration of Cultural Property，ICCROM），简称为"The Rome Centre"或"The International Centre for Conservation"；国际古迹遗址理事会（International Council on Monuments and Sites，ICOMOS）；世界自然保护联盟（International Union for Conservation of Nature，IUCN）。

联合国教科文组织，为联合国教育、科学及文化组织的简称，1945年建立，总部设在法国巴黎。联合国教科文组织致力于推动各国在教育、科学和文化领域开展国际合作，以此共筑和平。联合国教科文组织是全球遗产保护的主要推动者，在目前主要的各类全球性遗产保护体系中发挥关键性作用。

保护世界文化和自然遗产政府间委员会，简称世界遗产委员会，1972年建立，1976年开始运行。世界遗产委员会由21个成员国组成，每年至少召开一次会议（6月或7月）。委员会设有主席团，在委员会常会期间召开会议，会议次数根据实际需求确定。联合国教科文组织于1992年创建了世界遗产中心，承担世界遗产委员会秘书处的职能。

世界遗产委员会的咨询机构包括：国际文化遗产保护与修复研究中心、国际古迹遗址理事会以及世界自然保护联盟。

国际文化遗产保护与修复研究中心，是一个政府间国际组织，总部设在意大利的罗马，由联合国教科文组织于1956年创建，1959年基于与意大利的协议，中心在罗马建立。该中心的作用是开展研究、记录，提供技术援助、培训和推行增强公众意识的项目，加强对可移动和不可移动文化遗产的保护。

国际文化遗产保护与修复研究中心是世界遗产委员会在文化遗产培训领域的重要合作伙伴，监督世界文化遗产保护状况，审查由缔约国提交的国际援助申请，以及为能力建设活动提供支持。

国际古迹遗址理事会是一个非政府国际组织，总部设在法国巴黎，创建于1965年。理事会的作用在于推广文化遗产保护理论、方法和科学技术的应用。

作为世界遗产委员会在文化遗产方面的咨询机构，国际古迹遗址理事会评估申报文化遗产的项目，监督世界文化遗产保护状况，审查由缔约国提交的国际援助申请，以及为能力建设活动出力献策和提供支持。

世界自然保护联盟，总部设在瑞士格朗，创建于1948年，为各国政府、非政府组织和科学工作者在世界范围的合作提供了平台。其使命在于影响、鼓励和协助世界各团体保护自然的完整性和多样性，并确保任何对自然资源的使用都是公平的，而且符合生态的可持续发展。世界自然保护联盟在一系列关键的国际公约的建立中发挥了基础性作用，如湿地公约、世界遗产公约、生物多样性公约等。

作为世界遗产委员会在自然遗产方面的咨询机构，世界自然保护联盟评估申报自然遗产的项目、监督世界自然遗产保护状况、审查由缔约国提交的国际援助申请，以及为能力建设活动出力献策并提供支持。

除了以上与世界遗产公约相关的组织，还有一些与遗产保护密切相关的全球国际组织也非常重要，如湿地公约（Ramsar Convention/Convention on Wetlands，RAMSAR）组织，1971年建立；世界地质公园网络（Global Geoparks Network，GGN），2004年建立；联合国粮农组织（全称"联合国粮食及农业组织"，Food and Agriculture Organization of the United Nations，FAO），1945年建立；以及自然和文化遗产的其他相关组织，如国际风景园林师联合会（International Federation of Landscape Architects，IFLA）、国际工业遗产保护委员会（International Committee for the Conservation of the Industrial Heritage，TICCIH）、国际博物馆协会（International Council of Museums，ICOM）等。

2. 遗产保护的相关国际文件

（1）概述

与世界遗产相关的国际文件主要是由联合国、联合国教科文组织等制定的相关公约、计划、指南、宪章、建议、宣言、决议等组成一个基本的国际保护体系框架。国迹古迹遗址理事会主要关注文化遗产的保护，以《威尼斯宪章》确立了文化遗产保护的基本普适原则，逐步扩展其广度和深度，并和其他一些国际组织合作（如国际风景园林师联合会、国际工业遗产保护委员会等），发展制定了针对各类文化遗产及其保护相关问题的宪章、准则、指南、原则等各种文件，对各类具有不同价值特点的文化遗产的保护进行了阐释和讨论，构建了逐步深入和全面的理论框架。世界自然保护联盟则侧重于自然遗产的保护，尤其关注自然遗产的完整性和多样性以及可持续利用。联合国粮农组织则侧重于农业遗产的保护，尤其强调可持续的农业遗产系统。另外，还有一些专门组织如国际风景园林师联合会、国际工业遗产保护委员会等也针对某类遗产进行了深入的探讨，并与其他国际组织共同合作。这些全球性国际组织制定了一些指南、准则以及与各类遗产保护相关的重要文件，共同建立了保护的理论基础。

除了上述的国际组织和国际文件外，还有全球性和区域性的其他众多国际组织及其达成共识的国际文件亦在国际层面的遗产保护领域发挥着重要的作用，各个国家和地区也在进行着多方面的共同努力，这些都推动了人类对遗产保护的认识、研究和实践不断向前发展。

表1是近一个世纪以来遗产保护相关的部分重要国际文件。

表1　遗产保护相关的部分重要国际文件

文件名称	制定的组织/大会	通过时间
关于历史性纪念物修复的雅典宪章	第一届历史古迹建筑师及技师国际会议	1931年
关于在武装冲突的情况下保护文化财产的公约	联合国教科文组织	1954年
关于适用于考古发掘的国际原则的建议	联合国教科文组织	1956年
关于保护景观和遗址的风貌与特性的建议	联合国教科文组织	1962年
关于古迹遗址保护与修复的国际宪章（威尼斯宪章）	第二届历史古迹建筑师及技师国际会议，国际古迹遗址理事会	1964年（国际古迹遗址理事会1965年采纳）
关于保护受公共或私人工程危害的文化财产的建议	联合国教科文组织	1968年
关于禁止和防止非法进出口文化财产和非法转让其所有权的方法的公约	联合国教科文组织	1970年
关于特别是作为水禽栖息地的国际重要湿地公约（湿地公约）	联合国教科文组织	1971年
联合国人类环境会议宣言	联合国	1972年
保护世界文化和自然遗产公约	联合国教科文组织	1972年
关于在国家一级保护文化和自然遗产的建议	联合国教科文组织	1972年
关于建筑遗产的欧洲宪章	欧洲委员会	1975年
关于文化财产国际交换的建议	联合国教科文组织	1976年
关于历史地区的保护及其当代作用的建议（内罗毕建议）	联合国教科文组织	1976年

(续)

文件名称	制定的组织/大会	通过时间
实施世界遗产公约操作指南	联合国教科文组织，世界遗产委员会，世界遗产中心	第一版：1977年 最新版：2019年
关于保护可移动文化财产的建议	联合国教科文组织	1978年
关于保护与保存活动图像的建议	联合国教科文组织	1980年
佛罗伦萨宪章	国际古迹遗址理事会—国际风景园林师联合会	1982年
世界自然宪章	联合国	1982年
保护欧洲建筑遗产公约	欧洲委员会	1985年
保护历史城镇与城区宪章（华盛顿宪章）	国际古迹遗址理事会	1987年
我们共同的未来	联合国	1987年
保护民间创作建议书	联合国教科文组织	1989年
考古遗产保护与管理宪章	国际古迹遗址理事会	1990年
保护考古遗产的欧洲公约	欧洲委员会	1992年
关于环境与发展的里约热内卢宣言	联合国	1992年
21世纪议程	联合国	1992年
生物多样性公约	联合国	1992年
气候变化框架公约	联合国	1992年
关于在发生严重干旱和/或荒漠化的国家特别是在非洲防治荒漠化的公约（防治荒漠化公约）	联合国	1994年
奈良真实性文件	与世界遗产公约相关的奈良真实性会议	1994年
生物圈保护区塞维利亚纲要	联合国教科文组织	1995年
世界生物圈保护区网络章程框架	联合国教科文组织	1995年
水下文化遗产保护与管理宪章	国际古迹遗址理事会	1996年
历史木结构建筑保护准则	国际古迹遗址理事会	1999年
关于乡土建筑遗产的宪章	国际古迹遗址理事会	1999年
国际文化旅游宪章——遗产地旅游管理原则	国际古迹遗址理事会	1999年
欧洲景观公约	欧洲委员会	2000年
保护水下文化遗产公约	联合国教科文组织	2001年
可持续发展问题世界首脑会议执行计划	联合国	2002年
建筑遗产分析、保护和结构修复原则	国际古迹遗址理事会	2003年
关于蓄意破坏文化遗产问题的宣言	联合国教科文组织	2003年
关于工业遗产的下塔吉尔宪章	国际工业遗产保护委员会	2003年
壁画保护、修复和保存原则	国际古迹遗址理事会	2003年
保护非物质文化遗产公约	联合国教科文组织	2003年
保存数字遗产宪章	联合国教科文组织	2003年
保护和促进文化表现形式多样性公约	联合国教科文组织	2005年
北京文件——关于东亚地区文物建筑保护与修复	东亚地区文物建筑保护理念与实践国际研讨会	2007年

(续)

文件名称	制定的组织/大会	通过时间
文化线路宪章	国际古迹遗址理事会	2008年
文化遗产阐释与展示宪章	国际古迹遗址理事会	2008年
关于城市历史景观的建议书	联合国教科文组织	2011年
关于维护与管理历史城镇与城区的瓦莱塔原则	国际古迹遗址理事会	2011年
保护工业遗产遗址、构筑物、区域和景观的原则（都柏林原则）	国际古迹遗址理事会—国际工业遗产保护委员会	2011年
我们希望的未来	联合国	2012年
保护地管理分类应用指南	世界自然保护联盟	最新版：2013年
教科文组织世界地质公园操作指南	联合国教科文组织	2015年
关于保存和获取包括数字遗产在内的文献遗产的建议书	联合国教科文组织	2015年
中国文物古迹保护准则	国际古迹遗址理事会中国国家委员会	第一版：2000年 修订版：2015年
全球重要农业遗产系统（GIAHS）	联合国粮农组织	2017年
木质建成遗产保护准则	国际古迹遗址理事会	2017年
历史城市公园文件	国际古迹遗址理事会—国际风景园林师联合会	2017年
关于乡村景观遗产的准则	国际古迹遗址理事会—国际风景园林师联合会	2017年
公共考古遗址管理的塞拉莱指南	国际古迹遗址理事会	2017年
教科文组织世界记忆计划——通用指南	联合国教科文组织	最新版：2017年

（2）《世界遗产公约》及相关文件

1972年11月16日，联合国教科文组织第十七届大会通过了《保护世界文化和自然遗产公约》，并在同一天通过了《关于在国家一级保护文化和自然遗产的建议》。

《保护世界文化和自然遗产公约》，简称《世界遗产公约》，确定了文化遗产和自然遗产的定义，界定了公约缔约国对于国家保护和国际保护的责任，并对世界遗产委员会的机构和议事规则，以及如何将遗产列入遗产名录和濒危名录进行了规定，设立了保护世界文化和自然遗产基金以及相关章程，明确了国际援助的条件和程序，制定了相应的教育计划，并规定了缔约国和委员会提交报告等相关条款。截至2020年，共有194个国家加入了《世界遗产公约》。《世界遗产公约》极大地推动了全球的自然和文化遗产的保护。

由于文化和自然遗产的确定、保护、保存、展出和遗传后代，主要是有关缔约国的责任，《关于在国家一级保护文化和自然遗产的建议》这份文件对于缔约国的责任进行了更为详细清晰的界定以及提出了相应的导则。该《建议》首先重申了文化遗产和自然遗产的定义，对遗产的概念、缔约国保护遗产的政策等提出了一些总则，对遗产保护相关的行政组织设定了共同的标准，在科学、技术、行政、法律、财政等各方面提出了基本的措施，以确保文化和自然遗产得到保护，并提出了促进教育和文化行动以及国际合作的建议。

《实施〈世界遗产公约〉操作指南》由世界遗产委员会制定和修改，最早一版于1977年在第一届世界遗产大会上通过。该指南逐步更新，目前最新版本于2019年世界遗产大会通过。该文件对《世界遗产公约》的相关机构，建立和管理《世界遗产名录》《濒危世界遗产名录》，和以世界遗产基金的形式提供国际援助的标准和程序等作了详细、明确的规定。该指南中有关自然和文化遗产的评估标准，以及遗产真实性和完整性的界定，对于遗产的评定和保护有着重要的指导意义。

（3）文化遗产保护的相关文件

第一个专门讨论关于文化遗产保护的国际性文件是1931年在雅典举行的第一届历史古迹建筑师及技师国际会议上通过的，即《关于历史性纪念物修复的雅典宪章》，简称《雅典宪章》。在这份宪章里，提出了修复和保护的一些基本原则，奠定了后来的文化遗产保护文件的基础，其中一些重要原则的精神在后来的《威尼斯宪章》里得到了延续和充分体现。

由于20世纪上半叶战争对遗产的普遍破坏，国际社会认识到武装冲突对于文化财产的巨大威胁，1954年5月14日，联合国教科文组织在海牙举行的政府间会议上订立了《关于在武装冲突的情况下保护文化财产的公约》，简称《海牙公约》。在这个公约里，认识到保存文化遗产对全世界人民的极大重要性，确立了关于武装冲突的情况下保护文化财产的一般原则和责任，文化财产特别保护的措施，文化财产运输的原则，以及相关国际事务的程序，并且制定了相应的议定书。在1999年，又制定了公约的第二议定书。

1964年，在威尼斯举行的第二届历史古迹建筑师及技师国际会议通过了《关于古迹遗址保护与修复的国际宪章》，简称《威尼斯宪章》。在这篇标志性的文件里，确立了一个非常重要的文化遗产保护的核心原则，那便是"真实性"。宪章明确了历史古迹的定义和保护修复古迹的宗旨，提出了保护、修复、发掘、记录出版的基本原则，而这些原则始终贯彻的就是"真实性"这一要旨。1965年，国际古迹遗址理事会采纳了《威尼斯宪章》。这个宪章对文化遗产的保护与修复影响深远，其基本原则至今仍受到广泛尊重。

在第二次世界大战后的一段时间，由于工业化和城市化的逐步发展，众多的古迹和具有艺术、历史或科学价值的建筑开始日益受到公共和私人工程的威胁，协调文化遗产的保护和社会经济的发展所带来的变化刻不容缓。1968年11月19日，联合国教科文组织第十五届大会在巴黎通过了《关于保护受公共或私人工程危害的文化财产的建议》。这个文件对文化财产进行了定义，提出了受到公共或私人工程危害的文化财产的保护总则，保护和抢救文化财产的措施，立法、财政和行政措施，以及教育计划等。

文化财产非法进出口和所有权非法转让是造成原主国文化遗产枯竭的主要原因之一。为使文化财产免受偷盗、秘密发掘和非法出口的危险，为了在国家和国际范围进行组织以及密切合作，有效地保护文化遗产，1970年11月14日，联合国教科文组织第十六届大会在巴黎通过了《关于禁止和防止非法进出口文化财产和非法转让其所有权的方法的公约》。该公约对缔约国的责任进行了明确界定，并就国际合作制定了框架。公约为防止文物非法转让以及促进国际流失文物追索和文物返还本国提供了有力的依据。由于公约针对的流散文物的时间限制，早期流散文物的流通还无法通过此公约控制，但此公约体现的精神促进了国际共识的积极向前发展。

为了扩大和增进文化交流，尊重构成全人类文化遗产的其他民族文化的价值，在防止非法买卖的基础上促进文化财产的合理国际交换，1976年11月26日，联合国教科文组织第十九届大会在内罗毕通过《关于文化财产国际交换的建议》，为文物、文献、标本、艺术作品、档案、文件等文化财产的国际交换建立了国际合作的框架。

由于代表不同文化的可移动文化财产是人类共同遗产的重要组成部分，为了加强国际社会对可移动文化财产的有效保护，1978年11月28日，联合国教科文组织第二十届大会在巴黎通过了《关于保护可移动文化财产的建议》。文件制定了保护可移动文化财产的总则，提出了各级风险预防措施、控制措施、资金措施、以及国际合作等建议。

对于威尼斯宪章提出的首要原则——真实性，在不同的文化背景中有着广泛讨论。1994年11月1日至6日，联合国教科文组织、国际文化遗产保护与修复研究中心和国际古迹遗址理事会在奈良举行会议，就真实性问题进行了专门的探讨，通过了《奈良真实性文件》。文件重申《威尼斯宪章》所提出的"真实性"是遗产有关价值的基本要素,但由于文化价值及相关信息来源可信度的判断可能存在文化差异,强调出于对文化多样性和遗产多样性的尊重,需在相关文化背景下对遗产评判其真实性。《奈良真实性文件》对于真实性的批判性思考为真实性的深入讨论奠定了一个具有多维视野的基础。

鉴于震动了整个国际社会的阿富汗塔利班摧毁巴米扬大佛的悲剧性事件（2001年）,以及蓄意破坏文化遗产的行为不断出现,2003年10月17日,联合国教科文组织第三十二届大会在巴黎通过了《关于蓄意破坏文化遗产问题的宣言》。该宣言重申文化遗产的重要性,提出反对蓄意破坏文化遗产的措施,敦促各国加入《海牙公约》,并呼吁开展保护文化遗产的国际合作。时至今日,局部的冲突和战争仍然时常损害人类共同的遗产,蓄意破坏历史古迹的情况在全球仍时有发生,这个问题依然是文化遗产保护的极大威胁。

上述文件是国际社会对于文化遗产的总体共识的重要部分。下面对各类文化遗产的相关重要国际文件进行讨论。

建筑遗产

除了前述的《威尼斯宪章》作为建筑遗产保护的基础文件外,还有一些国际文件专门讨论建筑遗产的保护。

1975年9月,欧洲委员会（Council of Europe,CoE）通过并在10月举行的欧洲建筑遗产大会上公布了《关于建筑遗产的欧洲宪章》,对于建筑遗产保护提出了十条基本原则,促进在欧洲社会协调一致进行建筑遗产的整体性保护。

1985年10月,欧洲委员会进而在西班牙格拉纳达通过了《保护欧洲建筑遗产公约》,这是第一份关于整体保护建筑遗产的国际条约。该公约肯定了欧洲团结合作保护建筑遗产的必要性,确立了"欧洲协调保护政策"的原则,加强和促进了欧洲遗产的整体保护和成员国间的合作。

1999年10月,国际古迹遗址理事会第十二届大会在墨西哥通过了《历史木结构建筑保护准则》。这个文件对于木质建筑遗产的保护提出了基本的原则。2017年,国际古迹遗址理事会第十九届大会在印度新德里针对1999年的《历史木结构建筑保护准则》进行了补充和更新,于12月15日通过了《木质建成遗产保护准则》。这个文件强调木质建成遗产的价值,以及其保护的特殊性、包含的传统和技艺的重要性,并就检查、勘察和研究,分析和评估,干预措施,当今材料和技术的运用,记录和建档,监测和维护,历史森林保护区,教育和培训等方面,提出了较为全面的基本原则和建议。

由于乡土建筑的重要性和特殊价值,它是一种可识别的、与环境适应的、具有地方特征的建筑型制,也是世界文化多样性的表现,1999年10月,国际古迹遗址理事会第十二届大会在墨西哥通过了《关于乡土建筑遗产的宪章》。宪章明确了乡土建筑的特点,系统提出了乡土建筑的保护原则和保护实践中的指导方针,强调对其文化价值和传统特色的尊重,而由于乡土性几乎不可能通过单体建筑来表现,建议各个地区经由维持和保存有典型特征的建筑群和村落来保护乡土性。

建筑遗产的保护、加固和修复需要多学科的符合其文化背景的综合方法,2003年,国际古迹遗址理事会第十四届大会于津巴布韦的维多利亚瀑布市通过了《建筑遗产分析、保护和结构修复原则》,确立了建筑遗产结构的保护、研究、诊断、治疗和控制的一系列原则和措施,并明确提出最好的治疗是预防性维护。

景观和园林遗产

为了保护景观和遗址的文化、艺术、科学价值及其风貌特征不受损害,1962年12月11日,联合国教科文组织第十二届大会在巴黎通过了《关于保护景观和遗址的风貌与特性的建议》,提出了不论是自然的或人工的,自然、乡村及城市景观和遗址的任何部分都应进行保护,并从其保护总则、保护措施及其实施、公共教育等各方面提出了基本的框架。这个文件以及之前1954年的《海牙公约》等文件为后来的《世界遗产公约》奠定了基础。

1981年5月，国际古迹遗址理事会和国际风景园林师联合会的国际历史园林委员会于佛罗伦萨举行会议，起草了一份关于保护历史园林的宪章，作为《威尼斯宪章》的扩展，并以该城命名。国际古迹遗址理事会在1982年12月15日通过了这份针对历史园林保护的文件，即《佛罗伦萨宪章》。宪章明确了历史园林的定义、要素、内涵，对于历史园林的维护、保护、修复、重建，以及历史园林的利用提出了重要的基本原则，并提出了法律和行政保护的框架。

2000年10月20日，同样在佛罗伦萨，欧洲委员会通过了《欧洲景观公约》，亦称《佛罗伦萨公约》。在这个公约里提出的景观（Landscape）这一宽广的视野涵盖了自然的、乡村的、城市的和城郊的区域，不仅关注杰出的景观，亦关注日常的和退化的景观。在景观的保护、管理和规划方面，公约提出了缔约国在国家层面的措施以及欧洲层面的合作措施。公约认为景观的质量和多样性是欧洲共同的资源，必须加强欧洲整体的合作。《欧洲景观公约》的理念对于全球保护和改善景观的认识是十分积极的促进。

历史城市公园是城镇和住区不可分割的重要组成部分。国际风景园林师联合会和国际古迹遗址理事会合作，针对历史城市公园的保护进行了进一步的研究和探讨。国际古迹遗址理事会第十九届大会于2017年12月15日在印度新德里通过了《ICOMOS-IFLA历史城市公园文件》，界定了历史城市公园的定义、价值，对历史城市公园中决定特征的各种要素，以及历史城市公园的研究、保护和管理等方面提出了较为详细和具体的导则。

而对于乡村景观遗产这种延续性的文化景观，国际古迹遗址理事会第十九届大会还通过了《ICOMOS-IFLA关于乡村景观遗产的准则》。这个文件确定了乡村景观的定义、重要性、威胁、挑战、效益以及可持续性，提出了一系列基本行动标准，以促进对乡村景观遗产价值的欣赏，促进乡村景观遗产作为人类社会和文化的组成部分以及世界范围内重要资源的理解、有效保护、可持续管理和交流传播。

历史地区

1976年11月26日，联合国教科文组织第十九届大会在内罗毕通过了《关于历史地区的保护及其当代作用的建议》，简称《内罗毕建议》。历史地区为文化、宗教及社会活动的多样化提供了最确切的生动见证，为了使历史地区免受它们所面临的退化甚至全部毁坏的危险，《内罗毕建议》认为应采取全面有力的政策，将保护和恢复历史地区及周围环境作为国家、地区、或地方规划的组成部分。该文件认为历史地区及其环境是不可替代的世界遗产的组成部分，提出了保护历史地区的总则，国家、地区和地方政策，保护措施，以及促进研究、教育和国际合作的建议。

1987年10月，国际古迹遗址理事会第八届大会在华盛顿通过了《保护历史城镇与城区宪章》，即《华盛顿宪章》。《华盛顿宪章》对历史城镇和城区进行了定义，提出了保护历史城镇和城区的原则和目标，明确了保护历史城镇和城区所包含的要素，提出了保护历史城镇和城区的方法和手段，为保护历史城镇和城区建立了一个基本框架。

2011年11月10日，联合国教科文组织第三十六届大会在巴黎通过了《关于城市历史景观的建议书》。该文件强调历史地区的维护、管理及规划的重要性，历史地区是我们共同的文化遗产中最为丰富和多样的表现之一。该《建议书》为识别、保护和管理历史区域提出了一种景观方法，提出的"城市历史景观"超越了"历史中心"或"整体"的概念，纳入了更广泛的城市背景及地理环境，文件对于城市历史景观面临的挑战和机遇，维护城市历史景观的政策和手段，能力建设，研究、信息和传播，以及国际合作等方面提出了纲领性的建议。

基于前面的两个文件——《内罗毕建议》和《华盛顿宪章》，国际古迹遗址理事会的国际历史村镇委员会（CIVVIH）对保护历史城镇与城区维护和管理相关的原则和方法进行了修订。同样在2011年，国际古迹遗址理事会第十七届大会于11月28日在巴黎通过了《关于维护与管理历史城镇与城区的瓦莱塔原则》。文件加深了对历史城镇和城区的全面认识，并强调可持续发展的理念，在历史城镇和城区的内涵，各种要素的融合，其变化与自然环境、建筑环境、社会环境以及无形遗产的关系，维护和管理的方法及策略等方面都有所扩展。

考古遗产

1956年12月5日，联合国教科文组织第九届大会在新德里通过了《关于适用于考古发掘的国际原则的建议》，就考古遗产的保护、考古发掘、考古收藏、公众教育提出了一般总则，对考古发掘的国际合作创立了规则，确定了发掘者的权利与义务，对古物贸易进行了规定，并制定了防止秘密发掘和非法出口的原则。

考古遗产构成记载人类过去活动的基本材料，在以《威尼斯宪章》的准则为依据的基础上，1990年10月，国际古迹遗址理事会第九届大会在洛桑通过了《考古遗产保护与管理宪章》。该宪章规定了有关考古遗产管理的一系列原则，其中包括公共当局和立法者的责任，有关遗产的勘察、勘测、发掘、档案记录、研究、维护、保护、保存、重建、信息资料、展出、培训以及对外开放与公众利用等的专业操作程序规则。

1992年1月16日，欧洲委员会在马耳他的瓦莱塔通过了《保护考古遗产的欧洲公约》，也称《瓦莱塔公约》，它替代了1969年的《伦敦公约》。该公约将保护和加强考古遗产作为城市和区域规划政策的目标之一，制定了考古遗产的保护措施、资金筹措、调查研究、防止非法流通的准则，还涉及公众对考古遗址的访问，以及相应的教育行动，建立了欧洲就考古遗产开展合作的框架。

世界各地的国家公园系统和世界遗产地中的考古遗址，如今都面临特别的挑战，因为旅游业将其作为首要目的地之一。针对向公众开放的考古遗址的管理，2017年12月15日，国际古迹遗址理事会第十九届大会在印度新德里通过了《公共考古遗址管理的塞拉莱指南》。该指南中的建议来自许多国家和不同地区参与管理向公众开放的考古遗址人员的集体经验。指南的宗旨是建立可持续的管理框架，包括确定清单和进行评估，确立遗址边界和管理区，进行环境影响评估和研究，监测规划、考古研究计划、阐释方案、管理设施、人员计划、社区参与计划、总体管理规划，以及相应的管理实施等各方面。指南还重申了2015年《塞拉莱建议》中提出的"考古遗址公园"的概念，提出考古遗址公园应作为其他包含重要文化和自然资源的脆弱遗址提供一个如何实现可持续管理的范本。

水下文化遗产

1996年10月，国际古迹遗址理事会第十一届大会在保加利亚索菲亚通过了《水下文化遗产保护与管理宪章》。宪章认为，水下文化遗产应理解为处于水下环境中或已从水下环境中移出的考古遗产，它包括水下遗址和构造、沉船遗址和残骸及其考古的和自然的环境。水下文化遗产的很大一部分位于国际环境中。水下文化遗产可能受到改变海岸和海床或改变水流、沉积物和污染物的建筑工程的威胁。水下文化遗产也可能受到对生物和非生物资源的盲目开发的威胁。这个文件对于水下文化遗产的调查计划，研究目标、方法和技术，调查和记录，文物保护和保管，遗址管理和维护，传播和国际合作等提出了基本原则。

由于水下文化遗产是各国人民和各民族的历史中非常重要的一部分，更是共同遗产的关系史上一个极为重要的内容，2001年11月2日，联合国教科文组织第三十一届大会在巴黎通过了《保护水下文化遗产公约》，以促进对水下文化遗产的认识、欣赏和保护。在此公约中界定了水下文化遗产的定义为："水下文化遗产"系指至少100年来，周期性地或连续地，部分或全部位于水下的具有文化、历史或考古价值的所有人类生存的遗迹，如：遗址、建筑、房屋、工艺品和人的遗骸，及其有考古价值的环境和自然环境；

船只、飞行器、其他运输工具或上述三类的任何部分，所载货物或其他物品，及其有考古价值的环境和自然环境；具有史前意义的物品。公约确立了水下文化遗产保护的目标和总则，强调国际协作和共同保护；公约明确了关于内水、领海中的水下文化遗产，毗连区的水下文化遗产，专属经济区和大陆架上的水下文化遗产等的相关缔约国的责任。

工业遗产

国际工业遗产保护委员会是保护工业遗产的世界组织，也是国际古迹遗址理事会在工业遗产保护方面的专门顾问机构。国际工业遗产保护委员会于2003年7月17日在莫斯科通过了《关于工业遗产的下塔吉尔宪章》，这是第一份指导工业遗产保护和保存的国际性文件。该宪章界定了工业遗产的定义，工业遗产的价值，并对工业遗产的鉴定、记录和研究，工业遗产的保护和维护，相关的教育、培训以及阐释等给出了建议。

在此基础上，国际工业遗产保护委员会提交文件至国际古迹遗址理事会审议，国际古迹遗址理事会第十七届大会于2011年11月28日在巴黎通过了《ICOMOS-TICCIH保护工业遗产遗址、构筑物、区域和景观的原则》，简称《都柏林原则》。这个文件对于记录并理解工业遗产的构筑物、遗址、区域和景观及其价值，确保有效保护、保存和维护工业构筑物、遗址、区域和景观，展示和传播其遗产维度和价值，提高公众意识，支持培训和研究等层面建立了全面的原则框架。

文化线路

由于文化遗产保护科学的发展，文化线路的新概念体现了文化遗产视野的演变，以及与文化遗产环境和地域规模相关的价值日渐重要，展示了不同层次的遗产宏观结构。文化线路代表了人类跨文化联系互动的、动态的和演变的过程，反映了不同民族对文化遗产贡献的丰富多样性。鉴于保护文化线路的重要意义，2008年10月4日，国际古迹遗址理事会第十六届大会在加拿大魁北克通过了《文化线路宪章》。该宪章确定了文化线路及其要素的全面定义，明确了文化线路的类型及其完整性和真实性，提出了文化线路的研究、资金、保护、评估、保存、可持续利用、管理、公众参与、国际合作等一系列原则。

文化遗产其他相关文件

自然和文化遗产、多样性和生活文化是主要的旅游吸引力，过度的或没有妥善管理的旅游和与旅游相关的发展会威胁到它们的有形本质、真实性和重要特征。为了促进文化遗产的保护和管理，1999年10月，国际古迹遗址理事会第十二届大会在墨西哥通过了《国际文化旅游宪章——遗产地旅游管理原则》。这个文件对促进关于遗产重要性及其保护的公共意识的提高，管理古迹遗址与旅游业的动态关系，古迹保护和旅游规划给游客带来有价值的体验，社区参与古迹保护和旅游规划，旅游和保护使当地社区受益，以及负责任的旅游推广计划等提出了一系列的原则。文件体现的理念是可持续的旅游与遗产保护形成良性的相互作用和积极的相互促进。

壁画贯穿了人类的历史，它们是一种特别的文化表现形式，其损坏或破坏是文化遗产中重要部分的损失。2003年国际古迹遗址理事会第十四届大会在津巴布韦的维多利亚瀑布市通过了《壁画保护、修复和保存原则》，对壁画的调查，记录，预防性保护、维护和遗址管理，修复，紧急措施，研究和公共信息，专业培训，国际合作等提出了基本原则。

在众多保存下来的物质遗存和昔日社会与文明的无形价值的广阔范围中，选择保护什么、如何保护以及如何向公众展示，这些都是遗产阐释的要素。因此，为遗产"阐释与展示"制定明确的理论依据、标准术语和广泛认可的专业准则的必要性显而易见。2008年10月4日，国际古迹遗址理事会第十六届大会在加拿大魁北克通过了《文化遗产阐释与展示宪章》。该宪章建立了七项主要原则,包括接触渠道和理解、信息源、文脉和背景环境、真实性、可持续性、涵盖与包容面、研究、培训和评估等。

2007年5月24日至28日,"东亚地区文物建筑保护理念与实践国际研讨会"在北京召开。大会通过了《北京文件——关于东亚地区文物建筑保护与修复》,就东亚地区木结构为主的历史建筑的保护与修复,在强调和尊重之前的国际共识文件的基础上,进行了进一步的阐释和讨论,提出了基于东亚历史和文化的真实性和完整性保护的具体措施,特别是档案记录、保养与维修、木结构油漆彩画的表面处理、以及相关的保护管理等方面。《北京文件》对文化多样性的理解及其在东亚文物建筑保护中的具体阐释,对于东亚文物建筑的科学保护是一个积极的推动。

基于诸多国际文件的原则和精神,结合中国的文化背景、理论探索和保护实践,国际古迹遗址理事会中国国家委员会(ICOMOS CHINA,亦称中国古迹遗址保护协会)于2000年制定了《中国文物古迹保护准则》,2015年进行了修订。该准则科学构建了中国文化遗产保护从价值认知到保护原则,再到保护管理措施以及合理利用的完整体系。这个准则已被国际古迹遗址理事会认可。这个准则不仅对于中国文化遗产保护而且对于国际文化遗产保护的发展都具有十分积极的意义。

(4) 自然遗产保护的相关文件

早在20世纪60年代,一些国家和非政府组织关注到日渐消失和退化的水禽湿地栖息地。经过长时间的协商,1971年2月,18个国家的代表在伊朗小城拉姆萨尔举行会议,于2月2日通过了《关于特别是作为水禽栖息地的国际重要湿地公约》,简称《湿地公约》,1975年开始正式实施。这是现代最早的全球政府间的环境协议,后经1982年、1987年、1994年三次修订。《湿地公约》确定了湿地的定义,界定了缔约国的责任,建立了"国际重要湿地名录"这一保护体系,制定了缔约国会议的规则和制度。到2020年,《湿地公约》已有170个缔约国。《湿地公约》对于全球各种类型的重要湿地及其生态系统的保护起到了至关重要的作用。

联合国人类环境会议于1972年6月5日至16日在瑞典斯德哥尔摩召开,6月16日通过了《联合国人类环境会议宣言》,也称《斯德哥尔摩宣言》。宣言制定了共26条基本原则,以激发和指引全世界的人民来保护和改善人类环境。这是人类历史上第一次提出保护和改善人类环境的全球性建议。这次会议还促成了联合国环境规划署(United Nations Environment Programme,UNEP)的设立。

在《斯德哥尔摩宣言》之后,全球对环境问题的认识显著提高。十年后,由于认识到为了今世和后代的利益,保护自然系统、维持自然的平衡和质量以及养护自然资源的极端重要性,联合国第三十七届大会于1982年10月28日通过了《世界自然宪章》。该宪章确立了一系列保护自然的原则,以确保自然系统适当发挥功能,并提出了实施措施。

根据联合国大会1983年的决议,联合国设立了世界环境和发展委员会,基于四年的研究在1987年提交给联合国大会一份报告《我们共同的未来》,也称《布伦特兰报告》,提出了可持续发展的主题。在《斯德哥尔摩宣言》发布20年后,联合国环境与发展会议于1992年6月3日至14日在巴西里约热内卢召开,也被称为"地球高峰会议",或"里约会议"。这次会议于6月14日通过了可持续发展的《21世纪议程》,这个议程意味着一个全新的人类发展方式——可持续发展的开始。通过这次会议,联合国设立了可持续发展委员会。近30年来,可持续发展的理念已延伸到社会、经济、文化发展和资源、环境保护管理的各个层面,并在全球各个领域进行了逐步深入的探讨和实践。

这次高峰会议于6月14日还通过了《关于环境与发展的里约热内卢宣言》,在1972年《斯德哥尔摩宣言》的基础上更进一步,可持续发展的主题贯穿了这份《里约宣言》。

另外,本次会议于6月5日还通过了一项非常重要的公约——《生物多样性公约》。该公约强调生物多样性对进化和保持生物圈的生命维持系统的重要性,生物多样性的保护是全人类的共同关切事项,各国有责任保护生物多样性，并以可持续的方式使用生物资源。这一公约的主要目标是保护生物多样性、持续利用生物资源和公平合理地分享因开发利用遗传资源产生的惠益。该公约制定了保护和持续利用的一般措施、就地保护、移地保护、研究和培训、公众教育和认识、减少不利影响、遗传资源的取得、技术的取得和转让、信息交流、技术和科学合作、生物技术的处理及其惠益的分配、财务机制、缔约国会议等一系列框架。

由于地球气候的变化及其不利影响是人类共同关心的问题，人类活动已大幅增加大气中温室气体的浓度，这使得自然温室效应增强，将引起地球表面和大气进一步增温，并可能对自然生态系统和人类产生不利影响。1992年5月9日，联合国气候变化框架公约政府间委员会在纽约通过了《联合国气候变化框架公约》，目标是根据本公约的各项有关规定，将大气中温室气体的浓度稳定在防止气候系统受到危险的人为干扰的水平上，使得生态系统能够自然地适应气候变化，经济发展能够可持续地进行。在1992年6月的"里约会议"上，《联合国气候变化框架公约》开放签字。其后，基于《联合国气候变化框架公约》，经过政府间谈判，陆续通过了1997年的《京都议定书》和2015年的《巴黎协定》等文件，推动全球共同应对气候变化。

荒漠化和干旱是全球性的问题，影响到世界所有区域，需要国际社会联合行动，防治荒漠化或缓解干旱所带来的影响。1994年6月17日，联合国防治荒漠化公约政府间委员会在巴黎通过了《联合国关于在发生严重干旱和/或荒漠化的国家特别是在非洲防治荒漠化的公约》，简称《防治荒漠化公约》。该公约确立了缔约国的一般义务、受影响国家的义务、发达国家的义务等总则，提出了行动方案、科学和技术合作以及支持措施，并明确了机构章程。

生物圈保护区的概念是1974年由联合国教科文组织人与生物圈计划（Man and the Biosphere Programme of UNESCO，MAB）的工作小组提出的。1995年3月，联合国教科文组织在西班牙塞维利亚举行生物圈保护区国际会议，起草了《世界生物圈保护区网络章程框架》和《生物圈保护区塞维利亚纲要》。这两个文件提交联合国教科文组织第二十八届大会，于1995年11月通过。《塞维利亚纲要》提出了利用生物圈保护自然和文化多样性，作为土地管理和可持续发展途径的样板，开展研究、监测、教育和培训，以及生物圈保护区概念的实施等重大目标。《世界生物圈保护区网络章程框架》确定了生物圈保护区的标准、认定程序、生物圈网络合作、定期评估、机构等框架。

在可持续发展《21世纪议程》和《里约宣言》发布10年后，2002年9月4日，联合国的可持续发展问题世界首脑会议（又称为里约十周年特别会议）在南非约翰内斯堡通过了《可持续发展问题世界首脑会议执行计划》。由于自然资源对于可持续发展至关重要，在该计划中第四章专门讨论保护和管理经济和社会发展的自然资源基础，提出了保护和管理土地、水资源，以及保护海洋、海岸、湿地、山地、森林等各种生态系统，应对气候变化，促进可持续的产业发展等各级行动计划。

2012年6月22日，联合国可持续发展大会（又称为里约二十周年特别会议）在巴西里约热内卢通过了决议《我们希望的未来》，提出了经济、社会、环境的可持续未来的共同愿景，并作出一系列承诺促进和加强可持续发展。

自然景观和地质构造是地球演变的重要见证，在1990年代中期国际上产生了地质公园的概念，它响应了保护和增加地球历史上具有地质意义地区的价值的需要。2004年，在联合国教科文组织的支持下，欧洲地质公园网络的17个成员及8个中国地质公园共同创建了世界地质公园网络（Global Geoparks Network，GGN）。联合国教科文组织第三十八届大会于2015年11月17日在巴黎通过《教科文组织世界地质公园操作指南》，对世界地质公园的标准、地质公园相关的机构规则、世界地质公园的申请程序、能力建设等确立了基本的框架。

作为世界遗产委员会在自然遗产方面的咨询机构，以及在自然遗产的保护领域最为重要的国际组织，世界自然保护联盟就全球的各种保护地进行分类和研究，制定了《保护地管理分类应用指南》，目前的最新分类是 2013 年的版本，将各类保护地分为六大类，即 Ⅰa：严格的自然保护地；Ⅰb：荒野保护地；Ⅱ：国家公园；Ⅲ：自然历史遗迹或地貌；Ⅳ：栖息地 / 物种管理区；Ⅴ：陆地景观 / 海洋景观；Ⅵ：自然资源可持续利用保护地。联合国环境规划署与世界自然保护联盟合作建立了世界保护地数据库（World Database on Protected Areas，WDPA），由联合国环境规划署的世界保护监督中心（World Conservation Monitoring Centre，WCMC）管理，并与世界自然保护联盟的世界保护地委员会（World Commission on Protected Areas，WCPA）以及各国政府和非政府组织、学术界、行业等共同协作。

（5）其他国际文件

农业遗产

在世界许多地方，农民、渔民和牧民利用经过时间检验的技术开发了复杂、多样和适应当地的农业系统，形成了突出的农村景观、全球重要的农业生物多样性和独特的文化。为了应对传统农业系统受到侵蚀的全球趋势，在 2002 年约翰内斯堡召开的可持续发展问题世界首脑会议上，联合国粮农组织提出了全球重要农业遗产系统（Globally Important Agricultural Heritage Systems，GIAHS）的计划。在联合国粮农组织于 2017 年 1 月公布的《全球重要农业遗产系统（GIAHS）》文件中，明确了全球重要农业遗产系统的五项遴选标准，并提出遗产地应制定的可持续性行动计划的框架，以促进全球重要农业遗产系统的动态保护。

无形文化遗产

民间创作是人类共同的遗产，是各国人民的文化特性的重要表现形式，在社会、经济、文化和政治方面具有重要意义。1989 年 11 月 15 日，联合国教科文组织第二十五届大会在巴黎通过了《保护民间创作建议书》。该文件对民间创作的定义、鉴别、保存、保护、传播、维护和国际合作提出了一系列建议。

考虑到非物质文化遗产与物质文化遗产和自然遗产之间的内在相互依存关系，非物质文化遗产的价值和作用是不可估量的，为了在国家和国际层面有效地保护非物质文化遗产，2003 年 10 月 17 日，联合国教科文组织第三十二届大会在巴黎通过了《保护非物质文化遗产公约》[①]。该公约确定了非物质文化遗产的定义，缔约国大会和政府间保护非物质文化遗产委员会的基本章程，提出了在国家一级保护非物质文化遗产的措施，在国际一级建立"人类非物质文化遗产代表作名录"等措施，以及在国际合作与援助、非物质文化遗产基金等方面确立了基本框架。截至 2020 年，共有 180 个国家加入该公约。

和生物多样性一样，文化多样性是人类共同的遗产，应当为了全人类的利益对其加以珍爱和维护。文化在不同时间和空间具有多样形式和内容，体现为人类各民族和各社会文化特征和文化表现形式的独特性和多元性，因此成为各社区、各民族和各国可持续发展的一股主要推动力。为了在全球化进程中确保对文化多样性的尊重并推动其保护，2005 年 10 月 20 日，联合国教科文组织第三十三届大会在巴黎通过了《保护和促进文化表现形式多样性公约》，公约明确了目标、指导原则和相关定义，缔约方的权利、义务，确立了促进和保护文化表现形式多样性的措施、为促进可持续发展而开展合作、文化多样性国际基金以及公约机构等系列框架。

文献遗产

活动图像是各国人民文化特性的一种表达方式，并且由于其教育、文化、艺术、科学和历史价值，

[①] 非物质文化遗产，英文原文为 intangible cultrual heritage，原意为"无形文化遗产"，因公约中文版以及广泛使用的名称是"非物质文化遗产"，故此处仍用此名称。

形成了一个国家文化遗产不可分割的一部分。1980年10月27日,联合国教科文组织二十一届大会在巴黎通过了《关于保护与保存活动图像的建议》。该文件对电影、电视、录像等活动图像作品提出了相关保护措施。

信息和创造性表达方式方面的资源的生产、传播、使用和保存越来越多地采用数字形式,从而产生了一种新的遗产,即数字遗产,而这种遗产正濒临消失的危险,为当代人和后代人保存这种遗产是全世界关注的紧迫问题。2003年10月15日,联合国教科文组织第三十二届大会在巴黎通过了《保存数字遗产宪章》。该宪章就数字遗产的界定、防止数字遗产消失的行动必要性和保护措施、会员国的职责、国际合作等建立了基本框架。

为了防止集体记忆不可逆转的损失,联合国教科文组织于1992年开始设立"世界记忆"(Memory of the World, MoW)计划,目标是保护文献遗产,促进其保存、获取和传播,并提高公众对文献遗产重要性和保护文献遗产必要性的认识。最新的《通用指南》是2017年12月批准的版本。指南对世界记忆计划及其目标、战略和架构进行了阐释,界定了文献遗产的相关定义,并明确了世界记忆名录的登录标准,包括真实性和完整性,首要标准和比较标准等。

文献遗产记录了人类思想与活动的演变和语言、文化、民族及其对世界认识的发展。随着时间的推移,大量文献遗产已经因为自然或人为灾害而消失,或者因为技术的快速变革而逐渐变得不可获取。为了保护、保存、获取、提高文献遗产的价值,基于之前的文件和行动基础,2015年11月17日,联合国教科文组织第三十八届大会在巴黎通过了《关于保存和获取包括数字遗产在内的文献遗产的建议书》。该建议书对文献遗产的确认、保存、获取,国家的政策措施,以及国家和国际合作等提出了框架建议。

3. 结语

自1972年《世界遗产公约》签署以来,遗产保护在全球范围开展已近半个世纪。从自然和文化遗产保护相关国际文件的发展脉络我们可以看到,遗产保护的广度和深度,理论和实践拓展的范围,已逐步扩大,国际社会对遗产保护的理念和认识逐步加深,多个保护体系也得到了建立、促进和发展。从历史的遗存到自然的遗存;从不可移动的遗产到可移动的遗产;从以建筑、考古遗产为中心到对各类遗产的关注和研究;从单一的遗产到历史地区、文化线路的整体保护;从以文化遗产为主到强调自然遗产的保护;从自然和文化遗产的分野到自然与文化遗产的融合;从有形遗产到无形遗产;从实体遗产到人类记忆;这些发展和进步,不仅仅是国际认知和共识的扩展,更是人类对于历史和自然其过去、现在和未来的重新审视,是对可持续发展的深刻思考,也是和谐发展的未来保证。

世界遗产

保护世界文化和自然遗产公约[①]

（联合国教科文组织第十七届大会 1972 年 11 月 16 日在巴黎通过）

联合国教科文组织大会于 1972 年 10 月 17 日至 11 月 21 日在巴黎举行的第十七届会议，

注意到文化遗产和自然遗产越来越受到破坏的威胁，一方面因年久腐变所致，同时变化中的社会和经济条件使情况恶化，造成更加难以对付的损害或破坏现象；

考虑到任何文化或自然遗产的坏变或丢失都有使全世界遗产枯竭的有害影响；

考虑到国家一级保护这类遗产的工作往往不很完善，原因在于这项工作需要大量手段而列为保护对象的财产的所在国却不具备充足的经济、科学和技术力量；

回顾本组织《组织法》规定，本组织将通过保存和维护世界遗产和建议有关国家订立必要的国际公约来维护、增进和传播知识；

考虑到现有关于文化和自然遗产的国际公约、建议和决议表明，保护不论属于哪国人民的这类罕见且无法替代的财产，对全世界人民都很重要；

考虑到部分文化或自然遗产具有突出的重要性，因而需作为全人类世界遗产的一部分加以保护；

考虑到鉴于威胁这类遗产的新危险的规模和严重性，整个国际社会有责任通过提供集体性援助来参与保护具有突出的普遍价值的文化和自然遗产；这种援助尽管不能代替有关国家采取的行动，但将成为它的有效补充；

考虑到为此有必要通过采用公约形式的新规定，以便为集体保护具有突出的普遍价值的文化和自然遗产建立一个根据现代科学方法制定的永久性的有效制度；

在大会第十六届会议上，曾决定应就此问题制订一项国际公约，于 1972 年 11 月 16 日通过本公约。

Ⅰ. 文化和自然遗产的定义

第 1 条

在本公约中，以下各项为"文化遗产"：

文物：从历史、艺术或科学角度看具有突出的普遍价值的建筑物、碑雕和碑画、具有考古性质成份或结构、铭文、窟洞以及联合体；

建筑群：从历史、艺术或科学角度看在建筑式样、分布均匀或与环境景色结合方面具有突出的普遍价值的单立或连接的建筑群；

遗址：从历史、审美、人种学或人类学角度看具有突出的普遍价值的人类工程或自然与人联合工程以及考古地址等地方。

第 2 条

在本公约中，以下各项为"自然遗产"：

[①] 引自：世界遗产中心（WHC）官网，whc.unesco.org。

从审美或科学角度看具有突出的普遍价值的由物质和生物结构或这类结构群组成的自然面貌；

从科学或保护角度看具有突出的普遍价值的地质和自然地理结构以及明确划为受威胁的动物和植物生境区；

从科学、保护或自然美角度看具有突出的普遍价值的天然名胜或明确划分的自然区域。

第 3 条

本公约缔约国均可自行确定和划分上面第 1 条和第 2 条中提及的、本国领土内的文化和自然财产。

Ⅱ. 文化和自然遗产的国家保护和国际保护

第 4 条

本公约缔约国均承认，保证第 1 条和第 2 条中提及的、本国领土内的文化和自然遗产的确定、保护、保存、展出和遗传后代，主要是有关国家的责任。该国将为此目的竭尽全力，最大限度地利用本国资源，必要时利用所能获得的国际援助和合作，特别是财政、艺术、科学及技术方面的援助和合作。

第 5 条

为保证为保护、保存和展出本国领土内的文化和自然遗产采取积极有效的措施，本公约各缔约国应视本国具体情况尽力做到以下几点：

（a）通过一项旨在使文化和自然遗产在社会生活中起一定作用并把遗产保护工作纳入全面规划计划的总政策；

（b）如本国内尚未建立负责文化和自然遗产的保护、保存和展出的机构，则建立一个或几个此类机构，配备适当的工作人员和为履行其职能所需的手段；

（c）发展科学和技术研究，并制订出能够抵抗威胁本国文化或自然遗产的危险的实际方法；

（d）采取为确定、保护、保存、展出和恢复这类遗产所需的适当的法律、科学、技术、行政和财政措施；

（e）促进建立或发展有关保护、保存和展出文化和自然遗产的国家或地区培训中心，并鼓励这方面的科学研究。

第 6 条

1. 本公约缔约国，在充分尊重第 1 条和第 2 条中提及的文化和自然遗产的所在国的主权，并不使国家立法规定的财产权受到损害的同时，承认这类遗产是世界遗产的一部分，因此，整个国际社会有责任合作予以保护。

2. 缔约国根据本公约的规定，应有关国家的要求帮助该国确定、保护、保存和展出第 11 条第 2 和 4 段中提及的文化和自然遗产。

3. 本公约各缔约国不得故意采取任何可能直接或间接损害本公约其他缔约国领土的、第 1 条和第 2 条中提及的文化和自然遗产的措施。

第 7 条

在本公约中，世界文化和自然遗产的国际保护应被理解为建立一个旨在支持本公约缔约国保存和确定这类遗产的努力的国际合作和援助系统。

Ⅲ. 保护世界文化和自然遗产政府间委员会

第 8 条

1. 在联合国教科文组织内，要建立一个保护具有突出的普遍价值的文化和自然遗产政府间委员会，称为"世界遗产委员会"。委员会由联合国教科文组织大会常会期间召集的本公约缔约国大会选出的 15 个缔约国组成。委员会成员国的数目将在至少 40 个缔约国实施本公约之后的大会常会之日起增至 21 个。

2. 委员会委员的选举须保证均衡地代表世界的不同地区和不同文化。
3. 国际文物保护与修复研究中心（罗马中心）的一名代表、国际古迹遗址理事会的一名代表以及国际自然及资源保护联盟的一名代表可以咨询者身份出席委员会的会议，此外，应联合国教科文组织大会常会期间举行大会的本公约缔约国提出的要求，其他具有类似目标的政府间或非政府组织的代表亦可以咨询者身份出席委员会的会议。

第9条

1. 世界遗产委员会成员国的任期自当选之应届大会常会结束时起至应届大会后第三次常会闭幕时止。
2. 但是，第一次选举时指定的委员中，有三分之一的委员的任期应于当选应届大会后第一次常会闭幕时截止；同时指定的委员中，另有三分之一的委员的任期应于当选之应届大会后第二次常会闭幕时截止。这些委员由联合国教科文组织大会主席在第一次选举后抽签决定。
3. 委员会成员国应选派在文化或自然遗产方面有资历的人员担任代表。

第10条

1. 世界遗产委员会应通过其议事规则。
2. 委员会可随时邀请公共或私立组织或个人参加其会议，以就具体问题进行磋商。
3. 委员会可设立它认为为履行其职能所需的咨询机构。

第11条

1. 本公约各缔约国应尽力向世界遗产委员会递交一份关于本国领土内适于列入本条第2段所述《世界遗产目录》的、组成文化和自然遗产的财产的清单。这份清单不应看作是齐全的，它应包括有关财产的所在地及其意义的文献资料。
2. 根据缔约国按照第1段规定递交的清单，委员会应制订、更新和出版一份《世界遗产目录》，其中所列的均为本公约第1条和第2条确定的文化遗产和自然遗产的组成部分，也是委员会按照自己制订的标准认为是具有突出的普遍价值的财产。一份最新目录应至少每两年分发一次。
3. 把一项财产列入《世界遗产目录》需征得有关国家同意。当几个国家对某一领土的主权或管辖权均提出要求时，将该领土内的一项财产列入《目录》不得损害争端各方的权利。
4. 委员会应在必要时制订、更新和出版一份《处于危险的世界遗产目录》，其中所列财产均为载于《世界遗产目录》之中、需要采取重大活动加以保护并为根据本公约要求给予援助的财产。《处于危险的世界遗产目录》应载有这类活动的费用概算，并只可包括文化和自然遗产中受到下述严重的特殊危险威胁的财产，这些危险是：蜕变加剧、大规模公共或私人工程、城市或旅游业迅速发展计划造成的消失威胁；土地的使用变动或易主造成的破坏；未知原因造成的重大变化；随意摈弃；武装冲突的爆发或威胁；灾害和灾变；严重火灾、地震、山崩；火山爆发；水位变动、洪水和海啸等。委员会在紧急需要时可随时在《处于危险的世界遗产目录》中增列新的条目并立即予以发表。
5. 委员会应确定属于文化或自然遗产的财产可被列入本条第2和4段中提及的目录所依据的标准。
6. 委员会在拒绝一项要求列入本条第2和4段中提及的目录之一的申请之前，应与有关文化或自然财产所在缔约国磋商。
7. 委员会经与有关国家商定，应协调和鼓励为拟订本条第2和4段中提及的目录所需进行的研究。

第12条

未被列入第11条第2和4段提及的两个目录的属于文化或自然遗产的财产，决非意味着在列入这些目录的目的之外的其他领域不具有突出的普遍价值。

第13条

1. 世界遗产委员会应接收并研究本公约缔约国就已经列入或可能适于列入第11条第2和4段中提及的目录的本国领土内成为文化或自然遗产的财产要求国际援助而递交的申请。这种申请的目的可能是保证这类财产得到保护、保存、展出或恢复。

2. 本条第 1 段中提及的国际援助申请还可能涉及鉴定哪些财产属于第 1 和 2 条所确定的文化或自然遗产，当初步调查表明此项调查值得进行下去。

3. 委员会应就对这些申请所需采取的行动作出决定，必要时应确定其援助的性质和程度，并授权以它的名义与有关政府作出必要的安排。

4. 委员会应制订其活动的优先顺序并在进行这项工作时应考虑到需予保护的财产对世界文化和自然遗产各具的重要性、对最能代表一种自然环境或世界各国人民的才华和历史的财产给予国际援助的必要性、所需开展工作的迫切性、拥有受到威胁的财产的国家现有的资源、特别是这些国家利用本国资源保护这类财产的能力大小。

5. 委员会应制订、更新和发表已给予国际援助的财产目录。

6. 委员会应就本公约第 15 条下设立的基金的资金使用问题作出决定。委员会应设法增加这类资金，并为此目的采取一切有益的措施。

7. 委员会应与拥有与本公约目标相似的目标的国际和国家级政府组织和非政府组织合作。委员会为实施其计划和项目，可约请这类组织；特别是国际文物保护与修复研究中心（罗马中心）、国际古迹遗址理事会和国际自然及自然资源保护联盟并可约请公共和私立机构与个人。

8. 委员会的决定应经出席及参加表决的委员的三分之二多数通过。委员会委员的多数构成法定人数。

第 14 条

1. 世界遗产委员会应由联合国教科文组织总干事任命组成的一个秘书处协助工作。

2. 联合国教科文组织总干事应尽可能充分利用国际文物保护与修复研究中心（罗马中心）、国际古迹遗址理事会和国际自然及自然资源保护联盟在各自职权范围内提供的服务，以为委员会准备文件资料，制订委员会会议议程，并负责执行委员会的决定。

Ⅳ. 保护世界文化和自然基金

第 15 条

1. 现设立一项保护具有突出的普遍价值的世界文化和自然遗产基金，称为"世界遗产基金"。

2. 根据联合国教科文组织《财务条例》的规定，此项基金应构成一项信托基金。

3. 基金的资金采源应包括：

（a）本公约缔约国义务捐款和自愿捐款；

（b）下列方面可能提供的捐款、赠款或遗赠：

（ⅰ）其他国家；

（ⅱ）联合国教科文组织、联合国系统的其他组织（特别是联合国开发计划署）或其他政府间组织；

（ⅲ）公共或私立机构或个人；

（c）基金款项所得利息；

（d）募捐的资金和为本基金组织的活动的所得收入；

（e）世界遗产委员会拟订的基金条例所认可的所有其他资金。

4. 对基金的捐款和向委员会提供的其他形式的援助只能用于委员会限定的目的。委员会可接受仅用于某个计划或项目的捐款，但以委员会业已决定实施该计划或项目为条件，对基金的捐款不得带有政治条件。

第 16 条

1. 在不影响任何自愿补充捐款的情况下；本公约缔约国每两年定期向世界遗产基金纳款，本公约缔约国大会应在联合国教科文组织大会届会期间开会确定适用于所有缔约国的一个统一的纳款额百分比，缔约国大会关于此问题的决定，需由未作本条第2段中所述声明的、出席及参加表决的缔约国的多数通过。本公约缔约国的义务纳款在任何情况下都不得超过对联合国教科文组织正常预算纳款的百分之一。

2. 然而，本公约经第31条或第32条中提及的国家均可在交存批准书、接受书或加入书时声明不受本条第1段的约束。

3. 已作本条第2段中所述声明的本公约缔约国可随时通过通知联合国教科文组织总干事收回所作声明。然而，收回声明之举在紧接的一届本公约缔约国大会之日以前不得影响该国的义务纳款。

4. 为使委员会得以有效地规划其活动，已作本条第2段中所述声明的本公约缔约国应至少每两年定期纳款，纳款不得少于它们如受本条第1段规定约束所须交纳的款额。

5. 凡拖延交付当年和前一日历年的义务纳款或自愿捐款的本公约缔约国不能当选为世界遗产委员会成员，但此项规定不适用于第一次选举。属于上述情况但已当选委员会成员的缔约国的任期应在本公约第8条第1段规定的选举之时截止。

第17条

本公约缔约国应考虑或鼓励设立旨在为保护本公约第1和2条中所确定的文化和自然遗产募捐的国家、公共及私立基金会或协会。

第18条

本公约缔约国应对在联合国教科文组织赞助下为世界遗产基金所组织的国际募捐运动给予援助。它们应为第15条第3段中提及的机构为此目的所进行的募款活动提供便利。

V. 国际援助的条件和安排

第19条

凡本公约缔约国均可要求对本国领土内组成具有突出的普遍价值的文化或自然遗产之财产给予国际援助。它在递交申请时还应按照第21条规定所拥有的有助于委员会作出决定的文件资料。

第20条

除第13条第2段、第22条（c）分段和第23条所述情况外，本公约规定提供的国际援助仅限于世界遗产委员会业已决定或可能决定列入第11条第2和4段中所述目录的文化和自然遗产的财产。

第21条

1. 世界遗产委员会应制订对向它提交的国际援助申请的审议程序，并应确定申请应包括的内容，即打算开展的活动、必要的工程、工程的预计费用和紧急程度以及申请国的资源不能满足所有开支的原因所在。这类申请须尽可能附有专家报告。

2. 对因遭受灾难或自然灾害而提出的申请，由于可能需要开展紧急工作，委员会应立即给予优先审议，委员会应掌握一笔应急储备金。

3. 委员会在作出决定之前，应进行它认为必要的研究和磋商。

第22条

世界遗产委员会提供的援助可采取下述形式：

（a）研究在保护、保存、展出和恢复本公约第11条第2和4段所确定的文化和自然遗产方面所产生的艺术、科学和技术性问题；

（b）提供专家、技术人员和熟练工人，以保证正确地进行已批准的工作；

（c）在各级培训文化和自然遗产的鉴定、保护、保存、展出和恢复方面的工作人员和专家；

（d）提供有关国家不具备或无法获得的设备；

（e）提供可长期偿还的低息或无息贷款；
（f）在例外和特殊情况下提供无偿补助金。

第 23 条

世界遗产委员会还可向培训文化和自然遗产的鉴定、保护、保存、展出和恢复方面的各级工作人员和专家的国家或地区中心提供国际援助。

第 24 条

在提供大规模的国际援助之前，应先进行周密的科学、经济和技术研究。这些研究应考虑采用保护、保存、展出和恢复自然和文化遗产方面最先进的技术，并应与本公约的目标相一致。这些研究还应探讨合理利用有关国家现有资源的手段。

第 25 条

原则上，国际社会只担负必要工程的部分费用。除非本国资源不许可，受益于国际援助的国家承担的费用应构成用于各项计划或项目的资金的主要份额。

第 26 条

世界遗产委员会和受援国应在他们签订的协定中确定享有根据本公约规定提供的国际援助的计划或项目的实施条件。应由接受这类国际援助的国家负责按照协定制订的条件对如此卫护的财产继续加以保护、保存和展出。

Ⅵ. 教育计划

第 27 条

1. 本公约缔约国应通过一切适当手段，特别是教育和宣传计划，努力增强本国人民对本公约第 1 和 2 条中确定的文化和自然遗产的赞赏和尊重。
2. 缔约国应使公众广泛了解对这类遗产造成威胁的危险和根据本公约进行的活动。

第 28 条

接受根据本公约提供的国际援助的缔约国应采取适当措施，使人们了解接受援助的财产的重要性和国际援助所发挥的作用。

Ⅶ. 报告

第 29 条

1. 本公约缔约国在按照联合国教科文组织大会确定的日期和方式向该组织大会递交的报告中，应提供有关它们为实行本公约所通过的法律和行政规定和采取的其他行动的情况，并详述在这方面获得的经验。
2. 应提请世界遗产委员会注意这些报告。
3. 委员会应在联合国教科文组织大会的每届常会上递交 7 份关于其活动的报告。

Ⅷ. 最后条款

第 30 条

本公约以阿拉伯文、英文、法文、俄文和西班牙文拟订，五种文本同一作准。

第 31 条

1. 本公约应由联合国教科文组织会员国根据各自的宪法程序予以批准或接受。
2. 批准书或接受书应交存联合国教科文组织总干事。

第 32 条

1. 所有非联合国教科文组织会员的国家，经该组织大会邀请均可加入本公约。
2. 向联合国教科文组织总干事交存一份加入书后，加入方才有效。

第 33 条

本公约须在第二十份批准书、接受书或加入书交存之日的三个月之后生效，但这仅涉及在该日或之首交存各自批准书、接受书或加入书的国家。就任何其他国家而言，本公约应在这些国家交存其批准书、接受书或加入书的三个月之后生效。

第 34 条

下述规定须应用于拥有联邦制或非单一立宪制的本公约缔约国：

（a）关于在联邦或中央立法机构的法律管辖下实施的本公约规定，联邦或中央政府的义务应与非联邦国家的缔约国的义务相同；

（b）关于在无须按照联邦立宪制采取立法措施的联邦各个国家、地区、省或州法律管辖下实施的本公约规定，联邦政府应将这些规定连同其关于予以通过的建议一并通告各个国家、地区、省或州的主管当局。

第 35 条

1. 本公约缔约国均可通告废除本公约。
2. 废约通告应以一份书面文件交存联合国教科文组织的总干事。
3. 公约的废除应在接到废约通告一年后生效，废约在生效日之前不得影响退约国承担的财政义务。

第 36 条

联合国教科文组织总干事应将第 31 和 32 条规定交存的所有批准书、接受书和加入书和第 35 条规定的废约等事通告本组织会员国、第 32 条中提及的非本组织会员的国家以及联合国。

第 37 条

1. 本公约可由联合国教科文组织的大会修订。但任何修订只对将成为修订的公约缔约国具有约束力。
2. 如大会通过一项全部或部分修订本公约的新公约，除非新公约另有规定，本公约应从新的修订公约生效之日起停止批准、接受或加入。

第 38 条

按照《联合国宪章》第 102 条，本公约须应联合国教科文组织总干事的要求在联合国秘书处登记。

1972 年 11 月 23 日订于巴黎，两个正式文本均有大会第十七届会议主席和联合国教科文组织总干事的签字，由联合国教科文组织存档，并将证明无误之副本发送第 31 条和第 32 条述之所有国家以及联合国。

前文系联合国教科文组织大会在巴黎举行的，于一九七二年十一月二十一日宣布闭幕的第十七届会议通过的《公约》正式文本。

一九七二年十一月二十三日签字，以昭信守。

Convention concerning the Protection of the World Cultural and Natural Heritage[1]

Adopted by the UNESCO General Conference at its 17th Session, Paris, 16 November 1972

The General Conference of the United Nations Educational, Scientific and Cultural Organization meeting in Paris from 17 October to 21 November 1972, at its seventeenth session,

Noting that the cultural heritage and the natural heritage are increasingly threatened with destruction not only by the traditional causes of decay, but also by changing social and economic conditions which aggravate the situation with even more formidable phenomena of damage or destruction,

Considering that deterioration or disappearance of any item of the cultural or natural heritage constitutes a harmful impoverishment of the heritage of all the nations of the world,

Considering that protection of this heritage at the national level often remains incomplete because of the scale of the resources which it requires and of the insufficient economic, scientific, and technological resources of the country where the property to be protected is situated,

Recalling that the Constitution of the Organization provides that it will maintain, increase, and diffuse knowledge by assuring the conservation and protection of the world's heritage, and recommending to the nations concerned the necessary international conventions,

Considering that the existing international conventions, recommendations and resolutions concerning cultural and natural property demonstrate the importance, for all the peoples of the world, of safeguarding this unique and irreplaceable property, to whatever people it may belong,

Considering that parts of the cultural or natural heritage are of outstanding interest and therefore need to be preserved as part of the world heritage of mankind as a whole,

Considering that, in view of the magnitude and gravity of the new dangers threatening them, it is incumbent on the international community as a whole to participate in the protection of the cultural and natural heritage of outstanding universal value, by the granting of collective assistance which, although not taking the place of action by the State concerned, will serve as an efficient complement thereto,

Considering that it is essential for this purpose to adopt new provisions in the form of a convention establishing an effective system of collective protection of the cultural and natural heritage of outstanding universal value, organized on a permanent basis and in accordance with modern scientific methods,

Having decided at its sixteenth session, that this question should be made the subject of an international convention,

---

[1] from: UNESCO World Heritage Center, whc.unesco.org

Adopts this sixteenth day of November 1972 this Convention.

I. DEFINITION OF THE CULTURAL AND NATURAL HERITAGE

Article 1

For the purpose of this Convention, the following shall be considered as "cultural heritage":

monuments: architectural works, works of monumental sculpture and painting, elements or structures of an archaeological nature, inscriptions, cave dwellings and combinations of features, which are of outstanding universal value from the point of view of history, art or science;

groups of buildings: groups of separate or connected buildings which, because of their architecture, their homogeneity or their place in the landscape, are of outstanding universal value from the point of view of history, art or science;

sites: works of man or the combined works of nature and man, and areas including archaeological sites which are of outstanding universal value from the historical, aesthetic, ethnological or anthropological point of view.

Article 2

For the purposes of this Convention, the following shall be considered as "natural heritage":

natural features consisting of physical and biological formations or groups of such formations, which are of outstanding universal value from the aesthetic or scientific point of view;

geological and physiographical formations and precisely delineated areas which constitute the habitat of threatened species of animals and plants of outstanding universal value from the point of view of science or conservation;

natural sites or precisely delineated natural areas of outstanding universal value from the point of view of science, conservation or natural beauty.

Article 3

It is for each State Party to this Convention to identify and delineate the different properties situated on its territory mentioned in Articles 1 and 2 above.

II. NATIONAL PROTECTION AND INTERNATIONAL PROTECTION OF THE CULTURAL AND NATURAL HERITAGE

Article 4

Each State Party to this Convention recognizes that the duty of ensuring the identification, protection, conservation, presentation and transmission to future generations of the cultural and natural heritage referred to in Articles 1 and 2 and situated on its territory, belongs primarily to that State. It will do all it can to this end, to the utmost of its own resources and, where appropriate, with any international assistance and co-operation, in particular, financial, artistic, scientific and technical, which it may be able to obtain.

Article 5

To ensure that effective and active measures are taken for the protection, conservation and presentation of the cultural and natural heritage situated on its territory, each State Party to this Convention shall endeavor, in so far as possible, and as appropriate for each country:

(a) to adopt a general policy which aims to give the cultural and natural heritage a function in the life of the community and to integrate the protection of that heritage into comprehensive planning programmes;

(b) to set up within its territories, where such services do not exist, one or more services for the protection, conservation and presentation of the cultural and natural heritage with an appropriate staff and possessing the means to discharge their functions;

(c) to develop scientific and technical studies and research and to work out such operating methods as will make the State capable of counteracting the dangers that threaten its cultural or natural heritage;

(d) to take the appropriate legal, scientific, technical, administrative and financial measures necessary for the identification, protection, conservation, presentation and rehabilitation of this heritage; and

(e) to foster the establishment or development of national or regional centres for training in the protection, conservation and presentation of the cultural and natural heritage and to encourage scientific research in this field.

Article 6

1. Whilst fully respecting the sovereignty of the States on whose territory the cultural and natural heritage mentioned in Articles 1 and 2 is situated, and without prejudice to property right provided by national legislation, the States Parties to this Convention recognize that such heritage constitutes a world heritage for whose protection it is the duty of the international community as a whole to co-operate.

2. The States Parties undertake, in accordance with the provisions of this Convention, to give their help in the identification, protection, conservation and presentation of the cultural and natural heritage referred to in paragraphs 2 and 4 of Article 11 if the States on whose territory it is situated so request.

3. Each State Party to this Convention undertakes not to take any deliberate measures which might damage directly or indirectly the cultural and natural heritage referred to in Articles 1 and 2 situated on the territory of other States Parties to this Convention.

Article 7

For the purpose of this Convention, international protection of the world cultural and natural heritage shall be understood to mean the establishment of a system of international co-operation and assistance designed to support States Parties to the Convention in their efforts to conserve and identify that heritage.

III. INTERGOVERNMENTAL COMMITTEE FOR THE PROTECTION OF THE WORLD CULTURAL AND NATURAL HERITAGE

Article 8

1. An Intergovernmental Committee for the Protection of the Cultural and Natural Heritage of Outstanding Universal Value, called "the World Heritage Committee", is hereby established within the United Nations Educational, Scientific and Cultural Organization. It shall be composed of 15 States Parties to the Convention, elected by States Parties to the Convention meeting in general assembly during the ordinary session of the General Conference of the United Nations Educational, Scientific and Cultural Organization. The number of States members of the Committee shall be increased to 21 as from the date of the ordinary session of the General Conference following the entry into force of this Convention for at least 40 States.

2. Election of members of the Committee shall ensure an equitable representation of the different regions and cultures of the world.

3. A representative of the International Centre for the Study of the Preservation and Restoration of Cultural Property (Rome Centre), a representative of the International Council of Monuments and Sites (ICOMOS) and a representative of the International Union for Conservation of Nature and Natural Resources (IUCN), to whom

may be added, at the request of States Parties to the Convention meeting in general assembly during the ordinary sessions of the General Conference of the United Nations Educational, Scientific and Cultural Organization, representatives of other intergovernmental or non-governmental organizations, with similar objectives, may attend the meetings of the Committee in an advisory capacity.

Article 9

1. The term of office of States members of the World Heritage Committee shall extend from the end of the ordinary session of the General Conference during which they are elected until the end of its third subsequent ordinary session.

2. The term of office of one-third of the members designated at the time of the first election shall, however, cease at the end of the first ordinary session of the General Conference following that at which they were elected; and the term of office of a further third of the members designated at the same time shall cease at the end of the second ordinary session of the General Conference following that at which they were elected. The names of these members shall be chosen by lot by the President of the General Conference of the United Nations Educational, Scientific and Cultural Organization after the first election.

3. States members of the Committee shall choose as their representatives persons qualified in the field of the cultural or natural heritage.

Article 10

1. The World Heritage Committee shall adopt its Rules of Procedure.

2. The Committee may at any time invite public or private organizations or individuals to participate in its meetings for consultation on particular problems.

3. The Committee may create such consultative bodies as it deems necessary for the performance of its functions.

Article 11

1. Every State Party to this Convention shall, in so far as possible, submit to the World Heritage Committee an inventory of property forming part of the cultural and natural heritage, situated in its territory and suitable for inclusion in the list provided for in paragraph 2 of this Article. This inventory, which shall not be considered exhaustive, shall include documentation about the location of the property in question and its significance.

2. On the basis of the inventories submitted by States in accordance with paragraph 1, the Committee shall establish, keep up to date and publish, under the title of "World Heritage List", a list of properties forming part of the cultural heritage and natural heritage, as defined in Articles 1 and 2 of this Convention, which it considers as having outstanding universal value in terms of such criteria as it shall have established. An updated list shall be distributed at least every two years.

3. The inclusion of a property in the World Heritage List requires the consent of the State concerned. The inclusion of a property situated in a territory, sovereignty or jurisdiction over which is claimed by more than one State shall in no way prejudice the rights of the parties to the dispute.

4. The Committee shall establish, keep up to date and publish, whenever circumstances shall so require, under the title of "list of World Heritage in Danger", a list of the property appearing in the World Heritage List for the conservation of which major operations are necessary and for which assistance has been requested under this Convention. This list shall contain an estimate of the cost of such operations. The list may include only such property forming part of the cultural and natural heritage as is threatened by serious and specific dangers, such

as the threat of disappearance caused by accelerated deterioration, large-scale public or private projects or rapid urban or tourist development projects; destruction caused by changes in the use or ownership of the land; major alterations due to unknown causes; abandonment for any reason whatsoever; the outbreak or the threat of an armed conflict; calamities and cataclysms; serious fires, earthquakes, landslides; volcanic eruptions; changes in water level, floods and tidal waves. The Committee may at any time, in case of urgent need, make a new entry in the List of World Heritage in Danger and publicize such entry immediately.

5. The Committee shall define the criteria on the basis of which a property belonging to the cultural or natural heritage may be included in either of the lists mentioned in paragraphs 2 and 4 of this article.

6. Before refusing a request for inclusion in one of the two lists mentioned in paragraphs 2 and 4 of this article, the Committee shall consult the State Party in whose territory the cultural or natural property in question is situated.

7. The Committee shall, with the agreement of the States concerned, co-ordinate and encourage the studies and research needed for the drawing up of the lists referred to in paragraphs 2 and 4 of this article.

Article 12

The fact that a property belonging to the cultural or natural heritage has not been included in either of the two lists mentioned in paragraphs 2 and 4 of Article 11 shall in no way be construed to mean that it does not have an outstanding universal value for purposes other than those resulting from inclusion in these lists.

Article 13

1. The World Heritage Committee shall receive and study requests for international assistance formulated by States Parties to this Convention with respect to property forming part of the cultural or natural heritage, situated in their territories, and included or potentially suitable for inclusion in the lists mentioned referred to in paragraphs 2 and 4 of Article 11. The purpose of such requests may be to secure the protection, conservation, presentation or rehabilitation of such property.

2. Requests for international assistance under paragraph 1 of this article may also be concerned with identification of cultural or natural property defined in Articles 1 and 2, when preliminary investigations have shown that further inquiries would be justified.

3. The Committee shall decide on the action to be taken with regard to these requests, determine where appropriate, the nature and extent of its assistance, and authorize the conclusion, on its behalf, of the necessary arrangements with the government concerned.

4. The Committee shall determine an order of priorities for its operations. It shall in so doing bear in mind the respective importance for the world cultural and natural heritage of the property requiring protection, the need to give international assistance to the property most representative of a natural environment or of the genius and the history of the peoples of the world, the urgency of the work to be done, the resources available to the States on whose territory the threatened property is situated and in particular the extent to which they are able to safeguard such property by their own means.

5. The Committee shall draw up, keep up to date and publicize a list of property for which international assistance has been granted.

6. The Committee shall decide on the use of the resources of the Fund established under Article 15 of this Convention. It shall seek ways of increasing these resources and shall take all useful steps to this end.

7. The Committee shall co-operate with international and national governmental and non-governmental organizations having objectives similar to those of this Convention. For the implementation of its programmes and

projects, the Committee may call on such organizations, particularly the International Centre for the Study of the Preservation and Restoration of Cultural Property (the Rome Centre), the International Council of Monuments and Sites (ICOMOS) and the International Union for Conservation of Nature and Natural Resources (IUCN), as well as on public and private bodies and individuals.

8. Decisions of the Committee shall be taken by a majority of two-thirds of its members present and voting. A majority of the members of the Committee shall constitute a quorum.

Article 14

1. The World Heritage Committee shall be assisted by a Secretariat appointed by the Director-General of the United Nations Educational, Scientific and Cultural Organization.

2. The Director-General of the United Nations Educational, Scientific and Cultural Organization, utilizing to the fullest extent possible the services of the International Centre for the Study of the Preservation and the Restoration of Cultural Property (the Rome Centre), the International Council of Monuments and Sites (ICOMOS) and the International Union for Conservation of Nature and Natural Resources (IUCN) in their respective areas of competence and capability, shall prepare the Committee's documentation and the agenda of its meetings and shall have the responsibility for the implementation of its decisions.

IV. FUND FOR THE PROTECTION OF THE WORLD CULTURAL AND NATURAL HERITAGE

Article 15

1. A Fund for the Protection of the World Cultural and Natural Heritage of Outstanding Universal Value, called "the World Heritage Fund", is hereby established.

2. The Fund shall constitute a trust fund, in conformity with the provisions of the Financial Regulations of the United Nations Educational, Scientific and Cultural Organization.

3. The resources of the Fund shall consist of:

(a) compulsory and voluntary contributions made by States Parties to this Convention;

(b) contributions, gifts or bequests which may be made by:

 (i) other States;

 (ii) the United Nations Educational, Scientific and Cultural Organization, other organizations of the United Nations system, particularly the United Nations Development Programme or other intergovernmental organizations;

 (iii) public or private bodies or individuals;

(c) any interest due on the resources of the Fund;

(d) funds raised by collections and receipts from events organized for the benefit of the fund; and

(e) all other resources authorized by the Fund's regulations, as drawn up by the World Heritage Committee.

4. Contributions to the Fund and other forms of assistance made available to the Committee may be used only for such purposes as the Committee shall define. The Committee may accept contributions to be used only for a certain programme or project, provided that the Committee shall have decided on the implementation of such programme or project. No political conditions may be attached to contributions made to the Fund.

Article 16

1. Without prejudice to any supplementary voluntary contribution, the States Parties to this Convention

undertake to pay regularly, every two years, to the World Heritage Fund, contributions, the amount of which, in the form of a uniform percentage applicable to all States, shall be determined by the General Assembly of States Parties to the Convention, meeting during the sessions of the General Conference of the United Nations Educational, Scientific and Cultural Organization. This decision of the General Assembly requires the majority of the States Parties present and voting, which have not made the declaration referred to in paragraph 2 of this Article. In no case shall the compulsory contribution of States Parties to the Convention exceed 1% of the contribution to the regular budget of the United Nations Educational, Scientific and Cultural Organization.

2. However, each State referred to in Article 31 or in Article 32 of this Convention may declare, at the time of the deposit of its instrument of ratification, acceptance or accession, that it shall not be bound by the provisions of paragraph 1 of this Article.

3. A State Party to the Convention which has made the declaration referred to in paragraph 2 of this Article may at any time withdraw the said declaration by notifying the Director-General of the United Nations Educational, Scientific and Cultural Organization. However, the withdrawal of the declaration shall not take effect in regard to the compulsory contribution due by the State until the date of the subsequent General Assembly of States parties to the Convention.

4. In order that the Committee may be able to plan its operations effectively, the contributions of States Parties to this Convention which have made the declaration referred to in paragraph 2 of this Article, shall be paid on a regular basis, at least every two years, and should not be less than the contributions which they should have paid if they had been bound by the provisions of paragraph 1 of this Article.

5. Any State Party to the Convention which is in arrears with the payment of its compulsory or voluntary contribution for the current year and the calendar year immediately preceding it shall not be eligible as a Member of the World Heritage Committee, although this provision shall not apply to the first election.

The terms of office of any such State which is already a member of the Committee shall terminate at the time of the elections provided for in Article 8, paragraph 1 of this Convention.

Article 17

The States Parties to this Convention shall consider or encourage the establishment of national public and private foundations or associations whose purpose is to invite donations for the protection of the cultural and natural heritage as defined in Articles 1 and 2 of this Convention.

Article 18

The States Parties to this Convention shall give their assistance to international fund-raising campaigns organized for the World Heritage Fund under the auspices of the United Nations Educational, Scientific and Cultural Organization. They shall facilitate collections made by the bodies mentioned in paragraph 3 of Article 15 for this purpose.

V. CONDITIONS AND ARRANGEMENTS FOR INTERNATIONAL ASSISTANCE

Article 19

Any State Party to this Convention may request international assistance for property forming part of the cultural or natural heritage of outstanding universal value situated within its territory. It shall submit with its request such information and documentation provided for in Article 21 as it has in its possession and as will enable the Committee to come to a decision.

Article 20

Subject to the provisions of paragraph 2 of Article 13, sub-paragraph (c) of Article 22 and Article 23, international assistance provided for by this Convention may be granted only to property forming part of the cultural and natural heritage which the World Heritage Committee has decided, or may decide, to enter in one of the lists mentioned in paragraphs 2 and 4 of Article 11.

Article 21

1. The World Heritage Committee shall define the procedure by which requests to it for international assistance shall be considered and shall specify the content of the request, which should define the operation contemplated, the work that is necessary, the expected cost thereof, the degree of urgency and the reasons why the resources of the State requesting assistance do not allow it to meet all the expenses. Such requests must be supported by experts' reports whenever possible.

2. Requests based upon disasters or natural calamities should, by reasons of the urgent work which they may involve, be given immediate, priority consideration by the Committee, which should have a reserve fund at its disposal against such contingencies.

3. Before coming to a decision, the Committee shall carry out such studies and consultations as it deems necessary.

Article 22

Assistance granted by the World Heritage Fund may take the following forms:

(a) studies concerning the artistic, scientific and technical problems raised by the protection, conservation, presentation and rehabilitation of the cultural and natural heritage, as defined in paragraphs 2 and 4 of Article 11 of this Convention;

(b) provisions of experts, technicians and skilled labour to ensure that the approved work is correctly carried out;

(c) training of staff and specialists at all levels in the field of identification, protection, conservation, presentation and rehabilitation of the cultural and natural heritage;

(d) supply of equipment which the State concerned does not possess or is not in a position to acquire;

(e) low-interest or interest-free loans which might be repayable on a long-term basis;

(f) the granting, in exceptional cases and for special reasons, of non-repayable subsidies.

Article 23

The World Heritage Committee may also provide international assistance to national or regional centres for the training of staff and specialists at all levels in the field of identification, protection, conservation, presentation and rehabilitation of the cultural and natural heritage.

Article 24

International assistance on a large scale shall be preceded by detailed scientific, economic and technical studies. These studies shall draw upon the most advanced techniques for the protection, conservation, presentation and rehabilitation of the natural and cultural heritage and shall be consistent with the objectives of this Convention. The studies shall also seek means of making rational use of the resources available in the State concerned.

Article 25

As a general rule, only part of the cost of work necessary shall be borne by the international community. The contribution of the State benefiting from international assistance shall constitute a substantial share of the resources devoted to each programme or project, unless its resources do not permit this.

Article 26

The World Heritage Committee and the recipient State shall define in the agreement they conclude the conditions in which a programme or project for which international assistance under the terms of this Convention is provided, shall be carried out. It shall be the responsibility of the State receiving such international assistance to continue to protect, conserve and present the property so safeguarded, in observance of the conditions laid down by the agreement.

VI. EDUCATIONAL PROGRAMMES

Article 27

1. The States Parties to this Convention shall endeavor by all appropriate means, and in particular by educational and information programmes, to strengthen appreciation and respect by their peoples of the cultural and natural heritage defined in Articles 1 and 2 of the Convention.

2. They shall undertake to keep the public broadly informed of the dangers threatening this heritage and of the activities carried on in pursuance of this Convention.

Article 28

States Parties to this Convention which receive international assistance under the Convention shall take appropriate measures to make known the importance of the property for which assistance has been received and the role played by such assistance.

VII. REPORTS

Article 29

1. The States Parties to this Convention shall, in the reports which they submit to the General Conference of the United Nations Educational, Scientific and Cultural Organization on dates and in a manner to be determined by it, give information on the legislative and administrative provisions which they have adopted and other action which they have taken for the application of this Convention, together with details of the experience acquired in this field.

2. These reports shall be brought to the attention of the World Heritage Committee.

3. The Committee shall submit a report on its activities at each of the ordinary sessions of the General Conference of the United Nations Educational, Scientific and Cultural Organization.

VIII. FINAL CLAUSES

Article 30

This Convention is drawn up in Arabic, English, French, Russian and Spanish, the five texts being equally authoritative.

Article 31

1. This Convention shall be subject to ratification or acceptance by States members of the United Nations Educational, Scientific and Cultural Organization in accordance with their respective constitutional procedures.

2. The instruments of ratification or acceptance shall be deposited with the Director-General of the United Nations Educational, Scientific and Cultural Organization.

Article 32

1. This Convention shall be open to accession by all States not members of the United Nations Educational, Scientific and Cultural Organization which are invited by the General Conference of the Organization to accede to it.

2. Accession shall be effected by the deposit of an instrument of accession with the Director-General of the United Nations Educational, Scientific and Cultural Organization.

Article 33

This Convention shall enter into force three months after the date of the deposit of the twentieth instrument of ratification, acceptance or accession, but only with respect to those States which have deposited their respective instruments of ratification, acceptance or accession on or before that date. It shall enter into force with respect to any other State three months after the deposit of its instrument of ratification, acceptance or accession.

Article 34

The following provisions shall apply to those States Parties to this Convention which have a federal or non-unitary constitutional system:

(a) with regard to the provisions of this Convention, the implementation of which comes under the legal jurisdiction of the federal or central legislative power, the obligations of the federal or central government shall be the same as for those States parties which are not federal States;

(b) with regard to the provisions of this Convention, the implementation of which comes under the legal jurisdiction of individual constituent States, countries, provinces or cantons that are not obliged by the constitutional system of the federation to take legislative measures, the federal government shall inform the competent authorities of such States, countries, provinces or cantons of the said provisions, with its recommendation for their adoption.

Article 35

1. Each State Party to this Convention may denounce the Convention.

2. The denunciation shall be notified by an instrument in writing, deposited with the Director-General of the United Nations Educational, Scientific and Cultural Organization.

3. The denunciation shall take effect twelve months after the receipt of the instrument of denunciation. It shall not affect the financial obligations of the denouncing State until the date on which the withdrawal takes effect.

Article 36

The Director-General of the United Nations Educational, Scientific and Cultural Organization shall inform the States members of the Organization, the States not members of the Organization which are referred to in Article 32, as well as the United Nations, of the deposit of all the instruments of ratification, acceptance, or accession provided for in Articles 31 and 32, and of the denunciations provided for in Article 35.

Article 37

1. This Convention may be revised by the General Conference of the United Nations Educational, Scientific and Cultural Organization. Any such revision shall, however, bind only the States which shall become Parties to the revising convention.

2. If the General Conference should adopt a new convention revising this Convention in whole or in part, then, unless the new convention otherwise provides, this Convention shall cease to be open to ratification, acceptance or accession, as from the date on which the new revising convention enters into force.

Article 38

In conformity with Article 102 of the Charter of the United Nations, this Convention shall be registered with the Secretariat of the United Nations at the request of the Director-General of the United Nations Educational, Scientific and Cultural Organization.

Done in Paris, this twenty-third day of November 1972, in two authentic copies bearing the signature of the President of the seventeenth session of the General Conference and of the Director-General of the United Nations Educational, Scientific and Cultural Organization, which shall be deposited in the archives of the United Nations Educational, Scientific and Cultural Organization, and certified true copies of which shall be delivered to all the States referred to in Articles 31 and 32 as well as to the United Nations.

实施《世界遗产公约》操作指南[①]（节选）

联合国教科文组织，世界遗产委员会，世界遗产中心，2019年7月10日

Ⅱ.D.突出的普遍价值的评估标准[②]

77. 如果遗产符合下列一项或多项标准，委员会将会认为该遗产具有突出的普遍价值（见49-53段）。所申报遗产因而必须是：

（i）作为人类天才的创造力的杰作；

（ii）在一段时期内或世界某一文化区域内人类价值观的重要交流，对建筑、技术、古迹艺术、城镇规划或景观设计的发展产生重大影响；

（iii）能为延续至今或业已消逝的文明或文化传统提供独特的或至少是特殊的见证；

（iv）是一种建筑、建筑或技术整体、或景观的杰出范例，展现人类历史上一个（或几个）重要阶段；

（v）是传统人类居住地、土地使用或海洋开发的杰出范例，代表一种（或几种）文化或人类与环境的相互作用，特别是当它面临不可逆变化的影响而变得脆弱；

（vi）与具有突出的普遍意义的事件、活传统、观点、信仰、艺术或文学作品有直接或有形的联系（委员会认为本标准最好与其他标准一起使用）；

（vii）绝妙的自然现象或具有罕见自然美和美学价值的地区；

（viii）是地球演化史中重要阶段的突出例证，包括生命记载和地貌演变中的重要地质过程或显著的地质或地貌特征；

（ix）突出代表了陆地、淡水、海岸和海洋生态系统及动植物群落演变、发展的生态和生理过程；

（x）是生物多样性原址保护的最重要的自然栖息地，包括从科学和保护角度看，具有突出的普遍价值的濒危物种栖息地。

78. 只有同时具有完整性和/或真实性的特征，且有恰当的保护和管理机制确保遗产得到保护，遗产才能被视为具有突出的普遍价值。

Ⅱ.E.完整性和/或真实性

真实性

79. 依据标准（i）至（vi）申报的遗产须符合真实性的条件。附件4中包括了关于真实性的《奈良文件》，为评估相关遗产的真实性提供了操作基础，概要如下：

[①] 中国古迹遗址保护协会译。

[②] 这些标准起初分为两组，标准（i）至（vi）适用于文化遗产，标准（i）至（iv）适用于自然遗产。世界遗产委员会第6届特别会议决定将这十个标准合起来（第6 EXT.COM 5.1号决议）。

80. 理解遗产价值的能力取决于该价值信息来源的真实度或可信度。对历史上积累的，涉及文化遗产原始及发展变化的特征的信息来源的认识和理解，是评价真实性各方面的必要基础[①]。

81. 对于文化遗产价值和相关信息来源可信性的评价标准可因文化而异，甚至同一种文化内也存在差异。出于对所有文化的尊重，文化遗产的分析和判断必须首先在其所在的文化背景中进行。

82. 依据文化遗产类别及其文化背景，如果遗产的文化价值（申报标准所认可的）的下列特征真实可信，则被认为具有真实性：
- 外形和设计；
- 材料和实质；
- 用途和功能；
- 传统，技术和管理体系；
- 位置和环境；
- 语言和其他形式的非物质遗产；
- 精神和感觉；
- 其他内外因素。

83. 精神和感觉这样的属性在真实性评估中虽不易操作，却是评价一个遗产地特质和场所精神的重要指标，例如，在社区中保持传统和文化连续性。

84. 利用所有这些信息使我们对相关文化遗产在艺术、历史、社会和科学等特定领域的研究更加深入。"信息来源"指所有物质的、书面的、口头和图形的信息来源，从而使理解文化遗产的性质、特性、意义和历史成为可能。

85. 在考虑申报遗产的真实性时，缔约国首先要确认所有适用的真实性的重要载体。真实性声明应该评估真实性在每个载体特征上的体现程度。

86. 在真实性问题上，考古遗址或历史建筑及街区的重建只有在极个别情况才予以考虑。只有依据完整且详细的记载，不存在任何想象而进行的重建，才可以接受。

完整性

87. 所有申报列入《世界遗产名录》的遗产必须满足完整性条件[②]。

88. 完整性用来衡量自然和/或文化遗产及其特征的整体性和无缺憾性。因而，审查遗产完整性需要评估遗产符合以下特征的程度：
- a）包括所有表现其突出的普遍价值的必要因素；
- b）面积足够大，确保能完整地代表体现遗产价值的特色和过程；
- c）受到发展的负面影响和/或缺乏维护。

上述条件需要在完整性陈述中进行论述。

89. 依据标准（i）至（vi）申报的遗产，其物理构造和/或重要特征都必须保存完好，且侵劣化过程的影响得到控制。能表现遗产全部价值的绝大部分必要因素也要包括在内。文化景观、历史村镇或其他活遗产中体现其显著特征的种种关系和动态功能也应予保存[③]。

90. 所有依据标准（vii）至（x）申报的遗产，其生物物理过程和地貌特征应该相对完整。当然，由于任何区域都不可能完全保持天然，且所有自然区域都在变动之中，而且在某种程度上还会有人类的活动。包括传统社会和当地社区在内的人类活动在自然区域内时有发生。生物多样性和文化多样性可与人类活

[①] 第39 COM 11 号决议。

[②] 第20 COM IX.13 号决议。

[③] 将完整性条件应用于依据标准（i）至（vi）的申报的遗产之例证正在开发。

动密切联系，相互依存，例如传统社会、地方社区和原住民的活动等往往发生在自然区域。如果这些活动具有生态可持续性，也可以与同自然区域突出的普遍价值一致①。

91. 另外，对于依据标准（vii）至（x）申报的遗产来说，每个标准又有一个相应的完整性条件。

92. 依据标准（vii）申报的遗产应具备突出的普遍价值，且包括保持遗产美景所必须的关键地区。例如，某个遗产的景观价值在于瀑布，那么只有与维持遗产美景完整关系密切的临近的积水潭和下游地区也被涵盖在内，才能满足完整性条件。

93. 依据标准（viii）申报的遗产必须包括其自然关系中所有或大部分重要的相互联系、相互依存的因素。例如，"冰川期"遗址要满足完整性条件，则需包括雪地、冰河本身和凿面样本、沉积物和拓殖（例如，条痕、冰碛层及植物演替的先锋阶段等）。如果是火山，则岩浆层必须完整，且能代表所有或大部分火山岩种类和喷发类型。

94. 依据标准（ix）申报的遗产必须具有足够的规模，且包含能够展示长期保护其内部生态系统和生物多样性的重要过程的必要因素。例如，热带雨林地区要满足完整性条件，需要有一定的海拔层次、多样的地形和土壤种类、群落系统和自然形成的群落；同样，珊瑚礁必须包括诸如海草、红树林和其他为珊瑚礁提供营养沉积物的临近生态系统。

95. 依据标准（x）申报的遗产必须是对生物多样性保护至关重要的遗产。只有最具生物多样性和/或代表性的申报遗产才有可能满足该标准。遗产必须包括某生物区或生态系统内最具多样性的动植物特征的栖息地。例如：要满足完整性条件，热带草原需要具有完整的、共同进化的草食动物群和植物群；海岛生态系统则需要包括地方生态栖息地；包含多种物种的遗产必须足够大，能够包括确保这些物种生存的最重要的栖息地；如果某个地区有迁徙物种，则季节性的养育巢穴和迁徙路线，不管位于何处，都必须妥善保护。

Ⅳ.B.《濒危世界遗产名录》

列入《濒危世界遗产名录》的指南

177. 依照《公约》第 11 条第 4 段，当一项遗产满足以下要求时，委员会可将其列入《濒危世界遗产名录》。

a) 该遗产已列入《世界遗产名录》；

b) 该遗产面临严重的、具体的危险；

c) 该遗产的保护需要实施重大举措；

d) 已申请依据《公约》为该遗产提供援助。委员会认为，在某些情况下，传递对该遗产关注的信息可能是最有效的援助手段。将遗产地列入《濒危世界遗产名录》就是这样一种信息。此类援助申请可能由委员会成员或秘书处提起。

列入《濒危世界遗产名录》的标准

178. 当委员会查明一项世界遗产（如《公约》第 1 和第 2 条所定义）符合以下两种情况中至少一项时，该遗产可被列入《濒危世界遗产名录》。

179. 如属于文化遗产：

a) 已确知的危险——该遗产面临着具体的且确知即将来临的危险，例如

　ⅰ) 材料严重受损；

　ⅱ) 结构特征和/或装饰特色严重受损；

　ⅲ) 建筑和城镇规划的统一性严重受损；

---

① 第43 COM 11A决议。

ⅳ）城市或乡村空间，或自然环境严重受损；

ⅴ）历史真实性严重丧失；

ⅵ）文化意义严重丧失。

b）潜在的危险——该遗产面临可能会对其固有特性造成损害的威胁。此类威胁包括，如：

ⅰ）该遗产法律地位的改变引起的保护力度的削弱；

ⅱ）缺乏保护政策；

ⅲ）区域规划项目的威胁；

ⅳ）城镇规划的威胁；

ⅴ）武装冲突的爆发或威胁；

ⅵ）地质、气候或其他环境因素导致的威胁。

180. 如属于自然遗产[①]：

a）已确知的危险——该遗产面临着具体的且确知即将来临的危险，例如：

ⅰ）作为确立该项遗产法定保护地位依据的濒危物种或其他具有突出普遍价值的物种数量由于自然因素（例如疾病）或人为因素（例如偷猎）锐减；

ⅱ）遗产的自然美景和科学价值由于人类的定居、淹没遗产重要区域的水库的兴建、工农业的发展（包括杀虫剂和农药的使用，大型公共工程、采矿、污染、采伐、砍柴等）而遭受重大损害；

ⅲ）人类活动对保护范围或上游区域的侵蚀，威胁遗产的完整性。

b）潜在的危险——该遗产面临可能会对其固有特性造成损害的威胁。此类威胁包括：

ⅰ）该地区的法律保护地位发生变化；

ⅱ）在遗产范围内实施的，或虽在其范围外但足以波及和威胁到该遗产的移民或开发计划；

ⅲ）武装冲突的爆发或威胁；

ⅳ）管理规划或管理体系缺失、不完善或贯彻不彻底；

ⅴ）气候，地质或其他环境因素造成的威胁。

181. 另外，威胁遗产完整性的因素必须是人力可以补救的因素。对于文化遗产，自然因素和人为因素都可能构成威胁，而对于自然遗产来说，威胁其完整性的大多是人为因素，只有少数情况是由自然因素造成的（例如传染病）。某些情况下，对遗产完整性造成威胁的因素可通过行政或法律手段予以纠正，如取消某大型公共工程项目，加强法律地位[①]。

182. 审议是否将一项文化或自然遗产列入《濒危世界遗产名录》时，委员会可能要考虑到下列额外因素：

a）政府是在权衡各种因素后才做出影响世界遗产的决定。世界遗产委员会如能在遗产遭到威胁之前给予建议的话，该建议往往具有决定性。

b）尤其是对于已确知的危险，对遗产所遭受的物理和文化损害的判断应基于其影响程度，并应具体问题具体分析。

c）对于潜在的危险必须首先考虑：

ⅰ）结合遗产所处的社会和经济环境的常规进程对其所受到的威胁进行评估；

ⅱ）有些威胁对于文化和自然遗产的影响难以估量，例如武装冲突的威胁；

ⅲ）有些威胁在本质上不会立刻发生，而只能预见，例如人口的增长。

d）最后，委员会在进行评估时应将所有未知或无法预料的但可能危及文化或自然遗产的因素纳入考虑范围。

[①] 第39 COM 11号决议。

Operational Guidelines for the Implementation of the World Heritage Convention(excerpts)

UNESCO, WHC (World Heritage Committee), WHC (World Heritage Center), 10 July 2019

II. D Criteria for the assessment of Outstanding Universal Value[①]

77. The Committee considers a property as having Outstanding Universal Value (see paragraphs 49-53) if the property meets one or more of the following criteria. Nominated properties shall therefore:

(i) represent a masterpiece of human creative genius;

(ii) exhibit an important interchange of human values, over a span of time or within a cultural area of the world, on developments in architecture or technology, monumental arts, town-planning or landscape design;

(iii) bear a unique or at least exceptional testimony to a cultural tradition or to a civilization which is living or which has disappeared;

(iv) be an outstanding example of a type of building, architectural or technological ensemble or landscape which illustrates (a) significant stage(s) in human history;

(v) be an outstanding example of a traditional human settlement, land-use, or sea-use which is representative of a culture (or cultures), or human interaction with the environment especially when it has become vulnerable under the impact of irreversible change;

(vi) be directly or tangibly associated with events or living traditions, with ideas, or with beliefs, with artistic and literary works of outstanding universal significance. (The Committee considers that this criterion should preferably be used in conjunction with other criteria);

(vii) contain superlative natural phenomena or areas of exceptional natural beauty and aesthetic importance;

(viii) be outstanding examples representing major stages of earth's history, including the record of life, significant on-going geological processes in the development of landforms, or significant geomorphic or physiographic features;

(ix) be outstanding examples representing significant on-going ecological and biological processes in the evolution and development of terrestrial, fresh water, coastal and marine ecosystems and communities of plants and animals;

(x) contain the most important and significant natural habitats for in-situ conservation of biological diversity,

---

① These criteria were formerly presented as two separate sets of criteria - criteria (i) - (vi) for cultural heritage and (i) - (iv) for natural heritage. The 6th extraordinary session of the World Heritage Committee decided to merge the ten criteria (Decision 6 EXT.COM 5.1).

including those containing threatened species of Outstanding Universal Value from the point of view of science or conservation.

78. To be deemed of Outstanding Universal Value, a property must also meet the conditions of integrity and/or authenticity and must have an adequate protection and management system to ensure its safeguarding.

Ⅱ. E Authenticity and/or integrity

Authenticity

79. Properties nominated under criteria (i) to (vi) must meet the conditions of authenticity. Annex 4, which includes the Nara Document on Authenticity, provides a practical basis for examining the authenticity of such properties and is summarized below.

80. The ability to understand the value attributed to the heritage depends on the degree to which information sources about this value may be understood as credible or truthful. Knowledge and understanding of these sources of information, in relation to original and subsequent characteristics of the cultural heritage, and their meaning as accumulated over time, are the requisite bases for assessing all aspects of authenticity[①].

81. Judgments about value attributed to cultural heritage, as well as the credibility of related information sources, may differ from culture to culture, and even within the same culture. The respect due to all cultures requires that cultural heritage must be considered and judged primarily within the cultural contexts to which it belongs.

82. Depending on the type of cultural heritage, and its cultural context, properties may be understood to meet the conditions of authenticity if their cultural values (as recognized in the nomination criteria proposed) are truthfully and credibly expressed through a variety of attributes including:
- form and design;
- materials and substance;
- use and function;
- traditions, techniques and management systems;
- location and setting;
- language, and other forms of intangible heritage;
- spirit and feeling; and
- other internal and external factors.

83. Attributes such as spirit and feeling do not lend themselves easily to practical applications of the conditions of authenticity, but nevertheless are important indicators of character and sense of place, for example, in communities maintaining tradition and cultural continuity.

84. The use of all these sources permits elaboration of the specific artistic, historic, social, and scientific dimensions of the cultural heritage being examined. "Information sources" are defined as all physical, written, oral, and figurative sources, which make it possible to know the nature, specificities, meaning, and history of the cultural heritage.

85. When the conditions of authenticity are considered in preparing a nomination for a property, the State Party should first identify all of the applicable significant attributes of authenticity. The statement of authenticity

---

① Decision 39 COM 11.

should assess the degree to which authenticity is present in, or expressed by, each of these significant attributes.

86. In relation to authenticity, the reconstruction of archaeological remains or historic buildings or districts is justifiable only in exceptional circumstances. Reconstruction is acceptable only on the basis of complete and detailed documentation and to no extent on conjecture.

Integrity

87. All properties nominated for inscription on the World Heritage List shall satisfy the conditions of integrity[①].

88. Integrity is a measure of the wholeness and intactness of the natural and/or cultural heritage and its attributes. Examining the conditions of integrity, therefore requires assessing the extent to which the property:

a) includes all elements necessary to express its Outstanding Universal Value;

b) is of adequate size to ensure the complete representation of the features and processes which convey the property's significance;

c) suffers from adverse effects of development and/or neglect.

This should be presented in a statement of integrity.

89. For properties nominated under criteria (i) to (vi), the physical fabric of the property and/or its significant features should be in good condition, and the impact of deterioration processes controlled. A significant proportion of the elements necessary to convey the totality of the value conveyed by the property should be included. Relationships and dynamic functions present in cultural landscapes, historic towns or other living properties essential to their distinctive character should also be maintained[②].

90. For all properties nominated under criteria (vii) - (x), bio-physical processes and landform features should be relatively intact. However, it is recognized that no area is totally pristine and that all natural areas are in a dynamic state, and to some extent involve contact with people. Biological diversity and cultural diversity can be closely linked and interdependent and human activities, including those of traditional societies, local communities and indigenous peoples, often occur in natural areas. These activities may be consistent with the Outstanding Universal Value of the area where they are ecologically sustainable[③].

91. In addition, for properties nominated under criteria (vii) to (x), a corresponding condition of integrity has been defined for each criterion.

92. Properties proposed under criterion (vii) should be of Outstanding Universal Value and include areas that are essential for maintaining the beauty of the property. For example, a property whose scenic value depends on a waterfall, would meet the conditions of integrity if it includes adjacent catchment and downstream areas that are integrally linked to the maintenance of the aesthetic qualities of the property.

93. Properties proposed under criterion (viii) should contain all or most of the key interrelated and interdependent elements in their natural relationships. For example, an "ice age" area would meet the conditions of integrity if it includes the snow field, the glacier itself and samples of cutting patterns, deposition and colonization (e.g. striations, moraines, pioneer stages of plant succession, etc.); in the case of volcanoes, the magmatic series should be complete and all or most of the varieties of effusive rocks and types of eruptions be represented.

94. Properties proposed under criterion (ix) should have sufficient size and contain the necessary elements

---

① Decision 20 COM IX.13.

② Examples of the application of the conditions of integrity to properties nominated under criteria (i) - (vi) are under development.

③ Decision 43 COM 11A.

to demonstrate the key aspects of processes that are essential for the long term conservation of the ecosystems and the biological diversity they contain. For example, an area of tropical rain forest would meet the conditions of integrity if it includes a certain amount of variation in elevation above sea level, changes in topography and soil types, patch systems and naturally regenerating patches; similarly a coral reef should include, for example, seagrass, mangrove or other adjacent ecosystems that regulate nutrient and sediment inputs into the reef.

95. Properties proposed under criterion (x) should be the most important properties for the conservation of biological diversity. Only those properties which are the most biologically diverse and/or representative are likely to meet this criterion. The properties should contain habitats for maintaining the most diverse fauna and flora characteristic of the bio-geographic province and ecosystems under consideration. For example, a tropical savannah would meet the conditions of integrity if it includes a complete assemblage of co-evolved herbivores and plants; an island ecosystem should include habitats for maintaining endemic biota; a property containing wide ranging species should be large enough to include the most critical habitats essential to ensure the survival of viable populations of those species; for an area containing migratory species, seasonal breeding and nesting sites, and migratory routes, wherever they are located, should be adequately protected.

IV. B The List of World Heritage in Danger

Guidelines for the inscription of properties on the List of World Heritage in Danger

177. In accordance with Article 11, paragraph 4, of the *Convention*, the Committee may inscribe a property on the List of World Heritage in Danger when the following requirements are met:

a) the property under consideration is on the World Heritage List;

b) the property is threatened by serious and specific danger;

c) major operations are necessary for the conservation of the property;

d) assistance under the *Convention* has been requested for the property; the Committee is of the view that its assistance in certain cases may most effectively be limited to messages of its concern, including the message sent by inscription of a property on the List of World Heritage in Danger and that such assistance may be requested by any Committee member or the Secretariat.

Criteria for the inscription of properties on the List of World Heritage in Danger

178. A World Heritage property—as defined in Articles 1 and 2 of the *Convention*—can be inscribed on the List of World Heritage in Danger by the Committee when it finds that the condition of the property corresponds to at least one of the criteria in either of the two cases described below.

179. In the case of **cultural properties**:

a) <u>ASCERTAINED DANGER</u> —The property is faced with specific and proven imminent danger, such as:

    i) serious deterioration of materials;

    ii) serious deterioration of structure and/or ornamental features;

    iii) serious deterioration of architectural or town-planning coherence;

    iv) serious deterioration of urban or rural space, or the natural environment;

    v) significant loss of historical authenticity;

    vi) important loss of cultural significance.

b) <u>POTENTIAL DANGER</u> —The property is faced with threats which could have deleterious effects on its inherent characteristics. Such threats are, for example:

i) modification of juridical status of the property diminishing the degree of its protection;

ii) lack of conservation policy;

iii) threatening effects of regional planning projects;

vi) threatening effects of town planning;

v) outbreak or threat of armed conflict;

vi) threatening impacts of climatic, geological or other environmental factors.

180. In the case of **natural properties**[①] :

a) ASCERTAINED DANGER —The property is faced with specific and proven imminent danger, such as:

i) A serious decline in the population of the endangered species or the other species of Outstanding Universal Value for which the property was legally established to protect, either by natural factors such as disease or by human-made factors such as poaching.

ii) Severe deterioration of the natural beauty or scientific value of the property, as by human settlement, construction of reservoirs which flood important parts of the property, industrial and agricultural development including use of pesticides and fertilizers, major public works, mining, pollution, logging, firewood collection, etc.

iii) Human encroachment on boundaries or in upstream areas which threaten the integrity of the property.

b) POTENTIAL DANGER —The property is faced with major threats which could have deleterious effects on its inherent characteristics. Such threats are, for example:

i) a modification of the legal protective status of the area;

ii) planned resettlement or development projects within the property or so situated that the impacts threaten the property;

iii) outbreak or threat of armed conflict;

iv) the management plan or management system is lacking or inadequate, or not fully implemented;

v) threatening impacts of climatic, geological or other environmental factors.

181. In addition, the threats and/or their detrimental impacts on the integrity of the property must be those which are amenable to correction by human action. In the case of cultural properties, both natural factors and human-made factors may be threatening, while in the case of natural properties, most threats will be human-made and only very rarely a natural factor (such as an epidemic disease) will threaten the integrity of the property. In some cases, the threats and/or their detrimental impacts on the integrity of the property may be corrected by administrative or legislative action, such as the cancelling of a major public works project or the improvement of legal status[①].

182. The Committee may wish to bear in mind the following supplementary factors when considering the inclusion of a cultural or natural property in the List of World Heritage in Danger:

a) Decisions which affect World Heritage properties are taken by Governments after balancing all factors. The advice of the World Heritage Committee can often be decisive if it can be given before the property becomes threatened.

b) Particularly in the case of ascertained danger, the physical or cultural deteriorations to which a property has been subjected should be judged according to the intensity of its effects and analyzed case by case.

---

① Decision 39 COM 11.

c) Above all in the case of <u>potential danger</u> to a property, one should consider that:

    i) the threat should be appraised according to the normal evolution of the social and economic framework in which the property is situated;

    ii) it is often impossible to assess certain threats such as the threat of armed conflict as to their effect on cultural or natural properties;

    iii) some threats are not imminent in nature, but can only be anticipated, such as demographic growth.

d) Finally, in its appraisal the Committee should take into account <u>any cause of unknown or unexpected origin</u> which endangers a cultural or natural property.

关于在国家一级保护
文化和自然遗产的建议[①]

（联合国教科文组织第十七届大会1972年11月16日在巴黎通过）

联合国教科文组织大会于1972年10月17日至11月21日在巴黎举行第十七届会议。

考虑到在一个生活条件加速变化的社会里，就人类平衡和发展而言至关重要的是为人类保存一个合适的生活环境，以便人类在此环境中与自然及其前辈留下的文明痕迹保持联系。为此，应该使文化和自然遗产在社会生活中发挥积极的作用，并把当代成就、昔日价值和自然之美纳入一个整体政策；

考虑到这种与社会和经济生活的结合必定是地区发展和国家各级规划的一个基本方面；

考虑到我们这个时代特有的新现象所带来的异常严重的危险正威胁着文化和自然遗产，而这些遗产构成了人类遗产的一个基本特征，以及丰富和协调发展当代与未来文明的一种源泉；

考虑到每一项文化和自然遗产都是独一无二的，任何一项文化和自然遗产的消失都构成绝对的损失，并造成该遗产的不可逆转的枯竭；

考虑到在其领土上有文化和自然遗产组成部分的任何一个国家，有责任保护这一部分人类遗产并确保将它传给后代；

考虑到研究、认识及保护世界各国的文化遗产和自然遗产有利于人民之间的相互理解；

考虑到文化和自然遗产构成一个和谐的整体，其组成部分是不可分割；

考虑到经共同考虑和制定的保护文化和自然遗产的政策可能使成员国之间继续产生相互影响，并对联合国教科文组织在这一领域的活动产生决定性的影响；

考虑到大会已经通过了保护文化和自然遗产的国际文件，如，《关于适用于考古发掘的国际原则的建议》（1956）、《关于保护景观和遗址的风貌与特征的建议》（1962）以及《关于保护受到公共或私人工程危害的文化财产的建议》（1968）；

希望补充并扩大这类建议中所规定的标准和原则的适用范围；

收到有关保护文化遗产和自然遗产的建议，该问题作为第二十三项议案列入本届会议议程；

第十六届会议上决定：该问题应向成员国建议的形式制定为国际规章；

于1972年11月16日，通过本建议。

一. 文化和自然遗产的定义

1. 为本建议之目的，以下各项应被视为"文化遗产"：

（1）古迹：建筑物、不朽的雕刻和绘画作品，包括穴居和题记以及在考古、历史、艺术或科学方面

[①] 引自：联合国教科文组织世界遗产中心，国际古迹遗址理事会，国际文物保护与修复研究中心，中国国家文物局主编. 国际文化遗产保护文件选编[M]. 北京：文物出版社，2007.

具有特殊价值的组成部分或结构；

（2）建筑群：因其建筑、协调或在风景中的位置而具有特殊历史、艺术或科学价值的单独或相连建筑群；

（3）遗址：因风景秀丽或在考古、历史、人种或人类学方面的重要性而具有特殊价值的地形区，该地形区是人类与自然的共同产物。

2. 为本建议之目的，以下各项应被视为"自然遗产"：

在美学或科学方面具有特殊价值的、由物理和生物结构（群）所组成的自然风貌；

在科学或保护方面具有特殊价值的，或正面临威胁的构成动物和植物物种的栖息地或产地的地理和地文结构，以及准确划定的区域；

在科学、保护或自然风貌方面，或在其与人类和自然的共同产物的关系方面具有特殊价值的自然遗址或准确划定的自然地区。

二．国家政策

3. 各国应根据其司法和立法需要，尽可能制定、发展并应用一项其主要目的在于协调和利用一切可能得到的科学、技术、文化和其他资源的政策，以确保有效地保护、保存和展示文化和自然遗产。

三．总则

4. 文化遗产和自然遗产代表着财富。凡领土上有这些遗产的国家都有责任对其国民和整个国际社会保护、保存和展示这些遗产；成员国应采取履行该义务所需的相应行动。

5. 文化和自然遗产应被视为一个同种性质的整体，它不仅由具有巨大内在价值的作品组成，而且还包括随着时间流逝而具有文化或自然价值的较为一般的物品。

6. 任何一件作品和物品按一般原则都不应与其环境相分离。

7. 由于保护、保存和展示文化和自然遗产的最终目的是为了人类的发展，因此，各成员国应尽可能以不再把文化和自然遗产视为国家发展的障碍，而应视为决定因素这样一种方法来指导该领域的工作。

8. 应将保护、保存并有效地展示文化和自然遗产视为地区发展计划以及国家、地区和地方总体规划的重要方面之一。

9. 应制订一项保存文化和自然遗产并在社会生活中给其一席之地的积极政策。各成员国应安排公共和私人的一切有关部门采取行动，以制订并应用此政策。有关文化和自然遗产的预防和矫正措施应通过其他方面得到补充，其意图旨在使该遗产的每一组成部分都按照其文化或自然特性而发挥作用，从而成为现在和未来国家社会、经济、科学和文化生活的一部分。保护文化和自然遗产的行动应利用保护、保存和展示文化遗产或自然遗产所涉及的各个研究领域所取得的科学和技术进步。

10. 公共当局应尽可能为保护和展示文化和自然遗产提供日益增长的财政资源。

11. 将要采取的保护和保存措施，应与该地区的公众联系起来，并呼吁他们提出建议或给予帮助——特别是在对待和监督文化和自然遗产方面。也可以考虑从私人部门得到财政支持的可能性。

四．行政组织

12. 尽管由于行政组织的多样性使得各成员国无法采取一个统一的组织形式，然而还是应该遵循某些共同的标准。

专门的公共行政部门

13. 各成员国应根据各国的适当条件，在其尚无此类组织的领土上设立一个或多个专门的公共行政部门，负责有效地执行以下各项职能：

（1）制订和实施各种旨在保护、保存和展示本国文化和自然遗产并使其成为社会生活的一个积极因素的措施，并且先编纂一份文化和自然遗产的清单，建立相关的档案资料服务机构；

（2）培训并招聘所需的科学、技术和行政人员，由其负责文化和自然遗产的鉴定、保护、保存和其他综合计划，并指导其实施；

（3）组织各学科专家的紧密合作，研究文化和自然遗产的保护技术问题；

（4）利用或建立实验室，研究有关文化和自然遗产保护方面所涉及的各学科问题；

（5）确保遗产所有人或承租人进行必要的维修，并保持建筑物的最佳艺术和技术状况。

咨询机构

14. 专门的行政部门应与负责在准备文化和自然遗产有关措施方面提供咨询的专家机构合作。这类机构应包括专家、主要保护学会的代表以及有关行政部门的代表。

各机构间的合作

15. 从事保护、保存和展示文化和自然遗产的专门的行政部门应与其他公共行政部门一起在平等的基础上开展工作，特别是那些负责地区发展规划、主要公共工程、环境及经济和社会规划的部门。涉及文化和自然遗产的旅游发展计划的制订应审慎进行，以便不影响该遗产的内在特征和重要性，并应采取步骤在有关部门间建立适当的联系。

16. 凡涉及大型项目时，应组织专门的行政部门之间的、各种层次的不断合作并作好适当的协调安排，以便采取顾及有关各方利益的一致决定。从研究之初就应制订合作计划的规定，并确定解决冲突的机制。

中央、联邦地区和地方机构的权限

17. 考虑到保护、保存和展示文化和自然文化遗产所涉及的问题难以处理这一事实，有时需要专门知识，有时涉及艰难的抉择，并且也考虑到该领域不能得到足够的专业人员，因此，应根据各成员国的适当情况，在审慎平衡的基础上划分中央或联邦以及地区或地方当局之间有关制订和执行一般保护措施的一切职责。

五．保护措施

18. 各成员国应尽可能采取一切必要的科学、技术、行政、法律和财政措施，确保其领土上的文化和自然遗产得到保护。这些措施应根据各成员国的立法和组织而定。

科学和技术措施

19. 各成员国应经常对其文化和自然遗产进行精心维护，以避免因其退化而不得不进行的耗资巨大的项目。为此，各成员国应通过定期检查对其遗产的各部分经常进行监督。它们还应该依据现有科学、技术和财政手段精心制订能逐渐包括所有文化和自然遗产的保护和展示的计划项目。

20. 任何所需进行的工作应根据其重要性，都事先并同时进行彻底的研究。这种研究应同各有关领域的专家一起进行，或由有关领域的专家单独进行。

21. 各成员国应寻找有效的办法，对受到极为严重危险威胁的文化和自然遗产的组成部分给予更多的保护。此办法应考虑所涉及的且相互关联的科学、技术和艺术问题并能制订出适用的治理对策。

22. 另外在适当情况下，这些文化和自然遗产的组成部分应恢复其原有用途或赋予新的和更加恰当的用途，只要其文化价值并没有因此而受到贬损。

23. 对文化遗产所进行的任何工程都应旨在保护其传统原貌，并保护它免遭可能破坏它与周围环境之间总体或色彩关系的重建或改建。

24. 古迹与其周围环境之间由时间和人类所建立起来的和谐极为重要，通常不应受到干扰和毁坏，不应允许通过破坏其周围环境而孤立该古迹；也不应试图将古迹迁移，除非作为处理问题的一个例外方法，并证明这么做的理由是出于紧迫的考虑。

25. 各成员国应采取措施，保护文化和自然遗产免受标志现代文明的技术进步可能带来的有害影响。这些措施应旨在对付由机器和车辆所引起的震动和震颤的影响。还应采取措施防止污染和自然灾害和灾难，并对文化和自然遗产所受到的损坏进行修缮。

26. 由于建筑群的修复情况并非到处千篇一律，因此各成员国应在适当情况下进行社会科学调查，以便准确地确定有关建筑群所在的社区有何社会需要和文化需要。任何修复工程都应特别注意使人类能在已修复的环境中工作、发展并取得成就。

27. 各成员国应对各项自然遗产，如公园、野生生物、难民区或娱乐区或其他类似保护区进行地质和生态研究，以正确评估其科学价值，确定观众使用带来的影响，并观察各种相互关系，避免对遗产造成严重损害，并为动物和植物的管理提供足够的背景资料。

28. 各成员国应在运输、通迅、视听技术、数据自动处理和其他先进技术以及文化、娱乐发展趋势方面做到齐头并进，以便为科学研究和适合于各地而又不破坏自然资源的公共娱乐提供尽可能好的设备和服务。

行政措施

29. 各成员国应尽快制订出其文化和自然遗产的保护清单，其中包括那些虽不是至关重要但却与其环境不可分割并构成其特征的项目。

30. 通过对文化和自然遗产的这种勘查所获得的信息资料应以适当的形式予以收集，并定期更新。

31. 为了确保在各级规划中都能有效地确认文化和自然遗产，各成员国应准备涉及有关文化和自然财产的地图和尽可能详尽的资料。

32. 各成员国应考虑为不再用作原来用途的历史建筑群寻找合适的用途。

33. 应该为保护、保存、展示和修复具有历史和艺术价值的建筑群制订计划。它应包括边缘保护地带、规定土地使用条件并说明需要保护的建筑物及其保护条件。该计划应纳入有关地区的城镇和乡村整体规划的政策。

34. 修复计划应说明历史建筑物将作何用途以及修复地区与城市周围发展之间有何联系。在考虑指定一个修复区时，应同该地区的地方当局及居民代表进行磋商。

35. 任何可能导致改变保护区建筑物现状的工程须由城镇和乡村规划部门在听取负责文化和自然遗产保护的专门行政部门的意见并予以批准后方可进行。

36. 如果出于居住者生活的需要，并且只有在不会极大地改变古代寓所真实特性的条件下，才应允许对建筑群的内部进行改动以及安装现代化设施。

37. 各成员国应根据其自然遗产的清单，制订短期和长期计划以形成一套符合本国需要的保护系统。

38. 各成员国应就符合土地有效使用的国家保护政策提供咨询服务以指导民间组织及土地所有者。

39. 各成员国应为恢复因工业而遭废弃或人类活动而遭破坏的自然区域制定政策和计划。

法律措施

40. 文化和自然遗产的组成部分，应根据其本身的重要性，由与各国的权限和法律程序相一致的立法或法规单独地或集体地予以保护。

41. 通过制订新规定应对保护措施作必要的补充，以促进文化和自然遗产的保护，并有利于展示其组成部分。为此，保护措施的实施，应适用于拥有文化和自然遗产组成部分的个人或公共当局。

42. 未经专门行政部门批准，一律不准兴建新建筑物，也不准对位于保护区或附近的财产予以拆除、改造、修改或砍伐其树木。

43. 允许工业发展或公共和私人工程的规划之立法应考虑现有的有关保护的立法。负责保护文化和自然遗产的有关当局可以采取步骤，通过以下方法加快必要的保护工程，即或者向遗产所有者提供财政援助,或者代理所有者并行使其权力使工程竣工。有关当局有可能获得所有者通常原本应付的那部分费用的补偿。

44. 在出于保护财产之需要的情况下,可根据国内立法的规定赋予公共当局征用受保护的建筑物或自然遗址的权力。

45. 各成员国应制订法规,控制招贴画、霓虹灯和其他各类广告、商业招牌、野营、电线杆、高塔、电线或电话线、电视天线、各种交通运输停车场、路标和街头设施等,总之与装备或占据文化和自然遗产某一组成部分有关的一切事宜。

46. 无论所有权是否变更,为保护文化和自然遗产的任何组成部分所采取的措施应继续有效。如果一个受保护的建筑物或自然遗址被出售,应告诉买者它在被保护之列。

47. 对蓄意破坏、损害或毁坏被保护的古迹、建筑物群或遗址、或具有考古、历史、或艺术价值的遗产的人,应根据各国宪法、法律和权限予以惩罚或行政处罚。此外,对非法挖掘设备应予以没收。

48. 对其他任何破坏保护、保存和展示受保护的文化或自然遗产组成部分的行为负有责任者应给予惩罚和行政处罚。它应包括根据已有的科技标准将受影响的遗址修复至原状的规定。

财政措施

49. 中央和地方当局应根据构成文化和自然遗产组成部分的被保护财产的重要性,尽可能在预算中拨出一定比例的资金,以便维护、保护和展示其所拥有的被保护财产,并从财产上资助对公共或私人所有的其他被保护财产所进行的类似工程。

50. 因保护、保存和展示私人所有的文化和自然遗产所造成的开支应尽可能地由所有者或使用者负担。

51. 此类开支的减税或赠款或优惠贷款可以提供给被保护财产的私人所有者,条件是他们根据所同意的标准进行保护、保存、展示和修复其财产的工程。

52. 如有必要,应考虑向文化和自然遗产保护区所有者赔偿因保护计划而可能招致的损失。

53. 在适当情况下,给予私人所有者的财政优惠应取决于他们是否遵守为公共利益而规定的某些条件,如:允许人们进入公园、花园和遗址,游览部分或全部自然遗址及古迹和建筑群,允许拍照等。

54. 在公共部门的预算中,应为保护受大规模公共或私人工程的危害的文化和自然遗产划拨专项资金。

55. 为了增加可能得到的财政资源,各成员国可以设立一个或多个"文化和自然遗产基金会",它们如同合法设立的公共机构一样,有权接受私人馈赠、捐赠和遗赠,特别是来自工业和商业公司的捐款。

56. 对那些征集、修复或维护文化和自然遗产的特定组成部分的馈赠、捐赠或遗赠者应给予税务减让。

57. 为了有利于自然和文化遗产修复工程的进行,各成员国可以做出特别安排,特别是通过为更新和修复工程贷款的方式;各成员国也可以制定必要的法规,以避免由于不动产的投机而带来的物价上涨。

58. 为了避免因修缮给不得不搬出建筑物或建筑群的贫困居民带来的艰辛,可以考虑给予租金上涨的补偿,以使他们能够保留住宅。这种补偿应该是暂时性的,并应根据有关人员的收入而定,以使他们能够偿付由于进行工程而造成的不断增加的费用。

59. 各成员国可以为有利于文化和自然遗产各项工程的融资提供便利,即通过建立由公共机构和私人信贷部门支持的"信贷基金",负责向所有者提供低息长期贷款。

六. 教育和文化行动

60. 大学、各级教育机构及永久性教育机构应就艺术史、建筑、环境和城镇规划定期组织讲课、讲座、讨论会等。

61. 各成员国应开展教育运动以唤起公众对文化和自然遗产的广泛兴趣和尊重,还应继续努力以告知公众为保护文化和自然遗产现在正在做些什么,以及可做些什么,并谆谆教诲他们理解和尊重其所含价值。

为此，应动用一切所需之信息媒介。

62. 在不忽视文化和自然遗产的巨大经济和社会价值的情况下，应采取措施促进和增强该遗产的明显的文化和教育价值以服务于保护、保存和展示该遗产的基本目的。

63. 为文化和自然遗产组成部分所做的一切努力，都应考虑其代表一种环境，一种与人类及其地位相适应的建筑或城镇设计形式而自身蕴藏的内在的文化价值和教育价值。

64. 应建立志愿者机构以鼓励国家和地方当局充分利用其保护权力并向它们提供帮助及必要时替它们筹措资金。这些机构应该同地方历史学会、友好促进会、地方发展委员会以及旅游机构等保持联系，还可以组织其成员参观和游览文化和自然遗产的不同项目。

65. 为了说明已列入计划、正在进行的文化和自然遗产组成部分的修复工程，可设立信息中心、博物馆或举办展览。

七. 国际合作

66. 各成员国应就文化和自然遗产的保护、保存和展示进行合作，在必要情况下，从政府间和非政府间的国际组织寻求援助。这种多边或双边合作应认真予以协调，并采取以下形式的措施：

（1）交流信息及交换科技出版物；

（2）组织专题讨论会或工作小组；

（3）提供学习和旅游奖学金，提供科技行政人员与设备；

（4）通过让年轻研究人员和技术人员参加建筑项目、考古发掘和自然遗址的保护提供国外科技培训的便利；

（5）在一些成员国之间就保护、发掘、修复和修缮工程的大型项目进行协作，以推广所取得的经验。

Recommendation concerning the Protection, at National Level, of the Cultural and Natural Heritage[1]

Adopted by the UNESCO General Conference at its 17th Session, Paris, 16 November 1972

The General Conference of the United Nations Educational, Scientific and Cultural Organization, meeting in Paris, at its seventeenth session, from 17 October to 21 November 1972,

Considering that, in a society where living conditions are changing at an accelerated pace, it is essential for man's equilibrium and development to preserve for him a fitting setting in which to live, where he will remain in contact with nature and the evidences of civilization bequeathed by past generations, and that, to this end, it is appropriate to give the cultural and natural heritage an active function in community life and to integrate into an over-all policy the achievements of our time, the values of the past and the beauty of nature,

Considering that such integration into social and economic life must be one of the fundamental aspects of regional development and national planning at every level,

Considering that particularly serious dangers engendered by new phenomena peculiar to our times are threatening the cultural and natural heritage, which constitute an essential feature of mankind's heritage and a source of enrichment and harmonious development for present and future civilization,

Considering that each item of the cultural and natural heritage is unique and that the disappearance of any one item constitutes a definite loss and an irreversible impoverishment of that heritage,

Considering that every country in whose territory there are components of the cultural and natural heritage has an obligation to safeguard this part of mankind's heritage and to ensure that it is handed down to future generations,

Considering that the study, knowledge and protection of the cultural and natural heritage in the various countries of the world are conductive to mutual understanding among the peoples,

Considering that the cultural and natural heritage forms a harmonious whole, the components of which are indissociable,

Considering that a policy for the protection of the cultural and natural heritage, thought out and formulated in common, is likely to bring about a continuing interaction among Member States and to have a decisive effect on

---

[1] Records of the General Conference, 17th session, Paris, 17 October to 21 November 1972, v. 1: Resolutions, recommendations. UNESCO Document Code: 17 C/Resolutions + CORR.

the activities of the United Nations Educational, Scientific and Cultural Organization in this field,

Noting that the General Conference has already adopted international instruments for the protection of the cultural and natural heritage, such as the Recommendation on International Principles Applicable to Archaeological Excavations (1956), the Recommendation concerning the Safeguarding of the Beauty and Character of Landscapes and Sites (1962), and the Recommendation concerning the Preservation of Cultural Property Endangered by Public or Private Works (1968),

Desiring to supplement and extend the application of the standards and principles laid down in such recommendations,

Having before its proposals concerning the protection of the cultural and natural heritage, which question appears on the agenda of the session as item 23,

Having decided, at its sixteenth session, that this question should be made the subject of international regulations, to take the form of a recommendation to Member States,

Adopts, this sixteenth day of November 1972, this Recommendation.

I. DEFINITIONS OF THE CULTURAL AND THE NATURAL HERITAGE

1. For the purposes of this Recommendation, the following shall be considered as 'cultural heritage':

Monuments: architectural works, works of monumental sculpture and painting, including cave dwellings and inscriptions, and elements, groups of elements or structures of special value from the point of view of archaeology, history, art or science;

Groups of buildings: groups of separate or connected buildings which, because of their architecture, their homogeneity or their place in the landscape, are of special value from the point of view of history, art or science;

Sites: topographical areas, the combined works of man and of nature, which are of special value by reason of their beauty or their interest from the archaeological, historical, ethnological or anthropological points of view.

2. For the purposes of this Recommendation, the following shall be considered as 'natural heritage':

Natural features consisting of physical and biological formations or groups of such formations, which are of special value from the aesthetic or scientific point of view;

Geological and physiographical formations and precisely delineated areas which constitute the habitat of species of animals and plants, valuable or threatened, of special value from the point of view of science or conservation;

Natural sites or precisely delineated natural areas of special value from the point of view of science, conservation or natural beauty, or in their relation to the combined works of man and of nature.

II. NATIONAL POLICY

3. In conformity with their jurisdictional and legislative requirements, each State should formulate, develop and apply as far as possible a policy whose principal aim should be to co-ordinate and make use of all scientific, technical, cultural and other resources available to secure the effective protection, conservation and presentation of the cultural and natural heritage.

III. GENERAL PRINCIPLES

4. The cultural and natural heritage represents wealth, the protection, conservation and presentation of which impose responsibilities on the States in whose territory it is situated, both vis-a-vis their own nationals and vis-a-vis the international community as a whole; Member States should take such action as may be necessary to meet these responsibilities.

5. The cultural or natural heritage should be considered in its entirety as a homogeneous whole, comprising not only works of great intrinsic value, but also more modest items that have, with the passage of time, acquired cultural or natural value.

6. None of these works and none of these items should, as a general rule, be dissociated from its environment.

7. As the ultimate purpose of protecting, conserving and presenting the cultural and natural heritage is the development of man, Member States should, as far as possible, direct their work in this field in such a way that the cultural and natural heritage may no longer be regarded as a check on national development but as a determining factor in such development.

8. The protection, conservation and effective presentation of the cultural and natural heritage should be considered as one of the essential aspects of regional development plans, and planning in general, at the national, regional or local level.

9. An active policy for the conservation of the cultural and natural heritage and for giving it a place in community life should be developed. Member States should arrange for concerted action by all the public and private services concerned, with a view to drawing up and applying such a policy. Preventive and corrective measures relating to the cultural and natural heritage should be supplemented by others, designed to give each of the components of this heritage a function which will make it a part of the nation's social, economic, scientific and cultural life for the present and future, compatible with the cultural or natural character of the item in question. Action for the protection of the cultural and natural heritage should take advantage of scientific and technical advances in all branches of study involved in the protection, conservation and presentation of the cultural or natural heritage.

10. Increasingly significant financial resources should, as far as possible, be made available by the public authorities for the safeguarding and presentation of the cultural and natural heritage.

11. The general public of the area should be associated with the measures to be taken for protection and conservation and should be called on for suggestions and help, with particular reference to regard for and surveillance of the cultural and natural heritage. Consideration might also be given to the possibility of financial support from the private sector.

IV. ORGANIZATION OF SERVICES

12. Although their diversity makes it impossible for all Member States to adopt a standard form of organization, certain common criteria should nevertheless be observed.

Specialized public services

13. With due regard for the conditions appropriate to each country, Member States should set up in their territory, wherever they do not already exist, one or more specialized public services to be responsible for the

efficient discharge of the following functions:

(a) developing and putting into effect measures of all kinds designed for the protection, conservation and presentation of the country's cultural and natural heritage and for making it an active factor in the life of the community; and primarily, compiling an inventory of the cultural and natural heritage and establishing appropriate documentation services;

(b) training and recruiting scientific, technical and administrative staff as required, to be responsible for working out identification, protection, conservation and integration programmes and directing their execution;

(c) organizing close co-operation among specialists of various disciplines to study the technical conservation problems of the cultural and natural heritage;

(d) using or creating laboratories for the study of all the scientific problems arising in connection with the conservation of the cultural and natural heritage;

(e) ensuring that owners or tenants carry out the necessary restoration work and provide for the upkeep of the buildings in the best artistic and technical conditions.

Advisory bodies

14. The specialized services should work with bodies of experts responsible for giving advice on the preparation of measures relating to the cultural and natural heritage. Such bodies should include experts, representatives of the major preservation societies, and representatives of the administrations concerned.

Co-operation among the various bodies

15. The specialized services dealing with the protection, conservation and presentation of the cultural and natural heritage should carry out their work in liaison and on an equal footing with other public services, more particularly those responsible for regional development planning, major public works, the environment, and economic and social planning. Tourist development programmes involving the cultural and natural heritage should be carefully drawn up so as not to impair the intrinsic character and importance of that heritage, and steps should be taken to establish appropriate liaison between the authorities concerned.

16. Continuing co-operation at all levels should be organized among the specialized services when-ever large-scale projects are involved, and appropriate coordinating arrangements made so that decisions may be taken in concert, taking account of the various interests involved. Provision should be made for joint planning from the start of the studies and machinery developed for the settlement of conflicts.

Competence of central, federal, regional and local bodies

17. Considering the fact that the problems involved in the protection, conservation and presentation of the cultural and natural heritage are difficult to deal with, calling for special knowledge and sometimes entailing hard choices, and that there are not enough specialized staff available in this field, responsibilities in all matters concerning the devising and execution of protective measures in general should be divided among central or federal and regional or local authorities on the basis of a judicious balance adapted to the situation that exists in each State.

V. PROTECTIVE MEASURES

18. Member States should, as far as possible, take all necessary scientific, technical and administrative, legal and financial measures to ensure the protection of the cultural and natural heritage in their territories. Such

measures should be determined in accordance with the legislation and organization of the State.

Scientific and technical measures

19. Member States should arrange for careful and constant maintenance of their cultural and natural heritage in order to avoid having to undertake the costly operations necessitated by its deterioration; for this purpose, they should provide for regular surveillance of the components of their heritage by means of periodic inspections. They should also draw up carefully planned programmes of conservation and presentation work, gradually taking in all the cultural and natural heritage, depending upon the scientific, technical and financial means at their disposal.

20. Any work required should be preceded and accompanied by such thorough studies as its importance may necessitate. Such studies should be carried out in co-operation with or by specialists in all related fields.

21. Member States should investigate effective methods of affording added protection to those components of the cultural and natural heritage that are threatened by unusually serious dangers. Such methods should take account of the interrelated scientific, technical and artistic problems involved and make it possible to determine the treatment to be applied.

22. These components of the cultural and natural heritage should, in addition, be restored, wherever appropriate, to their former use or given a new and more suitable function, provided that their cultural value is not thereby diminished.

23. Any work done on the cultural heritage should aim at preserving its traditional appearance and protecting it from any new construction or remodeling which might impair the relations of mass or colour between it and its surroundings.

24. The harmony established by time and man between a monument and its surroundings is of the greatest importance and should not, as a general rule, be disturbed or destroyed. The isolation of a monument by demolishing its surroundings should not, as a general rule, be authorized; nor should the moving of a monument be contemplated save as an exceptional means of dealing with a problem, justified by pressing considerations.

25. Member States should take measures to protect their cultural and natural heritage against the possible harmful effects of the technological development characteristics of modern civilization. Such measures should be designed to counter the effects of shocks and vibrations caused by machines and vehicles. Measures should also be taken to prevent pollution and guard against natural disasters and calamities. and to provide for the repair of damage to the cultural and natural heritage.

26. Since the circumstances governing the rehabilitation of groups of buildings are not everywhere identical, Member States should provide for a social science inquiry in appropriate cases, in order to ascertain precisely what are the social and cultural needs of the community in which the group of buildings concerned is situated. Any rehabilitation operation should pay special attention to enabling man to work, to develop and to achieve fulfilment in the restored setting.

27. Member States should undertake studies and research on the geology and ecology of items of the natural heritage, such as park, wildlife, refuge or recreation areas, or other equivalent reserves, in order to appreciate their scientific value, to determine the impact of visitor use and to monitor interrelationships so as to avoid serious damage to the heritage and to provide adequate background for the management of the fauna and flora.

28. Member States should keep abreast of advances in transportation, communication, audio-visual techniques, automatic data-processing and other appropriate technology, and of cultural and recreational trends, so that the best possible facilities and services can be provided for scientific study and the enjoyment of the public, appropriate to the purpose of each area, without deterioration of the natural resources.

Administrative measures

29. Each Member State should draw up, as soon as possible, an inventory for the protection of its cultural and natural heritage, including items which, without being of outstanding importance, are inseparable from their environment and contribute to its character.

30. The information obtained by such surveys of the cultural and natural heritage should be collected in a suitable form and regularly brought up to date.

31. To ensure that the cultural and natural heritage is effectively recognized at all levels of planning, Member States should prepare maps and the fullest possible documentation covering the cultural and natural property in question.

32. Member States should give thought to finding suitable uses for groups of historic buildings no longer serving their original purpose.

33. A plan should be prepared for the protection, conservation, presentation and rehabilitation of groups of buildings of historic and artistic interest. It should include peripheral protection belts, lay down the conditions for land use, and specify the buildings to be preserved and the conditions for their preservation. This plan should be incorporated into the over-all town and country planning policy for the areas concerned.

34. Rehabilitation plans should specify the uses to which historic buildings are to be put, and the links there are to be between the rehabilitation area and the surrounding urban development. When the designation of a rehabilitation area is under consideration, the local authorities and representatives of the residents of the area should be consulted.

35. Any work that might result in changing the existing state of the buildings in a protected area should be subject to prior authorization by the town and country planning authorities, on the advice of the specialized services responsible for the protection of the cultural and natural heritage.

36. Internal alterations to groups of buildings and the installation of modern conveniences should be allowed if they are needed for the well-being of their occupants and provided they do not drastically alter the real characteristic features of ancient dwellings.

37. Member States should develop short-and long-range plans, based on inventories of their natural heritage, to achieve a system of conservation to meet the needs of their countries.

38. Member States should provide an advisory service to guide non-governmental organizations and owners of land on national conservation policies consistent with the productive use of the land.

39. Member States should develop policies and programmes for restoration of natural areas made derelict by industry, or otherwise despoiled by man's activities.

Legal measures

40. Depending upon their importance, the components of the cultural and natural heritage should be protected, individually or collectively, by legislation or regulations in conformity with the competence and the legal procedures of each country.

41. Measures for protection should be supplemented to the extent necessary by new provisions to promote the conservation of the cultural or natural heritage and to facilitate the presentation of its components. To that end, enforcement of protective measures should apply to individual owners and to public authorities when they are the owners of components of the cultural and natural heritage.

42. No new building should be erected, and no demolition, transformation, modification or deforestation carried out, on any property situated on or in the vicinity of a protected site, if it is likely to affect its appearance,

without authorization by the specialized services.

43. Planning legislation to permit industrial development, or public and private works should take into account existing legislation on conservation. The authorities responsible for the protection of the cultural and natural heritage might take steps to expedite the necessary conservation work, either by making financial assistance available to the owner, or by acting in the owner's place and exercising their powers to have the work done, with the possibility of their obtaining reimbursement of that share of the costs which the owner would normally have paid.

44. Where required for the preservation of the property, the public authorities might be empowered to expropriate a protected building or natural site subject to the terms and conditions of domestic legislation.

45. Member States should establish regulations to control bill-posting, neon signs and other kinds of advertisement, commercial signs, camping, the erection of poles, pylons and electricity or telephone cables, the placing of television aerials, all types of vehicular traffic and parking, the placing of indicator panels, street furniture, etc., and, in general, everything connected with the equipment or occupation of property forming part of the cultural and natural heritage.

46. The effects of the measures taken to protect any element of the cultural or natural heritage should continue regardless of changes of ownership. If a protected building or natural site is sold, the purchaser should be informed that it is under protection.

47. Penalties or administrative sanctions should be applicable, in accordance with the laws and constitutional competence of each State, to anyone who wilfully destroys, mutilates or defaces a protected monument, group of buildings or site, or one which is of archaeological, historical or artistic interest. In addition, equipment used in illicit excavation might be subject to confiscation.

48. Penalties or administrative sanctions should be imposed upon those responsible for any other action detrimental to the protection, conservation or presentation of a protected component of the cultural or natural heritage, and should include provision for the restoration of an affected site to its original state in accordance with established scientific and technical standards.

Financial measures

49. Central and local authorities should, as far as possible, appropriate, in their budgets, a certain percentage of funds, proportionate to the importance of the protected property forming part of their cultural or natural heritage, for the purposes of maintaining, conserving and presenting protected property of which they are the owners, and of contributing financially to such work carried out on other protected property by the owners, whether public bodies or private persons.

50. The expenditure incurred in protecting, conserving and presenting items of the privately owned cultural and natural heritage should, so far as possible, be borne by their owners or users.

51. Tax concessions on such expenditures, or grants or loans on favourable terms, could be granted to private owners of protected properties, on condition that they carry out work for the protection, conservation, presentation and rehabilitation of their properties in accordance with approved standards.

52. Consideration should be given to indemnifying, if necessary, owners of protected cultural and natural areas for losses they might suffer as a consequence of protective programmes.

53. The financial advantages accorded to private owners should, where appropriate, be dependent on their observance of certain conditions laid down for the benefit of the public, such as their allowing access to parks, gardens and sites, tours through all or parts of natural sites, monuments or groups of buildings, the taking of

photographs, etc.

54. Special funds should be set aside in the budgets of public authorities for the protection of the cultural and natural heritage endangered by large-scale public or private works.

55. To increase the financial resources available to them, Member States may set up one or more 'Cultural and Natural Heritage Funds', as legally established public agencies, entitled to receive private gifts, donations and bequests, particularly from industrial and commercial firms.

56. Tax concessions could also be granted to those making gifts, donations or bequests for the acquisition, restoration or maintenance of specific components of the cultural and natural heritage.

57. In order to facilitate operations for rehabilitation of the natural and cultural heritage, Member States might make special arrangements, particularly by way of loans for renovation and restoration work, and might also make the necessary regulations to avoid price rises caused by real-estate speculation in the areas under consideration.

58. To avoid hardship to the poorer inhabitants consequent on their having to move from rehabilitated buildings or groups of buildings, compensation for rises in rent might be contemplated so as to enable them to keep their accommodation. Such compensation should be temporary and determined on the basis of the income of the parties concerned, so as to enable them to meet the increased costs occasioned by the work carried out.

59. Member States might facilitate the financing of work of any description for the benefit of the cultural and natural heritage, by instituting 'Loan Funds', supported by public institutions and private credit establishments, which would be responsible for granting loans to owners at low interest rates and with repayment spread out over a long period.

VI. EDUCATIONAL AND CULTURAL ACTION

60. Universities, educational establishments at all levels and lifelong education establishments should organize regular courses, lectures, seminars, etc., on the history of art, architecture, the environment and town planning.

61. Member States should undertake educational campaigns to arouse widespread public interest in, and respect for, the cultural and natural heritage. Continuing efforts should be made to inform the public about what is being and can be done to protect the cultural or natural heritage and to inculcate appreciation and respect for the values it enshrines. For this purpose, all media of information should be employed as required.

62. Without overlooking the great economic and social value of the cultural and natural heritage, measures should be taken to promote and reinforce the eminent cultural and educational value of that heritage, furnishing as it does the fundamental motive for protecting, conserving and presenting it.

63. All efforts on behalf of components of the cultural and natural heritage should take account of the cultural and educational value inherent in them as representative of an environment, a form of architecture or urban design commensurate with man and on his scale.

64. Voluntary organizations should be set up to encourage national and local authorities to make full use of their powers with regard to protection, to afford them support and, if necessary, to obtain funds for them; these bodies should keep in touch with local historical societies, amenity improvement societies, local development committees and agencies concerned with tourism, etc., and might also organize visits to, and guided tours of, different items of the cultural and natural heritage for their members.

65. Information centres, museums or exhibitions might be set up to explain the work being carried out on components of the cultural and natural heritage scheduled for rehabilitation.

VII. INTERNATIONAL CO-OPERATION

66. Member States should co-operate with regard to the protection, conservation and presentation of the cultural and natural heritage, seeking aid, if it seems desirable, from international organizations, both intergovernmental and non-governmental. Such multilateral or bilateral co-operation should be carefully coordinated and should take the form of measures such as the following:

(a) exchange of information and of scientific and technical publications;

(b) organization of seminars and working parties on particular subjects;

(c) provision of study and travel fellowships, and of scientific, technical and administrative staff, and equipment;

(d) provision of facilities for scientific and technical training abroad, by allowing young research workers and technicians to take part in architectural projects, archaeological excavations and the conservation of natural sites;

(e) co-ordination, within a group of Member States, of large-scale projects involving conservation, excavations, restoration and rehabilitation work, with the object of making the experience gained generally available

文化遗产

关于历史性纪念物修复的雅典宪章[①]

(第一届历史古迹建筑师及技师国际会议1931年在雅典通过)

在雅典会议上通过了以下七项决议,它被称为"修复宪章":
1. 创立纪念物保护修复方面运作和咨询的国际组织;
2. 计划修复的项目应接受有见地的考评,以避免出现有损建筑特性和历史价值的错误;
3. 所有国家都要通过国家立法来解决历史古迹的保存问题;
4. 已发掘的遗址若不是立即修复的话应回填以利于保护;
5. 在修复工程中允许采用现代技术和材料;
6. 考古遗址将实行严格的"监护式"保护(custodial protection);
7. 应注意对历史古迹周边地区的保护。

雅典会议的概括性结论为:

第一条 学说和普遍原理

会议听取了有关纪念物保护的普遍原理和学说的陈述。

尽管具体案例多种多样,可能也会有不同的解决方案,会议注意到不同国家主流的解决办法都反映出同样的趋势,即应通过创立一个定期、持久的维护体系来有计划地保护建筑,从而摒弃整体重建的做法,以避免出现相应的危险。

当由于坍塌或破坏而必须进行修复时,大会建议,应该尊重过去的历史和艺术作品,不排斥任何一个特定时期的风格。

会议认为建筑物的使用有利于延续建筑的寿命,应继续使用他们,但使用功能必须以尊重建筑的历史和艺术特征为前提。

第二条 保护历史性纪念物的行政和立法措施

会议听取了为保护具有艺术、历史和科学价值的纪念物,不同国家在法律措施方面的建议。

在尊重私有权问题的同时,还要认可某些公共权力的存在,这一基本倾向得到会议的一致认同。

会议意识到不同国家法律措施间存在的差异,是由于在协调公法和私人利益之间存在困难。

因而,会议形成了这样一个共识:在赞同这些措施总体趋向的同时,相关措施应该顺应当地状况和公众意见,以便在实施过程中使阻力最小化。房产所有者为满足全局利益要求所做出的牺牲需得到应有的补偿。

会议建议每个国家的行政当局在面对紧急情况时,能够采取相应的保全措施。

大会热切的希望国际博物馆办事处(IMO)出版一份有关不同国家所施行法律的目录和比较性报表,并将这一信息不断更新。

[①] 译者:吴黎梅,张松。引自:联合国教科文组织世界遗产中心,国际古迹遗址理事会,国际文物保护与修复研究中心,中国国家文物局主编.国际文化遗产保护文件选编[M].北京:文物出版社,2007。

第三条 提升文物古迹的美学意义

会议认为,在建造过程中,新建筑的选址应尊重城市特征和周边环境,特别是当其邻近文物古迹时,应给予周边环境特别考虑。一些特殊的建筑群和风景如画的眺望景观也需要加以保护。

从保存其历史特征的角度出发,有必要研究某些纪念物或纪念物群适合配置何种装饰性花木。会议特别强调,在具有艺术和历史价值的纪念物的邻近地区,应杜绝设置任何形式的广告和树立有损景观的电杆,不许建设有噪音污染的工厂和高耸柱状物。

第四条 纪念物的修复

专家们听取了采用现代材料对文物古迹进行加固的各种意见,并赞成谨慎运用所有已掌握的现代技术资源,特别是钢筋混凝土。

专家们强调这样的加固工作应尽可能地隐藏起来,以保证修复后的纪念物其原有外观和特征得以保留。

专家们建议新材料的使用尤其适合于以下情况:当需要保护的部分采用新材料能够避免解体和复原的威胁时。

第五条 文物古迹的老化

会议注意到,在当前条件下,全世界的历史性纪念物都受到越来越严重的空气污染的威胁。

除了经常的预防和当前行之有效的用于保护纪念性雕塑的方法外,由于情况的复杂性和现有技术的局限性,不可能总结出一套普遍适用的法则来。

会议建议:

1. 每个国家的建筑师和纪念物的监管人都应该与物理、化学和自然科学专家合作,以便决定在特定的情况下采取相应措施;

2. 国际博物馆办事处(IMO)应及时被告知每个国家在这方面所取得的最新进展,并将其收入到办事处的出版物中。

关于纪念性雕塑的保护,会议认为原则上不鼓励将艺术品从原有的环境中迁出,会议建议只要这些艺术原作还存在,就必须采取一些防范措施来保护它们,一旦被证实其无法保护,才能采用浇铸的方法。

第六条 保护的技术

令人满意的是,会议在进行各项详细交流之前,在保护原则和技术方面就达成了共识,即:

对废墟遗址要小心谨慎地进行保护,必须尽可能地将找到的原物碎片进行修复,此做法称为原物归位(anastylosis)。为了这一目的所使用的新材料必须是可识别的。在发掘过程中当重见天日的废墟不可能被保护时,会议建议将其回填,并对回填之前的工作过程进行仔细记录。

毫无疑问,与发掘和保护文物古迹相关的技术工作,需要考古学家和建筑师的紧密合作。

至于其他纪念物,专家一致认为,在任何加固或局部修复行为实施之前,必须对其损坏和自然衰败进行全面的分析,他们认为,每个个案都要分别对待。

第七条 纪念物保护和国际协作

(一)技术上和理念上的合作

会议深信,保护具有艺术和考古价值的人类资产,是一个值得所有作为文明载体的国家应该关注的问题。

会议希望各国在《国际联盟公约》(CLN)的精神指导下,以更大的规模和更为具体的方式相互合作,以加强对具有艺术和历史价值的纪念物的保护。

在遵守国际法的前提下,将为那些对保护感兴趣、有资质的机构和组织提供各种机会,以保护那些代表了人类文明发展的最高峰、或面临毁灭威胁的艺术作品。

为实现国际协作这一共同目标,我们寄希望于国际智力合作组织联盟(ICOLN),同时也寄希望于各国的关注和重视。

在国际博物馆办事处（IMO）经过调查，并搜集了相关信息，尤其是来自国家智力合作委员会（NCIC）所关心的问题后，国际智力合作委员会（ICIC）应就拟采取步骤的合理性和每个案例中应遵循的规程表态。

大会成员在商议以及在当地所做的研究考察过程中，参观了大量被发现的遗址和古希腊纪念物，他们一致赞赏希腊政府的作为。多年来希腊政府一直担负着大量的保护工作，并且与来自不同国家的考古学家和专家开展合作。

大会成员在此看到了一个实践典范，它不但能够而且已经为实现智力合作作出了贡献，并在这一过程中使自身的努力得到证实。

（二）教育在保护过程中的作用

大会坚信，保护纪念物和艺术品最可靠的保证是人民大众对它们的珍惜和爱惜；公共当局通过恰当的举措可以在很大程度上提升这一感情。

会议建议教育工作者应劝阻孩子和年轻人做出污损各类纪念物外观的行为，并且教导他们在保护各个文明时期遗留下来的有形见证上，应该投入更大、更广泛的兴趣。

（三）国际文献的价值

大会表达了以下愿望：

1. 为实现这一目标，每个国家或者专门创立的有一定资质的相关机构，应出版一份有关文物古迹的详细清单，并附照片和文字注释；

2. 多国建立的官方档案中应包含本国历史性纪念物的所有文档；

3. 各国都应该在国际博物馆办事处存放有关艺术和历史性纪念物的出版物；

4. 办事处的出版物中应指定一部分篇幅用于详细介绍历史性纪念物保存的总体进展和方法；

5. 办事处将研究出一套最佳方法以使用这些收集来的资料。

The Athens Charter for the Restoration of Historic Monuments

Adopted at the First International Congress of Architects and Technicians of Historic Monuments, Athens, 1931

At the Congress in Athens the following seven main resolutions were made and called "Carta del Restauro":
1. International organizations for Restoration on operational and advisory levels are to be established.
2. Proposed Restoration projects are to be subjected to knowledgeable criticism to prevent mistakes which will cause loss of character and historical values to the structures.
3. Problems of preservation of historic sites are to be solved by legislation at national level for all countries.
4. Excavated sites which are not subject to immediate restoration should be reburied for protection.
5. Modern techniques and materials may be used in restoration work.
6. Historical sites are to be given strict custodial protection.
7. Attention should be given to the protection of areas surrounding historic sites.

General Conclusions of the Athens Conference.

I. DOCTRINES. GENERAL PRINCIPLES.

The Conference heard the statement of the general principles and doctrines relating to the protection of monuments.

Whatever may be the variety of concrete cases, each of which are open to a different solution, the Conference noted that there predominates in the different countries represented a general tendency to abandon restorations in toto and to avoid the attendant dangers by initiating a system of regular and permanent maintenance calculated to ensure the preservation of the buildings.

When, as the result of decay or destruction, restoration appears to be indispensable, it recommends that the historic and artistic work of the past should be respected, without excluding the style of any given period.

The Conference recommends that the occupation of buildings, which ensures the continuity of their life, should be maintained but that they should be used for a purpose which respects their historic or artistic character.

II. ADMINISTRATIVE AND LEGISLATIVE MEASURES REGARDING HISTORICAL MONUMENTS.

The Conference heard the statement of legislative measures devised to protect monuments of artistic, historic or scientific interest and belonging to the different countries.

It unanimously approved the general tendency which, in this connection, recognises a certain right of the community in regard to private ownership.

It noted that the differences existing between these legislative measures were due to the difficulty of reconciling public law with the rights of individuals.

Consequently, while approving the general tendency of these measures, the Conference is of opinion that they should be in keeping with local circumstances and with the trend of public opinion, so that the least possible opposition may be encountered, due allowance being made for the sacrifices which the owners of property may be called upon to make in the general interest.

It recommends that the public authorities in each country be empowered to take conservatory measures in cases of emergency.

It earnestly hopes that the International Museums Office will publish a repertory and a comparative table of the legislative measures in force in the different countries and that this information will be kept up to date.

III. AESTHETIC ENHANCEMENT OF ANCIENT MONUMENTS.

The Conference recommends that, in the construction of buildings, the character and external aspect of the cities in which they are to be erected should be respected, especially in the neighborhood of ancient monuments, where the surroundings should be given special consideration. Even certain groupings and certain particularly picturesque perspective treatment should be preserved.

A study should also be made of the ornamental vegetation most suited to certain monuments or groups of monuments from the point of view of preserving their ancient character. It specially recommends the suppression of all forms of publicity, of the erection of unsightly telegraph poles and the exclusion of all noisy factories and even of tall shafts in the neighborhood of artistic and historic monuments.

IV. RESTORATION OF MONUMENTS.

The experts heard various communications concerning the use of modern materials for the consolidation of ancient monuments. They approved the judicious use of all the resources at the disposal of modern technique and more especially of reinforced concrete.

They specified that this work of consolidation should whenever possible be concealed in order that the aspect and character of the restored monument may be preserved.

They recommended their adoption more particularly in cases where their use makes it possible to avoid the dangers of dismantling and reinstating the portions to be preserved.

V. THE DETERIORATION OF ANCIENT MONUMENTS.

The Conference noted that, in the conditions of present day life, monuments throughout the world were being threatened to an ever-increasing degree by atmospheric agents.

Apart from the customary precautions and the methods successfully applied in the preservation of monumental statuary in current practice, it was impossible, in view of the complexity of cases and with the knowledge at present available, to formulate any general rules.

The Conference recommends:

1. That, in each country, the architects and curators of monuments should collaborate with specialists in the physical, chemical, and natural sciences with a view to determining the methods to be adopted in specific cases;

2. That the International Museums Office should keep itself informed of the work being done in each country in this field and that mention should be made thereof in the publications of the Office.

With regard to the preservation of monumental sculpture, the Conference is of opinion that the removal of works of art from the surroundings for which they were designed is, in principle, to be discouraged. It recommends, by way of precaution, the preservation of original models whenever these still exist or if this proves impossible, the taking of casts.

VI. THE TECHNIQUE OF CONSERVATION.

The Conference is gratified to note that the principles and technical considerations set forth in the different detailed communications are inspired by the same idea, namely:

In the case of ruins, scrupulous conservation is necessary, and steps should be taken to reinstate any original fragments that may be recovered (anastylosis), whenever this is possible; the new materials used for this purpose should in all cases be recognisable. When the preservation of ruins brought to light in the course of excavations is found to be impossible, the Conference recommends that they be buried, accurate records being of course taken before filling-in operations are undertaken.

It should be unnecessary to mention that the technical work undertaken in connection with the excavation and preservation of ancient monuments calls for close collaboration between the archaeologist and the architect.

With regard to other monuments, the experts unanimously agreed that, before any consolidation or partial restoration is undertaken, a thorough analysis should be made of the defects and the nature of the decay of these monuments. They recognised that each case needed to be treated individually.

VII. THE CONSERVATION OF MONUMENTS AND INTERNATIONAL COLLABORATION.

a) Technical and moral co-operation.

The Conference, convinced that the question of the conservation of the artistic and archaeological property of mankind is one that interests the community of the States, which are wardens of civilisation,

Hopes that the States, acting in the spirit of the Covenant of the League of Nations, will collaborate with each other on an ever-increasing scale and in a more concrete manner with a view to furthering the preservation of artistic and historic monuments;

Considers it highly desirable that qualified institutions and associations should, without in any manner whatsoever prejudicing international public law, be given an opportunity of manifesting their interest in the protection of works of art in which civilisation has been expressed to the highest degree and which would seem to be threatened with destruction;

Expresses the wish that requests to attain this end, submitted to the Intellectual Co-operation Organisation of the League of Nations, be recommended to the earnest attention of the States.

It will be for the International Committee on Intellectual Co-operation, after an enquiry conducted by the International Museums Office and after having collected all relevant information, more particularly from the

National Committee on Intellectual Co-operation concerned, to express an opinion on the expediency of the steps to be taken and on the procedure to be followed in each individual case.

The members of the Conference, after having visited in the course of their deliberations and during the study cruise which they were able to make on this occasion, a number of excavation sites and ancient Greek monuments, unanimously paid a tribute to the Greek Government, which, for many years past, has been itself responsible for extensive works and, at the same time, has accepted the collaboration of archaeologists and experts from every country.

The members of the Conference there saw an example of activity which can but contribute to the realisation of the aims of intellectual co-operation, the need for which manifested itself during their work.

b) The role of education in the respect of monuments.

The Conference, firmly convinced that the best guarantee in the matter of the preservation of monuments and works of art derives from the respect and attachment of the peoples themselves;

Considering that these feelings can very largely be promoted by appropriate action on the part of public authorities;

Recommends that educators should urge children and young people to abstain from disfiguring monuments of every description and that they should teach them to take a greater and more general interest in the protection of these concrete testimonies of all ages of civilisation.

c) Value of international documentation.

The Conference expresses the wish that:

1. Each country, or the institutions created or recognised competent for this purpose, publish an inventory of ancient monuments, with photographs and explanatory notes;

2. Each country constitute official records which shall contain all documents relating to its historic monuments;

3. Each country deposit copies of its publications on artistic and historic monuments with the International Museums Office;

4. The Office devote a portion of its publications to articles on the general processes and methods employed in the preservation of historic monuments;

5. The Office study the best means of utilizing the information so centralised.

关于在武装冲突的情况下保护文化财产的公约[①]

(联合国教科文组织政府间会议 1954 年 5 月 14 日订立于海牙)

各缔约国：

认为文化财产在最近的一些冲突过程中遭受到严重的损害，并由于战争技术的发展，这些财产越来越受到摧毁的威胁；

确信鉴于各国人民均对世界文化作出了贡献，对文化财产（不管它属于哪国人民）的损害将构成对整个人类文化遗产的破坏；

考虑到保存文化遗产对全世界人民的极大重要性，务须确保这种遗产得到国际保护；

在 1899 年和 1907 年《海牙公约》以及 1935 年 4 月 15 日《华盛顿条约》中制订的关于在武装冲突情况下保护文化财产的原则指导下；

考虑到除非在和平时期即已采取国家性和国际性措施，否则，在武装冲突情况下的此种保护工作无法取得成效；

决心为保护文化财产采取一切可能的措施；

兹就下述条款达成协议：

第 I 章 关于保护的一般规则

第 1 条 文化财产之定义

为本公约之目的，下列财产被视为文化财产，而不论其来源或所有权归属：

a）对各国人民文化遗产具有很大重要性的财产（可移动或不可移动财产），诸如建筑、艺术或历史古迹（宗教的或世俗的）；考古遗址；本身具有历史或艺术意义的建筑群；艺术作品；手稿、书籍和其他具有艺术、历史或考古价值的物品，以及科学收藏品和书籍、档案或上述财产复制件等重要收藏物；

b）其主要和实际目的在于保存或展出 a）项规定之可移动文化财产的建筑物，如博物馆、大图书馆、档案储存室，以及在发生武装冲突情况下用于保护 a）项规定的可移动文化财产的保护所；

c）容有 a）、b）项规定的大量文化财产的中心，即"古迹中心"。

第 2 条 文化财产之保护

为本公约之目的，保护文化财产包括维护和尊重此种文化财产。

第 3 条 文化财产之维护

各缔约国保证为维护其本国领土上的文化财产免于武装冲突的可预见的影响，在和平时期即采取适

[①] 引自：Final act of the Intergovernmental Conference on the Protection of Cultural Property in the Event of Armed Conflict, The Hague, 1954(chi)。

当措施，预作准备。

第 4 条　文化财产之尊重

1. 各缔约国保证，既要尊重本国领土的文化财产，也要尊重其他缔约国领土内的文化财产，不得为利用这些财产及其毗邻地区，利用保护财产的规定为可能在武装冲突情况下使财产遭到摧毁或破坏的目的服务，不得采取任何针对此种财产的敌视行动。

2. 只有在军事上绝对需要的情况下，本条第 1 段提及之义务方可暂停执行。

3. 各缔约国保证禁止、防止，并在必要时制止任何形式的盗窃、劫掠或滥用文化财产的活动，以及对文化财产的任何破坏。各缔约国不得征用处于另一缔约国领土内的可移动文化财产。

4. 各缔约国不得采取任何针对文化财产的报复性措施。

5. 任何缔约国不得以另一缔约国未执行第 3 条规定的维护措施为理由拒不履行本条规定的对另一缔约国的义务。

第 5 条　占领

1. 全部或部分占领另一缔约国领土的缔约国应尽可能支持被占领土的主管国家当局维护和保存其文化财产的努力。

2. 如为保存被占领土内受到军事行动破坏的文化财产，紧急干预势在必行，而主管国家当局却无力采取措施时，占领国应尽最大可能和这些当局紧密合作，采取最为必要的各种保存措施。

3. 其政府被一抵抗运动各成员视为合法政府的任何缔约国应在可能时指请这些抵抗运动成员注意遵守公约中有关尊重文化财产诸条款的义务。

第 6 条　文化财产之特殊标记

根据第 16 条规定，文化财产可载有特殊标记，以利辨认。

第 7 条　军事措施

1. 各缔约国保证，在和平时期即应在其军事规章或指令中制定确保遵守本公约的条款，并向其武装部队人员灌输尊重文化和各国人民文化财产的精神。

2. 各缔约国保证，在和平时期即在其武装力量中筹建以确保尊重文化财产，并与负责维护这些财产的民政当局合作为宗旨的机构或调配专门人员。

第 II 章　特别保护

第 8 条　特别保护之提供

1. 在武装冲突情况下用于掩藏可移动文化财产的有限量的保护所、古迹中心及其他具有极大重要性的不可动文化财产可置于特别保护之下，只要它们：

a) 距离大工业中心或构成敏感地区的重要军事目标如机场、广播电台、国防机构，具有一定重要性的港口或火车站或交通干线等尚有相当的距离；

b) 并非用于军事目的。

2. 可移动文化财产的保护所，无论设于何处，只要其构筑得当，在任何情况下均不会为轰炸所破坏，则亦可置于特别保护之下。

3. 古迹中心一经用于军事人员或军事物资之调动（即使从中穿行）则须被视用于军事目的。如在中心内进行与军事行动、驻扎军事人员或生产战争物资直接有关的活动，则亦须被视为用于军事目的。

4. 由特设武装保卫人员实行第 1 段提及的对文化财产的保护，或由通常负责维护公共秩序的警察部队在文化财产所在地区驻守，不得视为用于军事目的。

5. 本条第 1 段所列文化财产如位于此段述及的一个重要军事目标附近地区，则亦可置于特别保护之下，但要求保护的缔约国须保证在武装冲突情况下不使用该军事目标，并在特别涉及港口、车站或机场时，保证不得用于任何交通运输。在此种情况下，改变交通线路工作需在和平时期准备就绪。

6. 对在"国际特别保护文化财产名册"上登记的文化财产须提供特别保护。此种注册在符合本公约条款并执行规则规定的条件下方可办理。

第9条 特别保护下文化财产之豁免

各缔约国应确保特别保护下文化财产的豁免权，并自此种财产在"国际文化财产名册"上注册之日起，不得对之采取任何敌对行为，亦不得将此种财产或其邻近地区用于军事目的（第8条第5段规定除外）。

第10条 标记和监督

在武装冲突过程中置于特别保护下的文化财产须载有第16条所述的特殊标记，并须接受本公约执行规则中规定的国际监督。

第11条 豁免权之取消

1. 如缔约一方对置于特别保护下的文化财产犯了第9条规定的义务，则只要此种违犯现象一直存在，其敌对的另一方则不受确保文化财产享受豁免的义务。然而，凡可能情况下后者首先要求在合理时间内停止此种违犯活动。

2. 除本条第1段规定的情况外，只有在无法避免的军事需要的特别情况下，对置于特别保护下的文化财产的豁免方可停止实施，并得在需要不再存在时即行恢复，此种需要只能由相当于或高于师一级的部队首长予以确定。凡情况允许时，停止豁免权的决定应尽可能提前通知敌对的另一方。

3. 停止实施豁免的缔约国须尽快书面通知本公约执行规则中规定的文化财产专员，说明停止豁免的原因。

第Ⅲ章 文化财产的运输

第12条 特别保护下之运输

1. 专门用于转移文化财产之运输（不论在本国领土内还是在另一国领土内进行），可应有关缔约国的要求，按本公约执行规则规定的条件在特别保护下进行。

2. 特别保护下的运输须在执行规则规定的国际监督下进行，并须载有第16条所述的特殊标记。

3. 各缔约国不得对特别保护下的运输采取任何敌视行动。

第13条 紧急情况下之运输

1. 如一缔约国认为，为了保证安全，需要对某文化财产进行转移，并认为此事紧急，不能遵循第12条中规定的程序（尤其在武装冲突的开始阶段），可在拟转移的文化财产上载列第16条规定的特殊标记，但须是在第12条中提到的豁免申请尚未提出并遭到拒绝的情况下方可这样做。应尽可能将转移一事通知敌对之另一方。但将文化财产转运至另一国领土可不需载有特殊标记，除非已明确予以豁免。

2. 缔约国应尽可能采取必要预防措施，避免针对本条第1段所述将予转移并载有特殊标记的文化财产的敌视行为。

第14条 免受没收、缴获和捕获

1. 须实行免受没收、缴获或捕获的有：

（1）享受第12条或第13条所规定的保护的文化财产；

（2）专门用于转移此类文化财产的运输工具；

2. 本条规定将丝毫不限制检查和搜查的权利。

第Ⅳ章 人员

第15条 人员

在符合安全需要的限度内,从保护文化财产的利益出发,从事保护文化财产的人员应受到尊重,如他们落到敌对国手中,只要他们所负责的文化财产也落到敌对国手中,就应允许他们继续履行其职责。

第Ⅴ章 特殊标记

第16条 公约之标记

1. 本公约的特殊标记为盾形,尖朝下,兰、白色相间(盾的下方为一品蓝色正方形,其一角为盾尖,上方为一品蓝色三角形,西侧各为一白色三角形)。
2. 此标记须单独使用,或根据第17条规定的条件,重复三次构成一三角形(一盾位于下方)。

第17条 标记之使用

1. 特殊标记只有作为确定下述情况的手段,方可重复三次:
（a）享受特别保护的不可动文化财产;
（b）根据第12条和第13条规定的条件运输文化财产的工具;
（c）根据公约执行规则规定的条件设立临时保护所。
2. 特殊标记只有作为确定下述情况的手段,方可单独使用:
（a）不享受特别保护的文化财产;
（b）根据公约执行规则负责监督的人员;
（c）文化财产保护人员;
（d）公约执行规则中提及的身份证。
3. 在武装冲突期间,在本条前几段未提及的其他情况下,均禁止使用特殊标记,并禁止出于任何目的使用类似特殊标记的标志。
4. 任何不可动文化财产,只有载有经缔约国主管当局正式签署和注明日期的认可标志,方可载有特殊标记。

第Ⅵ章 本公约之应用范围

第18条 公约之应用

1. 除在和平时期有效的条款外,本公约还适用于在两个或几个缔约国之间可能发生的已宣告的战争或其他武装冲突(即便其中一个或几个缔约国并未承认战争状态)。
2. 本公约还适用于对一个缔约国领土实行部分或全部占领的一切情况,即便该占领并未遇到武装抵抗。
3. 如冲突国家的一方不是本公约缔约国,属本公约缔约国的另一方则仍应在其相互关系中受本公约条款的约束。而且,如前者已宣布接受本公约条款并付诸实施,则后者在与其关系中应受本公约条款的约束。

第19条 非国际性冲突

1. 凡在一缔约国领土内发生非国际性武装冲突的情况下,冲突各方至少须实施本公约有关尊重文化财产的规定。

2. 冲突各方应通过特别安排，努力实施本公约其他所有或部分规定。
3. 联合国教科文组织可向冲突各方提供服务。
4. 上述条款的实施不得影响冲突各方的法律地位。

第Ⅶ章 公约之执行

第20条 公约执行规则
本公约执行规则确定了实施公约所需遵循的程序，因而构成本公约的组成部分之一。

第21条 保护国
本公约及其执行规则须在负责维护冲突各方利益的保护国的合作下实行。

第22条 调解程序
1. 当保护国认为由他们出面斡旋对文化财产可能有益时，特别在冲突各方对本公约或其执行规则条款的实施或解释出现分歧的情况下，保护国须提供斡旋服务。
2. 为此，各保护国可在一方或联合国教科文组织总干事的要求下，或自己主动向冲突各方建议，召集一次由各方代表尤其是有负责文化财产保护当局参加的会议，地点可在经适当选择的中立领土上。冲突各方有义务响应召开会议的建议。各保护国须提名一位中立国人士或一位联合国教科文组织总干事提出的人士，提请冲突各方批准作为主席参加此种会议。

第23条 教科文组织之协助
1. 在组织保护自己的文化财产或有关实施本公约及其执行规则的任何问题上，各缔约国可要求联合国教科文组织提供技术协助。本组织在其计划与可能的限度内提供此种协助。
2. 本组织有权主动就此问题向各缔约国提供建议。

第24条 特别协议
1. 各缔约国可就其认为宜于单独解决的任何问题达成特别协议。
2. 不得达成将削弱本公约对文化财产及其保护人员之保护的任何特别协议。

第25条 公约之传播
各缔约国保证在和平时期与武装冲突时期在各自国家内尽可能广泛地传播本公约及其执行规则的文本。各缔约国尤应保证将对公约及其执行规则的研究列入军事训练和民政训练（如可能）计划中，以使有关原则能为全体人民尤其是武装力量和文化财产保护人员所了解。

第26条 翻译本与报告
1. 各缔约国须通过联合国教科文组织总干事彼此送交本公约及其执行规则的正式译本。
2. 各缔约国还须至少每四年向总干事递交一份报告，就其各自主管部门实施本公约及其执行规则方面已采取、准备采取或正在考虑的措施，介绍自己认为适宜的情况。

第27条 会议
1. 联合国教科文组织总干事可在执行局的同意下召开各缔约国代表会议。如不少于五分之一的缔约国提出要求，总干事则必须召集此种会议。
2. 在不危害本公约或执行规则赋予的其他职能的情况下，会议的任务是研究与公约及其执行规则的实施有关的各项问题，并提出相应建议。
3. 如有多数缔约国出席，会议还可根据第39条规定修订公约或执行规则。

第28条 制裁
各缔约国保证在自己的刑法体制内采取一切必要措施，以便以刑罚或纪律制裁追究和打击一切违犯或下令违犯本公约者而不论其属何国籍。

最后条款

第29条 语文
1. 本公约用英文、西班牙文、法文和俄文制定，四种文本具有同等效力。
2. 联合国教科文组织须作出安排，将本公约译为大会其他正式语文。

第30条 签字
本公约的日期为1954年5月14日，但在1954年12月31日之前，应邀参加1954年4月21日至5月14日海牙会议的所有国家均可签字。

第31条 批准
1. 本公约须经签字国根据其各自立法程序予以批准。
2. 批准书须交联合国教科文组织总干事保存。

第32条 加入
自生效之日起，本公约将向第30条提及的未签字国和应联合国教科文组织执行局邀请加入的任何其他国家开放，供其加入。将加入书交联合国教科文组织总干事保存即为加入。

第33条 生效
1. 本公约在五份批准书交存三个月后即行生效。
2. 此后，本公约在每个缔约国递交批准书或加入书三个月后即对之生效。
3. 第18条和第19条所述形势如有出现，冲突各方在战争或占领开始之前或之后递交的批准和加入书须立即生效。在此种情况下，联合国教科文组织总干事须以最迅速的方式发出第38条提及的通知。

第34条 有效执行
1. 缔约国在公约生效之日即应采取一切必要措施以保证公约生效后六个月内得以有效执行。
2. 对公约生效后交存批准书或加入书的国家而言，这六个月的限期系从交存批准书或加入书之日算起。

第35条 公约扩大应用之领土范围
任何缔约国均可在批准或加入时在尔后的任何时候，书面通知联合国教科文组织总干事宣布本公约扩大到其国际关系由它负责的所有或任何一块领土。上述通知于收到三个月后即行生效。

第36条 与以前诸公约之关系
1. 凡受有关陆战法与惯例（Ⅳ）和有关战时海上轰炸（Ⅸ）的海牙公约（无论是1899年7月29日的海牙公约或是1907年10月18日的海牙公约）约束并系本公约缔约国的国家，在其相互关系中，本公约乃是对上述公约（Ⅸ）和上述公约（Ⅳ）所附规则的补充，并在本公约及其执行规则规定使用特殊标记的情况下，本公约第16条所确定的标记将取代上述公约（Ⅸ）第5条所确定的标记。
2. 凡受1935年4月15日保护艺术、科学机构与历史古迹的华盛顿条约（洛里奇条约）约束，并系本公约缔约国的国家，在其相互关系中，本公约是对华盛顿条约的补充，并在本公约及其执行规则规定使用特殊标记的情况下，本公约第16条所确定的标记将取代上述条约第Ⅲ条所确定的标志旗。

第37条 退约
1. 任何缔约国均可以本国名义或以其国际关系由它负责的任何一块领土的名义宣布退出本公约。
2. 退约通知须以书面形式交联合国教科文组织总干事保存。
3. 在收到退约书一年后退约生效。然而，如一年到期时，退约国正卷入一场武装冲突，则退约需待战事结束，或待归还文化财产的行动已告完成，以其中居后者计时方可生效。

第 38 条　通知

联合国教科文组织总干事须将第 31 条、第 32 条和第 39 条规定的批准书、加入书或接受书以及第 35 条、第 37 条和第 39 条规定的通知和退约书的交存情况,通知第 30 条和第 32 条提及的国家和联合国组织。

第 39 条　对公约及其执行规则的修订

1. 任何缔约国均可提出对本公约及其执行规则的修正案。提出的任何修正案文本均须通知联合国教科文组织总干事,由总干事转发各缔约国,同时请他们在四个月内就以下问题表明自己的意见:(a)他们是否希望召开一次大会来研究所提的修正案;(b)他们是否赞成不召开大会,即接受所提的修正案;(c)他们是否赞成不召开大会即驳回所提的修正案。

2. 总干事须将按本条第 1 段收到的答复转告所有缔约国。

3. 如所有缔约国均在规定时间内按本条第 1 b)段向联合国教科文组织总干事表示了自己的意见,通知他们赞成不召开大会即通过修正案,总干事则应按第 38 条将他们的决定通知各缔约国。修正将于发出此类通知的 90 天期满之日对所有缔约国生效。

4. 如有三分之一以上的缔约国提出要求,总干事须召集缔约各方开会,对所提出的修正案进行审议。

5. 前一段中所提对本公约或执行规则的修正案,只有在缔约各方代表参加的大会上一致通过并被每个缔约国接受后,方可生效。

6. 缔约各方对第 4、5 段中所提大会通过的对本公约和执行规则的修正的接受,须在向联合国教科文组织总干事递交一份正式接受书后方可有效。

7. 在对本公约或执行规则的修正生效后,只有业经修正的本公约或执行规则的文本才继续开放,供批准或加入。

第 40 条　登记

按照《联合国宪章》规定,根据联合国教科文组织总干事的要求,本公约须在联合国秘书处登记。

为此,下列签署人经正式授权签署本公约,以昭信守。

1954 年 5 月 14 日订于海牙,计一份,应保存于联合国教科文组织档案馆中,其经证明无误的副本应分送第 30 条和第 32 条所提及的所有国家和联合国组织。

Convention for the Protection of Cultural Property in the Event of Armed Conflict[①]

Adopted by the UNESCO Intergovernmental Conference on the Protection of Cultural Property in the Event of Armed Conflict, The Hague, 14 May 1954

The High Contracting Parties,

Recognizing that cultural property has suffered grave damage during recent armed conflicts and that, by reason of the developments in the technique of warfare, it is in increasing danger of destruction;

Being convinced that damage to cultural property belonging to any people whatsoever means damage to the cultural heritage of all mankind, since each people makes its contribution to the culture of the world;

Considering that the preservation of the cultural heritage is of great importance for all peoples of the world and that it is important that this heritage should receive international protection;

Guided by the principles concerning the protection of cultural property during armed conflict, as established in the Conventions of The Hague of 1899 and of 1907 and in the Washington Pact of 15 April, 1935;

Being of the opinion that such protection cannot be effective unless both national and international measures have been taken to organize it in time of peace;

Being determined to take all possible steps to protect cultural property;

Have agreed upon the following provisions:

CHAPTER I. GENERAL PROVISIONS REGARDING PROTECTION

ARTICLE 1. DEFINITION OF CULTURAL PROPERTY

For the purposes of the present Convention, the term "cultural property" shall cover, irrespective of origin or ownership:

(a) movable or immovable property of great importance to the cultural heritage of every people, such as monuments of architecture, art or history, whether religious or secular; archaeological sites; groups of buildings which, as a whole, are of historical or artistic interest; works of art; manuscripts, books and other objects of artistic, historical or archaeological interest; as well as scientific collections and important collections of books or archives or of reproductions of the property defined above;

(b) buildings whose main and effective purpose is to preserve or exhibit the movable cultural property defined in sub-paragraph (a) such as museums, large libraries and depositories of archives, and refuges intended to

---

[①] Final Act of the Intergovernmental Conference on the Protection of Cultural Property in the Event of Armed Conflict, The Hague, 1954.

shelter, in the event of armed conflict, the movable cultural property defined in sub-paragraph (a);

(c) centers containing a large amount of cultural property as defined in sub-paragraphs (a) and (b), to be known as "centers containing monuments".

ARTICLE 2. PROTECTION OF CULTURAL PROPERTY

For the purposes of the present Convention, the protection of cultural property shall comprise the safeguarding of and respect for such property.

ARTICLE 3. SAFEGUARDING OF CULTURAL PROPERTY

The High Contracting Parties undertake to prepare in time of peace for the safeguarding of cultural property situated within their own territory against the foreseeable effects of an armed conflict, by taking such measures as they consider appropriate.

ARTICLE 4. RESPECT FOR CULTURAL PROPERTY

1. The High Contracting Parties undertake to respect cultural property situated within their own territory as well as within the territory of other High Contracting Parties by refraining from any use of the property and its immediate surroundings or of the appliances in use for its protection for purposes which are likely to expose it to destruction or damage in the event of armed conflict; and by refraining from any act of hostility directed against such property.

2. The obligations mentioned in paragraph 1 of the present Article may be waived only in cases where military necessity imperatively requires such a waiver.

3. The High Contracting Parties further undertake to prohibit, prevent and, if necessary, put a stop to any form of theft, pillage or misappropriation of, and any acts of vandalism directed against, cultural property. They shall refrain from requisitioning movable cultural property situated in the territory of another High Contracting Party.

4. They shall refrain from any act directed by way of reprisals against cultural property.

5. No High Contracting Party may evade the obligations incumbent upon it under the present Article, in respect of another High Contracting Party, by reason of the fact that the latter has not applied the measures of safeguard referred to in Article 3.

ARTICLE 5. OCCUPATION

1. Any High Contracting Party in occupation of the whole or part of the territory of another High Contracting Party shall as far as possible support the competent national authorities of the occupied country in safeguarding and preserving its cultural property.

2. Should it prove necessary to take measures to preserve cultural property situated in occupied territory and damaged by military operations, and should the competent national authorities be unable to take such measures, the Occupying Power shall, as far as possible, and in close co-operation with such authorities, take the most necessary measures of preservation.

3. Any High Contracting Party whose government is considered their legitimate government by members of a resistance movement, shall, if possible, draw their attention to the obligation to comply with those provisions of the Convention dealing with respect for cultural property.

ARTICLE 6. DISTINCTIVE MARKING OF CULTURAL PROPERTY

In accordance with the provisions of Article 16, cultural property may bear a distinctive emblem so as to facilitate its recognition.

ARTICLE 7. MILITARY MEASURES

1. The High Contracting Parties undertake to introduce in time of peace into their military regulations or

instructions such provisions as may ensure observance of the present Convention, and to foster in the members of their armed forces a spirit of respect for the culture and cultural property of all peoples.

2. The High Contracting Parties undertake to plan or establish in peace-time, within their armed forces, services or specialist personnel whose purpose will be to secure respect for cultural property and to co-operate with the civilian authorities responsible for safeguarding it.

CHAPTER II. SPECIAL PROTECTION

ARTICLE 8. GRANTING OF SPECIAL PROTECTION

1. There may be placed under special protection a limited number of refuges intended to shelter movable cultural property in the event of armed conflict, of centres containing monuments and other immovable cultural property of very great importance, provided that they:

(a) are situated at an adequate distance from any large industrial centre or from any important military objective constituting a vulnerable point, such as, for example, an aerodrome, broadcasting station, establishment engaged upon work of national defense, a port or railway station of relative importance or a main line of communication;

(b) are not used for military purposes.

2. A refuge for movable cultural property may also be placed under special protection, whatever its location, if it is so constructed that, in all probability, it will not be damaged by bombs.

3. A center containing monuments shall be deemed to be used for military purposes whenever it is used for the movement of military personnel or material, even in transit. The same shall apply whenever activities directly connected with military operations, the stationing of military personnel, or the production of war material are carried on within the center.

4. The guarding of cultural property mentioned in paragraph I above by armed custodians specially empowered to do so, or the presence, in the vicinity of such cultural property, of police forces normally responsible for the maintenance of public order shall not be deemed to be used for military purposes.

5. If any cultural property mentioned in paragraph 1 of the present Article is situated near an important military objective as defined in the said paragraph, it may nevertheless be placed under special protection if the High Contracting Party asking for that protection undertakes, in the event of armed conflict, to make no use of the objective and particularly, in the case of a port, railway station or aerodrome, to divert all traffic therefrom. In that event, such diversion shall be prepared in time of peace.

6. Special protection is granted to cultural property by its entry in the "International Register of Cultural Property under Special Protection". This entry shall only be made, in accordance with the provisions of the present Convention and under the conditions provided for in the Regulations for the execution of the Convention.

ARTICLE 9. IMMUNITY OF CULTURAL PROPERTY UNDER SPECIAL PROTECTION

The High Contracting Parties undertake to ensure the immunity of cultural property under special protection by refraining, from the time of entry in the International Register, from any act of hostility directed against such property and, except for the cases provided for in paragraph 5 of Article 8, from any use of such property or its surroundings for military purposes.

ARTICLE 10. IDENTIFICATION AND CONTROL

During an armed conflict, cultural property under special protection shall be marked with the distinctive emblem described in Article 16, and shall be open to international control as provided for in the Regulations for the execution of the Convention.

ARTICLE 11. WITHDRAWAL OF IMMUNITY

1. If one of the High Contracting Parties commits, in respect of any item of cultural property under special protection, a violation of the obligations under Article 9, the opposing Party shall, so long as this violation persists, be released from the obligation to ensure the immunity of the property concerned. Nevertheless, whenever possible, the latter Party shall first request the cessation of such violation within a reasonable time.

2. Apart from the case provided for in paragraph 1 of the present Article, immunity shall be withdrawn from cultural property under special protection only in exceptional cases of unavoidable military necessity, and only for such time as that necessity continues. Such necessity can be established only by the officer commanding a force the equivalent of a division in size or larger. Whenever circumstances permit, the opposing Party shall be notified, a reasonable time in advance, of the decision to withdraw immunity.

3. The Party withdrawing immunity shall, as soon as possible, so inform the Commissioner-General for cultural property provided for in the Regulations for the execution of the Convention, in writing, stating the reasons.

CHAPTER III. TRANSPORT OF CULTURAL PROPERTY

ARTICLE 12. TRANSPORT UNDER SPECIAL PROTECTION

1. Transport exclusively engaged in the transfer of cultural property, whether within a territory or to another territory, may, at the request of the High Contracting Party concerned, take place under special protection in accordance with the conditions specified in the Regulations for the execution of the Convention.

2. Transport under special protection shall take place under the international supervision provided for in the aforesaid Regulations and shall display the distinctive emblem described in Article 16.

3. The High Contracting Parties shall refrain from any act of hostility directed against transport under special protection.

ARTICLE 13. TRANSPORT IN URGENT CASES

1. If a High Contracting Party considers that the safety of certain cultural property requires its transfer and that the matter is of such urgency that the procedure laid down in Article 12 cannot be followed, especially at the beginning of an armed conflict, the transport may display the distinctive emblem described in Article 16, provided that an application for immunity referred to in Article 12 has not already been made and refused. As far as possible, notification of transfer should be made to the opposing Parties. Nevertheless, transport conveying cultural property to the territory of another country may not display the distinctive emblem unless immunity has been expressly granted to it.

2. The High Contracting Parties shall take, so far as possible, the necessary precautions to avoid acts of hostility directed against the transport described in paragraph 1 of the present Article and displaying the distinctive emblem.

ARTICLE 14. IMMUNITY FROM SEIZURE, CAPTURE AND PRIZE

1. Immunity from seizure, placing in prize, or capture shall be granted to:

(a) cultural property enjoying the protection provided for in Article 12 or that provided for in Article 13;

(b) the means of transport exclusively engaged in the transfer of such cultural property.

2. Nothing in the present Article shall limit the right of visit and search.

CHAPTER Ⅳ. PERSONNEL

ARTICLE 15. PERSONNEL

As far as is consistent with the interests of security, personnel engaged in the protection of cultural property shall, in the interests of such property, be respected and, if they fall into the hands of the opposing Party, shall be allowed to continue to carry out their duties whenever the cultural property for which they are responsible has also fallen into the hands of the opposing Party.

CHAPTER Ⅴ. THE DISTINCTIVE EMBLEM

ARTICLE 16. EMBLEM OF THE CONVENTION

1. The distinctive emblem of the Convention shall take the form of a shield, pointed below, per saltire blue and white (a shield consisting of a royal-blue square, one of the angles of which forms the point of the shield, and of a royal-blue triangle above the square, the space on either side being taken up by a white triangle).

2. The emblem shall be used alone or repeated three times in a triangular formation (one shield below), under the conditions provided for in Article 17.

ARTICLE 17. USE OF THE EMBLEM

1. The distinctive emblem repeated three times may be used only as a means of identification of:

(a) immovable cultural property under special protection;

(b) the transport of cultural property under the conditions provided for in Articles 12 and 13;

(c) improvised refuges, under the conditions provided for in the Regulations for the execution of the Convention.

2. The distinctive emblem may be used alone only as a means of identification of:

(a) cultural property not under special protection;

(b) the persons responsible for the duties of control in accordance with the Regulations for the execution of the Convention;

(c) the personnel engaged in the protection of cultural property;

(d) the identity cards mentioned in the Regulations for the execution of the Convention.

3. During an armed conflict, the use of the distinctive emblem in any other cases than those mentioned in the preceding paragraphs of the present Article, and the use for any purpose whatever of a sign resembling the distinctive emblem, shall be forbidden.

4. The distinctive emblem may not be placed on any immovable cultural property unless at the same time there is displayed an authorization duly dated and signed by the competent authority of the High Contracting Party.

CHAPTER Ⅵ. SCOPE OF APPLICATION OF THE CONVENTION

ARTICLE 18. APPLICATION OF THE CONVENTION

1. Apart from the provisions which shall take effect in time of peace, the present Convention shall apply in the event of declared war or of any other armed conflict which may arise between two or more of the High Contracting Parties, even if the state of war is not recognized by one or more of them.

2. The Convention shall also apply to all cases of partial or total occupation of the territory of a High Contracting Party, even if the said occupation meets with no armed resistance.

3. If one of the Powers in conflict is not a Party to the present Convention, the Powers which are Parties thereto shall nevertheless remain bound by it in their mutual relations. They shall furthermore be bound by the Convention, in relation to the said Power, if the latter has declared that it accepts the provisions thereof and so long as it applies them.

ARTICLE 19. CONFLICTS NOT OF AN INTERNATIONAL CHARACTER

1. In the event of an armed conflict not of an international character occurring within the territory of one of the High Contracting Parties, each party to the conflict shall be bound to apply, as a minimum, the provisions of the present Convention which relate to respect for cultural property.

2. The parties to the conflict shall endeavour to bring into force, by means of special agreements, all or part of the other provisions of the present Convention.

3. The United Nations Educational, Scientific and Cultural Organization may offer its services to the parties to the conflict.

4. The application of the preceding provisions shall not affect the legal status of the parties to the conflict.

CHAPTER VII. EXECUTION OF THE CONVENTION

ARTICLE 20. REGULATIONS FOR THE EXECUTION OF THE CONVENTION

The procedure by which the present Convention is to be applied is defined in the Regulations for its execution, which constitute an integral part thereof.

ARTICLE 21. PROTECTING POWERS

The present Convention and the Regulations for its execution shall be applied with the co-operation of the Protecting Powers responsible for safeguarding the interests of the Parties to the conflict.

ARTICLE 22. CONCILIATION PROCEDURE

1. The Protecting Powers shall lend their good offices in all cases where they may deem it useful in the interests of cultural property, particularly if there is disagreement between the Parties to the conflict as to the application or interpretation of the provisions of the present Convention or the Regulations for its execution.

2. For this purpose, each of the Protecting Powers may, either at the invitation of one Party, of the Director-General of the United Nations Educational, Scientific and Cultural Organization, or on its own initiative, propose to the Parties to the conflict a meeting of their representatives, and in particular of the authorities responsible for the protection of cultural property, if considered appropriate on suitably chosen neutral territory. The Parties to the conflict shall be bound to give effect to the proposals for meeting made to them. The Protecting Powers shall propose for approval by the Parties to the conflict a person belonging to a neutral Power or a person presented by the Director-General of the United Nations Educational, Scientific and Cultural Organization, which person shall be invited to take part in such a meeting in the capacity of Chairman.

ARTICLE 23. ASSISTANCE OF UNESCO

1. The High Contracting Parties may call upon the United Nations Educational, Scientific and Cultural Organization for technical assistance in organizing the protection of their cultural property, or in connection with any other problem arising out of the application of the present Convention or the Regulations for its execution. The Organization shall accord such assistance within the limits fixed by its programme and by its

resources.

2. The Organization is authorized to make, on its own initiative, proposals on this matter to the High Contracting Parties.

ARTICLE 24. SPECIAL AGREEMENTS

1. The High Contracting Parties may conclude special agreements for all matters concerning which they deem it suitable to make separate provision.

2. No special agreement may be concluded which would diminish the protection afforded by the present Convention to cultural property and to the personnel engaged in its protection.

ARTICLE 25. DISSEMINATION OF THE CONVENTION

The High Contracting Parties undertake, in time of peace as in time of armed conflict, to disseminate the text of the present Convention and the Regulations for its execution as widely as possible in their respective countries. They undertake, in particular, to include the study thereof in their programmes of military and, if possible, civilian training, so that its principles are made known to the whole population, especially the armed forces and personnel engaged in the protection of cultural property.

ARTICLE 26. TRANSLATIONS, REPORTS

1. The High Contracting Parties shall communicate to one another, through the Director-General of the United Nations Educational, Scientific and Cultural Organization, the official translations of the present Convention and of the Regulations for its execution.

2. Furthermore, at least once every four years, they shall forward to the Director-General a report giving whatever information they think suitable concerning any measures being taken, prepared or contemplated by their respective administrations in fulfilment of the present Convention and of the Regulations for its execution.

ARTICLE 27. MEETINGS

1. The Director-General of the United Nations Educational, Scientific and Cultural Organization may, with the approval of the Executive Board, convene meetings of representatives of the High Contracting Parties. He must convene such a meeting if at least one-fifth of the High Contracting Parties so request.

2. Without prejudice to any other functions which have been conferred on it by the present Convention or the Regulations for its execution, the purpose of the meeting will be to study problems concerning the application of the Convention and of the Regulations for its execution, and to formulate recommendations in respect thereof.

3. The meeting may further undertake a revision of the Convention or the Regulations for its execution if the majority of the High Contracting Parties are represented, and in accordance with the provisions of Article 39.

ARTICLE 28. SANCTIONS

The High Contracting Parties undertake to take, within the framework of their ordinary criminal jurisdiction, all necessary steps to prosecute and impose penal or disciplinary sanctions upon those persons, of whatever nationality, who commit or order to be committed a breach of the present Convention.

FINAL PROVISIONS

ARTICLE 29. LANGUAGES

1. The present Convention is drawn up in English, French, Russian and Spanish, the four texts being equally authoritative.

2. The United Nations Educational, Scientific and Cultural Organization shall arrange for translations of the Convention into the other official languages of its General Conference.

ARTICLE 30. SIGNATURE

The present Convention shall bear the date of 14 May, 1954 and, until the date of 31 December, 1954, shall remain open for signature by all States invited to the Conference which met at The Hague from 21 April, 1954 to 14 May, 1954.

ARTICLE 31. RATIFICATION

1. The present Convention shall be subject to ratification by signatory States in accordance with their respective constitutional procedures.

2. The instruments of ratification shall be deposited with the Director-General of the United Nations Educational, Scientific and Cultural Organization.

ARTICLE 32. ACCESSION

From the date of its entry into force, the present Convention shall be open for accession by all States mentioned in Article 30 which have not signed it, aswell as any other State invited to accede by the Executive Board of the United Nations Educational, Scientific and Cultural Organization. Accession shall be affected by the deposit of an instrument of accession with the Director-General of the United Nations Educational, Scientific and Cultural Organization.

ARTICLE 33. ENTRY INTO FORCE

1. The present Convention shall enter into force three months after five instruments of ratification have been deposited.

2. Thereafter, it shall enter into force, for each High Contracting Party, three months after the deposit of its instrument of ratification or accession.

3. The situations referred to in Articles 18 and 19 shall give immediate effect to ratifications or accessions deposited by the Parties to the conflict either before or after the beginning of hostilities or occupation. In such cases the Director-General of the United Nations Educational, Scientific and Cultural Organization shall transmit the communications referred to in article 38 by the speediest method.

ARTICLE 34. EFFECTIVE APPLICATION

1. Each State Party to the Convention on the date of its entry into force shall take all necessary measures to ensure its effective application within a period of six months after such entry into force.

2. This period shall be six months from the date of deposit of the instruments of ratification or accession for any State which deposits its instrument of ratification or accession after the date of the entry into force of the Convention.

ARTICLE 35. TERRITORIAL EXTENSION OF THE CONVENTION

Any High Contracting Party may, at the time of ratification or accession, or at any time, thereafter, declare by notification addressed to the Director General of the United Nations Educational, Scientific and Cultural Organization, that the present Convention shall extend to all or any of the territories for whose international relations it is responsible. The said notification shall take effect three months after the date of its receipt.

ARTICLE 36. RELATION TO PREVIOUS CONVENTIONS

1. In the relations between Powers which are bound by the Conventions of The Hague concerning the Laws and Customs of War on Land (Ⅳ) and concerning Naval Bombardment in Time of War (Ⅸ), whether those of 29 July, 1899 or those of 18 October, 1907, and which are Parties to the present Convention, this last Convention shall be supplementary to the aforementioned Convention (Ⅸ) and to the Regulations annexed to the aforementioned Convention (Ⅳ) and shall substitute for the emblem described in Article 5 of the aforementioned Convention (Ⅸ)

the emblem described in Article 16 of the present Convention, in cases in which the present Convention and the Regulations for its execution provide for the use of this distinctive emblem.

2. In the relations between Powers which are bound by the Washington Pact of 15 April, 1935 for the Protection of Artistic and Scientific Institutions and of Historic Monuments (Roerich Pact) and which are Parties to the present Convention, the latter Convention shall be supplementary to the Roerich Pact and shall substitute for the distinguishing flag described in Article III of the Pact the emblem defined in Article 16 of the present Convention, in cases in which the present Convention and the Regulations for its execution provide for the use of this distinctive emblem.

ARTICLE 37. DENUNCIATION

1. Each High Contracting Party may denounce the present Convention, on its own behalf, or on behalf of any territory for whose international relations it is responsible.

2. The denunciation shall be notified by an instrument in writing, deposited with the Director-General of the United Nations Educational, Scientific and Cultural Organization.

3. The denunciation shall take effect one year after the receipt of the instrument of denunciation. However, if, on the expiry of this period, the denouncing Party is involved in an armed conflict, the denunciation shall not take effect until the end of hostilities, or until the operations of repatriating cultural property are completed, whichever is the later.

ARTICLE 38. NOTIFICATIONS

The Director-General of the United Nations Educational, Scientific and Cultural Organization shall inform the States referred to in Articles 30 and 32, as well as the United Nations, of the deposit of all the instruments of ratification, accession or acceptance provided for in Articles 31, 32 and 39 and of the notifications and denunciations provided for respectively in Articles 35, 37 and 39.

ARTICLE 39. REVISION OF THE CONVENTION AND OF THE REGULATIONS FOR ITS EXECUTION

1. Any High Contracting Party may propose amendments to the present Convention or the Regulations for its execution. The text of any proposed amendment shall be communicated to the Director-General of the United Nations Educational, Scientific and Cultural Organization who shall transmit it to each High Contracting Party with the request that such Party reply within four months stating whether it:

(a) desires that a Conference be convened to consider the proposed amendment;

(b) favours the acceptance of the proposed amendment without a Conference; or

(c) favours the rejection of the proposed amendment without a Conference.

2. The Director-General shall transmit the replies, received under paragraph 1 of the present Article, to all High Contracting Parties.

3. If all the High Contracting Parties which have, within the prescribed time-limit, stated their views to the Director-General of the United Nations Educational. Scientific and Cultural Organization, pursuant to paragraph 1 (b) of this Article, inform him that they favour acceptance of the amendment without a Conference, notification of their decision shall be made by the Director-General in accordance with Article 38. The amendment shall become effective for all the High Contracting Parties on the expiry of ninety days from the date of such notification.

4. The Director-General shall convene a Conference of the High Contracting Parties to consider the proposed amendment if requested to do so by more than one-third of the High Contracting Parties.

5. Amendments to the Convention or to the Regulations for its execution, dealt with under the provisions of the preceding paragraph, shall enter into force only after they have been unanimously adopted by the High

Contracting Parties represented at the Conference and accepted by each of the High Contracting Parties.

6. Acceptance by the High Contracting Parties of amendments to the Convention or to the Regulations for its execution, which have been adopted by the Conference mentioned in paragraphs 4 and 5, shall be affected by the deposit of a formal instrument with the Director-General of the United Nations Educational, Scientific and Cultural Organization.

7. After the entry into force of amendments to the present Convention or to the Regulations for its execution, only the text of the Convention or of the Regulations for its execution thus amended shall remain open for ratification or accession.

ARTICLE 40. REGISTRATION

In accordance with Article 102 of the Charter of the United Nations, the present Convention shall be registered with the Secretariat of the United Nations at the request of the Director-General of the United Nations Educational, Scientific and Cultural Organization.

In faith whereof the undersigned, duly authorized, have signed the present Convention.

Done at The Hague, this fourteenth day of May, 1954, in a single copy which shall be deposited in the archives of the United Nations Educational, Scientific and Cultural Organization, and certified true copies of which shall be delivered to all the States referred to in Articles 30 and 32 as well as to the United Nations.

关于古迹遗址保护与修复的国际宪章
（威尼斯宪章）[①]

（第二届历史古迹建筑师及技师国际会议1964年在威尼斯通过，国际古迹遗址理事会1965年采纳）

世世代代人民的历史古迹，饱含着过去岁月的信息留存至今，成为人们古老的活的见证。人们越来越意识到人类价值的统一性，并把古代遗迹看作共同的遗产，认识到为后代保护这些古迹的共同责任。将它们真实地、完整地传下去是我们的职责。

古代建筑的保护与修复指导原则应在国际上得到公认并作出规定，这一点至关重要。各国在各自的文化和传统范畴内负责实施这一规划。

1931年的雅典宪章第一次规定了这些基本原则，为一个国际运动的广泛发展作出了贡献，这一运动所采取的具体形式体现在各国的文件之中，体现在国际博物馆协会和联合国教科文组织的工作之中，以及在由后者建立的国际文物保护与修复研究中心之中。一些已经出现并在继续变得更为复杂和多样化的问题已越来越受到注意，并展开了紧急研究。现在，重新审阅宪章的时候已经来临，以便对其所含原则进行彻底研究，并在一份新文件中扩大其范围。

为此，1964年5月25日至31日在威尼斯召开了第二届历史古迹建筑师及技师国际会议，通过了以下文本：

定　义

第一条　历史古迹的要领不仅包括单个建筑物，而且包括能从中找出一种独特的文明、一种有意义的发展或一个历史事件见证的城市或乡村环境。这不仅适用于伟大的艺术作品，而且亦适用于随时光流逝而获得文化意义的过去一些较为朴实的艺术品。

第二条　古迹的保护与修复必须求助于对研究和保护考古遗产有利的一切科学技术。

宗　旨

第三条　保护与修复古迹的目的旨在把它们既作为历史见证，又作为艺术品予以保护。

保　护

第四条　古迹的保护至关重要的一点在于日常的维护。

第五条　为社会公用之目的使用古迹永远有利于古迹的保护。因此，这种使用合乎需要，但决不能

[①] 引自：联合国教科文组织世界遗产中心，国际古迹遗址理事会，国际文物保护与修复研究中心，中国国家文物局主编. 国际文化遗产保护文件选编[M]. 北京：文物出版社，2007。

改变该建筑的布局或装饰。只有在此限度内才可考虑或允许因功能改变而需做的改动。

第六条 古迹的保护包含着对一定规模环境的保护。凡传统环境存在的地方必须予以保存，决不允许任何导致改变主体和颜色关系的新建、拆除或改动。

第七条 古迹不能与其所见证的历史和其产生的环境分离。除非出于保护古迹之需要，或因国家或国际之极为重要利益而证明有其必要，否则不得全部或局部搬迁该古迹。

第八条 作为构成古迹整体一部分的雕塑、绘画或装饰品，只有在非移动而不能确保其保存的唯一办法时方可进行移动。

修 复

第九条 修复过程是一个高度专业性的工作，其目的旨在保存和展示古迹的美学与历史价值，并以尊重原始材料和确凿文献为依据。一旦出现臆测，必须立即予以停止。此外，即使如此，任何不可避免的添加都必须与该建筑的构成有所区别，并且必须要有现代标记。无论在什么情况下，修复之前及之后必须对古迹进行考古及历史研究。

第十条 当传统技术被证明为不适用时，可采用任何经科学数据和经验证明为有效的现代建筑及保护技术来加固古迹。

第十一条 各个时代为一古迹之建筑物所做的正当贡献必须予以尊重，因为修复的目的不是追求风格的统一。当一座建筑物含有不同时期的重叠作品时，揭示底层只有在特殊情况下，在被去掉的东西价值甚微，而被显示的东西具有很高的历史、考古或美学价值，并且保存完好足以说明这么做的理由时才能证明其具有正当理由。评估由此涉及的各部分的重要性以及决定毁掉什么内容不能仅仅依赖于负责此项工作的个人。

第十二条 缺失部分的修补必须与整体保持和谐，但同时须区别于原作，以使修复不歪曲其艺术或历史见证。

第十三条 任何添加均不允许，除非它们不至于贬低该建筑物的有趣部分、传统环境、布局平衡及其与周围环境的关系。

第十四条 古迹遗址必须成为专门照管对象，以保护其完整性，并确保用恰当的方式进行清理和开放。在这类地点开展的保护与修复工作应得到上述条款所规定之原则的鼓励。

发 掘

第十五条 发掘应按照科学标准和联合国教科文组织1956年通过的适用于考古发掘国际原则的建议予以进行。

遗址必须予以保存，并且必须采取必要措施，永久地保存和保护建筑风貌及其所发现的物品。此外，必须采取一切方法促进对古迹的了解，使它得以再现而不曲解其意。

然而对任何重建都应事先予以制止，只允许重修，也就是说，把现存但已解体的部分重新组合。所用粘结材料应永远可以辨别，并应尽量少用，只需确保古迹的保护和其形状的恢复之用便可。

出 版

第十六条 一切保护、修复或发掘工作永远应有用配以插图和照片的分析及评论报告这一形式所做的准确的记录。

清理、加固、重新整理与组合的每一阶段，以及工作过程中所确认的技术及形态特征均应包括在内。这一记录应存放于一公共机构的档案馆内，使研究人员都能查到。该记录应建议出版。

International Charter for the Conservation and Restoration of Monuments and Sites
(The Venice Charter)

IInd International Congress of Architects and Technicians of Historic Monuments, Venice, 1964.
Adopted by ICOMOS in 1965

Imbued with a message from the past, the historic monuments of generations of people remain to the present day as living witnesses of their age-old traditions. People are becoming more and more conscious of the unity of human values and regard ancient monuments as a common heritage. The common responsibility to safeguard them for future generations is recognized. It is our duty to hand them on in the full richness of their authenticity.

It is essential that the principles guiding the preservation and restoration of ancient buildings should be agreed and be laid down on an international basis, with each country being responsible for applying the plan within the framework of its own culture and traditions.

By defining these basic principles for the first time, the Athens Charter of 1931 contributed towards the development of an extensive international movement which has assumed concrete form in national documents, in the work of ICOM and UNESCO and in the establishment by the latter of the International Centre for the Study of the Preservation and the Restoration of Cultural Property. Increasing awareness and critical study have been brought to bear on problems which have continually become more complex and varied; now the time has come to examine the Charter afresh in order to make a thorough study of the principles involved and to enlarge its scope in a new document.

Accordingly, the IInd International Congress of Architects and Technicians of Historic Monuments, which met in Venice from May 25th to 31st 1964, approved the following text:

DEFINITIONS

Article 1.

The concept of a historic monument embraces not only the single architectural work but also the urban or rural setting in which is found the evidence of a particular civilization, a significant development or a historic event. This applies not only to great works of art but also to more modest works of the past which have acquired cultural significance with the passing of time.

Article 2.

The conservation and restoration of monuments must have recourse to all the sciences and techniques which can contribute to the study and safeguarding of the architectural heritage.

Article 3.

The intention in conserving and restoring monuments is to safeguard them no less as works of art than as historical evidence.

CONSERVATION

Article 4.

It is essential to the conservation of monuments that they be maintained on a permanent basis.

Article 5.

The conservation of monuments is always facilitated by making use of them for some socially useful purpose. Such use is therefore desirable but it must not change the lay-out or decoration of the building. It is within these limits only that modifications demanded by a change of function should be envisaged and may be permitted.

Article 6.

The conservation of a monument implies preserving a setting which is not out of scale. Wherever the traditional setting exists, it must be kept. No new construction, demolition or modification which would alter the relations of mass and colour must be allowed.

Article 7.

A monument is inseparable from the history to which it bears witness and from the setting in which it occurs. The moving of all or part of a monument cannot be allowed except where the safeguarding of that monument demands it or where it is justified by national or international interest of paramount importance.

Article 8.

Items of sculpture, painting or decoration which form an integral part of a monument may only be removed from it if this is the sole means of ensuring their preservation.

RESTORATION

Article 9.

The process of restoration is a highly specialized operation. Its aim is to preserve and reveal the aesthetic and historic value of the monument and is based on respect for original material and authentic documents. It must stop at the point where conjecture begins, and in this case moreover any extra work which is indispensable must be distinct from the architectural composition and must bear a contemporary stamp. The restoration in any case must be preceded and followed by an archaeological and historical study of the monument.

Article 10.

Where traditional techniques prove inadequate, the consolidation of a monument can be achieved by the use of any modern technique for conservation and construction, the efficacy of which has been shown by scientific data and proved by experience.

Article 11.

The valid contributions of all periods to the building of a monument must be respected, since unity of style is not the aim of a restoration. When a building includes the superimposed work of different periods, the revealing of the underlying state can only be justified in exceptional circumstances and when what is removed is of little interest and the material which is brought to light is of great historical, archaeological or aesthetic value, and its state of preservation good enough to justify the action. Evaluation of the importance of the elements involved and the decision as to what may be destroyed cannot rest solely on the individual in charge of the work.

Article 12.

Replacements of missing parts must integrate harmoniously with the whole, but at the same time must be distinguishable from the original so that restoration does not falsify the artistic or historic evidence.

Article 13.

Additions cannot be allowed except in so far as they do not detract from the interesting parts of the building, its traditional setting, the balance of its composition and its relation with its surroundings.

HISTORIC SITES

Article 14.

The sites of monuments must be the object of special care in order to safeguard their integrity and ensure that they are cleared and presented in a seemly manner. The work of conservation and restoration carried out in such places should be inspired by the principles set forth in the foregoing articles.

EXCAVATIONS

Article 15.

Excavations should be carried out in accordance with scientific standards and the recommendation defining international principles to be applied in the case of archaeological excavation adopted by UNESCO in 1956.

Ruins must be maintained and measures necessary for the permanent conservation and protection of architectural features and of objects discovered must be taken. Furthermore, every means must be taken to facilitate the understanding of the monument and to reveal it without ever distorting its meaning.

All reconstruction work should however be ruled out "*a priori*". Only anastylosis, that is to say, the reassembling of existing but dismembered parts can be permitted. The material used for integration should always be recognizable and its use should be the least that will ensure the conservation of a monument and the reinstatement of its form.

PUBLICATION

Article 16.

In all works of preservation, restoration or excavation, there should always be precise documentation in the form of analytical and critical reports, illustrated with drawings and photographs. Every stage of the work of clearing, consolidation, rearrangement and integration, as well as technical and formal features identified during the course of the work, should be included. This record should be placed in the archives of a public institution and made available to research workers. It is recommended that the report should be published.

关于保护受公共或私人工程危害的文化财产的建议[①]

(联合国教科文组织第十五届大会 1968 年 11 月 19 日在巴黎通过)

联合国教科文组织大会于 1968 年 10 月 15 日至 11 月 20 日在巴黎举行第十五届会议。

考虑到当代文明及未来之发展除了有赖于其他因素外,还有赖于全世界人民的文化传统、创造力以及社会与经济的发展;

考虑到文化财产是昔日不同传统和精神成就的产物和见证,因此,它是全世界人民民族特征的重要组成部分;

考虑到根据文化财产的历史和艺术价值尽量予以保护的必要性,以使有关文化财产的意义和信息成为人们据此可以了解自己本身的价值的精神生活的一部分;

考虑到根据联合国教科文组织 1966 年 11 月 4 日第十四次会议通过的《国际文化合作原则宣言》的精神保护文化遗产并对人们开放,构成鼓励各国人民互相了解的方法,从而有利于和平事业;

考虑到各国人民的兴盛特别有赖于一个有利的、起促进作用的环境,而对历史上各个时期的文化财产的保护则直接有利于这一环境;

另一方面,**认识到**世界文明的趋向——工业化在人类发展及其精神的和民族的完善方面发挥作用;

但也**考虑到**由于工业的发展和城市化的趋势,那些远古的、史前的及历史的古迹遗址以及诸多具有艺术、历史或科学价值的现代建筑正日益受到公共和私人工程的威胁;

考虑到各国政府有责任像促进社会和经济发展那样,尽力确保人类文化遗产的保护和保存;

考虑到协调文化遗产的保护和社会经济的发展所带来的变化刻不容缓,因此,应努力以宽厚的理解精神并根据可靠的规划来满足这两方面的要求;

同样**也考虑到**适当保护并对人们开放文化财产非常有利于拥有这些人类宝藏的国家和地区通过发展民族和国际旅游业促进其社会和经济的发展;

最后**考虑到**保护文化财产的最可靠的保障在于人类本身对它们的尊重和感情,并且相信通过各成员国采取适当的措施可极大地加强这种感情。

已收到关于保护受到公共或私人工程危害的文化财产的议案,作为本届会议第十六项议程。

第十三届会议已决定此项议案应以向各成员国建议的形式形成一国际文件。

兹于 1968 年 11 月 19 日通过本建议。

大会**建议**各国成员应采取为在其各自领土内实施本建议所规定的原则和规范所可能需要的任何立法或其他步骤,以适用下述各项规定。

[①] 引自:联合国教科文组织世界遗产中心,国际古迹遗址理事会,国际文物保护与修复研究中心,中国国家文物局主编. 国际文化遗产保护文件选编[M]. 北京:文物出版社,2007.

大会**建议**各成员国应把本建议提请负责公共或私人工程的当局或行政部门以及负责保存与保护古迹和历史、艺术、考古和科学遗址的机构的注意和重视。

大会**也建议**应同样把此建议通知制定教育和旅游发展规划的机构。

大会**建议**各成员国应接待由大会确定的日期和方式向大会报告它们为实施本建议所采取的行动。

一．定　义

1. 为本建议之目的，"文化财产"一词适用于：

（1）不可移动之物体，无论宗教的或世俗的，诸如考古、历史或科学遗址、建筑或其他具有历史、科学、艺术或建筑价值的特征，包括传统建筑群、城乡建筑区内的历史住宅区以及仍以有效形式存在的早期文化的民族建筑。它既适用于地下发现的考古或历史遗存，又适用于地上现存的不可移动的遗址。文化财产一词也包括此类财产周围的环境。

（2）具有文化价值的可移动财产，包括存在于或发掘于不可移动财产中的物品，以及埋藏于地下、可能会在考古或历史遗址或其他地方发现的物品。

2. "文化财产"一词不仅包括已经确定的和列入目录的建筑、考古及历史遗址和建筑，而且也包括未列入目录的或尚未分类的古代遗迹，以及具有艺术或历史价值的近代遗址和建筑。

二．总　则

3. 保护文化财产的措施应广泛用于一个成员国的全部领土，而不应只局限于某些古迹和遗址。

4. 无论是已列入目录或尚未列入目录的重要的文化财产的保护清单均应予以保留。若无此种清单，应优先在文化财产受到公共或私人工程威胁的地区，对此类财产进行全面调查，以建立此种清单。

5. 根据以下要求协定采取措施时，要充分考虑有关文化财产的相对意义：

（1）保护整个遗址、建筑或其他形式的不可移动文化财产免受私人或公共工程的影响；

（2）如果发现有文化财产的地区将由于公共或私人工程而遭到改变，并且所涉及的全部或部分文化财产将予以保存或搬迁，则应对该文化财产进行抢救或拯救。

6. 抢救措施应根据文化财产的特点、大小和位置以及它所受到的危害的性质而有所不同。

7. 保护或抢救文化财产的措施应具有预防性和矫正性。

8. 预防性和矫正性措施应旨在保护或抢救可能受公共或私人工程损坏或毁坏的文化财产，如：

（1）城市扩建和更新工程；尽管这些工程也许会保留列入目录的古迹，但是有时会迁移一些不甚重要的建筑，结果却破坏了历史关系和历史居住区的环境；

（2）在一些地区所进行的类似工程；该地区的传统建筑群作为一个整体具有文化价值，但由于缺乏一个已列入目录的古迹而有被毁坏的危险；

（3）对单个历史建筑物的不适当的修改和修缮；

（4）修建或改建对遗址、具有历史意义的重要建筑物或建筑群构成特别威胁的高速公路；

（5）修建灌溉、水力发电站或防洪大坝；

（6）铺设管道以及动力线和输电线；

（7）农田耕作，包括深耕、排水和灌溉，土地的清理和平整以及植树造林；

（8）因工业的发展以及工业化社会的技术进步所需的工程，如机场、采矿和采石以及河道和港口的疏浚和拓展。

9. 为保持历史的联系和延续性，各成员国应对受到公共和私人工程危害的文化遗产"就地保护"所需的措施给予适当的优先考虑。当经济或社会形势需要必须迁移、放弃或毁掉文化财产时，抢救或拯救行动总应包括对所涉及的文化遗产进行仔细研究并准备详细记录。

10. 为相关的抢救行动——尤其在不可移动文化财产的全部或大部分已被放弃或毁掉时——所进行的具有科学或历史价值的研究结果，应予以公布，或以其他方式提供给人们，供今后研究之用。

11. 为了免遭公共或私人工程毁坏而迁移的重要建筑和其他古迹，应安置在与其原来的位置、自然、历史或艺术相联系的及相似的地点或环境中。

12. 重要的可移动文化财产，包括从考古发掘中发现的、从抢救行动中获得的具有代表性的样品，应为研究之目的而予以保存，或放在诸如博物馆（包括遗址博物馆）或大学等机构中展览。

三．保护和抢救措施

13. 对受到公共或私人工程威胁的文化财产的保护或抢救应通过采取以下措施得到保障，具体的措施将由成员国的立法和组织机构来决定：

（1）立法；

（2）财政；

（3）行政措施；

（4）保护和抢救文化财产的程序；

（5）处罚；

（6）修缮；

（7）奖励；

（8）咨询；

（9）教育计划。

四．立　法

14. 各成员国应根据本建议所述准则和原则，制定或维护确保受到公共或私人工程危害的文化财产的保护或抢救所需的国家和地方立法措施。

五．财　政

15. 各成员国应保证有足够的预算用于保护或抢救受到公共或私人工程危害的文化财产。尽管法律制度和传统的差异以及财力的不同有碍于采取统一措施，但以下各点应予以考虑：

（1）负责保护文化财产的国家或地方当局应有足够的预算对受到公共或私人工程危害文化财产进行保护或抢救；或者

（2）保护或抢救受到公共或私人工程危害的文化财产的费用，包括初步的考古研究费用，应作为建设预算的一部分；或者

（3）应提供结合上述第（1）款和第（2）款所述两种方法的可行性。

16. 如果由于所需工程巨大并且复杂而引起的特殊开支，应有可能通过立法、特别补助、国家古迹资金或其他适当途径得到额外资金。负责保护文化财产的行政部门，应被授权管理或使用保护或抢救受到公共或私人工程危害的文化财产所需的这笔预算外捐款。

17. 各成员国应鼓励重要的历史或艺术建筑（包括构成传统建筑群一部分的建筑）所有者，或城乡建筑区内具有历史意义的街区的居民，通过以下方法保护其文化财产特征及其美学特点，否则它们将受到公共或私人工程的危害：

（1）优惠的税率；或者

（2）通过适当的立法编制一项预算，以赠款、贷款或其他方式帮助地方当局、团体和具有艺术、考古、科学或历史重要性建筑(包括传统建筑群)的私人所有者维护这些建筑或使之适应当代社会所需的作用；

（3）提供结合上述第(1)款和第(2)款所述两种方法的可能性；

18. 如果文化财产尚未被列入目录或相反已得到保护，其所有者应有可能向有关当局要求此种帮助。

19. 国家或地方当局以及私人所有者在为保护受到公共或私人工程危害的文化财产编制预算时，应考虑到文化财产的内在价值及其因对游客的吸引力而可能产生的经济收益。

六. 行政措施

20. 保护或抢救受到公共或私人工程危害的文化财产的责任应委托给适当的官方机构。只要已经存在保护文化财产的官方机构或行政部门，就应赋予它们保护文化财产免受公共或私人工程危害的责任。如果不存在这种行政部门，就应该设立特别机构或行政部门以保护受公共或私人工程危害的文化财产。尽管宪法规定和传统的差异有碍于采取统一体系，但某些共同的原则，应予以采纳：

（1）应设立一个协调或咨询机构，由负责保护文化财产、负责公共和私人工程、负责城市规划部门的代表以及研究和教育机构的代表组成。这些代表应能就保护受到公共或私人工程危害的文化财产、特别是就公共或私人工程的需求与保护抢救文化财产之间的利益冲突方面提出建议；

（2）省、市或其他形式的地方政府也应设有负责保护或抢救受到公共或私人工程危害的文化财产的行政部门。这些行政部门应能根据自己的职能和需要，请求国家行政部门或其他有关机构的帮助；

（3）负责保护文化财产的行政部门应配备足够的保护或抢救受到公共或私人工程危害的文化财产所需的专家，如建筑师、城市规划师、考古学家、历史学家、督导员以及其他专家和技师；

（4）应采取行政措施，对负责保护文化财产的各个行政部门和其他负责公共和私人工程的行政部门以及凡其职责涉及保护或抢救受到公共或私人工程危害的文化财产之问题的任何其他机构或行政部门之间的工作进行协调；

（5）应采取行政措施，在需要保护免受公共或私人工程危害的、已列入或未列入目录的历史居住区、遗址和古迹的所有社区内设立一个负责城市发展规划的主管部门或委员会。

21. 凡涉及在认为具有文化价值或可能存在重要考古和历史物品的地区进行的建设项目，在其初步勘查阶段，应准备几个地区或市一级的不同的工程方案，然后再做决定。应在全面比较分析的基础上对这些方案进行选择，以便能够采取既经济又能保护或抢救文化财产的最佳解决方案。

保护和抢救文化财产的程序

22. 早在进行任何可能危及文化财产安全的公共或私人工程之前，应进行充分的勘察，以确定：

（1）就地保护重要文化财产所要采取的措施；

（2）抢救行动可能需要的工作量，如选择需要发掘的考古遗址、需要迁移的建筑以及需要抢救的可移动文化财产等。

23. 保护或抢救文化财产的措施应早在公共或私人工程之前采取。重要的考古或文化地区，如历史城镇、村庄、遗址或街区，都应根据各国的立法进行保护，在这些地区开始新工程应以进行初步考古发掘为先决条件。如有必要，工程应予以推延，以确保采取充分的保护或抢救有关文化财产的措施。

24. 可能受到公共或私人工程危害的重要考古遗址、特别是难以确认的史前遗址、城乡地区的历史居住区、传统建筑群、早期文化的民族建筑以及其他不可移动的文化财产，应通过划分区域或列入目录予以保护；

（1）应划定考古保留区并将其列入目录，如有必要，买下不可移动的财产，以便能够对遗址内的遗物进行全面发掘或保护。

（2）应划定城乡中心的历史居住区和传统建筑群，并制定适当的规章以保护其环境及其特性，比如：

对重要历史或艺术建筑能够翻修的程度以及新建筑可以采用的式样和设计实行控制。保护古迹应是对任何设计良好的城市再发展规划的绝对要求,特别是在历史城镇或地区。类似规章应包括列入目录的古迹或遗址的周围地区及其环境,以保持其联系性和特征。对适用于新建项目的一般规定应允许进行适当修改。当新建筑被引入一历史区域时,这些规定应予以中止。用招贴画和灯光告示做一般性商业广告应予以禁止,但是可允许商业性机构通过适当的显示标志表明其存在。

25. 各成员国应规定,公共或私人工程中发现考古遗存者有义务尽快向主管行政部门申报,该行政部门应进行认真检查,如果遗址非常重要,应延迟施工以便能够进行全面发掘。对于因此而招致的延误,应给予适当的补贴或赔偿。

26. 各成员国应制定由国家或地方政府和其他有关机构通过购买获得受公共或私人工程危害的重要文化财产的规定。必要时应能通过征用的方式获得这些文化财产。

处罚

27. 各成员国应采取步骤,以确保根据各自刑法典严厉惩罚那些对受公共或私人工程危害的文化财产的故意或过失犯罪。这些刑法应包括罚款、监禁或二者兼有。此外,还可以采取以下措施:

(1) 如有可能,由对损坏遗址或建筑负有责任者出资进行修复;

(2) 如属偶然考古发现的情况下,当不可移动文化财产遭到损害、毁坏或忽视,应向国家交纳损害赔偿费;当一件可移动物品被藏匿时,应无偿予以没收。

修缮

28. 如果财产本身性质允许,各成员国应采取必要措施以确保对受到公共或私人工程危害的文化财产的修缮、修复或重建。各成员国也应预见,要求地方当局和重要文化财产的私人所有者进行修缮或修复的可能性,如有必要,可给予技术和财政援助。

奖励

29. 各成员国应鼓励个人、协会及市政当局,参加保护或抢救受到公共或私人工程危害的文化财产的计划。为此采取的措施可包括:

(1) 对举报或交出藏匿的考古发现物的个人给予优厚的报酬;

(2) 对为保护或抢救受公共或私人工程危害的文化财产作出突出贡献的个人——即使他们隶属政府行政部门、协会、社会机构或市政当局——授予证书、奖章或其他形式的奖励。

咨询

30. 各成员国应向缺乏必要经验和工作人员的个人、协会和市政当局提供技术咨询或监督,以便维持保护或抢救受到公共或私人工程威胁的文化财产的适当标准。

教育计划

31. 各成员国应本着国际合作的精神,采取措施激励和培养其国民对本国昔日文化遗产和其他传统的兴趣和尊重,以便保护或抢救受到公共或私人工程威胁的文化财产。

32. 专门出版物、报刊文章、广播和电视应该宣传由于不当的公共或私人工程给文化财产带来的危险性以及保护和抢救文化财产的成功实例。

33. 教育机构、历史和文化协会、与旅游业有关的公共团体以及公共教育学会应制订计划,宣传因为目光短浅的公共或私人工程对文化财产所带来的危险,并强调这样一个事实:保护文化财产的项目有助于国际间相互了解。

34. 博物馆、教育机构和其他有关组织应就不加控制的公共或私人工程对文化财产所带来的危害以及为保护或抢救已受到危害的文化财产所采取的措施筹办展览。

Recommendation concerning the Preservation of Cultural Property Endangered by Public or Private Works

Adopted by the UNESCO General Conference at its 15th Session, Paris, 19 November 1968

The General Conference of the United Nations Educational, Scientific and Cultural Organization, meeting in Paris from 15 October to 20 November 1968, at its fifteenth session,

Considering that contemporary civilization and its future evolution rest upon, among other elements, the cultural traditions of the peoples of the world, their creative force and their social and economic development,

Considering that cultural property is the product and witness of the different traditions and of the spiritual achievements of the past and thus is an essential element in the personality of the peoples of the world,

Considering that it is indispensable to preserve it as much as possible, according to its historical and artistic importance, so that the significance and message of cultural property become a part of the spirit of peoples who thereby may gain consciousness of their own dignity,

Considering that preserving cultural property and rendering it accessible constitute, in the spirit of the Declaration of the Principles of International Cultural Co-operation adopted on 4 November 1966 in the course of its fourteenth session, means of encouraging mutual understanding among peoples and thereby serve the cause of peace,

Considering also that the well-being of all peoples depends, *inter alia,* upon the existence of a favourable and stimulating environment and that the preservation of cultural property of all periods of history contributes directly to such an environment,

Recognizing, on the other hand, the role that industrialization, towards which world civilization is moving, plays in the development of peoples and their spiritual and national fulfilment,

Considering, however, that the prehistoric, protohistoric and historic monuments and remains, as well as numerous recent structures having artistic, historic or scientific importance are increasingly threatened by public and private works resulting from industrial development and urbanization,

Considering that it is the duty of governments to ensure the protection and the preservation of the cultural heritage of mankind, as much as to promote social and economic development,

Considering in consequence that it is urgent to harmonize the preservation of the cultural heritage with the

---

① Records of the General Conference, fifteenth session, Paris, 1968, v. 1: Resolutions. UNESCO Document Code: 15 C/Resolutions.

changes which follow from social and economic development, making serious efforts to meet both requirements in a broad spirit of understanding, and with reference to appropriate planning,

Considering equally that adequate preservation and accessibility of cultural property constitute a major contribution to the social and economic development of countries and regions which possess such treasures of mankind by means of promoting national and international tourism,

Considering finally that the surest guarantee for the preservation of cultural property rests in the respect and the attachment felt for it by the people themselves, and persuaded that such feelings may be greatly strengthened by adequate measures carried out by Member States,

Having *before it* proposals concerning the preservation of cultural property endangered by public or private works, which constitute item 16 on the agenda of the session,

Having *decided* at its thirteenth session that proposals on this item should be the subject of an international instrument in the form of a recommendation to Member States,

Adopts on this nineteenth day of November 1968 this recommendation.

The General Conference recommends that Member States should apply the following provisions by taking whatever legislative or other steps may be required to give effect within their respective territories to the norms and principles set forth in this recommendation.

The General Conference recommends that Member States should bring this recommendation to the attention of the authorities or services responsible for public or private works as well as to the bodies responsible for the conservation and the protection of monuments and historic, artistic, archaeological and scientific sites. It recommends that authorities and bodies which plan programmes for education and the development of tourism be equally informed.

The General Conference recommends that Member States should report to it, on the dates and in a manner to be determined by it, on the action they have taken to give effect to this recommendation.

I. Definition

1. For the purpose of this recommendation, the term 'cultural property' applies to:

(a) Immovables, such as archaeological and historic or scientific sites, structures or other features of historic, scientific, artistic or architectural value, whether religious or secular, including groups of traditional structures, historic quarters in urban or rural built-up areas and the ethno-logical structures of previous cultures still extant in valid form. It applies to such immovables constituting ruins existing above the earth as well as to archaeological or historic remains found within the earth. The term cultural property also includes the setting of such property;

(b) Movable property of cultural importance including that existing in or recovered from immovable property and that concealed in the earth, which may be found in archaeological or historical sites or elsewhere.

2. The term 'cultural property' includes not only the established and scheduled architectural, archaeological and historic sites and structures, but also the unscheduled or unclassified vestiges of the past as well as artistically or historically important recent sites and structures.

II. General principles

3. Measures to preserve cultural property should extend to the whole territory of the State and should not be confined to certain monuments and sites.

4. Protective inventories of important cultural property, whether scheduled or unscheduled, should be maintained. Where such inventories do not exist, priority should be given in their establishment to the thorough survey of cultural property in areas where such property is endangered by public or private works.

5. Due account should be taken of the relative significance of the cultural property concerned when determining measures required for the:

(a) Preservation of an entire site, structure, or other forms of immovable cultural property from the effects of private or public works;

(b) Salvage or rescue of cultural property if the area in which it is found is to be transformed by public or private works, and the whole or a part of the property in question is to be preserved and removed.

6. Measures should vary according to the character, size and location of the cultural property and the nature of the dangers with which it is threatened.

7. Measures for the preservation or salvage of cultural property should be preventive and corrective.

8. Preventive and corrective measures should be aimed at protecting or saving cultural property from public or private works likely to damage and destroy it, such as:

(a) Urban expansion and renewal projects, although they may retain scheduled monuments while sometimes removing less important structures, with the result that historical relations and the setting of historic quarters are destroyed;

(b) Similar projects in areas where groups of traditional structures having cultural value as a whole risk being destroyed for the lack of a scheduled individual monument;

(c) Injudicious modifications and repair of individual historic buildings;

(d) The construction or alteration of highways which are a particular danger to sites or to historically important structures or groups of structures;

(e) The construction of dams for irrigation, hydro-electric power or flood control;

(f) The construction of pipelines and of power and transmission lines of electricity;

(g) Farming operations including deep ploughing, drainage and irrigation operations, the clearing and levelling of land and afforestation;

(h) Works required by the growth of industry and the technological progress of industrialized societies such as airfields, mining and quarrying operations and dredging and reclamation of channels and harbours.

9. Member States should give due priority to measures required for the preservation *in situ* of cultural property endangered by public or private works in order to preserve historical associations and continuity. When overriding economic or social conditions require that cultural property be transferred, abandoned or destroyed, the salvage or rescue operations should always include careful study of the cultural property involved and the preparations of detailed records.

10. The results of studies having scientific or historic value carried out in connexion with salvage operations, particularly when all or much of the immovable cultural property has been abandoned or destroyed, should be published or otherwise made available for future research.

11. Important structures and other monuments which have been transferred in order to save them from destruction by public or private works should be placed on a site or in a setting which resembles their former position and natural, historic or artistic associations.

12. Important movable cultural property, including representative samples of objects recovered from archaeological excavations, obtained from salvage operations should be preserved for study or placed on

exhibition in institutions such as museums, including site museums, or universities.

III. Preservation and salvage measures

13. The preservation or salvage of cultural property endangered by public or private works should be ensured through the means mentioned below, the precise measures to be determined by the legislation and organizational system of the State: (a) Legislation; (b) Finance; (c) Administrative measures; (d) Procedures to preserve and to salvage cultural property; (e) Penalties; (f) Repairs; (g) Awards; (h) Advice; (i) Educational programmes.

Legislation

14. Member States should enact or maintain on the national as well as on the local level the legislative measures necessary to ensure the preservation or salvage of cultural property endangered by public or private works in accordance with the norms and principles embodied in this recommendation.

Finance

15. Member States should ensure that adequate budgets are available for the preservation or salvage of cultural property endangered by public or private works, although differences in legal systems and traditions as well as disparity in resources preclude the adoption of uniform measures, the following should be considered:

(a) The national or local authorities responsible for the safeguarding of cultural property should have adequate budgets to undertake the preservation or salvage of cultural property endangered by public or private works; or

(b) The costs of preserving or salvaging cultural property endangered by public or private works, including preliminary archaeological research, should form part of the budget of construction costs; or

(c) The possibility of combining the two methods mentioned in sub-paragraphs (a) and (b) above should be provided for.

16. In the event of unusual costs due to the size and complexity of the operations required, there should be possibilities of obtaining additional funds through enabling legislation, special subventions, a national fund for monuments or other appropriate means. The services responsible for the safeguarding of cultural property should be empowered to administer or to utilize these extra-budgetary contributions required for the preservation or salvage of cultural property endangered by public or private works.

17. Member States should encourage proprietors of artistically or historically important structures, including structures forming part of a traditional group, or residents in a historic quarter in urban or rural built-up areas to preserve the character and aesthetic qualities of their cultural property which would otherwise be endangered by public or private works, through:

(a) Favourable tax rates; or

(b) The establishment, through appropriate legislation, of a budget to assist, by grants, loans or other measures, local authorities, institutions and private owners of artistically, architecturally, scientifically or historically important structures including groups of traditional structures to maintain or to adapt them suitably for functions which would meet the needs of contemporary society; or

(c) The possibility of combining the two methods mentioned in sub-paragraphs (a) and (b) above should be provided for.

18. If the cultural property is not scheduled or otherwise protected it should be possible for the owner to request such assistance from the appropriate authorities.

19. National or local authorities, as well as private owners, when budgeting for the preservation of cultural property endangered by public or private works, should take into account the intrinsic value of cultural property and also the contribution it can make to the economy as a tourist attraction.

Administrative measures

20. Responsibility for the preservation or salvage of cultural property endangered by public or private works should be entrusted to appropriate official bodies. Whenever official bodies or services already exist for the protection of cultural property, these bodies or services should be given responsibility for the preservation of cultural property against the dangers caused by public or private works. If such services do not exist, special bodies or services should be created for the purpose of the preservation of cultural property endangered by public or private works; and although differences of constitutional provisions and traditions preclude the adoption of a uniform system, certain common principles should be adopted.

(a) There should be a co-ordinating or consultative body, composed of representatives of the authorities responsible for the safeguarding of cultural property, for public and private works, for town planning, and of research and educational institutions, which should be competent to advise on the preservation of cultural property endangered by public or private works and, in particular, on conflicts of interest between requirements for public or private works and the preservation or salvage of cultural property.

(b) Provincial, municipal or other forms of local government should also have services responsible for the preservation or salvage of cultural property endangered by public or private works. These services should be able to call upon the assistance of national services or other appropriate bodies in accordance with their capabilities and requirements.

(c) The services responsible for the safeguarding of cultural property should be adequately staffed with the specialists required for the preservation or salvage of cultural property endangered by public or private works, such as architects, urbanists, archaeologists, historians, inspectors and other specialists and technicians.

(d) Administrative measures should be taken to co-ordinate the work of the different services responsible for the safeguarding of cultural property with that of other services responsible for public and private works and that of any other department or service whose responsibilities touch upon the problem of the preservation or salvage of cultural property endangered by public or private works.

(e) Administrative measures should be taken to establish an authority or commission in charge of urban development programmes in all communities having scheduled or unscheduled historic quarters, sites and monuments which need to be preserved against public and private construction.

21. At the preliminary survey stage of any project involving construction in a locality recognized as being of cultural interest or likely to contain objects of archaeological or historical importance, several variants of the project should be prepared, at regional or municipal level, before a decision is taken. The choice between these variants should be made on the basis of a comprehensive comparative analysis, in order that the most advantageous solution, both economically and from the point of view of preserving or salvaging cultural property, may be adopted.

Procedures to preserve and to salvage cultural property

22. Thorough surveys should be carried out well in advance of any public or private works which might endanger cultural property to determine:

(a) The measures to be taken to preserve important cultural property *in situ;*

(b) The amount of salvage operations which would be required such as the selection of archaeological sites to be excavated, structures to be transferred and movable cultural property salvaged, etc.

23. Measures for the preservation or salvage of cultural property should be carried out well in advance of public or private works. In areas of archaeological or cultural importance, such as historic towns, villages, sites and districts, which should be protected by the legislation of every country, the starting of new work should be made conditional upon the execution of preliminary archaeological excavations. If necessary, work should be delayed to ensure that adequate measures are taken for the preservation or salvage of the cultural property concerned.

24. Important archaeological sites, and, in particular, prehistoric sites as they are difficult to recognize, historic quarters in urban or rural areas, groups of traditional structures, ethnological structures of previous cultures and other immovable cultural property which would otherwise be endangered by public or private works should be protected by zoning or scheduling:

(a) Archaeological reserves should be zoned or scheduled and, if necessary, immovable property purchased, to permit thorough excavation or the preservation of the ruins found at the site.

(b) Historic quarters in urban or rural centres and groups of traditional structures should be zoned and appropriate regulations adopted to preserve their setting and character, such as the imposition of controls on the degree to which historically or artistically important structures can be renovated and the type and design of new structures which can be introduced. The preservation of monuments should be an absolute requirement of any well-designed plan for urban redevelopment especially in historic cities or districts. Similar regulations should cover the area surrounding a scheduled monument or site and its setting to preserve its association and character. Due allowance should be made for the modification of ordinary regulations applicable to new construction; these should be placed in abeyance when new structures are introduced into an historical zone. Ordinary types of commercial advertising by means of posters and illuminated announcements should be forbidden, but commercial establishments could be allowed to indicate their presence by means of judiciously presented signs.

25. Member States should make it obligatory for persons finding archaeological remains in the course of public or private works to declare them at the earliest possible moment to the competent service. Careful examination should be carried out by the service concerned and, if the site is important, construction should be deferred to permit thorough excavation, due allowance or compensation being made for the delays incurred.

26. Member States should have provisions for the acquisition, through purchase, by national or local governments and other appropriate bodies of important cultural property endangered by public or private works. When necessary, it should be possible to effect such acquisition through expropriation.

Penalties

27. Member States should take steps to ensure that offences, through intent or negligence, against the preservation or salvage of cultural property endangered by public or private works are severely punished by their Penal Code, which should provide for fines or imprisonment or both.

In addition, the following measures could be applied:

(a) Whenever possible, restoration of the site or structure at the expense of those responsible for the damage to it;

(b) In the case of a chance archaeological find, payment of damages to the State when immovable cultural property has been damaged, destroyed or neglected; confiscation without compensation when a movable object has been concealed.

Repairs

28. Member States should, when the nature of the property so allows, adopt the necessary measures to ensure

the repair, restoration or reconstruction of cultural property damaged by public orprivate works. They should also foresee the possibility of requiring local authorities and private owners of important cultural property to carry out repairs or restorations, with technical and financial assistance if necessary.

Awards

29. Member States should encourage individuals, associations and municipalities to take part in programmes for the preservation or salvage of cultural property endangered by public or private works. Measures to that effect could include:

(a) *Ex* gratia payments to individuals reporting or surrendering hidden archaeological finds;

(b) Awards of certificates, medals or other forms of recognition to individuals, even if they belong to government service, associations, institutions or municipalities which have carried out outstanding projects for the preservation or salvage of cultural property endangered by public or private works.

Advice

30. Member States should provide individuals, associations or municipalities lacking the required experience or staff with technical advice or supervision to maintain adequate standards for the preservation or salvage of cultural property endangered by public or private works.

Educational programmes

31. In a spirit of international collaboration, Member States should take steps to stimulate and develop among their national interest in, and respect for, the cultural heritage of the past of their own and other traditions in order to preserve or to salvage cultural property endangered by public or private works.

32. Specialized publications, articles in the press and radio and television broadcasts should publicize the nature of the dangers to cultural property arising from ill-conceived public or private works as well as cases where cultural property has been successfully preserved or salvaged.

33. Educational institutions, historical and cultural associations, public bodies concerned with the tourist industry and associations for popular education should have programmes to publicize the dangers to cultural property arising from short-sighted public or private works, and to underline the fact that projects to preserve cultural property contribute to international understanding.

34. Museums and educational institutions and other interested organizations should prepare special exhibitions on the dangers to cultural property arising from uncontrolled public or private works and on the measures which have been used to preserve or to salvage cultural property which has been endangered.

关于禁止和防止非法进出口文化财产和非法转让其所有权的方法的公约[①]

(联合国教科文组织第十六届大会1970年11月14日在巴黎通过)

联合国教科文组织于1970年10月12日至11月14日在巴黎召开第十六届大会,

忆及其第十四届大会通过的《国际文化合作原则宣言》所载规定的重要性,

考虑到各国间为科学、文化及教育目的而进行的文化财产交流增进了对人类文明的认识、丰富了各国人民的文化生活并激发了各国之间的相互尊重和了解,

考虑到文化财产实为构成文明和民族文化的一大基本要素,只有尽可能充分掌握有关其起源、历史和传统背景的知识,才能理解其真正价值,

考虑到各国有责任保护其领土上的文化财产免受偷盗、秘密发掘和非法出口的危险,

考虑到为避免这些危险,各国必须日益认识到其尊重本国及其他所有国家的文化遗产的道义责任,

考虑到博物馆、图书馆和档案馆作为文化机构应保证根据普遍公认的道义原则汇集其收藏品,

考虑到非法进出口文化财产和非法转让其所有权阻碍了各国之间的谅解,教科文组织的一部分职责就是通过向有关国家推荐这方面的各项国际公约以促进这一谅解,

考虑到有各国在国家和国际范围上进行组织,密切合作,才能有效保护文化遗产,

考虑到教科文组织大会在1964年就此通过了一项建议,

已收到关于禁止和防止非法进出口文化财产和非法转让其所有权的方法的各项进一步建议,这一问题业已作为第十九项议程项目列入本届会议议程,

第十五届会议已决定就这一问题制订一项国际公约,

在1970年11月14日通过本公约。

第一条 为了本公约的目的,"文化财产"一词系指每个国家,根据宗教的或世俗的理由,明确指定为具有重要考古、史前史、历史、文学、艺术或科学价值的财产并属于下列各类者:

1. 动物群落、植物群落、矿物和解剖以及具有古生物学意义的物品的稀有收集品和标本;

2. 有关历史,包括科学、技术、军事及社会史,有关国家领袖、思想家、科学家、艺术家之生平以及有关国家重大事件的财产;

3. 考古发掘(包括正常的和秘密的)或考古发现的成果;

4. 业已肢解的艺术或历史古迹或考古遗址之构成部分;

5. 一百年以前的古物,如铭文、钱币和印章;

6. 具有人种学意义的文物;

[①] 原载国家文物局官网 http://www.ncha.gov.cn。

7. 有艺术价值的财产，如：
（1）全部是手工完成的图画、绘画和绘图，不论其装帧框座如何，也不论所用的是何种材料（不包括工业设计图及手工装饰的工业产品）；
（2）用任何材料制成的雕塑艺术和雕刻的原作；
（3）版画、印片和平版画的原件；
（4）用任何材料组集或拼集的艺术品原件；

8. 稀有手稿和古版书籍，有特殊意义的（历史、艺术、科学、文学等）古书、文件和出版物，不论是单本的或整套的；

9. 邮票、印花税票及类似的票证，不论是单张的或成套的；

10. 档案，包括有声、照相和电影档案；

11. 一百年以前的家具物品和古乐器。

第二条

1. 本公约缔约国承认文化财产非法进出口和所有权非法转让是造成这类财产的原主国文化遗产枯竭的主要原因之一，并承认国际合作是保护各国文化财产免遭由此产生的各种危险的最有效方法之一。

2. 为此目的，缔约国承担利用现有手段，特别是通过消除其根源、制止现有做法和帮助给予必要的补偿来反对这种做法。

第三条 本公约缔约国违反本公约所列的规定而造成的文化财产之进出口或所有权转让均属非法。

第四条 本公约缔约国承认，为了本公约的宗旨，凡属以下各类财产均为每个缔约国的文化遗产的一部分：

1. 有关国家的国民的个人或集体天才所创造的文化财产和居住在该国领土境内的外国国民或无国籍人在该国领土内创造的对有关国家具有重要意义的文化财产；

2. 在国家领土内发现的文化财产；

3. 经此类财产原主国主管当局的同意，由考古学、人种学或自然科学团体所获得的文化财产；

4. 经由自由达成协议实行交流的文化财产；

5. 经此类财产原主国主管当局的同意，作为赠送品而接收的或合法购置的文化财产。

第五条 为确保保护文化财产免于非法进出口和所有权的非法转让，本公约缔约国承担若尚未设立保护文化遗产的国家机构，可根据本国的情况，在其领土之内建立一个或一个以上的国家机构，配备足够人数的合格工作人员，以有效地行使下述职责：

1. 协助制订旨在切实保护文化遗产特别是防止重要文化财产的非法进出口和非法转让的法律和规章草案；

2. 根据全国受保护财产清册，制订并不断更新一份其出口将造成文化遗产的严重枯竭的重要的公共及私有文化财产的清单；

3. 促进发展或成立为保证文化财产的保存和展出所需之科学及技术机构（博物馆、图书馆、档案馆、实验室、工作室……）；

4. 组织对考古发掘的监督，确保在原地保存某些文化财产，并保护某些地区，供今后考古研究之用；

5. 为有关各方面（博物馆长、收藏家、古董商等）的利益，制订符合于本公约所规定道德原则的规章，并采取措施保证遵守这些规章；

6. 采取教育措施，鼓励并提高对各国文化遗产的尊重，并传播关于本公约规定的知识；

7. 注意对任何种类的文化财产的失踪进行适当宣传。

第六条 本公约缔约国承担：

1. 发放适当证件，出口国将在该证件中说明有关文化财产的出口已经过批准。根据规定出口的各种文化财产，均须附有此种证件；

2. 除非附有上述出口证件，禁止文化财产从本国领土出口；

3. 通过适当方法宣传这种禁止，特别要在可能出口或进口文化财产的人们中间进行宣传。

第七条 本公约缔约国承担：

1. 采取与本国立法相一致的必要措施防止本国领土内的博物馆及类似机构获取来源于另一缔约国并于本公约在有关国家生效后非法出口的文化财产。本公约对两国均已生效后，尽可能随时把自两国中的原主缔约国非法运出文化财产的建议通知该原主缔约国。

2.（1）本公约对有关国家生效后，禁止进口从本公约另一缔约国的博物馆或宗教的或世俗的公共纪念馆或类似机构中窃取的文化财产，如果该项财产业已用文件形式列入该机构的财产清册；

（2）本公约对有关两个国家生效后，根据两国中的原主缔约国的要求，采取适当措施收回并归还进口的此类文化财产，但要求国须向不知情的买主或对该财产具有合法权利者给予公平的赔偿。要求收回和归还失物必须通过外交部门进行，提出要求一方应提供使确定其收回或归还失物的要求的必要文件及其他证据，费用自理。各方不得对遵照本条规定而归还的文化财产征收关税或其他费用。归还和运送文化财产过程中所需的一切费用均由提出要求一方负担。

第八条 本公约缔约国承担对触犯上述第六条2和第七条2所列的禁止规定负有责任者予以惩处或行政制裁。

第九条 本公约的任一缔约国在其文化遗产由于考古或人种学的材料遭受掠夺而处境危殆时得向蒙受影响的其他缔约国发出呼吁。在此情况下，本公约缔约国承担参与协调一致的国际努力，以确定并实施必要的具体措施，包括对有关的特定物资的进出口及国际贸易实行管制。在尚未达成协议之前，有关各国应在可能范围内采取临时性措施，以便制止对提出要求的国家的文化遗产造成不可弥补的损失。

第十条 本公约缔约国承担：

1. 通过教育、情报和防范手段，限制非法从本公约缔约国运出的文化财产的移动，并视各国情况，责成古董商保持一份记录，载明每项文化财产的来源、提供者的姓名与住址以及每项售出的物品的名称与价格，并须把此类财产可能禁止出口的情况告知该项文化财产的购买人，违者须受刑事或行政制裁；

2. 努力通过教育手段，使公众心目中认识到，并进一步理解文化财产的价值和偷盗、秘密发掘与非法出口对文化财产造成的威胁。

第十一条 一个国家直接或间接地由于被他国占领而被迫出口文化财产或转让其所有权应被视为非法。

第十二条 本公约缔约国应尊重由其负责国际关系的领土内的文化财产，并应采取一切适当措施禁止并防止在这些领土内非法进出口文化财产和非法转让其所有权。

第十三条 本公约缔约国还应在符合其本国法律的情况下承担：

1. 通过一切适当手段防止可能引起文化财产的非法进出口的这一类财产的所有权转让；

2. 保证本国的主管机关进行合作，使非法出口的文化财产尽早归还其合法所有者；

3. 受理合法所有者或其代表提出的关于找回失落的或失窃的文化财产的诉讼；

4. 承认本公约缔约国有不可取消的权利规定并宣布某些文化财产是不能让与的，因而据此也不能出口，若此类财产已经出口务须促使这类财产归还给有关国家。

第十四条 为防止非法出口、履行本公约所规定的义务，本公约各缔约国应在可能范围内为其负责保护文化遗产的国家机关提供足够的预算并在必要时为此目的设立一项基金。

第十五条 在本公约对有关国家生效前，本公约之任何规定不应妨碍缔约国之间自行缔结有关归还从其原主国领土上不论以何种理由搬走之文化财产的特别协定，或制止它们继续执行业已缔结的有关协定。

第十六条 本公约缔约国应在向联合国教科文组织大会提交的定期报告中，提供它们已经通过的立法和行政规定和它们为实施本公约所采取的其他行动以及在此领域内取得的详尽经验的资料，报告的日期及方式由大会决定。

第十七条

1. 本公约缔约国可以向联合国教科文组织请求给予技术援助，特别是有关：

（1）情报和教育；

（2）咨询和专家建议；

（3）协调和斡旋。

2. 联合国教科文组织可以主动进行有关非法转移文化财产问题的研究并出版研究报告。

3. 为此，联合国教科文组织可以请求任何非政府的主管组织予以合作。

4. 联合国教科文组织可以主动向本公约缔约国提出有关本公约的实施的建议。

5. 经对本公约的实施有争议的两个以上的本公约缔约国的请求，联合国教科文组织得进行斡旋，使它们之间的争端得到解决。

第十八条 本公约以英文、法文、俄文和西班牙文制定，四种文本具有同等效力。

第十九条

1. 本公约须经联合国教科文组织会员国按各国宪法程序批准或接受。

2. 批准书或接受书，应交存联合国教科文组织总干事。

第二十条

1. 本公约应开放给非联合国教科文组织成员但经本组织执行局邀请加入本公约的所有国家加入。

2. 加入书交存联合国教科文组织总干事后，加入即行生效。

第二十一条 本公约在收到第三份批准书、接受书或加入书后的三个月开始生效，但这只对那些在该日或该日之前业已交存其各自的批准书、接受书或加入书的国有生效。对于任何其他国家，本公约则在其批准书、接受书或加入书交存后三个月开始生效。

第二十二条 本公约缔约国承认，本公约不仅适用于其本国领土，而且也适用于在国际关系上由其负责的一切领土；如有必要，缔约国须在批准、接受或加入之时或以前与这些领土的政府或其他主管当局进行磋商，以便保证本公约在这些领土的适用，并将本公约适用的领土通知联合国教科文组织总干事，该通知在收到之日起三个月生效。

第二十三条

1. 本公约之每一缔约国可以代表本国或代表由其负责国际关系的任何领土退出本公约。

2. 退约须以书面文件通知，该退约书交存联合国教科文组织总干事处。

3. 退约在收到退约通知书后十二个月生效。

第二十四条 联合国教科文组织总干事须将第十九条和二十条中规定的有关批准书、接受书和加入书的交存情况以及第二十二条和第二十三条分别规定的通知和退约告知本组织会员国、第二十条中所述的非本组织会员的国家以及联合国。

第二十五条

1. 本公约可经联合国教科文组织大会予以修正。任何这样的修正只对修正公约的缔约国具有约束力。

2. 如大会通过一项全面或部分地修订本公约的新公约，则除非新公约另有规定，本公约在新的修订公约生效之日起停止一切批准、接受或加入。

第二十六条 经联合国教科文组织总干事的要求，本公约应按照《联合国宪章》第一百零二条的规定在联合国秘书处登记。

1970年11月17日订于巴黎。两个正式文本均有大会第十六届会议主席和联合国教科文组织总干事的签名，将交存于联合国教科文组织的档案库中。验证无误之副本将分送第十九条到第二十条所述之所有国家和联合国。

以上乃1970年11月14日在巴黎召开的联合国教科文组织大会第十六届会议正式通过之公约的作准文本。

我们于1970年11月17日签字，以昭信守。

Convention on the Means of Prohibiting and Preventing the Illicit Import, Export and Transfer of Ownership of Cultural Property

Adopted by the UNESCO General Conference at its 16th Session, Paris, 14 November 1970

The General Conference of the United Nations Educational, Scientific and Cultural Organization, meeting in Paris from 12 October to 14 November 1970, at its sixteenth session,

Recalling the importance of the provisions contained in the Declaration of the Principles of International Cultural Co-operation, adopted by the General Conference at its fourteenth session,

Considering that the interchange of cultural property among nations for scientific, cultural and educational purposes increases the knowledge of the civilization of Man, enriches the cultural life of all peoples and inspires mutual respect and appreciation among nations,

Considering that cultural property constitutes one of the basic elements of civilization and national culture, and that its true value can be appreciated only in relation to the fullest possible information regarding its origin, history and traditional setting,

Considering that it is incumbent upon every State to protect the cultural property existing within its territory against the dangers of theft, clandestine excavation, and illicit export,

Considering that, to avert these dangers, it is essential for every State to become increasingly alive to the moral obligations to respect its own cultural heritage and that of all nations,

Considering that, as cultural institutions, museums, libraries and archives should ensure that their collections are built up in accordance with universally recognized moral principles,

Considering that the illicit import, export and transfer of ownership of cultural property is an obstacle to that understanding between nations which its part of UNESCO's mission to promote by recommending to interested States, international conventions to this end,

Considering that the protection of cultural heritage can be effective only if organized both nationally and internationally among States working in close co-operation,

Considering that the UNESCO General Conference adopted a Recommendation to this effect in 1964,

Having before it further proposals on the means of prohibiting and preventing the illicit import, export and transfer of ownership of cultural property, a question which is on the agenda for the session as item 19,

Having decided at its fifteenth session, that this question should be made the subject of an international convention,

Adopts this Convention on the fourteenth day of November 1970.

Article 1

For the purposes of this Convention, the term "cultural property" means property which, on religious or secular grounds, is specifically designated by each State as being of importance for archaeology, prehistory, history, literature, art or science and which belongs to the following categories:

(a) Rare collections and specimens of fauna, flora, minerals and anatomy, and objects of palaeontological interest;

(b) property relating to history, including the history of science and technology and military and social history, to the life of national leaders, thinkers, scientists and artist and to events of national importance;

(c) products of archaeological excavations (including regular and clandestine) or of archaeological discoveries;

(d) elements of artistic or historical monuments or archaeological sites which have been dismembered;

(e) antiquities more than one hundred years old, such as inscriptions, coins and engraved seals;

(f) objects of ethnological interest;

(g) property of artistic interest, such as:

    (i) pictures, paintings and drawings produced entirely by hand on any support and in any material (excluding industrial designs and manufactured articles decorated by hand);

    (ii) original works of statuary art and sculpture in any material;

    (iii) original engravings, prints and lithographs ;

    (iv) original artistic assemblages and montages in any material;

(h) rare manuscripts and incunabula, old books, documents and publications of special interest (historical, artistic, scientific, literary, etc.) singly or in collections ;

(i) postage, revenue and similar stamps, singly or in collections;

(j) archives, including sound, photographic and cinematographic archives;

(k) articles of furniture more than one hundred years old and old musical instruments.

Article 2

1. The States Parties to this Convention recognize that the illicit import, export and transfer of ownership of cultural property is one of the main causes of the impoverishment of the cultural heritage of the countries of origin of such property and that international co-operation constitutes one of the most efficient means of protecting each country's cultural property against all the dangers resulting therefrom.

2. To this end, the States Parties undertake to oppose such practices with the means at their disposal, and particularly by removing their causes, putting a stop to current practices, and by helping to make the necessary reparations.

Article 3

The import, export or transfer of ownership of cultural property effected contrary to the provisions adopted under this Convention by the States Parties thereto, shall be illicit.

Article 4

The States Parties to this Convention recognize that for the purpose of the Convention property which belongs to the following categories forms part of the cultural heritage of each State:

(a) Cultural property created by the individual or collective genius of nationals of the State concerned, and cultural property of importance to the State concerned created within the territory of that State by foreign nationals or stateless persons resident within such territory;

(b) cultural property found within the national territory;

(c) cultural property acquired by archaeological, ethnological or natural science missions, with the consent of the competent authorities of the country of origin of such property;

(d) cultural property which has been the subject of a freely agreed exchange;

(e) cultural property received as a gift or purchased legally with the consent of the competent authorities of the country of origin of such property.

Article 5

To ensure the protection of their cultural property against illicit import, export and transfer of ownership, the States Parties to this Convention undertake, as appropriate for each country, to set up within their territories one or more national services, where such services do not already exist, for the protection of the cultural heritage, with a qualified staff sufficient in number for the effective carrying out of the following functions:

(a) contributing to the formation of draft laws and regulations designed to secure the protection of the cultural heritage and particularly prevention of the illicit import, export and transfer of ownership of important cultural property;

(b) establishing and keeping up to date, on the basis of a national inventory of protected property, a list of important public and private cultural property whose export would constitute an appreciable impoverishment of the national cultural heritage;

(c) promoting the development or the establishment of scientific and technical institutions (museums, libraries, archives, laboratories, workshops...) required to ensure the preservation and presentation of cultural property;

(d) organizing the supervision of archaeological excavations, ensuring the preservation "in situ" of certain cultural property, and protecting certain areas reserved for future archaeological research;

(e) establishing, for the benefit of those concerned (curators, collectors, antique dealers, etc.) rules in conformity with the ethical principles set forth in this Convention; and taking steps to ensure the observance of those rules;

(f) taking educational measures to stimulate and develop respect for the cultural heritage of all States, and spreading knowledge of the provisions of this Convention;

(g) seeing that appropriate publicity is given to the disappearance of any items of cultural property.

Article 6

The States Parties to this Convention undertake:

(a) To introduce an appropriate certificate in which the exporting State would specify that the export of the cultural property in question is authorized. The certificate should accompany all items of cultural property exported in accordance with the regulations;

(b) to prohibit the exportation of cultural property from their territory unless accompanied by the above-mentioned export certificate;

(c) to publicize this prohibition by appropriate means, particularly among persons likely to export or import cultural property.

Article 7

The States Parties to this Convention undertake:

(a) To take the necessary measures, consistent with national legislation, to prevent museums and similar institutions within their territories from acquiring cultural property originating in another State Party which has been illegally exported after entry into force of this Convention, in the States concerned. Whenever possible, to inform a State of origin Party to this Convention of an offer of such cultural property illegally removed from that State after the entry into force of this Convention in both States;

(b) (i) to prohibit the import of cultural property stolen from a museum or a religious or secular public monument or similar institution in another State Party to this Convention after the entry into force of this Convention for the States concerned, provided that such property is documented as appertaining to the inventory of that institution;

(ii) at the request of the State Party of origin, to take appropriate steps to recover and return any such cultural property imported after the entry into force of this Convention in both States concerned, provided, however, that the requesting State shall pay just compensation to an innocent purchaser or to a person who has valid title to that property. Requests for recovery and return shall be made through diplomatic offices. The requesting Party shall furnish, at its expense, the documentation and other evidence necessary to establish its claim for recovery and return. The Parties shall impose no customs duties or other charges upon cultural property returned pursuant to this Article. All expenses incident to the return and delivery of the cultural property shall be borne by the requesting Party.

Article 8

The States Parties to this Convention undertake to impose penalties or administrative sanctions on any person responsible for infringing the prohibitions referred to under Articles 6(b) and 7(b) above.

Article 9

Any State Party to this Convention whose cultural patrimony is in jeopardy from pillage of archaeological or ethnological materials may call upon other States Parties who are affected. The States Parties to this Convention undertake, in these circumstances, to participate in a concerted international effort to determine and to carry out the necessary concrete measures, including the control of exports and imports and international commerce in the specific materials concerned. Pending agreement each State concerned shall take provisional measures to the extent feasible to prevent irremediable injury to the cultural heritage of the requesting State.

Article 10

The States Parties to this Convention undertake:

(a) To restrict by education, information and vigilance, movement of cultural property illegally removed from any State Party to this Convention and, as appropriate for each country, oblige antique dealers, subject to penal or administrative sanctions, to maintain a register recording the origin of each item of cultural property, names and addresses of the supplier, description and price of each item sold and to inform the purchaser of the cultural property of the export prohibition to which such property may be subject;

(b) to endeavour by educational means to create and develop in the public mind a realization of the value of cultural property and the threat to the cultural heritage created by theft, clandestine excavations and illicit exports.

Article 11

The export and transfer of ownership of cultural property under compulsion arising directly or indirectly from the occupation of a country by a foreign power shall be regarded as illicit.

Article 12

The States Parties to this Convention shall respect the cultural heritage within the territories for the international relations of which they are responsible, and shall take all appropriate measures to prohibit and prevent the illicit import, export and transfer of ownership of cultural property in such territories.

Article 13

The States Parties to this Convention also undertake, consistent with the laws of each State:

(a) to prevent by all appropriate means transfers of ownership of cultural property likely to promote the illicit import or export of such property;

(b) to ensure that their competent services co-operate in facilitating the earliest possible restitution of illicitly exported cultural property to its rightful owner;

(c) to admit actions for recovery of lost or stolen items of cultural property brought by or on behalf of the rightful owners;

(d) to recognize the indefeasible right of each State Party to this Convention to classify and declare certain cultural property as inalienable which should therefore ipso facto not be exported, and to facilitate recovery of such property by the State concerned in cases where it has been exported.

Article 14

In order to prevent illicit export and to meet the obligations arising from the implementation of this Convention, each State Party to the Convention should, as far as it is able, provide the national services responsible for the protection of its cultural heritage with an adequate budget and, if necessary, should set up a fund for this purpose.

Article 15

Nothing in this Convention shall prevent States Parties thereto from concluding special agreements among themselves or from continuing to implement agreements already concluded regarding the restitution of cultural property removed, whatever the reason, from its territory of origin, before the entry into force of this Convention for the States concerned.

Article 16

The States Parties to this Convention shall in their periodic reports submitted to the General Conference of the United Nations Educational, Scientific and Cultural Organization on dates and in a manner to be determined by it, give information on the legislative and administrative provisions which they have adopted and other action which they have taken for the application of this Convention, together with details of the experience acquired in this field.

Article 17

1. The States Parties to this Convention may call on the technical assistance of the United Nations Educational, Scientific and Cultural Organization, particularly as regards:

(a) Information and education;

(b) consultation and expert advice;

(c) co-ordination and good offices.

2. The United Nations Educational, Scientific and Cultural Organization may, on its own initiative conduct research and publish studies on matters relevant to the illicit movement of cultural property.

3. To this end, the United Nations Educational, Scientific and Cultural Organization may also call on the co-operation of any competent non-governmental organization.

4. The United Nations Educational, Scientific and Cultural Organization may, on its own initiative, make proposals to States Parties to this Convention for its implementation.

5. At the request of at least two States Parties to this Convention which are engaged in a dispute over its

implementation, UNESCO may extend its good offices to reach a settlement between them.

Article 18

This Convention is drawn up in English, French, Russian and Spanish, the four texts being equally authoritative.

Article 19

1. This Convention shall be subject to ratification or acceptance by States members of the United Nations Educational, Scientific and Cultural Organization in accordance with their respective constitutional procedures.

2. The instruments of ratification or acceptance shall be deposited with the Director-General of the United Nations Educational, Scientific and Cultural Organization.

Article 20

1. This Convention shall be open to accession by all States not members of the United Nations Educational, Scientific and Cultural Organization which are invited to accede to it by the Executive Board of the Organization.

2. Accession shall be effected by the deposit of an instrument of accession with the Director-General of the United Nations Educational, Scientific and Cultural Organization.

Article 21

This Convention shall enter into force three months after the date of the deposit of the third instrument of ratification, acceptance or accession, but only with respect to those States which have deposited their respective instruments on or before that date. It shall enter into force with respect to any other State three months after the deposit of its instrument of ratification, acceptance or accession.

Article 22

The States Parties to this Convention recognize that the Convention is applicable not only to their metropolitan territories but also to all territories for the international relations of which they are responsible; they undertake to consult, if necessary, the governments or other competent authorities of these territories on or before ratification, acceptance or accession with a view to securing the application of the Convention to those territories, and to notify the Director-General of the United Nations Educational, Scientific and cultural Organization of the territories to which it is applied, the notification to take effect three months after the date of its receipt.

Article 23

1. Each State Party to this Convention may denounce the Convention on its own behalf or on behalf of any territory for whose international relations it is responsible.

2. The denunciation shall be notified by an instrument in writing, deposited with the Director-General of the United Nations Educational, Scientific and Cultural Organization.

3. The denunciation shall take effect twelve months after the receipt of the instrument of denunciation.

Article 24

The Director-General of the United Nations Educational, Scientific and Cultural Organization shall inform the States members of the Organization, the States not members of the Organization which are referred to in Article 20, as well as the United Nations, of the deposit of all the instruments of ratification, acceptance and accession provided for in Articles 19 and 20, and of the notifications and denunciations provided for in Articles 22 and 23 respectively.

Article 25

1. This Convention may be revised by the General Conference of the United Nations Educational, Scientific and Cultural Organization. Any such revision shall, however, bind only the States which shall become Parties to

the revising convention.

2. If the General Conference should adopt a new convention revising this Convention in whole or in part, then, unless the new convention otherwise provides, this Convention shall cease to be open to ratification, acceptance or accession, as from the date on which the new revising convention enters into force.

Article 26

In conformity with Article 102 of the Charter of the United Nations, this Convention shall be registered with the Secretariat of the United Nations at the request of the Director-General of the United Nations Educational, Scientific and Cultural Organization.

Done in Paris this seventeenth day of November 1970, in two authentic copies bearing the signature of the President of the sixteenth session of the General Conference and of the Director-General of the United Nations Educational, Scientific and Cultural Organization, which shall be deposited in the archives of the United Nations Educational, Scientific and Cultural Organization, and certified true copies of which shall be delivered to all the States referred to in Articles 19 and 20 as well as to the United Nations.

The foregoing is the authentic text of the Convention duly adopted by the General Conference of the United Nations Educational, Scientific and Cultural Organization during its sixteenth session, which was held in Paris and declared closed the fourteenth day of November 1970.

IN FAITH WHEREOF we have appended our signatures this seventeenth day of November 1970.

奈良真实性文件[①]

（与世界遗产公约相关的奈良真实性会议 1994 年 11 月 1 日至 6 日在奈良通过）

序　言

1. 作为奈良（日本）会议全体专家，我等兹在此感谢日本当局的慷慨精神与学术勇气，为我们适时提供了此论坛，使我们得以挑战遗产保护领域的传统思想，并就拓展视野的方式与手段展开辩论，以使得我们在遗产保护实践中赋予文化与遗产多样性更多的尊重。

2. 我们也希望，借此对世界遗产委员会所提出的讨论框架的价值表示认可。该框架旨在以全面尊重所有社会的社会与文化价值的方式来验证真实性，并检验被列入《世界遗产名录》的文化资产的普遍性价值。

3.《奈良真实性文件》乃是孕育于 1964 年《威尼斯宪章》的精神，并以此为基础加以了延伸，以响应当代世界文化遗产关注与利益范围的不断拓展。

4. 在一个日益受到全球化以及同质化力量影响的世界，在一个时有借由侵略性民族主义与压制少数民族的文化以获取文化认同的世界，在保护实践中纳入真实性考虑具有重要的作用，可厘清并阐明人类的集体记忆。

文化多样性与遗产多样性

1. 整个世界的文化与遗产多样性对所有人类而言都是一项无可替代的丰富的精神与知识源泉。我们必须积极推动世界文化与遗产多样性的保护和强化，将其作为人类发展不可或缺的一部分。

2. 文化遗产的多样性存在于时间与空间之中，需要对其他文化及其信仰系统的各个方面予以尊重。在文化价值出现冲突的情况下，对文化多样性的尊重则意味着需要认可所有各方的文化价值的合理性。

3. 所有的文化与社会都是根植于以有形与无形手段表现出来的特殊形式和方法，这些形式和方法构成了他们的遗产，应该受到尊重。

4. 其中至关重要的是强调任何一种文化遗产都是所有人类的共同遗产这一联合国教科文组织的基本原则。对文化遗产的责任和管理首先应该是归属于其所产生的文化社区，接着是照看这一遗产的文化社区。然而，除这些责任之外，在决定相关原则与责任时，还应该遵守为文化遗产保护而制订的国际公约与宪章。所有社区都需要尽量在不损伤其基本文化价值的情况下，在自身的要求与其他文化社区的要求之间达成平衡。

价值与真实性

1. 对文化遗产的所有形式与历史时期加以保护是遗产价值的根本。我们了解这些价值的能力部分取

[①] 引自：联合国教科文组织世界遗产中心，国际古迹遗址理事会，国际文物保护与修复研究中心，中国国家文物局主编. 国际文化遗产保护文件选编[M]. 北京：文物出版社，2007.

决于这些价值的信息来源是否真实可靠。对这些与文化遗产的最初与后续特征有关的信息来源及其意义的认识与了解是全面评估真实性的必备基础。

2.《威尼斯宪章》所探讨及认可的真实性是有关价值的基本要素。对于真实性的了解在所有有关文化遗产的科学研究、保护与修复规划以及《世界遗产公约》与其他遗产名单收录程序中都起着至关重要的基本作用。

3. 一切有关文化项目价值以及相关信息来源可信度的判断都可能存在文化差异，即使在相同的文化背景内，也可能出现不同。因此不可能基于固定的标准来进行价值性和真实性评判。反之，出于对所有文化的尊重，必须在相关文化背景之下来对遗产项目加以考虑和评判。

4. 因此，在每一种文化内部就其遗产价值的具体性质以及相关信息来源的真实性和可靠性达成共识就变得极为重要和迫切。

5. 取决于文化遗产的性质、文化语境、时间演进，真实性评判可能会与很多信息来源的价值有关。这些来源可包括很多方面，譬如形式与设计、材料与物质、用途与功能、传统与技术、地点与背景、精神与感情以及其他内在或外在因素。使用这些来源可对文化遗产的特定艺术、历史、社会和科学维度加以详尽考察。

附录一

后续建议（由 H. Stovel 提议）

1. 对文化与遗产多样性的尊重需要有意识的努力，避免在试图界定或判断特定纪念物或历史场所的真实性时套用机械化的公式或标准化的程序。

2. 以尊重文化与遗产多样性的态度来判断真实性需要采取一定的方法，鼓励不同文化针对其性质和需求制订出特定的分析过程与工具。这些方法可能会有以下共同点：

- 努力确保在真实性评估中纳入跨学科合作，恰当利用所有可用的专业技术和知识；
- 努力确保相关价值真正代表了一个文化与其兴趣的多样性，尤其是纪念物与历史场所；
- 努力清晰记录有关纪念物与历史场所的真实性的特殊性质，作为未来开展处理与监控的实用性指南；
- 努力根据不断变化的价值和环境对真实性评估加以更新。

3. 尤其重要的是努力确保相关价值受到尊重，且尽量在决策中形成与这些价值有关的跨学科及社区统一意见。

4. 这些方法还应该建立在有志于文化遗产保护的所有各方的国际合作基础上，并进一步推动这一合作，以促进全世界对每一种文化的多样化表达和价值的尊重与了解。

5. 将此对话延伸并拓展到全世界不同区域与文化是提升人类共同遗产保护的真实性的实用价值的必要前提。

6. 增进公众对遗产的了解对于获得保护历史痕迹的切实措施很有必要。这意味着在增进对这些文化资产自身价值的了解的同时，也要尊重这些纪念物与历史场所在当代社会所扮演的角色。

附录二

定 义

保护：是指所有旨在了解一项遗产，掌握其历史和意义，确保其自然形态，并在必要时进行修复和增强的行为（文化遗产包括《世界遗产公约》第一条所定义的具有文化价值的纪念物、建筑群与历史场所）。

信息来源：可使人了解文化遗产的性质、规范、意义与历史的所有物质的、书面的、口述的与图像的来源。

The Nara Document on Authenticity

Nara Conference on Authenticity in Relation to the World Heritage Convention, Nara, 1-6 November, 1994

PREAMBLE

1. We, the experts assembled in Nara (Japan), wish to acknowledge the generous spirit and intellectual courage of the Japanese authorities in providing a timely forum in which we could challenge conventional thinking in the conservation field, and debate ways and means of broadening our horizons to bring greater respect for cultural and heritage diversity to conservation practice.

2. We also wish to acknowledge the value of the framework for discussion provided by the World Heritage Committee's desire to apply the test of authenticity in ways which accord full respect to the social and cultural values of all societies, in examining the outstanding universal value of cultural properties proposed for the World Heritage List.

3. The Nara Document on Authenticity is conceived in the spirit of the Charter of Venice, 1964, and builds on it and extends it in response to the expanding scope of cultural heritage concerns and interests in our contemporary world.

4. In a world that is increasingly subject to the forces of globalization and homogenization, and in a world in which the search for cultural identity is sometimes pursued through aggressive nationalism and the suppression of the cultures of minorities, the essential contribution made by the consideration of authenticity in conservation practice is to clarify and illuminate the collective memory of humanity.

CULTURAL DIVERSITY AND HERITAGE DIVERSITY

1. The diversity of cultures and heritage in our world is an irreplaceable source of spiritual and intellectual richness for all humankind. The protection and enhancement of cultural and heritage diversity in our world should be actively promoted as an essential aspect of human development.

2. Cultural heritage diversity exists in time and space, and demands respect for other cultures and all aspects of their belief systems. In cases where cultural values appear to be in conflict, respect for cultural diversity demands acknowledgment of the legitimacy of the cultural values of all parties.

3. All cultures and societies are rooted in the particular forms and means of tangible and intangible expression which constitute their heritage, and these should be respected.

4. It is important to underline a fundamental principle of UNESCO, to the effect that the cultural heritage of each is the cultural heritage of all. Responsibility for cultural heritage and the management of it belongs, in the first place, to the cultural community that has generated it, and subsequently to that which cares for it.

However, in addition to these responsibilities, adherence to the international charters and conventions developed for conservation of cultural heritage also obliges consideration of the principles and responsibilities flowing from them. Balancing their own requirements with those of other cultural communities is, for each community, highly desirable, provided achieving this balance does not undermine their fundamental cultural values.

VALUES AND AUTHENTICITY

1. Conservation of cultural heritage in all its forms and historical periods is rooted in the values attributed to the heritage. Our ability to understand these values depends, in part, on the degree to which information sources about these values may be understood as credible or truthful. Knowledge and understanding of these sources of information, in relation to original and subsequent characteristics of the cultural heritage, and their meaning, is a requisite basis for assessing all aspects of authenticity.

2. Authenticity, considered in this way and affirmed in the Charter of Venice, appears as the essential qualifying factor concerning values. The understanding of authenticity plays a fundamental role in all scientific studies of the cultural heritage, in conservation and restoration planning, as well as within the inscription procedures used for the World Heritage Convention and other cultural heritage inventories.

3. All judgements about values attributed to cultural properties as well as the credibility of related information sources may differ from culture to culture, and even within the same culture. It is thus not possible to base judgements of values and authenticity within fixed criteria. On the contrary, the respect due to all cultures requires that heritage properties must be considered and judged within the cultural contexts to which they belong.

4. Therefore, it is of the highest importance and urgency that, within each culture, recognition be accorded to the specific nature of its heritage values and the credibility and truthfulness of related information sources.

5. Depending on the nature of the cultural heritage, its cultural context, and its evolution through time, authenticity judgements may be linked to the worth of a great variety of sources of information. Aspects of the sources may include form and design, materials and substance, use and function, traditions and techniques, location and setting, and spirit and feeling, and other internal and external factors. The use of these sources permits elaboration of the specific artistic, historic, social, and scientific dimensions of the cultural heritage being examined.

APPENDIX 1

Suggestions for follow-up (proposed by H. Stovel)

1. Respect for cultural and heritage diversity requires conscious efforts to avoid imposing mechanistic formulae or standardized procedures in attempting to define or determine authenticity of particular monuments and sites.

2. Efforts to determine authenticity in a manner respectful of cultures and heritage diversity requires approaches which encourage cultures to develop analytical processes and tools specific to their nature and needs. Such approaches may have several aspects in common:

• efforts to ensure assessment of authenticity involve multidisciplinary collaboration and the appropriate utilization of all available expertise and knowledge;

• efforts to ensure attributed values are truly representative of a culture and the diversity of its interests, in particular monuments and sites;

• efforts to document clearly the particular nature of authenticity for monuments and sites as a practical guide to future treatment and monitoring;

- efforts to update authenticity assessments in light of changing values and circumstances.

3. Particularly important are efforts to ensure that attributed values are respected, and that their determination includes efforts to build, as far as possible, a multidisciplinary and community consensus concerning these values.

4. Approaches should also build on and facilitate international co-operation among all those with an interest in conservation of cultural heritage, in order to improve global respect and understanding for the diverse expressions and values of each culture.

5. Continuation and extension of this dialogue to the various regions and cultures of the world is a prerequisite to increasing the practical value of consideration of authenticity in the conservation of the common heritage of humankind.

6. Increasing awareness within the public of this fundamental dimension of heritage is an absolute necessity in order to arrive at concrete measures for safeguarding the vestiges of the past. This means developing greater understanding of the values represented by the cultural properties themselves, as well as respecting the role such monuments and sites play in contemporary society.

APPENDIX 2

Definitions

Conservation: all efforts designed to understand cultural heritage, know its history and meaning, ensure its material safeguard and, as required, its presentation, restoration and enhancement. (Cultural heritage is understood to include monuments, groups of buildings and sites of cultural value as defined in article one of the World Heritage Convention).

Information sources: all material, written, oral and figurative sources which make it possible to know the nature, specifications, meaning and history of the cultural heritage.

教科文组织关于蓄意破坏文化遗产问题的宣言[①]

(联合国教科文组织第三十二届大会2003年10月17日在巴黎通过)

联合国教科文组织大会于2003年在巴黎举行的第三十二届会议，

忆及震动了整个国际社会的摧毁巴米扬大佛的悲剧性事件；

对蓄意破坏文化遗产行为呈上升趋势表示严重关注；

参照教科文组织《组织法》第Ⅰ2c)条有关教科文组织具有通过"保证对图书、艺术作品及历史和科学文物等世界遗产之保存与维护，并建议有关国家订立必要之国际公约"，维护、增进及传播知识之职责的规定；

忆及教科文组织所有保护文化遗产的公约、建议书、宣言和宪章所确定的原则；

铭记文化遗产是社会、群体和个人的文化特性和社会凝聚力的重要组成部分，因此蓄意破坏文化遗产会对人的尊严和人权造成不利影响；

重申1954年《关于在武装冲突情况下保护文化财产的海牙公约》序言中提出的一条基本原则，即"鉴于各国人民均对世界文化作出了贡献，对文化财产（不管它属于哪国人民）的损害将构成对整个人类文化遗产的破坏"；

忆及1899年和1907年的《海牙公约》确定的关于在武装冲突情况下保护文化遗产的原则，特别是1907年《第四项海牙公约》第27和第56条以及后来的其他协定所确定的原则；

牢记还得到相关的判例法确认的有关在和平时期及在武装冲突情况下保护文化遗产的习惯国际法条款发生了变化；

还忆及与蓄意破坏文化遗产行为有关的《国际刑事法院罗马规约》第8(2)(b)(ix)条和第8(2)(e)(iv)条的规定，以及《前南斯拉夫问题国际刑事法庭规约》第3(d)条的规定（在适用时）；

重申本《宣言》和其他有关文化遗产的国际文书没有充分谈及的问题仍将继续遵循国际法的原则、人道的原则和受公共良心的支配；

通过并庄严宣布本宣言：

Ⅰ. 承认文化遗产的重要性

国际社会承认保护文化遗产的重要性，并重申要与任何形式的蓄意破坏文化遗产的行为做斗争，使文化遗产能够代代相传的决心。

[①] 引自：UNESCO决议32 C/15。

Ⅱ. 适用范围

1. 本宣言针对文化遗产，包括与自然景观相关的文化遗产的蓄意破坏问题。
2. 本宣言中的"蓄意破坏"系指故意违反国际法或无理违反人道的原则和公共良心的要求，整个或部分地毁坏文化遗产，使其完整性受到破坏的行为。故意无理违反人道的原则和公共良心的要求的做法，系指国际法的基本原则目前尚未作出规定的破坏行为。

Ⅲ. 反对蓄意破坏文化遗产行为的措施

1. 各国应采取一切适当措施，预防、避免、制止和打击蓄意破坏无论是何地的文化遗产的行为。
2. 各国应根据自己的经济能力，为保护文化遗产采取适当的法律、行政、教育和技术措施，并定期修订这些措施，使它们与不断变化的各国和国际文化遗产保护标准相一致。
3. 各国应采取一切适当手段，特别是通过实施教育、提高认识和宣传方面的计划，确保文化遗产受到社会的尊重。
4. 各国应：

（a）加入（如它们尚未加入的话）1954年《关于在武装冲突情况下保护文化财产的海牙公约》及其1954年和1999年的两项《议定书》，以及1949年的四项《日内瓦公约》的第一和第二项《附加议定书》；

（b）促进制定并通过完善的法律文件，提高保护文化遗产的标准；并

（c）促进协调实施现有的和今后将制定的有关保护文化遗产的各种文书。

Ⅳ. 在和平时期开展活动时保护文化遗产

在和平时期开展活动时，各国应当采取一切适当的措施，使自己的行为符合保护文化遗产的要求，尤其是符合1972年《保护世界文化和自然遗产公约》、1956年《关于国际考古发掘原则的建议书》、1968年《关于保护公共或私人工程危及的文化财产的建议书》、1972年《关于在国家一级保护文化和自然遗产的建议书》和1976年《关于保护历史或传统建筑群及其在现代生活中的作用的建议书》所确定的原则和宗旨。

Ⅴ. 在武装冲突，包括占领的情况下保护文化遗产

在卷入国际或非国际性武装冲突，包括占领的情况下，有关各国应采取一切适当的措施，使自己的行为符合保护文化遗产的要求，符合习惯国际法以及有关在敌对时期保护这类遗产的各项国际协定和教科文组织建议书的原则和宗旨。

Ⅵ. 有关国家的责任

蓄意破坏对人类具有重要意义的文化遗产，或故意不采取适当措施禁止、防止、制止和惩罚一切蓄意破坏行为的国家，不论该遗产是否列入教科文组织或其他国际组织的保护名录，均应在国际法规定的范围内对该破坏行为承担责任。

Ⅶ. 个人的刑事责任

各国应根据国际法采取一切适当的措施，确立有关的司法管辖权，并对那些犯有或下令犯有蓄意破

坏对人类具有特别重要意义之文化遗产行为的个人予以有效的刑事制裁，不论该文化遗产是否列入教科文组织或其他国际组织的保护名录。

Ⅷ. 保护文化遗产的合作

1. 各国应相互合作并与教科文组织开展合作，保护文化遗产免遭蓄意破坏。这种合作的基本要求是：(ⅰ)提供和交流有可能出现的蓄意破坏文化遗产问题的有关情况的信息；(ⅱ)在文化遗产的确受到或即将遭到破坏的情况下进行磋商；(ⅲ)应有关国家的要求，在促进开展预防和打击蓄意破坏文化遗产行为的教育计划、提高认识和能力方面考虑向它们提供援助；(ⅳ)应有关国家的要求，在打击蓄意破坏文化遗产的行为时，向它们提供有关的司法和行政援助。

2. 为了进行更加全面的保护，鼓励各国根据国际法采取各种适当的措施与其他有关国家进行合作，以便确立有关的司法管辖权，并对那些犯有或下令犯有上述行为（Ⅶ. 个人的刑事责任）并在该国领土被发现的个人（不论其国籍如何以及该行为在何处发生）予以有效的刑事制裁。

Ⅸ. 人权和国际人道主义法

实施本宣言，各国承认必须遵守有关将严重违反人权和国际人道主义法行为定为犯罪行为的国际规章，特别是在蓄意破坏文化遗产行为与这些违反行为有关联的情况下更应如此。

Ⅹ. 公众宣传

各国应采取各种适当的措施，特别是通过组织公众宣传运动，确保在公众和目标群体中最广泛地宣传本宣言。

UNESCO Declaration concerning the Intentional Destruction of Cultural Heritage[①]

Adopted by the UNESCO General Conference at its 32nd Session, Paris, 17 October 2003

The General Conference of the United Nations Educational, Scientific and Cultural Organization meeting in Paris at its thirty-second session in 2003,

Recalling the tragic destruction of the Buddhas of Bamiyan that affected the international community as a whole,

Expressing serious concern about the growing number of acts of intentional destruction of cultural heritage,

Referring to Article I (2)(c) of the Constitution of UNESCO that entrusts UNESCO with the task of maintaining, increasing and diffusing knowledge by "assuring the conservation and protection of the world's inheritance of books, works of art and monuments of history and science, and recommending to the nations concerned the necessary international conventions",

Recalling the principles of all UNESCO's conventions, recommendations, declarations and charters for the protection of cultural heritage,

Mindful that cultural heritage is an important component of the cultural identity of communities, groups and individuals, and of social cohesion, so that its intentional destruction may have adverse consequences on human dignity and human rights,

Reiterating one of the fundamental principles of the Preamble of the 1954 Hague Convention for the Protection of Cultural Property in the Event of Armed Conflict providing that "damage to cultural property belonging to any people whatsoever means damage to the cultural heritage of all mankind, since each people makes its contribution to the culture of the world",

Recalling the principles concerning the protection of cultural heritage in the event of armed conflict established in the 1899 and 1907 Hague Conventions and, in particular, in Articles 27 and 56 of the Regulations of the 1907 Fourth Hague Convention, as well as other subsequent agreements,

Mindful of the development of rules of customary international law as also affirmed by the relevant case-law, related to the protection of cultural heritage in peacetime as well as in the event of armed conflict,

Also recalling Articles 8(2)(b)(ix) and 8(2)(e)(iv) of the Rome Statute of the International Criminal Court, and, as appropriate, Article 3(d) of the Statute of the International Criminal Tribunal for the former Yugoslavia, related to the intentional destruction of cultural heritage,

---

[①] Records of the General Conference, 32nd session, Paris, 29 September to 17 October 2003, v. 1: Resolutions. UNESCO Document Code: 32 C/Resolutions.

Reaffirming that issues not fully covered by the present Declaration and other international instruments concerning cultural heritage will continue to be governed by the principles of international law, the principles of humanity and the dictates of public conscience,

Adopts and solemnly proclaims the present Declaration:

Ⅰ. Recognition of the importance of cultural heritage

The international community recognizes the importance of the protection of cultural heritage and reaffirms its commitment to fight against its intentional destruction in any form so that such cultural heritage may be transmitted to the succeeding generations.

Ⅱ. Scope

1. The present Declaration addresses intentional destruction of cultural heritage including cultural heritage linked to a natural site.

For the purposes of this Declaration "intentional destruction" means an act intended to destroy in whole or in part cultural heritage, thus compromising its integrity, in a manner which constitutes a violation of international law or an unjustifiable offence to the principles of humanity and dictates of public conscience, in the latter case in so far as such acts are not already governed by fundamental principles of international law.

Ⅲ. Measures to combat intentional destruction of cultural heritage

1. States should take all appropriate measures to prevent, avoid, stop and suppress acts of intentional destruction of cultural heritage, wherever such heritage is located.

2. States should adopt the appropriate legislative, administrative, educational and technical measures, within the framework of their economic resources, to protect cultural heritage and should revise them periodically with a view to adapting them to the evolution of national and international cultural heritage protection standards.

3. States should endeavour, by all appropriate means, to ensure respect for cultural heritage in society, particularly through educational, awareness-raising and information programmes.

4. States should:

(a) become parties to the 1954 Hague Convention for the Protection of Cultural Property in the Event of Armed Conflict and its two 1954 and 1999 Protocols and the Additional Protocols Ⅰ and Ⅱ to the four 1949 Geneva Conventions, if they have not yet done so;

(b) promote the elaboration and the adoption of legal instruments providing a higher standard of protection of cultural heritage, and

(c) promote a coordinated application of existing and future instruments relevant to the protection of cultural heritage.

Ⅳ. Protection of cultural heritage when conducting peacetime activities

When conducting peacetime activities, States should take all appropriate measures to conduct them in such a manner as to protect cultural heritage and, in particular, in conformity with the principles and objectives of the

1972 Convention for the Protection of the World Cultural and Natural Heritage, of the 1956 Recommendation on International Principles Applicable to Archaeological Excavations, the 1968 Recommendation concerning the Preservation of Cultural Property Endangered by Public or Private Works, the 1972 Recommendation concerning the Protection, at National Level, of the Cultural and Natural Heritage and the 1976 Recommendation concerning the Safeguarding and Contemporary Role of Historic Areas.

V. Protection of cultural heritage in the event of armed conflict, including the case of occupation

When involved in an armed conflict, be it of an international or non-international character, including the case of occupation, States should take all appropriate measures to conduct their activities in such a manner as to protect cultural heritage, in conformity with customary international law and the principles and objectives of international agreements and UNESCO recommendations concerning the protection of such heritage during hostilities.

VI. State responsibility

A State that intentionally destroys or intentionally fails to take appropriate measures to prohibit, prevent, stop, and punish any intentional destruction of cultural heritage of great importance for humanity, whether or not it is inscribed on a list maintained by UNESCO or another international organization, bears the responsibility for such destruction, to the extent provided for by international law.

VII. Individual criminal responsibility

States should take all appropriate measures, in accordance with international law, to establish jurisdiction over, and provide effective criminal sanctions against, those persons who commit, or order to be committed, acts of intentional destruction of cultural heritage of great importance for humanity, whether or not it is inscribed on a list maintained by UNESCO or another international organization.

VIII. Cooperation for the protection of cultural heritage

1. States should cooperate with each other and with UNESCO to protect cultural heritage from intentional destruction. Such cooperation should entail at least: (i) provision and exchange of information regarding circumstances entailing the risk of intentional destruction of cultural heritage; (ii) consultation in the event of actual or impending destruction of cultural heritage; (iii) consideration of assistance to States, as requested by them, in the promotion of educational programmes, awareness-raising and capacity-building for the prevention and repression of any intentional destruction of cultural heritage; (iv) judicial and administrative assistance, as requested by interested States, in the repression of any intentional destruction of cultural heritage.

2. For the purposes of more comprehensive protection, each State is encouraged to take all appropriate measures, in accordance with international law, to cooperate with other States concerned with a view to establishing jurisdiction over, and providing effective criminal sanctions against, those persons who have committed or have ordered to be committed acts referred to above (VII-Individual criminal responsibility) and who are found present on its territory, regardless of their nationality and the place where such act occurred.

IX. Human rights and international humanitarian law

In applying this Declaration, States recognize the need to respect international rules related to the criminalization of gross violations of human rights and international humanitarian law, in particular, when intentional destruction of cultural heritage is linked to those violations.

X. Public awareness

States should take all appropriate measures to ensure the widest possible dissemination of this Declaration to the general public and to target groups, *inter alia*, by organizing public awareness-raising campaigns.

·建筑遗产·

关于乡土建筑遗产的宪章[①]

(国际古迹遗址理事会第十二届大会1999年10月在墨西哥通过)

前 言

乡土建筑遗产在人类的情感和自豪中占有重要的地位。它已经被公认为是有特征的和有魅力的社会产物。它看起来是不拘于形式的,但却是有秩序的。它是有实用价值的,同时又是美丽和有趣味的。它是那个时代生活的聚焦点,同时又是社会史的记录。它是人类的作品,也是时代的创造物。如果不重视保存这些组成人类自身生活核心的传统性和谐,将无法体现人类遗产的价值。

乡土建筑遗产是重要的;它是一个社会文化的基本表现,是社会与其所处地区关系的基本表现,同时也是世界文化多样性的表现。

乡土建筑是社区自己建造房屋的一种传统和自然方式。为了对社会和环境的约束做出反应,乡土建筑包含必要的变化和不断适应的连续过程。这种传统的幸存物在世界范围内遭受着经济、文化和建筑同一化力量的威胁。如何抵制这些威胁是社区、政府、规划师、建筑师、保护工作者以及多学科专家团体必须熟悉的基本问题。

由于文化和全球社会经济转型的同一化,面对忽视、内部失衡和解体等严重问题,全世界的乡土建筑都非常脆弱。

因此,有必要建立管理和保护乡土建筑遗产的原则,以补充《威尼斯宪章》。

一般性问题

1. 乡土性可以由下列各项确认:
某一社区共有的一种建造方式;
一种可识别的、与环境适应的地方或区域特征;
风格、形式和外观一致,或者使用传统上建立的建筑型制;
非正式流传下来的用于设计和施工的传统专业技术;
一种对功能、社会和环境约束的有效回应;
一种对传统的建造体系和工艺的有效应用。

[①] 译者:赵巍。引自:联合国教科文组织世界遗产中心,国际古迹遗址理事会,国际文物保护与修复研究中心,中国国家文物局主编. 国际文化遗产保护文件选编[M]. 北京:文物出版社,2007.

2. 正确地评价和成功地保护乡土建筑遗产要依靠社区的参与和支持，依靠持续不断地使用和维护。

3. 政府和主管机关必须确认所有的社区有保持其生活传统的权利，通过一切可利用的法律、行政和经济手段来保护生活传统并将其传给后代。

保护原则

传统建筑的保护必须在认识变化和发展的必然性和认识尊重社区已建立的文化特色的必要性时，借由多学科的专门知识来实行。

当今对乡土建筑、建筑群和村落所做的工作应该尊重其文化价值和传统特色。

乡土性几乎不可能通过单体建筑来表现，最好是各个地区经由维持和保存有典型特征的建筑群和村落来保护乡土性。

乡土性建筑遗产是文化景观的组成部分，这种关系在保护方法的发展过程中必须予以考虑。

乡土性不仅在于建筑物、构筑物和空间的实体构成形态，也在于使用它们和理解它们的方法，以及附着在它们身上的传统和无形的联想。

实践中的指导方针

1. 研究和文献编辑工作

任何对乡土建筑进行的实际工作都应该谨慎，并且事先要对其形态和结构做充分的分析。这种文件应该存放于公众可以使用的档案里。

2. 场所、景观和建筑群

对乡土建筑进行干预时，应该尊重和维护场所的完整性、维护它与物质景观和文化景观的联系以及建筑和建筑之间的关系。

3. 传统建筑体系

与乡土性有关的传统建筑体系和工艺技术对乡土性的表现至为重要，也是修复和复原这些建筑物的关键。这些技术应该被保留、记录，并在教育和训练中传授给下一代的工匠和建造者。

4. 材料和部件的更换

为适应目前需要而做的合理的改变应该考虑到所引入的材料能保持整个建筑的表情、外观、质地和形式的一贯，以及建筑物材料的一致。

5. 改造

为了与可接受的生活水平相协调而改造和再利用乡土建筑时，应该尊重建筑的结构、性格和形式的完整性。在乡土形式不间断地连续使用的地方，存在于社会中的道德准则可以作为干预的手段。

6. 变化和定期修复

随着时间流逝而发生的一些变化，应作为乡土建筑的重要方面得到人们的欣赏和理解。乡土建筑工作的目标，并不是把一幢建筑的所有部分修复得像同一时期的产物。

7. 培训

为了保护乡土建筑所表达的文化价值，政府、主管机关、各种团体和机构必须在如下方面给予重视：

（1）按照乡土性原则实施对保护工作者的教育计划；

（2）帮助社区制定维护传统建造体系、材料和工艺技能方面的培训计划；

（3）通过信息传播，提高公众特别是年青一代的乡土建筑意识；

（4）用于交换专业知识和经验的有关乡土建筑区域性工作网络。

Charter on the Built Vernacular Heritage

Ratified by the 12th ICOMOS General Assembly, Mexico, October 1999

INTRODUCTION

The built vernacular heritage occupies a central place in the affection and pride of all peoples. It has been accepted as a characteristic and attractive product of society. It appears informal, but nevertheless orderly. It is utilitarian and at the same time possesses interest and beauty. It is a focus of contemporary life and at the same time a record of the history of society. Although it is the work of man it is also the creation of time. It would be unworthy of the heritage of man if care were not taken to conserve these traditional harmonies which constitute the core of man's own existence.

The built vernacular heritage is important; it is the fundamental expression of the culture of a community, of its relationship with its territory and, at the same time, the expression of the world's cultural diversity.

Vernacular building is the traditional and natural way by which communities house themselves. It is a continuing process including necessary changes and continuous adaptation as a response to social and environmental constraints. The survival of this tradition is threatened world-wide by the forces of economic, cultural and architectural homogenisation. How these forces can be met is a fundamental problem that must be addressed by communities and also by governments, planners, architects, conservationists and by a multidisciplinary group of specialists.

Due to the homogenisation of culture and of global socio-economic transformation, vernacular structures all around the world are extremely vulnerable, facing serious problems of obsolescence, internal equilibrium and integration.

It is necessary, therefore, in addition to the Venice Charter, to establish principles for the care and protection of our built vernacular heritage.

GENERAL ISSUES

1. Examples of the vernacular may be recognised by:

a) A manner of building shared by the community;

b) A recognisable local or regional character responsive to the environment;

c) Coherence of style, form and appearance, or the use of traditionally established building types;

d) Traditional expertise in design and construction which is transmitted informally;

e) An effective response to functional, social and environmental constraints;

f) The effective application of traditional construction systems and crafts.

2. The appreciation and successful protection of the vernacular heritage depend on the involvement and

support of the community, continuing use and maintenance.

3. Governments and responsible authorities must recognise the right of all communities to maintain their living traditions, to protect these through all available legislative, administrative and financial means and to hand them down to future generations.

PRINCIPLES OF CONSERVATION

1. The conservation of the built vernacular heritage must be carried out by multidisciplinary expertise while recognising the inevitability of change and development, and the need to respect the community's established cultural identity.

2. Contemporary work on vernacular buildings, groups and settlements should respect their cultural values and their traditional character.

3. The vernacular is only seldom represented by single structures, and it is best conserved by maintaining and preserving groups and settlements of a representative character, region by region.

4. The built vernacular heritage is an integral part of the cultural landscape and this relationship must be taken into consideration in the development of conservation approaches.

5. The vernacular embraces not only the physical form and fabric of buildings, structures and spaces, but the ways in which they are used and understood, and the traditions and the intangible associations which attach to them.

GUIDELINES IN PRACTICE

1. Research and documentation

Any physical work on a vernacular structure should be cautious and should be preceded by a full analysis of its form and structure. This document should be lodged in a publicly accessible archive.

2. Siting, landscape and groups of buildings

Interventions to vernacular structures should be carried out in a manner which will respect and maintain the integrity of the siting, the relationship to the physical and cultural landscape, and of one structure to another.

3. Traditional building systems

The continuity of traditional building systems and craft skills associated with the vernacular is fundamental for vernacular expression, and essential for the repair and restoration of these structures. Such skills should be retained, recorded and passed on to new generations of craftsmen and builders in education and training.

4. Replacement of materials and parts

Alterations which legitimately respond to the demands of contemporary use should be effected by the introduction of materials which maintain a consistency of expression, appearance, texture and form throughout the structure and a consistency of building materials.

5. Adaptation

Adaptation and reuse of vernacular structures should be carried out in a manner which will respect the integrity of the structure, its character and form while being compatible with acceptable standards of living. Where there is no break in the continuous utilisation of vernacular forms, a code of ethics within the community can serve as a tool of intervention.

6. Changes and period restoration

Changes over time should be appreciated and understood as important aspects of vernacular architecture. Conformity of all parts of a building to a single period, will not normally be the goal of work on vernacular structures.

7. Training

In order to conserve the cultural values of vernacular expression, governments, responsible authorities, groups and organisations must place emphasis on the following:

a) Education programmes for conservators in the principles of the vernacular;

b) Training programmes to assist communities in maintaining traditional building systems, materials and craft skills;

c) Information programmes which improve public awareness of the vernacular especially amongst the younger generation;

d) Regional networks on vernacular architecture to exchange expertise and experiences.

建筑遗产分析、保护和结构修复原则[1]

(国际古迹遗址理事会第十四届大会2003年在津巴布韦维多利亚瀑布市通过)

文件目的

建筑遗产结构，因为其十分具有自然性和历史性（材料和组合），用限于现代合理的代码和建筑标准去诊断和修复就体现出了许多挑战。确保与文化背景相适应的合理分析方法和修复方法的建议就显得十分必要[2]。

这些建议对涉及保护和修复问题的一切是有用的，但是无论如何不能取代从文化和科学讯息中获得的专业知识。

本文件中提出的建议分为两部分：原则，提出了保护的基本概念；指南，讨论了设计者应遵循的规则和方法。只有原则部分为通过ICOMOS认可的文件。

指南部分为独立的英语文本。

原 则

1. 总标准

1.1 建筑遗产的保护、加固和修复需要采用多学科综合方法。

1.2 建筑遗产的价值和真实性不能建立在固定标准的基础上，因为尊重文化多样性要求物质遗产需在其所属的文化背景中被考虑。

1.3 建筑遗产的价值不仅体现在其表面，而且还体现在其所有构成作为所处时代特有建筑技术的独特产物的完整性。特别是仅为维持外观而去除内部构件并不符合保护标准。

1.4 当使用或功能上的任何改变被提出，将必须仔细考虑所有保护工作需求和安全状况。

1.5 建筑遗产构件的修复并不以其自身为结果，而是达到目的的手段，其目的是修复作为整体的整个建筑。

1.6 具有复杂历史的遗产结构特性要求在每一精确步骤中组织研究和提议，这类似于医学中采用的方法。既往病史、诊断、治疗和控制均要寻找重要数据和信息、损害和朽坏的原因、治疗措施的选择以及干涉效果的控制。在建筑遗产以合理方式使用可利用资金可以达到发挥成本效率和最小影响的目的，重复此步骤的研究通常是有必要的。

1.7 如果没有确定建筑遗产可能出现的利害，则不应采取任何措施，除非为了避免构架即将崩塌而采

---

[1] 引自：联合国教科文组织世界遗产中心，国际古迹遗址理事会，国际文物保护与修复研究中心，中国国家文物局主编. 国际文化遗产保护文件选编[M]. 北京：文物出版社，2007.

[2] 编者根据英文原文对此句译文进行了少量修改。

取必要的紧急安全措施（例如地震灾害之后）；但是紧急措施应尽可能避免以不可逆方式更改结构。

2. 研究和诊断

2.1 通常考虑问题的类型和范围时，一个包含多学科的团队，应该从研究的第一步——遗址的初步检测和调查活动的准备——开始就一起工作。

2.2 数据和信息应初步大概处理，从而建立与构件真正问题相称的全面行动计划。

2.3 在保护工作中要求充分理解结构和材料特点。关于原始和更早状态中的结构、建设中采用的技术、变更及其影响、已经出现的现象以及现状的信息是必要的。

2.4 考古现场由于知识不够完备，发掘过程中构件又必须稳定，因此可能会出现各种具体问题[①]。"重新发现"的建筑的结构反应可能与"暴露"的建筑的状况大不相同。紧急的现场——结构——解决方案要求构件在发掘出土时就对其进行稳定，不应妥协于发现完整建筑的观念形式和用途。

2.5 诊断是基于历史的、定性的和定量的方法；定性方法主要基于结构损坏和材料糟朽的直接观察，以及历史和考古研究；定量方法主要基于材料和结构检测、监控和结构分析。

2.6 在决定结构干预前，首先必须确定损坏和糟朽的原因，然后评估结构的安全程度。

2.7 安全评估是诊断中的最后一个步骤，如果决定需要采取处理措施，应协调定性与定量分析：直接观察、历史研究、结构分析和（如果需要的话）实验和测试。

2.8 如果并非不可能，新建筑设计中同等安全水平的应用需要超出一般的措施。在这种情况下，特定分析和适当的考虑可调整不同方法至其安全。

2.9 所获信息的所有方面，包括安全评估在内的诊断，以及干预的决定都应在"说明性报告"中加以阐述。

3. 治疗措施和控制手段

3.1 治疗应治本而不是治标。

3.2 最好的治疗是预防性维护。

3.3 安全评估和结构重要性理解应是保护和加固措施的基础。

3.4 如果没有证明其绝对必要性则不应采取措施。

3.5 每次干预应与安全目标相称，这样可保持最少干预，从而最小伤害遗产价值，保证其安全和耐久性。

3.6 干预设计应建立对干预后造成损坏和糟朽的各种行为和结构分析中所考虑的行为有清楚认识的基础上；因为设计将会取决于它们。

3.7 根据所记住的安全性和耐久性要求，"传统"和"创新"技术间的选择应在一个个案例的基础上进行估量得出，并优先考虑那些对遗产价值有最小侵入性和最大谐调性的选择。

3.8 有时评估真正安全级别的难度和干预的可能好处可建议为"观察性方法"，即从最小级干预开始可进行增加的方法，可采取一系列增补或调整措施。

3.9 如果可能，任何被采取的措施应是"可逆的"，当获得新的认识时，可将其取消或代之以更合适的措施。如果并非完全可逆，现有的干预不应限制进一步的干预。

3.10 用于修复工作的材料（特别是新材料）的特性及其与现有材料的兼容性应得以完全确定。这必须包括长期影响，从而避免不合需要的副作用。

3.11 在原始或更早状态中的结构及其环境的可区别性质不应被破坏。

3.12 每次干预应尽可能远地考虑观念、技术以及将来可认识到的结构及其他证据的原始和早期状态的历史价值。

3.13 干预应该是重视建筑、结构、安装和功能性的不同方面的全面完整计划的结果。

---

① 编者根据英文原文对此句译文进行了少量修改。

3.14 只要可能,应避免任何历史材料或有特色的建筑特征的去除或改变。

3.15 只要可能,损毁的构件应被修复,而不是被取代。

3.16 当不完整和改变已经成为结构历史的一部分时,应将其维持下来,由此它们则不会危及安全要求。

3.17 当其他保护方式不可行,有危害时,则在材料和结构本质上要求一种措施时才能进行分解和重新组装。

3.18 干预中采用的临时保护系统应显示其没有对遗产价值造成任何伤害的目的和功能。

3.19 当工作在进行中时,尽量使任何干预建议都附带有将要开展的控制计划。

3.20 不应允许采取执行中无法控制的措施。

3.21 应展开干预中和干预后的检查和监测,从而确保有好的效果。

3.22 所有检查和监测活动应有文件记录,使其成为结构历史的一部分保存下来。

Principles for the Analysis, Conservation and Structural Restoration of Architectural Heritage

Ratified by the 14th ICOMOS General Assembly, Victoria Falls, Zimbabwe, 2003

PURPOSE OF THE DOCUMENT

Structures of architectural heritage, by their very nature and history (material and assembly), present a number of challenges in diagnosis and restoration that limit the application of modern legal codes and building standards. Recommendations are desirable and necessary to both ensure rational methods of analysis and repair methods appropriate to the cultural context.

These Recommendations are intended to be useful to all those involved in conservation and restoration problems, but cannot in anyway replace specific knowledge acquired from cultural and scientific texts.

The Recommendations presented in the complete document are in two sections: Principles, where the basic concepts of conservation are presented; Guidelines, where the rules and methodology that a designer should follow are discussed. Only the Principles have the status of an approved/ratified ICOMOS document.

The guidelines are available in English in a separate document.

PRINCIPLES

1. General criteria

1.1 Conservation, reinforcement and restoration of architectural heritage requires a multi-disciplinary approach.

1.2 Value and authenticity of architectural heritage cannot be based on fixed criteria because the respect due to all cultures also requires that its physical heritage be considered within the cultural context to which it belongs.

1.3 The value of architectural heritage is not only in its appearance, but also in the integrity of all its components as a unique product of the specific building technology of its time. In particular the removal of the inner structures maintaining only the façades does not fit the conservation criteria.

1.4 When any change of use or function is proposed, all the conservation requirements and safety conditions have to be carefully taken into account.

1.5 Restoration of the structure in Architecture Heritage is not an end in itself but a means to an end, which is the building as a whole.

1.6 The peculiarity of heritage structures, with their complex history, requires the organisation of studies and proposals in precise steps that are similar to those used in medicine. Anamnesis, diagnosis, therapy and controls, corresponding respectively to the searches for significant data and information, individuation of the causes of damage and decay, choice of the remedial measures and control of the efficiency of the interventions. In order to achieve cost effectiveness and minimal impact on architectural heritage using funds available in a rational way; it is usually necessary that the study repeats these steps in an iterative process.

1.7 No action should be undertaken without having ascertained the achievable benefit and harm to the architectural heritage, except in cases where urgent safeguard measures are necessary to avoid the imminent collapse of the structures (e.g. after seismic damages); those urgent measures, however, should when possible avoid modifying the fabric in an irreversible way.

2. Researches and diagnosis

2.1 Usually a multidisciplinary team, to be determined in relation to the type and the scale of the problem, should work together from the first steps of a study-as in the initial survey of the site and the preparation of the investigation programme.

2.2 Data and information should first be processed approximately, to establish a more comprehensive plan of activities in proportion to the real problems of the structures.

2.3 A full understanding of the structural and material characteristics is required in conservation practice. Information is essential on the structure in its original and earlier states, on the techniques that were used in the construction, on the alterations and their effects, on the phenomena that have occurred, and, finally, on its present state.

2.4 In archaeological sites specific problems may be posed because structures have to be stabilised during excavation when knowledge is not yet complete. The structural responses to a "rediscovered" building may be completely different from those to an "exposed" building. Urgent site-structural-solutions, required to stabilise the structure as it is being excavated, should not compromise the complete building's concept form and use.

2.5 Diagnosis is based on historical, qualitative and quantitative approaches; the qualitative approach being mainly based on direct observation of the structural damage and material decay as well as historical and archaeological research, and the quantitative approach mainly on material and structural tests, monitoring and structural analysis.

2.6 Before making a decision on structural intervention it is indispensable to determine first the causes of damage and decay, and then to evaluate the safety level of the structure.

2.7 The safety evaluation, which is the last step in the diagnosis, where the need for treatment measures is determined, should reconcile qualitative with quantitative analysis: direct observation, historical research, structural analysis and, if it is the case, experiments and tests.

2.8 Often the application of the same safety levels as in the design of new buildings requires excessive, if not impossible, measures. In these cases specific analyses and appropriate considerations may justify different approaches to safety.

2.9 All aspects related to the acquired information, the diagnosis including the safety evaluation, and the decision to intervene should be described in an "EXPLANATORY REPORT".

3. Remedial measures and controls

3.1 Therapy should address root causes rather than symptoms.

3.2 The best therapy is preventive maintenance

3.3 Safety evaluation and an understanding of the significance of the structure should be the basis for conservation and reinforcement measures.

3.4 No actions should be undertaken without demonstrating that they are indispensable.

3.5 Each intervention should be in proportion to the safety objectives set, thus keeping intervention to the minimum to guarantee safety and durability with the least harm to heritage values.

3.6 The design of intervention should be based on a clear understanding of the kinds of actions that were the cause of the damage and decay as well as those that are taken into account for the analysis of the structure after intervention; because the design will be dependent upon them.

3.7 The choice between "traditional" and "innovative" techniques should be weighed up on a case-by-case basis and preference given to those that are least invasive and most compatible with heritage values, bearing in mind safety and durability requirements.

3.8 At times the difficulty of evaluating the real safety levels and the possible benefits of interventions may suggest "an observational method", i.e. an incremental approach, starting from a minimum level of intervention, with the possible subsequent adoption of a series of supplementary or corrective measures.

3.9 Where possible, any measures adopted should be "reversible" so that they can be removed and replaced with more suitable measures when new knowledge is acquired. Where they are not completely reversible, interventions should not limit further interventions.

3.10 The characteristics of materials used in restoration work (in particular new materials) and their compatibility with existing materials should be fully established. This must include long-term impacts, so that undesirable side-effects are avoided.

3.11 The distinguishing qualities of the structure and its environment, in their original or earlier states, should not be destroyed.

3.12 Each intervention should, as far as possible, respect the concept, techniques and historical value of the original or earlier states of the structure and leaves evidence that can be recognised in the future.

3.13 Intervention should be the result of an overall integrated plan that gives due weight to the different aspects of architecture, structure, installations and functionality.

3.14 The removal or alteration of any historic material or distinctive architectural features should be avoided whenever possible.

3.15 Deteriorated structures whenever possible should be repaired rather than replaced.

3.16 Imperfections and alterations, when they have become part of the history of the structure, should be maintained so far so they do not compromise the safety requirements.

3.17 Dismantling and reassembly should only be undertaken as an optional measure required by the very nature of the materials and structure when conservation by other means impossible, or harmful.

3.18 Provisional safeguard systems used during the intervention should show their purpose and function without creating any harm to heritage values.

3.19 Any proposal for intervention must be accompanied by a programme of control to be carried out, as far as possible, while the work is in progress.

3.20 Measures that are impossible to control during execution should not be allowed.

3.21 Checks and monitoring during and after the intervention should be carried out to ascertain the efficacy of the results.

3.22 All the activities of checking and monitoring should be documented and kept as part of the history of the structure.

木质建成遗产保护准则[①]

（国际古迹遗址理事会第十九届大会 2017 年 12 月 15 日在印度新德里通过）

序　言

本准则是对 1999 年 10 月在墨西哥 ICOMOS 第 12 次全球代表大会上通过的"历史木构建筑保护准则"的补充及更新。此次更新过程始于墨西哥瓜达拉哈拉大会（2012），日本姬路大会（2013），并延续至瑞典法伦大会（2016）。

本文件力求与《威尼斯宪章》(1964)、《阿姆斯特丹宣言》(1975)、《巴拉宪章》(1979)、《奈良真实性文件》(1994) 的一般原则，以及联合国教科文组织和 ICOMOS 提出的有关木质建筑遗产保护的相关法规相适用。

本文件旨在尊重木质建成遗产文化意义的基础上，定义具有最大限度国际实例适用性的保护及保养的基本原则。

这里提到的"木质建成遗产"，是指所有类型的木质建筑，以及具有文化意义或作为历史区域一部分的其他木质构筑物，包括那些临时性的、可移动和持续演变的构筑物。

文件中提到的"价值"，指的是美学、人类学、考古学、文化、历史和科技的遗产价值。本准则适用于具有历史价值的木质建筑物和构筑物。并非所有建筑都完全由木材建造，由此也应考量木材与其他材料在建造中的相互作用。

原　则

- 认识并尊重木质建成遗产的重要性，它们的各个历史时期的结构体系和细节都是人类文化遗产的组成部分；
- 重视并尊重木质建成遗产的多样性以及任何与其相关的非物质遗产；
- 认识到木质遗产为手工艺者和建造者的技艺、以及他们掌握的传统的、文化的和祖传的知识提供物质证据；
- 理解文化价值随时间的持续演变，因而需要周期性回溯它们如何被定义，以及真实性如何被界定，以适应不断变化的认知和态度；
- 尊重不同的地方传统、建造实践和保护方法，并重视可以被应用于保护中的多样的方法与技术；
- 重视并尊重历史上采用的丰富多样的木材的种类和材质；
- 认识到从建筑物和构筑物整体来看，木构件是纪年信息的珍贵载体；
- 重视木结构能承受巨大外力（抗震）的优良性能；
- 认识到全木或半木结构在多变的气候环境条件下的脆弱性，易受（并不限于）温度和湿度变化、光照、

[①] 译者：郭瑞，胡玥，解立。中国古迹遗址保护协会 ICOMOS CHINA 提供。

真菌和昆虫、磨损风化、火灾、地震或其他自然灾害和人为损毁等因素的影响；

• 认识到因木构自身的脆弱性、不当利用、传统建筑设计和建造技艺的失传，以及对当地社区的精神和历史需求缺乏理解，越来越多的历史木构建筑在消失；

• 认识到木构建筑遗产保护中社区参与的相关性，保护与社会、环境变化的关系，及其对可持续发展的作用。

检查、勘察和研究

1. 在考虑实施任何干预前，应认真记录建筑结构及其各组成部分的现状，包括之前所有的干预工作。

2. 在任何干预行动前，必须实施全面、精确的诊断分析。分析内容需附有对建筑的建造和结构体系，现状及糟朽成因，损坏或结构故障，以及设计、定型或装配错误的分析。这些诊断必须以文献佐证、本体物理性勘察和分析为基础，若有必要，物理现状的检测应当采用无损测试，甚至必要时的实验室测试，也不排除在必要时采取微小干预和紧急保护措施。

3. 在检测对象被其他结构遮盖部位，上述检测方式可能不足以获得本体结构全部现状信息。在覆盖物价值允许的情况下，可以考虑局部临时性移除遮挡以实施检测，但必须在完成全面记录的基础上。

4. 木构件上"看不见"（隐藏着的）标记也应被记录。"看不见"的标记是指如木工的题记、水平线及被工匠用于施工（或后续工程或修缮中的）无意作为可见的建筑构成部分的其他标记。

分析和评估

5. 保护工作的首要任务是保留历史遗存的真实性，包括布局构造、材料、装配、完整性、建筑学及文化遗产价值，并尊重其历史变迁。而要做到这一点，则应尽可能保留所有界定遗产特征的要素。

界定遗产特征的要素可包含以下一项或多项内容：
a）整体结构系统；
b）非结构元素如立面、隔断、阶梯；
c）表面特征；
d）木工的装饰处理；
e）传统和工艺；
f）建筑材料，包括建材质量（或品级）和典型特征。

6. 必须对上述要素的价值进行评估和界定，以制定干预方案。

干预措施

7. 干预工作的第一步应制定建筑保护总体策略。这需要相关各方参与讨论并达成共识。

8. 干预策略须考虑当前的主流文化价值观。

9. 除干预规模过大、可能影响历史建筑真实性的情况外，建筑结构的原始功能应予以保留或修复。

10. 干预可采取如下形式：
a）使用传统木工工艺或兼容的现代固件的简单修复；
b）使用传统或兼容的材料和工艺的结构加固；
c）缓解现有结构荷载的补充结构的引入。

干预方式的选择应取决于是否能够最好地保护建筑结构的文化价值。

11. 干预最好能够做到：
a）以必要的最小干预来保证建筑或遗址的物理和结构稳定性及其本体和文化意义的长久保存；

b）遵循传统做法；
c）如技术可行，尽量可逆；
d）不影响或阻碍后续必要的保护工作；
e）不妨碍未来对显露或融入建筑中的证据的读取；
f）重视遗产环境。

12. 干预应遵循的标准是：能够确保建筑本体保存、尽可能多保留真实性和完整性、并使其持续安全地发挥功能的最小干预。但是，遇如下情形不排除部分拆卸甚至全部的结构解体（落架）：
a）采用原构件进行原址修缮时需要的干预程度过大；
b）变形严重以至于无法恢复其原有结构性能；
c）为维持已变形结构稳定需有不当添加。
任何拆卸工作的适当性均应结合其文化背景来考虑，且应以最好地保持建筑真实性为目标。
此外，干预决策的确定应考虑和评估拆卸过程中对木材以及木质和其他材质连接件（如钉子）等潜在的不可逆的破坏。

13. 应尽可能多地保留现有构件。当有必要替换整个或部分构件时，应首先尊重建筑的整体特性和价值。在特定文化背景下，如已有相关传统，其他老旧建筑中的构件也可能在干预过程中被利用。

14. 任何用于替换的木材应尽量满足如下条件：
a）与原构件属于同一木种；
b）与原木构件含水率相吻合；
c）可见的部分与原木构件有相似纹理特征；
d）加工时采用与原构件相似的工艺和工具。

15. 不应刻意将替换的木构件人工做旧。新构件不应在审美上影响整体外观。不应对替换构件上色以匹配整体色彩现状，但特殊情况如会对遗产建筑的艺术理解和文化意义造成严重负面影响时除外。

16. 新木构件可做谨慎的标记处理，以便后期可辨识。

17. 为评估诸如临时性和演进中的特定木质建成遗产的文化意义，需要对其更多特有的价值进行考量。

18. 在实施干预过程中，历史建筑应被视为一个整体。所有材料，包括结构性部件、填充性嵌木、防风板、屋顶、地面、门窗等，均应被同等重视。原则上，现存材料以及早期修缮，应在其不影响结构稳定性的情况下尽可能予以保留。保护对象还应包括各种建筑表层处理如地仗层、彩绘层、表面涂层、墙纸等。应尊重原材料、原工艺和原肌理。如建筑表面糟朽亟需更换时，宜采用兼容材料和工艺。

19. 考虑结构性部件时应注意如下几点：
a）若结构本身性能表现良好，且其使用情况、实际条件及承重系统均未变化时，可通过只简单维修/加固最近受损和失效的承重部分来有效增强其结构性能。
b）如近期产生过较大变动，或未来有可能的功能变更将会造成更大的负载时，在考虑实施任何加固措施前，应通过结构分析评估其潜在承载强度。

20. 任何情况下都不应仅仅为满足现代建筑规范要求而实施干预措施。

21. 一切干预措施均须建立在经充分验证的结构原则基础上。

22. 对于已经长期存在、无结构和功能影响的轻微偏移变形，不可一味地为迎合今天的审美倾向，而实施"纠偏"干预。

当今材料和技术

23. 对选择和使用当下新材料和技术应采取极端谨慎的态度，只有当这些材料和建造技术的耐久性和结构性能已经足够长的时间被证实表现良好时，方可考虑。

24. 实用设施的安装应考虑建成遗产的物质和非物质价值。

25. 新的设施的安装不应引起诸如温湿度等环境条件的巨大改变。

26. 化学性防腐剂的使用应当被谨慎控制和监测管理，且只有当公众和环境安全不受影响且有重要的长效提升等明确效果时方可使用。

记录和建档

27. 根据《威尼斯宪章》第16条以及《ICOMOS关于建筑、建筑群和遗址记录的准则》的规定，记录应包含干预措施和保护工作中涉及的所有材料。所有相关文献档案，包括从建筑中拆除的多余材料或构件的典型样品，以及传统技法和工艺的相关信息，均应被收集、编目、妥善保存且适当开放查阅。记录中应包括选择特定保护修复材料和方法的具体原因。

28. 既为了建筑今后的持续维护，也作为重要历史档案，所有上述记录应被妥善保存。

监测和维护

29. 必须制定一套清晰连贯的定期监测和日常维护的策略，以推迟更大的干预措施的实施，并确保对木质建成遗产及其文化价值的持续保护。

30. 监测工作须贯穿任何保护干预过程始终并持续进行，以确保采用方法的有效性以及木构件和其他材料的长期性能。

31. 日常维护和监测数据都应作为建筑历史资料的一部分妥善保存。

历史森林保护区

32. 因木构建筑非常脆弱，但作为持续贡献社会发展的活态遗产的一部分，涉及的木材的可得性对其保护至关重要。因此，森林保护区在木构建筑维护和修复的自我维持循环中发挥着非常关键的作用。这一点应当被充分重视。

33. 古迹遗址保护机构应当鼓励保护原始林区并建立风干木材仓库，以用于木质建成遗产的保护修缮。此项政策应预见到未来修复工作中对适用风干木材的大量需求。然而，这些政策并非要鼓励对历史建筑真实构件的大规模替换，而是为建筑必要的修缮和少量替换服务的储备型保护区。

教育和培训

34. 记录、保护和恢复历史木构建筑的传统知识和技艺是非常重要的。

35. 教育是通过推动对遗产价值和文化重要性的理解和认知，来提升木构建筑遗产保护意识的一个核心途径。教育是可持续的保护和发展政策的基础。一个综合、可持续的策略须涉及地方、区域、国家和国际层面，同时还应包括所有相关政府机构、领域、行业、社区和其他相关群体。

36. 应该鼓励开展有利于深入理解木质建成遗产的显著特征、其社会及人类学方面内容的研究项目（尤其是在区域层面）。

术语词汇表

建造、建筑（名词）：1.将材料有效排列、组合、统一构成一个整体的行为；2.建造的行为；3.建成物

（也见下文"构筑物"）；

文化意义：建筑或遗址中对过去、现在和未来世代具有的美学的、历史的、考古的、人类学的、科学的、技术的、社会的、精神的或其他非物质的遗产价值。

有机演进的建筑：那些在当今社会保持着活跃的社会角色而又与传统生活方式紧密相连，并且仍然在演变进程中的建筑。同时这些建筑是展示其历史演进过程的重要物证。

本体：建筑或遗址所有的物理材料，包括构成部分、固定装置、内容及其他实物。

非物质遗产：与木质建成遗产的建造和使用相关的各传统过程。

加固：增强建筑单个构件、构件组合或整体的结构性功效的行为。

修复：是指旨在恢复木构建筑遗产一部分或全部的结构性能、美学完整性的行为。这包括为了替换糟朽部分或保持建筑结构和材料的完整而对历史建筑本体采取的艰苦细致的干预工作。

构筑物（名词）：一个经过设计和建造的稳定的构件组合，它作为一个整体具有安全地支撑和传递使用荷载至地面的功能。

临时性结构：作为特定文化或民族的重要仪式或其他活动的一部分，体现其传统文化、工艺及传统知识，而被周期性建造、使用再拆除的结构。

Principles for the Conservation of Wooden Built Heritage

Adopted by the 19th ICOMOS General Assembly, New Delhi, India, 15 December 2017

PREAMBLE

These Principles have been written with the objective of updating the "Principles for the Preservation of Historic Timber Structures" adopted by ICOMOS at the 12th General Assembly in Mexico, October 1999. The updating process began in Guadalajara, Mexico (2012), Himeji, Japan (2013) and continued in Falun, Sweden (2016).

This document seeks to apply the general principles of the Venice Charter (1964), the Declaration of Amsterdam (1975), the Burra Charter (1979), the Nara Document on Authenticity (1994) and related UNESCO and ICOMOS doctrines concerning the protection and conservation of the wooden built heritage.

The purpose of this document is to define the basic principles and practices applicable in the widest variety of cases internationally for the protection and conservation of the wooden built heritage with respect to its cultural significance.

The words "wooden built heritage" refer here to all types of wooden buildings and other wooden structures that have cultural significance or are parts of historic places, and includes temporary, movable and evolving structures.

The word "values" in this document refers to aesthetic, anthropological, archaeological, cultural, historical, scientific and technological heritage values. These Principles apply to wooden architecture and structures with historic value. Not all buildings are made entirely of wood and due regard should be paid to the interaction of wood with other materials in the construction.

The Principles:

• recognize and respect the importance of the wooden built heritage, its structural systems and details from all periods as part of the cultural heritage of the world;

• take into account and respect the great diversity of the wooden built heritage, and any associated intangible heritage;

• recognize that wooden heritage provides evidence of the skills of craftworkers and builders and their traditional, cultural and ancestral knowledge;

• understand the continuous evolution of cultural values over time and the need to periodically review how they are identified and how authenticity is determined in order to accommodate changing perceptions and attitudes;

• respect different local traditions, building practices and conservation approaches, taking into account the great variety of methodologies and techniques that could be used in conservation;

• take into account and respect the various historically used species and qualities of wood;

• recognize that wood constructions provide a valuable record of chronological data concerning the whole building or structure;

• take into account the excellent behaviour of wood structures in withstanding seismic forces;

• recognize the vulnerability of structures made wholly or partially of wood in varying environmental and climatic conditions, caused by (among other things) temperature and humidity fluctuations, light, fungal and insect attacks, wear and tear, fire, earthquakes or other natural disasters, and destructive actions by humans;

• recognize the increasing loss of historic wooden structures due to vulnerability, misuse, loss of skills and knowledge of traditional design and construction technology, and the lack of understanding of the spiritual and historic needs of living communities;

• recognize the relevance of community participation in protection of the wooden heritage, its relation with social and environmental transformations, and its role in sustainable development.

INSPECTION, SURVEY AND RESEARCH

1. The condition of the structure and its components, including previous works, should be carefully recorded before considering any action.

2. A thorough and accurate diagnosis should precede any intervention. This should be accompanied by an understanding and analysis of the construction and structural system, of its condition and the causes of any decay, damage or structural failure as well as mistakes in conception, sizing or assembly. The diagnosis must be based on documentary evidence, physical inspection and analysis and, if necessary, measurements of physical conditions using non-destructive testing (NDT), and if necessary on laboratory testing. This does not preclude carrying out minor interventions and emergency measures where these are necessary.

3. This inspection may not be sufficient to assess the condition of the structure adequately where it is concealed by other elements of the fabric. Where the significance of the covering allows, consideration may be given to its local temporary removal to facilitate the investigation, but only after full recording has been carried out.

4. "Invisible" (hidden) marks on old wooden parts must also be recorded. "Invisible" marks refers to features such as scribe marks, level and other marks used by carpenters in setting out the work (or in subsequent works or repairs) and which were not intended to be visible features of the structure.

ANALYSIS AND EVALUATION

5. The primary aim of conservation is to maintain the authenticity of the historic fabric. This includes its configuration, materials, assembly, integrity, architectural and cultural heritage values, respecting changes through history. To do so one should retain as far as possible all its character-defining features.

Character-defining features may comprise one or more of the following:

a. the overall structural system;

b. non-structural elements such as facades, partitions, stairs;

c. surface features;

d. decorative treatment of the carpentry;

e. traditions and techniques;

f. the materials of construction, including their quality (or grade) and particular characteristics.

6. The value of these character-defining features must be determined in order to formulate any intervention plan.

INTERVENTIONS

7. The first stage in the process of intervention should be to devise a general strategy for the conservation of the building. This needs to be discussed and agreed by all parties involved.

8. The intervention strategy must take into account the prevailing cultural values.

9. The original function of a structure should be maintained or restored except in cases when the intervention would be too extensive and prejudicial to the authenticity of the structure.

10. Interventions may take the form of:

a. simple repairs using either traditional carpentry techniques or compatible modern fasteners;

b. the strengthening of the structure using traditional or compatible materials and techniques;

c. the introduction of a supplementary structure that will relieve the present structure of load.

The choice of which intervention to use should be determined by selecting that which best protects the structure's cultural significance.

11. Interventions should preferably:

a. be the minimum necessary to ensure the physical and structural stability and the long-term survival of the structure or site as well as its cultural significance;

b. follow traditional practices;

c. be reversible, if technically possible;

d. not prejudice or impede future conservation work should this become necessary;

e. not hinder the possibility of later access to evidence exposed and incorporated in the construction;

f. take environmental conditions into account.

12. Interventions should follow the criteria of the minimal intervention capable of ensuring the survival of the construction, saving as much as possible of its authenticity and integrity, and allowing it to continue to perform its function safely. However, that does not preclude the possible partial or even total dismantling of the structure if:

a. repairs carried out *in situ* and on original elements would require an unacceptable degree of intervention;

b. the distortion of the structure is such that it is not possible to restore its proper structural behaviour;

c. inappropriate additional work would be required to maintain it in its deformed state.

Decisions regarding the appropriateness of any dismantling should be considered within each cultural context, and should be aimed at best protecting the authenticity of the building.

In addition, decisions should always consider and evaluate the potential for irreversible damage to the wood, as well as to wood joints and connections (such as nails) during the dismantling intervention.

13. As much as possible of the existing members should be retained. Where replacement of a member or part of a member is necessary it should respect the character and significance of the structure. In cultures where the tradition exists, aged building parts from other structures might be used in the intervention.

14. Any replacement timber should preferably:

a. be of the same species as the original;

b. match the original in moisture content;

c. have similar characteristics of grain where it will be visible;

d. be worked using similar craft methods and tools as the original.

15. No attempt should be made to artificially age replacement timber. The new components should not aesthetically undermine the whole. Colouring the replaced members to match the current colour of the original may be permitted in specific cases when not doing so would unacceptably impair the aesthetic understanding and cultural significance of the structure.

16. New members or parts of members may be discreetly marked, so that they can be identified at a later date.

17. Consideration of specific values may be required to evaluate the cultural significance of some wooden built heritage, such as temporary and evolving buildings.

18. In the case of interventions, the historic structure should be considered as a whole. All materials, including structural members, in-fill panels, weather-boarding, roofs, floors, doors and windows, etc., should be given equal attention. In principle, as much as possible of the existing material, as well as earlier repair works, should be retained if they do not prejudice the stability of the structure. Conservation should also include surface finishes such as plaster, paint, coating, wall-paper, etc. The original materials, techniques and textures should be respected. If it is considered strictly necessary to renew or replace deteriorated surface finishes, the use of compatible materials and techniques is desirable.

19. When considering structural members it should be noted that:

a. if a structure has a satisfactory performance, and if the use, the actual conditions and loading regime are unchanged, the structure can be made adequately strong by simply repairing/stabilizing recent strength-reducing damage and failure;

b. if recent alterations have been made, or any proposed change of use would impose a more onerous loading, the potential load-bearing strength should be estimated by structural analysis before considering the introduction of any further reinforcement.

20. On no account should interventions be carried out simply to enable the structure to meet the requirements of modern building codes.

21. All interventions must be justified based upon sound structural principles and usage.

22. No attempt should be made to "correct" deflections that have occurred over time, and which have no structural significance, and present no difficulties of use, simply to address present-day aesthetic preferences.

PRESENT-DAY MATERIALS AND TECHNOLOGIES

23. Present-day materials and technologies should be chosen and used with the greatest caution and only in cases where the durability and structural behaviour of the materials and construction techniques have been satisfactorily proven over a sufficiently long period of time.

24. Utilities should be installed with respect for the tangible and intangible significance of the structure or site.

25. Installations should be designed so as not to cause changes to significant environmental conditions, such as temperature and humidity.

26. The use of chemical preservatives should be carefully controlled and monitored and should be used only where there is an assured benefit, where public and environmental safety will not be affected and where there is the expectation of significant long-term improvement.

RECORDING AND DOCUMENTATION

27. A record should be made of all materials used in interventions and treatments, in accordance with Article 16 of the Venice Charter and the ICOMOS Principles for the Recording of Monuments, Groups of Buildings and Sites. All relevant documentation, including characteristic samples of redundant materials or members removed from the structure, and information about relevant traditional skills and technologies, should be collected, catalogued, securely stored and made accessible as appropriate. The documentation should also include the specific reasons given for the choice of materials and methodologies in the conservation work.

28. All the above documentation must be retained both for future maintenance of the building and as an historical record.

MONITORING AND MAINTENANCE

29. A coherent strategy of regular monitoring and day-to-day maintenance must be established in order to delay the need for larger interventions and ensure the continuing protection of wooden built heritage and its cultural significance.

30. Monitoring should be carried out both during and after any intervention to ascertain the effectiveness of the methods used and to ensure the long-term performance of the timber and any other materials used.

31. Records of any maintenance and monitoring should be kept as part of the documented history of the structure.

HISTORIC FOREST RESERVES

32. Because wooden structures may be in a vulnerable state, but still part of a living heritage and contributing to society, the availability of suitable timbers is essential for their conservation. Therefore, the crucial role that forest reserves play in the self-sustaining cycles of maintenance and repair of these wooden structures should be recognized.

33. Institutions responsible for the conservation of monuments and sites should encourage the protection of original woodland reserves and establish stores of seasoned timber appropriate for the conservation and repair of the wooden built heritage. This policy should foresee the need for large properly seasoned wooden elements in future repairs. However, such policies should not encourage the extensive substitution of authentic elements of historic structures, but rather constitute a reserve for repairs and minor replacements.

EDUCATION AND TRAINING

34. It is essential to record, preserve and recover the traditional knowledge and skills used in constructing historic wooden architecture.

35. Educational programmes are an essential part of raising awareness of wooden heritage by encouraging

recognition and understanding of values and cultural significance. These programmes are the foundation of a sustainable conservation and development policy. A comprehensive and sustainable strategy must involve local, regional, national and international levels and should include all relevant officials, professions, trades, the community and other interested parties.

36. Research programmes (particularly at regional level) to identify the distinctive characteristics, and social and anthropological aspects of the wooden built heritage, buildings and sites, are to be encouraged.

GLOSSARY OF TERMS:

Construction (noun): the manner in which materials are ordered, assembled, and united into a whole[①]; the act of constructing; the thing built. (See also "Structure" below).

Cultural significance: the aesthetic, historical, archaeological, anthropological, scientific, technological, social, spiritual or other intangible heritage values of a structure or site for past, present or future generations.

Evolving buildings: those that retain an active social role in present-day society closely associated with a traditional way of life, and in which the evolutionary process is still in progress. At the same time such structures exhibit significant material evidence of their evolution over time.

Fabric: all the physical material of the structure or site including components, fixtures, contents and objects.

Intangible heritage: the traditional processes associated with the creation and use of the wooden built heritage.

Reinforcement: actions carried out to increase the structural efficiency of an element, an ensemble of elements, or a structure.

Repair: every action aimed at recovering the structural efficiency, aesthetic integrity and/or completion of them, of a part or the whole of a wooden built heritage. This involves a painstaking intervention in the historic fabric, aiming at replacing only decayed parts and otherwise leaving the structure and the materials intact.

Structure (noun): a stable assembly of elements designed and constructed to function as a whole in supporting and transmitting applied loads safely to the ground[②].

Temporary structures: those which are built, used and disassembled periodically as part of a culture's or nation's ceremonies or other activities and embody traditions, craftsmanship and traditional knowledge.

---

① Ching, Francis D K (1995) A Visual Dictionary of Architecture. New York: John Wiley & Sons.
② Ibid.

·景观和园林遗产·

关于保护景观和遗址的风貌与特性的建议[①]

(联合国教科文组织第十二届大会1962年12月11日在巴黎通过)

联合国教科文组织大会于1962年11月9日至12月12日在巴黎召开了第十二届会议,

考虑到人类在各个时期不时使构成其自然环境的组成部分的景观和遗址的风貌与特征遭到损坏,从而使得全世界各个地区的文化、艺术甚至极重要的遗产濒于枯竭;

考虑到因原始土地的开发,城市中心盲目的发展以及工商业与装备的巨大工程和庞大规划的实施,使现代文明加速了这种趋势,尽管其进程到上个世纪已相对减弱;

考虑到这种现象影响到不论其为自然的或人工的景观和遗址的艺术价值以及野生生物的文化和科学价值;

考虑到由于景观和遗址的风貌与特征,保护景观和遗址正如本建议所述,对人类生活必不可少,对人类而言,它们代表了一种有力的物质、道德和精神的再生影响,同时正如无数众所周知的事例所证明的也有利于人类文化和艺术生活;

进一步**考虑到**景观和遗址是许多国家经济和社会生活中的一个重要因素,而且大大有助于保障其居民的健康;

然而,**也认识到**应适当考虑社会生活及其演变以及技术进步的迅速发展之需要;

因此,**考虑到**只要尚有可能这样做,为保护各地的景观和遗址的风貌与特征,亟需紧急考虑和采取必要的措施;

已收到关于保护景观和遗址的风貌与特征的建议,该问题作为本届会议的第17.4.2项议程;

第十一届会议已决定此项建议应以向成员国建议的形式作为国际性文件的议题,于1962年12月11日通过本建议。

大会**建议**各成员国应通过国家法律或其他方式制定使本建议所体现的准则和原则在其所管辖的领土上生效的措施,以适用以下规定。

大会**建议**各成员国应将本建议提请与保护景观和遗址以及区域发展有关的部门和机构的注意,也提请受委托保护自然和发展旅游业的机构以及青年组织的注意。

大会**建议**各成员国应按待定的日期和形式向大会提交有关本建议执行情况的报告。

一. 定 义

1. 为本建议之目的,保护景观和遗址的风貌与特征系指保存并在可能的情况下修复无论是自然的或

[①] 引自:联合国教科文组织世界遗产中心,国际古迹遗址理事会,国际文物保护与修复研究中心,中国国家文物局主编. 国际文化遗产保护文件选编[M]. 北京:文物出版社,2007.

人工的，具有文化或艺术价值，或构成典型自然环境的自然、乡村及城市景观和遗址的任何部分。

2. 本建议的规定也拟作为保护自然的补充措施。

二. 总　则

3. 为保护景观和遗址所进行的研究和采取的措施应适用于一国之全部领土范围，并不应局限于某些选定的景观和遗址。

4. 在选择将采取的措施时，应适当考虑有关景观与遗址的相关意义。这些措施可根据景观与遗址的特征、大小、位置以及它们所面临威胁的性质而有所区别。

5. 保护不应只局限于自然景观与遗址，而应扩展到那些全部或部分由人工形成的景观与遗址。因此，应制定特别规定确保对那些受威胁最大、特别是因建筑施工和土地买卖而受到威胁的某些城市中的景观和遗址进行保护。对进入古迹应采取特别保护措施。

6. 为保护景观和遗址所采取的措施应既是预防性的，又是矫正性的。

7. 预防性措施应旨在保护遗址免受可能威胁它们的危险。这些措施尤其应包括对可能损坏景观和遗址的工程和活动进行监督，例如：

（1）建各类公私建筑，其设计应符合建筑本身的某些艺术要求，并且在避免简单模仿某些传统的和独特的形式的同时，应与它将保护的一般环境相协调；

（2）修建道路；

（3）高、低压电线、电力生产和输送工厂和设施、飞机场、广播电台和电视台等；

（4）加油站；

（5）广告招牌以及灯光招牌；

（6）砍伐森林，包括破坏构成景观风貌的树木，尤其是主干道或林荫道两旁成行的树木；

（7）空气和水的污染；

（8）采矿、采石及其废弃物的处理；

（9）喷泉管道、灌溉工程、水坝、隧道、沟渠、治理河流工程等；

（10）宿营地；

（11）废弃物和垃圾以及家庭、商业和工业废物的倾倒。

8. 在保护景观和遗址的风貌与特征时，也应考虑到因某些工作和现代生活的某些活动而引起的噪声所造成的危害。

9. 对可能损坏以其他方式列入保护目录或受到保护的地区内的景观和遗址的活动应施以制裁，除非为公共或社会利益所迫切需要。

10. 矫正性措施应旨在修缮对景观和遗址所造成的损坏，并尽可能使其恢复至原状。

11. 为促进各国负责保护景观和遗址的各种公共服务机构的工作，应建立科学研究机构，以便与主管当局合作，收集和编纂适用于这方面的法律和规定。这些规定和研究机构所从事的工作成果应定期及时刊登于单独的行政刊物上。

三. 保护措施

12. 景观和遗址的保护应通过使用以下方法予以确保：

（1）由主管当局进行全面监督；

（2）将责任列入城市发展规划以及区域、乡村和城市的各级规划；

（3）"通过划区"列出大面积景观区保护目录；

（4）列出零散的遗址保护目录；

（5）建立和维护自然保护区与国家公园；

（6）由社区获得遗址。

全面监督

13. 对全国范围内可能损坏景观和遗址的工程和活动，应实行全面监督。

城市规划与乡村规划方案

14. 城市规划与乡村规划方案应包括明确那些应强制执行、以确保位于所涉及地区内的甚至未列入保护目录的景观和遗址的保护义务的规定。

15. 城市和乡村规划方案应根据轻重缓急和顺序予以制定，特别是对处在迅速发展过程中的城市或地区，为保护该城市或地区的艺术或优美特征制定此种方案是正确的。

"通过划区"列出大面积景观区保护目录

16. 大面积景观区"通过划区"列入保护目录。

17. 在一个已列入保护目录的区域内，当艺术特征为头等重要时，列入保护目录的应包括：控制土地，遵循美学要求——包括材料的使用、颜色以及高度标准，采取预防措施以消除因筑坝和采石所造成的动土影响，制定管理树木砍伐的法规等。

18. "通过划区"列出的目录应予以公布，并应制订和公布为保护已列入目录的景观所应遵守的一般规则。

19. 一般来说，"通过划区"列出保护目录，不应涉及赔偿费的支付。

列出零散遗址保护目录

20. 对无论位于自然中还是位于城市内的零散小遗址，连同具有特殊意义的景观的各个部分，均应列出保护目录。对景色优美的地区，以及著名古迹周围的地区和建筑物，也应列出保护目录。凡列入保护目录的每一个遗址、地区和建筑物都须经特别行政决定并应及时通知其所有者。

21. 列入保护目录应意味着未经保护遗址的主管当局许可，禁止其所有者毁坏遗址，或改变其状况或外观。

22. 当得到此种许可，应同时附有保护遗址所需的一切条件。但对于正常的农业活动以及建筑物的正常维修无需此种许可。

23. 有关当局的征用以及在一列入保护目录的遗址内进行公共工程应征得负责该遗址保护的主管当局的同意。按规定，在列入保护目录的遗址内任何人不应获得可能改变该遗址特征或外观的权利。未经主管当局的同意，该遗址所有者不应通过签订协议授权他人。

24. 制定保护目录应包括禁止一切形式的对地面、空气或水的污染，同样，采矿也须经过特别许可。

25. 在列入保护目录的地区内及其邻近地带应禁止张贴任何广告，或者仅限于负责保护遗址的主管当局所指定的特定区域。

26. 在列入保护目录的遗址内宿营原则上应予以回绝，或者仅限于负责主管当局所确定的地区，并应接受其检查。

27. 遗址列入保护目录可以使遗址所有者有权对由此造成的直接的和确切的损失要求赔偿。

自然保护区和国家公园

28. 条例适宜时，各成员国应将其用于公共教育和娱乐的国家公园，或严格控制的或特定的自然保护区纳入受保护的区域和遗址之中。这类自然保护区和国家公园应构成一组还将用于研究景观的形成与修复以及自然保护的试验区。

由社区获得遗址

29. 各成员国应鼓励社区获得那些需要保护的构成景观或遗址组成部分的地区。必要时，应能够通过征用来实现这种获得。

四. 保护措施的实施

30. 各成员国保护景观和遗址的基本标准和原则应具有法律效力，其实施措施应在法律所赋予的权限范围内委托给负责的主管当局。

31. 各成员国应设立具有管理或咨询性质的专门机构。

32. 管理机构应是受委托实施保护措施的中央或地方的专门部门。因此，这些部门应有能力研究保护和制定保护目录的问题，开展实地考察，准备即将采取的决定并监督其实施。这些部门同样应受委托对旨在减少某些工程进行中或对由此种工程造成的损坏进行修复中可能涉及的危险提出建议措施。

33. 咨询机构应由国家、地区或地方各级委员组成，并被授予研究有关保护问题以及就这些问题向中央或地区主管当局或有关地方社区提出意见的任务。在任何情况下，特别是在大规模公益工程，诸如修建公路、安装水利技术或新型工业设施等规划的初期，应及时征求这些委员会的意见。

34. 各成员国应促进国家和地方非政府机构的设立及其运转，这些机构的职责之一是与第31、32和33条中所述机构合作，特别是通过这样一种方式合作，即把威胁景观和遗址的危险告知公众，并告诫有关部门。

35. 如违反保护景观和遗址的有关规定，应对损坏予以赔偿，或承担将该遗址尽可能修复至原状的义务。

36. 对故意损坏景观和遗址的行为，应给予行政或刑事处罚。

五. 公共教育

37. 教育活动应在校内、外进行，以激发与培养公众对景观和遗址的尊重，宣传为确保对名胜和古迹的保护所制定的规章。

38. 受委托承担这项任务的学校教员应在中、高等院校接受专门课程的特殊培训。

39. 各成员国也应促进现有博物馆的工作，以加强它们为此业已开展的教育活动，并应考虑建立专门博物馆，或在现有博物馆内设立专门部门的可能性，以便研究和展示特定地区的自然和文化风貌。

40. 校外公共教育应是新闻界、保护景观和遗址或保护自然的私人组织、有关旅游机构以及青年或大众教育组织的任务。

41. 各成员国应促进公共教育，并通过提供物资援助和通过让从事教育任务的学会、机构和组织以及普通教育工作者利用适当宣传媒介，例如：电影、广播和电视节目，永久性、临时性或流动性展览材料，以及适合于广泛传播并专为教育界设计的手册和书籍，促进它们的工作，还可以通过报刊、杂志以及地方期刊进行广泛宣传。

42. 各种国内、国际"节日"、竞赛和类似活动应专门用于鼓励对自然或人工景观和遗址的鉴赏，从而引导民众注意这样一个事实：保护景观和遗址的风貌与特征对社区而言至关重要。

Recommendation concerning the Safeguarding of the Beauty and Character of Landscapes and Sites[1]

Adopted by the UNESCO General Conference at its 12th Session, Paris, 11 December 1962

The General Conference of the United Nations Educational, Scientific and Cultural Organization, meeting in Paris from 9 November to 12 December 1962, in its twelfth session:

Considering that at all periods men have sometimes subjected the beauty and character of landscapes and sites forming part of their natural environment to damage which has impoverished the cultural, aesthetic and even vital heritage of whole regions in all parts of the world,

Considering that by the cultivation of virgin land, the sometimes ill-regulated development of urban centres, the carrying out of extensive works and vast plans for industrial and commercial development and equipment, modern civilizations have accelerated this trend whose progress was relatively slow up to the last century,

Considering that this phenomenon affects the aesthetic value of landscapes and sites, natural or man-made, and the cultural and scientific importance of wildlife,

Considering that, on account of their beauty and character, the safeguarding of landscapes and sites, as defined in this recommendation, is necessary to the life of men for whom they represent a powerful physical, moral and spiritual regenerating influence, while at the same time contributing to the artistic and cultural life of peoples, as innumerable and universally known examples bear witness,

Considering furthermore that landscapes and sites are an important factor in the economic and social life of many countries, and are largely instrumental in ensuring the health of their inhabitants,

Recognizing, however, that due account should be taken of the needs of community life, its evolution and the rapid development of technical progress,

Considering, therefore, that it is highly desirable and urgent to consider and adopt the necessary steps with a view to safeguarding the beauty and character of landscapes and sites everywhere, whenever it is still possible to do so,

Having before it proposals concerning the safeguarding of the beauty and character of landscapes and sites, this questions forming item 17.4.2 of the session's agenda,

Having decided at its eleventh session that proposals on this item should be the subject of an international

---

[1] Records of the General Conference, twelfth session, Paris, 1962: Resolutions. UNESCO Document Code: 12 C/Resolutions.

instrument in the form of a recommendation to Member States,

Adopts, on this eleventh day of December 1962, this recommendation.

The General Conference recommends that Member States should apply the following provisions by adopting, in the form of a national law or in some other way, measures designed to give effect in the territories under their jurisdiction to the norms and principles embodied in this recommendation.

The General Conference recommends that Member States should bring this recommendation to the attention of the authorities and bodies concerned with the protection of landscapes and sites and with regional development, and of bodies entrusted with the protection of nature and the development of the tourist trade, together with youth organizations.

The General Conference recommends that Member States should, on dates and in a form to be determined, submit to it reports concerning the implementation of this recommendation.

Ⅰ. DEFINITION

1. For the purpose of this recommendation, the safeguarding of the beauty and character of landscapes and sites is taken to mean the preservation and, where possible, the restoration of the aspect of natural, rural and urban landscapes and sites, whether natural or man-made, which have a cultural or aesthetic interest or form typical natural surroundings.

2. The provisions of this recommendation are also intended to supplement measures for the protection of nature.

Ⅱ. GENERAL PRINCIPLES

3. The studies and measures to be adopted with a view to the safeguarding of landscapes and sites should extend to the whole territory of a State, and should not be confined to certain selected landscapes or sites.

4. In choosing the measures to be adopted, due account should be taken of the relative significance of the landscapes and sites concerned. These measures might vary in accordance with the character and size of the landscapes and sites, their location and the nature of the dangers with which they are threatened.

5. Protection should not be limited to natural landscapes and sites, but should also extend to landscapes and sites whose formation is due wholly or in part to the work of man. Thus, special provisions should be made to ensure the safeguarding of certain urban landscapes and sites which are, in general, the most threatened, especially by building operations and land speculation. Special protection should be accorded to the approaches to monuments.

6. Measures taken for the safeguarding of landscapes and sites should be both preventive and corrective.

7. Preventive measures should be aimed at protecting sites from dangers which may threaten them. These measures should include, in particular, the supervision of works and activities likely to damage landscapes and sites, for example:

a. The construction of all types of public and private buildings. These should be designed so as to meet certain aesthetic requirements in respect of the building itself and, while avoiding a facile imitation of certain traditional and picturesque forms, should be in harmony with the general atmosphere which it is desired to safeguard;

b. The construction of roads;

c. High or low tension electric lines, power production and transmission plant and equipment, aerodromes, broadcasting and television stations, etc.;

 d. Petrol filling stations;

 e. Advertising hoardings and illuminated signs;

 f. Deforestation, including the destruction of trees contributing to the beauty of the landscape, particularly those lining thoroughfares or avenues;

 g. Pollution of the air and water;

 h. Working of mines and quarries and the disposal of their waste products;

 i. Piping of spring water, irrigation works, dams, channels, aqueducts, river regulation works, etc.;

 j. Camping;

 k. Dumping of worn-out material and waste, and domestic, commercial or industrial scrap.

 8. In safeguarding the beauty and character of landscapes and sites, allowance should also be made for the dangers resulting from certain forms of work and certain activities of present-day life, by reason of the noise which they occasion.

 9. Activities likely to mar landscapes or sites in areas that are scheduled or protected in some other way should be sanctioned only if the public or social welfare imperatively requires it.

 10. Corrective measures should be aimed at repairing the damage caused to landscapes and sites and, as far as possible, restoring them to their original condition.

 11. In order to facilitate the task of the various public services responsible for the safeguarding of landscapes and sites in each State, scientific research institutes should be set up to co-operate with the competent authorities with a view to the alignment and codification of the laws and regulations applicable in this matter. These provisions and the results of the work carried out by the research institutes should be published in a single administrative publication brought periodically up to date.

III. PROTECTIVE MEASURES

 12. The safeguarding of landscapes and sites should be ensured by use of the following methods:

 a. General supervision by the responsible authorities;

 b. Insertion of obligations into urban development plans and planning at all levels: regional, rural and urban;

 c. Scheduling of extensive landscapes "by zones" ;

 d. Scheduling of isolated sites;

 e. Creation and maintenance of natural reserves and national parks;

 f. Acquisition of sites by communities.

GENERAL SUPERVISION

 13. General supervision should be exercised over works and activities likely to damage landscapes and sites throughout the whole territory of the State.

TOWN PLANNING AND RURAL PLANNING SCHEMES

 14. Urban and rural planning schemes should embody provisions defining the obligations which should be imposed to ensure the safeguarding of landscapes and sites, even unscheduled ones, situated on the territory affected.

 15. Urban and rural planning schemes should be drawn up in order of urgency, specifically for towns or regions in process of rapid development, where the protection of the aesthetic or picturesque character of the town

or region justifies the establishment of such schemes.

SCHEDULING OF EXTENSIVE LANDSCAPES "BY ZONES"

16. Extensive landscapes should be scheduled "by zones".

17. When, in a scheduled zone, the aesthetic character is of prime importance, scheduling "by zones" should involve control of plots and observation of certain general requirements of an aesthetic order covering the use of materials, and their colour, height standards, precautions to be taken to conceal disturbances of the soil resulting from the construction of dams and the operation of quarries, and regulations governing the cutting down of trees, etc.

18. Scheduling "by zones" should be publicized, and general rules to be observed for the safeguarding of scheduled landscapes should be enacted and made public.

19. Scheduling "by zones" should not, as a rule, involve payment of compensation.

SCHEDULING OF ISOLATED SITES

20. Isolated small sites, whether natural or urban, together with portions of a landscape of particular interest, should be scheduled. Areas which provide a fine view, and areas and buildings surrounding an outstanding monument should also be scheduled. Each of these scheduled sites, areas and buildings should be the subject of a special administrative decision of which the owner should be duly notified.

21. Scheduling should mean that the owner is prohibited from destroying the site, or altering its condition or aspect, without permission from the authorities responsible for its protection.

22. When such permission is granted, it should be accompanied by all the conditions necessary to the safeguarding of the site. No permission should be needed, however, for normal agricultural activities, nor for normal maintenance work on buildings.

23. Expropriation by the authorities, together with the carrying out of public works in a scheduled site, should be subject to the agreement of the authorities responsible for its protection. No-one should be able to acquire, by prescription, within a scheduled site, rights likely to change the character or aspect of the site. No conventionary rights should be granted by the owner without the agreement of the responsible authorities.

24. Scheduling should involve a prohibition on the pollution of the ground, air or water in any way whatsoever, while the extraction of minerals should like-wise be subject to special permission.

25. All advertising should be forbidden in a scheduled area and its immediate surroundings, or be limited to special emplacements to be decided by the authorities responsible for the protection of the site.

26. Permission to camp in a scheduled site should, in principle, be refused, or granted only within an area fixed by the responsible authorities and subject to their inspection.

27. Scheduling of a site may entitle the owner to compensation in cases of direct and definite prejudice resulting therefrom.

NATURAL RESERVES AND NATIONAL PARKS

28. When conditions are suitable, Member States should incorporate in the zones and sites to be protected, national parks intended for the education and recreation of the public, or natural reserves, strict or special. Such natural reserves and national parks should form a group of experimental zones intended also for research into the formation and restoration of the landscape and the protection of nature.

ACQUISITION OF SITES BY COMMUNITIES

29. Member States should encourage the acquisition by communities of areas forming part of a landscape or site which it is desired to protect. When necessary, it should be possible to effect such acquisition by expropriation.

IV. APPLICATION OF PROTECTIVE MEASURES

30. The fundamental norms and principles governing the protection of landscapes and sites in each Member State should have the force of law, and the measures for their application should be entrusted to the responsible authorities within the framework of the powers conferred on then by law.

31. Member States should set up specialized bodies of an administrative or advisory nature.

32. The administrative bodies should be specialized central or regional departments entrusted with carrying out protective measures. Accordingly, those departments should be in a position to study problems of protection and scheduling, to undertake surveys on the spot, to prepare decisions to be taken and to supervise their implementation. They should likewise be entrusted with proposing measures designed to reduce the dangers which may be involved in carrying out certain types of work or repairing damage caused by such work.

33. The advisory bodies should consist of commissions at national, regional or local level, entrusted with the task of studying questions relating to protection and giving their opinion on those questions to the central or regional authorities or to the local communities concerned. The opinion of these commissions should be sought in all cases and in good time, particularly at the stage of preliminary planning, in the case of large-scale works of public interest, such as the building of highways, the setting up of hydro-technical or new industrial installations, etc.

34. Member States should facilitate the formation and operation of national and local non-governmental bodies, one of whose functions would be to collaborate with the bodies mentioned in paragraphs 31, 32 and 33, particularly by informing the public and warning the appropriate departments of dangers threatening landscapes and sites.

35. Violation of the rules governing the protection of landscapes and sites should involve payment of damages or the obligation to restore the site to its former condition, as far as possible.

36. Administrative or criminal prosecutions should be provided for in the case of deliberate damage to protected landscapes and sites.

V. EDUCATION OF THE PUBLIC

37. Educational action should be taken in school and out of school with a view to arousing and developing public respect for landscapes and sites and publicizing the regulations laid down to ensure their protection.

38. Teachers to be entrusted with this task in schools should undergo special training in the form of specialized courses in institutions of secondary and higher education.

39. Member States should also facilitate the work of existing museums, with a view to intensifying the educational action they have already undertaken to this end, and should consider the possibility of establishing special museums, or specialized departments in existing museums, for the study and display of the natural and cultural features of particular regions.

40. The education of the public outside schools should be the task of the press, of private associations for the protection of landscapes and sites or for the protection of nature, of bodies concerned with the tourist trade and of youth or popular education organizations.

41. Member States should facilitate the education of the public and promote the work of associations, bodies

and organizations devoted to this task by the supply of material assistance and by making available to them and to educationists in general appropriate publicity media such as films, radio and television programmes, material for permanent, temporary or mobile exhibitions, pamphlets and books suitable for wide distribution and planned on educational lines. Wide publicity could be provided through journals and magazines and regional periodicals.

42. National and international "days", competitions and similar occasions should be devoted to encouraging the appreciation of natural or man-made landscapes and sites in order to direct public attention to the fact that the protection of their beauty and character is of prime importance to the community.

佛罗伦萨宪章[1]

（国际古迹遗址理事会于 1982 年 12 月 15 日登记）

国际古迹遗址理事会与国际风景园林师联合会的国际历史园林委员会于 1981 年 5 月 21 日在佛罗伦萨召开会议[2]，决定起草一份以该城市命名的历史园林保护宪章。本宪章即由该委员会起草，并由国际古迹遗址理事会于 1982 年 12 月 15 日登记作为涉及有关具体领域的《威尼斯宪章》的附件。

定义与目标

第一条 "历史园林指从历史或艺术角度而言民众所感兴趣的建筑和园艺构造。"鉴此，它应被看做是一古迹。

第二条 "历史园林是一主要由植物组成的建筑构造，因此它是具有生命力的，即指有死有生。"因此，其面貌反映着季节循环、自然生死与园林艺人，希望将其保持永恒不变的愿望之间的永久平衡。

第三条 作为古迹，历史园林必须根据威尼斯宪章的精神予以保存。然而，既然它是一个活的古迹，其保存必须根据特定的规则进行，此乃本宪章之议题。

第四条 历史园林的建筑构造包括：

a. 其平面和地形；

b. 其植物，包括品种、面积、配色、间隔以及各自高度；

c. 其结构和装饰特征；

d. 其映照天空的水面，死水或活水。

第五条 这种园林作为文明与自然直接关系的表现，作为适合于思考和休息的娱乐场所，因而具有理想世界的巨大意义，用词源学的术语来表达就是"天堂"，并且也是一种文化、一种风格、一个时代的见证，而且常常还是具有创造力的艺术家的独创性的见证。

第六条 "历史园林"这一术语同样适用于不论是正规的，还是风景的小园林和大公园。

第七条 历史园林不论是否与某一建筑物相联系——在此情况下它是其不可分割的一部分——它不能隔绝于其本身的特定环境，不论是城市的还是农村的，亦不论是自然的还是人工的。

第八条 一历史遗址是与一值得纪念的历史事件相联系的特定风景区，例如：一主要历史事件、一著名神话、一场具有历史意义的战斗或一幅名画的背景。

第九条 历史园林的保存取决于对其鉴别和编目情况。对它们需要采取几种行动，即维护、保护和修复。

维护、保护、修复、重建

第十条 在对历史园林或其中任何一部分的维护、保护、修复和重建工作中，必须同时处理其所有

---

[1] 引自：联合国教科文组织世界遗产中心，国际古迹遗址理事会，国际文物保护与修复研究中心，中国国家文物局主编. 国际文化遗产保护文件选编[M]. 北京：文物出版社，2007。

[2] 编者根据英文原文对此句的译文进行了修改。

的构成特征。把各种处理孤立开来将会损坏其整体性。

维护与保护

第十一条 对历史园林不断进行维护至为重要。既然主要物质是植物，在没有变化的情况下，保存园林既要求根据需要予以及时更换，也要求有一个长远的定期更换计划（彻底地砍伐并重播成熟品种）。

第十二条 定期更换的树木、灌木、植物和花草的种类必须根据各个植物和园艺地区所确定和确认的实践经验加以选择，目的在于确定那些已长成雏形的品种并将它们保存下来。

第十三条 构成历史园林整体组成部分的永久性的或可移动的建筑、雕塑或装饰特征，只有在其保护或修复之必要范围内方可予以移动或替代。任何具有这种危险性质的替代和修复必须根据威尼斯宪章的原则予以实施，并且必须说明任何全部替代的日期。

第十四条 历史园林必须保存在适当的环境之中，任何危及生态平衡的自然环境变化必须加以禁止。所有这些适用于基础设施的任何方面（排水系统、灌溉系统、道路、停车场、栅栏、看守设施以及游客舒畅的环境等）。

修复与重建

第十五条 在未经彻底研究，以确保此项工作能科学地实施，并对该园林以及类似园林进行相关的发掘和资料收集等所有一切事宜之前，不得对某一历史园林进行修复，特别是不得进行重建。在任何实际工作开展之前，任何项目必须根据上述研究进行准备，并须将其提交一专家组予以联合审查和批准。

第十六条 修复必须尊重有关园林发展演变的各个相继阶段。原则上说，对任何时期均不应厚此薄彼，除非在例外情况下，由于损坏或破坏的程度影响到园林的某些部分，以致决定根据尚存的遗迹或根据确凿的文献证据对其进行重建。为了在设计中体现其重要意义，这种重建工作尤其可在园林内最靠近该建筑物的某些部分进行。

第十七条 在一园林彻底消失或至多只存在其相继阶段的推测证据的情况下，重建物不能被认为是一历史园林。

利　用

第十八条 虽然任何历史园林都是为观光或散步而设计的，但是其接待量必须限制在其容量所能承受的范围，以便其自然构造物和文化信息得以保存。

第十九条 由于历史园林的性质和目的，历史园林是一个有助于人类的交往、宁静和了解自然的安宁之地。它的日常利用概念必须与它在节日时偶尔所起的作用形成反差。因此，为了能使任何这种节日本身用来提高该园林的视觉影响，而不是对其进行滥用或损坏。这种偶尔利用一历史园林的情况必须予以明确规定。

第二十条 虽然历史园林适合于一些娴静的日常游戏，但也应毗连历史园林划出适合于生动活泼的游戏和运动的单独地区，以便可以满足民众在这方面的需要，不损害园林和风景的保护。

第二十一条 根据季节而确定时间的维护和保护工作，以及为了恢复该园林真实性的主要工作应优先于民众利用的需要。对参观历史园林的所有安排必须加以规定，以确保该地区的精神能得以保存。

第二十二条 如果一历史园林修有围墙，在对可能导致其气氛变化和影响其保存的各种可能后果进行检查之前，其围墙不得予以拆除。

法律和行政保护

第二十三条 根据具有资格的专家的建议，采取适当的法律和行政措施对历史园林进行鉴别、编目和保护是有关负责当局的任务。这类园林的保护必须规定在土地利用计划的基本框架之中，并且这类规定必须在有关地区性的或当地规划的文件中正式指出。根据具有资格的专家的建议，采取有助于维护、保护和修复以及在必要情况下重建历史园林的财政措施，亦是有关负责当局的任务。

第二十四条 历史园林是遗产特征之一，鉴于其性质，它的生存需要受过培训的专家长期不断的精心护理。因此，应该为这种人才，不论是历史学家、建筑学家、环境美化专家、园艺学家还是植物学家提供适当的培训课程。还应注意确保维护或恢复所需之各种植物的定期培植。

第二十五条 应通过各种活动激发对历史园林的兴趣。这种活动能够强调历史园林作为遗产一部分的真正价值，并且能够有助于提高对它们的了解和欣赏，即促进科学研究、信息资料的国际交流和传播、出版（包括为一般民众设计的作品）、鼓励民众在适当控制下接近园林以及利用宣传媒介树立对自然和历史遗产需要给予应有的尊重之意识。应建议将最杰出的历史园林列入世界遗产清单。

注 释

以上建议适用于世界上所有历史园林。

适用于特定类型的园林的附加条款可以附于本宪章之后，并对所述类型加以简要描述。

Historic Gardens (The Florence Charter)

Adopted by ICOMOS on 15 December 1982

PREAMBLE

The ICOMOS-IFLA International Committee for Historic Gardens, meeting in Florence on 21 May 1981, decided to draw up a charter on the preservation of historic gardens which would bear the name of that town. The present Florence Charter was drafted by the Committee and registered by ICOMOS on 15 December 1982 as an addendum to the Venice Charter covering the specific field concerned.

DEFINITIONS AND OBJECTIVES

Article 1.

"A historic garden is an architectural and horticultural composition of interest to the public from the historical or artistic point of view". As such, it is to be considered as a monument.

Article 2.

"The historic garden is an architectural composition whose constituents are primarily vegetal and therefore living, which means that they are perishable and renewable". Thus its appearance reflects the perpetual balance between the cycle of the seasons, the growth and decay of nature and the desire of the artist and craftsman to keep it permanently unchanged.

Article 3.

As a monument, the historic garden must be preserved in accordance with the spirit of the Venice Charter. However, since it is a living monument, its preservation must be governed by specific rules which are the subject of the Present charter.

Article 4.

The architectural composition of the historic garden includes:
- Its plan and its topography.
- Its vegetation, including its species, proportions, colour schemes, spacing and respective heights.
- Its structural and decorative features.
- Its water, running or still, reflecting the sky.

Article 5.

As the expression of the direct affinity between civilisation and nature, and as a place of enjoyment suited to meditation or repose, the garden thus acquires the cosmic significance of an idealised image of the world, a "paradise" in the etymological sense of the term, and yet a testimony to a culture, a style, an age, and often to the originality of a creative artist.

Article 6.

The term "historic garden" is equally applicable to small gardens and to large parks, whether formal or "landscape".

Article 7.

Whether or not it is associated with a building in which case it is an inseparable complement, the historic garden cannot be isolated from its own particular environment, whether urban or rural, artificial or natural.

Article 8.

A historic site is a specific landscape associated with a memorable act, as, for example, a major historic event; a well-known myth; an epic combat; or the subject of a famous picture.

Article 9.

The preservation of historic gardens depends on their identification and listing. They require several kinds of action, namely maintenance, conservation and restoration. In certain cases, reconstruction may be recommended. The authenticity of a historic garden depends as much on the design and scale of its various parts as on its decorative features and on the choice of plant or inorganic materials adopted for each of its parts.

MAINTENANCE, CONSERVATION, RESTORATION, RECONSTRUCTION

Article 10.

In any work of maintenance, conservation, restoration or reconstruction of a historic garden, or of any part of it, all its constituent features must be dealt with simultaneously. To isolate the various operations would damage the unity of the whole.

MAINTENANCE AND CONSERVATION

Article 11.

Continuous maintenance of historic gardens is of paramount importance. Since the principal material is vegetal, the preservation of the garden in an unchanged condition requires both prompt replacements when required and a long-term programme of periodic renewal (clear felling and replanting with mature specimens).

Article 12.

Those species of trees, shrubs, plants and flowers to be replaced periodically must be selected with regard for established and recognised practice in each botanical and horticultural region, and with the aim to determine the species initially grown and to preserve them.

Article 13.

The permanent or movable architectural, sculptural or decorative features which form an integral part of the historic garden must be removed or displaced only insofar as this is essential for their conservation or restoration. The replacement or restoration of any such jeopardised features must be effected in accordance with the principles of the Venice Charter, and the date of any complete replacement must be indicated.

Article 14.

The historic garden must be preserved in appropriate surroundings. Any alteration to the physical environment which will endanger the ecological equilibrium must be prohibited. These applications are applicable to all aspects of the infrastructure, whether internal or external (drainage works, irrigation systems, roads, car parks, fences, caretaking facilities, visitors' amenities, etc.).

RESTORATION AND RECONSTRUCTION

Article 15.

No restoration work and, above all, no reconstruction work on a historic garden shall be undertaken without thorough prior research to ensure that such work is scientifically executed and which will involve everything from excavation to the assembling of records relating to the garden in question and to similar gardens. Before any practical work starts, a project must be prepared on the basis of said research and must be submitted to a group of experts for joint examination and approval.

Article 16.

Restoration work must respect the successive stages of evolution of the garden concerned. In principle, no one period should be given precedence over any other, except in exceptional cases where the degree of damage or destruction affecting certain parts of a garden may be such that it is decided to reconstruct it on the basis of the traces that survive or of unimpeachable documentary evidence. Such reconstruction work might be undertaken more particularly on the parts of the garden nearest to the building it contains in order to bring out their significance in the design.

Article 17.

Where a garden has completely disappeared or there exists no more than conjectural evidence of its successive stages a reconstruction could not be considered a historic garden.

USE

Article 18.

While any historic garden is designed to be seen and walked about in, access to it must be restricted to the extent demanded by its size and vulnerability, so that its physical fabric and cultural message may be preserved.

Article 19.

By reason of its nature and purpose, a historic garden is a peaceful place conducive to human contacts, silence and awareness of nature. This conception of its everyday use must contrast with its role on those rare occasions when it accommodates a festivity. Thus, the conditions of such occasional use of a historic garden should be clearly defined, in order that any such festivity may itself serve to enhance the visual effect of the garden instead of perverting or damaging it.

Article 20.

While historic gardens may be suitable for quiet games as a daily occurrence, separate areas appropriate for active and lively games and sports should also be laid out adjacent to the historic garden, so that the needs of the public may be satisfied in this respect without prejudice to the conservation of the gardens and landscapes.

Article 21.

The work of maintenance and conservation, the timing of which is determined by season and brief operations which serve to restore the garden's authenticity, must always take precedence over the requirements of public use. All arrangements for visits to historic gardens must be subjected to regulations that ensure the spirit of the place is preserved.

Article 22.

If a garden is walled, its walls may not be removed without prior examination of all the possible consequences liable to lead to changes in its atmosphere and to affect its preservation.

LEGAL AND ADMINISTRATIVE PROTECTION

Article 23.

It is the task of the responsible authorities to adopt, on the advice of qualified experts, the appropriate legal and administrative measures for the identification, listing and protection of historic gardens. The preservation of such gardens must be provided for within the framework of land-use plans and such provision must be duly mentioned in documents relating to regional and local planning. It is also the task of the responsible authorities to adopt, with the advice of qualified experts, the financial measures which will facilitate the maintenance, conservation and restoration, and, where necessary, the reconstruction of historic gardens.

Article 24.

The historic garden is one of the features of the patrimony whose survival, by reason of its nature, requires intensive, continuous care by trained experts. Suitable provision should therefore be made for the training of such persons, whether historians, architects, landscape architects, gardeners or botanists. Care should also be taken to ensure that there is regular propagation of the plant varieties necessary for maintenance or restoration.

Article 25.

Interest in historic gardens should be stimulated by every kind of activity capable of emphasizing their true value as part of the patrimony and making for improved knowledge and appreciation of them: promotion of scientific research; international exchange and circulation of information; publications, including works designed for the general public; the encouragement of public access under suitable control and use of the media to develop awareness of the need for due respect for nature and the historic heritage. The most outstanding of the historic gardens shall be proposed for inclusion in the World Heritage List.

Nota Bene

The above recommendations are applicable to all the historic gardens in the world.

Additional clauses applicable to specific types of gardens may be subsequently appended to the present Charter with brief descriptions of the said types.

ICOMOS-IFLA 历史城市公园文件[①]

(国际古迹遗址理事会第十九届大会 2017 年 12 月 15 日在印度新德里通过)

前 言

历史城市公园是许多城镇和住区的传统和规划中不可分割的重要组成部分。本文件的主要目的是强调它们应作为历史遗址得到保护,以供今世和后代使用和享有。

为了所有人的福祉,历史城市公园得以创建或开放。长期以来,它们一直被视为"保留地",即"填充"了或用于特定群体的活动,而这些公园起初并不是为这些活动设计的。许多历史城市公园经历了有损于其历史特质、设计、植被、特质和用途的变化。19 世纪和 20 世纪初,人们认识到将公园纳入城市规划体系的重要性,所以许多公园都是从那个时代开始建造的,但是一些城市公园可能更古老或者更年轻。

漫步道、林荫大道、林荫路、林荫街、运河等概念的定义,必要时可由各自国家的主管部门和公园管理部门添加作为文件的脚注。

历史城市公园——定义

1. "公园"的概念是基于所有人都可以参观和享受的开放性和可达性原则。这个概念不受公园大小的限制或规定。

2. 公园通常是公有的,代表着"共同的财产"。它们可能由一个或多个公共机构或公共基金会所有,这些机构或基金会负责对它们的监督、专业的管护以及管理。

3. "公园"的概念有时与花园、广场或类似的表达同义(相反地,"公园"一词在某些语言中可以表示"场地")。历史城市公园的基本特征是基于植被、建筑、水体、道路和地形等要素构成。这些要素形成公园的特点、季节性的趣味、明暗以及空间和视觉特性。

注意,有些公园和广场,公众没有进入的权利,但是,它们确实有助于城市的生态、舒适和历史形态;这些仍然可以被视为历史城市公园,尽管不是公共空间。

4. 历史漫步道、林荫大道、林荫路和林荫街不是公园,而是一种特殊类型的公共空间。充分保持它们独有的特征十分重要。

5. 在许多情况下,历史城市公园可能位于林荫大道或林荫街旁,或者由林荫大道或林荫街连接起来(参见上一段)。它们形成了绿色干道,可以连接公园和其他公共空间。它们及其组成部分必须加以保护,即使某些部分可能是在不同的时期创建的。

[①] 译者:曹新。

历史城市公园——价值

6. 历史城市公园通常积累了一系列价值,包括当地或更大范围的社区的社会价值和无形价值;其设计的或特质的美学价值;园艺和生态价值;以及作为公众抗议或大型集会(如庆祝活动等)的场所的公民价值,等等。由于历史城市公园对于社区的价值,应该阐释、颂扬和保护这些价值、意义和功能,这些常常是为什么公园对于人们一直重要的核心。

历史城市公园的决定特征的要素

空间,风景,种植和透景线

7. 历史城市公园可包括一个或多个限定的空间。必须了解这些空间的大小、关系和比例,无论是大的还是小的,狭窄的、开放的还是封闭的,以及了解它们的组成部分,应认识它们的初始目的和意义,并给予恰当的保护或保存。

8. 历史城市公园中还包含风景、焦点和视点,这些是其设计不可或缺的组成部分,形成其特性并有助于对它的欣赏。

9. 历史城市公园是有明确边界的地方,但它们的视觉尺度往往超出了它们的边界。它们具有的远处全景、视线、透景线和风景是决定其遗产特征的要素中不可或缺的重要部分。透景线和风景甚至可能是公园最初形成的原因,也是它们被数代人参观和欣赏的原因。历史城市公园的风景通常是历史街道的重要组成部分,也是城市或城镇更广泛特征的重要组成部分。

10. 历史透景线、风景和视点应加以保护;新植被的种植,以及公园外要素的设置或重新选址,如建筑、艺术作品、水景或纪念活动,不得干扰它们。基础设施(如公共汽车候车亭、方向标识、接线柱和接线盒)以及其他城市设施(如广告牌),这些设施将阻碍或减损决定遗产特征的透景线或历史特征,不得在核心风景内建造。说明牌应该位于游客可见的地方,但不要干扰公园的重要风景或影响其他体验的品质。公园及其作为缓冲区的周边区域,不得设有自动售货机、变压器和其他会损害其环境的构筑物。

11. 历史城市公园的植被必须能被周围区域的人们自由地看到。因此,朝向公园的视野不得被广告牌、大型交通标识、立体停车场或其他基础设施等因素阻挡或削弱。公园还包含对其特征具有重要意义的植被,例如有的会给公园一种强烈的围合感。一个历史城市公园在周围的建成环境中形成了一个实体的和视觉上的缓冲,对于路人来说,看到和享受植物的动态、色彩、声音和树荫是很重要的。积极的更新和再植方案在历史城市公园的管理中发挥重要的作用。

12. 在某些情况下,历史城市公园是与邻近的城市空间、街道、运河或建筑相关而构思出来的。在某些情况下,历史城市公园的引入改变了在其周边发展的街区、空间和建筑的品质。因此,它们往往是历史城镇规划方案的内在组成部分。

在这些情况下,保护公园及其环境,在品质、设计和尺度方面都同等重要。相邻建筑高度或体量的变化会对空间关系、风景和透景线、小气候(阳光/阴影/风)以及主要的历史设计的真实特质产生不利影响,必须避免这些变化。相邻建筑物的高度增加会加大阴影或下灌风,对公园及其植被的健康和状况以及使用者的体验产生积极或消极的影响。

13. 同样,边缘条件要素,如街道宽度、铺装材料、行道树、照明和其他决定遗产特征的要素,也必须仔细考虑和保护。在与历史城市公园毗邻处选择使用的新元素和新材料时需要谨慎,以确保这些成为历史公园的特征的补充。

地形

14. 历史地貌、地形和坡度(如土丘和洼地)以及历史特征(如台地和假山)通常是历史城市公园的整体布局中不可分割的一部分，也是其特征的决定性要素。即使是其微小的改变也会对整体设计、韵律以及空间、风景和透景线之间的关系有损，应该避免。大型地下构造不应建在历史城市公园内。应尽可能避免或尽量减少基础设施升级（排水、电力或其他市政管道）引起的较大破坏。应进行研究并尽可能实施，将这些设施设置于历史城市公园范围之外。

灯光

15. 自然光线、阳光和荫凉是人们在公园和花园中寻求放松和慰藉的其中一些原因。对于许多城市居民而言，历史公园通常是在密集建造的城市中心享受这些自然品质的唯一机会。

如果要增加夜间照明，以便在天黑后公众能够愉快和安全地使用公园，灯柱和固定装置必须经过选择和择址，以增强公园的特征、空间关系、风景、透景线、视线和其他决定公园历史特征的要素，而不是减损它们。因此，应该使用经过协调性设计的灯柱和固定装置，而不是标准的路灯柱和固定装置。在一些区域，公园的夜景照明不应该扩展到夜空中。

环境

16. 历史城市公园对于城市生物多样性非常重要，可以支持一系列的生境和物种，并为城市居民提供直接接触自然的途径。公园的动植物群落应该得到认识和保护。在可能的情况下，只要与公园的特征相协调，就应该改善环境和生境，以增强相互联系的生态廊道。

许多历史城市公园都包含有源自世界其他地方的水景和植物。需要以可持续的方式管理水和能源的使用以保持这些特征。

历史研究、保护和管理

总论

17. 历史城市公园及其组成部分的管理必须基于仔细的研究、原始文件（如照片）以及对其现状和未来用途的评估。这些研究必须由合格或有适当经验的专家进行。同样重要的是研究历史公园及其环境的规划和发展的演变，以及它们对当地社区的重要性。建立并积极维护相关历史文件的档案也很重要，这些档案可作为其持续维护、管理和管护的基础。

所有这些工作都必须记录在案，记录必须存放和保管在可查阅的公共档案中，以有助于参考和理解，并确保造福后代。这种记录可以而且应该为未来的保护和管理决策以及行动提供信息。

18. 过度利用历史城市公园会对公园的享用和公园历史特征、品质及组成部分的保持产生负面影响。过度利用也会给植被带来压力。因此，必须建立适当的管理程序，根据每个公园及其中历史建筑的承载力来控制游客数量；这些应该定期计算和监控。限制游览人数和限制进入时间（或每小时的游人数量等）等选项应进行调查、测试和监控。为了减少历史公园的过度利用，市政当局应为其居民创建和维护精心设计的新公园。公园的规划应基于确定的承载力，以便在不对其造成不当损害的情况下使用。对承载力的定期检查和对损坏或其他影响的监控应为此类规划和管理决策提供信息。

19. 原有的和后来的协调性元素和设施，如栅栏、大门、灯柱、栏杆、铺装、垃圾箱、座椅、艺术作品和植被，在被损坏后或在其生命周期结束时，应进行保护和维修或实物替换。应定期重新评估非原有的、后期的和协调性元素的重要性，并为规划和管理决策提供信息。

20. 历史城市公园的一般保护原则与其他历史公园和花园的原则相同，如《ICOMOS-IFLA 佛罗伦萨历史园林宪章》（1981 年）中第 10 条所述。

通用的无障碍设计的适应性

21. 因为历史城市公园是公有的文化资源，所有人都应该可以使用，所以它们的一些组成部分或一些区域可能需要进行改造，以确保它们可以普遍使用，而不会对其遗产价值产生不利影响。推荐的方式应该是整合而不是隔离残障人士的需求。因此，设计专业人员应该使用综合的方法为所有使用者设计解决方案，而不是为那些残障人士创建单独的设施。任何新的无障碍设计的介入都应该易被感知而又不显眼地融入历史城市公园，而不损害它们的价值、特征的决定性要素和体验的品质。在进行任何改变或干预之前应积极研究，选择最小的改变，即，使新材料或标识的引入最小化。

普遍的应用

上述原则和建议适用于世界任何地方的所有历史城市公园。然而，在一些国家，如果这种改变或干预会对公园的历史完整性产生不利影响，可以免除法定要求。

ICOMOS-IFLA Document on Historic Urban Public Parks

Adopted by the 19th ICOMOS General Assembly, New Delhi, India, 15 December 2017

PREAMBLE

Historic urban public parks are an essential and inalienable part of the traditions and plans of many towns and settlements. It is the main purpose of this document to emphasize that they be preserved as historic sites for the use and enjoyment of present and future generations.

Historic urban public parks were created or made accessible for the well-being of all persons. They have for too long been regarded as 'reserve grounds', i.e. commodities to be 'filled' or used for events and activities of specific groups for which they were not designed. Many have undergone changes detrimental to their historic qualities, design, vegetation, character, and uses. The importance of integrating public parks in town planning schemes was acknowledged in the 19th and the early 20th centuries, so many of them date from that era, but some urban parks may be older or younger.

Definitions for concepts such as promenade, boulevard, avenue, tree-lined street, canal, etc. can be added as footnotes to the document by authorities and park management in their respective countries as necessary.

HISTORIC URBAN PUBLIC PARKS-DEFINITIONS

1. The concept 'public park' rests on the principle of openness and accessibility for all people to visit and enjoy. The concept is not limited or defined by size.

2. Public parks are typically in public ownership and represent 'common wealth'. They may be owned by one or more public bodies or public foundations that are responsible for their oversight, knowledgeable care, and stewardship.

3. The concept of 'park' is sometimes used synonymously with words such as garden, square, or similar expressions. (Conversely, the word 'park' can denote 'grounds' in some languages.) Fundamental to the identity of historic urban parks is their composition and dependency on such elements as vegetation, architectural elements, water features, paths, or topography. These elements contribute to their character, seasonal interest, shade, and spatial and visual identity.

Nota bene. There are parks and squares to which the general public do not have any rights of access, however, they do contribute to the ecology, amenity, and historic form of cities; these can be considered historic urban parks, though not public spaces.

4. Historic promenades, boulevards, avenues, and tree-lined streets are not public parks, but constitute a special category of public space. It is important that adequate care be taken to preserve their particular characteristics.

5. In many cases, historic urban public parks may be located along, or linked by, boulevards or tree-lined streets (see the previous passage). They form green arteries that can connect public parks with other public spaces. They and their component parts must be preserved, regardless of the fact that some parts may have been created at different times.

HISTORIC URBAN PUBLIC PARKS - VALUES

6. Historic urban public parks often accrue a range of values, including social and intangible values to local or wider communities; aesthetic values for their design or character; horticultural and ecological values; and civic value as places where public protests or major gatherings, such as celebrations, etc., have occurred. Due to their value to communities, these values, meanings, and functions should be explained, celebrated, and safeguarded. They often form the core of why public parks continue to matter to people.

SPECIAL CHARACTER-DEFINING ELEMENTS OF HISTORIC URBAN PUBLIC PARKS

Spaces, Views, Planting, and Vistas

7. An historic urban public park may include one or more defined spaces. The sizes, relationships, and proportions of these spaces, whether wide or small, narrow, open, or closed, and their component parts, must be understood, their original purposes and meanings recognized, and appropriately protected or conserved.

8. There may also be views, focal points, and viewpoints within historic urban public parks that are integral to their design and contribute to their identity and appreciation.

9. Historic urban public parks are places with defined perimeters, yet their visual dimensions often extend beyond their limits. The distant panoramas, sight-lines, vistas and views provided by them are typically part of their integral, heritage-character-defining elements. The vistas and views may even be the reason why the parks came into being in the first place, and why they have been visited and appreciated by generations. Views of historic urban public parks are often important parts of historic streets and the wider identity of the city or town.

10. Historic vistas, views, and viewpoints are to be preserved; the planting of new vegetation, as well as siting or re-siting of elements outside parks, such as built forms, art works, water features, or commemorations, must not interfere with them. Infrastructure, such as bus shelters, directional signs, utility posts and boxes, and other urban installations, such as billboards, that would obstruct or detract from heritage-character-defining vistas or historic character, must not be erected within key views. Interpretive signs should be located where they are visible to visitors, but not intrude on important views or the other experiential qualities of the park. Parks and their immediate surroundings - that serve as their buffer zones - must be kept free from vending machines, transformers, and other such structures that would detract from their ambiance.

11. The vegetation of historic urban public parks must be freely seen by people from the surrounding areas. Thus, the views towards parks must not be blocked or diminished by elements such as billboards, large traffic

signs, parking structures, or other infrastructure. Also parks have vegetation that is important to their character, for example giving them a strong sense of enclosure. An historic urban public park constitutes a physical, as well as visual, respite within the surrounding built environment and it is important for passers-by to see and to enjoy the movement, colours, sounds, and shade of the vegetation. Active programmes of renewal and replanting play an important part in its stewardship.

12. In some circumstances, historic urban public parks were conceived in relation to adjacent urban spaces, streets, canals, or buildings. In others, their introduction influenced the quality of the neighbourhoods, spaces, and built form that developed around them. They are thus often intrinsic components of historic town planning schemes.

Under these circumstances, the preservation of parks and their settings, in matters of quality, design, and scale, is equally important. Changes in the height or massing of adjacent buildings can adversely impact spatial relationships, views and vistas, microclimate (sun/shade/wind), and the authentic character of the primary historic design; such changes must be avoided. Increasing height of adjoining buildings can increase shade or wind downdraft, actively and negatively impacting on the health and condition of parks and their vegetation, as well as the experience of their users.

13. Similarly edge condition elements, such as street width, paving materials, street tree planting, lighting, and other heritage-character-defining elements must also be carefully considered and conserved. Care is required in selecting new elements and materials to be used adjacent to historic urban public parks to ensure that these complement their character.

Topography

14. Historic landforms, topography, and grades, such as mounds and swales, as well as historic features, such as terraces and rockeries, are often an integral part of the lay-out and character-defining elements of an historic urban public park. Even minor changes in these can be detrimental to the overall design, rhythm, and the relationships of spaces, views and vistas with each other, and should be avoided. Large underground structures should not be built within historic urban public parks. Major disruption for infrastructure upgrades (drainage, electricity, or other service pipelines) should be avoided or minimized where possible. Options to locate these outside historic urban public parks should be investigated and followed wherever possible.

Light

15. Natural light, sunshine, and shade are some of the reasons people find relaxation and solace in parks and gardens. For many urban dwellers, historic public parks offer the only opportunity to enjoy these natural qualities in densely built city centres.

If night lighting is to be added to enable enjoyable and safe public use after dark, lamp posts and fixtures must be selected and located so that they enhance the character, spatial relationships, views, vistas, sight-lines, and other historic-character-defining elements of parks, rather than detract from them. Thus compatibly-designed posts and fixtures should be used, rather than standard street light posts and fixtures. In some areas, night lighting of parks should not spill into the night sky.

Environment

16. Historic urban parks are important for urban biodiversity and can support a range of habitats and species and provide urban populations with direct access to nature. The flora and fauna of the park should be understood and protected. Where possible, and where compatible with the character of the park, the environment and habitat should be improved to enhance interconnected ecological corridors.

Many historic urban parks contain water features and planting originating in other parts of the world. The use of water and energy to maintain these features needs to be managed in a sustainable manner.

HISTORIC STUDY, PRESERVATION, AND MANAGEMENT

General Remarks

17. The stewardship of historic urban public parks and their component parts must be based on careful research, original documents, such as photographs, and evaluation of their condition in relation to an inventory of the existing park conditions and future uses. These studies must be done by qualified or appropriately experienced experts. It is equally important to research the evolution of the planning and development of historic parks and their settings, as well as their importance for local communities. It is also important to establish and actively maintain archives of related historic documents that can be used as the basis for their on-going maintenance, management, and stewardship.

All such work must be documented, and the records must be deposited and protected in accessible public archives to assist reference and understanding, and ensure the benefit to future generations. Such records can and should inform future conservation and management decisions and actions.

18. The overuse of historic urban public parks can adversely impact both the enjoyment of them and the retention of their historic character, quality, and component parts. Overuse can also stress their vegetation. Therefore, appropriate management procedures must be established to control the number of visitors based on the carrying capacity of each park and the historic buildings in them; these should be calculated and monitored regularly. Options such as restricting access and limiting hours of entry (or numbers per hour, etc.) should be investigated, tested and monitored. In order to alleviate the overuse of historic parks, municipalities should create and maintain well-designed new parks for their inhabitants, and park programming should be based on a determined carrying capacity, so that use can be supported without undue damage to them. Regular checks on carrying capacity and monitoring of damage or other impacts should inform such planning and management decisions.

19. Original and later compatible elements and furnishings, such as fences, gates, lamp posts, railings, paving materials, rubbish bins, seating, art works, and vegetation should be protected and repaired or replaced-in-kind when damaged or at the end of their life-cycles. Re-assessment of the significance of non-original, later, and compatible elements should be undertaken at regular intervals and inform planning and management decisions.

20. The general principles for the conservation of historic urban public parks are the same as those for other historic parks and gardens, as cited in the ICOMOS-IFLA Florence Charter on Historic Gardens (1981), Article 1.

UNIVERSALLY ACCESSIBLE DESIGN ADAPTATIONS

21. Because historic urban public parks are publicly-owned cultural resources that should be accessible to all, some of their components or areas may require modification in order to ensure that they are universally accessible without adversely impacting their heritage values. The recommended approach should integrate, rather than segregate, those who are physically challenged. Thus, design professionals should use an integrated approach to design solutions for all users, rather than creating separate facilities for those who are physically challenged. Any new accessible design interventions should fit sensitively and unobtrusively into historic urban public parks

without compromising their values, character-defining elements, and experiential qualities. Options to do so with minimal change - i.e. the minimal introduction of new materials or signage, should be actively investigated before any changes or interventions are made.

UNIVERSAL APPLICATION

The above principles and recommendations apply to all historic urban public parks anywhere in the world. However, in some countries, exemptions may be granted from statutory requirements, if such changes or interventions would adversely impact the historic integrity of the park.

ICOMOS-IFLA 关于乡村景观遗产的准则[①]

（国际古迹遗址理事会第十九届大会 2017 年 12 月 15 日在印度新德里通过）

序 言

乡村景观是人类遗产的重要组成部分，也是延续性文化景观中最常见的类型之一。全世界的乡村景观丰富多样，它们也代表了多样的文化和文化传统。乡村景观为人类社会提供多种经济和社会效益、多样化的功能、文化支持和生态系统服务。本文件旨在从国际到地方管理各级，和涉及的各个层面，就乡村景观系统的伦理、文化、环境和可持续转化，鼓励深入思考并提供指导。

认识到以文化为基础的食物生产与对可再生自然资源的利用所具有的全球重要性，以及在当代文化、环境、经济、社会及法律背景下面临的问题和挑战；

考虑到《联合国世界人权宣言（1948）》、《联合国生物多样性公约（1992）》、《联合国教科文组织世界文化多样性宣言（2001）》《联合国原住民权利宣言（2007）》、《粮食和农业的植物遗传资源国际条约》（粮食和农业组织，2011 年），2015 年联合国可持续发展目标（尤其是但不限于子目标 11.4[②]）等国际公约均阐明，所有人类都有权享受充足、健康和来源安全的食物和水；

考虑到《关于古迹遗址保护和修复的威尼斯宪章（1964）》、《联合国教科文组织保护世界文化和自然遗产公约（1972）》、《国际古迹遗址理事会—国际风景园林师联合会关于历史园林的佛罗伦萨宪章（1981）》、《国际古迹遗址理事会关于历史城镇和城区保护的华盛顿宪章（1987）》、《国际古迹遗址理事会关于真实性的奈良文件（1994）》、《联合国教科文组织保护非物质文化遗产公约（2003）》、《国际古迹遗址理事会关于保护文物建筑、遗址和遗产区域的背景环境的西安宣言（2005）》、《联合国教科文组织关于历史城市景观的建议（2011）》《国际古迹遗址理事会关于作为人类价值的遗产与景观的佛罗伦萨宣言（2014）》、《联合国教科文组织关于生物和文化多样性关联的佛罗伦萨宣言（2014）》、联合国教科文组织将可持续发展观纳入世界遗产公约议程的政策（2015）等国际文件都与景观的遗产和文化价值相关；

考虑到区域及国家层面诸多文件都与乡村景观有关，如《欧洲景观公约（2000）》、《欧洲乡村遗产观察指南（CEMAT，2003）》、《欧洲委员会关于文化遗产的社会价值的法罗公约（2005）》、《关于神圣自然遗产地和文化景观在生物和文化多样性保护中的作用的东京宣言（2005）》、《关于加勒比文化景观的古巴圣地亚哥宣言（2005）》、《拉丁美洲景观行动（LALI）（2012）》、《国际古迹遗址理事会澳大利亚国家委员会关于保护具有文化意义的场所的宪章（巴拉宪章）（1999—2013）》、《国际风景园林师联合会亚太地区景观宪章（2015）》；

考虑到联合国教科文组织世界遗产中心颁布的《实施保护世界遗产公约的操作指南（2015）》，自

[①] 译者：丁梦月，胡玥，解立。中国古迹遗址保护协会ICOMOS CHINA提供。

[②] "strengthen the efforts for the protection and safeguarding of the world's natural heritage"（United Nations Agenda 2030）."强化对世界自然与文化遗产的保护和防护"（联合国议程 2030）。

1992年以来就将乡村景观认定为"延续性的文化景观";

考虑到将乡村景观作为遗产的《国际古迹遗址理事会—国际风景园林师联合会文化景观科学委员会（ISCCL）关于乡村景观的米兰宣言（2014）》；

考虑到世界自然保护联盟（IUCN）在其管理体系中对第五类受保护陆地景观和海洋景观的认可，IUCN对维持传统游牧所做的努力（关于可持续畜牧业的全球倡议，2008），以及国际古迹遗址理事会（ICOMOS）与世界自然保护联盟（IUCN）联合倡议"自然与文化联合实践"，认识到人们与周围环境进行互动的方式维系了生物—文化多样性（包括农业生物多样性以及文化和精神价值）；

考虑到联合国粮食及农业组织（FAO）《全球重要农业遗产（GIAHS）》项目旨在确认和保护卓越的具有遗产价值和丰富的全球重要农业生物多样性及知识体系的土地利用系统和景观；

考虑了其他与乡村景观相关的文件，如《关于农业遗产的巴伊萨宪章（2012）》、在匈牙利托卡伊通过的《关于葡萄园文化景观的世界遗产主题专家会议的建议（2001）》以及其他关于将乡村文化景观作为遗产的主题专家会议；

国际古迹遗址理事会和国际风景园林师联合会

承诺将扩大双方的合作，通过传播和使用下述准则，来提升将乡村景观遗产作为人类社会和文化的组成部分以及世界范围内重要资源的理解、有效保护、可持续转化、传播和欣赏。

本准则旨在通过对乡村景观遗产价值的认知、保护和推广，寻求方法应对乡村景观及其相关社区所面临的损失和负面改变。目的是推动实现经济、社会、文化及环境各方之间的适度平衡。

Ⅰ. 准则

A. 定义

乡村景观：就本文件而言，乡村景观指在人与自然之间的相互作用下形成的陆地及水生区域，通过农业、畜牧业、游牧业、渔业、水产业、林业、野生食物采集、狩猎和其他资源开采（如盐），生产食物和其他可再生自然资源。乡村景观是多功能资源。同时，生活在这些乡村地区的人和社区还赋予其文化意义：一切乡村地区皆是景观。

乡村景观是变化着的活态体系，包括使用传统方法、技术、累积的知识、文化习俗等生产并管理的地区，以及那些传统生产方式业已改变的地区。乡村景观系统包括乡村元素、其内部及与更广泛背景的功能、生产、空间、视觉、象征和环境的关系。

乡村景观包括管理良好的、已退化或废弃但仍可再利用或开垦还原的区域，如广阔的乡村空间、城市边缘以及建成区域内的小型空间等。乡村景观涵盖地面、亚表土及资源、土地上空以及水域。

乡村景观遗产：指的是乡村地区的物质及非物质遗产。乡村景观遗产的物理特征包括生产性土地本身、结构形态、水、基础设施、植被、聚落、乡村建筑和中心区、本土建筑、交通和贸易网络等，以及更广阔的物理、文化、与环境关系及背景。乡村景观遗产还包括相关的文化知识、传统、习俗、当地社区身份及归属感的表达、过去和现代族群和社区赋予景观的文化价值和含义。乡村景观遗产包含涉及人与自然关系的技术、科学及实践知识。

乡村景观遗产反映了社会结构及功能组织，及其在过去和现在的形成、使用和变革。乡村景观遗产包括文化、精神和自然属性，这些都对生物文化多样性的延续意义重大。

独特或普通，传统还是被现代活动改变，所有乡村地区都可以被当作遗产解读：遗产以不同的类型和层次存在，与多个历史时期相关，如同羊皮纸上的文字，可以被重叠书写。

B. 重要性

乡村景观历经数千年得以形成，代表了地球上人类和环境发展史、生活方式及遗产的重要部分。世界许多地区对当地社区、原住民和参观者都是重要的食物、可再生自然资源、相应的世界观与福祉的源泉。用于生产和/或收获包括可食用资源的动植物资源的乡村景观，反映出广阔区域内人类与其他物种间的复杂关系。农业、林业、畜牧业、渔业和水产业、野生动植物资源以及其他资源活动的多样性对全球人类生活未来的适应力和复原力至关重要。

已有遗产名录认识到了乡村景观的遗产价值，如联合国教科文组织（UNESCO）世界遗产名录中的"延续性文化景观"。区域、国家及地方层面的遗产清单及保护区机制可能已识别出乡村景观的遗产价值。对乡村景观价值在任何级别的认识，都旨在提供对乡村景观中存在的物质及非物质特征和价值的意识，这也是推动这些地区的可持续保护、将其相关知识和文化意义传承后世的第一步，和必要的一步。

C. 威胁

不断增加的人口数量和气候变化导致乡村景观非常脆弱，面临损失和/或遗弃或巨变的风险。乡村景观受到的威胁反映出三种互相关联的变化类型：

1. 人口和文化（城市地区人口增长而乡村地区人口减少，城市扩张，密集的基础设施建设，开发压力，传统习俗、技艺、当地知识及文化的丧失）；

2. 结构（全球化，贸易及贸易关系的改变和增长，经济增长或衰退，农业实践和技术的强化，土地功能转变、天然牧场和驯化物种多样性的丧失）；

3. 环境（气候变化，污染和环境退化，包括不可持续资源的开采、对土壤、植被和空气质量的影响，生物多样性及农业生物多样性的丧失）。

D. 挑战

因其代表的重大价值，遗产应该在认识、保护和促进乡村景观和生物文化多样性上都发挥重要作用。通过支持乡村和城市居民、地方社区、政府、工业和集体，作为地区动态属性、威胁、风险、优势和潜力综合管理的一部分，遗产可以助力维护和增强乡村景观的适应性和应变力。保护乡村遗产的完整性和真实性，应集中确保在乡村景观内工作和生活的当地居民的生活水平和质量。与所有其他遗产一样，乡村遗产也是一种经济资源：应对其加以适当利用，为当地长期可持续发展提供重要支撑。

E. 效益

乡村景观是未来人类社会和世界环境发展的关键资源：它们提供了食物、原材料以及身份认同感；它们代表了经济、空间、环境、社会、文化、精神、健康、科学、技术以及，在某些区域，休闲娱乐的要素。除了提供食物和原材料外，乡村景观还有助于土地保护（自然、环境、土壤、水文网络），有助于将乡村文化（技艺、环境知识、文化传统等）传递给下一代。与遗产价值的提升和传播充分结合，乡村景观往往能创造独特的经济和旅游收益。

在过去的几十年里，环境和文化遗产越来越成为国际、跨学科的和学科间研究的对象。作为知识所有者的当地社区或地方行动，利益相关方、乡村和城市居民与专家学者之间的合作，都有助于乡村景观作为珍贵的共享资源的保护、认知和价值提升。许多国际、国家和地方管理机构已通过立法和政策来支持这一概念。

F. 乡村景观的可持续性

许多乡村体系已在长时间中被证明具备可持续性和发展弹性。这些乡村体系的多个方面，可为未来乡村活动管理提供参考，为保护和提高生物文化多样性提供支持，并有助于保障人们获得充足、优质食物和原材料的权利。

由于景观会经历持续的、不可逆的以及不可避免的变化过程，在制定乡村景观政策时，应将重点放在对可接受和适当的变化的管理，以及对遗产价值的保护、尊重和提升。

Ⅱ. 行动标准

具体措施是：理解、保护、可持续管理、交流传播景观及其遗产价值。

A. 理解乡村景观及其遗产价值

1. 认识到所有的乡村景观都具有遗产价值，无论被评估为突出还是一般价值，这些遗产价值在规模和特征上呈现出多样性（形状、材质、用途和功能、历史时期、变化等）。

2. 记录乡村景观的遗产价值，以此作为有效规划、决策制定和管理的基础。清单、目录、地图集、地图为乡村景观的空间规划、环境和遗产的保护与管理、景观设计和监测提供基础信息。

3. 形成关于乡村景观物理及文化特征的基线知识：乡村景观的现状；其历史演变及物质和非物质遗产的表现；对景观历史的、内在的及当代社会文化中的感知；乡村景观体系内不同要素之间（天然和人造，物质和非物质）存在的历史与当代联系（空间、文化、社会、生产及功能上的）；以及过去和当今涉及的利益相关方。清查和编目既是为描述乡村景观的现状也是为明确其历史变迁。

4. 制定不同层面的乡村景观（世界的、区域的、国家的、地方的）的清单目录。这些工具应整合当地、传统的和科学的知识体系，利用已有的、系统化的、适合专业和非专业人士使用的方法，以在国际及地方层面收集、比较乡村景观的信息。为建立有效的数据库，清单目录应考虑复杂性、人力成本、数据收集和整理时间安排等因素，并鼓励专家学者和当地居民的共同参与。

5. 形成相关知识体系以比较不同层级（世界、区域、国家、地方）的乡村景观，监测历史变化，支持共享学习，促进从地方到国际的合作，以及公共和私人利益相关方之间的合作。

6. 认识到当地居民是信息持有者，在很多情况下能够帮助塑造并维护景观，因此应积极参与到集体知识的创建中来。

7. 就研究、信息共享、技术支持，在各管理层级合作开展大范围知识创建活动等方面，推动公共机构、非政府组织和大学间展开广泛而持续的合作。

B. 保护乡村景观及其遗产价值

1. 审查并实施相关立法和政策框架，确保在应对来自全球、国家及地方的威胁、风险和机遇，利用和转化乡村景观时，保持生物文化发展的可持续性和适应性。

2. 落实政策：通过法律、法规、经济战略、监管方法、信息共享和文化支持。由于乡村景观具有较大的复杂性特征，为此必须形成详细的、跨领域的政策，从更广泛的层面考虑文化、社会、经济、环境等因素。

3. 明确动态保护、修复、创新、适应性转化、维护和长期管理的策略和行动。应寻求全球与当地方法间的平衡，确保在有效设计和日常管理过程中所有利益相关方和社区的参与和合作。

4. 考虑到乡村景观的遗产价值包括经济、社会、环境、文化、精神及空间等不同纬度，对每一乡村景观的价值的良好认知，将有助于对遗产未来适当和有效的转变的更好的管理。

5. 制定有效的方针政策，应先获取景观相关的地方知识、了解其强项和弱项，以及潜在的威胁和机遇。制定目标，选择适当的工具，形成项目行动计划，明确长、中、短期管理目标。

6. 明确监测策略，审查政策实施的有效性，重新评估与监测结果相关的短、中和长期目标。

7. 考虑到有效实施既定方针政策，有赖于公众有足够的知识和意识，能够支持所需的战略方针，并积极参与进来。有必要与其他行动相互补充。公共管理机构应支持积极主动的和自下而上的行动。

C. 持续管理乡村景观及其遗产价值

1. 考虑到食物和自然资源生产的生态文化权利。应实施有规划的管理方法，认识到景观具有动态特征，是活着的遗产，并尊重生活在其中的人类和非人类物种。尊重、珍视并支持文化多样性以及不同族群不同的与自然相处的方式。

2. 确认乡村景观的关键利益相关方，包括乡村居民、与当地有紧密联系的当地社区、原住民和移民群体；他们在塑造和维护景观中发挥的作用，以及他们关于自然和环境状况的知识、历史和当下的重要事件、当地文化和传统、以及数世纪以来不断试验和实施的科学和技术方案。承认乡村居民高标准高质量的生活将有助于促进乡村活动的开展、维护乡村景观、将乡村实践和文化传递至下一代，源远流长。

3. 考虑在制定作为遗产资源的乡村景观可持续管理战略时，大小规模景观在文化、自然、经济和社会等不同方面之间的关联。

4. 考虑乡村景观和城市景观的相互联系。乡村景观是全球都市居民提升生活品质（休闲娱乐、食物的品质和数量、木柴、水和洁净的空气、园艺种植等）的重要资源。城市可以为乡村景观出产的产品提供经济机会，并根据城市居民的需求融入其他休闲、教育、农业旅游等多样功能。应鼓励乡村、城郊以及城市居民积极合作和实践，促进共享乡村景观遗产知识和分担管理职责。

5. 在长期可持续（经济，社会，文化，环境）资源使用与遗产保护、乡村工人短期内提升生活品质的需求之间寻求平衡。这是维持和促进乡村景观活动的前提条件。生活品质包括收入、社会认同、教育等公共服务的供给、文化权利的认可等。这需要找到适当的方法和方式，使得活态遗产价值可以被认可，社会变革与遗产价值的保护、利用和传播能够相融合，与乡村景观遗产的经济增效相一致。

6. 支持对乡村景观实施公平治理，鼓励当地民众、利益相关方、城市及农村居民积极参与到乡村景观遗产的管理和监测中来，参与知识生产和传播，肩负相关责任。这是因为许多乡村景观包含私人、企业和政府等多种所有权形式，为此形成合作式工作关系是有必要的。

D. 乡村景观遗产和价值的沟通及传递

1. 通过协同分享活动来传播对乡村景观遗产价值的认知，如共享学习、教育、能力建设、遗产阐释和研究活动等。制订参与计划和实践方案，将民间团体、私营组织、公共管理机构等纳入进来，吸引城市及乡村居民的参与。

2. 提升人们对相关方式方法的认识，促进传统知识、技艺和实践的传承，开展相关案例研究，并推广最佳实践。

3. 使用各种工具、方法和文化实践活动支持共享学习、培训和研究，如文化地图、信息共享、教育、现场培训等，吸引当地社区、遗产专家、来自不同学科、学校和大学的专家学者等利益相关方以及媒体的积极参与。

注：该文件由国际古迹遗址理事会—国际风景园林师联合会文化景观国际科学委员会推广（世界乡村景观行动 http://www.worldrurallandscapes.org/）

ICOMOS-IFLA Principles concerning Rural Landscapes as Heritage

Adopted by the 19th ICOMOS General Assembly, New Delhi, India, 15 December 2017

PREAMBLE

Rural landscapes are a vital component of the heritage of humanity. They are also one of the most common types of continuing cultural landscapes. There is a great diversity of rural landscapes around the world that represent cultures and cultural traditions. They provide multiple economic and social benefits, multi- functionality, cultural support and ecosystem services for human societies. This document encourages deep reflection and offers guidance on the ethics, culture, environmental, and sustainable transformation of rural landscape systems, at all scales, and from international to local administrative levels.

Acknowledging the global importance of culturally-based food production and use of renewable natural resources, and the issues and threats challenging such activities within contemporary cultural, environmental, economic, social, and legal contexts;

Considering The United Nations *Universal Declaration of Human Rights* (1948), the United Nations *Convention on Biological Diversity* (1992), the *UNESCO Universal Declaration on Cultural Diversity* (2001), the United Nations *Declaration on the Rights of Indigenous People* (2007), the International Treaty on Plant Genetic *Resources for Food and Agriculture* (Food and Agriculture Organisation, 2011), and the United Nations *2015 Sustainable Development Goals* (in particular but not limited to Sub-Goal 11.4[①]), which state that all human beings have the right to adequate, healthy, and secure sources of food and water;

Considering international documents such as the *Venice Charter for the Conservation and Restoration of Monuments and Sites* (1964), the UNESCO *Convention Concerning the Protection of the World Cultural and Natural Heritage* (1972); the ICOMOS-IFLA *Florence Charter on Historic Gardens* (1981), the ICOMOS *Washington Charter for the Conservation of Historic Towns and Urban Areas* (1987), the ICOMOS *Nara Document on Authenticity* (1994), the UNESCO *Convention for the Safeguarding of the Intangible Heritage* (2003), the ICOMOS *Xi'an Declaration on the Conservation of the Setting of Heritage Structures, Sites and Areas* (2005), the UNESCO *Recommendation on the Historic Urban Landscape* (2011), the ICOMOS *Florence Declaration on Heritage and Landscape as Human Values* (2014), the UNESCO *Florence Declaration on the Links Between Biological and Cultural Diversity* (2014), and the UNESCO Policy to integrate a sustainable development

---

[①] "Strengthen the efforts for the protection and safeguarding of the world's natural and cultural heritage" (United Nations Agenda 2030).

perspective within the processes of the World Heritage Convention (2015) which relate to the heritage and cultural values of landscapes;

Considering regional and national documents related to rural landscapes, including *the European Landscape Convention* (2000), the *European Rural Heritage Observation Guide* (CEMAT, 2003), the Council of Europe's *Faro Convention on the Value of Cultural Heritage for Society* (2005), the Tokyo *Declaration on the Role of Sacred Natural Sites and Cultural Landscapes in the Conservation of Biological and Cultural Diversity* (2005), the *Santiago de Cuba Declaration on Cultural Landscape in the Caribbean* (2005), the *Latin American Landscape Initiative* (LALI) (2012), the Australia ICOMOS *Charter for Places of Cultural Significance* (*The Burra Charter*) (1999-2013), the IFLA *Asia Pacific Region Landscape Charter* (2015);

Considering the UNESCO World Heritage Centre *Operational Guidelines for the Implementation of the World Heritage Convention* (2015), which, from 1992, primarily designate rural landscapes as '*Continuing Cultural Landscapes*';

Considering the ICOMOS-IFLA ISCCL *Milano Declaration on Rural Landscapes* (2014) concerning rural landscapes as heritage;

Considering the International Union for the Conservation of Nature (IUCN) recognition of Category V Protected Landscapes and Seascapes in their management system, the IUCN efforts of sustaining pastoral nomadism (*World Initiative on Sustainable Pastoralism,* 2008), the joint ICOMOS-IUCN initiative "*Connecting Practice-nature and culture*" and the importance of people interacting with their environment in ways that sustain bio-cultural diversity (including agrobiodiversity, as well as cultural and spiritual values);

Considering the FAO *Globally Important Agricultural Heritage Systems* (*GIAHS*) programme that aims to identify and safeguard remarkable land-use systems and landscapes with heritage value and rich in globally significant agricultural biological diversity and knowledge systems;

Considering other documents solely related to aspects of rural landscapes, such as the *Charter of Baeza on Agrarian Heritage* (2012), the *Recommendations of the World Heritage Thematic Expert Meeting on Vineyard Cultural Landscapes,* Tokaj, Hungary (2001) and recommendations of many other thematic expert meetings on rural cultural landscapes as heritage;

ICOMOS and IFLA

Commit to expand their cooperative actions by adopting the dissemination and use of the following principles in order to promote the understanding, effective protection, sustainable transformation, and transmission and appreciation of rural landscape heritage as part of human societies and cultures and a crucial resource across the world.

The principles presented in this document seek to address loss and adverse changes to rural landscapes and their associated communities through the recognition, safeguarding, and promotion of their heritage values. Its goal is to promote an appropriate balance between economic, social, cultural, and environmental aspects.

I. PRINCIPLES

A. Definitions

Rural Landscape: For the purpose of this document, rural landscapes are terrestrial and aquatic areas co-produced by human-nature interaction used for the production of food and other renewable natural resources, via agriculture, animal husbandry and pastoralism, fishing and aquaculture, forestry, wild food gathering, hunting, and extraction of other resources, such as salt. Rural landscapes are multifunctional resources. At the same time, all rural areas have cultural meanings attributed to them by people and communities: all rural areas are landscapes.

Rural landscapes are dynamic, living systems encompassing places produced and managed through traditional methods, techniques, accumulated knowledge, and cultural practices, as well as those places where traditional approaches to production have been changed. Rural landscape systems encompass rural elements and functional, productive, spatial, visual, symbolic, environmental relationships among them and with a wider context.

Rural landscapes encompass both well-managed and degraded or abandoned areas that can be reused or reclaimed. They can be huge rural spaces, peri-urban areas as well as small spaces within built-up areas. Rural landscapes encompass land surfaces, subsurface soils and resources, the airspace above, and water bodies.

Rural Landscape as Heritage: Refers to the tangible and intangible heritage of rural areas. Rural landscape as heritage encompasses physical attributes–the productive land itself, morphology, water, infrastructure, vegetation, settlements, rural buildings and centers, vernacular architecture, transport, and trade networks, etc. – as well as wider physical, cultural, and environmental linkages and settings. Rural landscape as heritage also includes associated cultural knowledge, traditions, practices, expressions of local human communities' identity and belonging, and the cultural values and meanings attributed to those landscapes by past and contemporary people and communities. Rural landscapes as heritage encompass technical, scientific, and practical knowledge, related to human-nature relationships.

Rural Landscapes as Heritage are expressions of social structures and functional organizations, realizing, using and transforming them, in the past and in the present. Rural landscape as heritage encompasses cultural, spiritual, and natural attributes that contribute to the continuation of biocultural diversity.

All rural areas can be read as heritage, both outstanding and ordinary, traditional and recently transformed by modernization activities: heritage can be present in different types and degrees and related to many historic periods, as a palimpsest.

B. Importance

Rural landscapes have been shaped over millennia and represent significant parts of the earth's human and environmental history, ways of living, and heritage. Many areas of the world are vital sources of food, renewable natural resources, associated world view and wellbeing for local and indigenous communities, as well as for visitors and tourists. Landscapes used for the production and/or harvesting of plant and animal species, including edible resources, demonstrate the entangled connections between humans and other species across broad areas. The diversity of agricultural, forest, animal husbandry, fishery and aquaculture, wild-resource, and other resource practices is essential for the future adaptation and resilience of global human life.

The heritage values of rural landscapes are recognised in some heritage inventories, such as the UNESCO World Heritage List as '*continuing cultural landscapes*'. The values may be recognised in regional, national, and local heritage inventories and protected area regimes. Identification of rural landscapes values at any level aims to provide awareness of rural landscapes' tangible and intangible characters and values, and is the first and necessary step to promote the sustainable conservation of such areas and transmission of their associated knowledge and cultural meanings to future generations.

C. Threats

Increasing human populations and climate change make rural landscapes vulnerable to risks of loss and/or abandonment or radical change. The threats to rural landscapes reflect three inter-related types of change:

1. Demographic and cultural (population growth in urban areas and depopulation in rural areas, urban expansion, intensive infrastructure works, development pressures, loss of traditional practices, techniques, local knowledge, and cultures);

2. Structural (globalization, change and growth of trade and relations, economic growth or decline, intensification of agricultural practices and techniques, change of land and loss of native pastures and of domesticated species diversity);

3. Environmental (climate change, pollution and environmental degradation including non-sustainable resource mining, impacts on soil, vegetation, and air quality, and loss of biodiversity and agro-biodiversity).

D. Challenges

Heritage should play a significant role in the recognition, protection and promotion of rural landscapes and biocultural diversity due to the significant values it represents. Heritage can contribute to sustaining and increasing the adaptation and resilience of rural landscapes by supporting rural and urban inhabitants, local communities, governments, industries, and corporations as integral aspect to managing the dynamic nature, threats, risks, strengths, and potentialities of such areas. Conservation of the integrity and authenticity of the heritage should focus on assuring the standard and quality of living of local populations working and living in rural landscapes. As all heritage, rural heritage is an economic resource: its use should be appropriate and should provide vital support to its long-term sustainability.

E. Benefits

Rural landscapes are critical resources for the future of human society and the world environment: they provide food and raw materials as well as a sense of identity; they represent economic, spatial, environmental, social, cultural, spiritual, health, scientific, technical and, in some areas, recreational factors. In addition to food and raw materials, rural landscapes contribute to land conservation (nature, environment, soil, hydrographic networks) and the transmission of rural cultures (techniques, knowledge of environment, cultural traditions, etc.) to future generations. Rural landscapes often provide distinct economic and tourism benefits when closely associated with the communication and enhancement of their heritage values.

Over the past decades, environmental and cultural heritage have been the subject of increasing international, interdisciplinary, and transdisciplinary research. Communities as knowledge-holders or local initiatives and collaboration among stakeholders, rural and urban inhabitants, and professionals have contributed to conservation, awareness, and enhancement of rural landscapes as a valuable shared resource. Many international, national, and local public administrations have supported this idea through their legislation and policies.

F. Sustainability of rural landscapes

Many rural systems have proven to be sustainable and resilient over time. Various aspects of these systems can inform future management of rural activities and support conservation and improvement of biocultural diversity and peoples' rights to adequate quantities and good quality of food and raw materials.

As landscapes undergo continuous, irreversible, and inevitable processes of transformation, rural landscape policies should focus on managing acceptable and appropriate changes over time, dealing with conserving, respecting, and enhancing heritage values.

II. ACTION CRITERIA

Specific measures are: understand, protect, sustainably manage the transformation, communicate and transmit landscapes and their heritage values.

A. Understand rural landscapes and their heritage values

1. Recognise that all rural landscapes have heritage values, whether assessed to be of outstanding or ordinary values, and that such heritage values will vary with scale and character (shapes, materials, uses and functions, time periods, changes).

2. Document the heritage values of rural landscapes as a basis of effective planning, decision-making, and management. Inventories, catalogues, atlases and maps provide basic knowledge of rural landscapes to spatial planning, environmental and heritage protection and management tools, landscape design and monitoring.

3. Develop base-line knowledge of the physical and cultural characteristics of rural landscapes: the status of the rural landscape today; its historical transformations and expressions of tangible and intangible heritage; historic, inherited, and contemporary socio-cultural perceptions of the landscape; past and present links (spatial, cultural, social, productive, and functional) between all elements (natural and human-made, material and immaterial) of rural landscape systems; and the stakeholders involved in both their past and present. Inventorying and cataloguing aim to describe rural landscapes in the current state but also to identify changes over time.

4. Inventory and catalogue rural landscapes at all scales (world, regional, national, local). These tools should integrate local, traditional and scientific knowledge and use systematic methods that are readily achievable and suitable for use by both specialists and non-specialists in all countries in order to collect and compare rural landscapes internationally and locally. In order to achieve an effective database, inventorying and cataloguing activities should consider complexity, costs of human resources, timing of data collection and organisation, and involve both experts and local inhabitants.

5. Develop knowledge to enable comparison of rural landscapes at all levels (world, regional, national, local), monitoring historical changes to rural landscapes and support shared learning and collaboration from local to global scales and among all public and private stakeholders.

6. Recognize local populations as knowledge-holders who in many cases help to shape and maintain the landscape and should be involved to the building of collective knowledge.

7. Promote extensive and ongoing cooperation among public institutions, non-governmental organizations, and universities for research, information sharing, technical assistance, and coordination of a wide variety of knowledge building activities at all administrative levels.

B. Protect rural landscapes and their heritage values

1. Review and implement legal and policy frameworks to ensure biocultural sustainability and resilience in use and transformation of rural landscapes with respect to global, national, local threats, risks and opportunities.

2. Implement policies via laws, rules, economic strategies, governance solutions, information sharing, and cultural support. The complex character of rural landscapes necessitates development of both specific and cross-sectoral policies that consider broad cultural, social, economic, and environmental factors.

3. Define strategies and actions of dynamic conservation, repair, innovation, adaptive transformation, maintenance, and long-term management. These should seek to balance global and local approaches, and ensure the involvement and cooperation of all stakeholders and communities in their effective design and daily management.

4. Consider that rural landscape heritage values are economic, social, environmental, cultural, spiritual and spatial and that awareness of the values of each rural landscape enables the management of appropriate and effective future transformations.

5. Prepare effective policies based on informed local and other knowledge of the landscapes, their strengths and weaknesses, as well as potential threats and opportunities. Define objectives and tools. Programme actions with regard to long, medium, and short-term management goals.

6. Define monitoring strategies to review the effectivity of implemented policies and reassess short, medium and long-term goals, related to the monitoring results.

7. Consider that effective policy implementation is dependent on an informed and engaged public, on their support for required strategies and involvement on actions. It is essential to complement all other actions. Public administrations should support pro-active and bottom-up initiatives.

C. Sustainably manage rural landscapes and their heritage values

1. Consider bio-cultural rights within food and natural resource production. Implement planned management approaches that acknowledge the dynamic, living nature of landscapes and respect human and non-human species living within them. Respect, value, and support the diversities of cultures and various peoples' approaches to nature.

2. Recognize key stakeholders of rural landscapes, including rural inhabitants, and the local, indigenous, and migrant communities with connections and attachments to places, their role in shaping and maintaining the landscape, as well as their knowledge of natural and environmental conditions, past and present events, local cultures and traditions, and scientific and technical solutions trialed and implemented over the centuries. Acknowledge that the good standard and quality of living for rural inhabitants enables strengthening of rural activities, rural landscapes, and transmission and continuity of rural practices and cultures.

3. Consider the connections between cultural, natural, economic, and social aspects across large and small landscapes, in the development of sustainable management strategies for rural landscapes as heritage resource.

4. Consider the interconnections between rural and urban landscapes. Rural landscapes are a resource for urban inhabitants' quality of life (recreation, food quality and quantity, firewood, water and clean air quality, food gardening, etc.) in all metropolitan areas of the world. Urban areas can provide economic opportunities for rural landscape products and integrated other activities as recreation, education, agritourism, demanded by citizens (multifunctionality). Cooperation between rural, peri-urban, and urban inhabitants should be actively encouraged and practiced, both in sharing knowledge of rural landscapes' heritage and the responsibilities for their management.

5. Find a balance between long-term sustainable (economic, social, cultural, environmental) resource use and heritage conservation, and the short-term needs of rural workers' quality of living, which is a prerequisite for the continuation of activities that generate and sustain rural landscapes. Quality of living consists of both income and social appreciation, provision of public services including education, recognition of culture rights, etc. This requires finding appropriate ways and solutions in which living heritage values can be recognized so that change and adaptation are to be compatible with the conservation, use, and communication of heritage values, as well as with the economic enhancement of rural landscape heritage.

6. Support the equitable governance of rural landscapes, including and encouraging the active engagement of local populations, stakeholders, and rural and urban inhabitants, in both the knowledge of, and responsibilities for, the management and monitoring of rural landscape as heritage. Because many rural landscapes are a mosaic of private, corporate, and government ownership, collaborative working relationships are necessary.

D. Communicate and transmit the heritage and values of rural landscapes

1. Communicate awareness of the heritage values of rural landscapes through collaborative participatory actions, such as shared learning, education, capacity building, heritage interpretation and research activities. Develop participatory plans and practices that involve civil society, private organizations, public authorities, and amongst both urban and rural inhabitants.

2. Increase awareness of the means and methods for transmission of traditional and technical knowledge and practices and develop case studies to do so and disseminate best practices.

3. Support shared learning, training, and research using diverse tools, approaches and cultural practices, including cultural mapping, information-sharing, education, and on-site training involving stakeholders, such as local communities, heritage specialists, professionals of various disciplines, schools and universities, and the media.

NOTE: The document is promoted by *ICOMOS-IFLA International Scientific Committee on Cultural Landscapes* (*World Rural Landscapes Initiative* www.worldrurallandscapes.org).

历史地区

关于历史地区的保护及其当代作用的建议
（内罗毕建议）[1]

（联合国教科文组织第十九届大会 1976 年 11 月 26 日在内罗毕通过）

联合国教科文组织大会于 1976 年 10 月 26 日至 11 月 30 日在内罗毕举行第十九届会议。

考虑到历史地区是各地人类日常环境的组成部分，它们代表着形成其过去的生动见证，提供了与社会多样化相对应所需的生活背景的多样化，并且基于以上各点，它们获得了自身的价值，又得到了人性的一面；

考虑到自古以来，历史地区为文化、宗教及社会活动的多样化和财富提供了最确切的见证，保护历史地区并使它们与现代社会生活相结合是城市规划和土地开发的基本因素；

考虑到面对因循守旧和非个性化的危险，这些昔日的生动见证对于人类和对那些从中找到其生活方式缩影及其某一基本特征的民族，是至关重要的；

注意到整个世界在扩展或现代化的借口之下，拆毁（却不知道拆毁的是什么）和不合理不适当重建工程正给这一历史遗产带来严重的损害；

考虑到历史地区是不可移动的遗产，其损坏即使不会导致经济损失，也常常会带来社会动乱；

考虑到这种情况使每个公民承担责任，并赋予公共当局只有他们才能履行的义务；

考虑到为了使这些不可替代的财产免受它们所面临的退化甚至全部毁坏的危险，各成员国当务之急是采取全面而有力的政策，把保护和复原历史地区及其周围环境作为国家、地区或地方规划的组成部分；

注意到在许多情况下缺乏一套有关建筑遗产及其与城市规划、领土、地区或地方规划相互联系的相当有效而灵活的立法；

注意到大会已通过了保护文化和自然遗产的国际文件，如：《关于适用于考古发掘的国际原则的建议》（1956）、《关于保护景观和遗址的风貌与特征的建议》（1962）、《关于保护受到公共或私人工程威胁的文化财产的建议》（1972）；

希望补充并扩大这些国际文件所确定的标准和原则的适用范围；

收到关于历史地区的保护及其当代作用的建议，该问题作为本届会议第 27 项议程；

第十八次会议决定该问题应采取向各成员国的建议的形式。

于 1976 年 11 月 26 日通过本建议。

---

[1] 引自：联合国教科文组织世界遗产中心，国际古迹遗址理事会，国际文物保护与修复研究中心，中国国家文物局主编. 国际文化遗产保护文件选编[M]. 北京：文物出版社，2007.

大会**建议**各成员国应通过国家法律或其他方式制订使本建议所规定的原则和准则在其所管辖的领土上生效的措施，以适用以上规定。

大会**建议**各成员国应将本建议提请与保护历史地区及其周围环境有关的国家、地区和地方当局、事业单位、行政部门或机构以及各种协会的注意。

大会**建议**各成员国应按大会决定的日期和形式向大会提交有关本建议执行情况的报告。

一．定　义

1. 为本建议之目的：

（1）"历史和建筑（包括本地的）地区"系指包含考古和古生物遗址的任何建筑群、结构和空旷地，它们构成城乡环境中的人类居住地，从考古、建筑、史前史、历史、艺术和社会文化的角度看，其凝聚力和价值已得到认可。在这些性质各异的地区中，可特别划分为以下各类：史前遗址、历史城镇、老城区、老村庄、老村落以及相似的古迹群。不言而喻，后者通常应予以精心保存，维持不变。

（2）"环境"系指影响观察这些地区的动态、静态方法的、自然或人工的环境。

（3）"保护"系指对历史或传统地区及其环境的鉴定、保护、修复、修缮、维修和复原。

二．总　则

2. 历史地区及其环境应被视为不可替代的世界遗产的组成部分。其所在国政府和公民应把保护该遗产并使之与我们时代的社会生活融为一体作为自己的义务。国家、地区或地方当局应根据各成员国关于权限划分的情况，为全体公民和国际社会的利益，负责履行这一义务。

3. 每一历史地区及其周围环境应从整体上视为一个相互联系的统一体，其协调及特性取决于它的各组成部分的联合，这些组成部分包括人类活动、建筑物、空间结构及周围环境。因此一切有效的组成部分，包括人类活动，无论多么微不足道，都对整体具有不可忽视的意义。

4. 历史地区及其周围环境应得到积极保护，使之免受各种损坏，特别是由于不适当的利用、不必要的添建和诸如将会损坏其真实性的错误的或愚蠢的改变而带来的损害，以及由于各种形式的污染而带来的损害。任何修复工程的进行应以科学原则为基础。同样，也应十分注意组成建筑群并赋予各建筑群以自身特征的各个部分之间的联系与对比所产生的和谐与美感。

5. 在导致建筑物的规模和密度大量增加的现代城市化的情况下，历史地区除了遭受直接破坏的危险外，还存在一个真正的危险：新开发的地区会毁坏临近的历史地区的环境和特征。建筑师和城市规划者应谨慎从事，以确保古迹和历史地区的景色不致遭到破坏，并确保历史地区与当代生活和谐一致。

6. 当存在建筑技术和建筑形式的日益普遍化可能造成整个世界的环境单一化的危险时，保护历史地区能对维护和发展每个国家的文化和社会价值作出突出贡献。这也有助于从建筑上丰富世界文化遗产。

三．国家、地区和地方政策

7. 各成员国应根据各国关于权限划分的情况制定国家、地区和地方政策，以便使国家、地区和地方当局能够采取法律、技术、经济和社会措施，保护历史地区及其周围环境，并使之适应于现代生活的需要。由此制定的政策应对国家、地区或地方各级的规划产生影响，并为各级城市规划，以及地区和农村发展规划，为由此而产生的共构成制订目标和计划重要组成部分的活动、责任分配以及实施行为提供指导。在执行保护政策时，应寻求个人和私人协会的合作。

四．保护措施

8. 历史地区及其周围环境应按照上述原则和以下措施予以保护，具体措施应根据各国立法和宪法权限以及各国组织和经济结构来决定。

立法及行政措施

9. 保护历史地区及其周围环境的总政策之适用应基于对各国整体有效的原则。各成员国应修改现有规定，或必要时，制定新的法律和规章以便参照本章及下列章节所述之规定，确保对历史地区及其周围环境的保护。它们应鼓励修改或采取地区或地方措施以确保此种保护。有关城镇和地区规划以及住宅政策的法律应予以审议，以便使它们与有关保护建筑遗产的法律相协调、相结合。

10. 关于保护历史地区的制度的规定应确立关于制订必要的计划和文件的一般原则，特别是：适用于保护地区及其周围环境的一般条件和限制；

关于为保护和提供公共服务而制定的计划和行动说明；

将要进行的维护工作并为此指派负责人；

适用于城市规划，再开发以及农村土地管理的区域；

指派负责审批任何在保护范围内的修复、改动、新建或拆除的机构；

保护计划得到资金并得以实施的方式。

11. 保护计划和文件应确定：

被保护的区域和项目

对其适用的具体条件和限制；

在维护、修复和改进工作中所应遵守的标准；

关于建立城市或农村生活所需的服务和供应系统的一般条件；

关于新建项目的条件。

12. 原则上，这些法律也应包括旨在防止违反保护法的规定，以及防止在保护地区内财产价值的投机性上涨的规定，这一上涨可能危及为整个社会利益而计划的保护和维修。这些规定可以包括提供影响建筑用地价格之方法的城市规划措施，例如：设立邻里区或制定较小型的开发计划，授予公共机构优先购买权、在所有人不采取行动的情况下，为了保护、修复或自动干预之目的实行强制购买。这些规定可以确定有效的惩罚，如：暂停活动、强制修复和适当的罚款。

13. 个人和公共当局有义务遵守保护措施。然而，也应对武断的或不公正的决定提供上诉的机制。

14. 有关建立公共和私人机构以及公共和私人工程项目的规定应与保护历史地区及其周围环境的规定相适应。

15. 有关贫民区的房产和街区以及有补贴住宅之建设的规定，尤其应本着符合并有助于保护政策的目的予以制订或修改。因此，应拟定并调整已付补贴的计划，以便专门通过修复古建筑推动有补贴的住宅建筑和公共建设的发展。在任何情况下，一切拆除应仅限于没有历史或建筑价值的建筑物，并对所涉及的补贴应谨慎予以控制。另外，应将专用于补贴住宅建设的基金拨出一部分，用于旧建筑的修复。

16. 有关建筑物和土地的保护措施的法律后果应予以公开并由主管官方机构作出记录。

17. 考虑到各国的具体条件以及各个国家、地区和地方当局的责任划分，下列原则应构成保护机制运行的基础：

（1）应设有一个负责确保长期协调一切有关部门，如国家、地区和地方公共部门或私人团体的权力机构；

（2）跨学科小组一旦完成了事先一切必要的科学研究后，应立即制订保护计划和文件，这些跨学科小组特别应由以下人员组成：

保护和修复专家，包括艺术史学家；

建筑师和城市规划师；

社会学家和经济学家；

生态学家和风景建筑师；

公共卫生和社会福利的专家；

并且更广泛地说，所有涉及历史地区保护和发展学科方面的专家；

（3）这些机构应在传播有关民众的意见和组织他们积极参与方面起带头作用；

（4）保护计划和文件应由法定机构批准；

（5）负责实施保护规定和规划的国家、地区和地方各级公共当局应配有必要的工作人员和充分的技术、行政管理和财政来源。

技术、经济和社会措施

18. 应在国家、地区或地方一级制订保护历史地区及其周围环境的清单。该清单应确定重点，以使可用于保护的有限资源能够得到合理的分配。需要采取的任何紧急保护措施，不论其性质如何，均不应等到制订保护计划和文件后再采取。

19. 应对整个地区进行一次全面的研究，其中包括对其空间演变的分析。它还应包括考古、历史、建筑、技术和经济方面的数据。应制订一份分析性文件，以便确定哪些建筑物或建筑群应予以精心保护、哪些应在某种条件下予以保存，哪些应在极例外的情况下经全面记录后予以拆毁。这将能使有关当局下令停止任何与本建议不相符合的工程。此外，出于同样目的，还应制订一份公共或私人开阔地及其植被情况的清单。

20. 除了这种建筑方面的研究外，也有必要对社会、经济、文化和技术数据与结构以及更广泛的城市或地区联系进行全面的研究。如有可能，研究应包括人口统计数据以及对经济、社会和文化活动的分析、生活方式和社会关系、土地使用问题、城市基础设施、道路系统、通讯网络以及保护区域与其周围地区的相互联系。有关当局应高度重视这些研究并应牢记没有这些研究，就不可能制订出有效的保护计划。

21. 在完成上述研究之后，并在保护计划和详细说明制订之前，原则上应有一个实施计划，其中既要考虑城市规划、建筑、经济和社会问题，又要考虑城乡机构吸收与其具体特点相适应的功能的能力。实施计划应在使居住密度达到理想水平，并应规定分期进行的工作及其进行中所需的临时住宅，以及为那些无法重返先前住所的居民提供永久性的住房。该实施计划应由有关的社区和人民团体密切参与制订。由于历史地区及其周围环境的社会、经济及自然状态方面会随时间流逝而不断变化，因此，对其研究和分析应是一个连续不断的过程。所以，至关重要的是在能够进行研究的基础上制订保护计划并加以实施，而不是由于推敲计划过程而予以拖延。

22. 一旦制订出保护计划和详细说明并获得有关公共当局批准，最好由制订者本人或在其指导下予以实施。

23. 在具有几个不同时期特征的历史地区，保护应考虑到所有这些时期的表现形式。

24. 在有保护计划的情况下，只有根据该计划方可批准涉及拆除既无建筑价值和历史价值且结构又极不稳固、无法保存的建筑物的城市发展或贫民区治理计划，以及拆除无价值的延伸部分或附加楼层，乃至拆除有时破坏历史地区整体感的新建筑。

25. 保护计划未涉及地区的城市发展或贫民区治理计划应尊重具有建筑或历史价值的建筑物和其他组成部分及其附属建筑物。如果这类组成部分可能受到该计划的不利影响,应在拆除之前制订上述保护计划。

26. 为确保这些计划的实施不致有利于牟取暴利或与计划的目标相悖，有必要经常进行监督。

27. 任何影响历史地区的城市发展或贫民区治理计划应遵守适用于防止火灾和自然灾害的通用安全标准，只要这与适用于保护文化遗产的标准相符。如果确实出现了不符的情况，各有关部门应通力合作找出特别的解决方法，以便在不损坏文化遗产的同时，提供最大的安全保障。

28. 应特别注意对新建筑物制定规章并加以控制，以确保该建筑能与历史建筑群的空间结构和环境协调一致。为此，在任何新建项目之前，应对城市的来龙去脉进行分析，其目的不仅在于确定该建筑群的一般特征，而且在于分析其主要特征，如：高度、色彩、材料及造型之间的和谐、建筑物正面和屋顶建造方式的衡量、建筑面积与空间体积之间的关系及其平均比例和位置。特别应注意基址的面积，因为存在着这样一个危险，即基址的任何改动都可能带来整体的变化，均对整体的和谐不利。

29. 除非在极个别情况下并出于不可避免的原因，一般不应批准破坏古迹周围环境而使其处于孤立状态，也不应将其迁移他处。

30. 历史地区及其周围环境应得到保护，避免因架设电杆、高塔、电线或电话线、安置电视天线及大型广告牌而带来的外观损坏。在已经设置这些装置的地方，应采取适当措施予以拆除。张贴广告、霓虹灯和其他各种广告、商业招牌及人行道与各种街道设备应精心规划并加以控制，以使它们与整体相协调。应特别注意防止各种形式的破坏活动。

31. 各成员国及有关团体应通过禁止在历史地区附近建立有害工业，并通过采取预防措施消除由机器和车辆所带来的噪音、振动和颤动的破坏性影响，保护历史地区及其周围环境免受由于某种技术发展，特别是各种形式的污染所造成的日益严重的环境损害。另外还应作出规定，采取措施消除因旅游业的过分开发而造成的危害。

32. 各成员国应鼓励并帮助地方当局寻求解决大多数历史建筑群中所存在的一方面机动交通另一方面建筑规模以及建筑质量之间的矛盾的方法。为了解决这一矛盾并鼓励步行，应特别重视设置和开放既便于步行、服务通行又便于公共交通的外围乃至中央停车场和道路系统。许多诸如在地下铺设电线和其他电缆的修复工程，如果单独实施耗资过大，可以简单而经济地与道路系统的发展相结合。

33. 保护和修复工作应与振兴活动齐头并进。因此，适当保持现有的适当作用，特别是贸易和手工艺，并增加新的作用是非常重要的，这些新作用从长远来看，如果具有生命力，应与其所在的城镇、地区或国家的经济和社会状态相符合。保护工作的费用不仅应根据建筑物的文化价值而且应根据其经使用获得的价值进行估算。只有参照了这两方面的价值尺度，才能正确看待保护的社会问题。这些作用应满足居民的社会、文化和经济需要，而又不损坏有关地区的具体特征。文化振兴政策应使历史地区成为文化活动的中心并使其在周围社区的文化发展中发挥中心作用。

34. 在农村地区，所有引起干扰的工程和经济、社会结构的所有变化应严加控制，以使具有历史意义的农村社区保持其在自然环境中的完整性。

35. 保护活动应把公共当局的贡献同个人或集体所有者、居民和使用者单独或共同作出的贡献联系起来，应鼓励他们提出建议并充分发挥其积极作用。因此，特别应通过以下方法在社区和个人之间建立各种层次的经常性的合作：适合于某类人的信息资料，适合于有关人员的综合研究，建立附属于计划小组的顾问团体；所有者、居民和使用者在对公共企业机构发挥咨询作用方面的代表性。这些机构负责有关保护计划的决策、管理和组织实施的机构或负责创建参与实施计划。

36. 应鼓励建立自愿保护团体和非营利性协会以及设立荣誉或物质奖励，以使保护领域中各方面卓有成效的工作能得到认可。

37. 应通过中央、地区和地方当局足够的预算拨款，确保得到保护历史地区及其环境计划中所规定的用于公共投资的必要资金。所有这些资金应由受委托协调国家、地区或地方各级一切形式的财政援助、并根据全面行动计划发放资金的公共、私人或半公半私的机构集中管理。

38. 下述形式的公共援助应基于这样的原则：在适当和必要的情况下，有关当局采取的措施，应考虑到修复中的额外开支，即与建筑物新的市场价格或租金相比，强加给所有者的附加开支。

39. 一般来说，这类公共资金应主要用于保护现有建筑，特别包括低租金的住宅建筑，而不应划拨给新建筑的建设，除非后者不损害现有建筑物的使用和作用。

40. 赠款、补贴、低息贷款或税收减免应提供给按保护计划所规定的标准进行保护计划所规定的工程的私人所有者和使用者。这些税收减免、赠款和贷款可首先提供给拥有住房和商业财产的所有者或使用者团体，因为联合施工比单独行动更加节省。给予私人所有者和使用者的财政特许权，在适当情况下，应取决于要求遵守为公共利益而规定的某些条件的契约，并确保建筑物的完整，例如：允许参观建筑物、允许进入公园、花园或遗址，允许拍照等。

41. 应在公共或私人团体的预算中，拨出一笔特别资金，用于保护受到大规模公共工程和污染危害的历史建筑群。公共当局也应拨出专款，用于修复由于自然灾害所造成的损坏。

42. 另外，一切活跃于公共工程领域的政府部门和机构应通过既符合自己目的，又符合保护计划目标的融资，安排其计划与预算，以便为历史建筑群的修复作出贡献。

43. 为了增加可资利用的财政资源，各成员国应鼓励建立保护历史地区及其周围环境的公共和／或私人金融机构。这些机构应有法人地位，并有权接受来自个人、基金会以及有关工业和商业方面的赠款。对捐赠人可给予特别的税收减免。

44. 通过建立借贷机构为保护历史地区及其周围环境所进行的各种工程的融资工作，可由公共机构和私人信贷机构提供便利，这些机构将负责向所有者提供低息长期贷款。

45. 各成员国和其他有关各级政府部门可促进非赢利组织的建立。这些组织负责以周转资金购买，或如果合适在修复后出售建筑物。这笔资金是为了使那些希望保护历史建筑物、维护其特色的所有人能够在其中继续居住而专门设立的。

46. 保护措施不应导致社会结构的崩溃，这一点尤为重要。为了避免因翻修给不得不从建筑物或建筑群迁出的最贫穷的居民所带来的艰辛，补偿上涨的租金能使他们得以维持家庭住房、商业用房、作坊以及他们传统的生活方式和职业，特别是农村手工业、小型农业、渔业等。这项与收入挂钩的补偿，将会帮助有关人员偿付由于进行工程而导致的租金上涨。

五．研究、教育和信息

47. 为了提高所需技术工人和手工艺者的工作水平，并鼓励全体民众认识到保护的必要性并参与保护工作，各成员国应根据其立法和宪法权限，采取以下措施。

48. 各成员国和有关团体应鼓励系统地学习和研究：
城市规划中有关历史地区及其环境方面；
各级保护和规划之间的相互联系；
适用于历史地区的保护方法；
材料的改变；
现代技术在保护工作中的运用；
与保护不可分割的工艺技术。

49. 应采用并与上述问题有关的并包括实习培训期的专门教育。另外，至关重要的是鼓励培养专门从事保护历史地区，包括其周围的空间地带的专业技术工人和手工艺者。此外，还有必要振兴受工业化进程破坏的工艺本身。在这方面有关机构有必要与专门的国际机构进行合作，如在罗马的文化财产保护与修复研究中心、国际古迹遗址理事会和国际博物馆协会。

50. 对地方在历史地区保护方面发展中所需行政人员的教育，应根据实际需要，按照长远计划由有关当局提供资金并进行指导。

51. 应通过校外和大学教育，以及通过诸如书籍、报刊、电视、广播、电影和巡回展览等信息媒介增强对保护工作必要性的认识。还应提供不仅有关美学而且有关社会和经济得益于进展良好的保护历史地区及其周围环境的政策方面的、全面明确的信息。这种信息应在私人和政府专门机构以及一般民众中广为传播，以使他们知道为什么以及怎样才能按此方法改善他们的环境。

52. 对历史地区的研究应包括在各级教育之中，特别是在历史教学中，以便反复向青年人灌输理解和尊重昔日成就，并说明这些遗产在现代生活中的作用。这种教育应广泛利用视听媒介及参观历史建筑群的方法。

53. 为了帮助那些想了解历史地区的青年人和成年人，应加强教师和导游的进修课程以及对教师的培训。

六．国际合作

54. 各成员国应在历史地区及其周围环境的保护方面进行合作，如有必要，寻求政府间的和非政府间的国际组织的援助，特别是联合国教科文组织——国际博物馆协会——国际古迹遗址理事会文献中心的援助。此种多边或双边合作应认真予以协调，并应采取诸如下列形式的措施：

（1）交流各种形式的信息及科技出版物；

（2）组织专题研讨会或工作会；

（3）提供研究或旅行基金，派遣科技和行政工作人员并发送有关设备；

（4）采取共同行动以对付各种污染；

（5）实施大规模保护、修复与复原历史地区的项目，并公布已取得的经验。在边境地区，如果发展和保护历史地区及其周围的环境导致影响边境两边的成员国的共同问题，双方应协调其政策和行动，以确保文化遗产以尽可能的最佳方法得到利用和保护；

（6）邻国之间在保护共同感兴趣并具有本地区历史和文化发展特点的地区方面应互相协助。

55. 根据本建议的精神和原则，一成员国不应采取任何行动拆除或改变其所占领土之上的历史区段、城镇和遗址的特征。

Recommendation concerning the Safeguarding and Contemporary Role of Historic Areas [1]

Adopted by the UNESCO General Conference at its 19th session, Nairobi, 26 November 1976

The General Conference of the United Nations Educational, Scientific and Cultural Organization, meeting in Nairobi at its nineteenth session, from 26 October to 30 November 1976,

Considering that historic areas are part of the daily environment of human beings everywhere, that they represent the living presence of the past which formed them, that they provide the variety in life's background needed to match the diversity of society, and that by so doing they gain in value and acquire an additional human dimension,

Considering that historic areas afford down the ages the most tangible evidence of the wealth and diversity of cultural, religious and social activities and that their safeguarding and their integration into the life of contemporary society is a basic factor in town-planning and land development,

Considering that in face of the dangers of stereotyping and depersonalization, this living evidence of days gone by is of vital importance for humanity and for nations who find in it both the expression of their way of life and one of the cornerstones of their identity,

Noting that throughout the world, under the pretext of expansion or modernization, demolition ignorant of what it is demolishing, and irrational and inappropriate reconstruction work is causing serious damage to this historic heritage,

Considering that historic areas are an immovable heritage whose destruction may often lead to social disturbance, even where it does not lead to economic loss,

Considering that this situation entails responsibilities for every citizen and lays on public authorities obligations which they alone are capable of fulfilling,

Considering that in order to save these irreplaceable assets from the dangers of deterioration or even total destruction to which they are thus exposed, it is for each State to adopt, as a matter of urgency, comprehensive and energetic policies for the protection and revitalization of historic areas and their surroundings as part of national, regional or local planning,

Noting the absence in many cases of a legislation effective and flexible enough concerning the architectural

---

[1] Records of the General Conference, 19th session, Nairobi, 26 October to 30 November 1976, v. 1: Resolutions. UNESCO Document Code: 19 C/ Resolutions + CORR.

heritage and its interconnexion with town-planning, territorial, regional or local planning,

Noting that the General Conference has already adopted international instruments for the protection of the cultural and natural heritage such as the Recommendation on International Principles Applicable to Archaeological Excavations (1956), the Recommendation Concerning the Safe guarding of the Beauty and Character of Landscapes and Sites (1962), the Recommendation Concerning the Preservation of Cultural Property Endangered by Public or Private Works (1968), and the Recommendation Concerning the Protection, at National Level, of the Cultural and Natural Heritage (1972),

Desiring to supplement and extend the application of the standards and principles laid down in these international instruments,

Having before it proposals concerning the safeguarding and contemporary role of historic areas, which question appears on the agenda of the session as item 27,

Having decided at its eighteenth session that this question should take the form of a Recommendation to Member States,

Adopts, this twenty-sixth day of November 1976, the present Recommendation.

The General Conference recommends that Member States apply the above provisions by adopting, as a national law or in some other form, measures with a view to giving effect to the principles and norms set out in this Recommendation in the territories under their jurisdiction.

The General Conference recommends that Member States bring this Recommendation to the attention of the national, regional and local authorities and of institutions, services or bodies and associations concerned with the safeguarding of historic areas and their environment.

The General Conference recommends that Member States report to it, at the dates and in the form determined by it, on action taken by them on this Recommendation.

I . DEFINITIONS

1. For the purposes of the present recommendation:

(a) "Historic and architectural (including vernacular) areas" shall be taken to mean any groups of buildings, structures and open spaces including archaeological and paleontological sites, constituting human settlements in an urban or rural environment, the cohesion and value of which, from the archaeological, architectural, prehistoric, historic, aesthetic or socio-cultural point of view are recognized.

Among these "areas", which are very varied in nature, it is possible to distinguish the following in particular: prehistoric sites, historic towns, old urban quarters, villages and hamlets as well as homogeneous monumental groups, it being understood that the latter should as a rule be carefully preserved unchanged.

(b) The "environment" shall be taken to mean the natural or man-made setting which influences the static or dynamic way these areas are perceived or which is directly linked to them in space or by social, economic or cultural ties,

(c) "Safeguarding" shall be taken to mean the identification, protection, conservation, restoration, renovation, maintenance and revitalization of historic or traditional areas and their environment.

II . GENERAL PRINCIPLES

2. Historic areas and their surroundings should be regarded as forming an irreplaceable universal heritage, the governments and the citizens of the States in whose territory they are situated should deem it their duty to

safeguard this heritage and integrate it into the social life of our times. The national, regional or local authorities should be answerable for their performance of this duty in the interests of all citizens and of the international community, in accordance with the conditions of each Member State as regards the allocation of powers.

3. Every historic area and its surroundings should be considered in their totality as a coherent whole whose balance and specific nature depend on the fusion of the parts of which it is composed and which include human activities as much as the buildings, the spatial organization and the surroundings. All valid elements, including human activities, however modest, thus have significance in relation to the whole which must not be disregarded.

4. Historic areas and their surroundings should be actively protected against damage of all kinds, particularly that resulting from unsuitable use, unnecessary additions and misguided or insensitive changes such as will impair their authenticity, and from damage due to any form of pollution. Any restoration work undertaken should be based on scientific principles. Similarly, great attention should be paid to the harmony and aesthetic feeling produced by the linking or the contrasting of the various parts which make up the groups of buildings and which give to each group its particular character.

5. In the conditions of modern urbanization, which leads to a considerable increase in the scale and density of buildings, apart from the danger of direct destruction of historic areas, there is a real danger that newly developed areas can ruin the environment and character of adjoining historic areas. Architects and town-planners should be careful to ensure that views from and to monuments and historic areas are not spoilt and that historic areas are integrated harmoniously into contemporary life.

6. At a time when there is a danger that a growing universality of building techniques and architectural forms may create a uniform environment throughout the world, the preservation of historic areas can make an outstanding contribution to maintaining and developing the cultural and social values of each nation. This can contribute to the architectural enrichment of the cultural heritage of the world.

III. NATIONAL, REGIONAL AND LOCAL POLICY

7. In each Member State a national, regional and local policy should be drawn up, in conformity with the conditions of each State as regards the allocation of powers, so that legal, technical, economic and social measures may be taken by the national, regional or local authorities with a view to safeguarding historic areas and their surroundings and adapting them to the requirements of modern life. The policy thus laid down should influence planning at national, regional or local level and provide guidelines for town-planning and regional and rural development planning at all levels, the activities stemming from it forming an essential component in the formulation of aims and programmes, the assignment of responsibilities and the conduct of operations. The co-operation of individuals and private associations should be sought in implementing the safeguarding policy.

IV. SAFEGUARDING MEASURES

8. Historic areas and their surroundings should be safeguarded in conformity with the principles stated above and with the methods set out below, the specific measures being determined according to the legislative and constitutional competence and the organizational and economic structure of each State.

Legal and administrative measures

9. The application of an overall policy for safeguarding historic areas and their surroundings should be based on principles which are valid for the whole of each country. Member States should adapt the existing provisions,

or, where necessary, enact new laws and regulations, so as to secure the protection of historic areas and their surroundings taking into account the provisions contained in this chapter and in the following chapters. They should encourage the adaptation or the adoption of regional or local measures to ensure such protection. Laws concerning town and regional planning and housing policy should also be reviewed so as to co-ordinate and bring them into line with the laws concerning the safeguarding of the architectural heritage.

10. The provisions establishing a system for safeguarding historic areas should set out the general principles relating to the establishment of the necessary plans and documents and, in particular:

the general conditions and restrictions applicable to the protected areas and their surroundings;

a statement as to the programmes and operations to be planned for the purpose of conservation and provision of public services;

maintenance to be carried out and the designation of those to be responsible for it;

the fields to which town-planning, redevelopment and rural land management are applicable;

the designation of the body responsible for authorizing any restoration, modification, new construction or demolition within the protected perimeter;

the means by which the safeguarding programmes are to be financed and carried out.

11. Safeguarding plans and documents should define:

the areas and items to be protected;

the specific conditions and restrictions applicable to them;

the standards to be observed in the work of maintenance, restoration and improvements;

the general conditions governing the establishment of the supply systems and services needed in urban or rural life;

the conditions governing new constructions.

12. These laws should also in principle include provisions designed to prevent any infringement of the preservation laws, as well as any speculative rise in property values within the protected areas which could compromise protection and restoration planned in the interests of the community as a whole. These provisions could involve town-planning measures affording a means of influencing the price of building land, such as the establishment of neighbourhood or smaller development plans, granting the right of pre-emption to a public body, compulsory purchase in the interests of safeguarding or rehabilitation or automatic intervention in the case of failure to act on the part of the owners, and could provide for effective penalties such as the suspension of operations, compulsory restoration and/or a suitable fine.

13. Public authorities as well as individuals must be obliged to comply with the measures for safeguarding. However, machinery for appeal against arbitrary or unjust decisions should be provided.

14. The provisions concerning the setting up of public and private bodies and concerning public and private work projects should be adapted to the regulations governing the safeguarding of historic areas and their surroundings.

15. In particular, provisions concerning slum property and blocks and the construction of subsidized housing should be planned or amended both to fit in with the safeguarding policy and to contribute to it. The schedule of any subsidies paid should be drawn up and adjusted accordingly, in particular in order to facilitate the development of subsidized housing and public construction by rehabilitating old buildings. All demolition should in any case only concern buildings with no historic or architectural value and the subsidies involved should be carefully controlled. Further, a proportion of the funds earmarked for the construction of subsidized housing should be

allocated to the rehabilitation of old buildings.

16. The legal consequences of the protection measures as far as buildings and land are concerned should be made public and should be recorded by a competent official body.

17. Making due allowance for the conditions specific to each country and the allocation of responsibilities within the various national, regional and local authorities, the following principles should underline the operation of the safeguarding machinery:

(a) there should be an authority responsible for ensuring the permanent co-ordination of all those concerned, e.g. national, regional and local public services or groups of individuals;

(b) safeguarding plans and documents should be drawn up, once all the necessary advance scientific studies have been carried out, by multidisciplinary teams composed, in particular, of:

specialists in conservation and restoration, including art historians;

architects and town-planners;

sociologists and economists;

ecologists and landscape architects;

specialists in public health and social welfare;

and, more generally, all specialists in disciplines involved in the protection and enhancement of historic areas;

(c) the authorities should take the lead in sounding the opinions and organizing the participation of the public concerned;

(d) the safeguarding plans and documents should be approved by the body designated by law;

(e) the public authorities responsible for giving effect to the safeguarding provisions and regulations at all levels, national, regional and local, should be provided with the necessary staff and given adequate technical, administrative and financial resources.

Technical, economic and social measures

18. A list of historic areas and their surroundings to be protected should be drawn up at national, regional or local level. It should indicate priorities so that the limited resources available for protection may be allocated judiciously. Any protection measures, of whatever nature, that need to be taken as a matter of urgency should be taken without waiting for the safeguarding plans and documents to be prepared.

19. A survey of the area as a whole, including an analysis of its spatial evolution, should be made. It should cover archaeological, historical, architectural, technical and economic data. An analytical document should be drawn up so as to determine which buildings or groups of buildings are to be protected with great care, conserved under certain conditions, or, inquite exceptional and thoroughly documented circumstances, destroyed. This would enable the authorities to call a halt to any work incompatible with this recommendation. Additionally, an inventory of public and private open spaces and their vegetation should be drawn up for the same purposes.

20. In addition to this architectural survey, thorough surveys of social, economic, cultural and technical data and structures and of the wider urban or regional context are necessary. Studies should include, if possible, demographic data and an analysis of economic, social and cultural activities, ways of life and social relationships, land-tenure problems, the urban infrastructure, the state of the road system, communication networks and the reciprocal links between protected areas and surrounding zones. The authorities concerned should attach the greatest importance to these studies and should bear in mind that valid safeguarding plans cannot be prepared without them.

21. After the survey described above has been completed and before the safeguarding plans and specifications

are drawn up, there should in principle be a programming operation in which due account is taken both of town-planning, architectural, economic and social considerations and of the ability of the urban and rural fabric to assimilate functions that are compatible with its specific character. The programming operation should aim at bringing the density of settlement to the desired level and should provide for the work to be carried out in stages as well as for the temporary accommodation needed while it is proceeding, and premises for the permanent rehousing of those inhabitants who cannot return to their previous dwellings. This programming operation should be undertaken with the closest possible participation of the communities and groups of people concerned. Because the social, economic and physical context of historic areas and their surroundings may be expected to change over time, survey and analysis should be a continuing process. It is accordingly essential that the preparation of safeguarding plans and their execution be undertaken on the basis of studies available, rather than being postponed while the planning process is refined.

22. Once the safeguarding plans and specifications have been drawn up and approved by the competent public authority, it would be desirable for them to be executed either by their authors or under their authority.

23. In historic areas containing features from several different periods, preservation should be carried out taking into account the manifestations of all such periods.

24. Where safeguarding plans exist urban development or slum clearance programmes consisting of the demolition of buildings of no architectural or historic interest and which are structurally too unsound to be kept, the removal of extensions and additional storeys of no value, and sometimes even the demolition of recent buildings which break the unity of the area, may only be authorized in conformity with the plan.

25. Urban development or slum clearance programmes for areas not covered by safeguarding plans should respect buildings and other elements of architectural or historic value as well as accompanying buildings. If such elements are likely to be adversely affected by the programme, safeguarding plans as indicated above should be drawn up in advance of demolition.

26. Constant supervision is necessary to ensure that these operations are not conducive to excessive profits nor serve other purposes contrary to the objectives of the plan.

27. The usual security standards applicable to fire and natural catastrophes should be observed in any urban development or slum clearance programme affecting a historic area, provided that this be compatible with the criteria applicable to the preservation of the cultural heritage. If conflict does occur, special solutions should be sought, with the collaboration of all the services concerned, so as to provide the maximum security, while not impairing the cultural heritage.

28. Particular care should be devoted to regulations for and control over new buildings so as to ensure that their architecture adapts harmoniously to the spatial organization and setting of the groups of historic buildings. To this end, an analysis of the urban context should precede any new construction not only so as to define the general character of the group of buildings but also to analyse its dominant features, e.g. the harmony of heights, colours, materials and forms, constants in the way the facades and roofs are built, the relationship between the volume of buildings and the spatial volume, as well as their average proportions and their position. Particular attention should be given to the size of the lots since there is a danger that any reorganization of the lots may cause a change of mass which could be deleterious to the harmony of the whole.

29. The isolation of a monument through the demolition of its surroundings should not generally be authorized, neither should a monument be moved unless in exceptional circumstancesand for unavoidable reasons.

30. Historic areas and their surroundings should be protected from the disfigurement caused by the erection

of poles, pylons and electricity or telephone cables and the placing of television aerials and large-scale advertising signs. Where these already exist appropriate measures should be taken for their removal. Bill-posting, neon signs and other kinds of advertisement, commercial signs, street pavements and furniture, should be planned with the greatest care and controlled so that they fit harmoniously into the whole. Special efforts should be made to prevent all forms of vandalism.

31. Member States and groups concerned should protect historic areas and their surroundings against the increasingly serious environmental damage caused by certain technological developments-in particular the various forms of pollution-by banning harmful industries in the proximity of these areas and by taking preventive measures to counter the destructive effects of noise, shocks and vibrations caused by machines and vehicles. Provision should further be made for measures to counter the harm resulting from over-exploitation by tourism.

32. Member States should encourage and assist local authorities to seek solutions to the conflict existing in most historic groupings between motor traffic on the one hand and the scale of the buildings and their architectural qualities on the other. To solve the conflict and to encourage pedestrian traffic, careful attention should be paid to the placing of, and access to, peripheral and even central car parks and routing systems established which will facilitate pedestrian traffic, service access and public transport alike. Many rehabilitation operations such as putting electricity and other cables underground, too expensive if carried out singly, could then be coordinated easily and economically with the development of the road system.

33. Protection and restoration should be accompanied by revitalization activities. It would thus be essential to maintain appropriate existing functions, in particular trades and crafts, and establish new ones, which, if they are to be viable, in the long term, should be compatible with the economic and social context of the town, region or country where they are introduced. The cost of safeguarding operations should be evaluated not only in terms of the cultural value of the buildings but also in relation to the value they acquire through the use made of them, The social problems of safeguarding cannot be seen correctly unless reference is made to both these value scales. These functions should answer the social, cultural and economic needs of the inhabitants without harming the specific nature of the area concerned. A cultural revitalization policy should make historic areas centres of cultural activities and give them a central role to play in the cultural development of the communities around them.

34. In rural areas all works which cause disturbances and all changes of economic and social structure should be carefully controlled so as to preserve the integrity of historic rural communities within their natural setting.

35. Safeguarding activities should couple the public authorities' contribution with the contribution made by the individual or collective owners and the inhabitants and users, separately or together, who should be encouraged to put forward suggestions and generally play an active part. Constant co-operation between the community and the individual should thus be established at all levels particularly through methods such as: information adapted to the types of persons concerned; surveys adapted to the persons questioned; establishment of advisory groups attached to planning teams; representation of owners, inhabitants and users in an advisory function on bodies responsible for decision-making, management and the organization of operations connected with plans for safeguarding, or the creation of public corporations to play a part in the plan's implementation.

36. The formation of voluntary conservation groups and non-profit-making associations and the establishment of honorary or financial rewards should be encouraged so that especially meritorious work in all aspects of safeguarding may be recognized.

37. Availability of the necessary funds for the level of public investment provided for in the plans for the safeguarding of historic areas and their surroundings should be ensured by including adequate appropriations in

the budgets of the central, regional and local authorities. All these funds should be centrally managed by public, private or semi-public bodies entrusted with the co-ordination of all forms of financial aid at national, regional or local level and with the channeling of them according to an overall plan of action.

38. Public assistance in the forms described below should be based on the principle that, wherever this is appropriate and necessary, the measures taken by the authorities concerned should take into account the "extra cost" of restoration, i.e., the additional cost imposed on the owner as compared with the new market or rental value of the building.

39. In general, such public funds should be used primarily to conserve existing buildings including especially buildings for low rental housing and should not be allocated to the construction of new buildings unless the latter do not prejudice the use and functions of existing buildings.

40. Grants, subsidies, loans at favourable rates, or tax concessions should be made available to private owners and to users carrying out work provided for by the safeguarding plans and in conformity with the standards laid down in those plans. These tax concessions, grants and loans could be made first and foremost to groups of owners or users of living accommodation and commercial property, since joint operations are more economical than individual action. The financial concessions granted to private owners and users should, where appropriate, be dependent on covenants requiring the observance of certain conditions laid down in the public interest, and ensuring the integrity of the buildings such as allowing the buildings to be visited and allowing access to parks, gardens or sites, the taking of photographs, etc.

41. Special funds should be set aside in the budgets of public and private bodies for the protection of groups of historic buildings endangered by large-scale public works and pollution. Public authorities should also set aside special funds for the repair of damage caused by natural disasters.

42. In addition, all government departments and agencies active in the field of public works should arrange their programmes and budgets so as to contribute to the rehabilitation of groups of historic buildings by financing work which is both in conformity with their own aims and the aims of the safeguarding plan.

43. To increase the financial resources available to them, Member States should encourage the setting up of public and/or private financing agencies for the safeguarding of historic areas and their surroundings. These agencies should have corporate status and be empowered to receive gifts from individuals, foundations and industrial and commercial concerns. Special tax concessions may be granted to donors.

44. The financing of work of any description carried out for the safeguarding of historic areas and their surroundings by setting up a loans corporation, could be facilitated by public institutions and private credit establishments, which would be responsible for making loans to owners at reduced rates of interest with repayment spread out over a long period.

45. Member States and other levels of government concerned could facilitate the creation of non-profit-making associations responsible for buying and, where appropriate after restoration, selling buildings by using revolving funds established for the special purpose of enabling owners of historic buildings who wish to safeguard them and preserve their character to continue to reside there.

46. It is most important that safeguarding measures should not lead to a break in the social fabric. To avoid hardship to the poorest inhabitants consequent on their having to move from buildings or groups of buildings due for renovation, compensation for rises in rent could enable them to keep their homes, commercial premises and workshops and their traditional living patterns and occupations, especially rural crafts, small-scale agriculture, fishing, etc. This compensation, which would be income-related, would help those concerned to pay the increased

rentals resulting from the work carried out.

V. RESEARCH, EDUCATION AND INFORMATION

47. In order to raise the standard of work of the skilled workers and craftsmen required and to encourage the whole population to realize the need for safeguarding and to take part in it, the following measures should be taken by Member States, in accordance with their legal and constitutional competence.

48. Member States and groups concerned should encourage the systematic study of, and research on:

town-planning aspects of historic areas and their environment;

the interconnexions between safeguarding and planning at all levels;

methods of conservation applicable to historic areas;

the alteration of materials;

the application of modern techniques to conservation work;

the crafts techniques indispensable for safeguarding.

49. Specific education concerning the above questions and including practical training periods should be introduced and developed. In addition, it is essential to encourage the training of skilled workers and craftsmen specializing in the safeguarding of historic areas, including any open spaces surrounding them. Furthermore, it is necessary to encourage the crafts themselves, which are jeopardized by the processes of industrialization. It is desirable that the institutions concerned cooperate in this matter with specialized international agencies such as the Centre for the Study of the Preservation and Restoration of Cultural Property, in Rome, the International Council of Monuments and Sites (ICOMOS) and the International Council of Museums (ICOM).

50. The education of administrative staff for the needs of local development in the field of safeguarding of historic areas should be financed where applicable and needed and directed by the appropriate authorities according to a long-term programme.

51. Awareness of the need for safeguarding work should be encouraged by education in school, out of school and at university and by using information media such as books, the press, television, radio, cinema and travelling exhibitions. Clear, comprehensive information should be provided as to the advantages not only aesthetic, but also social and economic to be reaped from a well-conducted policy for the safeguarding of historic areas and their surroundings. Such information should be widely circulated among specialized private and government bodies and the general public so that they may know why and how their surroundings can be improved in this way.

52. The study of historic areas should be included in education at all levels, especially in history teaching, so as to inculcate in young minds an understanding of and respect for the works of the past and to demonstrate the role of this heritage in modern life. Education of this kind should make wide use of audio-visual media and of visits to groups of historic buildings.

53. Refresher courses for teachers and guides and the training of instructors should be facilitated so as to aid groups of young people and adults wishing to learn about historic areas.

VI. INTERNATIONAL CO-OPERATION

54. Member States should cooperate with regard to the safeguarding of historic areas and their surroundings, seeking aid, if it seems desirable, from international organizations, both intergovernmental and non-governmental, in particular that of the UNESCO-ICOM-ICOMOS Documentation Centre. Such multilateral or bilateral co-

operation should be carefully co-ordinated and should take the form of measures such as the following:

(a) exchange of information in all forms and of scientific and technical publications;

(b) organization of seminars and working parties on particular subjects;

(c) provision of study and travel fellowships, and the dispatch of scientific, technical and administrative staff, and equipment;

(d) joint action to combat pollution of all kinds;

(e) implementation of large-scale conservation, restoration and rehabilitation projects for historic areas and publication of the experience acquired. In frontier areas where the task of developing and safeguarding historic areas and their surroundings gives rise to problems jointly affecting Member States on either side of the frontier, they should co-ordinate their policies and activities to ensure that the cultural heritage is used and protected in the best possible way;

(f) mutual assistance between neighbouring countries for the preservation of areas of common interest characteristic of the historic and cultural development of the region.

55. In conformity with the spirit and the principles of this recommendation, a Member State should not take any action to demolish or change the character of the historic quarters, towns and sites, situated in territories occupied by that State.

保护历史城镇与城区宪章（华盛顿宪章）[1]

（国际古迹遗址理事会第八届大会1987年10月在华盛顿通过）

序言与定义

一、所有城市社区，不论是长期逐渐发展起来的，还是有意创建的，都是历史上各种各样的社会的表现。

二、本宪章涉及历史城区，不论大小，其中包括城市、城镇以及历史中心或居住区，也包括其自然的和人造的环境。除了它们的历史文献作用之外，这些地区体现着传统的城市文化的价值。今天，由于社会到处实行工业化而导致城镇发展的结果，许多这类地区正面临着威胁，遭到物理退化、破坏甚至毁灭。

三、面对这种经常导致不可改变的文化、社会甚至经济损失的惹人注目的状况，国际古迹遗址理事会认为有必要为历史城镇和城区起草一国际宪章，作为《国际古迹保护与修复宪章》（通常称之为《威尼斯宪章》）的补充。这个新文本规定了保护历史城镇和城区的原则、目标和方法。它也寻求促进这一地区私人生活和社会生活的协调方法，并鼓励对这些文化财产的保护。这些文化财产无论其等级多低，均构成人类的记忆。

四、正如联合国教科文组织1976年华沙—内罗毕会议《关于历史地区保护及其当代作用的建议》以及其他一些文件所规定的，"保护历史城镇与城区"意味着这种城镇和城区的保护、保存和修复及其发展并和谐地适应现代生活所需的各种步骤。

原则和目标

一、为了更加卓有成效，对历史城镇和其他历史城区的保护应成为经济与社会发展政策的完整组成部分，并应当列入各级城市和地区规划。

二、所要保存的特性包括历史城镇和城区的特征以及表明这种特征的一切物质的和精神的组成部分，特别是：

（一）用地段和街道说明的城市的形制；

（二）建筑物与绿地和空地的关系；

（三）用规模、大小、风格、建筑、材料、色彩以及装饰说明的建筑物的外貌，包括内部的和外部的；

（四）该城镇和城区与周围环境的关系，包括自然的和人工的；

（五）长期以来该城镇和城区所获得的各种作用。任何危及上述特性的威胁，都将损害历史城镇和城区的真实性。

---

[1] 引自：联合国教科文组织世界遗产中心，国际古迹遗址理事会，国际文物保护与修复研究中心，中国国家文物局主编. 国际文化遗产保护文件选编[M]. 北京：文物出版社，2007。

三、居民的参与对保护计划的成功起着重大的作用，应加以鼓励。历史城镇和城区的保护首先涉及它们周围的居民。

四、历史城镇和城区的保护需要认真、谨慎以及系统的方法和学科，必须避免僵化，因为，个别情况会产生特定问题。

方法和手段

五、在作出保护历史城镇和城区规划之前必须进行多学科的研究。保护规划必须反映所有相关因素，包括考古学、历史学、建筑学、工艺学、社会学以及经济学。

保护规划的主要目标应该明确说明达到上述目标所需的法律、行政和财政手段。

保护规划的目的应旨在确保历史城镇和城区作为一个整体的和谐关系。

保护规划应该决定哪些建筑物必须保存，哪些在一定条件下应该保存以及哪些在极其例外的情况下可以拆毁。在进行任何治理之前，应对该地区的现状作出全面的记录。

保护规划应得到该历史地区居民的支持。

六、在采纳任何保护规划之前，应根据本宪章和《威尼斯宪章》的原则和目的开展必要的保护活动。

七、日常维护对有效地保护历史城镇和城区至关重要。

八、新的作用和活动应该与历史城镇和城区的特征相适应。使这些地区适应现代生活需要认真仔细地安装或改进公共服务设施。

九、房屋的改进应是保存的基本目标之一。

十、当需要修建新建筑物或对现有建筑物改建时，应该尊重现有的空间布局，特别是在规模和地段大小方面。与周围环境和谐的现代因素的引入不应受到打击，因为，这些特征能为这一地区增添光彩。

十一、通过考古调查和适当展出考古发掘物，应使一历史城镇和城区的历史知识得到拓展。

十二、历史城镇和城区内的交通必须加以控制，必须划定停车场，以免损坏其历史建筑物及其环境。

十三、城市或区域规划中作出修建主要公路的规定时，这些公路不得穿过历史城镇或城区，但应改进接近它们的交通。

十四、为了保护这一遗产并为了居民的安全与安居乐业，应保护历史城镇免受自然灾害、污染和噪音的危害。不管影响历史城镇或城区的灾害的性质如何，必须针对有关财产的具体特性采取预防和维修措施。

十五、为了鼓励全体居民参与保护，应为他们制定一项普通信息计划，从学龄儿童开始。与遗产保护相关的行为亦应得到鼓励，并应采取有利于保护和修复的财政措施。

十六、对一切与保护有关的专业应提供专门培训。

Charter for the Conservation of Historic Towns and Urban Areas (The Washington Charter)

Adopted by the 8th ICOMOS General Assembly, Washington, DC, October 1987

PREAMBLE AND DEFINITIONS

All urban communities, whether they have developed gradually over time or have been created deliberately, are an expression of the diversity of societies throughout history.

This charter concerns historic urban areas, large and small, including cities, towns and historic centres or quarters, together with their natural and man-made environments. Beyond their role as historical documents, these areas embody the values of traditional urban cultures. Today many such areas are being threatened, physically degraded, damaged or even destroyed, by the impact of the urban development that follows industrialisation in societies everywhere.

Faced with this dramatic situation, which often leads to irreversible cultural, social and even economic losses, the International Council on Monuments and Sites (ICOMOS) deems it necessary to draw up an international charter for historic towns and urban areas that will complement the "International Charter for the Conservation and Restoration of Monuments and Sites", usually referred to as "The Venice Charter". This new text defines the principles, objectives, and methods necessary for the conservation of historic towns and urban areas. It also seeks to promote the harmony of both private and community life in these areas and to encourage the preservation of those cultural properties, however modest in scale, that constitute the memory of mankind.

As set out in the UNESCO "Recommendation Concerning the Safeguarding and Contemporary Role of Historic Areas" (Warsaw-Nairobi, 1976), and also in various other international instruments, "the conservation of historic towns and urban areas" is understood to mean those steps necessary for the protection, conservation and restoration of such towns and areas as well as their development and harmonious adaptation to contemporary life.

PRINCIPLES AND OBJECTIVES

1. In order to be most effective, the conservation of historic towns and other historic urban areas should be an integral part of coherent policies of economic and social development and of urban and regional planning at every level.

2. Qualities to be preserved include the historic character of the town or urban area and all those material and spiritual elements that express this character, especially:

a) Urban patterns as defined by lots and streets;

b) Relationships between buildings and green and open spaces;

c) The formal appearance, interior and exterior, of buildings as defined by scale, size, style, construction, materials, colour and decoration;

d) The relationship between the town or urban area and its surrounding setting, both natural and man-made; and

e) The various functions that the town or urban area has acquired over time.

Any threat to these qualities would compromise the authenticity of the historic town or urban area.

3. The participation and the involvement of the residents are essential for the success of the conservation programme and should be encouraged. The conservation of historic towns and urban areas concerns their residents first of all.

4. Conservation in a historic town or urban area demands prudence, a systematic approach and discipline. Rigidity should be avoided since individual cases may present specific problems.

METHODS AND INSTRUMENTS

5. Planning for the conservation of historic towns and urban areas should be preceded by multidisciplinary studies.

Conservation plans must address all relevant factors including archaeology, history, architecture, techniques, sociology and economics.

The principal objectives of the conservation plan should be clearly stated as should the legal, administrative and financial measures necessary to attain them.

The conservation plan should aim at ensuring a harmonious relationship between the historic urban areas and the town as a whole.

The conservation plan should determine which buildings must be preserved, which should be preserved under certain circumstances and which, under quite exceptional circumstances, might be expendable.

Before any intervention, existing conditions in the area should be thoroughly documented.

The conservation plan should be supported by the residents of the historic area.

6. Until a conservation plan has been adopted, any necessary conservation activity should be carried out in accordance with the principles and the aims of this Charter and the Venice Charter.

7. Continuing maintenance is crucial to the effective conservation of a historic town or urban area.

8. New functions and activities should be compatible with the character of the historic town or urban area. Adaptation of these areas to contemporary life requires the careful installation or improvement of public service facilities.

9. The improvement of housing should be one of the basic objectives of conservation.

10. When it is necessary to construct new buildings or adapt existing ones, the existing spatial layout should be respected, especially in terms of scale and lot size.

The introduction of contemporary elements in harmony with the surroundings should not be discouraged since such features can contribute to the enrichment of an area.

11. Knowledge of the history of a historic town or urban area should be expanded through archaeological investigation and appropriate preservation of archaeological findings.

12. Traffic inside a historic town or urban area must be controlled and parking areas must be planned so that they do not damage the historic fabric or its environment.

13. When urban or regional planning provides for the construction of major motorways, they must not penetrate a historic town or urban area, but they should improve access to them.

14. Historic towns should be protected against natural disasters and nuisances such as pollution and vibrations in order to safeguard the heritage and for the security and well-being of the residents. Whatever the nature of a disaster affecting a historic town or urban area, preventative and repair measures must be adapted to the specific character of the properties concerned.

15. In order to encourage their participation and involvement, a general information programme should be set up for all residents, beginning with children of school age.

16. Specialised training should be provided for all those professions concerned with conservation.

关于城市历史景观的建议书,包括定义汇编[1]

(联合国教科文组织第三十六届大会2011年11月10日在巴黎通过)

前 言

大会

考虑到历史城区是我们共同的文化遗产最为丰富和多样的表现之一,是一代又一代的人所缔造的,是通过空间和时间来证明人类的努力和抱负的关键证据;

还考虑到城市遗产对人类来说是一种社会、文化和经济资产,其特征是接连出现的文化和现有文化所创造的价值在历史上的层层积淀以及传统和经验的累积,这些都体现在其多样性中;

又考虑到城市化正以人类历史上前所未有的规模向其推进,并且正在全世界推动社会经济变革和发展,应在地方、国家、地区和国际各级对城市化加以控制;

承认活的城市的动态性质;

但注意到常常失控的高速发展正在改变城区及其环境,这可能在世界范围内导致城市遗产的破碎和恶化,对社区价值观产生深刻影响;

因此,考虑到要支持对自然遗产和文化遗产的保护,就必须重视把历史城区的维护、管理及规划战略纳入地方发展进程和城市规划,例如,当代建筑和基础设施的发展,在这方面运用景观法有助于保持城市的特征。

考虑到可持续发展原则规定了保护现有资源、积极保护城市遗产以及城市遗产的可持续管理是发展的一个必要条件;

忆及教科文组织关于历史区域保护问题的一系列准则性文件,包括各项公约、建议书和宪章[2],所有这些文件仍然有效;

但注意到由于人口迁移过程、全球市场的自由化和分散化、大规模旅游、对遗产的市场开发以及气候变化,条件已经发生了变化,城市承受着发展的压力和挑战,这些压力和挑战在1976年通过关于历史区域的教科文组织前一项建议书(《关于保护历史或传统建筑群及其在现代生活中的作用的建议书》)时并不存在;

---

[1] 引自:UNESCO 第36 C/15号决议。

[2] 特别是1972年教科文组织《保护世界文化和自然遗产公约》、2005年教科文组织《保护和促进文化表现形式多样性公约》、1962年教科文组织《关于保护景观和古迹之美及特色的建议书》、1968年教科文组织《关于保护公共或私人工程危及的文化财产的建议书》、1972年教科文组织《关于在国家一级保护文化和自然遗产的建议书》、1976年教科文组织《关于保护历史或传统建筑群及其在现代生活中的作用的建议书》、1964年国际古迹遗址理事会的《国际古迹遗址保护与修复宪章》(威尼斯宪章)、1982年国际古迹遗址理事会的《国际历史花园宪章》(佛罗伦萨宪章)以及1987年国际古迹遗址理事会的《保护历史名城和历史城区宪章》(华盛顿宪章)、2005年国际古迹遗址理事会关于保护遗产建筑物、古迹和历史区域的《西安宣言》以及2005年关于世界遗产与现代建筑设计——城市历史景观管理的《维也纳备忘录》。

还注意到通过地方倡议和国际会议①的联合行动,文化和遗产的概念以及其管理方式都发生了变化,这些地方倡议和国际会议对于指导世界各地的政策和实践发挥了有益的作用;

希望补充和拓展现有国际文书中规定的标准和原则的执行;

收到了关于城市历史景观作为城市遗产保护的一种方式的建议,该建议是大会第三十六届会议的议程项目8.1;

在其第三十五届会议上**决定**通过一份面向会员国的建议书来处理该问题;

1. 兹于2011年11月10日通过了关于城市历史景观的本《建议书》;

2. 建议会员国采纳适当的立法机构框架和措施,以期在其所管理的领土上执行本《建议书》中确立的原则和标准;

3. 还建议会员国要求地方、国家和地区当局以及与保护、维护和管理历史城区及其更广泛的地理环境有关的机构、部门或社团以及协会重视本《建议书》。

引　言

1. 我们的时代见证了历史上最大规模的人类迁徙。如今,全世界超过一半的人口生活在城区。作为发展的引擎、创新和创造的中心,城区日益变得重要;城市提供就业和教育的机会,满足人们的发展需求和向往。

2. 然而,无节制的快速城市化可能常常导致社会和空间的四分五裂以及城市及周边农村地区环境的急剧恶化。显然,这可能是由于建筑物密度过大、建筑物样式的趋同和单调、公共场所和福利设施缺乏、基础设施不足、严重的贫困现象、社会隔绝以及与气候有关的灾害风险加大等因素造成的。

3. 在提高城区的宜居性,以及在不断变化的全球环境中促进经济发展和社会融合方面,城市遗产,包括有形遗产和无形遗产,是一种重要的资源。由于人类的未来取决于有效规划和管理资源,保护就成为了一种战略,目的是在可持续的基础上实现城市发展与生活质量之间的平衡。

4. 在过去的半个世纪里,城市遗产保护成为了全世界公共政策的一个重要部分,这是为了满足维护共同价值观和获益于历史遗存的需要。然而,要实现从主要强调建筑遗迹向更广泛地承认社会、文化和经济进程在维护城市价值中的重要性这一重要观念的转变,需要努力调整现行政策,并为实现这一新的城市遗产理念创造新的手段。

5. 《建议书》提到有必要更好地设计城市遗产保护战略并将其纳入整体可持续发展的更广泛目标,以支持旨在维持和改善人类环境质量的政府行动和私人行动。通过考虑其自然形状的相互联系、其空间布局和联系、其自然特征和环境,以及其社会、文化和经济价值,《建议书》为在城市大背景下识别、保护和管理历史区域提出了一种景观方法。

6. 这一方法涉及政策、治理和管理方面要关心的问题,包含各利益攸关者,包括在地方、国家、地区、国际各级参与城市发展进程的政府和私人行动者。

7. 本《建议书》借鉴了以前与遗产保护有关的四份教科文组织《建议书》,承认其概念和原则在保护历史和实践中的重要性和有效性。此外,现代保护公约和宪章涉及文化和自然遗产的许多方面,为本《建议书》奠定了基础。

---

① 尤其是1982年在墨西哥城召开的世界文化政策会议、1994年奈良原真性会议、1995年世界文化和发展委员会首脑会议、1996年在伊斯坦布尔召开的第二次联合国人类住区会议(会议批准了《21世纪议程》)、1998年在斯德哥尔摩召开的教科文组织政府间文化政策促进发展会议、1998年世界银行和教科文组织关于可持续发展中的文化——投资于文化和自然方面的天赋资源的联合会议、2005年在维也纳召开的关于世界遗产与当代建筑的国际会议、2005年国际古迹遗址理事会在西安召开的关于古迹遗址的大会,以及2008年国际古迹遗址理事会在魁北克召开的关于遗产地精神的大会。

Ⅰ. 定义

8. 城市历史景观是文化和自然价值及属性在历史上层层积淀而产生的城市区域，其超越了"历史中心"或"整体"的概念，包括更广泛的城市背景及其地理环境。

9. 上述更广泛的背景主要包括遗址的地形、地貌、水文和自然特征；其建成环境，不论是历史上的还是当代的；其地上地下的基础设施；其空地和花园、其土地使用模式和空间安排；感觉和视觉联系；以及城市结构的所有其他要素。背景还包括社会和文化方面的做法和价值观、经济进程以及与多样性和特性有关的遗产的无形方面。

10. 这一定义为在一个可持续发展的大框架内以全面综合的方式识别、评估、保护和管理城市历史景观打下了基础。

11. 城市历史景观方法旨在维持人类环境的质量，在承认其动态性质的同时提高城市空间的生产效用和可持续利用，以及促进社会和功能方面的多样性。该方法将城市遗产保护目标与社会和经济发展目标相结合。其核心在于城市环境与自然环境之间、今世后代的需要与历史遗产之间可持续的平衡关系。

12. 城市历史景观方法将文化多样性和创造力看作是促进人类发展、社会发展和经济发展的重要资产，它提供了一种手段，用于管理自然和社会方面的转变，确保当代干预行动与历史背景下的遗产和谐地结合在一起，并且考虑地区环境。

13. 城市历史景观方法借鉴地方社区的传统和看法，同时也尊重国内和国际社会的价值观。

Ⅱ. 城市历史景观面临的挑战和机遇

14. 现有的教科文组织《建议书》承认历史城市区域在现代社会中的重要作用。这些《建议书》还查明了在保护历史城市区域方面面临的一些特殊威胁，并为应对这样的挑战提出了一般性原则、政策和准则。

15. 城市历史景观方法反映了一个事实，即城市遗产保护学科和实践在最近几十年里发生了显著的变化，使得政策制定者和管理者能够更有效地应对新的挑战和把握机遇。城市景观方法支持社区在保留与其历史、集体记忆和环境有关的特征和价值的同时，寻求发展和适应求变的努力。

16. 过去几十年里，由于世界城市人口的激增、大规模和高速度发展、不断变化的经济，使城市住区及其历史区域在世界许多地区成为了经济增长的中心和驱动力，在文化和社会生活中发挥着新的作用。正因为如此，城市住区也承受着各种各样的新压力，包括：

城市化和全球化

17. 城市发展正在改变许多历史城区的本质。全球化进程对社区赋予城区及其环境的价值、对居民和用户的看法和他们的现实生活有着深刻的影响。一方面，城市化提供了能够改善生活质量和城区传统特征的经济、社会和文化机遇；另一方面，城市密度和规模增长无节制的发展带来的改变会损害地方特质感、城市结构的完整性以及社区的特性。一些历史城区正在丧失其功能性、传统作用和人口。城市历史景观方法可以帮助控制和减轻这样的影响。

发展

18. 许多经济进程提供了减轻城市贫困和促进社会和人类发展的途径和手段。信息技术以及可持续的规划、设计和建筑方法等新事物的进一步普及能够改善城市区域，从而提高生活质量。如果通过城市历史景观方法得到妥善管理，服务和旅游等新功能可以在经济方面发挥重要的积极作用，增进社区的福利，促进对历史城区及其文化遗产的保护，同时确保城市经济和社会的多样性以及居住的功能。如果不能把握这些机遇，那么城市就失去了可持续性和宜居性，就好像对城市开发不当和不合时宜会导致遗产损毁，给后世子孙造成不可挽回的损失一样。

环境

19. 人类住区一直在发生改变以适应气候和环境的变化，包括灾害所导致的变化。然而，当前变化的强度和速度对我们复杂的城市环境构成了挑战。出于对环境，尤其是水和能源消费的担心，城市生活需要采取新的方式和模式，其基础是旨在加强城市生活的可持续性和质量的重视生态的政策和做法。不过，许多这类举措应统筹考虑自然遗产和文化遗产，把它们作为促进可持续发展的资源。

20. 历史城区发生的改变也可能源于突发灾害和武装冲突。这些灾害和冲突可能是短暂的，但会产生持久影响。城市历史景观方法可以帮助控制和减轻这样的影响。

Ⅲ. 政　策

21. 现有国际建议书和宪章中所反映的现代城市保护政策为维护历史城区创造了条件。然而，为了应对现在和未来的挑战，需要拟定和执行一批新的公共政策，查明和保护城市环境中文化和自然价值在历史上的层层积淀以及平衡。

22. 应将城市遗产的保护纳入一般性政策规划和实践以及与更广泛的城市背景相关的政策规划和实践。政策应提供在短期和长期平衡保护与可持续性的机制。应特别强调具有历史意义的城市结构与当代干预行动之间的协调整合。尤其是，各利益攸关方负有下述责任：

（a）会员国应按照城市历史景观方法，将城市遗产保护战略纳入国家发展政策和议程。在这一框架内，地方当局应拟定城市发展计划，计划应考虑区域价值，包括景观及其他遗产的价值及其相关特征；

（b）公共和私营部门的利益攸关者应通过例如伙伴关系开展合作，以确保城市历史景观方法的成功实施；

（c）处理可持续发展进程的国际组织应将城市历史景观方法纳入其战略、计划和行动；

（d）国内和国际非政府组织应参与为实施城市景观方法开发和传播工具和最佳做法。

23. 各级政府——地方、地区国家／联邦——应清楚自己的责任，为定义、拟定、执行和评估城市遗产保护政策作出贡献。这些政策应基于所有利益攸关者参与的方法，并且从机构和部门的角度加以协调。

Ⅳ. 手　段

24. 基于城市历史景观的方法意味着应用一系列适应当地环境的传统手段和创新手段。需作为涉及不同利益攸关者的程序的一部分加以开发的这些手段中的一些可能包括：

（a）公民参与手段应让各部门的利益攸关者参与进来，并赋予他们权力，让他们能够查明其所属城区的重要价值，形成反映城区多样性的愿景，确立目标，就保护期遗产和促进可持续发展的行动达成一致。作为城市治理动态的一个组成部分，这些手段应通过借鉴各个社区的历史、传统、价值观、需要和向往以及促进相互冲突的不同利益和群体间的调解和谈判，为文化间对话提供便利。

（b）知识和规划手段应有助于维护城市遗产属性的完整性和真实性。这些手段还应考虑到对文化意义及多样性的承认，规定对变化进行监督和管理以改善生活质量和城市空间的质量。这些手段将包括记录和绘制文化特征和自然特征。应利用遗产评估、社会评估和环境评估来支持和便利可持续发展框架内的决策工作。

（c）监管制度应反映当地条件，可包括旨在维护和管理城市遗产的有形和无形特征包括其社会、环境和文化价值的立法措施和监管措施。必要时应承认和加强传统和习俗。

（d）财务手段应旨在建设能力和支持植于传统的能创造收入的创新发展模式。除了来自国际机构的政府资金和全球资金,应有效利用财务手段来促进地方一级的私人投资。支持地方事业的小额贷款和其他灵活融资以及各种合作模式对于城市历史景观方法在财务方面的可持续性具有重要作用。

V. 能力建设、研究、信息和传播

25. 能力建设应包含主要的利益攸关者:社区、决策者以及专业人员和管理者,以促进对城市历史景观方法及其实施的理解。有效的能力建设取决于这些主要的利益攸关者的积极配合,以便根据地区环境因地制宜地落实本《建议书》,制定和完善地方战略和目标、行动框架以及资源动员计划。

26. 应针对城市住区复杂的层积现象进行研究,以查明价值,理解其对社区的意义,并全面展示给游客。应鼓励学术机构、大学机构以及其他研究中心就城市历史景观方法的方方面面开展科学研究,并在地方、国家、地区和国际各级开展合作。重要的是记录城区的状况及其演变,以便利对改革提案进行评价,改进保护和管理技能和程序。

27. 鼓励利用信息和传播技术来记录、了解和展示城区复杂的层积现象及其组成部分。这一数据的收集和分析是城区知识的一个重要部分。为了与社会各部门进行沟通,尤为重要的是接触青年和所有代表人数不足的群体,以鼓励其参与。

VI. 国际合作

28. 各会员国和国际政府组织和非政府组织应促进公众理解和参与城市历史景观方法的实施,办法是宣传最佳做法及从世界各地获取的经验教训,以加强知识共享和能力建设网络。

29. 会员国应促进地方当局之间的跨国合作。

30. 应鼓励各会员国的国际发展和合作机构、非政府组织以及基金会开发考虑城市历史景观方法的办法,并根据其关于城区的援助计划和项目调整这些办法。

附 件

定义汇编

历史区域/城市(引自教科文组织1976年《建议书》)

"历史和建筑(包括具有民间风格的)区域应被认为是指自然和生态环境中的任何建筑群、结构和空地的集合体,包括考古和古生物遗址,它们是人类在城市或农村环境中的居住地,其聚合力和价值从考古、建筑、史前、历史、美学或社会文化角度得到承认。在这些性质千变万化的"区域"中,特别可以区分以下几类:史前遗址、历史名城、古老的城市街区、乡村和小村庄以及同类纪念性建筑群,作为一项规则,应小心谨慎地使纪念性建筑群保持原貌。

历史城区(引自国际古迹遗址理事会《华盛顿宪章》)

历史城区,无论大小,包括城市、城镇和历史中心或街区,连同其自然和人工环境。除了起着历史文献的作用,这些区域还体现了传统城市文化的价值。

城市遗产〔引自欧盟第十六号报告(2004年):通过城市内部的积极整合来实现城市历史区域的可持续发展 –SUIT〕

城市遗产包括三大类:
- 具有特殊文化价值的遗迹;
- 并不独特但以协调的方式大量出现的遗产要素;
- 应考虑的新的城市要素(例如):

- 城市建成结构；
- 空地、街道、公共空地；
- 城市基础设施、重要网络和装备。

城市保护

城市保护不只是维护单个建筑物。城市保护把建筑看作是整个城市环境的一个要素，把它作为一个复杂和多面的学科。因此，按照定义，城市保护是城市规划的核心。

建成环境

建成环境指的是用于支持人类活动的人造的（对应于天然的）资源和基础设施，例如建筑物、道路、公园以及其他福利设施。

景观方法〔引自世界保护自然联盟（IUCN）和世界保护自然基金（WWF）〕

景观方法是作出景观保护决定的框架。景观方法有助于作出具体干预行动（例如新修道路或种植植物）的明智决定，能够为涉及整个景观的活动的规划、协商和执行提供便利。

城市历史景观

（见《建议书》第9段：定义）

环境（引自国际古迹遗址理事会《西安宣言》）

遗产建筑物、遗址或历史区域的环境被定义为其直接环境和延伸环境，该环境是其重要性和独特性的组成部分或是其重要性或独特性形成的原因之一。

文化意义（引自国际古迹遗址理事会《澳大利亚巴拉宪章》）

文化意义指的是对于过去、现在或未来的人的美学、历史、科学、社会或精神价值。文化意义蕴涵于地方本身，蕴涵于其结构、环境、用途、联系、含义、记录、相关地方和相关物品。地方对不同的人或人群而言可能具有一系列的价值。

Recommendation on the Historic Urban Landscape, Including a Glossary of Definitions [1]

Adopted by the UNESCO General Conference at its 36th Session, Paris, 10 November 2011

Preamble

The General Conference,

Considering that historic urban areas are among the most abundant and diverse manifestations of our common cultural heritage, shaped by generations and constituting a key testimony to humankind's endeavours and aspirations through space and time,

Also considering that urban heritage is for humanity a social, cultural and economic asset, defined by an historic layering of values that have been produced by successive and existing cultures and an accumulation of traditions and experiences, recognized as such in their diversity,

Further considering that urbanization is proceeding on an unprecedented scale in the history of humankind, and that throughout the world this is driving socio-economic change and growth, which should be harnessed at the local, national, regional and international levels,

Recognizing, the dynamic nature of living cities,

Noting, however, that rapid and frequently uncontrolled development is transforming urban areas and their settings, which may cause fragmentation and deterioration to urban heritage with deep impacts on community values, throughout the world,

Considering, therefore, that in order to support the protection of natural and cultural heritage, emphasis needs to be put on the integration of historic urban area conservation, management and planning strategies into local development processes and urban planning, such as, contemporary architecture and infrastructure development, for which the application of a landscape approach would help maintain urban identity,

Also considering that the principle of sustainable development provides for the preservation of existing resources, the active protection of urban heritage and its sustainable management is a condition *sine qua non* of development,

Recalling that a corpus of UNESCO standard-setting documents, including conventions, recommendations

---

[1] Records of the General Conference, 36th Session, Paris, 25 October - 10 November 2011, v. 1: Resolutions. UNESCO Document Code:3 6 C/ Resolutions + CORR.

and charters① exists on the subject of the conservation of historic areas, all of which remain valid,

Also noting, however, that under processes of demographic shifts, global market liberalization and decentralization, as well as mass tourism, market exploitation of heritage, and climate change, conditions have changed and cities are subject to development pressures and challenges not present at the time of adoption of the most recent UNESCO recommendation on historic areas in 1976 (Recommendation Concerning①, the Safeguarding and Contemporary Role of Historic Areas),

Further noting the evolution of the concepts of culture and heritage and of the approaches to their management, through the combined action of local initiatives and international meetings②, which have been useful in guiding policies and practices worldwide,

Desiring to supplement and extend the application of the standards and principles laid down in existing international instruments,

Having before it proposals concerning the historic urban landscape as an approach to urban heritage conservation, which appear on the agenda of the 36th session of the General Conference as item 8.1,

Having decided at its 35th session that this issue should be addressed by means of a recommendation to Member States,

1. *Adopts*, this 10th day of November 2011, the present Recommendation on the Historic Urban Landscape;

2. *Recommends* that Member States adopt the appropriate legislative institutional framework and measures, with a view to applying the principles and norms set out in this Recommendation in the territories under their jurisdiction;

3. *Also recommends* that Member States bring this Recommendation to the attention of the local, national and regional authorities, and of institutions, services or bodies and associations concerned with the safeguarding, conservation and management of historic urban areas and their wider geographical settings.

Introduction

1. Our time is witness to the largest human migration in history. More than half of the world's population now lives in urban areas. Urban areas are increasingly important as engines of growth and as centres of innovation and creativity; they provide opportunities for employment and education and respond to people's evolving needs and aspirations.

2. Rapid and uncontrolled urbanization, however, may frequently result in social and spatial fragmentation

---

① In particular, the 1972 Convention concerning the Protection of the World Cultural and Natural Heritage, the 2005 Convention on the Protection and Promotion of the Diversity of Cultural Expressions, the 1962 Recommendation concerning the Safeguarding of the Beauty and Character of Landscapes and Sites, the 1968 Recommendation concerning the Preservation of Cultural Property Endangered by Public or Private Works, the 1972 Recommendation concerning the Protection, at National Level, of the Cultural and Natural Heritage, the 1976 Recommendation concerningthe Safeguarding and Contemporary Role of Historic Areas, the 1964 ICOMOS International Charter for the Conservation and Restoration of Monuments and Sites (Venice Charter), the 1982 ICOMOS Historic Gardens (Florence Charter), and the 1987 ICOMOS Charter for the Conservation of Historic Towns and Urban Areas (Washington Charter), the 2005 ICOMOS Xi'an Declaration on the Conservation of the Setting of Heritage Structures, Sites and Areas, as well as the 2005 Vienna Memorandum on World Heritage and Contemporary Architecture – Managing the Historic Urban Landscape.

② In particular the 1982 World Conference on Cultural Policies in Mexico City, the 1994 Nara Meeting on Authenticity, the 1995 summit of the World Commission on Culture and Development, the 1996 HABITAT II Conference in Istanbul with ratification of Agenda 21, the 1998 UNESCO Intergovernmental Conference on Cultural Policies for Development in Stockholm, the 1998 joint World Bank-UNESCO Conference on Culture in Sustainable Development–Investing in Cultural and Natural Endowments, the 2005 International Conference on World Heritage and Contemporary Architecture in Vienna, the 2005 ICOMOS General Assembly on the Setting of Monuments and Sites in Xi'an, and the 2008 ICOMOS General Assembly on the Spirit of Place in Québec.

and in a drastic deterioration of the quality of the urban environment and of the surrounding rural areas. Notably, this may be due to excessive building density, standardized and monotonous buildings, loss of public space and amenities, inadequate infrastructure, debilitating poverty, social isolation, and an increasing risk of climate-related disasters.

3. Urban heritage, including its tangible and intangible components, constitutes a key resource in enhancing the livability of urban areas, and fosters economic development and social cohesion in a changing global environment. As the future of humanity hinges on the effective planning and management of resources, conservation has become a strategy to achieve a balance between urban growth and quality of life on a sustainable basis.

4. In the course of the past half century, urban heritage conservation has emerged as an important sector of public policy worldwide. It is a response to the need to preserve shared values and to benefit from the legacy of history. However, the shift from an emphasis on architectural monuments primarily towards a broader recognition of the importance of the social, cultural and economic processes in the conservation of urban values, should be matched by a drive to adapt the existing policies and to create new tools to address this vision.

5. This Recommendation addresses the need to better integrate and frame urban heritage conservation strategies within the larger goals of overall sustainable development, in order to support public and private actions aimed at preserving and enhancing the quality of the human environment. It suggests a landscape approach for identifying, conserving and managing historic areas within their broader urban contexts, by considering the interrelationships of their physical forms, their spatial organization and connection, their natural features and settings, and their social, cultural and economic values.

6. This approach addresses the policy, governance and management concerns involving a variety of stakeholders, including local, national, regional, international, public and private actors in the urban development process.

7. This Recommendation builds upon the four previous UNESCO recommendations concerning heritage preservation, and recognizes the importance and the validity of their concepts and principles in the history and practice of conservation. In addition, modern conservation conventions and charters address the many dimensions of cultural and natural heritage, and constitute the foundations of this Recommendation.

I. Definition

8. The historic urban landscape is the urban area understood as the result of a historic layering of cultural and natural values and attributes, extending beyond the notion of "historic centre" or "ensemble" to include the broader urban context and its geographical setting.

9. This wider context includes notably the site's topography, geomorphology, hydrology and natural features, its built environment, both historic and contemporary, its infrastructures above and below ground, its open spaces and gardens, its land use patterns and spatial organization, perceptions and visual relationships, as well as all other elements of the urban structure. It also includes social and cultural practices and values, economic processes and the intangible dimensions of heritage as related to diversity and identity.

10. This definition provides the basis for a comprehensive and integrated approach for the identification, assessment, conservation and management of historic urban landscapes within an overall sustainable development framework.

11. The historic urban landscape approach is aimed at preserving the quality of the human environment,

enhancing the productive and sustainable use of urban spaces, while recognizing their dynamic character, and promoting social and functional diversity. It integrates the goals of urban heritage conservation and those of social and economic development. It is rooted in a balanced and sustainable relationship between the urban and natural environment, between the needs of present and future generations and the legacy from the past.

12. The historic urban landscape approach considers cultural diversity and creativity as key assets for human, social and economic development, and provides tools to manage physical and social transformations and to ensure that contemporary interventions are harmoniously integrated with heritage in a historic setting and take into account regional contexts.

13. The historic urban landscape approach learns from the traditions and perceptions of local communities, while respecting the values of the national and international communities.

II. Challenges and opportunities for the historic urban landscape

14. The existing UNESCO recommendations recognize the important role of historic areas in modern societies. These recommendations also identify a number of specific threats to the conservation of historic urban areas, and provide general principles, policies and guidelines to meet such challenges.

15. The historic urban landscape approach reflects the fact that both the discipline and practice of urban heritage conservation have evolved significantly in recent decades, enabling policy-makers and managers to deal more effectively with new challenges and opportunities. The historic urban landscape approach supports communities in their quest for development and adaptation, while retaining the characteristics and values linked to their history and collective memory, and to the environment.

16. In the past decades, owing to the sharp increase in the world's urban population, the scale and speed of development, and the changing economy, urban settlements and their historic areas have become centres and drivers of economic growth in many regions of the world, and have taken on a new role in cultural and social life. As a result, they have also come under a large array of new pressures, including:

Urbanization and globalization

17. Urban growth is transforming the essence of many historic urban areas. Global processes have a deep impact on the values attributed by communities to urban areas and their settings, and on the perceptions and realities of their inhabitants and users. On the one hand, urbanization provides economic, social and cultural opportunities that can enhance the quality of life and traditional character of urban areas; on the other hand, the unmanaged changes in urban density and growth can undermine the sense of place, the integrity of the urban fabric, and the identity of communities. Some historic urban areas are losing their functionality, traditional role and populations. The historic urban landscape approach may assist in managing and mitigating such impacts.

Development

18. Many economic processes offer ways and means to alleviate urban poverty and to promote social and human development. The greater availability of innovations, such as information technology and sustainable planning, design and building practices, can improve urban areas, thus enhancing the quality of life. When properly managed through the historic urban landscape approach, new functions, such as services and tourism, are important economic initiatives that can contribute to the well-being of the communities and to the conservation of historic urban areas and their cultural heritage while ensuring economic and social diversity and the residential function. Failing to capture these opportunities leads to unsustainable and unviable cities, just as implementing

them in an inadequate and inappropriate manner results in the destruction of heritage assets and irreplaceable losses for future generations.

Environment

19. Human settlements have constantly adapted to climatic and environmental changes, including those resulting from disasters. However, the intensity and speed of present changes are challenging our complex urban environments. Concern for the environment, in particular for water and energy consumption, calls for approaches and new models for urban living, based on ecologically sensitive policies and practices aimed at strengthening sustainability and the quality of urban life. Many of these initiatives, however, should integrate natural and cultural heritage as resources for sustainable development.

20. Changes to historic urban areas can also result from sudden disasters and armed conflicts. These may be short lived but can have lasting effects. The historic urban landscape approach may assist in managing and mitigating such impacts.

III. Policies

21. Modern urban conservation policies, as reflected in existing international recommendations and charters, have set the stage for the preservation of historic urban areas. However, present and future challenges require the definition and implementation of a new generation of public policies identifying and protecting the historic layering and balance of cultural and natural values in urban environments.

22. Conservation of the urban heritage should be integrated into general policy planning and practices and those related to the broader urban context. Policies should provide mechanisms for balancing conservation and sustainability in the short and long terms. Special emphasis should be placed on the harmonious, integration of contemporary interventions into the historic urban fabric. In particular, the responsibilities of the different stakeholders are the following:

(a) Member States should integrate urban heritage conservation strategies into national development policies and agendas according to the historic urban landscape approach. Within this framework, local authorities should prepare urban development plans taking into account the area's values, including the landscape and other heritage values, and features associated therewith;

(b) Public and private stakeholders should cooperate, *inter alia*, through partnerships to ensure the successful application of the historic urban landscape approach;

(c) International organizations dealing with sustainable development processes should integrate the historic urban landscape approach into their strategies, plans and operations;

(d) National and international non-governmental organizations should participate in developing and disseminating tools and best practices for the implementation of the historic urban landscape approach.

23. All levels of government – local, regional, national/federal, – aware of their responsibility – should contribute to the definition, elaboration, implementation and assessment of urban heritage conservation policies. These policies should be based on a participatory approach by all stakeholders and coordinated from both the institutional and sectorial viewpoints.

IV. Tools

24. The approach based on the historic urban landscape implies the application of a range of traditional and

innovative tools adapted to local contexts. Some of these tools, which need to be developed as part of the process involving the different stakeholders, might include:

(a) **Civic engagement tools** should involve a diverse cross-section of stakeholders, and empower them to identify key values in their urban areas, develop visions that reflect their diversity, set goals, and agree on actions to safeguard their heritage and promote sustainable development. These tools, which constitute an integral part of urban governance dynamics, should facilitate intercultural dialogue by learning from communities about their histories, traditions, values, needs and aspirations, and by facilitating mediation and negotiation between groups with conflicting interests.

(b) **Knowledge and planning tools** should help protect the integrity and authenticity of the attributes of urban heritage. They should also allow for the recognition of cultural significance and diversity, and provide for the monitoring and management of change to improve the quality of life and of urban space. These tools would include documentation and mapping of cultural and natural characteristics. Heritage, social and environmental impact assessments should be used to support and facilitate decision-making processes within a framework of sustainable development.

(c) **Regulatory systems** should reflect local conditions, and may include legislative and regulatory measures aimed at the conservation and management of the tangible and intangible attributes of the urban heritage, including their social, environmental and cultural values. Traditional and customary systems should be recognized and reinforced as necessary.

(d) **Financial tools** should be aimed at building capacities and supporting innovative income-generating development, rooted in tradition. In addition to government and global funds from international agencies, financial tools should be effectively employed to foster private investment at the local level. Micro-credit and other flexible financing to support local enterprise, as well as a variety of models of partnerships, are also central to making the historic urban landscape approach financially sustainable.

Ⅴ. Capacity-building, research, information and communication

25. Capacity-building should involve the main stakeholders: communities, decision-makers, and professionals and managers, in order to foster understanding of the historic urban landscape approach and its implementation. Effective capacity-building hinges on an active collaboration of these main stakeholders, aimed at adapting the implementation of this Recommendation to regional contexts in order to define and refine the local strategies and objectives, action frameworks and resource mobilization schemes.

26. Research should target the complex layering of urban settlements, in order to identify values, understand their meaning for the communities, and present them to visitors in a comprehensive manner. Academic and university institutions and other centres of research should be encouraged to develop scientific research on aspects of the historic urban landscape approach, and cooperate at the local, national, regional and international level. It is essential to document the state of urban areas and their evolution, to facilitate the evaluation of proposals for change, and to improve protective and managerial skills and procedures.

27. Encourage the use of information and communication technology to document, understand and present the complex layering of urban areas and their constituent components. The collection and analysis of this data is an essential part of the knowledge of urban areas. To communicate with all sectors of society, it is particularly important to reach out to youth and all under-represented groups in order to encourage their participation.

VI. International cooperation

28. Member States and international governmental and non-governmental organizations should facilitate public understanding and involvement in the implementation of the historic urban landscape approach, by disseminating best practices and lessons learned from different parts of the world, in order to strengthen the network of knowledge-sharing and capacity-building.

29. Member States should promote multinational cooperation between local authorities.

30. International development and cooperation agencies of Member States, non-governmental organizations and foundations should be encouraged to develop methodologies which take into account the historic urban landscape approach and to harmonize them with their assistance programmes and projects pertaining to urban areas.

APPENDIX
Glossary of Definitions

Historic area/city (from the 1976 Recommendation)

"Historic and architectural (including vernacular) areas" shall be taken to mean any groups of buildings, structures and open spaces including archaeological and paleontological sites, constituting human settlements in an urban or rural environment, the cohesion and value of which, from the archaeological, architectural, prehistoric, historic, aesthetic or sociocultural point of view are recognized. Among these "areas", which are very varied in nature, it is possible to distinguish the following in particular: prehistoric sites, historic towns, old urban quarters, villages and hamlets as well as homogeneous monumental groups, it being understood that the latter should as a rule be carefully preserved unchanged.

Historic urban area (from the ICOMOS Washington Charter)

Historic urban areas, large and small, include cities, towns and historic centres or quarters, together with their natural and man-made environments. Beyond their role as historical documents, these areas embody the values of traditional urban cultures.

Urban heritage (from European Union research report N°. 16 (2004), *Sustainable development of Urban historical areas through and active Integration within Towns–SUIT*)

Urban heritage comprises three main categories:
- Monumental heritage of exceptional cultural value;
- Non-exceptional heritage elements but present in a coherent way with a relative abundance;
- New urban elements to be considered (for instance):
    - The urban built form;
    - The open space: streets, public open spaces;
    - Urban infrastructures: material networks and equipment.

Urban conservation

Urban conservation is not limited to the preservation of single buildings. It views architecture as but one element of the overall urban setting, making it a complex and multifaceted discipline. By definition, then, urban conservation lies at the very heart of urban planning.

Built environment

The built environment refers to human-made (versus natural) resources and infrastructure designed to support human activity, such as buildings, roads, parks, and other amenities.

Landscape approach (from the International Union for Conservation of Nature – IUCN, and the World Wildlife Fund – WWF)

The landscape approach is a framework for making landscape-level conservation decisions. The landscape approach helps to reach decisions about the advisability of particular interventions (such as a new road or plantation), and to facilitate the planning, negotiation and implementation of activities across a whole landscape.

Historic urban landscape

(see definition in paragraph 9 of the Recommendation)

Setting (from the ICOMOS Xi'an Declaration)

The setting of a heritage structure, site or area is defined as the immediate and extended environment that is part of, or contributes to, its significance and distinctive character.

Cultural significance (from the ICOMOS Australia Burra Charter)

Cultural significance means aesthetic, historic, scientific, social or spiritual value for past, present or future generations. Cultural significance is embodied in the place itself, its fabric, setting, use, associations, meanings, records, related places and related objects. Places may have a range of values for different individuals or groups.

关于维护与管理历史城镇与城区的瓦莱塔原则

(国际古迹遗址理事会第十七届大会 2011 年 11 月 28 日在巴黎通过)

前 言

当今时代,人类必须应对众多变化。这些变化总的来说与人类聚居地有关,尤其是历史城镇和城区。市场和生产方式的全球化,导致了地区之间以及通往城镇的人口迁移,尤其是大城市。政治监管和商业规范的变化,也要求城镇和城区建立新的结构和新的条件。除此之外,还有必要应对隔离和社会漂泊感,作为强化身份认同的部分手段。

在当前对城市保护所展开的反思这个国际框架下,人们正越来越多地认识到这些新的要求。主管遗产保护及其价值强化的组织需要发展他们的技能、工具和态度,在很多情况下,还包括他们在规划进程中的作用。

因此,CIVVIH(ICOMOS——国际历史村镇委员会)根据现有的一系列参考文件,对《华盛顿宪章》(1987)和《内罗毕建议》(1976)中所列出的方法和关注事项进行了修订。CIVVIH重新界定了目标、态度和所需的工具,将与历史城镇和城区维护和管理相关的定义和方法的重大沿革纳入了考虑范畴。

这些修订内容反映了对历史遗产问题更广泛的认识:在地区规模上,而不只是局限于城区;延续性和身份认同等非物质价值;传统的土地使用;公共空间在社区互动中的作用;以及其他社会经济因素,比如人口融合和环境因素。与景观作为共同基础的作用相关的问题,或者说城市景观的概念(包括地貌与天际线)变得前所未有的重要。另一个重要的修订内容,尤其是在快速发展的城市,则将大规模发展问题纳入了考虑范畴。这些问题改变了构成历史城市地貌的传统场所的规模。

从这个意义上来说,将遗产看作是一种基本资源,作为城市生态系统的一部分至关重要。要确保历史城镇及其背景的和谐发展,就必须严格尊重这一概念。

可持续发展的观念也变得更加重要,当前很多与建筑规划和介入相关的指导文件都是以旨在限制城市扩张和保护城市遗产的政策为基础。

这份文件的主要目标是,提出适用于历史城镇和城区的每一个介入行为的原则和策略。这些原则和策略旨在保护历史城镇及其背景的价值,以及它们与当今时代的社会、文化和经济生活的融合。

这些介入活动必须尊重物质和非物质遗产价值,以及居民生活品质。

这份关于维护历史城镇和城区及其背景的文件被分为四个部分:

1- 名词解释

2- 变化领域(挑战)

3- 介入标准

4- 建议和策略

1. 名词解释

a- 历史城镇与城区

历史城镇和城区由物质和非物质元素构成。除城市结构外，物质元素包括：建筑元素、城镇内和周边的景观、考古遗迹、全景图、天际线、视线和地标。非物质元素包括：构成它们的历史价值的实质的活动、象征和历史功能、文化行为、传统、记忆和文化参照物。

历史城镇和城区是表现一个社会及其文化身份的沿革的空间结构。它们是更广泛的自然或人造背景不可或缺的组成部分，必须将两者分开来考虑。历史城镇和城区是构成它们的过去的生动证据。

历史或传统地区构成了人类日常生活的一部分。它们的保护及其与当代社会的融合，构成了城镇规划和土地发展的基础。

b- 背景

背景指的是历史城市遗产所在的影响这些地区被感知、体验和（或）欣赏的静态或动态方式，或者是与它们有着直接的社会、经济或文化联系的自然和（或）人造背景。

c- 维护

历史城镇和城区及其周边环境的维护包括为它们的保护、保存、强化和管理以及连贯发展以及与当代生活的和谐适应而采取的必要的程序。

d- 保护城区

保护城区是城镇中任何一部分代表城镇某一个历史时期或发展阶段的部分，包括：纪念碑和真正的城市机构，在这些地方，建筑表现了场所之所以被保护的文化价值。

保护可能还包括城镇的历史发展，以及为其特有的城市、宗教和社会功能提供支持。

e- 缓冲区

缓冲区是位于保护区外的一个清晰界定的区域，其作用是为保护区的文化价值提供屏障，使其免于受到周边活动的影响。这个影响可以是物理的、视觉的或社会的。

f- 管理计划

管理计划是一份文件，该文件详尽地列出所有用于遗产保护的战略和工具，同时也对当代生活的需求做出回应，包括法律、财务、行政和管理文件，同时也包括保护和监管计划。

g- 场所精神

场所精神是为一个地区赋予特定身份、内涵、情感和神秘性的物质的和非物质的、物理的和精神的元素。精神创造了空间，反过来，空间又建造了精神，并为其赋予结构（《魁北克宣言》，2008年）。

2. 变化领域

作为有生命的有机体，历史城镇和城区总是不断经历变化。这些变化会影响到城镇的所有元素（自然、人工、物质和非物质）。

变化如果管理得当，可以成为以历史特征为基础改善历史城镇和城区品质的机会。

a- 变化与自然环境

《华盛顿宪章》已经关注了与自然环境变化相关的问题："为了保护这一遗产并为了居民的安全与安居乐业，应保护历史城镇（及其背景）免受自然灾害、污染和噪音的危害"（《华盛顿宪章》）。

在历史城镇和城区，变化应当建立在尊重自然平衡的基础上，避免破坏自然资源、浪费能源和打破自然循环的平衡。

变化应被用于：改善历史城镇和城区的环境背景；改善空气、水和土壤质量；鼓励绿色空间的拓展和可用性；避免给自然资源造成不恰当的压力。

应保护历史城镇及其背景免受气候变化以及日益频繁的自然灾害的影响。

气候变化可能给历史城镇和城区带来灾难性的影响，除了城市结构的脆弱性之外，很多建筑正遭到废弃，需要花费大量的资金去处理气候变化所导致的问题。

利用全球对气候变化的认识的增加及从中所产生的策略，将它们恰当地用于应对维护历史城镇的挑战。

b- 变化与建筑环境

关于现代建筑，《华盛顿宪章》指出："与周围环境和谐的现代因素的引入不应受到打击，因为，这些特征能为这一地区增添光彩。"

现代建筑元素的引进必须尊重古迹及其背景的价值。这些元素可以为城镇增添光彩，让城市的价值得以延续。从空间、视觉、非物质和功能角度来说，恰当的建筑介入的基础是对历史价值、模式和层次的尊重。

新建筑必须与历史区域的空间组织连贯一致，尊重其传统地貌，同时又恰当地表现当时当地的建筑潮流。无论采取何种风格和表现方式，所有新建筑都必须避免戏剧性或过度的对比、以及将城市结构和空间割裂和打破所带来的负面效果。

必须优先考虑构成的延续性，既不能给现有建筑造成负面影响，又能具有敏锐的创造力，蕴含场所的精神。

建筑师和城市规划师必须对城市历史背景有深入的理解。

c- 用途和社会环境的变化

传统用途和功能的失去和（或）被替代，比如某个地方社区的特定生活方式，可能对历史城镇和城区造成巨大的负面影响。如果不能认识这些变化的本质，就可能导致社区迁移，文化活动消失，这些被遗弃的场所也会随之失去身份和个性。还可能导致历史城镇和城区变成只从事休闲旅游的单一功能区，不再适合日常生活。

历史城镇保护需要采取措施保存传统活动、保护本地原住人口。

另一个重要的问题就是控制由于租金增加所带来的住宅高档化进程，以及城镇和城区房屋和公共空间的恶化。

重要的是认识到住宅高档化进程可能影响社区，导致社区失去可居住性，并最终失去其个性。

保留每一个场所的传统文化和经济多样性至关重要，尤其是当这种多样性正是该场所的特色所在的时候。

历史城镇和城区正面临着成为大众旅游消费品的风险，这可能导致它们的真实性和遗产价值的失落。因此，必须审慎管理新活动，避免交通冲突或交通拥堵造成的次要负面影响。

d- 变化和非物质遗产

非物质遗产的维护与建筑环境的保存和保护一样重要。

构成场所身份和精神的非物质元素需要被巩固和维护，因为它们有助于决定一个地区和场所的个性。

3. 介入标准

a- 价值

对历史城镇和城区的所有介入活动都必须尊重并参考其物质和非物质文化价值。

b- 质量

对历史城镇和城区的每一个介入活动都必须以改善当地人的生活质量以及环境质量为目标。

c- 数量

变化累积可能对历史城镇及其价值造成负面影响。

应避免大规模的量变和质变，除非它们能够明显地改善城市环境及其文化价值。

应控制和审慎管理城市增长固有的变化，将其对城市景观和建筑结构的物理和视觉影响降至最小。

d- 连贯性

关于"连贯性"，《内罗毕建议》第3条指出："每一历史地区及某周围环境应从整体上视为一个相互联系的统一体，其协调及特性取决于它的各组成部分的联合，这些组成部分包括人类活动、建筑物、空间结构及周围环境。因此一切有效的组成部分，包括人类活动，无论多么微不足道，都对整体具有不可忽视的意义。"

历史城镇和城区及其背景都应被看作是一个统一体。

它们的均衡和性质取决于其构成成份。然而，历史城镇和城区的维护必须成为对城市结构及其周边环境的整体认识不可或缺的一部分。这需要采取连贯一致的经济和社会发展政策，将历史城镇纳入到所有规划层面的思考之中，同时尊重它们的社会结构和文化多样性。

e- 均衡和匹配性

历史城镇的维护必须将维护空间、环境、社会、文化和经济的基本平衡作为必要条件。这需要采取一定的行动，让城市结构保留原有居民，欢迎新到来者（无论是作为居民还是历史城镇的使用者），同时还要在不造成拥堵的情况下为发展提供协助。

f- 时间

变化的速度应成为被控制的参数。过快的变化速度可能给历史城镇的所有价值的完整性造成负面影响。

在可行性研究和规划文件中，必须纳入介入活动的范围和频率，并与之匹配，同时遵守透明和有控制的介入流程。

g- 方法和科学训练

"通过考古调查和适当展出考古发掘物，应使历史城镇和城区的历史知识得到拓展。"（《华盛顿宪章》）

应以审慎的、系统性的方法和态度指导历史城镇或城区的维护和管理，遵守可持续发展原则。

维护和管理必须建立在初步的多学科研究的基础上，以决定需要保护的城市遗产元素和价值。必须对古迹及其背景拥有深厚的知识，为任何维护行为提供资料。

持之以恒的监测和维护对于历史城镇或城区的有效保护至关重要。

恰当的规划要求最新的准确归档和记录（背景分析、不同层级的研究、组成部件及影响的清册目录、城镇历史及发展阶段，等等）。

与居民和其他利益相关者的直接磋商和持续对话必不可少，因为历史城镇或城区的维护首先与他们有关。

h- 监管

良好的监管为组织所有利益相关者的广泛参与做出了规定：选举机构、自治服务、公共管理、专家、专业组织、志愿机构、大学、居民等等。这对于历史城镇和城区的成功维护、重置和可持续发展至关重要。

居民的参与可以通过信息传播、意识提高和培训来推动。传统的城市监管系统应当审查文化和社会多样性的所有方面，建立新的民主机构，以满足新的现实需要。

在城市规划历史城市维护流程中，必须为居民提供足够的信息和时间，以获得充分的反馈。

必须鼓励维护，并采取恰当的财务措施，推动私人领域的所有参与者之间在建筑环境保护和修复方面的合作。

i- 多学科性与合作

"在作出保护历史城镇和城区规划之前必须进行多学科的研究。"（《华盛顿宪章》）

从初级研究开始，历史城镇的保护就必须以众多不同学科的专家的有效合作为基础，在研究者、公共服务机构、私营企业和广大工作的合作下开展。

这些研究应当提出明确的建议，供政治决策者、社会和经济机构及居民采纳。

j- 文化多样性

在城市保护规划的背景下，必须尊重和重视历史上居住在历史城镇的不同社区的文化多样性。

建立敏感和共享的均衡对于维护历史遗产丰富的文化多样性至关重要。

4. 建议和策略

a- 需要保存的元素

1- 作为其最基本的特征，历史城镇的真实性和完整性是通过所有物质和非物质元素的性质和连贯性表现出来的，尤其是：

a- 通过街道网格、地块、绿地以及建筑和绿地及空地之间的关系所界定的城市格局；

"b- 用规模、大小、风格、建筑、材料、色彩以及装饰说明的建筑物的外貌，包括内部的和外部的；

c- 该城镇和城区与周围环境的关系，包括自然的和人工的；"（《华盛顿宪章》）

d- 城镇或城区随着时间的推移而发展出来的各种功能；

e- 文化传统、传统技巧、场所精神以及有助于决定场所身份的一切；

2- 场所[1]整体、其组成部分、背景以及构成背景的组成部分之间的关系；

3- 社会结构，文化多样性；

4- 不可更新的资源，将它们的消耗降至最低，鼓励它们的重复和循环使用。

b- 新功能

"新的作用和活动应该与历史城镇和城区的特征相适应。"（《华盛顿宪章》）

新活动的引进不能破坏传统活动的生存，或者是支持本地居民日常生活的任何事。这可以有助保存历史文化的多样性，以及在这一背景下的某些最有价值的元素。

在引进新活动之前，有必要考虑涉及到的使用者的数量、使用的长度、与其他现有活动是否相适应，以及对传统地方活动的影响。

这些新功能必须满足可持续发展的需要，与历史城镇作为一个独特的不可替代的生态系统的概念一致。

c- 当代建筑

如果必须要建造新建筑，或者是改造现有建筑，当代建筑必须要与历史城镇现有的空间规划以及整个城市环境保持一致。

当代建筑应在尊重场所规模，与现有建筑及其背景的发展模式和谐一致的前提下，找到自己的表达方式。

"应特别注意对新建筑物制定规章并加以控制，以确保该建筑能与历史建筑群的空间结构和环境协调一致。为此，在任何新建项目之前，应对城市的来龙去脉进行分析，其目的不仅在于确定该建筑群的一般特征，而且在于分析其主要特征，如：高度、色彩、材料及造型之间的和谐、建筑物正面和屋顶建造方式的衡量、建筑面积与空间体积之间的关系及其平均比例和位置。特别应注意基址的面积，因为存在着这样一个危险，即基址的任何改动都可能带来整体的变化，均对整体的和谐不利。"（《内罗毕建议》第28条）

视角、景观、焦点和视觉走廊都是历史空间认知不可或缺的部分。在采取新的介入活动时必须予以尊重。

在采取任何介入活动之前，应对现有背景进行仔细的分析和整理归档，应甄别、研究和维护看向新建筑及由新建筑看出的视锥。

应从正式的功能性的角度评估在历史背景或景观中引入新建筑的行为，尤其是当其涉及到新活动的时候。

d- 公共空间

历史城镇中的公共空间不仅是流通的重要资源[2]，也是供城中居民沉思、学习和欣赏的场所。其设计和布局，包括街道设备的选择以及其管理都必须保护某个性和魅力，促进其作为社会交流的公共场所的使用。

在采取新的介入行为和增加新的用途时，必须仔细分析和控制公共空地与建筑密集环境之间的均衡。

e- 设施和改造

维护历史城镇的城市规划必须将居民对设施的需要纳入考虑范畴。将新设施整合到历史建筑中是地方政府机构不能忽视的挑战。

f- 活动性

"历史城镇和城区内的交通必须加以控制。"（《华盛顿宪章》）

"城市或区域规划中作出修建主要公路的规定时，这些公路不得穿过历史城镇或城区，但应改进接近它们的交通。"（《华盛顿宪章》）

大多数城镇和城区都针对人行道和缓慢的交通形式设计。这些地方逐渐被汽车入侵，导致景观退化，与此同时也降低了生活质量。

交通基础设施（停车场、地铁站等）的规划不能破坏历史结构或其环境。历史城镇应鼓励开设足迹较小的交通方式。

鼓励步行交通也很重要。要做到这一点，应大幅度限制交通，减少停车设施。与此同时，还需要引入可持续发展的无污染的公共交通系统，推广软性流动。

应对道路加以研究和规划，给予人行道优先权。停车设施最好是位于保护区外，如果有可能最好是位于缓冲区外。

应规划地下设施（比如地铁）以避免破坏历史或考古结构或其环境。

主要高速公路网络必须避开保护区和缓冲区。

g- 旅游业

旅游业可以给历史城镇和城区的发展和复兴带来积极影响。历史城镇的旅游业发展应以为遗址及开阔空间增添光彩为基础；尊重和支持本地社区的身份认同及其文化和传统活动；维护地区和环境特征。旅游活动还必须尊重而不是干扰居民的日常生活。

太多旅游者涌入可能给遗址和历史城区的保护带来危险。

保护和管理计划必须考虑到旅游业可能带来的影响，并本着对遗产和本地居民有利的原则规范相关流程。

h- 风险

"不管影响历史城镇或城区的灾害的性质如何，必须针对有关财产的具体特性采取预防和维修措施。"（《华盛顿宪章》）

保护计划应为改善风险准备和推动环境管理和可持续原则提供机会。

i- 节约能源

对历史城镇和城区的所有介入活动，都应在尊重历史遗产个性的基础上，以提高能源效率和减少污染为目标。

应增加可再生能源的使用。

历史城区的任何新建筑都应尊重能源效率。应采用城市绿地、绿色走廊及其他措施，避免城市热岛。

j- 参与

"居民的参与对保护计划的成功起着重大的作用，应加以鼓励。历史城镇和城区的保护首先涉及它们周围的居民。"（《华盛顿宪章》，第 3 条）

历史城区的规划必须是所有利益相关者都参与其中的过程。

为了鼓励参与，应针对从学龄儿童开始的所有居民建立一整套沟通计划。必须鼓励保护协会等行为，采取恰当的财政措施，推动建筑环境的保护和修复。

基于公共意识的共同认知以及对地方社区与专业团体之间的共同目标的追求，是成功保护、复兴和发展历史城镇的基础。信息技术可以促进直接和即时的沟通，有利于本地团体积极负责的参与。

必须鼓励政府机构有兴趣维护历史城镇和城区，建立能够促进管理和改善计划成功的财务措施。

k- 保护规划

"保护规划的目的应旨在确保历史城镇和城区作为一个整体的和谐关系……"（《华盛顿宪章》，第 5 条）

保护规划应涵盖物质和非物质元素，在不阻碍沿革的前提下保护场所身份。

保护规划的主要目标"应该明确说明达到上述目标所需的法律、行政和财政手段"。（《华盛顿宪章》，第 5 条）

保护规划必须建立在对整个城镇的城市规划的基础上，包括对考古、历史、建筑、技术、社会和经济价值的分析。规划应指定保护项目，并结合一份管理计划和后续的持久监测。

保护规划应决定任何变化的条件、规则、目标和结果。"应该决定哪些建筑物必须保存，哪些在一定条件下应该保存以及哪些在极其例外的情况下可以拆毁。"（《华盛顿宪章》）

在采取任何介入行动之前，应对该地区的现状作出全面的记录。

保护规划必须指明并保护对城镇价值和特征有利的元素，以及丰富并（或）展现历史城镇和城区个性的组成部分。

保护规划中的建议必须以实际可行的方式从法律、财务和经济角度根据所需要的标准和限制清晰阐述出来。

"保护规划应得到该历史地区居民的支持。"（《华盛顿宪章》，第 5 条）

如果没有保护规划，历史城镇的所有必要的保护和发展活动都必须依据保护和强化的原则和目标执行。

l- 管理计划

应根据每一个历史城镇和城区的类型和特征及其文化和自然背景设计有效的管理系统。管理计划应整合传统活动，与当前正在使用的其他城市和地区规划工具协调。

管理计划是建立在对物质和非物质资源的了解、保护和强化的基础上。

因此，管理计划应：

- 决定文化价值；
- 指明利益相关者及其价值；
- 指明潜在冲突；
- 决定管理目标；
- 决定法律、财政、行政和技术方法和工具；
- 了解优势、劣势、机会和威胁；
- 界定恰当的策略、工作期限和具体行动。

类似管理计划的出台应该是一个广泛参与的过程。

除了地方政府机构、官员、现场调查和详尽的档案所提供的资料外，计划还应该在附录中放入利益相关者的讨论结果,以及对这些固有矛盾的冲突的分析[3]。

跟进工作

上述建议是 CIVVIH 共同劳动的结果,也是对 ICOMOS 所主持的更广泛的讨论的一点贡献。

这是一份开放的资源文件,可以随着话题讨论的发展而不断更新。

CIVVIH

国际历史村镇委员会(International Committee on Historic Towns and Villages,简称 CIVVIH)成立于 1982 年。

委员会致力于处理与历史村镇的规划和管理相关的问题。委员会成员由与历史城镇保护相关的不同专业背景的专家组成。

我们来自全球 ICOMOS 各成员国,致力于与这个领域的所有同行分享我们的知识和经验[4]。

编者注:[1]、[2]、[3]、[4],此处根据英文原文有少量修改。

The Valletta Principles for the Safeguarding and Management of Historic Cities, Towns and Urban Areas

Adopted by the 17th ICOMOS General Assembly, Paris, 28 November 2011

Preamble

Humanity today must confront a number of changes. These changes concern human settlements, in general, and historic towns and urban areas in particular. The globalization of markets and methods of production cause shifts in population between regions and towards towns, especially large cities. Changes in political governance and in business practices require new structures and new conditions in towns and urban areas. These are also necessary to counteract segregation and social rootlessness as part of attempts to reinforce identity.

Within what is now an international framework of reflection on urban conservation, there is an ever-increasing awareness of these new demands. The organizations charged with the conservation of heritage and the enhancement of its value need to develop their skills, their tools, their attitudes and, in many cases, their role in the planning process.

CIVVIH (ICOMOS-International Committee on Historic Towns and Villages) has therefore updated the approaches and considerations contained in the Washington Charter (1987) and the Nairobi Recommendation (1976), based on the existing set of reference documents. CIVVIH has redefined the objectives, attitudes and tools needed. It has taken into consideration the significant evolution in definitions and methodologies concerning the safeguarding and management of historic towns and urban areas.

The modifications reflect a greater awareness of the issue of historic heritage on a regional scale rather than just confined to urban areas; of intangible values such as continuity and identity; of traditional land use, the role of public space in communal interactions, and of other socioeconomic factors such as integration and environmental factors. Questions around the role of landscape as common ground, or conceptualizing the townscape, including its topography and skyline, as a whole, seem more important than before. Another important modification, particularly in fast-growing cities, takes into account the problems of large-scale developments, which alter the traditional lot sizes that help to define historic urban morphology.

In this sense, it is fundamental to consider heritage as an essential resource, as part of the urban ecosystem. This concept must be strictly respected in order to ensure harmonious development of historic towns and their settings.

The notion of sustainable development has gained such importance that many directives on architectural planning and interventions are now based on policies designed to limit urban expansion and to preserve urban heritage.

The main objective of this document is to propose principles and strategies applicable to every intervention in historic towns and urban areas. These principles and strategies are meant to safeguard the values of historic towns and their settings, as well as their integration into the social, cultural and economic life of our times.

These interventions must ensure respect for tangible and intangible heritage values, as well as for the quality of life of inhabitants.

This present document for the safeguarding of historic towns and urban areas and their settings, is divided into four parts:

1 - Definitions
2 - Aspects of change (Challenges)
3 - Intervention criteria
4 - Proposals and strategies

1-Definitions

a-Historic towns and urban areas

Historic towns and urban areas are made up of tangible and intangible elements. The tangible elements include, in addition to the urban structure, architectural elements, the landscapes within and around the town, archaeological remains, panoramas, skylines, view-lines and landmark sites. Intangible elements include activities, symbolic and historic functions, cultural practices, traditions, memories, and cultural references that constitute the substance of their historic value.

Historic towns and urban areas are spatial structures that express the evolution of a society and of its cultural identity. They are an integral part of a broader natural or man-made context and the two must be considered inseparable. Historic towns and urban areas are living evidence of the past that formed them.

Historical or traditional areas form part of daily human life. Their protection and integration into contemporary society are the basis for town-planning and land development.

b-Setting

Setting means the natural and/or man-made contexts (in which the historic urban heritage is located) that influence the static or dynamic way these areas are perceived, experienced and/or enjoyed, or which are directly linked to them socially, economically or culturally.

c-Safeguarding

The safeguarding of historic towns and urban areas, and their surroundings, includes the necessary procedures for their protection, conservation, enhancement and management as well as for their coherent development and their harmonious adaptation to contemporary life.

d-Protected urban area

A protected urban area is any part of a town that represents a historical period or stage of development of the town. It includes monuments and authentic urban fabric, in which buildings express the cultural values for which the place is protected.

The protection may also include the historical development of the town and support its characteristic civic, religious and social functions.

e-Buffer zone

A buffer zone is a well-defined zone outside the protected area whose role is to shield the cultural values of the protected zone from the impact of activities in its surroundings. This impact can be physical, visual or social.

f-Management Plan

A Management Plan is a document specifying in detail all the strategies and tools to be used for heritage protection and which at the same time responds to the needs of contemporary life. It contains legislative, financial, administrative and conservation documents, as well as Conservation and Monitoring Plans.

g-Spirit of place

Spirit of place is defined as the tangible and intangible, the physical and the spiritual elements that give the area its specific identity, meaning, emotion and mystery. The spirit creates the space and at the same time the space constructs and structures this spirit (Quebec Declaration, 2008).

2-Aspects of Change

Historic towns and urban areas, as living organisms, are subject to continual change. These changes affect all the elements of the town (natural, human, tangible and intangible).

Change, when appropriately managed, can be an opportunity to improve the quality of historic towns and urban areas on the basis of their historical characteristics.

a-Change and the natural environment

The Washington Charter has already focused on the problems linked to changes in the natural environment: "Historic towns (and their settings) should be protected against natural disasters and nuisances such as pollution and vibrations in order to safeguard the heritage and for the security and well-being of the residents". (Washington Charter)

In historic towns and urban areas, change should be based on respect for natural balance, avoiding the destruction of natural resources, waste of energy and disruption in the balance of natural cycles.

Change must be used to: improve the environmental context in historic towns and urban areas; improve the quality of air, water and soil; foster the spread and accessibility of green spaces; and to avoid undue pressure on natural resources.

Historic towns and their settings must be protected from the effects of climate change and from increasingly frequent natural disasters.

Climate change can have devastating consequences for historic towns and urban areas because, in addition to the fragility of the urban fabric, many buildings are becoming obsolete, requiring high levels of expenditure to tackle problems arising from climate change.

The aim should be to take advantage of strategies arising from growing global awareness of climate change and to apply them appropriately to the challenges of safeguarding historic towns.

b-Change and the built environment

On the subject of modern architecture, the Washington Charter states: "The introduction of contemporary elements in harmony with the surroundings should not be discouraged since such features can contribute to the enrichment of an area".

The introduction of contemporary architectural elements must respect the values of the site and its setting. It can contribute to the enrichment of the town, bringing alive the value of urban continuity.

The basis of appropriate architectural interventions in spatial, visual, intangible and functional terms should be respect for historical values, patterns and layers.

New architecture must be consistent with the spatial organisation of the historic area and respectful of its traditional morphology while at the same time being a valid expression of the architectural trends of its time and place. Regardless of style and expression, all new architecture should avoid the negative effects of drastic or excessive contrasts and of fragmentation and interruptions in the continuity of the urban fabric and space.

Priority must be given to a continuity of composition that does not adversely affect the existing architecture but at the same time allows a discerning creativity that embraces the spirit of the place.

Architects and urban planners must be encouraged to acquire a deep understanding of the historic urban context.

c-Change in use and social environment

The loss and/or substitution of traditional uses and functions, such as the specific way of life of a local community, can have major negative impacts on historic towns and urban areas. If the nature of these changes is not recognised, it can lead to the displacement of communities and the disappearance of cultural practices, and subsequent loss of identity and character for these abandoned places. It can result in the transformation of historic towns and urban areas into areas with a single function devoted to tourism and leisure and not suitable for day-to-day living.

Conserving a historic town requires efforts to maintain traditional practices and to protect the indigenous population.

It is also important to control the gentrification process arising from rent increases and the deterioration of the town or area's housing and public space.

It is important to recognise that the process of gentrification can affect communities and lead to the loss of a place's liveability and, ultimately, its character.

Retention of the traditional cultural and economic diversity of each place is essential, especially when it is characteristic of the place.

Historic towns and urban areas run the risk of becoming a consumer product for mass tourism, which may result in the loss of their authenticity and heritage value.

New activities must therefore be carefully managed to avoid secondary negative effects such as transport conflicts or traffic congestion.

d-Change and intangible heritage

The preservation of intangible heritage is as important as the conservation and protection of the built environment.

The intangible elements that contribute to the identity and spirit of places need to be established and preserved, since they help in determining the character of an area and its spirit.

3-Intervention Criteria

a-Values

All interventions in historic towns and urban areas must respect and refer to their tangible and intangible cultural values.

b-Quality

Every intervention in historic towns and urban areas must aim to improve the quality of life of the local residents and the quality of the environment.

c-Quantity

An accumulation of changes could have a negative effect on a historic town and its values.

Major quantitative and qualitative changes should be avoided, unless they will clearly result in the improvement of the urban environment and its cultural values.

Changes that are inherent to urban growth must be controlled and carefully managed to minimise physical and visual effects on the townscape and architectural fabric.

d-Coherence

On 'coherence' article 3 of the Nairobi Recommendation states: "Every historic area and its surroundings should be considered in their totality as a coherent whole whose balance and specific nature depend on the fusion of the parts of which it is composed and which include human activities as much as the buildings, the spatial organization and the surroundings. All valid elements, including human activities, however modest, thus have significance in relation to the whole which must not be disregarded".

Historic towns and urban areas as well as their settings must be considered in their totality.

Their balance and nature depend on their constituent parts.

However, the safeguarding of historic towns and urban areas must be an integral part of a general understanding of the urban structure and its surroundings. This requires coherent economic and social development policies that take historic towns into account at all planning levels, whilst always respecting their social fabric and cultural diversity.

e-Balance and compatibility

The safeguarding of historic towns must include, as a mandatory condition, the preservation of fundamental spatial, environmental, social, cultural and economic balances. This requires actions that allow the urban structure to retain the original residents and to welcome new arrivals (either as residents or as users of the historic town), as well as to aid development, without causing congestion.

f-Time

The speed of change is a parameter to be controlled. Excessive speed of change can adversely affect the integrity of all the values of a historic town.

The extent and frequency of intervention must be embedded in and compatible with feasibility and planning documents and studies, as well as adhering to transparent and regulated intervention procedures.

g-Method and scientific discipline

"Knowledge of the history of a historic town or urban area should be expanded through archaeological investigation and appropriate preservation of archaeological findings". (Washington Charter)

The safeguarding and management of a historic town or urban area must be guided by prudence, a systematic approach and discipline, in accordance with the principles of sustainable development.

Safeguarding and management must be based on preliminary multidisciplinary studies, in order to determine the urban heritage elements and values to be conserved. It is imperative to have a profound knowledge of the site and its setting to inform any safeguarding action.

Continuous monitoring and maintenance is essential to safeguard a historic town or urban area effectively.

Proper planning requires up-to-date precise documentation and recording (context analysis, study at different scales, inventory of component parts and of impact history of the town and its phases of evolution, etc.).

Direct consultation and continuous dialogue with the residents and other stakeholders is indispensable because the safeguarding of their historic town or area concerns them first and foremost.

h-Governance

Good governance makes provision for organizing broad orchestration amongst all stakeholders: elected authorities, municipal services, public administrations, experts, professional organizations, voluntary bodies, universities, residents, etc. This is essential for the successful safeguarding, rehabilitation and sustainable development of historic towns and urban areas.

Participation by the residents can be facilitated through distributing information, awareness raising and training. The traditional systems of urban governance should examine all aspects of cultural and social diversity, so as to establish new democratic institutions to suit the new reality.

Procedures for urban planning and safeguarding historic cities must provide sufficient information and time for residents to give fully informed responses.

Safeguarding needs to be encouraged and financial measures put in place, in order to facilitate partnerships with players from the private sector in the conservation and restoration of the built environment.

i-Multidisciplinary and cooperation

"Planning for the conservation of historic towns and urban areas should be preceded by multidisciplinary studies." (Washington Charter)

From the beginning of preliminary studies, the safeguarding of historic towns should be based on an effective collaboration between specialists of many different disciplines, and undertaken with the cooperation of researchers, public services, private enterprises and the broader public.

These studies should lead to concrete proposals that can be taken up by political decision-makers, social and economic agents and residents.

j-Cultural diversity

Within the context of urban conservation planning, the cultural diversity of the different communities that have inhabited historic towns over the course of time must be respected and valued.

It is essential to establish a sensitive and shared balance in order to maintain their historical heritage in the fullness of its cultural diversity.

4-Proposals and Strategies

a-Elements to be preserved

1-The authenticity and integrity of historic towns, whose essential character is expressed by the nature and coherence of all their tangible and intangible elements, notably:

a-Urban patterns as defined by the street grid, the lots, the green spaces and the relationships between buildings and green and open spaces;

"b-The form and appearance, interior and exterior, of buildings as defined by their structure, volume, style, scale, materials, colour and decoration;

c-The relationship between the town or urban area and its surrounding setting, both natural and man-made;" (Washington Charter)

d-The various functions that the town or urban area has acquired over time;

e-Cultural traditions, traditional techniques, spirit of place and everything that contributes to the identity of a place;

2-The relationships between the site in its totality, its constituent parts, the context of the site, and the parts that make up this context;

3-Social fabric, cultural diversity;

4-Non-renewable resources, minimising their consumption and encouraging their reuse and recycling.

b-New functions

"New functions and activities should be compatible with the character of the historic towns or urban area." (Washington Charter)

The introduction of new activities must not compromise the survival of traditional activities or anything that supports the daily life of the local inhabitants. This could help to preserve the historical cultural diversity and plurality, some of the most valuable elements in this context.

Before introducing a new activity, it is necessary to consider the number of users involved, the length of utilization, compatibility with other existing activities and the impact on traditional local practices.

Such new functions must also satisfy the need for sustainable development, in line with the concept of the historic town as a unique and irreplaceable ecosystem.

c-Contemporary architecture

When it is necessary to construct new buildings or to adapt existing ones, contemporary architecture must be coherent with the existing spatial layout in historic towns as in the rest of the urban environment. Contemporary architecture should find its expression while respecting the scale of the site and have a clear rapport with existing architecture and the development patterns of its context.

"Analysis of the urban context should precede any new construction not only so as to define the general character of the group of buildings but also to analyse its dominant features, e.g. the harmony of heights, colours, materials and forms, constants in the way the façades and roofs are built, the relationship between the volume of buildings and the spatial volume, as well as their average proportions and their position. Particular attention should be given to the size of the lots since there is a danger that any reorganization of the lots may cause a change of mass which could be deleterious to the harmony of the whole." (Nairobi Recommendation art. 28)

Perspectives, views, focal points and visual corridors are integral parts of the perception of historic spaces. They must be respected in the event of new interventions. Before any intervention, the existing context should be carefully analysed and documented. View cones, both to and from new constructions, should be identified, studied and maintained.

The introduction of a new building into a historical context or landscape must be evaluated from a formal and functional point of view, especially when it is designated for new activities.

d-Public space

Public space in historic towns is not just an essential resource for circulation, but is also a place for contemplation, learning and enjoyment of the town. Its design and layout, including the choice of street furniture, as well as its management, must protect its character and beauty, and promote its use as a public place dedicated to social communication.

The balance between public open space and the dense built environment must be carefully analyzed and controlled in the event of new interventions and new uses.

e-Facilities and modifications

Urban planning to safeguard historic towns must take into consideration the residents' need for facilities.

The integration of new facilities into historic buildings is a challenge that local authorities must not ignore.

f-Mobility

"Traffic inside a historic town or urban area must be strictly controlled by regulations." (Washington Charter)

"When urban or regional planning provides for the construction of major motorways, they must not penetrate a historic town or urban area, but they should improve access to them." (Washington Charter)

Most historic towns and urban areas were designed for pedestrians and slow forms of transport. Gradually these places were invaded by the car, causing their degradation. At the same time, quality of life has reduced.

Traffic infrastructure (car parks, subway stations, etc.) must be planned in ways that will not damage the historic fabric or its environment. A historic town should encourage the creation of transport with a light footprint.

It is important to encourage pedestrian circulation. To achieve this, traffic should be drastically limited and parking facilities reduced. At the same time, sustainable, non-polluting public transport systems need to be introduced, and soft mobility promoted.

Roadways should be studied and planned to give priority to pedestrians. Parking facilities should preferably be located outside protected zones and, if possible, outside buffer zones.

Underground infrastructure, such as subways, must be planned so as not to damage historic or archaeological fabric or its environment.

Major highway networks must avoid protected areas and buffer zones.

g-Tourism

Tourism can play a positive role in the development and revitalisation of historic towns and urban areas. The development of tourism in historic towns should be based on the enhancement of monuments and open spaces; on respect and support for local community identity and its culture and traditional activities; and on the safeguarding of regional and environmental character. Tourism activity must respect and not interfere with the daily life of residents.

Too great an influx of tourists is a danger for the preservation of monuments and historic areas.

Conservation and management plans must take into account the expected impact of tourism, and regulate the process, for the benefit of the heritage and of local residents.

h-Risks

"Whatever the nature of a disaster affecting a historic town or urban area, preventative and repair measures must be adapted to the specific character of the properties concerned." (Washington Charter)

Conservation plans offer an opportunity to improve risk preparedness and to promote environmental management and the principles of sustainability.

i-Energy saving

All interventions in historic towns and urban areas, while respecting historic heritage characteristics, should aim to improve energy efficiency and to reduce pollutants.

The use of renewable energy resources should be enhanced.

Any new construction in historic areas must be energy efficient. Urban green spaces, green corridors and other measures should be adopted to avoid urban heat islands.

j-Participation

"The participation and the involvement of the residents-and all local interest groups-are essential for the success of the conservation programme and should be encouraged. The conservation of historic towns and urban areas concerns their residents first of all." (Washington Charter art 3)

Planning in historic urban areas must be a participatory process, involving all stakeholders.

In order to encourage their participation and involvement, a general information programme should be set up for all residents, beginning with children of school age. The actions of conservation associations must be encouraged, and financial measures put in place, to facilitate the conservation and restoration of the built environment.

Mutual understanding, based on public awareness, and the search for common objectives between local communities and professional groups, is the basis of the successful conservation, revitalization and development of historic towns.

Information technology enables direct and immediate communication. This allows for active and responsible participation by local groups.

Authorities must be encouraged to take an interest in the safeguarding of historic towns and urban areas, in order to establish financial measures which will enable management and improvement plans to succeed.

k-Conservation Plan

"The conservation plan should aim at ensuring a harmonious relationship between historic urban areas..." (Washington Charter art. 5)

It covers both tangible and intangible elements, in order to protect a place's identity without impeding its evolution.

The principal objectives of the conservation plan "should be clearly stated as should the legal, administrative and financial measures necessary to attain them." (Washington Charter art. 5)

A conservation plan must be based on urban planning for the whole town, including analysis of archaeological, historical, architectural, technical, sociological and economical values. It should define a conservation project and be combined with a management plan and followed by permanent monitoring.

The conservation plan must determine the terms, rules, objectives and outcomes of any changes. It should determine which buildings and spaces must be preserved, which should be preserved under certain circumstances and which, "under quite exceptional circumstances, might be expendable." (Washington Charter)

Before any intervention, existing conditions should be rigorously documented.

The conservation plan must identify and protect the elements contributing to the values and character of the town, as well as the components that enrich and/or demonstrate the character of the historic town and urban area.

The proposals in the conservation plan must be articulated in a realistic fashion, from the legislative, financial and economic point of view, as well as with regard to the required standards and restrictions.

"The Conservation Plan should be supported by the residents of the historic area." (Washington Charter art 5)

When there is no conservation plan, all necessary conservation and development activities in a historic town must be carried out in accordance with the principles and objectives of conservation and enhancement.

l-Management Plan

An effective management system should be devised according to the type and characteristics of each historic town and urban area, and their cultural and natural context. It should integrate traditional practices and be coordinated with other urban and regional planning tools in force.

A management plan is based on the knowledge, conservation and enhancement of tangible and intangible resources.

Therefore, it must:
- determine the cultural values;

- identify stakeholders and their values;
- identify potential conflicts;
- determine conservation targets;
- determine legal, financial, methods and tools;
- understand strengths, weaknesses, opportunities and threats;
- define suitable strategies, deadlines for the work, and specific actions.

The production of such a management plan should be a participatory process.

In addition to the information provided by local authorities, officials, field survey and detailed documentation, the Plan should include, as an appendix, the conclusions from stakeholder discussions and an analysis of the conflicts arising in these inherently contradictory debates.

Follow Up

These recommendations are the outcome of collaborative work by CIVVIH, which intends them as a contribution to the wider discussions being led by ICOMOS. This is an open source document that can be updated in the light of the evolution of the issues discussed.

CIVVIH

The International Committee on Historic Towns and Villages (CIVVIH) was established in 1982.

The Committee deals with questions relevant to the planning and management of historic towns and villages. Its membership is made of experts who have different professional backgrounds related to historic town preservation.

We come from ICOMOS member countries all over the world to share their knowledge and experience with colleagues practicing in the field.

·考古遗产·

考古遗产保护与管理宪章[①]

(国际古迹遗址理事会第九届大会1990年10月在洛桑通过)

导 言

众所周知,认识和了解人类社会的起源与发展对人类鉴别其文化和社会根源有着极其重要的作用。

考古遗产构成记载人类过去活动的基本材料,因此,对其保护和合理的管理能对考古学家和其他学者代表人类当前和今后的利益对其进行研究和解释起到巨大的作用。

对这种遗产的保护不能仅仅依靠应用考古学方法,它需要较广泛的专业和科学知识与技能基础。有些考古遗产的构成是建筑结构的组成部分,在这种情况下,就必须根据1966年保护和修复古迹遗址的威尼斯宪章所规定的这类结构的保护标准进行保护,考古遗产的其他构成是当地人民生活习惯的组成部分,对于这类遗址和古迹,当地文化团体参与其保护和保存具有重要意义。

由于这些原因以及其他一些原因,考古遗产的保护必须依靠各学科专家的有效合作,它需要政府当局、学术研究人员、公私企业以及一般民众的合作。因此,本宪章规定了有关考古遗产管理不同方面的原则,其中包括公共当局和立法者的责任,有关遗产的勘察、勘测、发掘、档案记录、研究、维护、保护、保存、重建、信息资料、展览以及对外开放与公众利用等的专业操作程序规则以及考古遗产保护所涉及的专家之资格等。

本宪章受到了作为学者、专家以及政府的政策与实践思想的源泉与准则的威尼斯宪章的成功之鼓舞。

本宪章必须反映具有全球效力的基本原则和准则。鉴此,宪章不能考虑地区性的和国家的具体问题和可能性。因而,本宪章必须为此需要根据将来的原则与准则,在地区性和国家范围内加以补充。

第一条 定义与介绍

"考古遗产"是根据考古方法提供主要资料实物遗产部分,它包括人类生存的各种遗存,它是由与人类活动各种表现有关的地点、被遗弃的结构、各种各样的遗迹(包括地下和水下的遗址)以及与上述有关的各种可移动的文化资料所组成。

第二条 整体保护政策

考古遗产是一种容易损坏、不能再生的文化资源。因此,土地利用必须加以控制并合理开发,以便把对考古遗产的破坏减小到最低限度。

考古遗产的保护政策应该构成有关土地利用、开发和计划以及文化环境和教育政策的整体组成部分。

[①] 引自:联合国教科文组织世界遗产中心,国际古迹遗址理事会,国际文物保护与修复研究中心,中国国家文物局主编.国际文化遗产保护文件选编[M].北京:文物出版社,2007。

考古遗产的保护政策必须不断予以检查，以便跟上时代的发展，考古保护区的划定亦构成此种政策的一部分。

考古遗产的保护必须纳入国际的、国家的、区域的以及地方一级的规划政策。

一般民众的积极参与必须构成考古遗产保护政策的组成部分。涉及当地人民遗产时这点显得更加重要。参与必须以得到作出决定所需知识之机会为基础。因此，向一般民众提供信息资料是整体保护的重要组成部分。

第三条　立法和经济

考古遗产的保护应看做是全人类的道德义务，它是民众的一项集体责任。此项义务必须通过相应的立法以及支持遗产有效管理计划的足够资金的规定加以确认。

考古遗产为全人类社会所共有，因此，每个国家应有义务保证拨出足够的资金用于考古遗产的保护。

立法应该为适合于每个国家和地区的需要、历史和传统的考古遗产提供保护，提供就地保护和研究的法律需要。

立法应该以考古遗产是全人类和人类群体的遗产这个概念为基础，而不局限于某一个人或国家。

立法应该禁止在没有得到有关考古当局的同意而通过改变考古遗址或古迹或其环境对其进行毁坏、损坏和改变。

在批准毁掉考古遗产的情况下，原则上，立法应要求对其进行全面的考古研究和档案记录。

立法应要求并规定对考古遗产进行适当的维护、管理和保护。

对违反考古遗产法律的行为应制定适当的法律制裁措施。

如果立法仅仅只对那些登记在选择法定财产清单中的考古遗产的某些部分提供保护，对没有受到保护或新近发现的古迹和遗址必须制定暂时保护规定，直至对其作出考古评估。

开发项目构成对考古遗产的最大威胁之一。开发者有责任保证在开发计划实施之前对考古遗产影响进行研究，因此，该项责任应体现在适当的立法中，并规定此种研究经费应包括在项目经费之中。立法中还应该建立这样的原则，即：开放项目的设计应该将其对考古遗产的影响减小到最低限度。

第四条　勘察

对考古遗产的保护必须以对其范围和性质尽可能的全面了解为基础。因此，对考古资源进行全面的勘察是考古遗产保护与管理的一项基本义务。

同时，考古财产清单构成科学研究主要数据库，因此，编制考古财产清单应被认为是一个不断变化的过程。其结果是：考古财产清单应该包括各个重要和可靠阶段的资料，因为即使是表面的知识也能构成保护措施的起点。

第五条　调查研究

考古知识主要基于对考古遗产的科学调查研究。此种调查研究包括广泛的方法，从非破坏性的取样技术到全面发掘。

收集考古遗产的资料不应更多地毁坏为保护或科学研究目的所需的考古证据，这是一项最重要的原则。因此，与全面发掘相比，非破坏性技术、空中的地面勘测、取样等方法应在尽可能的范围内加以鼓励。

由于发掘总是意味着需要以失去其他资料甚至可能以毁坏整个遗址为代价来选择将要记录和保存的证据，因此只有在经过深思熟虑之后方可作出发掘的决定。

发掘应该在遭受发展规划、土地用途改变、掠夺和自然蜕化的威胁的古迹和遗址上进行。

作为例外情况，为了阐明研究问题或为了向民众展览而更有效地阐述古迹遗址，也可以对没有遭受威胁的遗址进行发掘。在这种情况下，发掘之前必须首先对遗址的重要性进行全面的科学评估。发掘应该是部分的，留一部分不受干扰，以便今后研究。

在发掘工作完成后的一段合理期间内，应该向科学团体提交一份符合既定标准的报告，报告应包括相应的考古财产清单。发掘工作应根据 1956 年联合国教科文组织关于适用于考古发掘的国际原则的建议所规定的原则以及既定的国际国内专业标准予以进行。

第六条　维护与保护

考古遗产管理的总体目标应是就地保存古迹和遗址，包括对一切相关的记录和藏品等进行适当的长期保护与保管。将遗产的任何组成部分转移至新的地点的任何行为即构成违反就地保存遗产的原则。这项原则强调适当维护、保护和管理的需要。它也坚持如果发掘考古遗产的适当维护和管理之规定得不到保障，则不应通过发掘或在发掘后暴露考古遗产的原则。

作为促进维护考古遗产的一种方法，应该积极寻求和鼓励当地承担义务及其参与。这一原则在处理当地人民和地方文化团体的遗产时特别重要。在某些情况下，把保护和管理古迹和遗址的责任委托给当地人民也许是适当的。

由于所能得到的资源难免有限，积极的维护不得不在有选择的基础上进行。因此，它应该在各种古迹遗址的重要性和代表性的科学评估基础上适用于其中的一个范例，而不应局限于那些比较著名并引人注目的遗址。

在考古遗产的维护和保护方面应适用 1956 年联合国教科文组织的建议所规定的相应原则。

第七条　展出、信息资料、重建

向民众展出考古遗产是促进了解现代社会起源和发展的至关重要的方法。同时，它也是促进了解对其进行保护需要的最重要的方法。

展出和信息资料应被看做是对当前知识状况的通俗解释，因此，必须经常予以修改。它应考虑到了解过去的其他多种方法。

重建起到两方面的作用：试验性的研究和解释。然而，重建应该非常细心谨慎，以免影响任何幸存的考古证据，并且，为了达到真实可靠，应该考虑所有来源的证据。在可能和适当的情况下，重建不应直接建在考古遗址之上，并应能够辨别出为重建物。

第八条　专业资格

在各个不同学科拥有至高学术水平对考古遗产的管理极为重要。因此，在相应的专业领域培养足够数量的合格专业人员是每个国家教育政策的重要目标。发展某些高尖端专业领域的技能之需要，要求进行国际合作。必须建立和维持专业培训和专业指导的标准。

考古学术培训的目标应该考虑到保护政策从发掘到就地保存的转变。它还应该考虑到这样的事实，即：在保存和了解考古遗产方面，研究当地人民的历史与研究著名的古迹和遗址同样重要。

考古遗产的保护是一个不断变化发展的过程。因此，应该使从事这方面工作的专业人员有时间更新他们的知识，应该制定专门侧重于考古遗产保护和管理的研究生培训计划。

第九条　国际合作

考古遗产是全人类共同遗产，因此，国际合作在制定和维持其管理标准方面极为重要。

为从事考古遗产管理的专业人员交流信息和经验，急需创建国际机构。它要求组织地区性和全球性的大会、研讨会、专题讨论会等，并建立地区性的研究生研究中心。国际古迹遗址理事会应通过其专业团体，在其中长期计划中促进这方面的工作。

作为提高考古遗产管理水平的一种方法，还应该发展专业人员的国际交流。在国际古迹遗址理事会的领导下，应制定出考古遗产管理方面的技术援助计划。

Charter for the Protection and Management of the Archaeological Heritage

Approved by the 9th ICOMOS General Assembly, Lausanne, 1990

INTRODUCTION

It is widely recognised that a knowledge and understanding of the origins and development of human societies is of fundamental importance to humanity in identifying its cultural and social roots.

The archaeological heritage constitutes the basic record of past human activities. Its protection and proper management is therefore essential to enable archaeologists and other scholars to study and interpret it on behalf of and for the benefit of present and future generations.

The protection of this heritage cannot be based upon the application of archaeological techniques alone. It requires a wider basis of professional and scientific knowledge and skills. Some elements of the archaeological heritage are components of architectural structures and in such cases must be protected in accordance with the criteria for the protection of such structures laid down in the 1966 Venice Charter on the Conservation and Restoration of Monuments and Sites. Other elements of the archaeological heritage constitute part of the living traditions of indigenous peoples, and for such sites and monuments the participation of local cultural groups is essential for their protection and preservation.

For these and other reasons the protection of the archaeological heritage must be based upon effective collaboration between professionals from many disciplines. It also requires the co-operation of government authorities, academic researchers, private or public enterprise, and the general public. This charter therefore lays down principles relating to the different aspects of archaeological heritage management. These include the responsibilities of public authorities and legislators, principles relating to the professional performance of the processes of inventorisation, survey, excavation, documentation, research, maintenance, conservation, preservation, reconstruction, information, presentation, public access and use of the heritage, and the qualification of professionals involved in the protection of the archaeological heritage.

The charter has been inspired by the success of the Venice Charter as guidelines and source of ideas for policies and practice of governments as well as scholars and professionals.

The charter has to reflect very basic principles and guidelines with global validity. For this reason, it cannot take into account the specific problems and possibilities of regions or countries. The charter should therefore be supplemented at regional and national levels by further principles and guidelines for these needs.

DEFINITION AND INTRODUCTION

Article 1.

The "archaeological heritage" is that part of the material heritage in respect of which archaeological methods provide primary information. It comprises all vestiges of human existence and consists of places relating to all manifestations of human activity, abandoned structures, and remains of all kinds (including subterranean and underwater sites), together with all the portable cultural material associated with them.

INTEGRATED PROTECTION POLICIES

Article 2.

The archaeological heritage is a fragile and non-renewable cultural resource. Land use must therefore be controlled and developed in order to minimise the destruction of the archaeological heritage.

Policies for the protection of the archaeological heritage should constitute an integral component of policies relating to land use, development, and planning as well as of cultural, environmental and educational policies. The policies for the protection of the archaeological heritage should be kept under continual review, so that they stay up to date. The creation of archaeological reserves should form part of such policies.

The protection of the archaeological heritage should be integrated into planning policies at international, national, regional and local levels.

Active participation by the general public must form part of policies for the protection of the archaeological heritage. This is essential where the heritage of indigenous peoples is involved. Participation must be based upon access to the knowledge necessary for decision-making. The provision of information to the general public is therefore an important element in integrated protection.

LEGISLATION AND ECONOMY

Article 3.

The protection of the archaeological heritage should be considered as a moral obligation upon all human beings; it is also a collective public responsibility. This obligation must be acknowledged through relevant legislation and the provision of adequate funds for the supporting programmes necessary for effective heritage management.

The archaeological heritage is common to all human society and it should therefore be the duty of every country to ensure that adequate funds are available for its protection.

Legislation should afford protection to the archaeological heritage that is appropriate to the needs, history, and traditions of each country and region, providing for in situ protection and research needs.

Legislation should be based on the concept of the archaeological heritage as the heritage of all humanity and of groups of peoples, and not restricted to any individual person or nation.

Legislation should forbid the destruction, degradation or alteration through changes of any archaeological site or monument or to their surroundings without the consent of the relevant archaeological authority.

Legislation should in principle require full archaeological investigation and documentation in cases where the destruction of the archaeological heritage is authorised.

Legislation should require, and make provision for, the proper maintenance, management and conservation of the archaeological heritage. Adequate legal sanctions should be prescribed in respect of violations of archaeological heritage legislation.

If legislation affords protection only to those elements of the archaeological heritage which are registered in a selective statutory inventory, provision should be made for the temporary protection of unprotected or newly discovered sites and monuments until an archaeological evaluation can be carried out.

Development projects constitute one of the greatest physical threats to the archaeological heritage. A duty for developers to ensure that archaeological heritage impact studies are carried out before development schemes are implemented, should therefore be embodied in appropriate legislation, with a stipulation that the costs of such studies are to be included in project costs. The principle should also be established in legislation that development schemes should be designed in such a way as to minimise their impact upon the archaeological heritage.

SURVEY

Article 4.

The protection of the archaeological heritage must be based upon the fullest possible knowledge of its extent and nature. General survey of archaeological resources is therefore an essential working tool in developing strategies for the protection of the archaeological heritage. Consequently archaeological survey should be a basic obligation in the protection and management of the archaeological heritage.

At the same time, inventories constitute primary resource databases for scientific study and research. The compilation of inventories should therefore be regarded as a continuous, dynamic process. It follows that inventories should comprise information at various levels of significance and reliability, since even superficial knowledge can form the starting point for protectional measures.

INVESTIGATION

Article 5.

Archaeological knowledge is based principally on the scientific investigation of the archaeological heritage. Such investigation embraces the whole range of methods from non-destructive techniques through sampling to total excavation.

It must be an overriding principle that the gathering of information about the archaeological heritage should not destroy any more archaeological evidence than is necessary for the protectional or scientific objectives of the investigation. Non-destructive techniques, aerial and ground survey, and sampling should therefore be encouraged wherever possible, in preference to total excavation.

As excavation always implies the necessity of making a selection of evidence to be documented and preserved at the cost of losing other information and possibly even the total destruction of the monument, a decision to excavate should only be taken after thorough consideration.

Excavation should be carried out on sites and monuments threatened by development, land-use change, looting, or natural deterioration.

In exceptional cases, unthreatened sites may be excavated to elucidate research problems or to interpret them more effectively for the purpose of presenting them to the public. In such cases excavation must be preceded by thorough scientific evaluation of the significance of the site. Excavation should be partial, leaving a portion undisturbed for future research.

A report conforming to an agreed standard should be made available to the scientific community and should be incorporated in the relevant inventory within a reasonable period after the conclusion of the excavation.

Excavations should be conducted in accordance with the principles embodied in the 1956 UNESCO Recommendations on International Principles Applicable to Archaeological Excavations and with agreed international and national professional standards.

MAINTENANCE AND CONSERVATION

Article 6.

The overall objective of archaeological heritage management should be the preservation of monuments and sites in situ, including proper long-term conservation and curation of all related records and collections etc. Any transfer of elements of the heritage to new locations represents a violation of the principle of preserving the heritage in its original context. This principle stresses the need for proper maintenance, conservation and management. It also asserts the principle that the archaeological heritage should not be exposed by excavation or left exposed after excavation if provision for its proper maintenance and management after excavation cannot be guaranteed.

Local commitment and participation should be actively sought and encouraged as a means of promoting the maintenance of the archaeological heritage. This principle is especially important when dealing with the heritage of indigenous peoples or local cultural groups. In some cases it may be appropriate to entrust responsibility for the protection and management of sites and monuments to indigenous peoples.

Owing to the inevitable limitations of available resources, active maintenance will have to be carried out on a selective basis. It should therefore be applied to a sample of the diversity of sites and monuments, based upon a scientific assessment of their significance and representative character, and not confined to the more notable and visually attractive monuments.

The relevant principles of the 1956 UNESCO Recommendations should be applied in respect of the maintenance and conservation of the archaeological heritage.

PRESENTATION, INFORMATION, RECONSTRUCTION

Article 7.

The presentation of the archaeological heritage to the general public is an essential method of promoting an understanding of the origins and development of modern societies. At the same time it is the most important means of promoting an understanding of the need for its protection.

Presentation and information should be conceived as a popular interpretation of the current state of knowledge, and it must therefore be revised frequently. It should take account of the multifaceted approaches to an understanding of the past.

Reconstructions serve two important functions: experimental research and interpretation. They should, however, be carried out with great caution, so as to avoid disturbing any surviving archaeological evidence, and they should take account of evidence from all sources in order to achieve authenticity. Where possible and appropriate, reconstructions should not be built immediately on the archaeological remains, and should be identifiable as such.

PROFESSIONAL QUALIFICATIONS

Article 8.

High academic standards in many different disciplines are essential in the management of the archaeological heritage. The training of an adequate number of qualified professionals in the relevant fields of expertise should therefore be an important objective for the educational policies in every country. The need to develop expertise in certain highly specialised fields calls for international co-operation. Standards of professional training and professional conduct should be established and maintained.

The objective of academic archaeological training should take account of the shift in conservation policies from excavation to in situ preservation. It should also take into account the fact that the study of the history of indigenous peoples is as important in preserving and understanding the archaeological heritage as the study of outstanding monuments and sites.

The protection of the archaeological heritage is a process of continuous dynamic development. Time should therefore be made available to professionals working in this field to enable them to update their knowledge. Postgraduate training programmes should be developed with special emphasis on the protection and management of the archaeological heritage.

INTERNATIONAL CO-OPERATION

Article 9.

The archaeological heritage is the common heritage of all humanity. International co-operation is therefore essential in developing and maintaining standards in its management.

There is an urgent need to create international mechanisms for the exchange of information and experience among professionals dealing with archaeological heritage management. This requires the organisation of conferences, seminars, workshops, etc. at global as well as regional levels, and the establishment of regional centres for postgraduate studies. ICOMOS, through its specialised groups, should promote this aspect in its medium and long-term planning.

International exchanges of professional staff should also be developed as a means of raising standards of archaeological heritage management.

Technical assistance programmes in the field of archaeological heritage management should be developed under the auspices of ICOMOS.

公共考古遗址管理的塞拉莱指南[①]

(国际古迹遗址理事会第十九届大会 2017 年 12 月 15 日在印度新德里通过)

序 言

考古遗址受到其所在国家和地区的利益相关者的正当控制。若这些利益相关者决定将一个考古遗址向公众开放,那么接下来的指南就是给他们的一些建议。**这些指南无意成为法规或标准,许多这些指南的制定参与方也特意声明我们反对将以下内容变成法规或标准。**指南中的建议是来自许多国家和世界不同地区的参与管理向公众开放的考古遗址的人员的集体经验。这些建议认同一个事实,即每个国家和地区是不同的,并且这种文化多样性丰富了全人类的生活。因此,本指南中所提出的任何与具体考古遗址(尤其是那些对游客开放的遗址)所在的区域和地方文化管理不相符合的建议,都可以修改。世界各地的国家公园系统和世界遗产地中的考古遗址都面临特别的挑战,因为旅游业将其作为首要目的地。自《保护世界文化和自然遗产公约》实施后的几十年里,这一现象变得尤其突出。类似问题持续出现在向公众开放的考古遗址中。本指南旨在减少类似问题在向公众开放的考古遗址中发生、发展和变得不可挽回的可能性。

本指南的宗旨和目标

本指南的宗旨是:

• 确定必要的研究,用以评估向公众开放或可能向公众开放的考古遗址建立可持续管理框架和系统的可行性;

• 参考上述可行性评估,指导可持续管理系统的建立。

本指南的根本目标概括如下:

• 在其背景环境中保存和维护考古遗迹、遗物和遗址,以能够用科学的方式研究它们;

• 为向公众开放的考古遗址中的文化和自然资源提供一个合理的可持续管理(包括利用)实践模型;

• 利用向公众开放的考古遗址,以互利共赢的方式使公众认识文化多样性的价值和文化间交流的力量;

• 保证考古遗址对可持续发展做出贡献。主要通过保存和必要时恢复其生态服务功能,并以不引起社会扰动的方式为当地居民提供机会和支持来获得经济效益。

考古遗址包含着实物证据,对其进行科学研究可以告诉我们有关人类的历史,正因如此,1964 年国际古迹遗址理事会《威尼斯宪章》以诗意的语言称它们"饱含着过去岁月的信息"。参观考古遗址使人以直观的方式了解人类的过去,这是其他方式不能提供的。因此,在不危及或毁坏历史实物证据的前提下,参观考古遗址的体验应该尽可能广泛地向公众提供。相比较而言,地上建筑能够从外观上进行修复,考

[①] 译者:李说,彭婷,孙田,解立。中国古迹遗址保护协会 ICOMOS CHINA 提供。

古遗址的历史和科学价值则完全依赖于调查原址中的原始材料的能力，这使得考古遗址与其他所有类型的遗产地区分开来。

参观考古遗址可以广泛的推进与遗产相关的收益，包括社会的、经济的和文化的。向公众开放、用心展示的遗产能够增强我们对人与自然之间现有关系的理解，也能增强对人类自我组织及与其他群体互动方式的普遍性和多样性的理解。这些都是当今的核心议题。遗产在构建集体认同方面具有基础作用。在遗产被以有利于某个特定群体的方式进行特权叙事时，根据考古调查及其实物证据进行的遗产研究能够恰如其分地挑战这些叙事。

向公众开放的考古遗址既能以可持续的也能以不可持续的方式产生经济效益。向公众开放的考古遗址的可持续管理要求了解公众的参观和体验是如何与促进该遗址保护联系起来的。可持续管理还要求清晰地确定向公众开放的发展可能会以何种方式伤害该遗址。顾名思义，不可持续的利用在遗址保护上妥协，也损害了以一种尽可能公正，因而也是有效的方式来呈现人类历史的努力。

本指南旨在面向所有对公众开放的考古遗址，但它们与世界遗产中的此类遗址尤其相关。列入《世界遗产名录》所产生的声誉促使游客参观量增加，并能促进当地经济的重大发展。

列入《世界遗产名录》的每一个遗产地都包含具有考古研究价值的物质遗存。世界遗产地包括了历史城市，它们都包含更早期的"城下之城"的考古遗存。由于自然资源的突出普遍价值而被列入名录的世界遗产地，也存在考古遗存。相对晚近的、被认为是天才的建筑或工程作品的建造物和景观也是考古学和相关学科的研究范畴。所有这些类型遗产地中的考古遗存，如果加以适当研究，都能产生丰富详细、引人入胜的发现，加深对该遗产地的理解。考古学以一种与我们当今生活密切相关的形式揭示了人类历史和人类过去的经验，包括人类冲突导致的社会和经济后果的证据、对环境过度利用后果的见证等。考古遗存作为历史信息的一种关键载体，它的保存可能在向公众开放的遗址上显得尤其重要，因为科学研究能够激活和显著增加该遗址已有的知识和内涵。而且，所有世界遗产地，拥有着突出普遍价值、非凡的特质和来自全球的关注，更应该成为可持续管理的范例。

指南的必要性

这些指南清晰地表达了一种必要性，即相比起评估一个地方值得公众关心和关注的理由是否恰当，应以相同的，在某些情况下甚至更多的关注和时间、金钱的投入，来评估建立向公众开放的考古遗址的可持续管理的可行性。对处理与世界遗产地管理相关的大量问题，已存在很多有用的文件。由于它们是世界范围内的，因此对本指南要实现的目的而言也都是有用的，并且其中一些和考古遗址相关。然而，本指南是专门应用于所有向公众开放的考古遗址的。这些遗址中,有的考古遗址本身就是《世界遗产名录》中的，还有一些可能被列入名录中（即《世界遗产公约》缔约国设立的《世界遗产预备名录》上的遗址）。《世界遗产名录》上的遗址应提供能够在其他地区适用的可持续管理模式。它们能示范如何建立机构和制定方案来保护所有文化和自然遗产地，以符合《世界遗产公约》第五章阐述的目标。

就恰当性而言，《世界遗产名录》上许多最著名的和标志性的遗址，包括但不限于佩特拉、马丘比丘、吴哥和庞贝，都是世界遗产名单上明显的选项。它们都无可置疑地符合一个或多个《实施世界遗产公约操作指南》中设置的标准，并且它们都拥有突出普遍价值。然而，列入的影响和列入后可持续管理的可行性在列入时并没有被充分理解。之后更多的世界遗产申报项目，依然没有充分的管理可行性研究来指导申报材料的准备。在尚未制定可持续管理的可行框架的情况下，申报遗产地的突出普遍价值，包括其完整性和真实性就是脆弱的。实际上，管理本身也是突出普遍价值的重要支撑之一。考古遗址向公众开放前忽视实施可持续管理的可行性只会导致这座科学和历史信息宝库的损耗和遗址参观体验的降级。

在遗产地向公众开放以后迅速地建立一套管理系统是一项艰巨的任务，特别是当开放导致游客数量显著增长时（这在遗产地被列入《世界遗产名录》时很常见）。缺乏区域规划和对区划的当地社区支持，遗产地内部和周边的发展对环境的破坏是很普遍的，且通常也会对遗址本身造成破坏。这种情况会非常迅速地发生，且破坏可能是不可逆的。一旦发生，不恰当占据遗产地的建筑和居民已被证明几乎不可能再被迁移。如同时还存在必要的技术、规定、管理、人员和财政资源的匮乏，这些问题将会加剧。结果通常对所有利益相关者都是差强人意的。

这里所指的"可行性"依赖于利益相关者为遗产地的保存和保护对公众参观所需的设备和服务的发展进行恰当规划的能力。这需要以设计和实施有效的管理框架和系统为前提。首先，管理系统必须要建立在所有参与者对遗址充分认识的基础上。它包括监测相关的能力建设，并有足以实施可持续管理的控制性计划或活动。管理的规划和实施应不仅只针对遗址本身，也应将遗址周边环境和计划开发游览区域考虑在内。

本指南为有效管理框架和系统的确立和发展提供了一份路线图，也可对已有的管理框架和系统提供必要的改进。

为向公众开放的考古遗址的管理制定公认的指南还有额外的战略价值。许多政府的和非营利发展协助项目可供申请，它们能为在可持续的经济发展方面寻求帮助的缔约国和机构提供资金。遵守已被认可的指南能够帮助这些项目的申请，并且为资金和技术支持的要求提供合理依据。为向公众开放的考古遗址的可持续管理建立一个可行的多年计划，为有效发展提供了一个结构。

前　情

本文件吸取了国际古迹遗址理事会过去的工作成果，特别是2002年在马阿甘(Ma'agan)所召开的会议，并充分尊重该会议的指导原则（Cleere 2010, 5），该会议将以下因素作为全部管理规划的核心内容：

a）各利益相关方对遗产价值有全面的理解和共识；
b）规划、实施、监测、评估和反馈的循环机制；
c）合作伙伴和利益相关方的参与；
d）必要资源的配置；
e）能力建设；
f）对管理制度运作有可信且透明的描述。

考古遗址公园的概念

本指南所称公园定义为：为公众参观、休闲和教育而设的保护区。这一定义与2015年2月23日至25日在阿曼苏丹国塞拉莱（Salalah, the Sultanate of Oman）举行的国际古迹遗址理事会考古遗址公园第一次国际会议的定义相一致。

如《塞拉莱（Salalah）建议》所述，考古遗址公园既包括地上遗存，也包括地下遗迹。《塞拉莱（Salalah）建议》指出考古遗址公园"一方面应被视为保护考古遗址的工具，另一方面它们的展示和阐释应被视为理解人类共同过去的一种手段"（http://whc.unesco.org/en/news/1256）。因此，它可以被视为推动了《世界遗产公约》的总体目标。由于它能反映人类共享的概念，它应该作为一种教学手段；并且，在得到可持续管理后，为其他存在重要文化和自然资源的脆弱遗址提供一个如何实现可持续管理的范本。

指　南

1. 管理规划

1.1　清单和评估。应努力将经济有效、非侵入性、非破坏型的技术手段用于文化与自然资源的清查和评估。这些技术手段应包括例如对遗址和资源的直接探测或为遗址和资源的分布建模。

1.1.1 文化资源。建立一个针对考古遗址、遗迹和景观的可持续管理制度，一份文化资源的清单和评估是确定其可行性的第一步。评估应了解文化资源的脆弱性、所受威胁及其重要性。

该地区的管理者应：

1.1.1.1 确保有专业资格、被业界认可、国际公认的考古学专家协助考古遗址、遗物和景观及所有相关材料的认定和评估工作；

1.1.1.2 确保存档完整的、国际公认的最佳实践得以执行，包括对考古遗产的田野研究、记录、评估和保护。

1.1.2 自然资源。对自然资源的清查和评估与文化资源的一样重要，并应能够确定那些现在或将来可能威胁考古资源的环境变化以及有利于当地人民的环境服务。

该地区的管理者应：

1.1.2.1 确保有资格的、被广泛认可、国际公认的相关领域的专家协助。自然资源的清单应当全面，并确定哪些是或可能是：

1.1.2.1.1 受到威胁或濒危的；

1.1.2.1.2 对包含考古遗址为其一部分的更大范围的环境景观极其重要的，特别是那些与考古遗存在其背景环境中的保存相关的；

1.1.2.1.3 与对当地人口的有价值的环境服务密不可分的。

1.1.3 基础设施。应提供竣工检验单、详细技术参数和全部基础设施现状条件，以及已知或估计的用户数量。基础设施包括所有的建筑、公共设施、道路、通讯网络及进入参观和旅游手段。

1.1.4 传统使用区域。应确定传统使用区域。传统使用区域是指对遗址及周边地区的当代居民有特殊价值的区域，包括那些可能被认为是神圣的或用于传统目的的区域（例如，特别视域，婚庆活动，或药用/营养植物的收集）。

向公众开放的考古遗址的管理者应：

1.1.4.1 确保有资格的、被广泛认可的和公认的传统使用区域的专家来识别和评估这些地区的考古遗产；

1.1.4.2 确保存档完整的、国际公认的最佳实践得以执行，包括田野研究、记录、评估和传统使用区域考古遗产的保护。

1.2 确立遗址边界和管理区

1.2.1 遗址边界。根据文化和自然资源清单准确确定可能向公众开放的考古遗址的拟定边界是至关重要的。

1.2.2 遗址规模和布局。遗址应具有足够的规模和合适的布局，使可持续的资源保护和游客休闲成为可能（应将拟定边界外资源的当前和潜在影响纳入考虑范围）。

1.2.3 考虑成本。遗址的独特性不应将负有管理责任的一方或多方实现有效管理和经营所能承担的合理成本排除在外。考虑因素包括：

1.2.3.1 遗址区内和缓冲区内外土地的当前和潜在用途；

1.2.3.2 土地所有权和合法使用权，包括可能的权利变更；

1.2.3.3 公众参观和休闲的潜力；

1.2.3.4 与采购、开发、修复、日常管理和操作相关的成本；

1.2.3.5 参观（例如，进出的路线，导引，流通和服务）；

1.2.3.6 对考古资源的现状恶化及原因的分析；

1.2.3.7 对考古资源当前和潜在的威胁；

1.2.3.8 地方和公众（例如企业，政府和土地所有者）支持的水平；

1.2.3.9 保护地位所产生的社会、政治、环境和经济影响；

1.2.3.10 公众考古遗址的建立对公共福利，如自然和社会环境质量、教育、健康和安全服务的提升方式和程度。

1.2.4 缓冲区。缓冲区边界也应当准确并且记录完整。

1.2.4.1 由于单独的缓冲区通常不足以确保免于被侵占，因此应与社区和政府实体沟通协商并达成协议，以实现这一目标。

1.2.5 管理区。每个遗址内，应建立管理区，并且应确认以下内容：

1.2.5.1 期望用途；

1.2.5.2 所需条件；

1.2.5.3 必要的游客服务；

1.2.5.4 阐释主题（即应在每个区域呈现的信息）。

1.3 环境影响评估或环境影响研究

1.3.1 环境影响。应对任何可能影响环境质量的开发活动进行环境影响评估或环境影响研究。

1.3.2 环境影响的经济后果。环境影响评估或环境影响研究应包括一份经济分析，分析个人、企业、社会团体以及地方的、区域的、国家的乃至全球的公众可能受到的潜在经济效益和经济负债。

1.4 监测规划

1.4.1 监测规划。监测规划应具体明确用来监测以下内容的技术、协议、工具、指标和标准：

1.4.1.1 各类文化资源的状况；

1.4.1.2 各类自然资源的状况；

1.4.1.3 游客数量、容量和满意度；

1.4.1.4 社区满意度；

1.4.1.5 设备和基础设施条件。

1.4.2 监测重点。监测重点的确定应通过考虑以下资源和体验：

1.4.2.1 对遗产自然或文化完整性以及享受遗址的机会具有关键作用；

1.4.2.2 对保持遗址曾符合突出普遍价值的标准具有关键作用；

1.4.2.3 在遗址一般管理规划或其他相关规划文件中被确定为重点。

1.5 考古研究计划

1.5.1 考古研究计划。应制定计划，包括研究重点，以研究减轻自然过程（如洪水）和人为活动（如掠夺或开发）对考古资源扰动。计划还应确定与遗址重要性相关的考古学研究，特别是可能与考古学领域、当代环境政策和国际关系的提升有重大关系的议题的研究。

1.6 阐释方案

1.6.1 阐释方案。应准备阐释方案，方案应确定一个最有助于实现遗址教学功能的阐释主题和子主题。方案应至少每五年更新一次。

1.7 管理设施

1.7.1 管理设施。管理设施包括实施考古遗址可持续管理必要的建筑构筑物、设施和设备。应明确那些对确保遗址的完整性、真实性和与其重要性相关的特点必不可少的设施，此外，也应确定对这些设施的具体要求。

1.8 人力计划

1.8.1 可持续管理需要各种训练有素的工作人员，通常包括对公众考古遗址中的自然和文化资源具有相关经验的科学家和考古学家、维护人员、能安排日程和预算的行政人员、向游客介绍遗址的讲解员、具有博物馆、策展和表达方面能力的人员、社区联络员、医务人员、执法人员以及能够协调发展、协调一切必要的政策、项目和活动的管理者。

岗位需求是多种多样的，因此，岗位计划应根据文化和自然资源的清单和评估、确定的这些资源的脆弱性和所受威胁，以及与向公众开放遗址的具体目标来制定。计划应包括一份组织结构图、所需岗位的任职要求、以及所有岗位的责任和义务。

1.9 社区参与计划

1.9.1 社区参与计划。社区参与计划应指出利益相关者要如何被认定、分类和参与。

1.10 总体管理规划

1.10.1 总体管理规划。鉴于前文和后文中所呈现的有效管理的核心要素，需要准备一份总体管理规划。规划应明确要采取的框架、结构、系统、政策和行动以确保可持续管理。每一措施都要设定标准、计划、指标和预算。

总体管理规划应包括第 1.1-1.9 节中所列的所有内容。更具体地说，它还应包括：

1.10.1.1 一份财务计划，其中应说明门票收入和其他费用应当如何配置给遗址管理，及其配置原理；

1.10.1.2 一份周期性维护计划，其中应说明适当的程序、所需人员、设备和供应需求以及设施设计；

1.10.1.3 一份安全计划，应包括灾难应对、搜索和救援协议，以及医疗设备的需求；

1.10.1.4 涵盖了如第 1.9 节概括的岗位计划，明确所需人员，确定每个工作人员必要的资质、作用和责任。人力计划应包括一份组织结构图。

2. 管理实施

2.1 监测

2.1.1 监测系统反馈。监测系统和程序的结果应作为遗址管理的决策支持工具。由监测支持的决定涵盖管理的所有方面，包括但不限于：周期性维护和改善资本状况、人员招募与管理、承载量的确定（应根据管理能力，随时间的推移而变化）和改变的可接受范围，以及有效的社区参与所需的政策、项目和活动。

2.2 透明

2.2.1 监测和管理中的透明。利益相关者，从地方社区团体到对遗址感兴趣的国际组织，与他们感兴趣的内容相关的任何管理项目和活动都应及时告知。监测结果应定期向所有利益相关者公开。

2.3 沟通

2.3.1 遗址管理者间的沟通和协调。建议公众考古遗址代表定期会晤，分享共同关心的问题，探讨有助于解决问题的途径、方案和活动。

Salalah Guidelines for the Management of Public Archaeological Sites

Adopted by the 19th ICOMOS General Assembly, New Delhi, India, 15 December 2017

PREAMBLE TO GUIDELINES

Archaeological sites are under the rightful control of stakeholders residing in the country and region in which they are located. The guidelines to follow are suggestions made to those stakeholders, should they decide to open an archaeological site to the public. *These guidelines are not intended to be regulations or standards, and the many parties that have participated in developing these guidelines hereby declare our opposition to transforming what follows into regulations or standards.* The suggestions made in these guidelines are drawn from the collective experience of those who have been engaged with management of publicly accessible archaeological sites in many countries and in different regions around the world. They are offered with the understanding that each country and region is different, and that this cultural diversity enriches the lives of all humans. Any suggestions made in these guidelines that are not consistent with the regional and local cultural stewardship of archaeological sites, and especially those open to visitors, can therefore be modified. Archaeological sites in national park systems around the world and those within World Heritage Sites present particular challenges because the tourism industry markets them as premier destinations. This has become clear in the decades since the ratification of the Convention Concerning the Protection of the World Cultural and Natural Heritage. Since then, similar sets of persistent problems have emerged at archaeological sites open to the public. These guidelines are intended to lessen the likelihood that such problems develop and become irremediable at archaeological sites opened to the public.

PURPOSES AND OBJECTIVES OF THESE GUIDELINES

The purposes of these guidelines are:
• To identify the studies necessary to assess the feasibility of establishing a sustainable management framework and system for archaeological sites that are, or are likely to become, open to the public; and
• To guide the development of a sustainable management system by reference to such a feasibility assessment.
The ultimate objectives of these guidelines are summarized as follows:
• Preserving and maintaining archaeological features, materials and sites in context until they can be studied in a scientific manner;
• Providing a model of sound sustainable management practice (including the use) for the cultural and natural

resources of archaeological sites that are open to the public;

• Making use of archaeological sites open to the public to build public awareness of the value of cultural diversity and the strength of interconnections between cultures in ways that can benefit all;

• Ensure that archaeological sites contribute to Sustainable Development by preserving and remediating where needed ecological services and providing opportunities and support for local populations to benefit economically in ways that do not incite social disruption.

Archaeological sites contain material evidence that when studied scientifically can inform us about the history of humanity; in that way, in the poetic language of the ICOMOS Venice Charter of 1964, they are "imbued with messages from the past". A visit to an archaeological site conveys the human past with an immediacy that cannot be provided by other means. Therefore, the experience of visiting an archaeological site should be available to as wide an audience as possible, with the proviso that this does not compromise or destroy the physical evidence of what transpired in the past. While a standing structure can be cosmetically repaired, the historic and scientific value of an archaeological site resides completely in the ability to investigate original material in original: this sets archaeological sites apart from all other heritage sites.

A visit to an archaeological site can advance the wide spectrum of benefits - social, economic, and cultural- associated with heritage. Publicly, conscientiously presented heritage enriches our understanding of the ongoing relationship between humans and nature, as well as the common and various means by which humans organize themselves and interact with other groups. These are critical contemporary issues. Heritage plays a fundamental role in developing collective identities. Where heritage is used to privilege narratives in ways that benefit certain groups, heritage studies drawn from archaeological research and its material evidence can just as surely be used to challenge these narratives.

Publicly accessible archaeological sites can generate economic benefit in ways that are both sustainable and unsustainable. Sustainable management of archaeological sites that are open to the public requires an understanding of how public access and experience combine to help protect the sites concerned. Sustainable management also requires the clear identification of how the development of public access might harm the sites concerned. By definition, unsustainable exploitation compromises sites that are open to the public and disrupts the endeavour to present human history in a manner that is as unbiased as possible, and thus in a useful way.

These guidelines are intended to apply to all archaeological sites open to the public, but they are of particular relevance to sites engaged with the World Heritage programme. The prestige that attends inscription on the World Heritage List encourages visitation and can foster important economic development locally.

Every site inscribed on the World Heritage List contains material remains of interest to the field of archaeology. World Heritage Sites include historic cities, all of which contain archaeological remains of the earlier "city below the city". Other World Heritage Sites, inscribed by virtue of the Outstanding Universal Value attached to natural resources can possess archaeological remains. Relatively recent structures and landscapes that are regarded as works of architectural or engineering genius are of interest to the study of archaeology and related disciplines. Archaeological materials from all these kinds of sites, if properly studied, can yield detailed and fascinating information that enriches understanding of the sites concerned. Archaeology reveals human history and human experience in the past in ways that are pertinent to contemporary life, including evidence for the social and economic consequences of human conflict and the repercussions of overexploitation of the environment. The preservation of archaeological material, as an essential repository of information, is perhaps of particular importance at sites that are open to the public as scientific study can enliven and significantly add to the established knowledge and narratives of the sites concerned. Furthermore, all World Heritage Sites, with their Outstanding Universal Value, extraordinary qualities and global visibility, should be exemplars of sustainable management.

THE NEED FOR THESE GUIDELINES

These guidelines explicitly address the necessity for assessing the feasibility of establishing sustainable management of archaeological sites open to the public with as much, or in some cases more, attention and investment of time and funds than has been given to assessing the suitability of designating a place a special one that deserves the special notice and regard of the public. There are many useful documents that deal with the myriad issues associated with the management of World Heritage Sites. Because they are international in scope, these are useful to the purposes of these guidelines and some are relevant to archaeological sites. The guidelines presented here are, however, specifically intended to apply to all archaeological sites that are open to the public. Among those are archaeological sites recognized explicitly as such on the World Heritage List or those that may be inscribed on the List (that is, sites on the World Heritage Tentative Lists that have been established by States Parties to the World Heritage Convention). Sites on the World Heritage List should provide models of sustainable management that can be used elsewhere. They can demonstrate how institutions and programmes can be developed to protect all cultural and natural heritage sites, in accord with the objectives presented in Article V of the World Heritage Convention.

Many of the most prominent places and iconic sites on the World Heritage List, including, but not limited to, Petra, Machu Picchu, Angkor, and Pompeii were obvious choices for World Heritage inscription in terms of *suitability*. They all undeniably meet one or more of the criteria laid out in the *Operational Guidelines for the Implementation of the World Heritage Convention*, and they all possess Outstanding Universal Value. Yet the impact of inscription and the *feasibility* of sustainably managing them following inscription was not adequately understood at the time of inscription. Other candidate World Heritage Sites continue to be presented for nomination with inadequate management feasibility studies to guide the preparation of dossiers. Where a feasible framework for sustainable management has not been developed, the Outstanding Universal Value including integrity and authenticity of nominated sites is vulnerable. Indeed, management itself is one of the pillars of Outstanding Universal Value. Inattention to the feasibility of putting in place sustainable management before inviting the public to archaeological sites can only lead to depletion of the storehouse of scientific and historical information at archaeological sites and degradation of the experience of visiting these sites.

It is a daunting task to rapidly assemble a management system after the public has been invited to visit, particularly if this results in a significant increase in visitors (often the case when sites are inscribed on the World Heritage List). In the absence of regional planning and community support for zoning, it is common for development around and in the site to degrade the environment, often in ways that are destructive to the site itself. This can occur very rapidly, and damage can be irreversible. Once in place, structures and populations that occupy them have proven almost impossible to relocate. These issues are exacerbated if there is limited access to the necessary technological, regulatory, administrative, personnel, and financial resources. The results too often are very unsatisfactory for all stakeholders.

Feasibility in this context is dependent upon the ability of stakeholders to plan appropriately for protection and conservation of the site and the development of facilities and services required by the public visiting it. This presupposes the design and implementation of a sound management framework and system. Management must be founded, first and foremost, on an adequate knowledge of the site by all involved. It involves establishing capacities for monitoring together with regulating programmes and activities that are adequate for sustainable management. Management planning and implementation should be linked not only for the site itself, but also for the immediate surroundings of the site and region where development is planned that is related to visitation.

These guidelines provide a roadmap for the identification and development of effective management frameworks and systems, and the necessary improvement to those already in place.

There is additional strategic value in establishing accepted guidelines for the management of archaeological sites that are open to the public. Numerous governmental and non-profit development assistance programmes are available that can provide funds for State Parties and agencies seeking assistance with sustainable economic development. Adherence to approved guidelines can assist applications to these programmes and provide a rationale for requests of funding and technical support. The development of a multi-year plan for the sustainable management of an archaeological site that is open to the public provides a structure for effective development.

ANTECEDENTS

This document takes note of the work undertaken by ICOMOS in the past, particularly at Ma'agan in 2002, and has full regard for the guiding principles of that meeting (Cleere 2010, 5), which identified the following elements as essential to all management planning:

a. A thorough shared understanding of the property by all stakeholders;
b. A cycle of planning, implementation, monitoring, evaluation and feedback;
c. The involvement of partners and stakeholders;
d. The allocation of necessary resources;
e. Capacity-building; and
f. An accountable, transparent description of how the management system functions.

THE CONCEPT OF THE ARCHAEOLOGICAL PARK

A park is defined for the purposes of these guidelines as a protected area set aside for public access, enjoyment, and education. This definition is compatible with *the Salalah Recommendation on Archaeological Parks and Sites*, developed at the First International Conference of ICOMOS on Archaeological Parks and Sites, 23-25 February 2015, in Salalah, the Sultanate of Oman.

As described in the Salalah Recommendation, archaeological parks contain both above-ground and below-ground archaeological remains and material. The Salalah Recommendation advises that the archaeological park should be seen "as a tool for conservation of archaeological sites on the one hand, and their presentation and interpretation as a means to understand the shared past of humanity on the other hand" (http://whc.unesco.org/en/news/1256). As such, it can be seen to advance the overall objectives of the World Heritage Convention. It should serve as a didactic device because it can reflect the concept of shared humanity and, if sustainably managed, provide an example of how sustainable management can be accomplished in other vulnerable places where important cultural and natural resources are present.

GUIDELINES

1. Management Planning

1.1 Inventory and evaluation

Every effort should be made to employ cost effective, non-intrusive, and non-destructive technologies for the inventory and evaluation of cultural and natural resources. These technologies shall include, for example, direct detection of sites and resources or modelling the distribution of sites and resources.

1.1.1 *Cultural resources.* An inventory and evaluation of cultural resources is the first step in establishing the feasibility of developing a sustainable management system for archaeological sites, features, and landscapes. The evaluation should address vulnerability and threats as well as importance of cultural resources.

Those with stewardship for the area in question should:

1.1.1.1 Retain credentialed, accredited and internationally recognized archaeological experts to assist in the identification and evaluation of archaeological sites, features, landscapes, and all associated material; and

1.1.1.2 Ensure that well-documented and internationally recognized best practices for field-based study, documentation, evaluation, and protection of archaeological heritage are implemented.

1.1.2 *Natural resources.* An inventory and evaluation of natural resources is as important as that which should be done for cultural resources, and should be done in ways that will identify environmental changes that might threaten archaeological resources and environmental services that benefit the local human population, or might do so in the future.

Stewards of the area should:

1.1.2.1 Retain credentialed, accredited and internationally recognized experts in relevant fields. The inventory should be comprehensive for natural resources and identify those that are or may be:

1.1.2.1.1 Threatened or endangered;

1.1.2.1.2 Of central importance to the greater landscape, of which the archaeological site is a part, in particular those that are related to the preservation of archaeological materials in context;

1.1.2.1.3 Integral to environmental services of value to local human populations.

1.1.3 *Infrastructure.* As-built surveys and specifications and current conditions of all infrastructure should be provided, along with known or estimated numbers of users. Infrastructure includes all buildings, utilities, roads, communication networks, and means of access and travel.

1.1.4 *Traditional use areas.* Traditional use areas should be identified. These are areas of particular value to contemporary inhabitants of the site and surrounding region, including those that might be considered sacred or are used for traditional purposes (e.g. view sheds, marriages or other celebrations, or the collection of medicinal or nutritional plants).

Those who have stewardship of archaeological sites open to the public should:

1.1.4.1 Retain credentialed, accredited and recognized experts on traditional use areas to identify and evaluate archaeological heritage in such areas; and

1.1.4.2 Ensure that well-documented and internationally recognized best practices for field-based study, documentation, evaluation and protection of archaeological heritage in traditional use areas are implemented.

1.2 Establish site boundaries and management zones

1.2.1 *Site boundaries.* It is essential that the proposed boundary of an archaeological site that might be opened to the public be accurately determined, as informed by the inventory of cultural and natural resources.

1.2.2 *Site size and configuration*. The site should be of sufficient size and appropriate configuration to render sustainable resource protection and visitor enjoyment possible and likely (taking into account current and potential impacts from sources beyond proposed boundaries).

1.2.3 *Cost considerations*. The characteristics of the site should not preclude efficient management and administration at a reasonable cost that can be borne by the party or parties with stewardship responsibility for the site.

Considerations should include:

1.2.3.1 Current and potential uses of the area within the site boundaries and surrounding lands within and beyond the buffer zone;

1.2.3.2 Land ownership and legal rights to use, including possible changes;

1.2.3.3 Public access and enjoyment potential;

1.2.3.4 Costs associated with acquisition, development, restoration, and day-to-day management and operation;

1.2.3.5 Access (e.g. routes in and out of the property, way-finding, circulation, and services);

1.2.3.6 Analysis of current degradation of the archaeological resources and its causes;

1.2.3.7 Current and potential threats to the archaeological resources;

1.2.3.8 The level of local and general public support (e.g. from businesses, governments, and landowners);

1.2.3.9 The social, political, environmental, and economic impacts of designation; and

1.2.3.10 The manner and degree to which public goods, such as the quality of the natural and social environments, education, and health and safety services, should be enhanced by the establishment of a public archaeological site.

1.2.4 *Buffer zones*. The boundaries of a buffer zone should also be accurate and well documented.

1.2.4.1 Because a buffer zone alone is usually not enough to ensure protection from encroachment, agreements with communities and government entities should be negotiated and formalized in order to accomplish this.

1.2.5 *Management Zones*. Within each site, Management Zones should be established, and for each the following should be identified:

1.2.5.1 Desired uses;

1.2.5.2 Desired conditions;

1.2.5.3 Essential visitor services;

1.2.5.4 Interpretive themes (the information that should be presented in each zone).

1.3 Environmental Impact Assessment or Environmental Impact Study

1.3.1 *Environmental impact*. An Environmental Impact Assessment or Environmental Impact Study should be performed for any proposed development activity that might affect the quality of the environment.

1.3.2 *Economic consequences of environmental impact*. An Environmental Impact Assessment or Environmental Impact Study should include an economic analysis of the potential economic benefits and liabilities that might accrue to private individuals, business interests, community groups, or local, regional, national, or global publics.

1.4 Monitoring Plan

1.4.1 *The monitoring plan*. The monitoring plan should specify the technologies, protocols, instruments, indicators, and standards that should monitor:

1.4.1.1 The condition of cultural resources of all types;

1.4.1.2 The condition of natural resources of all types;

1.4.1.3 Visitor numbers, circulation, and satisfaction;

1.4.1.4 Community satisfaction; and

1.4.1.5 The condition of facilities and infrastructure.

1.4.2 *Monitoring priorities*. Monitoring priorities should be set by considering which resources and experiences are:

1.4.2.1 Key to the natural or cultural integrity of the site and to the opportunities for enjoyment of the site;

1.4.2.2 Essential in order to maintain compliance with the criteria used to identify the site's Outstanding Universal Value; and

1.4.2.3 Identified in the site's general management plan or other relevant planning documents as significant.

1.5 Archaeological Research Plan

1.5.1 *The archaeological research plan*. A plan, including research priorities, should be developed to address needs for mitigation of archaeological resource disturbance from natural processes (e.g. flooding) as well as human activities (e.g. looting or development). The plan should also identify archaeological research that is relevant to the importance of the site, and especially research that might address issues of urgent concern to the field of archaeology, contemporary environmental policy, and improving international relations.

1.6 Interpretive Plan

1.6.1 *The interpretive plan*. An interpretive plan should be prepared that identifies the interpretive themes and sub-themes that best serve the didactic function of the site. The plan should be updated at least every five years.

1.7 Management Facilities

1.7.1 *Management facilities*. Management facilities include the structures, utilities, and equipment necessary for the sustainable management of the archaeological site. Those necessary to ensure the retention of the site's integrity, authenticity, and characteristics relating to its importance should be identified; further, the requirements for these facilities should be identified.

1.8 Staffing Plan

1.8.1 *Sustainable management will require the services of a variety of well-trained people*. These will typically include scientists and archaeologists with pertinent experience in the natural and cultural resources of the public archaeological site, maintenance staff, administrative staff having skills in budgeting and scheduling, interpreters to present the site to visitors, people with museum, curation and presentation skills, community liaisons, people trained in providing health and safety services, enforcement personnel, and managers who can coordinate develop and coordinate all necessary policies, programmes, and activities.

Staffing needs will vary; therefore, a staffing plan should be developed that is informed by the inventory and evaluation of cultural and natural resources and the identified vulnerability and threats to those resources, as well as the specific objectives associated with presenting the site to the public. The plan should include an organization chart, necessary qualifications for all required positions, and duties and responsibilities for all positions.

1.9 Community Engagement Plan

1.9.1 *The community engagement plan*. The community engagement plan should address how stakeholders should be identified, categorized, and engaged.

1.10 General Management Plan

1.10.1 *The General Management Plan*. Respecting the essential elements of effective management as presented above and below, a General Management Plan should be prepared. The plan should set out the framework, structure, system, policies, and actions that should be taken to ensure sustainable management. For each action, benchmarks, schedules, indicators, and budgets should be established.

The General Management Plan should include all the material described in Sections 1.1 through 1.9. More specifically, it should also include:

1.10.1.1 A financial plan, which should describe how entry fees and other fees should be allocated to the management of the site and a rationale for this;

1.10.1.2 A cyclical maintenance plan, which should describe appropriate programmes, staffing needs, equipment and supplies needs, and facility design;

1.10.1.3 A safety plan, which should include protocols for disaster response, search and rescue, and requirements for medical facilities; and

1.10.1.4 The inclusion of the staffing plan outlined above (1.9.), which presents required staff and identifies necessary qualifications, roles, and responsibilities for each staff member. The staffing plan should include an organization chart.

2 Management Implementation

2.1 Monitoring

2.1.1 *Monitoring system feedback.* The results of the monitoring system and programme should be used as decision support tools by site management. Decisions supported by monitoring should involve all aspects of management, including, but not limited to, cyclical maintenance and capital improvements; personnel acquisition and management; determination of carrying capacity (which should vary over time according to management capacity) and limits of acceptable change; and policy, programs, and activities needed for effective community involvement.

2.2 Transparency

2.2.1 *Transparency in monitoring and management.* Stakeholders, from local community groups to international organizations with an interest in the site, should be kept informed of any management programmes and activities related to their interest in the site. Monitoring results should be made available to all stakeholders on a regular basis.

2.3 Networking

2.3.1 *Communication and coordination among site managers.* It is recommended that representatives of public archaeological sites meet on a regular basis to share issues of common concern and the approaches, programmes, and activities that have helped resolve issues of common concern.

·水下文化遗产·

水下文化遗产保护与管理宪章[①]

(国际古迹遗址理事会第十一届大会1996年10月在保加利亚索菲亚通过)

引　言

　　本宪章旨在鼓励保护和管理内陆和近岸水域、浅海和深海的水下文化遗产。宪章专注于水下文化遗产的具体属性和情况,应被理解为对1990年国际古迹遗址理事会《保护和管理考古遗产宪章》的补充。1990年的《考古遗产宪章》将"考古遗产"定义为考古方法提供了主要信息的物质遗产的一部分,它包含了人类存在的所有残迹,其中包括与人类活动的所有现象有关的场所、废弃的构造和各种遗迹,以及与之相关的所有可移动的文化材料。就本宪章而言,水下文化遗产应理解为处于水下环境中或已从水下环境中移出的考古遗产。它包括水下遗址和构造、沉船遗址和残骸及其考古的和自然的环境。

　　水下文化遗产其特点是一种国际资源。水下文化遗产的很大一部分位于国际环境中,来自国际贸易和交流,在这种贸易和交流中,船只及其物品在远离其来源或目的地的地方丢失。

　　考古学关注环境保护;以资源管理的角度来看,水下文化遗产既是有限的,也是不可再生的。如果水下文化遗产有助于我们未来对环境的认识,那么我们现在就必须承担起个人和集体的责任,以确保其持续生存。

　　考古学是一项公共活动;每个人都有权利用过去来知晓自己的生活,任何试图限制对过去的了解的行为都是对个人自主权的侵犯。水下文化遗产有助于认同性的形成,对人们的社区意识非常重要。如果管理得当,水下文化遗产可以在促进游憩和旅游方面发挥积极作用。

　　考古学是由研究推动的,它增加了对历史上的人类文化多样性的了解,并为过去的生活提供了新的和富有挑战性的观点。这些知识和观点有助于理解今天的生活,从而预测未来的挑战。

　　许多海洋活动本身是有益和可取的,但如果其影响无法预见,可能会给水下文化遗产带来令人遗憾的后果。

　　水下文化遗产可能受到改变海岸和海床或改变水流、沉积物和污染物的建筑工程的威胁。水下文化遗产也可能受到对生物和非生物资源的盲目开发的威胁。此外,不恰当的到访形式和拿走"纪念品"的增量影响将会产生有害的作用。

　　通过早期咨询考古学家和实施缓和的项目,许多这种威胁都可消除或大大减少。本宪章旨在帮助迅速有效地利用高标准的考古专业知识应对水下文化遗产面临的这种威胁。

[①] 译者:曹新。

水下文化遗产也受到完全不可取的活动的威胁，因为这些活动的目的是以牺牲许多人的利益来获取少数人的利益。为贸易或投机目的对水下文化遗产进行商业开发，与遗产的保护和管理在根本上不相容。本宪章旨在确保所有调查在目标、方法和预期结果上都是明确的，这样每个项目的意图对所有人都是透明的。

第一条　基本原则

原地保护水下文化遗产应被视为第一选择。

应该鼓励对公众开放。

应鼓励非破坏性技术、非侵扰性调查和取样，而不是进行发掘。

调查对于水下文化遗产的负面影响不得超过项目的缓和性目标或研究目标的必需程度。

调查必须避免对人类遗骸或崇拜场所不必要的干扰。

调查必须同时有充分的记录。

第二条　项目设计

在调查之前，必须做项目设计，需要考虑：
- 项目的缓和性或研究目标；
- 采用的方法和运用的技术；
- 预期的资金；
- 完成项目的时间表；
- 调查组的构成、资质、责任和经验；
- 实体的保护；
- 遗址管理和维护；
- 与博物馆及其他机构合作的安排；
- 记录文件；
- 健康和安全；
- 报告编写；
- 保存档案，包括调查中移出的水下文化遗产；
- 传播，包括公众参与。

项目设计应根据需要进行修订和修正。

调查必须按照项目设计进行。项目设计应提供给考古界。

第三条　资金

在调查之前，必须确保有足够的资金来完成项目设计的所有阶段，包括保护、报告编写和传播。项目设计应包括应急计划，以确保在出现预期资金中断时保护水下文化遗产和支撑文件。

项目资金不得要求出售水下文化遗产或采用任何会导致水下文化遗产和支撑文件不可挽回地分散的策略。

第四条　时间计划

在调查之前，必须保证有足够的时间来完成项目设计的所有阶段，包括保护、报告编写和传播。项目设计应包括应急计划，以确保在预期时间计划中断时保护水下文化遗产和支撑文件。

第五条　研究目标、方法和技术

项目设计中必须确定研究目标以及所采用的方法和技术的细节。研究方法应符合调查的研究目标，所采用的技术必须尽可能不具有侵扰性。

田野工作后对于人工制品和记录的分析是所有调查的必要组成部分；在项目设计中必须为这种分析作出充分的准备。

第六条 资质、责任和经验

调查组中的所有人员必须具备适合其项目角色的资质和经验。他们必须充分了解和理解工作的要求。

对水下文化遗产的所有侵扰性调查仅在指定水下考古学家的指导和控制下进行，他们应具有经认可的资质和项目调查所需的经验。

第七条 初步调查

对水下文化遗产的所有侵扰性调查必须在评估该遗址的脆弱性、重要性和可能性基础上进行。

遗址评估必须包括现有的历史和考古证据的背景研究、遗址的考古和环境特征，以及侵扰对于调查区域的长期稳定性的影响。

第八条 记录

所有调查必须根据考古记录的现行专业标准进行彻底记录。

必须全面记录遗址，包括在调查过程中移动或移出的水下文化遗产的来源、现场记录、平面图和图纸、照片以及其他媒介的记录。

第九条 实体保护

实体保护方案必须规定在调查、运输和长期过程中对考古遗迹的处理措施。

实体保护必须按照现行的专业标准进行。

第十条 遗址管理和维护

必须制定遗址管理计划，详细说明在现场工作结束时原地保护和管理水下文化遗产的措施。该计划应包括公共信息，遗址加固以及防止干扰的监测和保护的合理措施。应促进公众对水下文化遗产原址的到访，除非到访与保护和管理不相容。

第十一条 健康和安全

调查组和第三方的健康和安全至关重要。调查组中的所有人员必须根据满足相关法定和专业要求的安全措施工作，并在项目设计中列出这些安全措施。

第十二条 报告

中期报告应根据项目设计中规定的时间表提交，并保存在相关公共记录中。

报告应包括：
- 目标说明；
- 所采用的方法和技术的说明；
- 所取得成果的说明；
- 关于调查期间移出的水下文化遗产的未来研究、遗址管理和保管的建议。

第十三条 保管

项目档案，包括在调查期间移出的水下文化遗产和所有支撑文件的副本，必须存放在一个能够供公众访问和永久保管该档案的机构。档案存放的安排应在调查开始前达成一致，并应在项目设计中列出。档案应根据当前的专业标准进行准备。

必须保证项目档案的科学完整性；在多家机构中的存放不得排除重新组装的可能性，以便进一步研究。水下文化遗产不得作为具有商业价值的物品进行交易。

第十四条 传播

应通过在各种媒体上进行大众演示，提高公众对调查结果和水下文化遗产重要性的认识。不应因高收费而阻碍广大观众观看此类演示。

应鼓励与当地社区和团体的合作，特别是与水下文化遗产相关的社区和团体的合作。调查应得到这些社区和团体的同意和认可。

调查组将努力让社区和利益相关团体参与调查，只要这种参与相容于保护和管理。在可行的情况下，调查组应通过培训和教育为公众提供培养考古技能的机会。

应鼓励与博物馆和其他机构的合作。合作机构应在调查之前提供条件以便访问、研究和撰写报告。

根据研究的复杂程度，必须尽快地提供调查的最终综合报告，并保存在相关公共记录中。

第十五条　国际合作

国际合作对于水下文化遗产的保护和管理至关重要，应该为了高标准的调查和研究而促进这种合作。应该鼓励国际合作，以便有效发挥专门研究水下文化遗产的考古学家和其他专业人员的作用。专业人员的交流计划应被视为传播最佳实践的一种手段。

Charter on the Protection and Management of Underwater Cultural Heritage

Ratified by the 11th ICOMOS General Assembly, Sofia, Bulgaria, October 1996

INTRODUCTION

This Charter is intended to encourage the protection and management of underwater cultural heritage in inland and inshore waters, in shallow seas and in the deep oceans. It focuses on the specific attributes and circumstances of cultural heritage under water and should be understood as a supplement to the ICOMOS Charter for the Protection and Management of Archaeological Heritage, 1990. The 1990 Charter defines the "archaeological heritage" as that part of the material heritage in respect of which archaeological methods provide primary information, comprising all vestiges of human existence and consisting of places relating to all manifestations of human activity, abandoned structures, and remains of all kinds, together with all the portable cultural material associated with them. For the purposes of this Charter underwater cultural heritage is understood to mean the archaeological heritage which is in, or has been removed from, an underwater environment. It includes submerged sites and structures, wreck-sites and wreckage and their archaeological and natural context.

By its very character the underwater cultural heritage is an international resource. A large part of the underwater cultural heritage is located in an international setting and derives from international trade and communication in which ships and their contents are lost at a distance from their origin or destination.

Archaeology is concerned with environmental conservation; in the language of resource management, underwater cultural heritage is both finite and non-renewable. If underwater cultural heritage is to contribute to our appreciation of the environment in the future, then we have to take individual and collective responsibility in the present for ensuring its continued survival.

Archaeology is a public activity; everybody is entitled to draw upon the past in informing their own lives, and every effort to curtail knowledge of the past is an infringement of personal autonomy. Underwater cultural heritage contributes to the formation of identity and can be important to people's sense of community. If managed sensitively, underwater cultural heritage can play a positive role in the promotion of recreation and tourism.

Archaeology is driven by research, it adds to knowledge of the diversity of human culture through the ages and it provides new and challenging ideas about life in the past. Such knowledge and ideas contribute to understanding life today and, thereby, to anticipating future challenges.

Many marine activities, which are themselves beneficial and desirable, can have unfortunate consequences for underwater cultural heritage if their effects are not foreseen.

Underwater cultural heritage may be threatened by construction work that alters the shore and seabed or alters the flow of current, sediment and pollutants. Underwater cultural heritage may also be threatened by insensitive exploitation of living and non-living resources. Furthermore, inappropriate forms of access and the incremental impact of removing "souvenirs" can have a deleterious effect.

Many of these threats can be removed or substantially reduced by early consultation with archaeologists and by implementing mitigatory projects. This Charter is intended to assist in bringing a high standard of archaeological expertise to bear on such threats to underwater cultural heritage in a prompt and efficient manner.

Underwater cultural heritage is also threatened by activities that are wholly undesirable because they are intended to profit few at the expense of many. Commercial exploitation of underwater cultural heritage for trade or speculation is fundamentally incompatible with the protection and management of the heritage. This Charter is intended to ensure that all investigations are explicit in their aims, methodology and anticipated results so that the intention of each project is transparent to all.

Article 1 - Fundamental Principles

The preservation of underwater cultural heritage in situ should be considered as a first option.

Public access should be encouraged.

Non-destructive techniques, non-intrusive survey and sampling should be encouraged in preference to excavation.

Investigation must not adversely impact the underwater cultural heritage more than is necessary for the mitigatory or research objectives of the project.

Investigation must avoid unnecessary disturbance of human remains or venerated sites.

Investigation must be accompanied by adequate documentation.

Article 2 - Project Design

Prior to investigation a project must be prepared, taking into account:
- the mitigatory or research objectives of the project;
- the methodology to be used and the techniques to be employed;
- anticipated funding;
- the time-table for completing the project;
- the composition, qualifications, responsibility and experience of the investigating team;
- material conservation;
- site management and maintenance;
- arrangements for collaboration with museums and other institutions;
- documentation;
- health and safety;
- report preparation;
- deposition of archives, including underwater cultural heritage removed during investigation;
- dissemination, including public participation.

The project design should be revised and amended as necessary.

Investigation must be carried out in accordance with the project design. The project design should be made available to the archaeological community.

Article 3 - Funding

Adequate funds must be assured in advance of investigation to complete all stages of the project design including conservation, report preparation and dissemination. The project design should include contingency plans that will ensure conservation of underwater cultural heritage and supporting documentation in the event of any interruption in anticipated funding.

Project funding must not require the sale of underwater cultural heritage or the use of any strategy that will cause underwater cultural heritage and supporting documentation to be irretrievably dispersed.

Article 4 - Time-table

Adequate time must be assured in advance of investigation to complete all stages of the project design including conservation, report preparation and dissemination. The project design should include contingency plans that will ensure conservation of underwater cultural heritage and supporting documentation in the event of any interruption in anticipated timings.

Article 5 - Research objectives, methodology and techniques

Research objectives and the details of the methodology and techniques to be employed must be set down in the project design. The methodology should accord with the research objectives of the investigation and the techniques employed must be as non-intrusive as possible.

Post-fieldwork analysis of artefacts and documentation is integral to all investigation; adequate provision for this analysis must be made in the project design.

Article 6 - Qualifications, responsibility and experience

All persons on the investigating team must be suitably qualified and experienced for their project roles. They must be fully briefed and understand the work required.

All intrusive investigations of underwater cultural heritage will only be undertaken under the direction and control of a named underwater archaeologist with recognised qualifications and experience appropriate to the investigation.

Article 7 - Preliminary investigation

All intrusive investigations of underwater cultural heritage must be preceded and informed by a site assessment that evaluates the vulnerability, significance and potential of the site.

The site assessment must encompass background studies of available historical and archaeological evidence, the archaeological and environmental characteristics of the site and the consequences of the intrusion for the long term stability of the area affected by investigations.

Article 8 - Documentation

All investigation must be thoroughly documented in accordance with current professional standards of archaeological documentation.

Documentation must provide a comprehensive record of the site, which includes the provenance of underwater cultural heritage moved or removed in the course of investigation, field notes, plans and drawings, photographs and records in other media.

Article 9 - Material conservation

The material conservation programme must provide for treatment of archaeological remains during investigation, in transit and in the long term.

Material conservation must be carried out in accordance with current professional standards.

Article 10 - Site management and maintenance

A programme of site management must be prepared, detailing measures for protecting and managing in situ underwater cultural heritage in the course of an upon termination of fieldwork. The programme should include public information, reasonable provision for site stabilisation, monitoring and protection against interference. Public access to in situ underwater cultural heritage should be promoted, except where access is incompatible with protection and management.

Article 11 - Health and safety

The health and safety of the investigating team and third parties is paramount. All persons on the investigating team must work according to a safety policy that satisfies relevant statutory and professional requirements and is set out in the project design.

Article 12 - Reporting

Interim reports should be made available according to a time-table set out in the project design and deposited in relevant public records.

Reports should include:
• an account of the objectives;
• an account of the methodology and techniques employed;
• an account of the results achieved;
• recommendations concerning future research, site management and curation of underwater cultural heritage removed during the investigation.

Article 13 - Curation

The project archive, which includes underwater cultural heritage removed during investigation and a copy of all supporting documentation, must be deposited in an institution that can provide for public access and permanent curation of the archive. Arrangements for deposition of the archive should be agreed before investigation commences and should be set out in the project design. The archive should be prepared in accordance with current professional standards.

The scientific integrity of the project archive must be assured; deposition in a number of institutions must not preclude reassembly to allow further research. Underwater cultural heritage is not to be traded as items of commercial value.

Article 14 - Dissemination

Public awareness of the results of investigations and the significance of underwater cultural heritage should be promoted through popular presentation in a range of media. Access to such presentations by a wide audience should not be prejudiced by high charges.

Co-operation with local communities and groups is to be encouraged, as is co-operation with communities and groups that are particularly associated with the underwater cultural heritage concerned. It is desirable that investigations proceed with the consent and endorsement of such communities and groups.

The investigation team will seek to involve communities and interest groups in investigations to the extent that such involvement is compatible with protection and management. Where practical, the investigation team should provide opportunities for the public to develop archaeological skills through training and education.

Collaboration with museums and other institutions is to be encouraged. Provision for visits, research and reports by collaborating institutions should be made in advance of investigation.

A final synthesis of the investigation must be made available as soon as possible, having regard to the complexity of the research, and deposited in relevant public records.

Article 15 - International co-operation

International co-operation is essential for protection and management of underwater cultural heritage and should be promoted in the interests of high standards of investigation and research. International co-operation should be encouraged in order to make effective use of archaeologists and other professionals who are specialised in investigations of underwater cultural heritage. Programmes for exchange of professionals should be considered as a means of disseminating best practice.

保护水下文化遗产公约

(联合国教科文组织第三十一届大会 2001 年 11 月 2 日在巴黎通过)

大会,

认识到水下文化遗产的重要性,它是人类文化遗产的组成部分,也是各国人民和各民族的历史及其在共同遗产方面的关系史上极为重要的一个内容;

认识到保护和保存水下文化遗产的重要性,所有国家都应负起这一责任;

注意到公众对水下文化遗产日益关心和重视;

深信研究、宣传和教育对保护和保存水下文化遗产极为重要;

深信公众只要以负责的和非闯入的方式进入仍在水下的水下文化遗产,就有权从中接受教育和得到娱乐,也深信公众接受的教育有助于他们认识、欣赏和保护这份遗产;

意识到水下文化遗产受到未经批准的开发活动的威胁,有必要采取更有力的措施阻止这些活动;

意识到合法开发水下文化遗产的活动也可能无意中对其造成不良后果,因而有必要对此作出相应的对策;

对水下文化遗产日益频繁的商业开发,尤其是对某些以买卖、占有或交换水下文化遗产为目的的活动**深感忧虑**;

意识到先进的技术为发现和进入水下文化遗产提供了便利;

认为国家、国际组织、科研机构、专业组织、考古学家、潜水员、其他有关方面和广大公众之间的合作对保护水下文化遗产是极为重要的;

考虑到水下文化遗产的勘测、挖掘和保护都必须掌握,并能应用特殊的科学方法,必须利用恰当的技术和设备,还必须具备高度的专业知识,所有这些说明必须有统一的标准;

认识到必须根据国际法和国际惯例,包括 1970 年 11 月 14 日的《教科文组织关于采取措施禁止并防止文化财产非法进出口和所有权非法转让公约》,1972 年 11 月 16 日的《教科文组织保护世界文化和自然遗产公约》和 1982 年 12 月 10 日的《联合国海洋法公约》,编纂有关保护和保存水下文化遗产的法典和逐步制定这方面的规章制度;

决心提高国际、地区和各国为就地保护水下文化遗产,或因科研及保护的需要,小心打捞水下文化遗产而采取的措施的有效性;

在其第二十九届大会**已决定**为此拟定一份国际公约的基础上,

于 2001 年 11 月 2 日**通过**本公约。

第 1 条 定义

在本公约中:

---

① 引自:UNESCO 决议 31 C/15。

1.（a）"水下文化遗产"系指至少100年来，周期性地或连续地，部分或全部位于水下的具有文化、历史或考古价值的所有人类生存的遗迹，比如：

（ⅰ）遗址、建筑、房屋、工艺品和人的遗骸，及其有考古价值的环境和自然环境；

（ⅱ）船只、飞行器、其他运输工具或上述三类的任何部分，所载货物或其他物品，及其有考古价值的环境和自然环境；

（ⅲ）具有史前意义的物品。

（b）海底铺设的管道和电缆不应视为水下文化遗产。

（c）海底铺设的管道和电缆以外的，且仍在使用的装置，不应视为水下文化遗产。

2.（a）"缔约国"系指同意接受本公约之约束和本公约对其具有约束力的国家。

（b）本公约经必要的改动后也适用于本公约第26条第2段（b）中所指的那些根据该条规定的条件成为本公约的缔约方的地区，从这个意义上说，"缔约国"也指这些地区。

3."教科文组织"系指联合国教科文组织。

4."总干事"即教科文组织总干事。

5."区域"系指国家管辖范围以外的海床和洋底及其底土。

6."开发水下文化遗产的活动"系指以水下文化遗产为其主要对象，并可能直接或间接对其造成损伤或破坏的活动。

7."无意中影响水下文化遗产的活动"系指尽管不以水下文化遗产为主要对象或对象之一，但可能对其造成损伤或破坏的活动。

8."国家的船只和飞行器"系指属于某国或由其使用，且在沉没时仅限于政府使用而非商用的，并经确定属实又符合水下文化遗产的定义的军舰和其他船只或飞行器。

9."规章"系指本公约第33条所指的《有关开发水下文化遗产之活动的规章》。

第2条 目标和总则

1. 本公约的目的是确保和加强对水下文化遗产的保护。
2. 缔约国应开展合作，保护水下文化遗产。
3. 缔约国应根据本公约的各项规定为全人类之利益保护水下文化遗产。
4. 缔约国应根据本公约和国际法，按具体情况单独或联合采取一切必要的措施来保护水下文化遗产，并应根据各自的能力，运用各自能用的最佳的可行手段。
5. 在允许或进行任何开发水下文化遗产的活动之前，就地保护应作为首选。
6. 打捞出来的水下文化遗产必须妥善存放和保管，以便长期保存。
7. 不得对水下文化遗产进行商业开发。
8. 本公约须与各国的惯例和包括《联合国海洋法公约》在内的国际法相一致，任何条款均不应被理解为对有关主权豁免的国际法和国家惯例的规定的修正，也不改变任何国家对本国的船只和飞行器拥有的权利。
9. 缔约国应确保对海域中发现的所有人的遗骸给予恰当的尊重。
10. 只要不妨碍对水下文化遗产的保护和管理，应当鼓励人们以负责的和非闯入方式进入仍在水下的水下文化遗产，以对其进行考察或建立档案资料，从而使公众认识到应当了解、欣赏和保护水下文化遗产。
11. 根据本公约采取的任何行动或开展的任何活动均不构成对国家主权或国家管辖权提出要求、支持或反对的理由。

第3条 本公约与《联合国海洋法公约》之间的关系

本公约中的任何条款均不得妨碍国际法，包括《联合国海洋法公约》，所赋予各国的权利、管辖权和义务。本公约应结合国际法,包括《联合国海洋法公约》,加以解释和执行,不得与之相悖。

第 4 条　与打捞法和打捞物法的关系

打捞法和打捞物法不适用于开发本公约所指的水下文化遗产的活动,除非它:

(a) 得到主管当局的批准,同时

(b) 完全符合本公约的规定,同时又

(c) 确保任何打捞出来的水下文化遗产都能得到最大程度的保护。

第 5 条　无意中影响水下文化遗产的活动

每个缔约国应采用它能用的最佳的可行手段防止或减轻其管辖范围内无意中影响水下文化遗产的活动可能造成的任何不良后果。

第 6 条　双边、地区或其他多边协定

1. 鼓励缔约国为保护水下文化遗产,签订双边、地区或其他多边协定,或对现有的协定加以补充。所有这些协定应完全符合本公约的规定,不得削弱本公约的普遍性。各国在这些协定中可提出能比本公约提出的规章更好地保护水下文化遗产的规章。

2. 这些双边、地区或其他多边协定的缔约方可邀请与有关的水下文化遗产确有联系,尤其是文化、历史或考古方面的联系的国家加入这些协定。

3. 本公约不得改变缔约国在本公约通过之前缔结的其他双边、地区或多边协定,尤其是与本公约的宗旨相一致的协定中规定的有关保护沉船的权利和义务。

第 7 条　内水、群岛水域和领海中的水下文化遗产

1. 缔约国在行使其主权时,拥有管理和批准开发其内水、群岛水域和领海中的水下文化遗产的活动的专属权利。

2. 在不违背其他有关保护水下文化遗产的国际协定和国际法准则的情况下,缔约国应要求开发内水、群岛水域和领海中的水下文化遗产的活动遵守《规章》中的各项规定。

3. 缔约国在其群岛水域和领海内行使其主权时,根据国与国之间的通行做法,为了在保护国家船只和飞行器的最佳办法方面进行合作,要向是本公约缔约国的船旗国,并根据情况,向与该水下文化遗产确有联系,尤其是文化、历史或考古方面的联系的其他国家通知发现可认出国籍的船只和飞行器的情况。

第 8 条　毗连区的水下文化遗产

在不违背第 9、10 两条的情况下,并在此两条之外,根据《联合国海洋法公约》第 303 条第 2 段的规定,缔约国可管理和批准在毗连区内开发水下文化遗产的活动。此时,缔约国应要求遵守《规章》的各项规定。

第 9 条　专属经济区和大陆架范围内的报告和通知

1. 所有缔约国都有责任按本公约保护其专属经济区内和大陆架上的水下文化遗产。因此:

(a) 当一缔约国的国民,或悬挂其国旗的船只发现或者有意开发该国专属经济区内或大陆架上的水下文化遗产时,该缔约国应要求该国国民或船主报告其发现或活动;

（b）在另一缔约国的专属经济区内或大陆架上：
　（i）缔约国应要求该国国民或船主向其，并向另一缔约国报告这些发现或活动；
　（ii）或，一缔约国应要求该国国民或船主向其报告这些发现或活动，并迅速有效地转告所有其他缔约国。

2. 在交存其批准、接受、赞同或加入文书时，一缔约国应说明本条第 1 段（b）中提到的报告的传达方式。

3. 缔约国应向总干事通报根据本条第 1 段向其报告的所有发现和活动。

4. 总干事应及时向所有缔约国通报根据本条第 3 段向其汇报的信息。

5. 任何缔约国都可以向在专属经济区内或大陆架上拥有水下文化遗产的缔约国表示愿意在有效保护这些水下文化遗产方面提供咨询。提出这种意愿的基础是这一缔约国必须与有关的水下文化遗产确有联系，尤其是文化、历史或考古方面的联系。

第 10 条　专属经济区内和大陆架上的水下文化遗产的保护

1. 在本条款许可范围之外，不得授权开发专属经济区内或大陆架上的水下文化遗产。

2. 缔约国有权依据包括《联合国海洋法公约》在内的国际法，为保护其主权权利和管辖权不受干涉而禁止或授权开发本国专属经济区内或大陆架上的文化遗产。

3. 当一缔约国在其专属经济区内或大陆架上发现水下文化遗产，或有意在其专属经济区或大陆架上开发水下文化遗产时，该缔约国应：

（a）与所有根据第 9 条第 5 段提出意愿的缔约国共同商讨如何最有效地保护这些水下文化遗产；

（b）作为"协调国"对这类商讨进行协调，除非该缔约国明确表示不愿做"协调国"；在这种情况下，其他根据第 9 条第 5 段表达参与商讨意愿的缔约国应另行指定一个"协调国"。

4. 在不妨碍缔约国遵照国际法采取各种可行措施来保护水下文化遗产，以防止水下文化遗产受到包括抢劫在内的紧急危险的情况下，如有必要，协调国可在协商之前遵照本《公约》采取一切可行的措施，和/或授权采取这些措施，以防止人类活动或包括抢劫在内的其他原因对水下文化遗产构成的紧急危险。在采取这些措施时，可请其他缔约国给予协助。

5. 协调国：

（a）应实施包括协调国在内的协商国一致同意的保护措施，除非包括协调国在内的协商国同意由另一个缔约国来实施这些措施；

（b）应为实施一致同意的符合《规章》的保护措施进行必要的授权，除非包括协调国在内的协商国同意由另一个缔约国来作出这些授权；

（c）可对水下文化遗产进行必要的初步研究，并为此进行必要的授权，并应及时向教科文组织总干事报告研究结果，总干事也应及时将这些信息通报其他缔约国。

6. 协调国在根据本条款协调缔约国之间的协商，对水下文化遗产采取保护措施，进行初步研究和/或进行授权时，应代表所有缔约国的整体利益，而不应只代表本国的利益。协调国在采取上述行动时不能就此认为自己享有包括《联合国海洋法公约》在内的国际法没有赋予它的优先权和管辖权。

7. 除本条款第 2 段和第 4 段所指的情况外，未经船旗国的同意和协调国的协作，不得对国家船只和飞行器采取任何行动。

第 11 条　"区域"内的报告和通知

1. 根据本公约和《联合国海洋法公约》第 149 条之规定，缔约国有责任保护"区域"内的水下文化遗产。据此，当一缔约国的国民或悬挂其国旗的船只在"区域"内发现水下文化遗产，或有意开发"区域"内的水下文化遗产时，该缔约国应要求其国民或船长向该缔约国报告他们的发现或活动。

2. 缔约国应向教科文组织总干事和国际海底管理局秘书长通知向他们报告的这些发现和活动。

3. 教科文组织总干事应及时将缔约国提供的这些信息通报给所有的缔约国。

4. 任何缔约国均可向教科文组织总干事表示愿意参与商讨如何有效地保护该水下文化遗产。提出这种意愿的基础是这一缔约国必须与有关的水下文化遗产确有联系，特别应考虑该遗产的文化、历史和考古起源国的优先权利。

第 12 条 "区域"内的水下文化遗产的保护

1. 在本条款许可范围之外，不得授权开发"区域"内的水下文化遗产。

2. 总干事应邀请根据第 11 条第 4 段提出愿意的缔约国商讨如何最有效地保护有关的水下文化遗产，并指定其中一个缔约国为"协调国"，协调商讨工作。教科文组织总干事还应邀请国际海底管理局参加此类协商。

3. 任何缔约国可依照本公约采取一切切实可行的措施，以防止人类活动或包括抢劫在内的其他原因对水下文化遗产造成的直接危害。必要时，可在与其他缔约国进行协商之前采取措施。

4. 协调国应：

（a）实施由包括协调国在内的协商国一致同意的保护措施，除非包括协调国在内的协商国同意由另一个缔约国来实施这些措施；和

（b）根据本公约之规定，为实施一致同意的措施进行必要的授权，除非包括协调国在内的协商国同意由另一缔约国进行这些授权。

5. 协调国可对水下文化遗产进行必要的初步研究，并为此进行必要的授权，并应及时向教科文组织总干事报告研究结果，总干事也应及时将这些信息通报其他缔约国。

6. 协调国在根据本条款协调缔约国之间的协商，对水下文化遗产采取保护措施，进行初步研究和 / 或进行授权时，应以全人类的利益为重，代表所有的缔约国。应特别考虑有关水下文化遗产的文化、历史和考古起源国的优先权利。

7. 任何缔约国未经船旗国的许可，不得对"区域"内的国家船只或飞行器采取任何行动。

第 13 条 主权豁免

享有主权豁免的军舰和其他政府船只或军用飞行器，在执行非商业性的和非针对水下文化遗产的正常任务时，没有根据本公约第 9、10、11 和 12 条之规定，报告发现水下文化遗产的义务。但是缔约国应采取适当措施，在不妨碍上述船只和飞行器执行任务或损害其执行任务的能力的情况下，确保上述船只和飞行器在合理和可行的范围内，遵守本公约的第 9、10、11 和 12 条。

第 14 条 限制进入领土，买卖和拥有

缔约国应采取措施，阻止非法出口和 / 或以违反本公约的方式非法打捞的水下文化遗产进入其领土，和在其领土上买卖或拥有这种水下文化遗产。

第 15 条 禁止使用缔约国管辖的区域

缔约国应采取措施禁止使用其领土，包括完全处于其管辖权和控制之下的海港及人工岛，设施和结构，进行违反本公约开发水下文化遗产的活动。

第 16 条 有关国民和船只的措施

缔约国应采取一切可行的措施，以确保其国民和悬挂其国旗的船只不进行任何不符合本公约的水下

文化遗产的开发活动。

第 17 条 制裁

1. 缔约国应对违反贯彻本公约的措施的行为进行制裁。

2. 对违反行为所作的制裁的力度应足以惩诫任何地方的违法行为，确保遵守本公约，并剥夺违反者从非法行为中获取的利益。

3. 缔约国应相互合作以确保根据本条款所采取的制裁措施得到实施。

第 18 条 水下文化遗产之扣押与处置

1. 缔约国应采取措施在其领土上扣押以违反本公约的方式打捞的水下文化遗产。

2. 缔约国应对根据本公约扣押的水下文化遗产进行登记和加以保护，并采取一切合理的措施使其保持原有状况。

3. 缔约国应向教科文组织总干事报告其依据本公约扣押的水下文化遗产，并通报任何与该水下文化遗产确有联系，尤其是文化、历史或考古方面的联系的缔约国。

4. 扣押了水下文化遗产的缔约国应确保对该文化遗产的处理方式符合公众的利益，要考虑对该遗产的保护和研究，散落文物之复原，向公众开放，展览和进行教育等问题，以及与该文化遗产确有联系，尤其是文化、历史或考古方面的联系的缔约国的利益。

第 19 条 合作与信息共享

1. 缔约国应依据本公约在水下文化遗产的保护和管理方面相互合作，互相帮助，有可能的话，也应在对这种遗产的调查、挖掘、记录、保存、研究和展出等方面开展协作。

2. 在不违反本公约宗旨的前提下，各缔约国要与其他缔约国分享有关水下文化遗产的信息，包括水下文化遗产的发现、所处位置、违反本公约或国际法或违反与这种遗产有关的其他国际法、有关的科学方法和技术以及有关法律挖掘或打捞的文化遗产。

3. 缔约国之间，或教科文组织与缔约国之间分享的有关水下文化遗产的发现或其位置的信息，只要泄露后可能危害水下文化遗产或危及水下文化遗产的保护工作，就应在不违反缔约国国内法律的前提下，作为只有缔约国主管当局了解的机密。

4. 缔约国应采取一切可行的措施，并在可行的情况下，包括利用有关的国际数据库，公布有关违反本公约或国际法挖掘或打捞的水下文化遗产的信息。

第 20 条 提高公众意识

缔约国应采取一切可行的措施，提高公众对水下文化遗产的价值与意义的认识、以及依照本公约保护水下文化遗产之重要性的认识。

第 21 条 水下考古培训

缔约国应开展合作，提供水下考古、水下文化遗产保存技术方面的培训，并按商定的条件进行与水下文化遗产有关的技术的转让。

第 22 条 主管机构

1. 为确保本公约的有效实施，缔约国应设立主管机构，已设立的要予以加强，负责水下文化遗产目录的编制、保存和更新工作，对水下文化遗产进行有效的保护、保存、展出和管理，并开展有关的科研和教育活动。

2. 缔约国应将其主管水下文化遗产的机构的名称和地址告知总干事。

第 23 条　缔约国会议

1. 总干事应在本公约生效一年之后召开一次缔约国会议，其后至少每两年召开一次。如大多数缔约国要求，总干事应召开缔约国特别会议。

2. 缔约国会议应确定其职能和责任。

3. 缔约国会议应有自己的《议事规则》。

4. 缔约国会议可以设立一个由缔约国提名的专家组成的科学与技术咨询委员会，该委员会的组成应充分考虑公平的地理分配原则和男女成员的适当比例。

5. 科学与技术咨询委员会应在实施《规章》中涉及的科学和技术问题方面，向缔约国会议提供必要的协助。

第 24 条　公约秘书处

1. 总干事应负责为本公约设立秘书处。

2. 秘书处的职能包括：

（a）根据第 23 条第 1 段的规定组织缔约国会议；

（b）协助缔约国落实缔约国会议的决定。

第 25 条　和平解决争端

1. 两个或两个以上缔约国在解释或实施本公约时出现的任何争端，都应以诚恳的协商或它们所选择的其他和平方式加以解决。

2. 如此类协商未能在合理的时间内解决争端，可经当事缔约国同意后，交由教科文组织调解。

3. 如未进行调解或调解无效，《联合国海洋法公约》第十五部分有关解决争端的条款，经必要修改后，可适用于本公约缔约国之间在解释或实施本公约中出现的任何争端，无论这些缔约国是否也是《联合国海洋法公约》的缔约国。

4. 本公约及《联合国海洋法公约》的缔约国依据《联合国海洋法公约》第 287 条所选择的任何程序，都适用于解决本条款中所说的争端，除非该缔约国在批准、接受、赞同或加入本公约之时或其后的任何时候，依据第 287 条选择了其他程序来解决因本公约引起的争端。

5. 没有加入《联合国海洋法公约》的本公约缔约国，在批准、接受、赞同或加入本公约之时或其后的任何时候，可以通过书面声明的方式，由自由选择《联合国海洋法公约》第 287 条第 1 段所规定的一种或多种方式，来解决本条款中所说的争端。第 287 条适用于这类声明，也适用于上述缔约国为当事一方，但是不在有效声明范围内的任何争端。依据《联合国海洋法公约》附件Ⅴ和附件Ⅶ，为了进行调解和仲裁，上述缔约国有权指定调解人和仲裁人，列入附件Ⅴ第 2 条和附件Ⅶ第 2 条提到的名单，以解决因本公约引起的争端。

第 26 条　批准、接受、赞同或加入

1. 教科文组织会员国可以批准、接受或赞同本公约。

2. 可以加入本公约的国家或地区包括：

（a）不是教科文组织会员国，但是联合国成员国或联合国系统内某一专门机构或国际原子能机构的会员国的国家，《国际法院规约》的缔约国，以及应教科文组织大会的邀请加入本公约的任何国家；

（b）没有完全独立，但根据联合国大会第 1514（XV）号决议被联合国承认为充分享有内部自治，并且有权处理本公约范围内的事宜，包括有权就这些事宜签署协议的地区。

3. 批准、接受、赞同或加入本公约的文书应交存于总干事处。

第 27 条 生效

在收到本公约第 26 条言及之第二十份文书三个月之后，本公约生效，但仅限于递交了文书的二十个国家或地区。其他任何国家或地区在递交其文书三个月后，本公约生效。

第 28 条 内陆水域声明

任何国家或地区，在批准、接受、赞同或加入本公约之时或其后的任何时候，都可以声明本公约之《规章》适用于其不具海洋性质的内陆水域。

第 29 条 地理范围的限定

任何国家或地区，在批准、接受、赞同或加入本公约之时，可向文书保管者声明，本公约不适用于其领土、内水、群岛水域或领海的某些特定部分，并在声明中阐述其理由。该国应尽其所能尽快地创造条件，使本公约适用于其声明中所指的特定区域，一旦条件成熟，应尽快全部或部分地撤回其声明。

第 30 条 保留

除第 29 条所指的情况外，对本公约不得持任何保留意见。

第 31 条 修正

1. 缔约国可书面通知教科文组织总干事，对本公约提出修正建议。总干事应将此通知转发给所有缔约国。如在通知发出之日起六个月内，有一半以上的缔约国答复赞成这一要求，总干事应将此建议提交下一次缔约国会议讨论，决定是否通过。
2. 对本公约的修正须经出席并参加表决的缔约国三分之二多数票通过。
3. 对本公约的修正一俟通过，可交由缔约国批准、接受、赞同或加入。
4. 对于批准、接受、赞同或加入修正案的缔约国来说，本公约修正案在三分之二的缔约国递交本条第 3 段所提及的文书之日三个月之后生效。此后，对任何批准、接受、赞同或加入修正案的国家或地区来说，在其递交批准、接受、赞同或加入文书之日三个月之后，本公约修正案即生效。
5. 依照本条第 4 段修正案生效后，本公约的缔约国或地区，在该国或地区未表示异议的情况下，应：
（a）被视为本公约业经修正之文本的缔约方；
（b）但在与不受修正案约束的任何缔约国的关系中，仍被视为未经修正之公约的缔约方。

第 32 条 退出

1. 缔约国可书面通知教科文组织总干事退出本公约。
2. 退出自接到通知之日起十二个月后生效，除非通知指定一个较后的日期。
3. 退出本公约决不意味着该缔约国可以不履行按照本公约以外的国际法应承担的与本公约的规定相同的一切义务。

第 33 条 规章

作为本公约之附件的《规章》是本公约的一个组成部分，除非另有明确说明，否则凡提及本公约时，均包括该《规章》。

第 34 条 备案
根据联合国宪章第102条，本公约应按总干事的要求在联合国秘书处备案。

第 35 条 有效文本
本公约用阿拉伯文、中文、英文、法文、俄文和西班牙文制定，这六种文本具有同等效力。

附 件

有关开发水下文化遗产之活动的规章

Ⅰ．一般原则

第 1 条 就地保护应作为保护水下文化遗产的首选方案。因此，批准开发水下文化遗产的活动必须看它是否符合保护该遗产之要求，在符合这种要求的情况下，可以批准进行一些有助于保护、认识或改善水下文化遗产的活动。

第 2 条 以交易或投机为目的而对水下文化遗产进行的商业性开发或造成的无法挽救的失散与保护和妥善管理这一遗产的精神是根本不相容的。水下文化遗产不得作为商品进行交易、买卖和以物换物。

本条不得解释为禁止下述活动：

（a）开展性质和目的完全符合本《公约》之规定，并经主管当局批准的专业考古工作或必要的辅助工作；

（b）保管在开展与本《公约》精神相符的研究项目时打捞的水下文化遗产，条件是这种保管不会损害打捞物的科学或文化价值，无损于其完整性或不会造成其无可挽回的失散，而且要符合第33和第34条的规定并经主管当局的批准。

第 3 条 开发水下文化遗产的活动对这一遗产造成的损坏必须以为完成项目而不得不造成的损坏为限。

第 4 条 开发水下文化遗产的活动应当优先考虑使用非破坏性的技术和勘测方法，而不是去打捞有关物品。如果为了科学研究或最终保护有关水下文化遗产而需要进行挖掘或打捞，那么所使用的技术和方法应尽可能不造成破坏，并有助于保存遗物。

第 5 条 开发水下文化遗产的活动应当避免不必要地侵扰人的遗骸或历史悠久的遗址。

第 6 条 开展开发水下文化遗产的活动应当严格按规定做好文化、历史和考古方面的资料工作。

第 7 条 应当鼓励向公众开放仍在水下的水下文化遗产，但不利于保护和管理的情况除外。

第 8 条 应鼓励在开展开发水下文化遗产的活动方面进行国际合作，以促进有效地交流或使用考古学家及其他有关的专业人员。

Ⅱ．项目说明

第 9 条 在开展开发水下文化遗产的活动之前，应当拟定一份项目说明，并提交主管当局批准和请同行进行必要的评议。

第 10 条 项目说明应当包括：

（a）对先前或初步研究的结果进行评估；

（b）项目说明和目标；

（c）准备采用的方法和技术；
（d）预计的资金；
（e）完成项目的时间表；
（f）项目小组的成员，每位成员的资历、责任和经验；
（g）实地考查工作后的分析工作和其他活动的计划；
（h）与主管当局密切合作拟定的文物和遗址保护计划；
（i）整个项目执行期间的遗址管理和保护政策；
（j）文献资料计划；
（k）安全措施；
（l）环境政策；
（m）与博物馆和其他机构，特别是与科研机构的合作安排；
（n）报告的编写；
（o）档案，包括打捞上来的水下文化遗产的存放计划；及
（p）出版计划。

第 11 条 应当根据主管当局批准的项目说明开展开发水下文化遗产的活动。

第 12 条 在出现未曾预料的发现或情况发生变化的情况下，项目说明应经主管当局批准予以复议和修订。

第 13 条 在出现紧急情况或意外发现时，即使没有项目说明，也可允许开展开发水下文化遗产的活动，包括短期的保护措施或活动，特别是稳定遗址方面的工作，以保护水下文化遗产。

III. 初步工作

第 14 条 第 10（a）条所说的初步工作包括一项评估工作，即评估水下文化遗产和周边自然环境的重要性和建议执行的项目会在多大程度上使其受损，以及收集符合项目目标的数据的可能性。

第 15 条 这项评估工作也应包括对现有的历史和考古资料，对有关遗址在考古和环境方面的特点，以及这些活动对有关水下文化遗产的长期稳定可能造成的侵扰的后果进行研究。

IV. 项目的目标和使用的方法及技术

第 16 条 所使用的方法应符合项目的目标，采用的技术应尽量不造成破坏。

V. 资　金

第 17 条 除水下文化遗产的紧急保护外，在开始进行任何开发活动之前，必须有足以完成项目说明中所有阶段所需的基本资金，包括对打捞的文物进行保护，登记造册和保管以及编写和散发报告所需的基本资金。

第 18 条 项目说明应表明有足够的能力，如获得一笔保证金，来资助该项目，直至全部完成。

第 19 条 项目说明应包括一项应急计划，确保在预计资金中断的情况下仍能保护水下文化遗产和编写有关的文献资料。

VI. 项目的期限-时间表

第 20 条 在开展开发水下文化遗产的活动之前，应拟定一份详细的时间表，以确保完成项目说明中

规定的各个阶段的活动，包括对打捞上来的水下文化遗产进行保护、登记和保管，以及编写和散发报告等工作。

第 21 条　项目说明应包括一项应急计划，确保在项目中断或终止执行的情况下仍能保护水下文化遗产和编写有关的文献资料。

Ⅶ. 专业水平和资历

第 22 条　开发水下文化遗产的活动只能在有一名具有项目所需的科学能力的合格的水下考古专家并经常在现场指导和监督的情况下才能开展。

第 23 条　项目小组的所有成员都应能胜任工作并具备完成各自的任务所需的专业技能。

Ⅷ. 文化保护与遗址管理

第 24 条　文物保护计划应提出在开展开发水下文化遗产的活动期间、在运输途中和在长时期内如何处理有关文物。保护工作应按现行的专业准则进行。

第 25 条　遗址管理计划应对水下文化遗产在现场开发期间及之后的就地保护和管理工作作出规定。这一计划应包括公众宣传，以及采取稳定遗址、对其进行监测和防止其受到侵扰的合理手段。

Ⅸ. 文献资料

第 26 条　文献资料计划应根据现行的考古文献工作的专业标准，详细记录开发水下文化遗产活动的全部情况，包括一份进度报告。

第 27 条　文献资料至少应包括一份遗址的详细介绍，包括在开发活动中被挪动的或打捞的水下文化遗产的来历、现场纪事、示意图、图样、截面图及照片或以其他手段保存的资料。

Ⅹ. 安　全

第 28 条　应制订一套安全措施，充分确保项目小组成员和第三方的安全与健康，并符合现行法律和职业方面的一切规定。

Ⅺ. 环　境

第 29 条　应制订一项环境政策，确保不过多地打乱海底和海洋生物的现状。

Ⅻ. 报　告

第 30 条　应根据项目说明中规定的工作时间表提交中期报告和最后报告，并应存放在有关的公共档案中。

第 31 条　报告应包括：
（a）目标的实现情况；
（b）方法和技术使用情况；
（c）已获得的结果；
（d）活动各阶段的主要图表与照片等文献资料；

(e)有关保护和保存遗址及所打捞的水下文化遗产的建议;
(f)有关今后活动的建议。

XIII.项目档案的保存

第32条 在开展任何开发活动之前,应当商定保存项目档案的措施,并应写入项目说明。

第33条 项目档案,包括所有被打捞的水下文化遗产和所有相关的文献资料必须尽量集中在一起,并保持其完好无损,以便于专业人员和公众使用和对这些档案的保存。这项工作应当尽快完成,至迟在项目结束之后的十年内完成,因为这符合保存有关水下文化遗产的精神。

第34条 项目档案应根据国际专业标准加以管理,并由主管当局认可。

XIV.宣 传

第35条 项目应包括对公众的教育,在有条件的情况下,还应向公众展出其活动的成果。

第36条 项目的最后综合报告应:
(a)在考虑到项目的复杂性和有关资料的保密性或敏感性的同时,尽早公布于众;
(b)存放在有关的国家档案中。

Convention on the Protection of the Underwater Cultural Heritage[1]

Adopted by the UNESCO General Conference at its 31st Session, Paris, 2 November 2001

The General Conference of the United Nations Educational, Scientific and Cultural Organization, meeting in Paris from 15 October to November 2001, at its thirty-fist session,

Acknowledging the importance of underwater cultural heritage as an integral part of the cultural heritage of humanity and a particularly important element in the history of peoples, nations, and their relations with each other concerning their common heritage,

Realizing the importance of protecting and preserving the underwater cultural heritage and that responsibility therefore rests with all States,

Noting growing public interest in and public appreciation of underwater cultural heritage,

Convinced of the importance of research, information and education to the protection and preservation of underwater cultural heritage,

Convinced of the public's right to enjoy the educational and recreational benefits of responsible non-intrusive access to *in situ* underwater cultural heritage, and of the value of public education to contribute to awareness, appreciation and protection of that heritage,

Aware of the fact that underwater cultural heritage is threatened by unauthorized activities directed at it, and of the need for stronger measures to prevent such activities,

Conscious of the need to respond appropriately to the possible negative impact on underwater cultural heritage of legitimate activities that may incidentally affect it,

Deeply concerned by the increasing commercial exploitation of underwater cultural heritage, and in particular by certain activities aimed at the sale, acquisition or barter of underwater cultural heritage,

Aware of the availability of advanced technology that enhances discovery of and access to underwater cultural heritage,

Believing that cooperation among States, international organizations, scientific institutions, professional organizations, archaeologists, divers, other interested parties and the public at large is essential for the protection of underwater cultural heritage,

Considering that survey, excavation and protection of underwater cultural heritage necessitate the availability and application of special scientific methods and the use of suitable techniques and equipment as well as a high

---

[1] Records of the General Conference, 31st session, Paris, 15 October to 3 November 2001, v. 1: Resolutions. UNESCO Document Code: 31 C/Resolutions + CORR.

degree of professional specialization, all of which indicate a need for uniform governing criteria,

Realizing the need to codify and progressively develop rules relating to the protection and preservation of underwater cultural heritage in conformity with international law and practice, including the UNESCO Convention on the Means of Prohibiting and Preventing the Illicit Import, Export and Transfer of Ownership of Cultural Property of 14 November 1970, the UNESCO Convention for the Protection of the World Cultural and Natural Heritage of 16 November 1972 and the United Nations Convention on the Law of the Sea of 10 December 1982,

Committed to improving the effectiveness of measures at international, regional and national levels for the preservation *in situ* or, if necessary for scientific or protective purposes, the careful recovery of underwater cultural heritage,

Having decided at its twenty-ninth session that this question should be made the subject of an international convention,

Adopts this second day of November 2001 this Convention.

Article 1 - Definitions

For the purposes of this Convention:

1. (a) "Underwater cultural heritage" means all traces of human existence having a cultural, historical or archaeological character which have been partially or totally under water, periodically or continuously, for at least 100 years such as:

>   (i) sites, structures, buildings, artifacts and human remains, together with their archaeological and natural context;

>   (ii) vessels, aircraft, other vehicles or any part thereof, their cargo or other contents, together with their archaeological and natural context; and

>   (iii) objects of prehistoric character.

(b) Pipelines and cables placed on the seabed shall not be considered as underwater cultural heritage.

(c) Installations other than pipelines and cables, placed on the seabed and still in use, shall not be considered as underwater cultural heritage.

2. (a) "States Parties" means States which have consented to be bound by this Convention and for which this Convention is in force.

(b) This Convention applies *mutatis mutandis* to those territories referred to in Article 26, paragraph 2(b), which become Parties to this Convention in accordance with the conditions set out in that paragraph, and to that extent "States Parties" refers to those territories.

3. "UNESCO" means the United Nations Educational, Scientific and Cultural Organization.

4. "Director-General" means the Director-General of UNESCO.

5. "Area" means the seabed and ocean floor and subsoil thereof, beyond the limits of national jurisdiction.

6. "Activities directed at underwater cultural heritage" means activities having underwater cultural heritage as their primary object and which may, directly or indirectly, physically disturb or otherwise damage underwater cultural heritage.

7. "Activities incidentally affecting underwater cultural heritage" means activities which, despite not having underwater cultural heritage as their primary object or one of their objects, may physically disturb or otherwise damage underwater cultural heritage.

8. "State vessels and aircraft" means warships, and other vessels or aircraft that were owned or operated by a State and used, at the time of sinking, only for government non-commercial purposes, that are identified as such and that meet the definition of underwater cultural heritage.

9. "Rules" means the Rules concerning activities directed at underwater cultural heritage, as referred to in Article 33 of this Convention.

Article 2 - Objectives and general principles

1. This Convention aims to ensure and strengthen the protection of underwater cultural heritage.

2. States Parties shall cooperate in the protection of underwater cultural heritage.

3. States Parties shall preserve underwater cultural heritage for the benefit of humanity in conformity with the provisions of this Convention.

4. States Parties shall, individually or jointly as appropriate, take all appropriate measures in conformity with this Convention and with international law that are necessary to protect underwater cultural heritage, using for this purpose the best practicable means at their disposal and in accordance with their capabilities.

5. The preservation *in situ* of underwater cultural heritage shall be considered as the first option before allowing or engaging in any activities directed at this heritage.

6. Recovered underwater cultural heritage shall be deposited, conserved and managed in a manner that ensures its long-term preservation.

7. Underwater cultural heritage shall not be commercially exploited.

8. Consistent with State practice and international law, including the United Nations Convention on the Law of the Sea, nothing in this Convention shall be interpreted as modifying the rules of international law and State practice pertaining to sovereign immunities, nor any State's rights with respect to its State vessels and aircraft.

9. States Parties shall ensure that proper respect is given to all human remains located in maritime waters.

10. Responsible non-intrusive access to observe or document *in situ* underwater cultural heritage shall be encouraged to create public awareness, appreciation, and protection of the heritage except where such access is incompatible with its protection and management.

11. No act or activity undertaken on the basis of this Convention shall constitute grounds for claiming, contending or disputing any claim to national sovereignty or jurisdiction.

Article 3 - Relationship between this Convention and the United Nations Convention on the Law of the Sea

Nothing in this Convention shall prejudice the rights, jurisdiction and duties of States under international law, including the United Nations Convention on the Law of the Sea. This Convention shall be interpreted and applied in the context of and in a manner consistent with international law, including the United Nations Convention on the Law of the Sea.

Article 4 - Relationship to law of salvage and law of finds

Any activity relating to underwater cultural heritage to which this Convention applies shall not be subject to the law of salvage or law of finds, unless it:

(a) is authorized by the competent authorities, and
(b) is in full conformity with this Convention, and
(c) ensures that any recovery of the underwater cultural heritage achieves its maximum protection.

Article 5 - Activities incidentally affecting underwater cultural heritage

Each State Party shall use the best practicable means at its disposal to prevent or mitigate any adverse effects that might arise from activities under its jurisdiction incidentally affecting underwater cultural heritage.

Article 6 - Bilateral, regional or other multilateral agreements

1. States Parties are encouraged to enter into bilateral, regional or other multilateral agreements or develop existing agreements, for the preservation of underwater cultural heritage. All such agreements shall be in full conformity with the provisions of this Convention and shall not dilute its universal character. States may, in such agreements, adopt rules and regulations which would ensure better protection of underwater cultural heritage than those adopted in this Convention.

2. The Parties to such bilateral, regional or other multilateral agreements may invite States with a verifiable link, especially a cultural, historical or archaeological link, to the underwater cultural heritage concerned to join such agreements.

3. This Convention shall not alter the rights and obligations of States Parties regarding the protection of sunken vessels, arising from other bilateral, regional or other multilateral agreements concluded before its adoption, and, in particular, those that are in conformity with the purposes of this Convention.

Article 7 - Underwater cultural heritage in internal waters, archipelagic waters and territorial sea

1. States Parties, in the exercise of their sovereignty, have the exclusive right to regulate and authorize activities directed at underwater cultural heritage in their internal waters, archipelagic waters and territorial sea.

2. Without prejudice to other international agreements and rules of international law regarding the protection of underwater cultural heritage, States Parties shall require that the Rules be applied to activities directed at underwater cultural heritage in their internal waters, archipelagic waters and territorial sea.

3. Within their archipelagic waters and territorial sea, in the exercise of their sovereignty and in recognition of general practice among States, States Parties, with a view to cooperating on the best methods of protecting State vessels and aircraft, should inform the flag State Party to this Convention and, if applicable, other States with a verifiable link, especially a cultural, historical or archaeological link, with respect to the discovery of such identifiable State vessels and aircraft.

Article 8 - Underwater cultural heritage in the contiguous zone

Without prejudice to and in addition to Articles 9 and 10, and in accordance with Article 303, paragraph 2, of the United Nations Convention on the Law of the Sea, States Parties may regulate and authorize activities directed at underwater cultural heritage within their contiguous zone. In so doing, they shall require that the Rules be applied.

Article 9 - Reporting and notification in the exclusive economic zone and on the continental shelf

1. All States Parties have a responsibility to protect underwater cultural heritage in the exclusive economic zone and on the continental shelf in conformity with this Convention.

Accordingly:

(a) a State Party shall require that when its national, or a vessel flying its flag, discovers or intends to engage in activities directed at underwater cultural heritage located in its exclusive economic zone or on its continental shelf, the national or the master of the vessel shall report such discovery or activity to it;

(b) in the exclusive economic zone or on the continental shelf of another State Party:

(i) States Parties shall require the national or the master of the vessel to report such discovery or activity to them and to that other State Party;

(ii) alternatively, a State Party shall require the national or master of the vessel to report such discovery or activity to it and shall ensure the rapid and effective transmission of such reports to all other States Parties.

2. On depositing its instrument of ratification, acceptance, approval or accession, a State Party shall declare the manner in which reports will be transmitted under paragraph 1(b) of this Article.

3. A State Party shall notify the Director-General of discoveries or activities reported to it under paragraph 1 of this Article.

4. The Director-General shall promptly make available to all States Parties any information notified to him under paragraph 3 of this Article.

5. Any State Party may declare to the State Party in whose exclusive economic zone or on whose continental shelf the underwater cultural heritage is located its interest in being consulted on how to ensure the effective protection of that underwater cultural heritage. Such declaration shall be based on a verifiable link, especially a cultural, historical or archaeological link, to the underwater cultural heritage concerned.

Article 10 - Protection of underwater cultural heritage in the exclusive economic zone and on the continental shelf

1. No authorization shall be granted for an activity directed at underwater cultural heritage located in the exclusive economic zone or on the continental shelf except in conformity with the provisions of this Article.

2. A State Party in whose exclusive economic zone or on whose continental shelf underwater cultural heritage is located has the right to prohibit or authorize any activity directed at such heritage to prevent interference with its sovereign rights or jurisdiction as provided for by international law including the United Nations Convention on the Law of the Sea.

3. Where there is a discovery of underwater cultural heritage or it is intended that activity shall be directed at underwater cultural heritage in a State Party's exclusive economic zone or on its continental shelf, that State Party shall:

(a) consult all other States Parties which have declared an interest under Article 9, paragraph 5, on how best to protect the underwater cultural heritage;

(b) coordinate such consultations as "Coordinating State", unless it expressly declares that it does not wish to do so, in which case the States Parties which have declared an interest under Article 9, paragraph 5, shall appoint a Coordinating State.

4. Without prejudice to the duty of all States Parties to protect underwater cultural heritage by way of all practicable measures taken in accordance with international law to prevent immediate danger to the underwater cultural heritage, including looting, the Coordinating State may take all practicable measures, and/or issue any necessary authorizations in conformity with this Convention and, if necessary prior to consultations, to prevent any immediate danger to the underwater cultural heritage, whether arising from human activities or any other cause, including looting. In taking such measures assistance may be requested from other States Parties.

5. The Coordinating State:

(a) shall implement measures of protection which have been agreed by the consulting States, which include the Coordinating State, unless the consulting States, which include the Coordinating State, agree that another State Party shall implement those measures;

(b) shall issue all necessary authorizations for such agreed measures in conformity with the Rules, unless the consulting States, which include the Coordinating State, agree that another State Party shall issue those authorizations;

(c) may conduct any necessary preliminary research on the underwater cultural heritage and shall issue all necessary authorizations therefor, and shall promptly inform the Director-General of the results, who in turn will make such information promptly available to other States Parties.

6. In coordinating consultations, taking measures, conducting preliminary research and/or issuing authorizations pursuant to this Article, the Coordinating State shall act on behalf of the States Parties as a whole and not in its own interest. Any such action shall not in itself constitute a basis for the assertion of any preferential or jurisdictional rights not provided for in international law, including the United Nations Convention on the Law of the Sea.

7. Subject to the provisions of paragraphs 2 and 4 of this Article, no activity directed at State vessels and aircraft shall be conducted without the agreement of the flag State and the collaboration of the Coordinating State.

Article 11 - Reporting and notification in the Area

1. States Parties have a responsibility to protect underwater cultural heritage in the Area in conformity with this Convention and Article 149 of the United Nations Convention on the Law of the Sea. Accordingly when a national, or a vessel flying the flag of a State Party, discovers or intends to engage in activities directed at underwater cultural heritage located in the Area, that State Party shall require its national, or the master of the vessel, to report such discovery or activity to it.

2. States Parties shall notify the Director-General and the Secretary-General of the International Seabed Authority of such discoveries or activities reported to them.

3. The Director-General shall promptly make available to all States Parties any such information supplied by States Parties.

4. Any State Party may declare to the Director-General its interest in being consulted on how to ensure the effective protection of that underwater cultural heritage. Such declaration shall be based on a verifiable link to the underwater cultural heritage concerned, particular regard being paid to the preferential rights of States of cultural, historical or archaeological origin.

Article 12 - Protection of underwater cultural heritage in the Area

1. No authorization shall be granted for any activity directed at underwater cultural heritage located in the Area except in conformity with the provisions of this Article.

2. The Director-General shall invite all States Parties which have declared an interest under Article 11, paragraph 4, to consult on how best to protect the underwater cultural heritage, and to appoint a State Party to coordinate such consultations as the "Coordinating State". The Director-General shall also invite the International Seabed Authority to participate in such consultations.

3. All States Parties may take all practicable measures in conformity with this Convention, if necessary prior to consultations, to prevent any immediate danger to the underwater cultural heritage, whether arising from human activity or any other cause including looting.

4. The Coordinating State shall:

(a) implement measures of protection which have been agreed by the consulting States, which include the Coordinating State, unless the consulting States, which include the Coordinating State, agree that another State Party shall implement those measures; and

(b) issue all necessary authorizations for such agreed measures, in conformity with this Convention, unless the consulting States, which include the Coordinating State, agree that another State Party shall issue those authorizations.

5. The Coordinating State may conduct any necessary preliminary research on the underwater cultural heritage and shall issue all necessary authorizations therefor and shall promptly inform the Director-General of the results, who in turn shall make such information available to other States Parties.

6. In coordinating consultations, taking measures, conducting preliminary research, and/or issuing authorizations pursuant to this Article, the Coordinating State shall act for the benefit of humanity as a whole, on behalf of all States Parties. Particular regard shall be paid to the preferential rights of States of cultural, historical or archaeological origin in respect of the underwater cultural heritage concerned.

7. No State Party shall undertake or authorize activities directed at State vessels and aircraft in the Area without the consent of the flag State.

Article 13 - Sovereign immunity

Warships and other government ships or military aircraft with sovereign immunity, operated for non-commercial purposes, undertaking their normal mode of operations, and not engaged in activities directed at underwater cultural heritage, shall not be obliged to report discoveries of underwater cultural heritage under Articles 9, 10, 11 and 12 of this Convention. However, States Parties shall ensure, by the adoption of appropriate measures not impairing the operations or operational capabilities of their warships or other government ships or military aircraft with sovereign immunity operated for non-commercial purposes, that they comply, as far as is reasonable and practicable, with Articles 9, 10, 11 and 12 of this Convention.

Article 14 - Control of entry into the territory, dealing and possession

States Parties shall take measures to prevent the entry into their territory, the dealing in, or the possession of, underwater cultural heritage illicitly exported and/or recovered, where recovery was contrary to this Convention.

Article 15 - Non-use of areas under the jurisdiction of States Parties

States Parties shall take measures to prohibit the use of their territory, including their maritime ports, as well as artificial islands, installations and structures under their exclusive jurisdiction or control, in support of any activity directed at underwater cultural heritage which is not in conformity with this Convention.

Article 16 - Measures relating to nationals and vessels

States Parties shall take all practicable measures to ensure that their nationals and vessels flying their flag do not engage in any activity directed at underwater cultural heritage in a manner not in conformity with this Convention.

Article 17 - Sanctions

1. Each State Party shall impose sanctions for violations of measures it has taken to implement this Convention.

2. Sanctions applicable in respect of violations shall be adequate in severity to be effective in securing compliance with this Convention and to discourage violations wherever they occur and shall deprive offenders of the benefit deriving from their illegal activities.

3. States Parties shall cooperate to ensure enforcement of sanctions imposed under this Article.

Article 18 - Seizure and disposition of underwater cultural heritage

1. Each State Party shall take measures providing for the seizure of underwater cultural heritage in its territory that has been recovered in a manner not in conformity with this Convention.

2. Each State Party shall record, protect and take all reasonable measures to stabilize underwater cultural heritage seized under this Convention.

3. Each State Party shall notify the Director-General and any other State with a verifiable link, especially a cultural, historical or archaeological link, to the underwater cultural heritage concerned of any seizure of underwater cultural heritage that it has made under this Convention.

4. A State Party which has seized underwater cultural heritage shall ensure that its disposition be for the public benefit, taking into account the need for conservation and research; the need for reassembly of a dispersed collection; the need for public access, exhibition and education; and the interests of any State with a verifiable link, especially a cultural, historical or archaeological link, in respect of the underwater cultural heritage concerned.

Article 19 - Cooperation and information-sharing

1. States Parties shall cooperate and assist each other in the protection and management of underwater cultural heritage under this Convention, including, where practicable, collaborating in the investigation, excavation, documentation, conservation, study and presentation of such heritage.

2. To the extent compatible with the purposes of this Convention, each State Party undertakes to share

information with other States Parties concerning underwater cultural heritage, including discovery of heritage, location of heritage, heritage excavated or recovered contrary to this Convention or otherwise in violation of international law, pertinent scientific methodology and technology, and legal developments relating to such heritage.

3. Information shared between States Parties, or between UNESCO and States Parties, regarding the discovery or location of underwater cultural heritage shall, to the extent compatible with their national legislation, be kept confidential and reserved to competent authorities of States Parties as long as the disclosure of such information might endanger or otherwise put at risk the preservation of such underwater cultural heritage.

4. Each State Party shall take all practicable measures to disseminate information, including where feasible through appropriate international databases, about underwater cultural heritage excavated or recovered contrary to this Convention or otherwise in violation of international law.

Article 20 - Public awareness

Each State Party shall take all practicable measures to raise public awareness regarding the value and significance of underwater cultural heritage and the importance of protecting it under this Convention.

Article 21 - Training in underwater archaeology

States Parties shall cooperate in the provision of training in underwater archaeology, in techniques for the conservation of underwater cultural heritage and, on agreed terms, in the transfer of technology relating to underwater cultural heritage.

Article 22 - Competent authorities

1. In order to ensure the proper implementation of this Convention, States Parties shall establish competent authorities or reinforce the existing ones where appropriate, with the aim of providing for the establishment, maintenance and updating of an inventory of underwater cultural heritage, the effective protection, conservation, presentation and management of underwater cultural heritage, as well as research and education.

2. States Parties shall communicate to the Director-General the names and addresses of their competent authorities relating to underwater cultural heritage.

Article 23 - Meetings of States Parties

1. The Director-General shall convene a Meeting of States Parties within one year of the entry into force of this Convention and thereafter at least once every two years. At the request of a majority of States Parties, the Director-General shall convene an Extraordinary Meeting of States Parties.

2. The Meeting of States Parties shall decide on its functions and responsibilities.

3. The Meeting of States Parties shall adopt its own Rules of Procedure.

4. The Meeting of States Parties may establish a Scientific and Technical Advisory Body composed of experts nominated by the States Parties with due regard to the principle of equitable geographical distribution and the desirability of a gender balance.

5. The Scientific and Technical Advisory Body shall appropriately assist the Meeting of States Parties in

questions of a scientific or technical nature regarding the implementation of the Rules.

Article 24 - Secretariat for this Convention

1. The Director-General shall be responsible for the functions of the Secretariat for this Convention.

2. The duties of the Secretariat shall include:

(a) organizing Meetings of States Parties as provided for in Article 23, paragraph 1; and

(b) assisting States Parties in implementing the decisions of the Meetings of States Parties.

Article 25 - Peaceful settlement of disputes

1. Any dispute between two or more States Parties concerning the interpretation or application of this Convention shall be subject to negotiations in good faith or other peaceful means of settlement of their own choice.

2. If those negotiations do not settle the dispute within a reasonable period of time, it may be submitted to UNESCO for mediation, by agreement between the States Parties concerned.

3. If mediation is not undertaken or if there is no settlement by mediation, the provisions relating to the settlement of disputes set out in Part XV of the United Nations Convention on the Law of the Sea apply *mutatis mutandis* to any dispute between States Parties to this Convention concerning the interpretation or application of this Convention, whether or not they are also Parties to the United Nations Convention on the Law of the Sea.

4. Any procedure chosen by a State Party to this Convention and to the United Nations Convention on the Law of the Sea pursuant to Article 287 of the latter shall apply to the settlement of disputes under this article, unless that State Party, when ratifying, accepting, approving or acceding to this Convention, or at any time thereafter, chooses another procedure pursuant to Article 287 for the purpose of the settlement of disputes arising out of this Convention.

5. A State Party to this Convention which is not a Party to the United Nations Convention on the Law of the Sea, when ratifying, accepting, approving or acceding to this Convention or at any time thereafter shall be free to choose, by means of a written declaration, one or more of the means set out in Article 287, paragraph 1, of the United Nations Convention on the Law of the Sea for the purpose of settlement of disputes under this Article. Article 287 shall apply to such a declaration, as well as to any dispute to which such State is party, which is not covered by a declaration in force. For the purpose of conciliation and arbitration, in accordance with Annexes V and VII of the United Nations Convention on the Law of the Sea, such State shall be entitled to nominate conciliators and arbitrators to be included in the lists referred to in Annex V, Article 2, and Annex VII, Article 2, for the settlement of disputes arising out of this Convention.

Article 26 - Ratification, acceptance, approval or accession

1. This Convention shall be subject to ratification, acceptance or approval by Member States of UNESCO.

2. This Convention shall be subject to accession:

(a) by States that are not members of UNESCO but are members of the United Nations or of a specialized agency within the United Nations system or of the International Atomic Energy Agency, as well as by States Parties to the Statute of the International Court of Justice and any other State invited to accede to this Convention by the General Conference of UNESCO;

(b) by territories which enjoy full internal self-government, recognized as such by the United Nations, but have not attained full independence in accordance with General Assembly resolution 1514 (XV) and which have competence over the matters governed by this Convention, including the competence to enter into treaties in respect of those matters.

3. The instruments of ratification, acceptance, approval or accession shall be deposited with the Director-General.

Article 27 - Entry into force

This Convention shall enter into force three months after the date of the deposit of the twentieth instrument referred to in Article 26, but solely with respect to the twenty States or territories that have so deposited their instruments. It shall enter into force for each other State or territory three months after the date on which that State or territory has deposited its instrument.

Article 28 - Declaration as to inland waters

When ratifying, accepting, approving or acceding to this Convention or at any time thereafter, any State or territory may declare that the Rules shall apply to inland waters not of a maritime character.

Article 29 - Limitations to geographical scope

At the time of ratifying, accepting, approving or acceding to this Convention, a State or territory may make a declaration to the depositary that this Convention shall not be applicable to specific parts of its territory, internal waters, archipelagic waters or territorial sea, and shall identify therein the reasons for such declaration. Such State shall, to the extent practicable and as quickly as possible, promote conditions under which this Convention will apply to the areas specified in its declaration, and to that end shall also withdraw its declaration in whole or in part as soon as that has been achieved.

Article 30 - Reservations

With the exception of Article 29, no reservations may be made to this Convention.

Article 31 - Amendments

1. A State Party may, by written communication addressed to the Director-General, propose amendments to this Convention. The Director-General shall circulate such communication to all States Parties. If, within six months from the date of the circulation of the communication, not less than one half of the States Parties reply favourably to the request, the Director-General shall present such proposal to the next Meeting of States Parties for discussion and possible adoption.

2. Amendments shall be adopted by a two-thirds majority of States Parties present and voting.

3. Once adopted, amendments to this Convention shall be subject to ratification, acceptance, approval or accession by the States Parties.

4. Amendments shall enter into force, but solely with respect to the States Parties that have ratified, accepted, approved or acceded to them, three months after the deposit of the instruments referred to in paragraph 3 of this Article by two thirds of the States Parties. Thereafter, for each State or territory that ratifies, accepts, approves or accedes to it, the amendment shall enter into force three months after the date of deposit by that Party of its instrument of ratification, acceptance, approval or accession.

5. A State or territory which becomes a Party to this Convention after the entry into force of amendments in conformity with paragraph 4 of this Article shall, failing an expression of different intention by that State or territory, be considered:

(a) as a Party to this Convention as so amended; and

(b) as a Party to the unamended Convention in relation to any State Party not bound by the amendment.

Article 32 - Denunciation

1. A State Party may, by written notification addressed to the Director-General, denounce this Convention.

2. The denunciation shall take effect twelve months after the date of receipt of the notification, unless the notification specifies a later date.

3. The denunciation shall not in any way affect the duty of any State Party to fulfil any obligation embodied in this Convention to which it would be subject under international law independently of this Convention.

Article 33 - The Rules

The Rules annexed to this Convention form an integral part of it and, unless expressly provided otherwise, a reference to this Convention includes a reference to the Rules.

Article 34 - Registration with the United Nations

In conformity with Article 102 of the Charter of the United Nations, this Convention shall be registered with the Secretariat of the United Nations at the request of the Director-General.

Article 35 - Authoritative texts

This Convention has been drawn up in Arabic, Chinese, English, French, Russian and Spanish, the six texts being equally authoritative.

Annex
Rules concerning activities directed at underwater cultural heritage

I. *General principles*

Rule 1. The protection of underwater cultural heritage through *in situ* preservation shall be considered as the first option. Accordingly, activities directed at underwater cultural heritage shall be authorized in a manner consistent with the protection of that heritage, and subject to that requirement may be authorized for the purpose of making a significant contribution to protection or knowledge or enhancement of underwater cultural heritage.

Rule 2. The commercial exploitation of underwater cultural heritage for trade or speculation or its irretrievable dispersal is fundamentally incompatible with the protection and proper management of underwater cultural heritage. Underwater cultural heritage shall not be traded, sold, bought or bartered as commercial goods.

This Rule cannot be interpreted as preventing:

(a) the provision of professional archaeological services or necessary services incidental thereto whose nature and purpose are in full conformity with this Convention and are subject to the authorization of the competent authorities;

(b) the deposition of underwater cultural heritage, recovered in the course of a research project in conformity with this Convention, provided such deposition does not prejudice the scientific or cultural interest or integrity of the recovered material or result in its irretrievable dispersal; is in accordance with the provisions of Rules 33 and 34; and is subject to the authorization of the competent authorities.

Rule 3. Activities directed at underwater cultural heritage shall not adversely affect the underwater cultural heritage more than is necessary for the objectives of the project.

Rule 4. Activities directed at underwater cultural heritage must use non-destructive techniques and survey methods in preference to recovery of objects. If excavation or recovery is necessary for the purpose of scientific studies or for the ultimate protection of the underwater cultural heritage, the methods and techniques used must be as non-destructive as possible and contribute to the preservation of the remains.

Rule 5. Activities directed at underwater cultural heritage shall avoid the unnecessary disturbance of human remains or venerated sites.

Rule 6. Activities directed at underwater cultural heritage shall be strictly regulated to ensure proper recording of cultural, historical and archaeological information.

Rule 7. Public access to *in situ* underwater cultural heritage shall be promoted, except where such access is incompatible with protection and management.

Rule 8. International cooperation in the conduct of activities directed at underwater cultural heritage shall be encouraged in order to further the effective exchange or use of archaeologists and other relevant professionals.

II. *Project design*

Rule 9. Prior to any activity directed at underwater cultural heritage, a project design for the activity shall be developed and submitted to the competent authorities for authorization and appropriate peer review.

Rule 10. The project design shall include:

(a) an evaluation of previous or preliminary studies;

(b) the project statement and objectives;

(c) the methodology to be used and the techniques to be employed;

(d) the anticipated funding;

(e) an expected timetable for completion of the project;

(f) the composition of the team and the qualifications, responsibilities and experience of each team member;

(g) plans for post-fieldwork analysis and other activities;

(h) a conservation programme for artefacts and the site in close cooperation with the competent authorities;

(i) a site management and maintenance policy for the whole duration of the project;

(j) a documentation programme;

(k) a safety policy;

(l) an environmental policy;

(m) arrangements for collaboration with museums and other institutions, in particular scientific institutions;

(n) report preparation;

(o) deposition of archives, including underwater cultural heritage removed; and

(p) a programme for publication.

Rule 11. Activities directed at underwater cultural heritage shall be carried out in accordance with the project design approved by the competent authorities.

Rule 12. Where unexpected discoveries are made or circumstances change, the project design shall be reviewed and amended with the approval of the competent authorities.

Rule 13. In cases of urgency or chance discoveries, activities directed at the underwater cultural heritage, including conservation measures or activities for a period of short duration, in particular site stabilization, may be authorized in the absence of a project design in order to protect the underwater cultural heritage.

III. *Preliminary work*

Rule 14. The preliminary work referred to in Rule 10 (a) shall include an assessment that evaluates the significance and vulnerability of the underwater cultural heritage and the surrounding natural environment to damage by the proposed project, and the potential to obtain data that would meet the project objectives.

Rule 15. The assessment shall also include background studies of available historical and archaeological evidence, the archaeological and environmental characteristics of the site, and the consequences of any potential intrusion for the long-term stability of the underwater cultural heritage affected by the activities.

IV. *Project objective, methodology and techniques*

Rule 16. The methodology shall comply with the project objectives, and the techniques employed shall be as non-intrusive as possible.

V. *Funding*

Rule 17. Except in cases of emergency to protect underwater cultural heritage, an adequate funding base shall be assured in advance of any activity, sufficient to complete all stages of the project design, including conservation, documentation and curation of recovered artefacts, and report preparation and dissemination.

Rule 18. The project design shall demonstrate an ability, such as by securing a bond, to fund the project through to completion.

Rule 19. The project design shall include a contingency plan that will ensure conservation of underwater cultural heritage and supporting documentation in the event of any interruption of anticipated funding.

VI. *Project duration–timetable*

Rule 20. An adequate timetable shall be developed to assure in advance of any activity directed at underwater cultural heritage the completion of all stages of the project design, including conservation, documentation and curation of recovered underwater cultural heritage, as well as report preparation and dissemination.

Rule 21. The project design shall include a contingency plan that will ensure conservation of underwater cultural heritage and supporting documentation in the event of any interruption or termination of the project.

VII. *Competence and qualifications*

Rule 22. Activities directed at underwater cultural heritage shall only be undertaken under the direction and control of, and in the regular presence of, a qualified underwater archaeologist with scientific competence appropriate to the project.

Rule 23. All persons on the project team shall be qualified and have demonstrated competence appropriate to their roles in the project.

VIII. *Conservation and site management*

Rule 24. The conservation programme shall provide for the treatment of the archaeological remains during the activities directed at underwater cultural heritage, during transit and in the long term. Conservation shall be carried out in accordance with current professional standards.

Rule 25. The site management programme shall provide for the protection and management *in situ* of underwater cultural heritage, in the course of and upon termination of fieldwork. The programme shall include public information, reasonable provision for site stabilization, monitoring, and protection against interference.

IX. *Documentation*

Rule 26. The documentation programme shall set out thorough documentation including a progress report of activities directed at underwater cultural heritage, in accordance with current professional standards of archaeological documentation.

Rule 27. Documentation shall include, at a minimum, a comprehensive record of the site, including the provenance of underwater cultural heritage moved or removed in the course of the activities directed at underwater cultural heritage, field notes, plans, drawings, sections, and photographs or recording in other media.

X. *Safety*

Rule 28. A safety policy shall be prepared that is adequate to ensure the safety and health of the project team and third parties and that is in conformity with any applicable statutory and professional requirements.

XI. *Environment*

Rule 29. An environmental policy shall be prepared that is adequate to ensure that the seabed and marine life are not unduly disturbed.

XII. *Reporting*

Rule 30. Interim and final reports shall be made available according to the timetable set out in the project design, and deposited in relevant public records.

Rule 31. Reports shall include:

(a) an account of the objectives;

(b) an account of the methods and techniques employed;

(c) an account of the results achieved;

(d) basic graphic and photographic documentation on all phases of the activity;

(e) recommendations concerning conservation and curation of the site and of any underwater cultural heritage removed; and

(f) recommendations for future activities.

XIII. *Curation of project archives*

Rule 32. Arrangements for curation of the project archives shall be agreed to before any activity commences, and shall be set out in the project design.

Rule 33. The project archives, including any underwater cultural heritage removed and a copy of all supporting documentation shall, as far as possible, be kept together and intact as a collection in a manner that is available for professional and public access as well as for the curation of the archives. This should be done as rapidly as possible and in any case not later than ten years from the completion of the project, in so far as may be compatible with conservation of the underwater cultural heritage.

Rule 34. The project archives shall be managed according to international professional standards, and subject to the authorization of the competent authorities.

XIV. *Dissemination*

Rule 35. Projects shall provide for public education and popular presentation of the project results where appropriate.

Rule 36. A final synthesis of a project shall be:

(a) made public as soon as possible, having regard to the complexity of the project and the confidential or sensitive nature of the information; and

(b) deposited in relevant public records.

·工业遗产·

关于工业遗产的下塔吉尔宪章[1]

（国际工业遗产保护委员会2003年7月17日在莫斯科通过）

导 言

人类的早期的历史是依据生产方式根本变革方面的考古学证据来界定的，保护和研究这些变革证据的重要性已得到普遍认同。

从中世纪到18世纪末，欧洲的能源利用和商业贸易的革新，带来了具有与新石器时代向青铜时代历史转变同样深远意义的变化，制造业的社会、技术、经济环境都得到了非常迅速而深刻的发展，足以称为一次革命。这次工业革命是一个历史现象的开端，它影响了有史以来最广泛的人口，以及地球上所有其他的生命形式，并一直延续至今。

这些具有深远意义的变革的物质见证，是全人类的财富，研究和保护它们的重要性必须得到认识。

因而，2003年聚集在俄罗斯召开的TICCIH大会上的代表们宣告：那些为工业活动而建造的建筑物和构筑物、其生产的过程与使用的生产工具，以及所在的城镇和景观，连同其他的有形的或无形的表现，都具有基本的重大价值。我们必须研究它们，让它们的历史为人所知，它们的内涵和重要性为众人知晓，为现在和未来的利用和利益，那些最为重要和最典型的实例应当依照《威尼斯宪章》的精神，进行鉴定、得以保护和修缮。

1. 工业遗产的定义

工业遗产是指工业文明的遗存，它们具有历史的、科技的、社会的、建筑的或科学的价值。这些遗存包括建筑、机械、车间、工厂、选矿和冶炼的矿场和矿区、货栈仓库，能源生产、输送和利用的场所，运输及基础设施，以及与工业相关的社会活动场所，如住宅、宗教和教育设施等。

工业考古学是对所有工业遗存证据进行多学科研究的方法，这些遗存证据包括物质的和非物质的，如为工业生产服务的或由工业生产创造的文件档案、人工制品、地层和工程结构、人居环境以及自然景观和城镇景观等。工业考古学采用了最适当的调查研究方法以增进对工业历史和现实的认识。

具有重要影响的历史时期始于18世纪下半叶的工业革命，直到当代，当然也要研究更早的前工业和原始工业起源。此外，也要注重对归属于科技史的产品和生产技术研究。

---

[1] 译者：顾承兵，周瑾，张松。引自：联合国教科文组织世界遗产中心，国际古迹遗址理事会，国际文物保护与修复研究中心，中国国家文物局主编，国际文化遗产保护文件选编[M]. 北京：文物出版社，2007。

2. 工业遗产的价值

（1）工业遗产是工业活动的见证，这些活动一直对后世产生着深远的影响。保护工业遗产的动机在于这些历史证据的普遍价值，而不仅仅是那些独特遗址的唯一性。

（2）工业遗产作为普通人们生活记录的一部分，并提供了重要的可识别性感受，因而具有社会价值。工业遗产在生产、工程、建筑方面具有技术和科学的价值，也可能因其建筑设计和规划方面的品质而具有重要的美学价值。

（3）这些价值是工业遗址本身、建筑物、构件、机器和装置所固有的，它存在于工业景观中，存在于成文档案中，也存在于一些无形记录，如人的记忆与习俗中。

（4）特殊生产过程的残存、遗址的类型或景观，由此产生的稀缺性增加了其特别的价值，应当被慎重地评价。早期或最先出现的例子更具有特殊的价值。

3. 鉴定、记录和研究的重要性

（1）每一国家或地区都需要鉴定、记录并保护那些需要为后代保存的工业遗存。

（2）对工业地区和工业类型进行调查研究以确定工业遗产的范围。利用这些信息，对所有已鉴定的遗址进行登记造册，其分类应易于查询，公众也能够免费获取这些信息。而利用计算机和因特网是一个颇有价值的方向性目标。

（3）记录是研究工业遗产的基础工作，在任何变动实施之前都应当对工业遗址的实体形态和场址条件做完整的记录、并存入公共档案。在一条生产线或一座工厂停止运转前，可以对很多信息进行记录。记录的内容包括文字描述、图纸、照片以及录像，以及相关的文献资料等。人们的记忆是独特的、不可替代的资源，也应当与尽可能地记录下来。

（4）考古学方法是进行历史性工业遗址调查、研究的基本技术手段，并将达到与其他历史和文化时期研究相同的高水准。

（5）为了制定保护工业遗产的政策，需要相关的历史研究计划。由于许多工业活动具有关联性，国际合作研究有助于鉴定具有世界意义的工业遗址及其类型。

（6）对工业建筑的评估标准应当被详细说明并予以公布，采用为广大公众所接受的、统一的标准。在适当研究的基础上，这些标准将用于鉴定那些最重要的遗存下来的景观、聚落、场址、原型、建筑、结构、机器和工艺过程。

（7）已认定的重要遗址和结构应当用强有力的法律手段保护起来，以确保其重要意义得到保护。联合国教科文组织的《世界遗产名录》，应给予给人类文化带来重大影响的工业文明以应有的重视。

（8）应明确界定重要工业遗址的价值，对将来的维修改造应制定导则。任何对保存其价值所必要的法律的、行政的和财政的手段应得以施行。

（9）应确定濒危的工业遗址，这样就可以通过适当的手段减少危险，并推动合适的维修和再利用的计划。

（10）从协调行动和资源共享方面考虑，国际合作是保护工业遗产特别合适的途径。在建立国际名录和数据库时需要制定适当的标准。

4. 法定保护

（1）工业遗产应当被视作普遍意义上文化遗产的整体组成部分。然而，对工业遗产的法定保护应当考虑其特殊性，要能够保护好机器设备、地下基础、固定构筑物、建筑综合体和复合体以及工业景观。

对废弃的工业区，在考虑其生态价值的同时也要重视其潜在的历史研究价值。

（2）工业遗产保护计划应同经济发展政策以及地区和国土规划整合起来。

（3）那些最重要的遗址应当被充分地保存，并且不允许有任何干涉危及建筑等实物的历史完整性和真实性。对于保存工业建筑而言，适当改造和再利用也许是一种合适且有效的方式，应当通过适当的法规控制、技术建议、税收激励和转让来鼓励。

（4）因迅速的结构转型而面临威胁的工业社区应当得到中央和地方政府的支持。因这一变化而使工业遗产面临潜在威胁，应能预知并通过事先的规划避免采取紧急行动。

（5）为防止重要工业遗址因关闭而导致其重要构件的移动和破坏，应当建立快速反应的机制。有相应能力的专业权威人士应当被赋予法定的权利，必要时应介入受到威胁的工业遗址保护工作中。

（6）政府应当有专家咨询团体，他们对工业遗产保存与保护的相关问题能提供独立的建议，所有重要的案例都必须征询他们的意见。

（7）在保存与保护地区的工业遗产方面，应尽可能地保证来自当地社区的参与和磋商。

（8）由志愿者组成的协会和社团，在遗址鉴定、促进公众参与、传播信息和研究等方面对工业遗产保护具有重要作用，如同剧场不能缺少演员一样。

5. 维护和保护

（1）工业遗产保护有赖于对功能完整性的保存，因此对一个工业遗址的改动应尽可能地着眼于维护。如果机器或构件被移走，或者组成遗址整体的辅助构件遭到破坏，那么工业遗产的价值和真实性会被严重削弱。

（2）工业遗址的保护需要全面的知识，包括当时建造的目的和效用，各种曾有的生产工序等。随着时间的变化可能都已经改变，但所有过去的使用情况都应被检测和评估。

（3）原址保护应当始终是优先考虑的方式。只有当经济和社会有迫切需要时，工业遗址才考虑拆除或者搬迁。

（4）为了实现对工业遗址的保护，赋予其新的使用功能通常是可以接受的，除非这一遗址具有特殊重要的历史意义。新的功能应当尊重原先的材料和保持生产流程和生产活动的原有形式，并且尽可能地同原先主要的使用功能保持协调。建议保留部分能够表明原有功能的地方。

（5）继续改造再利用工业建筑可以避免能源浪费并有助于可持续发展。工业遗产对于衰败地区的经济复兴具有重要作用，在长期稳定的就业岗位面临急剧减少的情况时，继续再利用能够维持社区居民心理上的稳定性。

（6）改造应具有可逆性，并且其影响应保持在最小限度内。任何不可避免的改动应当存档，被移走的重要元件应当被记录在案并完好保存。许多生产工艺保持着古老的特色，这是遗址完整性和重要性的重要组成内容。

（7）重建或者修复到先前的状态是一种特殊的改变。只有有助于保持遗址的整体性或者能够防止对遗址主体的破坏，这种改变才是适当的。

（8）许多陈旧或废弃的生产线里体现着人类的技能，这些技能是极为重要的资源，且不可再生，无可替代。它们应当被谨慎地记录下来并传给年轻一代。

（9）提倡对文献记录、公司档案、建筑设计资料以及生产样品的保护。

6. 教育与培训

（1）应从方法、理论和历史等方面对工业遗产保护开展专业培训，这类课程应在专科院校和综合性大学设置。

(2) 工业历史及其遗产专门的教育素材,应由中小学生们去搜集,并成为他们的教学内容之一。

7. 陈述与解释

(1) 公众对于工业遗产的兴趣与热情以及对其价值的鉴赏水平,是实施保护的有力保障。政府当局应积极通过出版、展览、广播电视、国际互联网及其他媒体向公众解释工业遗址的意义和价值,提供工业遗址持续的可达性,促进工业遗址地区的旅游发展。

(2) 建立专门的工业和技术博物馆和保护工业遗址,都是保护和阐释工业遗产的重要途径。

(3) 地区和国际的工业遗产保护途径,能够突显工业技术转型的持续性和引发大规模的保护运动。

The Nizhny Tagil Charter for the Industrial Heritage

TICCIH, Moscow, 17 July 2003

Preamble

The earliest periods of human history are defined by the archaeological evidence for fundamental changes in the ways in which people made objects, and the importance of conserving and studying the evidence of these changes is universally accepted.

From the Middle Ages, innovations in Europe in the use of energy and in trade and commerce led to a change towards the end of the 18th century just as profound as that between the Neolithic and Bronze Ages, with developments in the social, technical and economic circumstances of manufacturing sufficiently rapid and profound to be called a revolution. The Industrial Revolution was the beginning of a historical phenomenon that has affected an ever-greater part of the human population, as well as all the other forms of life on our planet, and that continues to the present day.

The material evidence of these profound changes is of universal human value, and the importance of the study and conservation of this evidence must be recognized.

The delegates assembled for the 2003 TICCIH Congress in Russia wish therefore to assert that the buildings and structures built for industrial activities, the processes and tools used within them and the towns and landscapes in which they are located, along with all their other tangible and intangible manifestations, are of fundamental importance. They should be studied, their history should be taught, their meaning and significance should be probed and made clear for everyone, and the most significant and characteristic examples should be identified, protected and maintained, in accordance with the spirit of the Venice Charter[1], for the use and benefit of today and of the future.

1. Definition of industrial heritage

Industrial heritage consists of the remains of industrial culture which are of historical, technological, social, architectural or scientific value. These remains consist of buildings and machinery, workshops, mills and factories, mines and sites for processing and refining, warehouses and stores, places where energy is generated, transmitted and used, transport and all its infrastructure, as well as places used for social activities related to industry such as housing, religious worship or education.

---

[1] The ICOMOS 'Venice Charter for the Conservation and Restoration of Monuments and Sites', 1964.

Industrial archaeology is an interdisciplinary method of studying all the evidence, material and immaterial, of documents, artefacts, stratigraphy and structures, human settlements and natural and urban landscapes[①], created for or by industrial processes. It makes use of those methods of investigation that are most suitable to increase understanding of the industrial past and present.

The *historical period* of principal interest extends forward from the beginning of the Industrial Revolution in the second half of the eighteenth century up to and including the present day, while also examining its earlier pre-industrial and proto-industrial roots. In addition it draws on the study of work and working techniques encompassed by the history of technology.

2. Values of industrial heritage

ⅰ. The industrial heritage is the evidence of activities which had and continue to have profound historical consequences. The motives for protecting the industrial heritage are based on the universal value of this evidence, rather than on the singularity of unique sites.

ⅱ. The industrial heritage is of social value as part of the record of the lives of ordinary men and women, and as such it provides an important sense of identity. It is of technological and scientific value in the history of manufacturing, engineering, construction, and it may have considerable aesthetic value for the quality of its architecture, design or planning.

ⅲ. These values are intrinsic to the site itself, its fabric, components, machinery and setting, in the industrial landscape, in written documentation, and also in the intangible records of industry contained in human memories and customs.

ⅳ. Rarity, in terms of the survival of particular processes, site typologies or landscapes, adds particular value and should be carefully assessed. Early or pioneering examples are of especial value.

3. The importance of identification, recording and research

ⅰ. Every territory should identify, record and protect the industrial remains that it wants to preserve for future generations.

ⅱ. Surveys of areas and of different industrial typologies should identify the extent of the industrial heritage. Using this information, inventories should be created of all the sites that have been identified. They should be devised to be easily searchable and should be freely accessible to the public. Computerisation and on-line access are valuable objectives.

ⅲ. Recording is a fundamental part of the study of industrial heritage. A full record of the physical features and condition of a site should be made and placed in a public archive before any interventions are made. Much information can be gained if recording is carried out before a process or site has ceased operation. Records should include descriptions, drawings, photographs and video film of moving objects, with references to supporting documentation. Peoples' memories are a unique and irreplaceable resource which should also be recorded when they are available.

ⅳ. Archaeological investigation of historic industrial sites is a fundamental technique for their study. It should be carried out to the same high standards as that of sites from other historical or cultural periods.

ⅴ. Programmes of historical research are needed to support policies for the protection of the industrial heritage. Because of the interdependency of many industrial activities, international studies can help identify sites

---

① For convenience, 'sites' will be taken to mean landscapes, complexes, buildings, structures and machines unless these terms are used in a more specific way.

and types of sites of world importance.

ⅵ. The criteria for assessing industrial buildings should be defined and published so as to achieve general public acceptance of rational and consistent standards. On the basis of appropriate research, these criteria should be used to identify the most important surviving landscapes, settlements, sites, typologies, buildings, structures, machines and processes.

ⅶ. Those sites and structures that are identified as important should be protected by legal measures that are sufficiently strong to ensure the conservation of their significance. The World Heritage List of UNESCO should give due recognition to the tremendous impact that industrialisation has had on human culture.

ⅷ. The value of significant sites should be defined and guidelines for future interventions established. Any legal, administrative and financial measures that are necessary to maintain their value should be put in place.

ⅸ. Sites that are at risk should be identified so that appropriate measures can be taken to reduce that risk and facilitate suitable schemes for repairing or re-using them.

ⅹ. International co-operation is a particularly appropriate approach to the conservation of the industrial heritage through co-ordinated initiatives and sharing resources. Compatible criteria should be developed to compile international inventories and databases.

4. Legal protection

ⅰ. The industrial heritage should be seen as an integral part of the cultural heritage in general. Nevertheless, its legal protection should take into account the special nature of the industrial heritage. It should be capable of protecting plant and machinery, below-ground elements, standing structures, complexes and ensembles of buildings, and industrial landscapes. Areas of industrial waste should be considered for their potential archaeological as well as ecological value.

ⅱ. Programmes for the conservation of the industrial heritage should be integrated into policies for economic development and into regional and national planning.

ⅲ. The most important sites should be fully protected and no interventions allowed that compromise their historical integrity or the authenticity of their fabric. Sympathetic adaptation and re-use may be an appropriate and a cost-effective way of ensuring the survival of industrial buildings, and should be encouraged by appropriate legal controls, technical advice, tax incentives and grants.

ⅳ. Industrial communities which are threatened by rapid structural change should be supported by central and local government authorities. Potential threats to the industrial heritage from such changes should be anticipated and plans prepared to avoid the need for emergency actions.

ⅴ. Procedures should be established for responding quickly to the closure of important industrial sites to prevent the removal or destruction of significant elements. The competent authorities should have statutory powers to intervene when necessary to protect important threatened sites.

ⅵ. Government should have specialist advisory bodies that can give independent advice on questions relating to the protection and conservation of industrial heritage, and their opinions should be sought on all important cases.

ⅶ. Every effort should be made to ensure the consultation and participation of local communities in the protection and conservation of their local industrial heritage.

ⅷ. Associations and societies of volunteers have an important role in identifying sites, promoting public participation in industrial conservation and disseminating information and research, and as such are indispensable actors in the theatre of industrial heritage.

5. Maintenance and conservation

ⅰ. Conservation of the industrial heritage depends on preserving functional integrity, and interventions to an industrial site should therefore aim to maintain this as far as possible. The value and authenticity of an industrial site may be greatly reduced if machinery or components are removed, or if subsidiary elements which form part of a whole site are destroyed.

ⅱ. The conservation of industrial sites requires a thorough knowledge of the purpose or purposes to which they were put, and of the various industrial processes which may have taken place there. These may have changed over time, but all former uses should be examined and assessed.

ⅲ. Preservation *in situ* should always be given priority consideration. Dismantling and relocating a building or structure are only acceptable when the destruction of the site is required by overwhelming economic or social needs.

ⅳ. The adaptation of an industrial site to a new use to ensure its conservation is usually acceptable except in the case of sites of especial historical significance. New uses should respect the significant material and maintain original patterns of circulation and activity, and should be compatible as much as possible with the original or principal use. An area that interprets the former use is recommended.

ⅴ. Continuing to adapt and use industrial buildings avoids wasting energy and contributes to sustainable development. Industrial heritage can have an important role in the economic regeneration of decayed or declining areas. The continuity that re-use implies may provide psychological stability for communities facing the sudden end a long-standing sources of employment.

ⅵ. Interventions should be reversible and have a minimal impact. Any unavoidable changes should be documented and significant elements that are removed should be recorded and stored safely. Many industrial processes confer a patina that is integral to the integrity and interest of the site.

ⅶ. Reconstruction, or returning to a previous known state, should be considered an exceptional intervention and one which is only appropriate if it benefits the integrity of the whole site, or in the case of the destruction of a major site by violence.

ⅷ. The human skills involved in many old or obsolete industrial processes are a critically important resource whose loss may be irreplaceable. They need to be carefully recorded and transmitted to younger generations.

ⅸ. Preservation of documentary records, company archives, building plans, as well as sample specimens of industrial products should be encouraged.

6. Education and training

ⅰ. Specialist professional training in the methodological, theoretical and historical aspects of industrial heritage should be taught at technical and university levels.

ⅱ. Specific educational material about the industrial past and its heritage should be produced by and for students at primary and secondary level.

7. Presentation and interpretation

ⅰ. Public interest and affection for the industrial heritage and appreciation of its values are the surest ways to conserve it. Public authorities should actively explain the meaning and value of industrial sites through publications, exhibitions, television, the Internet and other media, by providing sustainable access to important sites and by promoting tourism in industrial areas.

ⅱ. Specialist industrial and technical museums and conserved industrial sites are both important means of protecting and interpreting the industrial heritage.

ⅲ. Regional and international routes of industrial heritage can highlight the continual transfer of industrial technology and the large-scale movement of people that can be caused by it.

ICOMOS-TICCIH 保护工业遗产遗址、构筑物、区域和景观的原则（都柏林原则）[①]

（国际古迹遗址理事会第十七届大会 2011 年 11 月 28 日在巴黎通过）

前　言

在世界各地，各种各样的遗址、构筑物、综合体、城市和聚落、区域、景观和线路见证了人类的工业开采和生产活动。在许多地方，这种遗产仍在使用，工业化仍是一个具有历史连续性的积极过程；而在另一些地方，这种遗产提供了过去的工业活动和技术的考古证据。除了与工业技术和工艺流程、工程、建筑和城市规划相关的有形遗产外，这种遗产还包括体现在工人及其社区的技能、记忆和社会生活中的许多无形层面。

过去两个世纪可见的全球工业化进程构成了人类历史的一个重要阶段，这使得其遗产对现代世界尤为重要和关键。通过仍然活跃的或考古的遗址，工业化的先兆和开端在世界许多地方都可追溯到远古时代，我们的注意力延伸到这种过程及其遗产的任何案例。然而，就我们的目的而言，这些共同的原则主要关注的内容与现代工业革命的共同理念相一致，其特点是独特和专门的生产、运输以及能源开发，或优化流程和技术、贸易和商业互动以及新的社会和文化模式。

工业遗产非常脆弱，常常面临危险，往往由于缺乏认识、文献、认可或保护而消失，也因为不断变化的经济趋势、负面看法、环境问题或其巨大的规模和复杂性而消失。然而，通过延长现有构筑物的生命周期以及扩展其内在活力，保护建成的工业遗产，能有助于在地方、国家和国际各层级实现可持续发展的目标。它涉及社会、物质和环境等方面的发展，应该得到承认。

在过去的几十年里，不断发展的研究、国际间和跨学科合作以及社区行动极大地促进了对工业遗产更好的理解以及管理方、利益相关者和专业人员之间更多的合作。这一进展得益于国际古迹遗址理事会编制的一系列国际参考文献和指南，以及联合国教科文组织 1972 年通过的《世界遗产公约》等国际建议和法律文件的实施。2003 年，国际保护工业遗产委员会通过了《关于工业遗产的下塔吉尔宪章》，这是第一份受到承认的国际参考文本，用以指导该领域的遗产保护和保存。

认识到工业遗产的特殊性质，以及由于当代经济、法律、文化和环境背景与工业遗产的关系而产生影响遗产的问题和威胁，国际古迹遗址理事会和国际保护工业遗产委员会希望通过促进传播和运用以下原则来扩大合作，以有助于将工业遗产作为世界各地人类社会遗产的一部分来记录、保护、保存和欣赏。

1. 定义：工业遗产包括场所、构筑物、综合体、区域和景观，以及相关的机器、物件或文件，这些提供了过去或仍在进行中的工业生产过程、原材料提取、原材料转化为商品以及相关的能源和运输基础

[①] 译者：曹新。

设施的证据。工业遗产反映了文化和自然环境之间的深刻联系，因为工业过程，无论是古代的还是现代的，都依赖于源自自然的原材料、能源和运输网络来生产产品并将产品分销到更广阔的市场。它既包括物质资产——不动产和动产，也包括无形因素，如专有技术，工作和工人的组织，以及塑造社区生活并给整个社会和整个世界带来重大组织变革的复杂的社会和文化遗产。

2. 工业遗产地的目的、设计和随时间推移的演变非常多样化。许多遗产代表了生产流程、技术以及地区的或历史时期的状况，有一些则代表了具有全球影响力的杰出成就。还有一些是工业综合体和多场所的运营系统，其许多组成部分是相互依赖的，经常呈现不同的技术和不同的历史时期。工业遗产的意义和价值是构筑物或遗址本身、其物质结构、组成部分、机械装置和环境等所固有的，表现在工业景观、书面文献里，也包含在记忆、艺术和习俗的无形记录中。

Ⅰ. 记录并理解工业遗产构筑物、遗址、区域和景观及其价值

3. 研究和记录工业构筑物、遗址、景观和相关的机械、设备、记载或无形的要素，这对识别、保护它们和欣赏其遗产意义及价值非常重要。过去的工业流程中包含的人类技能和知识是需要保护的至关重要的资源，必须在遗产评估过程中加以考虑。

4. 研究和记录工业遗产遗址和构筑物必须考虑它们的历史、技术和社会经济层面，从而为保护和管理提供一个综合的基础。它需要跨学科的研究和教育计划的支持，以确定工业遗产遗址或构筑物的重要性。它应得益于多样的专业知识和信息来源，包括现场调查和记录、历史和考古调查、材料和景观分析、口述历史和/或公共、团体或私人档案的研究。应鼓励研究和保存文献记录、公司档案、建筑规划和工业产品样本。文献评估应由相关行业适当的专家进行，以确定其遗产意义。社区和其他利益相关方的参与也是这项工作不可或缺的组成部分。

5. 全面了解一个地区或国家的工业和社会经济史，或者它们与世界其他地区的联系，对于理解工业遗产遗址或构筑物的意义是必要的。带有比较性的，针对关键工业部门或技术的，单一工业背景、类型学或区域性的研究，对于认识个体的构筑物、遗址、区域或景观中固有的遗产价值非常有益。公众、学者和管理者都应该能够访问和搜索到这些相关研究。

Ⅱ. 确保有效保护和保存工业遗产构筑物、遗址、区域和景观

6. 需要采取和充分执行适当的政策、法律和行政措施，以保护和保存工业遗产遗址和构筑物，包括其机械和记录。这些措施必须处理工业遗产、工业生产和经济之间的密切关系，特别是关于企业和投资、贸易或知识产权（如专利）的规则，以及适用于有效的工业经营的标准。

7. 应编制构筑物、遗址、区域、景观及其环境和相关物件、文件、图件和档案或非物质遗产的综合清单，并将其作为有效的管理和保护政策及保护措施的一部分。这些应受益于法律认可、充分的保护和管理，以确保它们的重要性、完整性和真实性得到维护。如果工业遗产是通过偶然发现确定的，应给予临时保护，以留出必要的时间对遗产进行适当的文件编制和研究。

8. 就具有遗产意义的活跃的工业构筑物或遗址而言，必须认识到，作为一种活态的生产或开采设施，它们的继续使用和功能发挥会承载某些遗产意义，并将提供充分的条件来实现物质和经济的可持续性。当实施当代法规，如建筑法规、环境要求或降低风险的策略等，以应对自然或人为灾害时，需要尊重它们的具体技术特征和特性。

9. 保护措施应运用于建筑物及其组成部分，因为完整性或功能的整体性对工业遗产构筑物和遗址的意义尤为重要。如果移除机械或其他重要部件，或者如果构成整个遗址一部分的附属元素被破坏，它们的遗产价值可能会受到极大的损害或降低。应制定法律和行政框架，使管理部门能够对关闭运营中的工

业遗址和建筑群做出快速反应，以防止机械、工业物品或相关记录等重要元素被移除或破坏。

Ⅲ. 保护和维护工业遗产构筑物、遗址、区域和景观

10. 合宜的原有或替代的以及适应性的利用是确保工业遗产遗址或构筑物得到保护的最常见方式，也常是最可持续的方式。新的用途应该尊重重要的材料、组成部分以及循环和运行的模式。专业技能是必要的，以确保在管理这些工业遗产遗址和构筑物的可持续利用时，考虑并尊重其遗产的意义。建筑规范、降低风险要求、环境或工业法规以及其他标准应当以适应性的方式实施，以便在通过物理干预实施这些法规时考虑遗产层面。

11. 只要有可能，物理干预应该是可逆的，并尊重年代价值和重要的痕迹或标记。变更应记录在案。在特殊情况下，出于教育目的，并且必须基于彻底的研究和完整的文献，恢复到以前已知的状态是可以接受的。只有在特别情况下，客观情况证明势不可挡的经济或社会需求必须破坏遗址，拆解和迁移才是可以接受的。

12. 如果工业遗产遗址或构筑物有预期的冗余、停产和／或改造，应记录这些过程，例如，部件必须拆除、机器必须移除的情况。作为工业流程的一部分，它们的物质形式以及它们的功能和位置应详尽地记录下来。还应收集与工作流程相关人的口头和／或书面故事。

Ⅳ. 展示和传播工业构筑物、遗址、区域和景观的遗产维度和价值，以提高公众和团体意识，并支持培训和研究

13. 工业遗产是学习的源泉，需要从多个维度进行传播。它体现了地方、国家和国际历史的重要方面以及不同时代和文化之间的相互作用。它展示了与科学和技术发展以及与社会和艺术运动相关的创造性才智。公众和团体对工业遗产的认识和理解是成功保护工业遗产的重要手段。

14. 应制定和维持各种计划和设施，如参观活跃的工业遗产地，展示其运行情况，以及与其历史、机械和工业流程、工业或城市博物馆和解说中心、展览、出版物、网站、区域或跨区域游线相关的故事和非物质遗产，以此提高对当代社会具有丰富意义的工业遗产的认识和欣赏。理想情况下，这些设施应该设置于工业化进程已经发生的遗址本身，能够进行最好的传播。在可能的情况下，应授权研究和保护遗产的国家和国际机构将遗产用作普通公众和专业团体的教育设施。

Joint ICOMOS-TICCIH Principles for the Conservation of Industrial Heritage Sites, Structures, Areas and Landscapes
(The Dublin Principles)

Adopted by the 17th ICOMOS General Assembly, Paris, 28 November 2011

PREAMBLE

Around the World, a great diversity of sites, structures, complexes, cities and settlements, areas, landscapes and routes bear witness to human activities of industrial extraction and production. In many places, this heritage is still in use and industrialisation is still an active process with a sense of historical continuity, while in other places it offers archaeological evidence of past activities and technologies. Besides the tangible heritage associated with industrial technology and processes, engineering, architecture and town-planning, it includes many intangible dimensions embodied in the skills, memories and social life of workers and their communities.

The global process of industrialisation observed over the past two centuries constitutes a major stage of human history, making its heritage particularly important and critical to the Modern World. Precursors and beginnings of industrialisation can be recognized in many parts of the world well back into ancient times through active or archaeological sites, and our attention extends to any examples of such process and its heritage. However, for our purposes, these joint principles' primary interests coincide with the common notions of the Modern Era Industrial Revolution, marked by distinctive and dedicated production, transportation and power-generating or harnessing processes and technologies, trade and commercial interactions, and new social and cultural patterns.

The industrial heritage is highly vulnerable and often at risk, often lost for lack of awareness, documentation, recognition or protection but also because of changing economic trends, negative perceptions, environmental issues or its sheer size and complexity. Yet, by extending the life-cycle of existing structures and their embodied energy, conservation of the built industrial heritage, can contribute to achieving the goals of sustainable development at the local, national and international levels. It touches the social as well as the physical and environmental aspects of development and should be acknowledged as such.

Over the past decades, growing research, international and interdisciplinary cooperation as well as community initiatives have greatly contributed to a better appreciation of the industrial heritage and increased collaboration between stewards, stakeholders and professionals. This progress has benefitted from the development of a corpus of international references and guidelines by ICOMOS–the International Council on Monuments and Sites, and the implementation of international recommendations and instruments such as the World Heritage Convention adopted by UNESCO in 1972. In 2003, The International Committee for the Conservation of Industrial Heritage (TICCIH) adopted its Nizhny Tagil Charter for the Industrial Heritage, a first international reference text of such recognition to guide protection and conservation in the field.

Acknowledging the particular nature of the industrial heritage and the issues and threats affecting it as a result of its relation to the contemporary economic, legal, cultural and environmental contexts, ICOMOS and TICCIH wish to expand their cooperation by adopting and promoting the dissemination and use of the following Principles to assist in the documentation, protection, conservation and appreciation of industrial heritage as part of the heritage of human societies around the World.

1. Definition: The industrial heritage consists of sites, structures, complexes, areas and landscapes as well as the related machinery, objects or documents that provide evidence of past or ongoing industrial processes of production, the extraction of raw materials, their transformation into goods, and the related energy and transport infrastructures. Industrial heritage reflects the profound connection between the cultural and natural environment, as industrial processes—whether ancient or modern—depend on natural sources of raw materials, energy and transportation networks to produce and distribute products to broader markets. It includes both material assets—immovable and movable—, and intangible dimensions such as technical know-how, the organisation of work and workers, and the complex social and cultural legacy that shaped the life of communities and brought major organizational changes to entire societies and the world in general.

2. Industrial heritage sites are very diversified in terms of their purpose, design and evolution over time. Many are representative of processes, technologies as well as regional or historical conditions while others constitute outstanding achievements of global influence. Others are complexes and multiple site operations or systems whose many components are interdependent, with different technologies and historical periods frequently present. The significance and value of industrial heritage is intrinsic to the structures or sites themselves, their material fabric, components, machinery and setting, expressed in the industrial landscape, in written documentation, and also in the intangible records contained in memories, arts and customs.

I. Document and understand industrial heritage structures, sites, areas and landscapes and their values

3. Researching and documenting industrial structures, sites, landscapes and the related machinery, equipment, records or intangible aspects is essential to their identification, conservation, and the appreciation of their heritage significance and value. Human skills and knowledge involved in old industrial processes are a critically important resource in conservation and must be considered in the heritage evaluation process.

4. Researching and documenting industrial heritage sites and structures must address their historical, technological and socio-economical dimensions to provide an integrated base for conservation and management. It requires an interdisciplinary approach supported by interdisciplinary research and educational programmes to identify the significance of industrial heritage sites or structures. It should benefit from a diversity of sources of expertise and information including site surveys and recording, historical and archaeological investigation, material and landscape analysis, oral history and/or research in public, corporate or private archives. Research

and preservation of documentary records, company archives, building plans, and specimens of industrial products should be encouraged. The evaluation and assessment of documents should be undertaken by an appropriate specialist in the industry to which they relate to determine their heritage significance. The participation of communities and other stakeholders is also an integral part of this exercise.

5. Thorough knowledge of the industrial and socio-economic history of an area or country or their links to other parts of the world is necessary to understand the significance of industrial heritage sites or structures. Single industry context, typological or regional studies, with a comparative component, aimed at key industrial sectors or technologies are very useful in recognizing the heritage values inherent in individual structures, sites, areas or landscapes. They should be accessible and searchable by the public, scholars as well as managers.

II. Ensure effective protection and conservation of the industrial heritage structures, sites, areas and landscapes

6. Appropriate policies, legal and administrative measures need to be adopted and adequately implemented to protect and ensure the conservation of industrial heritage sites and structures, including their machinery and records. These measures have to address the close relation between the industrial heritage, industrial production and the economy, in particular with respect to rules for corporations and investments, trades or intellectual property such as patents, and standards applicable to active industrial operations.

7. Integrated inventories and lists of structures, sites, areas, landscapes their setting and associated objects, documents, drawings and archives or intangible heritage should be developed and used as part of these effective management and conservation policies and protection measures. These should benefit from a legal recognition, adequate conservation and management to ensure that their significance, integrity and authenticity are maintained. In the case of industrial heritage identified through fortuitous discovery, temporary protection should be granted to allow time necessary for proper heritage documentation and research.

8. In the case of active industrial structures or sites of heritage significance, it must be recognized that their continued use and function might carry some of their heritage significance and provide adequate conditions for their physical and economic sustainability as a living production or extraction facilities. Their specific technical characteristics and features need to be respected while implementing contemporary regulations such as building codes, environmental requirements or risk reduction strategies to address hazards of natural or human origin.

9. Protection measures should apply to buildings and their contents since completeness or functional integrity is especially important to the significance of industrial heritage structures and sites. Their heritage value may be greatly jeopardized or reduced if machinery or other significant components are removed, or if subsidiary elements which form part of a whole site are destroyed. Legal and administrative frameworks should be developed to enable authorities to respond quickly to the closure of operating industrial heritage sites and complexes to prevent removal or destruction of significant elements such as machinery, industrial objects or related records

III. Conserve and maintain the industrial heritage structures, sites, areas and landscapes

10. Appropriate original or alternative and adaptive use is the most frequent way and often the most

sustainable way of ensuring the conservation of industrial heritage sites or structures. New uses should respect significant material, components and patterns of circulation and activity. Specialist skills are necessary to ensure that the heritage significance is taken into account and respected in managing the sustainable use of these industrial heritage sites and structures. Building codes, risk mitigation requirements, environmental or industrial regulations, and other standards should be implemented in an adapted way to take heritage dimensions into account when they are enforced through physical interventions.

11. Wherever possible, physical interventions should be reversible, and respect the age value and significant traces or marks. Changes should be documented. Reverting to a previous known state may be acceptable under exceptional circumstances for educational purposes, and must be based on thorough research and documentation. Dismantling and relocating are only acceptable in extraordinary cases when the destruction of the site is required by objectively proved overwhelming economic or social needs.

12. In case of prospective redundancy, decommissioning, and / or adaptation of industrial heritage sites or structures, the processes should be recorded including, for example, where components have to be demolished and machinery has to be removed. Their material form as well as their functioning and location as part of the industrial processes should be exhaustively documented. Oral and / or written stories of people connected with work processes should also be collected.

IV. Present and communicate the heritage dimensions and values of industrial structures, sites, areas and landscapes to raise public and corporate awareness, and support training and research

13. The industrial heritage is a source of learning which needs to be communicated in its multiple dimensions. It illustrates important aspects of local, national and international history and interactions over times and cultures. It demonstrates the inventive talents related to scientific and technological developments, as well as social and artistic movements. Public and corporate awareness and understanding for the industrial heritage are important means for its successful conservation.

14. Programmes and facilities such as visits of active industrial heritage sites and the presentation of their operations as well as the stories and intangible heritage associated with their history, machinery and industrial processes, industrial or city museums and interpretation centres, exhibitions, publications, websites, regional or trans-boundary itineraries should be developed and sustained as means to raise awareness and appreciation for the industrial heritage in the full richness of its meaning for contemporary societies. These should ideally be located at the heritage sites itself where the process of industrialisation has taken place and can be best communicated. Wherever possible, national and international institutions in the field of research and conservation of heritage should be empowered to use them as educational facilities for the general public and the professional communities.

文化线路

文化线路宪章[①]

(国际古迹遗址理事会第十六届大会2008年10月4日在加拿大魁北克通过)

前 言

由于文化遗产保护科学的发展,"文化线路"的新概念体现了文化遗产视野的演变,以及与其环境和地域规模相关的价值日渐重要,在不同层面展示了遗产的宏观结构。这个概念引入了一种新的保护伦理的范式,将这些遗产视为超越国家界线的并且需要共同努力的共同遗产。通过尊重每个单体要素的固有价值,文化线路承认和强调作为整体中独立存在部分的所有要素的价值。这也有助于体现当代社会的理念,即文化遗产的价值是可持续的社会和经济发展的资源。

文化遗产这个更为扩展的概念需要在一个更广阔的背景中用新的方法去描述和保护它与其直接关联的自然、文化和历史环境的重要关系。在此发展中,文化线路的概念是创新的、复合的、以及多维度的。对于文化遗产保护的理论和实践,它带来和呈现了一个定性的新方法。

文化线路代表了人类跨文化联系互动的、动态的和演变的过程,反映了不同民族对文化遗产贡献的丰富多样性。

虽然文化线路在历史上既是和平又是敌对的相逢结果,但它们反映了许多超越其最初功能的共有层面,基于共同的历史纽带,也基于相关社区呈现出包容、尊重和欣赏文化多样性的特征,文化线路为和平文化提供了一个特殊的背景。

将文化线路视为一个新概念或新类别,与其他类别或类型的文化遗产既没有冲突,也没有重叠,如古迹、城市、文化景观、工业遗产等,那些遗产可能存在于特定文化线路的轨迹内。文化线路只是将它们包含在一个联合系统中,从而增强了它们的重要性。这一综合、跨学科和共享的框架通过创新的科学视角在它们之间建立了新的联系,提供了一个多边的、更完整的和更准确的历史视野。这种方法不仅促进了世界各民族之间的理解和交流,而且加强了保护文化遗产的合作。

"文化线路"的概念创新地揭示了人类流动和交流这一特定现象的遗产内容,这种现象是通过促进其流动的交流路线发展起来的,并且被用于或有意服务于一个具体和特殊的目的。文化线路可能是特意为实现这一目的而创建的线路,也可能是用作不同目的的一些已有道路的部分的或全部而形成的线路。但是,除了它作为一种交流或运输方式的特性之外,它作为一种文化线路的存在和意义,只能通过它在很长一段历史时期用于这种特定目的,并产生了与其相关的遗产价值和文化属性来说明,而这些价值和属性反

[①] 译者:曹新。

映了不同文化群体之间由于其自身独特的动态关系而产生的相互影响。

因此，文化线路不是简单的交流和运输方式，它可能包括不同的文化遗产，连接不同的民族。文化线路是特殊的历史现象，不可能通过个体的想象和意志来创造，从而建立一系列碰巧具有共同特征的相关文化遗产。

文化线路有时是作为人类意志预先计划的一个项目出现的，它有足够的力量承担特定的目的（例如印加和罗马帝国大道）。在其他情况下，它们是长期演化过程的结果，在这一过程中，不同人为因素的集体介入共同作用，并被引向一个共同的目的（例如通往圣地亚哥的线路、非洲贸易商队线路或丝绸之路）。在这两种情况下，它们都是源于人类意志实现特定目标的过程。

鉴于其文化丰富性和多样性，包括与文化线路存在原因直接相关的相互联系和特色遗产（如古迹、考古遗迹、历史城镇、乡土建筑、无形遗产、工业和技术遗产、公共工程、文化和自然景观、交通方式和其他运用特定知识和专门技术的实例），它们的研究和管理需要一种多学科的方法，以论证和推进科学假设，并丰富历史、文化、技术和艺术知识。

宪章的目标

- 制定针对文化线路类别的基本研究原则和方法，这些原则和方法与其他先前建立和研究的文化遗产类别相关。
- 提出基本机制以发展文化线路的评估、保护、维护、管理和保存的相关知识。
- 确定基本指南、原则和标准，以正确利用文化线路作为可持续的社会和经济发展资源，尊重其真实性、完整性、恰当的保存和历史意义。
- 为国家和国际合作奠定基础，这对于开展与文化线路相关的研究、保护和发展项目及其所需的筹资至关重要。

定　义

任何交流线路，无论是陆路、水路还是其他类型，有明确的物理界限，其特征还在于具有自己特别的动态的功能和历史的功能，以服务于特定和明确的目的，必须满足以下条件：

a) 它必须产生于并反映了人们互动的活动，以及不同民族、国家、地区或大陆之间在很长一段时间内多个维度的、持续和互惠的商品、思想、知识和价值观的交流；

b) 因此，它一定促进了受其影响的不同文化在空间和时间上的交互滋养，这反映在它们的有形和无形遗产中；

c) 它必须已将与其存在相关的历史关系和文化遗产整合成一个动态系统。

文化线路要素的定义：
背景，内容，作为一个整体的跨文化意义，动态特征和环境

1. **背景**：文化线路发生在自然和/或文化背景中，它们对背景产生影响，并且作为互动过程的一部分，它们以新的维度来塑造背景的特征和丰富背景。

2. **内容**：一条文化线路必须要由有形要素支撑，这些要素见证其文化遗产，并提供其存在的实物证明。任何无形的要素都给构成整体的各种要素赋予含义和意义。

（1）决定文化线路存在的不可或缺的物质因素是交流线路本身，它作为工具服务于设计的项目，或

是产生于人类活动而实现特定的目标。

（2）其他基本的实质性要素是与历史线路的功能相关的有形遗产（中转站、海关、存储、休息和住宿场所，医院，市场，港口，防御工事，桥梁，通讯和运输工具；工业、矿业或其他设施，以及反映不同时代的技术、科学和社会应用及进步、与制造业和贸易相关的设施；城市中心、文化景观、圣地、礼拜和虔敬的场所，等等）以及无形遗产要素，这些要素见证了文化线路沿途涉及的人们之间的交流和对话过程。

3. 作为一个整体的跨文化意义：文化线路的概念意味着作为一个整体的价值，它大于其各部分的总和，并赋予线路以意义。

（1）文化线路构成一种文化资产，这种文化资产因其所滋养的不同文化而变得充实，并通过大量的共同特征和价值体系，在整体价值上超越了它们。

（2）在其整体特性之内，其各部分的价值在于它们共同的、共享的、多方面的意义。

（3）它更大规模地使民族、国家、地区和大陆之间的文化联系成为可能。

（4）从包含的范围到包含的各种遗产要素综合管理的角度来看，这种规模的幅度是很重要的。与此同时，它所暗含的文化多样性为文化同质化过程提供了另外一种可能。

4. 动态特征：除了呈现其历史路径的实体证据以及文化遗产要素之外，文化线路还包括一个动态因素，即作为互惠的文化影响的流动导体或渠道。

（1）文化线路的动态演变不遵循自然规律或偶然现象，而只遵循人类的进程和利益，因此只能作为一种文化现象来理解。

（2）这种重要的文化流动不仅体现在物质或有形的方面，也体现在构成文化线路的无形遗产的精神和传统方面。

（3）将一条文化线路理解为各民族之间文化交流的一系列动态要素，可以从其真正的空间和历史维度来欣赏其文化遗产，从而能对整个线路的保护采取综合的和可持续的方法。

5. 环境：文化线路与其环境密切相关，并构成其不可分割的一部分。

（1）地理环境有助于塑造文化线路，或者确定其路径，或者随着时间的推移影响其发展。

（2）无论是自然环境还是文化环境（城市或乡村的），都为文化线路提供了框架，赋予其特殊的环境，其特征是物质的和无形的要素和价值，对于理解、保护和享有文化线路至关重要。

（3）一条文化线路将地形和十分多样的遗产关联和联结在一起，形成一个统一的整体。文化线路及其环境与它们不同的自然或文化景观相关，但这些景观只是文化线路的组成部分之一，而基于文化线路经过的不同区域和地区，这些景观有自己独特的特征和特性。这些不同的景观使得组成线路整体的不同部分各具特色，丰富了线路的多样性。

（4）在文化线路的一些部分，与自然的关系特别紧密；在另一些部分，与城市或农村环境的关系特别紧密，而在那些分布有独立于其他建筑的古迹区域（如教堂、修道院、喷泉、桥梁、边界线等），是这些古迹与其景观环境的关系塑造了文化线路这一部分的特质。

（5）保护和保存文化线路需要对其周围的历史、自然和文化特征有深刻的了解。任何必要的干预措施都必须适应这一背景，尊重其典型特征，促进对文化线路的理解，不能扭曲传统的景观，无论其是自然景观、文化景观还是综合景观。

（6）必须确定文化线路的背景环境，清晰标记明确的界线、受监管的缓冲区边界，以使其中包含的物质和非物质文化价值完全真实、完整地得到保护。这种保护必须包括不同景观的价值，这些景观构成文化线路的不同部分，形成文化线路的特有环境。

具体指标

作为适用于文化线路类别的基本区分指标,应考虑以下因素:路线的结构及其物质基础,以及关于其用于实现特定目标的历史数据;与文化线路的具体目的和功能相关的任何物质结构;交流要素,以及在沿途(或确定地点)共同起源的文化表现形式,例如实践、传统、习俗以及共同的宗教、仪式、语言、节日、烹饪或相似特质;在音乐、文学、建筑、美术、手工艺、科学发展、技术和技能,以及其他物质和非物质文化资产方面的相互影响,这些文化资产由文化线路的历史功能而衍生。

文化线路的类型

文化线路可以按以下分类:
- 根据其地域范畴:地方、国家、地区、大陆或洲际。
- 根据其文化范畴:在确定的文化区域内或跨越不同的地理区域,这些区域在文化价值的形成或演化过程中已经或继续相互影响。
- 根据其目标或功能:社会、经济、政治或文化。这些特征在一个多维背景中共享。
- 根据其持续时间:那些不再使用的,和那些在社会经济、政治和文化交流影响下继续发展的。
- 根据其结构形态:线形、圆形、十字形、放射状或网状。
- 根据其自然环境:陆地、水生、混合或其他自然环境。

鉴别,完整性和真实性

- 初步指标

出于鉴别和评估的目的,以下方面首先可被视为文化线路存在的初步证据、非决定性证据:
- 动态的社会、经济、政治和文化进程的表达,这些进程在相关领域的不同文化群体之间引发了交流;
- 由历史纽带连接的不同地理和文化区域所共有的显著特征;
- 不同文化的民族或种族群体之间的流动和联系的证据;
- 植根于不同社区的传统生活的特定文化特征;
- 与线路的意义和功能相关的遗产元素和文化实践,如代表一个或多个特定文化和历史区域内不同社区共同价值观的仪式、节日和宗教庆典。

- 鉴别程序

鉴别文化线路的程序必须考虑其服务于具体和确定目的的特定功能,由于相互的文化影响而动态地产生遗产的有形和无形价值,其结构形态,整体的地理和历史背景,自然和文化环境(无论是城市还是乡村的),及其相应的特有的环境价值,其与景观的关系,持续的时间,以及其象征性和精神性的维度,所有这些都将有助于鉴别并理解文化线路的重要性。

文化线路的无形资产对于理解其重要性及其相关的遗产价值至关重要。因此,必须始终结合其他无形的价值来研究物质层面。

为了进行比较评估,还应考虑线路不同部分相对于整体的持续时间和历史意义。

就一条现存的文化线路而言,即使历史过程已随时间经历了变化,新的元素已被纳入,与具体的、确定的目的相关的联系和动态功能也应进行维护,这种联系和功能使得线路兴起并用于定义和确定线路。这些新元素应在其与文化线路的功能关系的框架内进行评估,并且可能发生以下情况:有些本身具有遗产价值的遗产,由于并不构成文化线路的一部分,而不能被视为文化线路的组成要素。

- **真实性**

每一条文化线路都应符合真实性标准，基于自然和文化环境，并就其物质和非物质的决定性要素和显著特征，以可论证和可信的方式表达其价值：

- 这些标准应适用于所研究的每个路段，以评估其在整个历史发展过程中相对于线路总体意义的重要性，并通过其路径的遗迹验证其结构布局的真实性。
- 基于分析和评估，真实性也应该在线路每一段的自然和文化背景中显而易见，以及在其历史功能和环境中包含的其他有形和无形遗产要素中显而易见。
- 即使在某些部分，文化线路的物质痕迹没有被清晰地保存下来，它在这些地区的存在也可以通过史学的、无形的要素和非物质的信息源来证明它们作为该线路整体的组成部分的真正意义，并证明它的真实性。
- 用于保护、保存和管理文化线路的技术和方法，无论是传统的还是新的应用，都必须尊重真实性标准。

- **完整性**

对文化线路完整性的确认必须基于一系列具有充分代表性的有形和无形的证据和要素，这些证据和要素见证了作为一个整体的文化线路的全球意义和价值，并确保完整体现了产生文化线路的历史进程的特征和重要性。

证明文化线路的独特性所必需的关于历史联系和动态功能的证据应该得到保存。此外，必须考虑其实体结构和/或重要特征是否状态良好，退化过程的影响是否得到控制，以及线路是否反映了因开发、废弃或忽视引起的任何可能的不良影响。

方法论

文化线路的概念要求对其研究、评估、保护、维护、保存、使用和管理采用特别的方法。鉴于文化线路的广度和整体价值及其地域范围，需要建立一个协调和整体管理的行动系统。

首先必须确定整个线路及其各个部分，并列出组成线路的遗产清单，分析其保护状况，这将有助于制定保护线路的战略计划。该计划必须包括制定措施，以提高公共和私人机构对该线路的认识和关注。还要求制定协调措施和具体法律措施，以保护、利用和管理作为整个线路价值和意义的实质性部分的所有要素。

1. 研究

对文化线路的研究可能扩展到不同的地理区域，这些区域可能彼此相距甚远。因此，建议在线路的主要特征点设立几个研究小组。

研究方法，以及实践和附加指标，用以正确鉴别和评估文化线路不同部分的遗产价值时，不应忽视线路作为一个整体的意义，以避免线路意义或历史重要性的任何损失。

从事这类文化遗产工作的研究小组应该具有多学科和合作的性质。应建立共同的工作标准，基于这样的原则，即从各部分调查开始，但不能忽视项目整体。同样，应使用事先标准化的通用方法工具来收集数据。项目计划应包括协调机制，以促进研究人员之间的沟通与合作，从而实现每个团队的工作和成果的数据交换。

研究人员应该牢记，文化线路沿线存在各种类型的文化遗产，这并不意味着它们必然是该线路的组成部分，或者是与之相关的恰当的研究对象。在对文化线路的科学调研中，唯一应该强调的要素是那些与线路的特定目标相关的要素，以及与功能的动态变化引发的影响相关的要素。

2. 资金

鉴于确定和强调一条广阔的文化线路的价值所涉及的任务范围，应分阶段获得资金，以便在研究项目以及与其各个部分相关的维护、利用和管理项目中取得平衡、协调的进展。可取的做法是对要保存的价值进行联合评估，以便确定行动的优先次序和相应战略的实施。这要求通过双边或多边合作协定以获得资金，以及通过建立专门研究和重视文化线路价值的机构获得资金。同样，其管辖权完全或部分叠合文化线路的历史路径的地区机构应确定如何才能最好地激发有关国家的兴趣并获得它们的合作。如果可能，吸引慈善机构和私人捐助者的合作也很重要。

3. 保护——评估——维护 / 保存

文化线路及其环境需要新的评估、保护、保存和评价方法。仅仅保证对其遗产要素的部分或随机的保护是不够的。应制定这些要素的严格清单，并对其真实性和完整性进行评估，以确定对文化线路价值的影响，从而确定对文化线路重要性的影响。还必须控制退化过程的影响，并制定策略防止因开发和忽视而产生的不利影响。所有这一切都需要建立一个体系，包括协调的法律措施和适当的方法，以保证这条线路得到维护，并以整体的方式突出其价值和意义。在对文化线路进行任何可能影响 / 改变其重要性的干预之前，理解遗产价值是至关重要的。

4. 可持续利用——与旅游活动的关系

就其利用而言，文化线路可用于促进那些对于稳定的发展极其重要的具有社会和经济价值的活动。

应特别注意避免混淆旅游线路和文化线路的概念，即使是那些有文化价值的旅游线路。然而，还应该认识到，文化线路是一个现实存在，对区域凝聚力和可持续发展非常重要。从这一角度来看，应努力促进对文化线路的了解，并将其恰当和可持续地用于旅游目的，同时始终采取旨在消除风险的适当措施。为此，文化线路的保护和促进应协调整合附属基础设施，用于旅游活动、交通线路、信息、阐释和展示，其必要条件是不损害文化线路历史价值的意义、真实性和完整性，而这些是向游客传达的关键要素。

应根据先前的环境影响研究、公众使用和社区参与计划，以及旨在防止旅游业负面影响的控制和监测措施，合理管理游客参观。

为旅游目的开发文化线路在任何情况下都应保证当地社区以及当地旅游公司和所在地区旅游公司的优先参与。应竭尽全力防止大型国际公司制造垄断，或是文化线路的历史路径所经过的较发达国家的大公司制造垄断。

鉴于文化线路是一种合作和理解的工具，它提供了对于形成文化线路的文化和文明碰撞的整体解读，我们还应铭记，不管其每一部分的相对重要性如何，促进每一部分的积极发展，都会有利于文化线路，并有利于其他部分的发展。

5. 管理

"理解文化线路的意义"是管理文化线路的基本 / 根本原则。这意味着要确保以协调的及和谐的方式开展与其研究、评估和知识的社会传播有关的所有活动。这也需要交叉协调，保证与保护、维护、保存、区域组织、可持续发展、利用、旅游等有关的政策相整合。因此，需要制定联合项目，确保国家（省、地区、地方等）和国际范围的可持续发展，以及设置旨在保护该线路抵御自然灾害和各种风险影响的管理措施，这些灾害和风险可能会影响该文化线路的完整性和真实性，从而影响其重要意义。

6. 公众参与

保护、保存 / 维护、振兴和管理文化线路需要激发公众意识，并需要共享该线路的不同地区的居民参与。

国际合作

有一些著名的文化线路的例子，其历史路径涉及不同的国家。因此，国际合作对于研究、评估和保护构成国际文化线路的遗产是必需的。

当文化线路涉及不同发展程度的国家时，建议较发达的国家提供经济、技术和组织合作的方法，以及在信息、经验和研究人员交流方面的援助。

非常希望联合国教科文组织和其他国际组织建立合作机制（财政、技术和组织），帮助促进和实施与文化线路有关的项目，这些项目对不止一个国家都有利。

文化线路应被视为各民族融合的象征。沿着文化线路发展起来的历史纽带有助于推动民族间新的合作，他们在过去曾分享某些价值观和知识。

The ICOMOS Charter on Cultural Routes

Ratified by the 16th ICOMOS General Assembly, Québec, Canada, 4 October 2008

Preamble

As a result of the development of the sciences of conservation of cultural heritage, the new concept of Cultural Routes shows the evolution of ideas with respect to the vision of cultural properties, as well as the growing importance of values related to their setting and territorial scale and reveals the macrostructure of heritage on different levels. This concept introduces a model for a new ethics of conservation that considers these values as a common heritage that goes beyond national borders, and which requires joint efforts. By respecting the intrinsic value of each individual element, the Cultural Route recognizes and emphasizes the value of all of its elements as substantive parts of a whole. It also helps to illustrate the contemporary social conception of cultural heritage values as a resource for sustainable social and economic development.

This more extensive notion of cultural heritage requires new approaches to its treatment within a much wider context in order to describe and protect its significant relationships directly associated with its natural, cultural and historical setting. Within this advance, the concept of the Cultural Route is innovative, complex and multidimensional. It introduces and represents a qualitatively new approach to the theory and practice of conservation of the cultural heritage.

Cultural Routes represent interactive, dynamic, and evolving processes of human intercultural links that reflect the rich diversity of the contributions of different peoples to cultural heritage.

Though Cultural Routes have resulted historically from both peaceful and hostile encounters, they present a number of shared dimensions which transcend their original functions, offering an exceptional setting for a culture of peace based on the ties of shared history as well as the tolerance, respect, and appreciation for cultural diversity that characterize the communities involved.

The consideration of Cultural Routes as a new concept or category does not conflict nor overlap with other categories or types of cultural properties—monuments, cities, cultural landscapes, industrial heritage, etc.—that may exist within the orbit of a given Cultural Route. It simply includes them within a joint system which enhances their significance. This integrated, interdisciplinary and shared framework creates new relationships among them by means of an innovative scientific perspective that provides a multilateral, more complete, and more accurate vision of history. This approach stimulates not only understanding and communication among the peoples of the world, but also increases cooperation to preserve cultural heritage.

The innovation introduced by the concept of "Cultural Routes" reveals the heritage content of a specific phenomenon of human mobility and exchange that developed via communication routes that facilitated their flow and which were used or deliberately served a concrete and peculiar purpose. A Cultural Route can be a road that was expressly created to serve this purpose or a route that takes advantage either totally of partially of preexisting roads used for different purposes. But beyond its character as a way of communication or transport, its existence and significance as a Cultural Route can only be explained by its use for such specific purpose throughout a long period of history and by having generated heritage values and cultural properties associated to it which reflect reciprocal influences between different cultural groups as a result of its own peculiar dynamics.

Therefore, Cultural Routes are not simple ways of communication and transport which may include cultural properties and connect different peoples, but special historic phenomena that cannot be created by applying one's imagination and will to the establishment of a set of associated cultural assets that happen to possess features in common.

Cultural Routes have sometimes arisen as a project planned a priori by the human will which had sufficient power to undertake a specific purpose (for example, the Incan and the Roman Empire Routes). On other occasions, they are the result of a long evolutionary process in which the collective interventions of different human factors coincide and are channeled towards a common purpose (such as in the Route to Santiago, the African trade caravan routes, or the Silk Route). In both cases, they are processes arising from the human will to achieve a specific objective.

Given the cultural richness and variety of both the interrelationships and the characteristic assets directly associated with the reason for the existence of Cultural Routes (such as monuments, archaeological remains, historic towns, vernacular architecture, intangible, industrial and technological heritage, public works, cultural and natural landscapes, transportation means and other examples of the application of specific knowledge and technical skills), their study and management requires a multidisciplinary approach that illustrates and reinvigorates scientific hypotheses and stimulates increased historic, cultural, technical and artistic knowledge.

Objectives of the Charter

• To establish the basic principles and methods of research specific to the category of Cultural Route as they relate to other previously established and studied categories of cultural heritage assets.

• To propose the basic mechanisms for the development of knowledge about, evaluation, protection, preservation, management and conservation of Cultural Routes.

• To define the basic guidelines, principles and criteria for correct use of Cultural Routes as resources for sustainable social and economic development, respecting their authenticity and integrity, appropriate preservation and historical significance.

• To establish the bases for national and international cooperation that will be essential for undertaking research, conservation and development projects related to Cultural Routes, as well as the financing required for these efforts.

Definition

Any route of communication, be it land, water, or some other type, which is physically delimited and is also characterized by having its own specific dynamic and historic functionality to serve a specific and well-determined purpose, which must fulfill the following conditions:

(a) It must arise from and reflect interactive movements of people as well as multi-dimensional, continuous, and reciprocal exchanges of goods, ideas, knowledge and values between peoples, countries, regions or continents over significant periods of time;

(b) It must have thereby promoted a cross-fertilization of the affected cultures in space and time, as reflected both in their tangible and intangible heritage;

(c) It must have integrated into a dynamic system the historic relations and cultural properties associated with its existence.

Defining elements of Cultural Routes:

context, content, cross-cultural significance as a whole, dynamic character, and setting.

1. *Context*: Cultural Routes occur in a natural and /or cultural context upon which they exert an influence and which they help to characterize and enrich with new dimensions as part of an interactive process.

2. *Content*: A Cultural Route must necessarily be supported by tangible elements that bear witness to its cultural heritage and provide a physical confirmation of its existence. Any intangible elements serve to give sense and meaning to the various elements that make up the whole.

1) The indispensable physical element that determines the existence of a Cultural Route is the communication route itself as an instrument serving a project designed or arising through human activity to accomplish specific goals.

2) Other basic substantive elements are the tangible assets related to its functionality as a historic route (staging posts, customs offices, places for storage, rest, and lodging, hospitals, markets, ports, defensive fortifications, bridges, means of communication and transport; industrial, mining or other establishments, as well as those linked to manufacturing and trade, that reflect the technical, scientific and social applications and advances in its various eras; urban centers, cultural landscapes, sacred sites, places of worship and devotion, etc.) as well as intangible heritage elements that bear witness to the process of exchange and dialogue between the peoples involved along its path.

3. *Cross-cultural significance as a whole:* The concept of Cultural Route implies a value as a whole which is greater than the sum of its parts and gives the Route its meaning.

1) The cultural route constitutes a cultural asset enriched by the different cultures it has fertilized and which transcends them in overall value by offering a substantial number of shared characteristics and value systems.

2) Within its overall identity, the value of its parts resides in their common, shared, multi-faceted significance.

3) Its wider scale permits a cultural linking of peoples, countries, regions, and continents.

4) This breadth of scale is important from the point of view of both the territory included and of the comprehensive management of the various heritage elements included in it. At the same time the cultural diversity it implies provides an alternative to a process of cultural homogenization.

4. *Dynamic character:* In addition to presenting physical evidences of its historic path, along with cultural heritage elements, Cultural Routes include a dynamic factor that acts as a conductor or channel through which the reciprocal cultural influences have flowed.

1) The dynamic of a Cultural Route does not obey natural laws or casual phenomena, but rather exclusively human processes and interests, and is therefore understandable only as a cultural phenomenon.

2) This vital fluid of culture is manifested not only in material or tangible aspects, but also in the spirit and traditions making up the intangible heritage of Cultural Routes.

3) By understanding a Cultural Route as a set of dynamic elements of cultural communication between peoples, its cultural heritage assets can be appreciated in their true spatial and historical dimensions, which allows for a comprehensive and sustainable approach to the conservation of the Route as a whole.

5. *Setting*: The cultural route is closely linked to its setting and forms an inseparable part of it.

1) The geographical setting has helped to shape the Cultural Route, either determining its path or influencing its development over time.

2) The territorial setting, whether natural or cultural (urban or rural), provides the framework of the Cultural Route, gives it its particular atmosphere, characterized by elements and values of both physical and intangible nature, and is fundamental for the comprehension, conservation and enjoyment of the route.

3) A Cultural Route connects and interrelates geography and very diverse heritage properties, forming a unified whole. Cultural Routes and their setting are related to their different landscapes, natural or cultural, which are but just one of their components and have their own distinctive characteristics and identity depending on the different areas and regions they pass through in their course. The different landscapes contribute to characterize the diverse sections of the Route as a whole, enriching it with their diversity.

4) The relationship with nature is especially sensitive in some sections, in others it is the relationship with the urban or rural environment, and in the areas with monuments that are isolated from other buildings (such as chapels, monasteries, fountains, bridges, boundary crosses, etc.), it is the relationship of these monuments with their landscape setting which shapes the nature of that section of the Cultural Route.

5) The protection and conservation of the Cultural Routes requires a profound knowledge of the historic, natural and cultural characteristics of their surroundings. Any interventions that may be necessary must fit in with this context and respect its defining features by facilitating their understanding and not distorting the traditional landscape, whether it is natural, cultural or combined.

6) A delineation of the setting must be provided for the Cultural Route, clearly marking the boundaries of a well-defined, regulated buffer zone, which should allow the material and immaterial cultural values included in it to be preserved in their full authenticity and integrity. Such protection must include the values of the different landscapes forming part of the Cultural Route and providing its characteristic atmosphere.

Specific indicators

As basic differentiating indicators applicable to the category of Cultural Route, the following should be considered: the structure of the route and its physical substratum as well as historical data about its use to accomplish a specific goal; any physical structures associated with the concrete purpose and functionality of the Cultural Route; communication elements, and the existence of cultural manifestations of shared origin along (or at given points of) the route such as practices, traditions, customs, and common uses of a religious, ritual, linguistic, festival, culinary, or similar nature; reciprocal influences in music, literature, architecture, fine arts, handicrafts, scientific advances, technical and technological skills, and other material and immaterial cultural assets whose full understanding derives from the historic function of the Cultural Route.

Types of Cultural Routes

Cultural routes can be classified as follows:

• According to their territorial scope: local, national, regional, continental, or intercontinental.

• According to their cultural scope: within a given cultural region or extended across different geographical areas that have shared or continue to share a process of reciprocal influences in the formation or evolution of cultural values.

• According to their goal or function: social, economic, political, or cultural. These characteristics can be found shared across a multi-dimensional context.

• According to their duration in time: those that are no longer used versus those that continue to develop

under the influence of socio-economic, political, and cultural exchanges.
- According to their structural configuration: linear, circular, cruciform, radial or network.
- According to their natural environment: land, aquatic, mixed, or other physical setting.

Identification, Integrity and Authenticity

- *Prima facie indicators*

For identification and assessment purposes, the following aspects may initially be considered as *prima facie*, non-conclusive evidence of the existence of a Cultural Route:

- Expressions of dynamic social, economic, political, and cultural processes which have generated exchanges between different cultural groups of related areas;
- Distinguishing characteristics that are shared by different geographical and cultural areas connected by historical bonds;
- Evidences of mobility and of relationships forged between peoples or ethnic groups of different cultures;
- Specific cultural features rooted in the traditional life of different communities;
- Heritage elements and cultural practices—such as ceremonies, festivals and religious celebrations representative of shared values for different communities within (a) specific cultural and historic area(s)—related to the significance and functionality of the Route.

- *Identification process*

The process for identifying a Cultural Route will necessarily take into account its specific functionality to serve a concrete and well-determined purpose, the tangible and intangible values of its heritage dynamically generated as a results of reciprocal cultural influences, its structural configuration, its whole geographic and historic context, its natural and cultural setting, whether the latter is urban or rural, and its corresponding characteristic environmental values, its relationships to the landscape, its duration in time, and its symbolic and spiritual dimension, all of which will contribute to its identification and to the understanding of its significance.

The intangible assets of a Cultural Route are fundamental for understanding its significance and its associative heritage values. Therefore, material aspects must always be studied in connection with other values of an intangible nature.

For the purpose of its comparative evaluation, the temporal duration and historic significance of the different sections of the Route in relation to the whole should also be taken into account.

In the case of a living Cultural Route, the relationships and dynamic functions associated with the specific and well-determined purpose that gave rise to its existence and serves to define and identify the route should be maintained, even if the historic processes have undergone change over time and new elements have been incorporated. These new elements should be evaluated within the framework of their functional relationship to the Cultural Route, and the case may occur where properties that have heritage values in themselves cannot be considered as components of the Cultural Route because they do not form part of it.

- *Authenticity*

Every Cultural Route should fulfill authenticity criteria demonstrably and credibly expressing its value in terms of both its natural and cultural environment, and concerning both its defining elements and its distinctive features of a material and immaterial nature:

- These criteria should be applied to each section under study to assess its significance in relation to the overall meaning of the Route throughout its historical development, and to verify the authenticity of its structural layout through the vestiges of its path.

• Authenticity should also be evident in the natural and cultural context of each stretch of the Route subject to analysis and assessment, as well as in the other tangible and intangible heritage elements included within its historic functionality and its setting.

• Even if in certain sections the material traces of a Cultural Route are not clearly preserved, its existence in these areas could be shown through historiography, intangible elements and immaterial sources of information that prove their real meaning as integral components of that Route and evidence its authenticity.

• The techniques and methodologies used for the protection, conservation and management of the Cultural Routes, whether traditional or newly implemented, must respect the authenticity criteria.

• *Integrity*

The verification of the integrity of a Cultural Route must necessarily be based on a sufficiently representative set of both tangible and intangible evidences and elements that witness to its global significance and values as a whole and ensure the complete representation of the features and importance of the historic processes which generated the Cultural Route.

Evidences of the historic relationships and dynamic functions essential to the distinctive character of the Cultural Route should be maintained. In addition, regard must be had for whether its physical fabric and/or its significant features are in good condition and the impact of deterioration processes controlled, and whether or not the Route reflects any possible side effects of development, abandonment or neglect.

Methodology

The concept of Cultural Route requires a specific methodology for its research, assessment, protection, preservation, conservation, use and management. Given its breadth and its value as a whole, as well as its territorial dimensions, this methodology requires the establishment of a system of coordinated and integrally managed activities.

It is essential to start with the identification both of the Route as a whole and of its individual sections, along with an inventory of the assets that comprise it and an analysis of their state of conservation which will facilitate the elaboration of a strategic plan for its preservation. This plan should necessarily include measures for raising awareness of the Route and creating interest in it among public and private entities. It also requires the formulation of coordinated measures and specific legal instruments for the protection, use and management of all of its elements as substantive parts of the value and significance of the Route as awhole.

1. Research

The study of cultural routes may extend across different geographical areas, possibly widely separated from each other. It is therefore advisable to set up several research teams located at the main characteristic points of the Route under study.

The research methodology, along with the adoption of practices and the attachment of indicators for proper identification and assessment of the heritage values in the different sections of a Cultural Route, should never lose sight of the meaning of the Route as a whole, in order to avoid any loss in the meaning or historic significance of the route.

Research teams working on this cultural heritage category should be of a multidisciplinary and co-operative nature. Common working criteria should be established based on the principle of starting with an investigation of the parts, but without losing sight of the project as a whole. Similarly, common methodological instruments—standardized in advance—should be used for the collection of data. The project plan should include coordinating mechanisms that will facilitate communication and cooperation among the researchers in order to make it possible to transmit data about the work and achievements of each team.

Researchers should keep in mind that the presence of various types of cultural heritage properties along the path of a Cultural Route does not, in and of itself, imply that they are necessarily integral components of that route or are appropriate objects of study in relation to it. The only elements that should be highlighted in the scientific investigation of a Cultural Route are those related to the specific goal of the Route and any influences arising from its functional dynamic.

2. Funding

Given the scope of the tasks involved in identifying and highlighting the value of a vast Cultural Route, funding should be obtained in stages that will allow for balanced, coordinated progress in the research projects as well as the preservation, use, and management projects related to its various sections. It is advisable to establish a joint estimation of the values to be preserved so as to allow the setting of a scale of priorities for action and the implementation of the corresponding strategies. This requires that funding be obtained through bilateral or multilateral cooperation agreements, as well as through the creation of bodies specifically devoted to researching and highlighting the value of the Route. Along the same lines, regional bodies whose jurisdictions coincide totally or partially with the historic path of a Cultural Route should determine how they can best gain the interest of the States involved and obtain their cooperation. It is also important to attract, if possible, the cooperation of philanthropic institutions and private donors.

3. Protection – Assessment – Preservation / Conservation

Cultural Routes and their setting require new instruments for their assessment, protection, conservation and evaluation. It is not sufficient to guarantee protection of their heritage elements on a partial or random basis. The preparation of rigorous inventories of these elements, as well as an assessment of their authenticity and integrity should take place in order to identify impacts on the values of the Cultural Route and therefore impacts on its significance. It is also necessary to control the impact of deterioration processes, and to develop a strategy to prevent the adverse effects of development and neglect. All of this requires the establishment of a system of coordinated legal measures and appropriate instruments that guarantee that the Route will be preserved, and its value and significance highlighted in a holistic fashion. Understanding heritage values is fundamental prior to any intervention on Cultural Routes that may impact/change their significance.

4. Sustainable Use–Relationship to Tourist Activities

With regard to its use, a Cultural Route can be used to promote an activity of social and economic interest of extraordinary importance for stable development.

Special care should be taken to avoid confusion between the concepts of tourist routes — even including those of cultural interest — and Cultural Routes. However, it should also be recognized that a Cultural Route is a reality that can have great importance for territorial cohesion and sustainable development. From this point of view, efforts should be made to promote knowledge about Cultural Routes, along with their appropriate and sustainable use for tourism purposes, always with the adoption of appropriate measures aimed at eliminating risks. For this purpose, protection and promotion of a Cultural Route should harmoniously integrate a supplementary infrastructure — for tourist activities, access routes, information, interpretation and presentation — with the essential condition that it does not jeopardize the meaning, authenticity and integrity of the historic values of the Cultural Route as key elements to be conveyed to visitors.

Tourist visits should be managed on a rational basis in accordance with prior environmental impact studies and with plans for public use and community participation, as well as control and monitoring measures intended to prevent the negative impacts of tourism.

The development of a Cultural Route for tourism purposes should guarantee in any case that priority is given to the participation of the local community and to local and regional tourist companies. Every effort should be made to prevent the creation of monopolies by large international companies or by powerful companies based in the more developed countries through which the historic path of the Cultural Route passes.

Given the fact that a Cultural Route is an instrument for cooperation and understanding which provides a holistic reading of the encounter of cultures and civilization that form that Route, we should also keep in mind that independently of the relative importance of each one of its parts, the promotion of positive developments in each one, leads to increased interest on the Route and benefits for the other parts.

5. Management

"Understanding of Cultural Routes Significance" becomes the basic/fundamental principle associated to management of cultural routes. This implies ensuring that all activities related to their research, assessment and social dissemination of knowledge about them are carried out in a coordinated and harmonious manner. This also requires a cross coordination that guarantees the combination of policies relating to protection, preservation, conservation, territorial organization, sustainable development, use and tourism. Therefore, joint projects need to be prepared that ensure sustainable development on a national (at the provincial, regional, local level, etc.) and international scale, as well as the establishment of management tools designed to protect the Route against natural disasters and all kinds of risks which could impact on the integrity and authenticity of the Cultural Route and therefore on its significance.

6. Public participation

The protection, conservation/preservation, promotion and management of a Cultural Route calls for the stimulation of public awareness, and the participation of the inhabitants of the areas which share the Route.

International cooperation

There are notable examples of Cultural Routes whose historic paths involve various countries. For this reason, international cooperation is essential for research, assessment, and preservation of the assets that make up international Cultural Routes.

When Cultural Routes exist which involve countries with different degrees of development, it is recommended that the more developed countries provide the means for economic, technical, and logistic cooperation as well as assistance in the exchange of information, experience, and researchers.

It is highly desirable that UNESCO and other international organizations should establish mechanisms of cooperation (financial, technical, and logistic) to help foster and implement projects related to Cultural Routes that are of interest to more than one country.

Cultural Routes should be seen as symbols of union between peoples. The historic ties developed along Cultural Routes can serve to promote projects based on renewed cooperation between peoples who shared certain values and knowledge in the past.

·文化遗产其他文件·

国际文化旅游宪章——遗产地旅游管理原则①

(国际古迹遗址理事会第十二届大会1999年10月在墨西哥通过)

导 言

宪章的精神

从最广泛的程度上来说,自然和文化遗产属于所有人。我们每个人都有权利和责任理解、欣赏和保护其普遍价值。

遗产是一个很宽泛的概念,包括自然和文化的环境。它包括景观、历史遗址、场地和环境,还有生物多样性、收藏、过去和正在进行的文化活动、知识和生活经历。它记录和表达了历史发展的漫长过程,是构成不同国家、地区、民族和当地特征的本质,并且是现代生活的一个必要组成部分。它是生动的社会参照点和发展变化的积极手段。每一社区或场所特别的遗产和集体的记忆是不可取代的,是现在和将来发展的一个重要基础。

在全球化进程日益加剧的时代,对文化遗产和任何一个特殊地区或场所的文化多样性进行保护、讲解和展示,对任何地方的人来说,都是一个重要的挑战。但是,在国际认可的框架内和恰当地使用标准下管理遗产通常是特别社区或监护团体的责任。

管理文化遗产的一个主要目标是使文化遗产的重要性和保护它的必要性在东道主社区和旅游者中广为传播。合理妥善管理有形的、知识的或感情的通往文化遗产和文化发展的通道是权利也是荣幸。它带来对遗产价值、今天遗产所在社区的利益和公正待遇、历史财产的原住民监护方或拥有者以及诞生遗产的景观和文化进行尊重的义务。

旅游和文化遗产之间的作用

国内和国际旅游继续作为文化交流最重要的工具之一,也提供了历经沧桑的人生经历和不同社会当代生活的体验。它正日益成为自然和文化保护的积极力量。旅游可以为文化遗产创造经济利益,并通过

---

① 引自:联合国教科文组织世界遗产中心,国际古迹遗址理事会,国际文物保护与修复研究中心,中国国家文物局主编. 国际文化遗产保护文件选编[M]. 北京:文物出版社,2007. 编者根据英文原文对标题稍作修改。

创造资金、教育社区和影响政策来实现以保护为目的的管理。它是许多国家和地区经济的主要部分，如果成功管理，可以成为发展中的一个重要因素。

旅游本身已经成为一个日益复杂的现象，纵横政治、经济、生物、物理、生态和美学的各个领域。旅游者的期望和东道主社区的期望之间可能会产生冲突，要实现两者之间有价值的相互影响，面临许多挑战，也会产生许多机遇。

自然和文化遗产、多样性和生活文化是主要的旅游吸引力。过度的或没有妥善管理的旅游和与旅游相关的发展可以威胁到它们的有形本质、真实性和重要特征。东道主社区的生态、文化和生活方式以及旅游者在其地的经历也可能被降格。

旅游应该为东道主社区带来经济效益，为他们提供一个重要的途径和动力，来重视保护他们的遗产和文化活动。当地原住民社区代表、古迹保护积极分子、旅游业经营者、资产主人、制定政策方、国家发展计划制定者和场地管理者之间的合作非常必要，以实现可持续发展的旅游业，为子孙后代促进遗产资源的保护。

ICOMOS，即国际古迹遗址理事会，作为此宪章的起草者，和其他国际组织以及旅游业一起，将全力以赴投身挑战。

宪章的目标

国际文化旅游宪章的目标是：

促进和鼓励参与文化遗产保护和管理的工作，使这些遗产的重要性为东道主社区和旅游者充分理解。

促进和鼓励旅游业，以尊重和改善文化遗产及东道主社区生活文化的方式来推广和管理旅游业。

促进和鼓励保护文物各方和旅游业之间的对话，讨论遗迹场所、收藏和生活文化的重要性和脆弱的本质，包括将来它们可持续发展的需要。

鼓励计划和政策的制定者在保护和修缮文物的宗旨下发展具体的可衡量的有关文物场所和文化活动展示和揭示的目标和策略。

另外，宪章支持国际古迹遗址理事会、其他国际组织和旅游业更广泛的积极努力，来维护遗产管理和保护的完整性。

宪章鼓励所有相关的或时有冲突的利益、责任和义务各方来参与实现这些目标。

宪章鼓励感兴趣的各方制定具体的指南，促进原则在特殊场合的实施，或满足特殊组织和社区的要求。

宪章的原则

原则一：鼓励公众意识

由于国内和国际旅游是文化交流最重要的途径之一，对话应该为东道主社区成员和旅游者提供负责任的和管理良好的机会，使他们可以通过第一手经历来了解社区的遗产和文化。

1.1 自然和文化遗产是一个物质和精神的资源，提供了对历史发展的叙述。它在现代生活中是一个重要的角色，并应该在有形的、知识的或感情的各方面向公众开放。我们应该建立保护这些遗产的计划，方便东道主社区和游客以平等和可承担的方式，去理解和领略遗产的重要性。这些计划应宣传保护这些遗产有形的品质、无形的方面、当代文化表现和广泛的应用环境。

1.2 自然和文化遗产的各个方面有不同程度的重要性，有一些具有普遍价值，其他的一些在国家、地区或地方层面有价值。阐释计划应该将重要性以一种相关和可及的方法，通过适当的、启发性的当代教育形式、媒体、科技和个人对历史、环境和文化信息的解释，向东道主社区和旅游者展现。

1.3 阐释和演示的计划应该促进和鼓励高度的公众意识,支持自然和文化遗产长期生存的必要条件。

1.4 阐释的计划应该在过去的经历和现在该地区和东道主社区的多样性中展现古迹、传统和文化活动的重要性,包括一些少数民族的文化或语言群体。我们应该始终告知游客不同的文化价值,这些文化价值可以被归类为某种特殊的遗产资源。

原则二:管理动态的关系

古迹遗址和旅游业之间的关系是瞬息万变的,随时可能包含有冲突的价值。我们应该以一种可持续发展的方式来理顺这些关系,为我们也为后人造福。

2.1 具有文化遗产重要性的处所,作为一个文化多样化和社会发展的重要基础,其存在对所有人都有一个内在的价值。对生活文化、历史遗迹、收藏、它们形态和生态的完整及其环境背景的长期保护和修缮,应该是社会、经济、政治、法律、文化和旅游发展政策的一个重要组成部分。

2.2 文化遗产资源或价值和旅游业之间的交流是充满活力和瞬息万变的,机会和挑战同时产生,还有潜在的冲突。旅游项目、活动和发展应该实现积极的结果,最大限度减少对遗产和东道主社区生活方式的不良影响,同时响应旅游者的需要和期望。

2.3 计划应该建立在对细致的、但通常也是复杂或互相冲突的遗产各个方面的综合理解上。持续的研究和咨询对深入理解和领略文化遗产的重要性是重要的。

2.4 保留历史遗迹和收藏的真实性是重要的。它是体现文化意义的一个重要元素,其真实性可以通过有形的物质、记忆和从过去一直流传下来的无形传统来表现。宣传计划应该体现和解释场所和文化经历的真实性,提高对文化遗产的欣赏和理解程度。

2.5 旅游发展和基建项目应该考虑到美学、社会和文化各方面、自然和文化的景观、生态多样性的特征和遗产场所更广泛的视觉背景。应该优先考虑使用当地材料,考虑当地的建筑风格或当地语言传统。

2.6 在古迹场所被推广或发展来满足日益增长的旅游需要之前,管理计划应该评估资源的自然和文化价值。它们应该为可接受的变化确立恰当的限度,特别是和访问人数对其有形特征、完整性、生态多样性、当地交通系统和社区的社会、经济和文化稳定发展的影响有关的方面。如果变化的可能程度是不可接受的,发展计划应该予以改进。

2.7 应该有持续的计划来评估旅游活动和发展对特别场所或社区循序渐进的影响。

原则三:确保带给游客一段有价值的经历

古迹保护和旅游规划应该确保带给游客一段有价值的、满意的和愉悦的经历。

3.1 古迹保护和旅游的计划应该提供游客高质量的信息,以确保游客最清楚地了解遗产的重要特征和保护其需要,使他们能够以恰当的方式享受在当地的旅游。

3.2 旅游者应该能够以他们自己希望的速度和方式游览古迹遗址。可能需要安排特殊的交通路线来尽量减少对估计的完整性、实际构造、自然和文化特点的影响。

3.3 尊重有精神意义的古迹、活动和传统的神圣性对古迹管理者、旅游者、政策制定者、规划者和旅游活动经营者来说是一个需要重点考虑的方面。应该鼓励游客成为受当地欢迎的游客,并尊重东道主社区的价值和生活方式,抵制任何潜在的对文化财产的盗窃或非法交易,这样可以使其在下一次访问时仍然受到欢迎。

3.4 旅游活动的规划应该在不破坏古迹的显著特征或生态特点的基础上,提供恰当的设施,可以保障游客的舒适和安全,并提高旅游的享受程度。

原则四:让东道主和原住民社区一起参与

东道主社区和原住民应该参与到保护古迹和旅游的规划中。

4.1 旅游区的地方权利和利益、古迹财产拥有者和相关的、对土地和重要遗址拥有权利和义务的原住民，应该得到尊重。在旅游背景下，他们应该参与到为遗产资源、文化活动和当代文化表达制定目标、策略、政策和条约的工作中。

4.2 任何特殊场所或地区的古迹可以有个通用的范围界限，应该尊重一些社区或原住民要限制或管理通向一些文化活动、知识、信仰、活动、人造物或场所的通道的需要和愿望。

原则五：为东道主社区提供利益

旅游和保护活动应该使东道主社区受益。

5.1 政策制定者应该推广在国家或地区公正分配旅游业利润的方法，提高社会经济发展的水平，并为减少贫困作贡献。

5.2 通过教育、培训和创立全职就业机会，古迹保护管理和旅游活动应该为东道主或当地社区各个层次提供公正的经济、社会和文化利益。

5.3 从旅游计划中获得收入的一大部分应该被用于古迹场所的保护、修缮和展示工作，包括它们的自然和文化环境。可能的话，应该告知游客这些收入的分配情况。

5.4 旅游计划应该鼓励培训和雇佣来自东道主社区的导游和古迹地址讲解员，来提高当地人们展示和解释其文化价值的技巧。

5.5 在东道主社区中展开文化遗产的阐释和教育计划应该鼓励当地的讲解员积极参与。计划应该鼓励对文化遗产的了解和尊重，鼓励当地人们对保护文化遗产产生直接的兴趣。

5.6 维护管理和旅游计划应该包括为政策制定者、规划师、研究者、设计者、建筑师、讲解员、维护者和旅游经营者提供教育和就业机会。我们应该鼓励参与者主动地理解相关事宜、机遇，并帮助解决一些同时遭遇到的问题。

原则六：负责任的推广计划

旅游推广计划应该保护和改善自然和文化遗产的特征。

6.1 旅游推广计划应该创造现实的期望，负责任地告知游客关于东道主社区内特定的文化遗产的特点，鼓励他们做出恰当的举动。

6.2 重要的古迹和收藏应该以保护其真实性和改善旅游者经历的方法来推广和管理，可以通过尽量减少到达旅游点游客量的波动和避免同一时刻过多游客的到访来提高旅游质量。

6.3 旅游推广计划应该提供更广泛的利益分配，减轻一些热点旅游场所的压力，鼓励游客感受更多方面的当地文化和自然遗产。

6.4 当地手工艺品和其他产品的推广、分配和销售应该为东道主社区提供一个合理的社会和经济效益，同时确保其文化的完整性不被破坏。

International Cultural Tourism Charter: Managing Tourism at Places of Heritage Significance

Adopted by the 12th ICOMOS General Assembly, Mexico, October 1999

INTRODUCTION

The Charter Ethos

At the broadest level, the natural and cultural heritage belongs to all people. We each have a right and responsibility to understand, appreciate and conserve its universal values.

Heritage is a broad concept and includes the natural as well as the cultural environment. It encompasses landscapes, historic places, sites and built environments, as well as bio-diversity, collections, past and continuing cultural practices, knowledge and living experiences. It records and expresses the long processes of historic development, forming the essence of diverse national, regional, indigenous and local identities and is an integral part of modern life. It is a dynamic reference point and positive instrument for growth and change. The particular heritage and collective memory of each locality or community is irreplaceable and an important foundation for development, both now and into the future.

At a time of increasing globalisation, the protection, conservation, interpretation and presentation of the heritage and cultural diversity of any particular place or region is an important challenge for people everywhere. However, management of that heritage, within a framework of internationally recognised and appropriately applied standards, is usually the responsibility of the particular community or custodian group.

A primary objective for managing heritage is to communicate its significance and need for its conservation to its host community and to visitors. Reasonable and well managed physical, intellectual and/or emotive access to heritage and cultural development is both a right and a privilege. It brings with it a duty of respect for the heritage values, interests and equity of the present-day host community, indigenous custodians or owners of historic property and for the landscapes and cultures from which that heritage evolved.

The Dynamic Interaction between Tourism and Cultural Heritage

Domestic and international tourism continues to be among the foremost vehicles for cultural exchange, providing a personal experience, not only of that which has survived from the past, but of the contemporary life and society of others. It is increasingly appreciated as a positive force for natural and cultural conservation. Tourism can capture the economic characteristics of the heritage and harness these for conservation by generating funding, educating the community and influencing policy. It is an essential part of many national and regional economies and can be an important factor in development, when managed successfully.

Tourism itself has become an increasingly complex phenomenon, with political, economic, social, cultural, educational, bio-physical, ecological and aesthetic dimensions. The achievement of a beneficial inter-action between the potentially conflicting expectations and aspirations of visitors and host or local communities, presents many challenges and opportunities.

The natural and cultural heritage, diversities and living cultures are major tourism attractions. Excessive or poorly-managed tourism and tourism related development can threaten their physical nature, integrity and significant characteristics. The ecological setting, culture and lifestyles of host communities may also be degraded, along with the visitor's experience of the place.

Tourism should bring benefits to host communities and provide an important means and motivation for them to care for and maintain their heritage and cultural practices. The involvement and co-operation of local and/or indigenous community representatives, conservationists, tourism operators, property owners, policy makers, those preparing national development plans and site managers is necessary to achieve a sustainable tourism industry and enhance the protection of heritage resources for future generations.

ICOMOS, the International Council on Monuments and Sites, as the author of this Charter, other international organisations and the tourism industry, are dedicated to this challenge.

Objectives of the Charter

The Objectives of the International Cultural Tourism Charter are:

• To facilitate and encourage those involved with heritage conservation and management to make the significance of that heritage accessible to the host community and visitors.

• To facilitate and encourage the tourism industry to promote and manage tourism in ways that respect and enhance the heritage and living cultures of host communities.

• To facilitate and encourage a dialogue between conservation interests and the tourism industry about the importance and fragile nature of heritage places, collections and living cultures, including the need to achieve a sustainable future for them.

• To encourage those formulating plans and policies to develop detailed, measurable goals and strategies relating to the presentation and interpretation of heritage places and cultural activities, in the context of their preservation and conservation.

In addition,

• The Charter supports wider initiatives by ICOMOS, other international bodies and the tourism industry in maintaining the integrity of heritage management and conservation.

• The Charter encourages the involvement of all those with relevant or at times conflicting interests, responsibilities and obligations to join in achieving its objectives.

• The Charter encourages the formulation of detailed guidelines by interested parties, facilitating the implementation of the Principles to their specific circumstances or the requirements of particular organisations and communities.

PRINCIPLES OF THE CULTURAL TOURISM CHARTER

Principle 1
Since domestic and international tourism is among the foremost vehicles for cultural exchange, conservation should provide responsible and well managed opportunities for members of the host community and visitors to experience and understand that community's heritage and culture at first hand.

    1.1 The natural and cultural heritage is a material and spiritual resource, providing a narrative of historical development. It has an important role in modern life and should be made physically, intellectually and/or emotively accessible to the general public. Programmes for the protection and conservation of the physical attributes, intangible aspects, contemporary cultural expressions and broad context, should facilitate an understanding and appreciation of the heritage significance by the host community and the visitor, in an equitable and affordable manner.

    1.2 Individual aspects of natural and cultural heritage have differing levels of significance, some with universal values, others of national, regional or local importance. Interpretation programmes should present that significance in a relevant and accessible manner to the host community and the visitor, with appropriate, stimulating and contemporary forms of education, media, technology and personal explanation of historical, environmental and cultural information.

    1.3 Interpretation and presentation programmes should facilitate and encourage the high level of public awareness and support necessary for the long term survival of the natural and cultural heritage.

    1.4 Interpretation programmes should present the significance of heritage places, traditions and cultural practices within the past experience and present diversities of the area and the host community, including that of minority cultural or linguistic groups. The visitor should always be informed of the differing cultural values that may be ascribed to a particular heritage resource.

Principle 2
The relationship between Heritage Places and Tourism is dynamic and may involve conflicting values. It should be managed in a sustainable way for present and future generations.

    2.1 Places of heritage significance have an intrinsic value for all people as an important basis for cultural diversity and social development. The long term protection and conservation of living cultures, heritage places, collections, their physical and ecological integrity and their environmental context, should be an essential component of social, economic, political, legislative, cultural and tourism development policies.

    2.2 The interaction between heritage resources or values and tourism is dynamic and ever changing, generating both opportunities and challenges, as well as potential conflicts. Tourism projects, activities and developments should achieve positive outcomes and minimise adverse impacts on the heritage and lifestyles of the host community, while responding to the needs and aspirations of the visitor.

    2.3 Conservation, interpretation and tourism development programmes should be based on a comprehensive understanding of the specific, but often complex or conflicting aspects of heritage significance of the particular place. Continuing research and consultation are important to furthering the evolving understanding and appreciation of that significance.

    2.4 The retention of the authenticity of heritage places and collections is important. It is an essential element of their cultural significance, as expressed in the physical material, collected memory and intangible traditions that remain from the past. Programmes should present and interpret the authenticity of places and cultural experiences to enhance the appreciation and understanding of that cultural heritage.

2.5 Tourism development and infrastructure projects should take account of the aesthetic, social and cultural dimensions, natural and cultural landscapes, bio-diversity characteristics and the broader visual context of heritage places. Preference should be given to using local materials and take account of local architectural styles or vernacular traditions.

2.6 Before heritage places are promoted or developed for increased tourism, management plans should assess the natural and cultural values of the resource. They should then establish appropriate limits of acceptable change, particularly in relation to the impact of visitor numbers on the physical characteristics, integrity, ecology and biodiversity of the place, local access and transportation systems and the social, economic and cultural well-being of the host community. If the likely level of change is unacceptable the development proposal should be modified.

2.7 There should be on-going programmes of evaluation to assess the progressive impacts of tourism activities and development on the particular place or community.

Principle 3

Conservation and Tourism Planning for Heritage Places should ensure that the Visitor Experience will be worthwhile, satisfying and enjoyable.

3.1 Conservation and tourism programmes should present high quality information to optimise the visitor's understanding of the significant heritage characteristics and of the need for their protection, enabling the visitor to enjoy the place in an appropriate manner.

3.2 Visitors should be able to experience the heritage place at their own pace, if they so choose. Specific circulation routes may be necessary to minimise impacts on the integrity and physical fabric of a place, its natural and cultural characteristics.

3.3 Respect for the sanctity of spiritual places, practices and traditions is an important consideration for site managers, visitors, policy makers, planners and tourism operators. Visitors should be encouraged to behave as welcomed guests, respecting the values and lifestyles of the host community, rejecting possible theft or illicit trade in cultural property and conducting themselves in a responsible manner which would generate a renewed welcome, should they return.

3.4 Planning for tourism activities should provide appropriate facilities for the comfort, safety and well-being of the visitor, that enhance the enjoyment of the visit but do not adversely impact on the significant features or ecological characteristics.

Principle 4

Host communities and indigenous peoples should be involved in planning for conservation and tourism.

4.1 The rights and interests of the host community, at regional and local levels, property owners and relevant indigenous peoples who may exercise traditional rights or responsibilities over their own land and its significant sites, should be respected. They should be involved in establishing goals, strategies, policies and protocols for the identification, conservation, management, presentation and interpretation of their heritage resources, cultural practices and contemporary cultural expressions, in the tourism context.

4.2 While the heritage of any specific place or region may have a universal dimension, the needs and wishes of some communities or indigenous peoples to restrict or manage physical, spiritual or intellectual access to certain cultural practices, knowledge, beliefs, activities, artefacts or sites should be respected.

Principle 5

Tourism and conservation activities should benefit the host community.

5.1   Policy makers should promote measures for the equitable distribution of the benefits of tourism to be shared across countries or regions, improving the levels of socio-economic development and contributing where necessary to poverty alleviation.

5.2   Conservation management and tourism activities should provide equitable economic, social and cultural benefits to the men and women of the host or local community, at all levels, through education, training and the creation of full-time employment opportunities.

5.3   A significant proportion of the revenue specifically derived from tourism programmes to heritage places should be allotted to the protection, conservation and presentation of those places, including their natural and cultural contexts. Where possible, visitors should be advised of this revenue allocation.

5.4   Tourism programmes should encourage the training and employment of guides and site interpreters from the host community to enhance the skills of local people in the presentation and interpretation of their cultural values.

5.5   Heritage interpretation and education programmes among the people of the host community should encourage the involvement of local site interpreters. The programmes should promote a knowledge and respect for their heritage, encouraging the local people to take a direct interest in its care and conservation.

5.6   Conservation management and tourism programmes should include education and training opportunities for policy makers, planners, researchers, designers, architects, interpreters, conservators and tourism operators. Participants should be encouraged to understand and help resolve the at times conflicting issues, opportunities and problems encountered by their colleagues.

Principle 6

Tourism promotion programmes should protect and enhance Natural and Cultural Heritage characteristics.

6.1   Tourism promotion programmes should create realistic expectations and responsibly inform potential visitors of the specific heritage characteristics of a place or host community, thereby encouraging them to behave appropriately.

6.2   Places and collections of heritage significance should be promoted and managed in ways which protect their authenticity and enhance the visitor experience by minimising fluctuations in arrivals and avoiding excessive numbers of visitors at any one time.

6.3   Tourism promotion programmes should provide a wider distribution of benefits and relieve the pressures on more popular places by encouraging visitors to experience the wider cultural and natural heritage characteristics of the region or locality.

6.4   The promotion, distribution and sale of local crafts and other products should provide a reasonable social and economic return to the host community, while ensuring that their cultural integrity is not degraded.

壁画保护、修复和保存原则[①]

(国际古迹遗址理事会第十四届大会2003年在津巴布韦维多利亚瀑布市通过)

导言与定义

从最开始的岩画等形式发展到今天的壁画,壁画已成为贯穿历史的人类创造的文化表现形式。它们的变质、无意或有意破坏成为世界文化遗产中重要部分的损失。《威尼斯宪章》(1964)为文化遗产的保护修复提供了总原则。介绍综合保护理念的《阿姆斯特丹宣言》(1975)和处理文化多样性问题的《奈良真实性文件》(1994)都扩充了这些原则。考虑到这些和其他相关贡献,例如《国际博物馆协会保存维护委员会道德原则》(1984)、《帕维亚文件》(1997)和《欧洲保护师与修复师组织联合会专业指南》(1997)等,本文件的目的是为了提供壁画保护、保存和保护修复的详细原则。因此,本文件反映了基本的和普遍适用的原则和实践,并未考虑某个地区或国家的特殊问题,可在必要时针地区或国家补充提供进一步建议。

壁画的丰富性建立在文化表现和美学成就多样性,以及从古至今所使用的材料和技术的多样性基础上。以下条例是关于在无机支撑体上创作的壁画,例如石膏砖、黏土和石头;不包括有机支撑体上创作的壁画,例如木头、纸张和帆布。很多历史建筑的合成材料是在本文件之外需要特殊考虑的。具有历史、美学和技术价值的建筑表面及其最后完工的表层必须作为历史古迹中相当重要的部分加以考虑。

壁画是古迹遗址的一个主要部分,应进行原址保存。影响壁画的很多问题都与建筑或构件的恶劣环境、不恰当使用、缺乏维护、频繁修补和更改有关。另外,频繁修补、不必要的暴露,以及不适当的方法和材料的使用都会造成不可挽回的伤害。不合规格和不适当的实践工作和专业资质已经导致了令人遗憾的结果。因此,有必要制定一份关于正确保护修复壁画原则的文件。

第一条 保护方针

保护文化和宗教壁画的一个必要途径是列出包括壁画在内的古迹遗址的详细清单,即便它们已模糊不清。文化遗产保护法规必须禁止壁画及其环境的破坏、退化或更改。立法不应仅为壁画保护作准备,而且还为研究、专业处理和监测提供可用资源,并为社会对其有形和无形价值的肯定作准备。

如果需要干预,应在具备全面知识和相关机构同意的条件下进行干预行动。任何违反此类规定的行为应受到法律制裁。法律规定也应考虑到新发现及其未确定正式保护方案的保存。影响壁画的地区、城市或建筑发展项目,例如道路和水坝建设、建筑物改建等,如果没有初始影响评估研究和为其安全提供补救措施,则不应开展。

在不违背真实性的条件下,必须在不同机构的合作中做出特别努力,以适应并尊重宗教壁画的祭礼功能。

第二条 调查

所有保护项目应从实质性的学术调查开始。调查的目的是为了尽可能多地找出结构构造及其历史、

[①] 引自:联合国教科文组织世界遗产中心,国际古迹遗址理事会,国际文物保护与修复研究中心,中国国家文物局主编.国际文化遗产保护文件选编[M].北京:文物出版社,2007.

美学和技术叠加层。这应该包含壁画的所有物质和非物质价值，包括历史变更、添加物和修复。这就是所谓的多学科交叉方法。

调查方法应尽可能是非破坏的。应特别考虑可能隐藏在石灰水、漆层和石膏等等之下的壁画。任何保护计划的先决条件都是对宏观和微观范围内的腐朽机理、材料分析和环境诊断进行的科学调查。

第三条　文档

同意《威尼斯宪章》，壁画的保护修复必须附有以分析评论报告形式做出的精确计划文件，同时配有素描、摹本、照片和地图等插图。壁画的环境、关于制作过程的技术特点及其历史都必须记录下来。此外，保护修复的每一阶段，所采用的材料和方法也应备有文件。该报告应存放于公共机构的档案室，并使其对感兴趣的公众有用。此类文档的副本也应在原址存放，或由对古迹负责的机构所持有。同时建议出版工作结果。根据这样的调查、诊断和处理，该文档应考虑到区域定义单元。手写和绘图文档的传统方法可由数字方法进行补充。但是，如果不考虑技术，记录的永久性和文档在将来的有效性都是极其重要的。

第四条　预防性保护、维护和遗址管理

预防性保护的目的是为了创造使朽坏最小化的有利条件，并避免不必要的补救措施，从而延长壁画的寿命。环境的适当监测和控制都是预防性保护的主要部分。不适当的气候条件和湿度可导致变质和生物破坏。监测可探查出壁画或支撑结构朽坏的初始过程，从而阻止进一步损害。变形和结构性破坏甚至可能导致的支撑结构崩塌可在早期得以识别。建筑或构件的定期维护是壁画安全的最好保证。

有壁画的古迹遗址的不恰当或不可控制的公共事业会导致损害。这种情况下有必要限制游客，并在某些时候暂时关闭向公众开放的渠道。但是，如果能让游客体验和欣赏作为文化遗产一部分的壁画则更好。因此，将遗迹管理规划中的开放和使用、保存，以及古迹遗址的有形和无形价值结合起来很重要。

由于各种社会、意识形态和经济原因，很多壁画经常处于被隔离的环境中，成为故意破坏和偷窃行为的牺牲品。在这种情况下，相关机构应采取特别的预防措施。

第五条　保护——修复处理

壁画是建筑或构件的一个主要部分。因此，其保护应和建筑实体及其环境结构结合起来考虑。

任何对古迹的干预必须考虑壁画的特性及其保存期。所有干预，例如加固、清洗和拼合，应在必须的情况下，在最小的范围内进行，从而避免降低材料和画面的真实性。只要可能，应对能证明壁画历史的地层学样品在原址上加以保存保护。自然老化是时间流逝的迹象，对此应加以重视。如果对其进行移动有伤害性的话，不可逆的化学和物理变化应被保存下来。之前进行的修复、添加物和覆盖绘画层都是壁画历史的一部分。应将其视为历史表现的证据并进行评价。在壁画保护修复中使用的方法和材料应考虑到将来处理的可能性。新材料和方法的使用必须基于全面的科学数据和实验室及遗址现场测试的积极结果。但是，必须记住用于壁画的新材料和方法的长期有效性是未知的，也可能是有害的。因此，如果壁画成分和周围结构相一致，应该鼓励使用传统材料。

当说到原始创造和历史时，修复的目的是为了进一步理解壁画的形式和内容。美学式重新拼合可减小危害的可见性，应开始就在非原始材料上进行。润饰和修补应以能区别于原始状态的方式进行，所有添加物应易于去除，必须避免重绘。壁画的未覆盖部分要求考虑到历史状态和可能丢失的东西的评估。该操作应仅在环境、尺寸和价值初步调查后才能执行，并考虑如果没有造成损害则什么时候可能进行。最近未覆盖的画面不应暴露在不利的环境中。在一些情况下，有图饰的壁画或彩色建筑表面的修补是保护修复项目的一部分。这使得真正的碎片保护成为必需，并使其全部或部分覆盖保护层成为必要。一个备有充分文件并可执行的专业性修补使用传统材料和技术可证明表面和内部的历史面貌。

保护修复项目的正确方向应在所有阶段都得以维持，并得到相关机构的认可。这要求项目的独立监督受保于对结果没有商业兴趣的有能力的机构或组织。与管理决定相应的工作必须为指定性的，并且必须由具备相应知识和技能的专业人员来执行。

第六条 紧急措施

在紧急情况下,即时紧急处理对保护壁画来说是必要的。使用的材料和技术必须允许进行稍后的处理。适当的保护措施必须尽快在相关机构的许可下进行。

拆分和转移是危险的、激烈的和不可逆的操作,会极大地影响壁画的物理成分、材料结构和美学特点。因此,这些操作只有在所有原址处理选择都不可行的极端情况下才能进行。如果将发生此类情况,包括拆分和转移在内的决定应始终由专业人员团队来作出,而不是开展保护工作的个人来作出。如果可能的话,被拆分的壁画应放置在其原始位置。

应采取特别措施来保护和维护被拆分的壁画,预防偷窃和散落。

隐藏图饰的覆盖层的应用应在预防暴露在不安全环境里造成伤害和损坏的打算中进行,应在材料与壁画相容,允许将来不覆盖的情况下执行。

第七条 研究和公众信息

壁画保护修复领域研究项目的确定是持续保护政策的本质要求。建立在研究基础上,有可能对恶化过程有更多了解的调查应得以鼓励。可扩大我们知识面的原始绘画技术,以及过去修复工作的材料和方法研究在适当保护项目的执行中是必要的。该研究也涉及艺术和科学的相关学科。对重要结构进行研究或取样都应最小化。

知识的传播是研究的重要特征,应在专业级和普通级上进行。公众信息可充分增强壁画保护需要的意识,即使保护修复工作可造成暂时的不便。

第八条 专业资质和培训

壁画保护修复在遗产保护领域是一个专门学科。因为这项工作要求有特殊的知识、技能、经验和职责,此类文化财产的保护修复师应受过专业化教育和培训,应由国际博物馆协会保存维护委员会的道德原则(1984)和欧洲保护师和修复师联合会(E.C.C.O.)和欧洲保护修复教育网(ENCoRE)联合推荐。

第九条 更新的传统

在世界上的很多地区,画家和工匠的真实绘画工作是由采用传统材料和技术的反复的历史装饰和肖像绘画活动延续着的。这些满足宗教文化要求并符合奈良原则的传统应被延续下来。然而,尽管保护这些特殊知识如此重要,但这并不意味着保护修复壁画的处理会由工匠或画家进行。

第十条 国际合作

共同关注遗产一个可接受的全国性和国际性观念。因此,有必要鼓励知识交流和传播各种信息。在多学科合作的精神指导下,壁面保护修复师需要和其他国家的同伴以及全世界的相关机构和专家保持联络。

ICOMOS Principles for the Preservation and Conservation-Restoration of Wall Paintings

Ratified by the 14th ICOMOS General Assembly, Victoria Falls, Zimbabwe, 2003

Introduction and Definition

Wall paintings have been cultural expressions of human creation throughout history, from the earliest beginnings, such as rock art, extending up to present day murals. Their deterioration, accidental or intentional destruction constitutes a loss affecting a significant part of the world's cultural heritage. The Venice Charter (1964) has provided general principles for the conservation-restoration of cultural heritage. The Amsterdam Declaration (1975) introducing the concept of integrated conservation, and the Nara Document on Authenticity (1994) dealing with cultural diversity, have expanded these principles. Taking into account these and additional relevant contributions, such as the ICOM-CC Code of Ethics (1984), Document of Pavia (1997), and E.C.C.O. Professional Guidelines (1997), the aim of this document is to provide more specific principles for the protection, preservation and the conservation-restoration of wall paintings. This document, therefore, reflects basic and universally applicable principles and practices, and does not take into account particular problems of regions or countries, which can be supplemented at regional and national level by providing further recommendations where necessary.

The richness of wall paintings is founded on the variety of cultural expressions, aesthetic achievements, and the diversity of materials and techniques used from ancient until present times. The following articles refer to paintings created on inorganic supports, such as plaster, brick, clay and stone, and do not include paintings executed on organic supports, such as wood, paper and canvas. Composite materials in many historic buildings need special consideration outside the scope of this document. Architectural surfaces and their finishing layers, with their historical, aesthetic and technical values have to be considered as equally important components of historic monuments.

Wall paintings are an integral part of monuments and sites and should be preserved in situ. Many of the problems affecting wall paintings are linked to the poor condition of the building or structure, its improper use, lack of maintenance, frequent repairs and alterations. Also, frequent restorations, unnecessary uncovering, and use of inappropriate methods and materials can result in irreparable damage. Substandard and inadequate practices and professional qualifications have led to unfortunate results. It is for this reason that an appropriate document covering the principles of proper conservation-restoration of wall paintings is necessary.

Article 1: Protection Policy

A necessary approach to the protection of wall paintings of every culture and religion is to list and make inventories of monuments and sites including wall paintings, even in cases when they are not presently visible. Laws and regulations for the protection of cultural heritage must prohibit the destruction, the degradation or alteration of wall paintings, including their surroundings. Legislation should not only provide for the protection of wall paintings, but also make available resources for research, professional treatment and monitoring, and provide for the appreciation of their tangible and intangible values by society.

If interventions are required, these should be carried out with the full knowledge and the consent of the authorities responsible. Legal sanctions should be provided for any violation of such regulations. Legal provisions should also consider new discoveries and their preservation pending formal protection. Regional, urban or architectural development projects, such as the construction of roads, dams, conversion of buildings, etc. affecting wall paintings should not be carried out without an initial impact assessment study and without providing appropriate remedies for their safeguard.

Special efforts must be made through the co-operation of various authorities to accommodate and respect the cult function of religious paintings without compromising their authenticity.

Article 2: Investigation

All conservation projects should begin with substantial scholarly investigations. The aim of such investigations is to find out as much as possible about the fabric of the structure and its superimposed layers with their historical, aesthetic and technical dimensions. This should encompass all material and incorporeal values of the painting, including historic alterations, additions and restorations. This calls for an interdisciplinary approach.

The methods of investigation should be as far as possible non-destructive. Special consideration should be given to wall paintings that may be hidden under whitewash, paint layers, plaster, etc. Prerequisites for any conservation program are the scientific investigation of decay mechanisms on macro and micro scale, the material analysis and the diagnosis of the condition.

Article 3: Documentation

In agreement with the Venice Charter, the conservation-restoration of wall paintings must be accompanied by a precise program of documentation in the form of an analytical and critical report, illustrated with drawings, copies, photographs, mapping, etc. The condition of the paintings, the technical and formal features pertaining to the process of the creation and the history of the object must be recorded. Furthermore, every stage of the conservation-restoration, materials and methodology used should be documented. This report should be placed in the archives of a public institution and made available to the interested public. Copies of such documentation should also be kept in situ, or in the possession of those responsible for the monument. It is also recommended that the results of the work should be published. This documentation should consider definable units of area in terms of such investigations, diagnosis and treatment. Traditional methods of written and graphic documentation can be supplemented by digital methods. However, regardless of the technique, the permanence of the records and the future availability of the documentation is of utmost importance.

Article 4: Preventive Conservation, Maintenance and Site Management

The aim of preventive conservation is to create favourable conditions minimising decay, and to avoid unnecessary remedial treatments, thus prolonging the life span of wall paintings. Appropriate monitoring and the control of the environment are both essential components of preventive conservation. Inappropriate climatic conditions and moisture problems can cause deterioration and biological attacks. Monitoring can detect initial processes of decay of the painting or the supporting structure, thus preventing further damage. Deformation and structural failure leading even to possible collapse of the supporting structure, can be recognised at an early stage. Regular maintenance of the building or the structure is the best guarantee for the safeguard of the wall paintings.

Inappropriate or uncontrolled public uses of monuments and sites with wall paintings can lead to their damage. This may necessitate the limitation of visitors and, in certain cases, involve temporary closure to public access. However, it is preferable that the public should have the opportunity to experience and appreciate wall paintings as being part of the common cultural heritage. It is, therefore, important to incorporate into the site management careful planning of access and use, preserving, as far as possible, the authentic tangible and intangible values of the monuments and sites.

Due to various sociological, ideological and economic reasons many wall paintings, often situated in isolated locations, become the victims of vandalism and theft. In these cases, the responsible authorities should take special preventive measures.

Article 5: Conservation-Restoration Treatments

Wall paintings are an integral part of the building or structure. Therefore, their conservation should be considered together with the fabric of the architectural entity and surroundings. Any intervention in the monument must take into account the specific characteristics of wall paintings and the terms of their preservation. All interventions, such as consolidation, cleaning and reintegration, should be kept at a necessary minimal level to avoid any reduction of material and pictorial authenticity. Whenever possible, samples of stratigraphic layers testifying to the history of the paintings should be preserved, preferably in situ.

Natural ageing is a testimony to the trace of time and should be respected. Irreversible chemical and physical transformations are to be preserved if their removal is harmful. Previous restorations, additions and over-painting are part of the history of the wall painting. These should be regarded as witnesses of past interpretations and evaluated critically.

All methods and materials used in conservation and restoration of wall paintings should take into account the possibility of future treatments. The use of new materials and methods must be based on comprehensive scientific data and positive results of testing in laboratories as well as on sites. However, it must be kept in mind that the long-term effects of new materials and methods on wall paintings are unknown and could be harmful. Therefore, the use of traditional materials, if compatible with the components of the painting and the surrounding structure, should be encouraged.

The aim of restoration is to improve the legibility of form and content of the wall painting, while respecting the original creation and its history. Aesthetic reintegration contributes to minimising the visibility of damage and should primarily be carried out on non-original material. Retouching and reconstructions should be carried out in a way that is discernible from the original. All additions should be easily removable. Over-painting must be avoided.

Uncovering of wall paintings requires the respect of the historic situation and the evaluation of what might be lost. This operation should be executed only after preliminary investigations of their condition, extent and value, and when this is possible without incurring damage. The newly uncovered paintings should not be exposed to unfavourable conditions.

In some cases, reconstruction of decorative wall paintings or coloured architectural surfaces can be a part of a conservation-restoration program. This entails the conservation of the authentic fragments and may necessitate their complete or partial covering with protective layers. A well-documented and professionally executed reconstruction using traditional materials and techniques can bear witness to the historic appearances of facades and interiors.

Competent direction of conservation-restoration projects should be maintained at all stages and have the approval of the relevant authorities. It would be desirable that independent supervision of the project were insured by competent authorities or institutions without commercial interest in the outcome. Those responsible for management decisions must be named, and the work must be implemented by professionals with appropriate knowledge and skills.

Article 6: Emergency Measures

In urgent cases, immediate emergency treatment is necessary for the safeguard of wall paintings. Materials and techniques employed must permit later treatment. Appropriate conservation measures must follow as soon as possible with the permission of the relevant authorities.

Detachment and transfer are dangerous, drastic and irreversible operations that severely affect the physical composition, material structure and aesthetic characteristics of wall paintings. These operations are, therefore, only justifiable in extreme cases when all options of in situ treatment are not viable. Should such situations occur, decisions involving detachment and transfer should always be taken by a team of professionals, rather than by the individual who is carrying out the conservation work. Detached paintings should be replaced in their original location whenever possible.

Special measures should be taken for the protection and maintenance of detached paintings, and for the prevention of their theft and dispersion.

The application of a covering layer concealing an existing decoration, carried out with the intention of preventing damage or destruction by exposure to an inhospitable environment, should be executed with materials compatible with the wall painting, and in a way that will permit future uncovering.

Article 7: Research and Public Information

The establishment of research projects in the field of conservation-restoration of wall paintings is an essential requisite of sustainable preservation policy. Investigations based on research questions, which have potential to add to the knowledge of degradation processes should be encouraged. Research that will expand our knowledge of the original painting techniques, as well as materials and methods of past restoration practices are essential in the implementation of appropriate conservation projects. This research is also relevant to related disciplines of the arts and sciences. The disturbance of significant fabric for study, or to obtain samples, should be minimised.

Dissemination of knowledge is an important feature of research and should be done on both the professional and popular levels. Public information can substantially advance awareness of the need for preservation of wall paintings, even if conservation-restoration work may cause temporary inconveniences.

Article 8: Professional Qualifications and Training

Conservation-restoration of wall paintings is a specialised discipline in the field of heritage preservation. As this work requires specific knowledge, skills, experience and responsibility, conservators-restorers of this kind of cultural property should be professionally educated and trained, as recommended by the Code of Ethics of the ICOM-Committee of Conservation (1984) and by associations such as E.C.C.O. (European Confederation of Conservator-Restorers' Organisations) and ENCoRE (European Network for Conservation-Restoration Education).

Article 9: Traditions of Renewal

In many regions of the world, the authentic painting practices of artists and craftsmen are continued by repeating historic decorative and iconographic programs using traditional materials and techniques. These traditions, satisfying religio-cultural needs and keeping to the Nara principles, should be sustained. However, as important as it is to preserve this special knowledge, this does not imply that the conservation-restoration treatments of wall paintings are to be carried out by craftsmen or artists.

Article 10: International Co-operation

Sharing the care for common heritage is nationally and internationally an accepted concept. It is therefore necessary to encourage the exchange of knowledge and to disseminate information at every level. In the spirit of interdisciplinary collaboration, conservators-restorers of wall paintings need to liaise with their colleagues in other countries and with relevant institutions and specialists around the world.

文化遗产阐释与展示宪章

(国际古迹遗址理事会第十六届大会 2008 年 10 月 4 日在加拿大魁北克通过)

序 言

作为致力于文化遗产地的研究、记录和保护的国际遗产专家组织,国际古迹遗址理事会自 1965 年成立以来努力在其所有工作中发扬遗产保护的职业道德,促进公众对人类物质文化遗产的所有形式和多样性的理解。

正如《威尼斯宪章》(1964)中提到的,"有必要在国际范围内协商和制定指导古建筑保护和修复的原则,并由各个国家负责在本国文化和传统的框架内实施。"此后的 ICOMOS 宪章继承了这一使命,针对具体保护问题建立了专业指导准则,并鼓励在世界各地有效地宣传遗产保护的重要性。

这些 ICOMOS 宪章强调公众交流(也称"传播"、"推广"、"展示"和"阐释")的重要性在于它是更大规模的保护程序的必要组成部分。这些宪章也间接地说明,各种遗产保护行为(在世界所有文化传统中),本质上都是交流行为。

在众多保存下来的物质遗存和昔日社会与文明的无形价值的广阔范围中,选择保护什么、如何保护以及如何向公众展示,这些都是遗产阐释的要素。这些要素体现了各代人对什么是有意义的、什么是重要的,以及为什么要将过去的物质遗存传承于后世等方面的不同见解。

因此,为遗产"阐释与展示"制定明确的理论依据、标准术语和广泛认可的专业准则的必要性显而易见。近年来,许多文化遗产地阐释工作的巨大发展,高精尖阐释技术的引进,以及宣传和经营文化遗产地而引入的新经济策略,都带来了新的复杂性,并对世界范围内文化遗产保护与公众理解这两个目标提出了以下核心问题:

——关于文化遗产地阐释与展示的公认的、可接受的目标是什么?

——哪些原则有助于确定什么样的技术方式和方法适用于特定的文化和遗产背景?

——哪些道德和专业考虑有助于根据各种特定的形式和技术进行"阐释与展示"?

因此,本宪章的目的是定义"阐释与展示"的基本原则。这些基本原则是遗产保护工作的必要组成部分,也是增进公众对文化遗产地理解的一个方法。[①]

定 义

就本宪章而言,

阐释:指一切可能的、旨在提高公众意识、增进公众对文化遗产地理解的活动。这些可包含印刷品和电子出版物、公共讲座、现场及场外设施、教育项目、社区活动,以及对阐释过程本身的持续研究、

---

① 虽然本宪章的原则和目标同样适用于异地阐释,但主要用于遗产地或其周边地区的阐释与展示。

培训和评估。

展示：尤其指在文化遗产地通过对阐释信息的安排、直接的接触，以及展示设施等有计划地传播阐释内容。可通过各种技术手段传达信息，包括（但不限于）信息板、博物馆展览、精心设计的游览路线、讲座和参观讲解、多媒体应用和网站等。

阐释设施：指专门用于阐释与展示，包括通过创新技术和现有技术进行的支持阐释的、在文化遗产地或与之相连的区域内的实物装置、设施和空间。

遗产地讲解员：指文化遗产地长期或临时的职员或志愿者，负责向大众讲解遗产地的价值和重要性。

文化遗产地：指被公认为具有重要历史和文化意义而通常受到法律保护的遗迹、区域、自然景观、居民区、建筑群、考古遗址或建筑构造物。

目　标

在认识到阐释与展示是文化遗产保护和管理整个过程的组成部分的情况下，本宪章尝试建立七项主要原则，根据特定情况所采取的适当的、无论何种形式或媒介的阐释与展示，都应以此为基础。

原则 1：接触渠道和理解
原则 2：信息源
原则 3：重视背景环境和文脉
原则 4：保持真实性
原则 5：可持续性规划
原则 6：关注涵盖与包容面
原则 7：研究、培训和评估的重要性

根据这七项原则，得出本宪章的目标是：

1. 促进对文化遗产地的理解和欣赏，培养文化遗产保护所需的公众意识及公众参与。

2. 认真记录从公认的科学和学术方法，以及从现存的文化传统中识别的遗产地的价值，并向各方受众宣传文化遗产地的意义和内涵。

3. 保护文化遗产地在其自然和文化背景以及社会环境下的有形和无形价值。

4. 通过向公众展示文化遗产地的历史结构和文化价值，并通过保护使其免受有害的展示设施、旅游压力、不准确或不恰当的阐释等带来的不利影响，达到尊重文化遗产地真实性的目的。

5. 通过促进公众对现行保护工作的理解、参与，并通过对展示设施的长期维护和阐释内容的定期检查，促进文化遗产地的可持续保护。

6. 在阐释项目的设计和实施过程中，促进利益相关者和相关团体的参与，增进文化遗产地阐释的涵盖和包容面。

7. 制定与发展遗产阐释与展示的技术与专业指导原则，包括技术、研究和培训。这些指导方针符合其社会背景并具有可持续性。

原　则

原则 1：接触渠道和理解

阐释与展示项目应促进公众接触文化遗产本体和相关知识。

1.1 有效的阐释与展示应能增强个人体验，提高公众对文化遗产地的尊重和理解，宣传对其保护的重要性。

1.2 阐释与展示应鼓励个人和团体反思自身对遗产地的认识，帮助他们建立有意义的联系。目的是激发更深层次的兴趣、学习、体验和探索。

1.3 阐释与展示项目应从人口统计和文化方面识别并分析其受众，力求向各方受众宣讲遗产地的价值和意义。

1.4 展示基础设施应当考虑到参观者以及遗产地相关社区语言的多样性。

1.5 阐释与展示活动应形式多样，并能够实实在在地接近公众。

1.6 若由于保护需要、文化敏感性、改造再利用或安全考虑限制参观，则应提供场外的阐释与展示。

原则 2：信息源

阐释与展示应以通过公认的科学和学术方法以及从现行的文化传统中搜集的证据为依据。

2.1 阐释应说明口头和书面信息、物质遗存、传统和遗产地意义等的范围。信息来源应进行记录、归档，并提供给公众。

2.2 阐释应以对遗产地及其周边环境所进行的详尽的多学科研究为基础。也应当认识到，客观且有意义的阐释也有必要反映其他历史假设、当地传统和民间传说。

2.3 如果文化遗产地的传统故事或历史参与者的回忆，为展现遗产地价值提供了重要的信息来源，阐释活动则应包含这些口头证据。可通过展示设施间接进行，也可通过相关社区成员作为讲解员在现场直接参与。

2.4 对遗产地的视觉再现，无论是由艺术家、建筑师或计算机模拟实现，都应以对环境、考古、建筑以及历史数据的详细系统分析为基础，包括对书面、口头、图像材料和照片的分析。应准确记录这些视觉表现所依据的信息来源。如果能够获取基于相同证据构建的其他影像，也应用做比较。

2.5 阐释与展示方案及活动也应全面记录并存档，用于将来的参考和反思。

原则 3：文脉和背景环境

文化遗产地的阐释与展示应结合其广泛的社会、文化、历史以及自然的发展脉络和背景环境。

3.1 阐释应当探究遗产地在其历史、政治、精神和艺术等多层面发展脉络中的意义。应考虑遗产地文化、社会和环境等所有方面的意义和价值。

3.2 向公众进行文化遗产地阐释应当清晰地指出遗产地发展演变过程中经历的各个阶段和影响，并注明时间。应尊重各个时期在遗产地价值形成中做出的贡献。

3.3 遗产阐释也应当考虑到对遗产地历史和文化重要性有贡献的所有群体。

3.4 遗产地周边景观、自然环境和地理背景都是遗产地历史文化价值的必要组成部分，因此，也应在阐释时加以考虑。

3.5 遗产的无形元素如：文化和精神传统、传说、音乐、舞蹈、戏剧、文学、视觉艺术、当地风俗和烹饪传统等，在遗产地阐释过程中都应加以考虑。

3.6 遗产地在跨文化方面的重要性以及以学术研究、历史记录和现行传统为基础的各种认识角度，都应在制定阐释方案时加以考虑。

原则 4：真实性

文化遗产地的阐释与展示必须遵守《奈良文件》(1994)中关于真实性的基本原则。

4.1 文化遗产的真实性既关乎物质遗存，也关乎所在社区。在设计遗产地阐释项目时，应当尊重遗产地的传统社会职能、以及当地居民和相关社区的文化实践及尊严。

4.2 阐释与展示应通过宣传文化遗产地的价值帮助保护其真实性，避免对其文化价值造成不利影响、或给遗产结构本身带来不可逆转的变化。

4.3 所有可视的阐释设施（如问讯亭、步行路线和信息板等）必须在易于辨认的同时，与遗产地的整体特点、背景环境、以及遗产地的文化和自然价值相协调。

4.4 现场音乐会、戏剧表演和其他的阐释活动，必须经过精心策划，以保护遗产地的价值和周边环境，并使对当地居民的干扰最小化。

原则 5：可持续性

文化遗产地的阐释规划必须尊重遗产地的自然和文化环境，其核心目标应包括社会、经济和环境的可持续性。

5.1 阐释与展示项目的设计和实施应当是文化遗产地总体规划、预算和管理过程的必要组成部分。

5.2 在遗产影响评估研究中，必须全面考虑到阐释设施和游客数量对遗产地的文化价值、外部特征、完整性和自然环境的潜在影响。

5.3 阐释与展示应广泛地为保护、教育和文化目标服务。阐释性项目的成功与否不应单纯的以游客人数和旅游收入来衡量。

5.4 阐释与展示应是遗产保护过程不可缺少的组成部分，它能够增进公众对遗产地面临的特定保护问题的认识，并向公众更好地解释为保护遗产地完整性和真实性所做的努力。

5.5 被确定为遗产地阐释基础设施中永久性组成部分的任何技术要素，都应以适当的方式进行设计和构建，以保证有效的定期维护。

5.6 阐释性项目的目标应为：通过提供教育、培训和就业机会，为遗产地所有的利益相关者带来公平的、可持续的经济、社会和文化利益。

原则 6：涵盖与包容面

文化遗产地的阐释与展示必须是遗产专家、遗产地负责机构和相关社区，以及其他利益相关者共同的有意义合作的结果。

6.1 在阐释与展示项目的制定过程中，应当整合学者、社区成员、遗产保护专家、政府机构、遗产地管理者和讲解员、旅游经营者和其他专业人士的多学科专业知识。

6.2 在策划遗产地阐释与展示项目时，应当注意并尊重所有者、使用者和相关社区的传统权利、责任和利益。

6.3 阐释与展示项目的扩展和修订计划应接纳公众意见，鼓励参与。发表意见和观点是每个人的权利和责任。

6.4 由于知识产权和传统文化权益的问题与遗产阐释过程及其传播媒介（如现场多媒体展示、数字媒体和印刷材料）关系密切，因此，图像、文字以及其他阐释性材料的法定所有权和使用权均应在设计规划过程中探讨、明确并达成共识。

原则 7：研究、培训和评估

不断进行研究、培训和评估是文化遗产地阐释工作必不可少的组成部分。

7.1 文化遗产地阐释工作不应随着具体展示设施的完工而告结束。持续的研究和咨询对增进人们对遗产地价值的理解和正确评价起着重要作用。定期审查应当是每个遗产地阐释项目必不可少的要素。

7.2 阐释性项目和基础设施的设计和建造应便于对阐释内容的不断修订和/或扩展。

7.3 应当持续监测和评估阐释与展示项目对遗产地的影响，并根据科学和学术分析以及公众的反馈信息，作定期调整。参观者、所在社区成员以及遗产专家都应参与到此评估过程中。

7.4 每个阐释项目都应成为各年龄层次的公众教育资源。项目的设计应考虑其应用在学校课程、非正式和终生学习项目、通信和信息媒体、特殊活动、大型活动中的可能性，以及季节性志愿者的参与。

7.5 在遗产地阐释与展示各个专门领域，如内容创建、管理、技术、导游和教育等领域培养合格的专业人员是一个关键目标。此外，在遗产保护专业教学基础课中应设置阐释与展示的课程。

7.6 现场的培训项目和课程，应当以向相关社区、各级遗产保护和阐释工作者宣传该领域新的发展和创新成果为目标。

7.7 国际合作以及经验分享对于制定和保持阐释方法与技术的高标准是非常必要的。为此，应鼓励召开国际会议、专业人员的研讨和交流，以及全国和地方会议。这些都将为定期分享各地区和各种文化背景下的多元阐释方法和经验提供机会。

The ICOMOS Charter for the Interpretation and Presentation of Cultural Heritage Sites

Ratified by the 16th ICOMOS General Assembly, Québec, Canada, 4 October 2008

PREAMBLE

Since its establishment in 1965 as a worldwide organisation of heritage professionals dedicated to the study, documentation, and protection of cultural heritage sites, ICOMOS has striven to promote the conservation ethic in all its activities and to help enhance public appreciation of humanity's material heritage in all its forms and diversity.

As noted in the Charter of Venice (1964) "It is essential that the principles guiding the preservation and restoration of ancient buildings should be agreed and be laid down on an international basis, with each country being responsible for applying the plan within the framework of its own culture and traditions." Subsequent ICOMOS charters have taken up that mission, establishing professional guidelines for specific conservation challenges and encouraging effective communication about the importance of heritage conservation in every region of the world.

These earlier ICOMOS charters stress the importance of public communication as an essential part of the larger conservation process (variously describing it as "dissemination" "popularization" "presentation" and "interpretation"). They implicitly acknowledge that every act of heritage conservation—within all the world's cultural traditions—is by its nature a communicative act.

From the vast range of surviving material remains and intangible values of past communities and civilisations, the choice of what to preserve, how to preserve it, and how it is to be presented to the public are all elements of site interpretation. They represent every generation's vision of what is significant, what is important, and why material remains from the past should be passed on to generations yet to come.

The need for a clear rationale, standardised terminology, and accepted professional principles for Interpretation and Presentation is evident. In recent years, the dramatic expansion of interpretive activities at many cultural heritage sites and the introduction of elaborate interpretive technologies and new economic strategies for the marketing and management of cultural heritage sites have created new complexities and aroused basic questions that are central to the goals of both conservation and the public appreciation of cultural heritage sites throughout the world:

—What are the accepted and acceptable goals for the Interpretation and Presentation of cultural heritage sites?

—What principles should help determine which technical means and methods are appropriate in particular cultural and heritage contexts?

—What general ethical and professional considerations should help shape Interpretation and Presentation in light of its wide variety of specific forms and techniques?

The purpose of this Charter is therefore to define the basic principles of Interpretation and Presentation as essential components of heritage conservation efforts and as a means of enhancing public appreciation and understanding of cultural heritage sites[①].

DEFINITIONS

For the purposes of the present Charter,

Interpretation refers to the full range of potential activities intended to heighten public awareness and enhance understanding of cultural heritage site. These can include print and electronic publications, public lectures, on-site and directly related off-site installations, educational programmes, community activities, and ongoing research, training, and evaluation of the interpretation process itself.

Presentation more specifically denotes the carefully planned communication of interpretive content through the arrangement of interpretive information, physical access, and interpretive infrastructure at a cultural heritage site. It can be conveyed through a variety of technical means, including, yet not requiring, such elements as informational panels, museum-type displays, formalized walking tours, lectures and guided tours, and multimedia applications and websites.

Interpretive infrastructure refers to physical installations, facilities, and areas at, or connected with a cultural heritage site that may be specifically utilised for the purposes of interpretation and presentation including those supporting interpretation via new and existing technologies.

Site interpreters refers to staff or volunteers at a cultural heritage site who are permanently or temporarily engaged in the public communication of information relating to the values and significance of the site.

Cultural Heritage Site refers to a place, locality, natural landscape, settlement area, architectural complex, archaeological site, or standing structure that is recognized and often legally protected as a place of historical and cultural significance.

OBJECTIVES

In recognizing that interpretation and presentation are part of the overall process of cultural heritage conservation and management, this Charter seeks to establish seven cardinal principles, upon which Interpretation and Presentation—in whatever form or medium is deemed appropriate in specific circumstances—should be based.

Principle 1: Access and Understanding

Principle 2: Information Sources

Principle 3: Attention to Setting and Context

Principle 4: Preservation of Authenticity

Principle 5: Planning for Sustainability

Principle 6: Concern for Inclusiveness

---

① Although the principles and objectives of this Charter may equally apply to off-site interpretation, its main focus is interpretation and presentation at, or in the immediate vicinity of, cultural heritage sites.

Principle 7: Importance of Research, Training, and Evaluation

Following from these seven principles, the objectives of this Charter are to:

1. **Facilitate understanding and appreciation** of cultural heritage sites and foster public awareness and engagement in the need for their protection and conservation.

2. **Communicate the meaning** of cultural heritage sites to a range of audiences through careful, documented recognition of significance, through accepted scientific and scholarly methods as well as from living cultural traditions.

3. **Safeguard the tangible and intangible values** of cultural heritage sites in their natural and cultural settings and social contexts.

4. **Respect the authenticity** of cultural heritage sites, by communicating the significance of their historic fabric and cultural values and protecting them from the adverse impact of intrusive interpretive infrastructure, visitor pressure, inaccurate or inappropriate interpretation.

5. **Contribute to the sustainable conservation** of cultural heritage sites, through promoting public understanding of, and participation in, ongoing conservation efforts, ensuring long-term maintenance of the interpretive infrastructure and regular review of its interpretive contents.

6. **Encourage inclusiveness** in the interpretation of cultural heritage sites, by facilitating the involvement of stakeholders and associated communities in the development and implementation of interpretive programmes.

7. **Develop technical and professional guidelines** for heritage interpretation and presentation, including technologies, research, and training. Such guidelines must be appropriate and sustainable in their social contexts.

PRINCIPLES

Principle 1: Access and Understanding

Interpretation and presentation programmes should facilitate physical and intellectual access by the public to cultural heritage sites.

1. Effective interpretation and presentation should enhance personal experience, increase public respect and understanding, and communicate the importance of the conservation of cultural heritage sites.

2. Interpretation and presentation should encourage individuals and communities to reflect on their own perceptions of a site and assist them in establishing a meaningful connection to it. The aim should be to stimulate further interest, learning, experience, and exploration.

3. Interpretation and presentation programmes should identify and assess their audiences demographically and culturally. Every effort should be made to communicate the site's values and significance to its varied audiences.

4. The diversity of language among visitors and associated communities connected with a heritage site should be taken into account in the interpretive infrastructure.

5. Interpretation and presentation activities should also be physically accessible to the public, in all its variety.

6. In cases where physical access to a cultural heritage site is restricted due to conservation concerns, cultural sensitivities, adaptive re-use, or safety issues, interpretation and presentation should be provided off-site.

Principle 2: Information Sources

Interpretation and presentation should be based on evidence gathered through accepted scientific and scholarly methods as well as from living cultural traditions.

1. Interpretation should show the range of oral and written information, material remains, traditions, and meanings attributed to a site. The sources of this information should be documented, archived, and made accessible to the public.

2. Interpretation should be based on a well researched, multidisciplinary study of the site and its surroundings. It should also acknowledge that meaningful interpretation necessarily includes reflection on alternative historical hypotheses, local traditions, and stories.

3. At cultural heritage sites where traditional storytelling or memories of historical participants provide an important source of information about the significance of the site, interpretive programmes should incorporate these oral testimonies—either indirectly, through the facilities of the interpretive infrastructure, or directly, through the active participation of members of associated communities as on-site interpreters.

4. Visual reconstructions, whether by artists, architects, or computer modelers, should be based upon detailed and systematic analysis of environmental, archaeological, architectural, and historical data, including analysis of written, oral and iconographic sources, and photography. The information sources on which such visual renderings are based should be clearly documented and alternative reconstructions based on the same evidence, when available, should be provided for comparison.

5. Interpretation and presentation programmes and activities should also be documented and archived for future reference and reflection.

Principle 3: Context and Setting

The Interpretation and Presentation of cultural heritage sites should relate to their wider social, cultural, historical, and natural contexts and settings.

1. Interpretation should explore the significance of a site in its multi-faceted historical, political, spiritual, and artistic contexts. It should consider all aspects of the site's cultural, social, and environmental significance and values.

2. The public interpretation of a cultural heritage site should clearly distinguish and date the successive phases and influences in its evolution. The contributions of all periods to the significance of a site should be respected.

3. Interpretation should also take into account all groups that have contributed to the historical and cultural significance of the site.

4. The surrounding landscape, natural environment, and geographical setting are integral parts of a site's historical and cultural significance, and, as such, should be considered in its interpretation.

5. Intangible elements of a site's heritage such as cultural and spiritual traditions, stories, music, dance, theater, literature, visual arts, local customs and culinary heritage should be considered in its interpretation.

6. The cross-cultural significance of heritage sites, as well as the range of perspectives about them based on scholarly research, ancient records, and living traditions, should be considered in the formulation of interpretive programmes

Principle 4: Authenticity

The Interpretation and Presentation of cultural heritage sites must respect the basic tenets of authenticity

in the spirit of the Nara Document (1994).

1. Authenticity is a concern relevant to human communities as well as material remains. The design of a heritage interpretation programme should respect the traditional social functions of the site and the cultural practices and dignity of local residents and associated communities.

2. Interpretation and presentation should contribute to the conservation of the authenticity of a cultural heritage site by communicating its significance without adversely impacting its cultural values or irreversibly altering its fabric.

3. All visible interpretive infrastructures (such as kiosks, walking paths, and information panels) must be sensitive to the character, setting and the cultural and natural significance of the site, while remaining easily identifiable.

4. On-site concerts, dramatic performances, and other interpretive programmes must be carefully planned to protect the significance and physical surroundings of the site and minimise disturbance to the local residents.

Principle 5: Sustainability

The interpretation plan for a cultural heritage site must be sensitive to its natural and cultural environment, with social, financial, and environmental sustainability among its central goals.

1. The development and implementation of interpretation and presentation programmes should be an integral part of the overall planning, budgeting, and management process of cultural heritage sites.

2. The potential effect of interpretive infrastructure and visitor numbers on the cultural value, physical characteristics, integrity, and natural environment of the site must be fully considered in heritage impact assessment studies.

3. Interpretation and presentation should serve a wide range of conservation, educational and cultural objectives. The success of an interpretive programme should not be evaluated solely on the basis of visitor attendance figures or revenue.

4. Interpretation and presentation should be an integral part of the conservation process, enhancing the public's awareness of specific conservation problems encountered at the site and explaining the efforts being taken to protect the site's physical integrity and authenticity.

5. Any technical or technological elements selected to become a permanent part of a site's interpretive infrastructure should be designed and constructed in a manner that will ensure effective and regular maintenance.

6. Interpretive programmes should aim to provide equitable and sustainable economic, social, and cultural benefits to all stakeholders through education, training and employment opportunities in site interpretation programmes.

Principle 6: Inclusiveness

The Interpretation and Presentation of cultural heritage sites must be the result of meaningful collaboration between heritage professionals, host and associated communities, and other stakeholders.

1. The multidisciplinary expertise of scholars, community members, conservation experts, governmental authorities, site managers and interpreters, tourism operators, and other professionals should be integrated in the formulation of interpretation and presentation programmes.

2. The traditional rights, responsibilities, and interests of property owners and host and associated

communities should be noted and respected in the planning of site interpretation and presentation programmes.

3. Plans for expansion or revision of interpretation and presentation programmes should be open for public comment and involvement. It is the right and responsibility of all to make their opinions and perspectives known.

4. Because the question of intellectual property and traditional cultural rights is especially relevant to the interpretation process and its expression in various communication media (such as on-site multimedia presentations, digital media, and printed materials), legal ownership and right to use images, texts, and other interpretive materials should be discussed, clarified, and agreed in the planning process.

Principle 7: Research, Training, and Evaluation

Continuing research, training, and evaluation are essential components of the interpretation of a cultural heritage site.

1. The interpretation of a cultural heritage site should not be considered to be completed with the completion of a specific interpretive infrastructure. Continuing research and consultation are important to furthering the understanding and appreciation of a site's significance. Regular review should be an integral element in every heritage interpretation programme.

2. The interpretive programme and infrastructure should be designed and constructed in a way that facilitates ongoing content revision and/or expansion.

3. Interpretation and presentation programmes and their physical impact on a site should be continuously monitored and evaluated, and periodic changes made on the basis of both scientific and scholarly analysis and public feedback. Visitors and members of associated communities as well as heritage professionals should be involved in this evaluation process.

4. Every interpretation programme should be considered as an educational resource for people of all ages. Its design should take into account its possible uses in school curricula, informal and lifelong learning programmes, communications and information media, special activities, events, and seasonal volunteer involvement.

5. The training of qualified professionals in the specialised fields of heritage interpretation and presentation, such as content creation, management, technology, guiding, and education, is a crucial objective. In addition, basic academic conservation programmes should include a component on interpretation and presentation in their courses of study.

6. On-site training programmes and courses should be developed with the objective of updating and informing heritage and interpretation staff of all levels and associated and host communities of recent developments and innovations in the field.

7. International cooperation and sharing of experience are essential to developing and maintaining standards in interpretation methods and technologies. To that end, international conferences, workshops and exchanges of professional staff as well as national and regional meetings should be encouraged. These will provide an opportunity for the regular sharing of information about the diversity of interpretive approaches and experiences in various regions and cultures.

中国文物古迹保护准则

(国际古迹遗址理事会中国国家委员会制定,2015 年修订)

第一章 总 则

第 1 条
本准则适用对象统称为文物古迹。它是指人类在历史上创造或遗留的具有价值的不可移动的实物遗存,包括古文化遗址、古墓葬、古建筑、石窟寺、石刻、近现代史迹及代表性建筑、历史文化名城、名镇、名村和其中的附属文物;文化景观、文化线路、遗产运河等类型的遗产也属于文物古迹的范畴。

第 2 条
准则的宗旨是对文物古迹实施有效保护。保护是指为保存文物古迹及其环境和其他相关要素进行的全部活动。保护的目的是通过技术和管理措施真实、完整地保存其历史信息及其价值。

第 3 条
文物古迹的价值包括历史价值、艺术价值、科学价值以及社会价值和文化价值。
社会价值包含了记忆、情感、教育等内容,文化价值包含了文化多样性、文化传统的延续及非物质文化遗产要素等相关内容。文化景观、文化线路、遗产运河等文物古迹还可能涉及相关自然要素的价值。

第 4 条
保护必须按照本《准则》规定的程序进行。价值评估应置于首位,保护程序的每一步骤都实行专家评审制度。

第 5 条
研究应贯穿保护工作全过程,所有保护程序都要以研究成果为依据。研究成果应当通过有效的途径公布或出版,促进文物古迹保护研究,促进公众对文物古迹价值的认识。

第 6 条
文物古迹的利用必须以文物古迹安全为前提,以合理利用为原则。利用必须坚持突出社会效益,不允许为利用而损害文物古迹的价值。

第 7 条
文物古迹的从业人员应具有相关的专业教育背景,并经过专业培训取得相应资格。获取资格的从业人员,应定期接受培训,提高工作能力。

第 8 条
文物古迹的保护是一项社会事业,需要全社会的共同参与。全社会应当共享文物古迹保护的成果。

第二章 保护原则

第 9 条
不改变原状:是文物古迹保护的要义。它意味着真实、完整地保护文物古迹在历史过程中形成的价值及体现这种价值的状态，有效地保护文物古迹的历史、文化环境，并通过保护延续相关的文化传统。

第 10 条

真实性：是指文物古迹本身的材料、工艺、设计及其环境和它所反映的历史、文化、社会等相关信息的真实性。对文物古迹的保护就是保护这些信息及其来源的真实性。与文物古迹相关的文化传统的延续同样也是对真实性的保护。

第 11 条

完整性：文物古迹的保护是对其价值、价值载体及其环境等体现文物古迹价值的各个要素的完整保护。文物古迹在历史演化过程中形成的包括各个时代特征、具有价值的物质遗存都应得到尊重。

第 12 条

最低限度干预：应当把干预限制在保证文物古迹安全的程度上。为减少对文物古迹的干预，应对文物古迹采取预防性保护。

第 13 条

保护文化传统：当文物古迹与某种文化传统相关联，文物古迹的价值又取决于这种文化传统的延续时，保护文物古迹的同时应考虑对这种文化传统的保护。

第 14 条

使用恰当的保护技术：应当使用经检验有利于文物古迹长期保存的成熟技术，文物古迹原有的技术和材料应当保护。对原有科学的、利于文物古迹长期保护的传统工艺应当传承。所有新材料和工艺都必须经过前期试验，证明切实有效，对文物古迹长期保存无害、无碍，方可使用。

所有保护措施不得妨碍再次对文物古迹进行保护，在可能的情况下应当是可逆的。

第 15 条

防灾减灾：及时认识并消除可能引发灾害的危险因素，预防灾害的发生。要充分评估各类灾害对文物古迹和人员可能造成的危害，制定应对突发灾害的应急预案，把灾害发生后可能出现的损失减到最低程度。对相关人员进行应急预案培训。

第三章　保护和管理工作程序

第 16 条

文物古迹保护和管理工作程序分为六步，依次是调查、评估、确定文物保护单位等级、制订文物保护规划、实施文物保护规划、定期检查文物保护规划及其实施情况。

第 17 条

调查：包括普查、复查和重点调查。一切历史遗迹和有关的文献，以及周边环境都应当列为调查对象。遗址应进行考古勘查，确定遗址范围和保存状况。

第 18 条

评估：包括对文物古迹的价值、保存状态、管理条件和威胁文物古迹安全因素的评估，也包括对文物古迹研究和展示、利用状况的评估。评估对象为文物古迹本体以及所在环境。评估应以勘查、发掘及相关研究为依据。

第 19 条

确定文物古迹的保护等级：文物古迹根据其价值实行分级管理。价值评估是确定文物古迹保护等级的依据。各级政府应根据文物古迹的价值及时公布文物保护单位名单。公布为文物保护单位的文物古迹应落实保护范围，建立说明标志，完善记录档案，设置专门机构或专人负责管理。保护范围以外应划定建设控制地带，以缓解周边建设或生产活动对文物古迹造成的威胁。

第 20 条

编制文物保护规划：文物古迹所在地政府应委托有相应资质的专业机构编制文物古迹保护规划。规划应符合相关行业规范和标准。规划编制单位应会同相关专业人员共同编制。涉及考古遗址时，应有负责考古工作的单位和人员参与编制。

文物古迹的管理者也应参与规划的编制，熟悉规划的相关内容。规划涉及的单位和个人应参与规划编制的过程并了解规划内容。在规划编制过程中应征求公众意见。

文物保护规划应与当地相关规划衔接。文物保护规划一经公布，则具有法律效力。

第 21 条

实施文物保护规划：通过审批的文物保护规划应向社会公布。文物古迹所在地政府是文物保护规划的实施主体。文物古迹保护管理机构负责执行规划确定的工作内容。

应通过实施专项设计落实文物保护规划。列入规划的保护项目、游客管理、展陈和教育计划、考古研究及环境整治应根据文物古迹的具体情况编制专项设计。规划中的保护工程专项设计必须符合各类工程规范，由具有相应资质的专业机构承担，由相关专业的专家组成的委员会评审。

第 22 条

定期评估：管理者应定期对文物保护规划及其实施进行评估。文物行政管理部门应对文物保护规划实施情况予以监督，并鼓励公众通过质询、向文物行政管理部门反映情况等方式对文物保护规划的实施进行监督。当文物古迹及其环境与文物保护规划的价值评估或现状评估相比出现重大变化时，经评估、论证，文物古迹所在地政府应委托有相应资质的专业机构对文物保护规划进行调整，并按原程序报批。

第 23 条

管理：是文物古迹保护的基本工作。管理包括通过制定具有前瞻性的规划，认识、宣传和保护文物古迹的价值；建立相应的规章制度；建立各部门间的合作机制；及时消除文物古迹存在的隐患；控制文物古迹建设控制地带内的建设活动；联络相关各方和当地社区；培养高素质管理人员；对文物古迹定期维护；提供高水平的展陈和价值阐释；收集、整理档案资料；管理旅游活动；保障文物古迹安全；保证必要的保护经费来源。

第四章 保护措施

第 24 条

保护措施是通过技术手段对文物古迹及环境进行保护、加固和修复，包括保养维护与监测、加固、修缮、保护性设施建设、迁移以及环境整治。所有技术措施在实施之前都应履行立项程序，进行专项设计。所有技术和管理措施都应记入档案。相关的勘查、研究、监测及工程报告应由文物古迹管理部门公布、出版。

第 25 条

保养维护及监测：是文物古迹保护的基础。保养维护能及时消除影响文物古迹安全的隐患，并保证文物古迹的整洁。应制定并落实文物古迹保养制度。

监测是认识文物古迹蜕变过程及时发现文物古迹安全隐患的基本方法。对于无法通过保养维护消除的隐患，应实行连续监测，记录、整理、分析监测数据，作为采取进一步保护措施的依据。

保养维护和监测经费由文物古迹管理部门列入年度工作计划和经费预算。

第 26 条

加固：是直接作用于文物古迹本体，消除蜕变或损坏的措施。加固是针对防护无法解决的问题而采取的措施，如灌浆、勾缝或增强结构强度以避免文物古迹的结构或构成部分蜕变损坏。加固措施应根据评估，消除文物古迹结构存在的隐患，并确保不损害文物古迹本体。

第 27 条

修缮：包括现状整修和重点修复。

现状整修主要是规整歪闪、坍塌、错乱和修补残损部分，清除经评估为不当的添加物等。修整中被清除和补配部分应有详细的档案记录，补配部分应当可识别。

重点修复包括恢复文物古迹结构的稳定状态，修补损坏部分，添补主要的缺失部分等。

对传统木结构文物古迹应慎重使用全部解体的修复方法。经解体后修复的文物古迹应全面消除隐患。修复工程应尽量保存各个时期有价值的结构、构件和痕迹。修复要有充分依据。

附属文物只有在不拆卸则无法保证文物古迹本体及附属文物安全的情况下才被允许拆卸，并在修复后按照原状恢复。

由于灾害而遭受破坏的文物古迹，须在有充分依据的情况下进行修复，这些也属于修缮的范畴。

第 28 条

保护性设施建设：通过附加防护设施保障文物古迹和人员安全。保护性设施建设是消除造成文物古迹损害的自然或人为因素的预防性措施，有助于避免或减少对文物古迹的直接干预，包括设置保护设施，在遗址上搭建保护棚罩等。

监控用房、文物库房及必要的设备用房等也属于保护性设施。它们的建设、改造须依据文物保护规划和专项设计实施，把对文物古迹及环境影响控制在最低程度。

第 29 条

迁建：是经过特殊批准的个别的工程，必须严格控制。迁建必须具有充分的理由，不允许仅为了旅游观光而实施此类工程。迁建必须经过专家委员会论证，依法审批后方可实施。必须取得并保留全部原状资料，详细记录迁建的全过程。

第 30 条

环境整治：是保证文物古迹安全，展示文物古迹环境原状，保障合理利用的综合措施。整治措施包括：对保护区划中有损景观的建筑进行调整、拆除或置换，清除可能引起灾害的杂物堆积，制止可能影响文物古迹安全的生产及社会活动，防止环境污染对文物造成的损伤。

绿化应尊重文物古迹及周围环境的历史风貌，如采用乡土物种，避免因绿化而损害文物古迹和景观环境。

第 31 条

油饰彩画保护：必须在科学分析、评估其时代、题材、风格、材料、工艺、珍稀性和破坏机理的基础上，根据价值和保存状况采取现状整修或重点修复的保护措施。

油饰彩画保护的目的是通过适当的加固措施尽可能保存原有彩画。若通过评估需要重绘时，重绘部分必须尊重原设计、使用原工艺并尽可能使用原材料。

工程的每一步骤必须有详尽的档案记录。有重要价值但无法在原位保存的彩画应在采取保护措施后，作为文物或档案资料保存。

第 32 条

壁画保护：对石窟、寺庙、墓葬壁画所采取的保护措施必须经过研究、分析和试验，保证切实有效。

壁画保护首先应采取防护措施。只有在充分认识壁画的退化机理的前提下，才能进行加固。

复原可能破坏壁画的真实性，不适合壁画的保护。只有在原有环境中确实难以保护的情况下，壁画才允许迁移保护。

第 33 条

彩塑保护：首先应保证彩塑结构稳定、安全，对彩塑所采取的保护措施，必须经过研究、分析和试验，证明切实有效。

彩塑保护应注意保存不同时代彩妆的信息，避免或杜绝为展示某一特定时代特征而消除其他时代信息的做法。

第 34 条

石刻保护：应以物理防护为主，首先保证石刻安全。任何直接接触石刻表面的防护和保护措施都必须经过研究、分析和试验，证明对石刻文物无害方可使用。

第 35 条

考古遗址保护：考古发掘应优先考虑面临发展规划、土地用途改变、自然退化威胁的遗址和墓葬。有计划或抢救性考古发掘、包括因国家重大工程建设进行的考古发掘，都应制定发掘中和发掘后的保护预案，在发掘现场对遗址和文物提取做初步的保护，避免或减轻由于环境变化对遗址和文物造成的损害。

经发掘的遗址和墓葬不具备展示条件的，应尽量实施原地回填保护，并防止人为破坏。经过评估，无条件在原址保存的遗址和墓葬，方可迁移保护。

规模宏大、价值重大、影响深远的大型考古遗址（大遗址）应整体保护。在确保遗址安全的前提下，可采取多种展示方式进行合理利用。具有一定资源条件、社会条件和可视性的大型考古遗址可建设为考古遗址公园。

第 36 条

近现代史迹及代表性建筑的保护：近现代建筑、工业遗产和科技遗产的保护应突出考虑原有材料的基本特征，尽可能采用不改变原有建筑及结构特征的加固措施。增加的加固措施应当可以识别，并尽可能可逆，或至少不影响以后进一步的维修保护。

第 37 条

纪念地的保护：应突出对于体现纪念地价值的环境特征的保护。

第 38 条

文化景观、文化线路、遗产运河的保护：必须在对各构成要素保护的基础上突出对文物古迹整体的保护。一定范围内的环境和自然景观是这些文物古迹本体的构成要素，对这部分环境和自然景观的保护和修复即是对文物古迹本体的保护。

第 39 条

历史文化名城、名镇、名村的保护：除了对文物古迹各构成要素的保护，还须考虑对整体的城镇历史景观的保护。保护不仅要考虑城市肌理和建筑体量、密度、高度、色彩、材料等因素，同时也应保护、延续仍保持活力的文化传统。

从环境景观的角度还需考虑对视线通廊、周围山水环境等体现城镇、村落选址、景观设计意图等要素的保护。

第五章　合理利用

第 40 条

合理利用是文物古迹保护的重要内容。应根据文物古迹的价值、特征、保存状况、环境条件，综合考虑研究、展示、延续原有功能和赋予文物古迹适宜的当代功能的各种利用方式。利用应强调公益性和可持续性，避免过度利用。

第 41 条

鼓励以文物古迹为资料，进行相关研究工作。

文物古迹是历史变迁、文化发展的实物例证，是历史、文化研究的重要对象。对文物古迹的研究是实现文物古迹价值的重要方式。

第 42 条

鼓励对文物古迹进行展示，对其价值做出真实、完整、准确地阐释。展示应基于对文物古迹全面、深入的研究。要避免对文物古迹及相关历史、文化作不准确的表述。展示应针对不同背景的群体采用易于理解的方式。

展示和游客服务设施的选址应根据文物保护规划和专项设计进行，须符合文物古迹保护、价值阐释、保证游客安全、对原有环境影响最小等要求。服务性设施应尽可能远离文物古迹本体。展陈、游览设施应统一设计安置。

第 43 条

不提倡原址重建的展示方式。考古遗址不应重建。鼓励根据考古和文献资料通过图片、模型、虚拟展示等科技手段和方法对遗址进行展示。

第 44 条

对仍保持原有功能，特别是这些功能已经成为其价值组成部分的文物古迹，应鼓励和延续原有的使用方式。

第 45 条

赋予文物古迹新的当代功能必须根据文物古迹的价值和自身特点，确保文物古迹安全和价值不受损害。利用必须考虑文物古迹的承受能力，禁止超出文物古迹承受能力的利用。

因利用而增加的设施必须是可逆的。

第六章 附 则

第 46 条

针对新的文物古迹类型，鼓励遵循《准则》的原则探索适合特定类型的文物古迹的保护方法。

第 47 条

本《准则》由中国古迹遗址保护协会制定、通过，中国国家文物局批准向社会公布。中国古迹遗址保护协会负责对本《准则》及其附件进行解释。在需要进行修订时也要履行相同程序。

Principles for the Conservation of Heritage Sites in China

ICOMOS CHINA, revised 2015

Chapter 1 General Principles

Article 1

Heritage sites. These Principles can serve as guidelines in conservation practice for everything commonly referred to as heritage sites. Heritage sites are the immovable physical remains that were created during the history of humankind and that have significance; they include archaeological sites and ruins, tombs, traditional architecture, cave temples, stone carvings, sculpture, inscriptions, stele, and petroglyphs, modern and contemporary sites and architecture, and historically and culturally famous cities, towns and villages together with their original components. Cultural landscapes and heritage routes and canals are also deemed to be heritage sites.

Article 2

Purpose. The purpose of the Principles is to ensure good practice in the conservation of heritage sites. Conservation refers to all measures carried out to preserve a site, its setting and associated elements. The aim of conservation is to preserve and protect the authenticity and integrity of the site, its historic information and values, using both technical and management measures.

Article 3

Values. The heritage values of a site are its historic, artistic, and scientific values, as well as its social and cultural values. Social value encompasses memory, emotion and education. Cultural value comprises cultural diversity, the continuation of traditions, and essential components of intangible cultural heritage. Cultural landscapes and heritage routes and canals may also have important natural values.

Article 4

Conservation process. Conservation needs to be carried out in sequence according to the process prescribed in these Principles. An assessment of the values and significance of a site is the first step that should be undertaken. The system for review by experts of each step of the process must be followed.

Article 5

Research. Research is fundamental to every aspect of conservation. Each step in the conservation process should be based on the results of research. Research results should be made public through an effective channel or published so as to promote further research into the conservation of heritage sites and assist the public to gain an appreciation of their values.

Article 6

Use. Use of a heritage site must comply with the principle of appropriate use while ensuring its protection. Use of a site for the benefit of society is important, but such use should not diminish the site's values.

Article 7

Training. All personnel at a heritage site should have received training or an education in a relevant discipline and should gain professional qualifications prior to commencement of duty. Qualified personnel should undertake regular training to enhance their capabilities.

Article 8

Participation. Conservation of heritage sites is a social undertaking that requires broad community participation. The public should derive social benefit from heritage conservation.

Chapter 2 Conservation Principles

Article 9

Historic condition. An essential requirement in the conservation of a heritage site is to preserve its historic condition. The historic condition of a site embodies its values, authenticity and integrity as they have evolved during the course of its history. Through good conservation practice, a site's historic and cultural context and its cultural traditions are preserved and retained for the future.

Article 10

Authenticity. Authenticity resides in the original materials, workmanship and design of a site and its setting, as well as in its historical, cultural, and social characteristics and qualities. Respecting these aspects through conservation retains authenticity. The continuation of long-established cultural traditions associated with a particular site is also a means of retaining its authenticity.

Article 11

Integrity. Integrity derives from preserving the entirety and full range of a heritage site's values, including those embodied in the physical fabric and setting. Sites evolve over the course of history and significant features and physical remnants from a site's different periods should be respected.

Article 12

Minimal intervention. Intervention to a heritage site should be restricted to the minimum necessary to ensure its preservation. Preventive conservation measures should be undertaken to reduce the need for interventions.

Article 13

Cultural traditions. When a heritage site's values depend on the continuation of associated cultural traditions, consideration needs to be given to preserving these traditions along with the site itself.

Article 14

Appropriate technology. The use of appropriate conservation technology refers to technology that is tried and proven and is beneficial to the long-term preservation of a site. Evidence of original technology and historic materials should be conserved. Traditional craftsmanship that contributes to the site's long-term preservation should be maintained. New materials and techniques may only be used after they have been tested and proven effective, and should not be detrimental or cause long-term damage. Conservation measures should not preclude future interventions and should be reversible when conditions permit.

Article 15

Disaster preparedness. Disaster prevention and preparedness requires a timely understanding and elimination, where possible, of threats. A comprehensive assessment of threats to a site and people should be undertaken and response plans developed to minimize damage should a disaster occur. Training in how to carry out these plans should be offered to relevant individuals.

Chapter 3 Conservation and Management Process

Article 16

Conservation and management process. The conservation and management process involves six steps undertaken in the following order:

(1) identification and investigation; (2) assessment; (3) formal proclamation as an officially protected site and its level of protection; (4) preparation of a conservation master plan; (5) implementation of the master plan; and (6) periodic review of the plan and its implementation.

Article 17

Identification and investigation: The process of identification and investigation of heritage sites comprises a national level survey and inventory, an investigation of selected sites in greater depth, and a detailed investigation of the most significant ones. These investigations must examine all historic vestiges and traces and relevant extant documentation, as well as the immediate setting. Survey should be undertaken at archaeological sites to determine the site boundaries and state of preservation.

Article 18

Assessment: Assessment consists of determining the values of a site, its threats and state of preservation, and its management context, as well as the status of research, presentation and interpretation, and use. Assessment includes both the site and its setting and should be based on site inspection, excavation, and research.

Article 19

Formal proclamation. Sites are managed by government according to their level of protection as determined through an assessment of significance. Each level of government (national, provincial, and local) should expeditiously proclaim a list of protected sites under its jurisdiction. Officially protected sites must ensure that boundaries are demarcated, a plaque erected declaring the site's status as an officially protected entity, archives and records maintained, and supplemented, and a dedicated organization established or person appointed to manage the site. A buffer zone should be established around the site's boundary to control development and production activities.

Article 20

Master planning: Local government shall assign master plan preparation to a suitably qualified professional organization. The master plan should conform to relevant industry standards. The organization entrusted to write the plan should work with professionals from relevant disciplines. Organizations and professionals responsible for archaeological work should also participate in the writing of plans for archaeological sites.

Site management staff should participate in the writing of the plan and be familiar with its contents. Stakeholders should take part in the planning process and should be aware the plan's contents. During the plan's drafting the public should be given an opportunity to provide feedback.

The master plan for a site should be linked to local government plans. After promulgation, conservation master plans are legally binding.

Article 21

Implementation. Approved master plans should be made public. Local government has primary responsibility to ensure that legal requirements are adhered to by site management, which is responsible for implementing work programs specified in the plan. Master plans are realized through the implementation of sub-plans, which should be developed for conservation projects, visitor management, presentation and interpretation, and education, as well as archaeological research and treatment of the setting. Sub-plans written for major conservation interventions must be developed by qualified professional organizations, comply with relevant technical standards, and be reviewed by a committee of experts with appropriate specialist background.

Article 22

Periodic review. Site management is responsible for regular review of a master plan and its implementation. The government entity at the appropriate level of the heritage site should oversee the implementation and encourage public scrutiny of the plan's implementation through inquiries and feedback. If there are significant changes to the condition and values of a site or its setting from the original assessment, local government should authorize a qualified organization to revise those elements in the plan after reassessment and evaluation. The revised master plan should go through the same approval process as the original.

Article 23

Site management. Management is fundamental to the conservation of heritage sites. The role of site management is to understand, promote and protect the site's values through long-term planning and vision, establishing policies and regulations, coordinating activities among departments, identifying and taking action to eliminate potential threats, controlling development in the buffer zones, liaising with stakeholders and local community, providing site staff with educational and training opportunities, regular maintenance of the site, providing quality exhibitions and interpretation, collecting and compiling archival documents, managing tourism, providing security, and ensuring sources of finance.

Chapter 4 Conservation Measures

Article 24

Conservation measures. Conservation measures refer to technical interventions and treatments to protect, stabilize or restore a site and its setting. These include regular maintenance and monitoring, strengthening and stabilization measures, repair, protective structures, relocation, and treatment of the setting. Technical interventions should go through project design and associated approval processes prior to implementation. All technical and management interventions should be documented and archived. Related surveying, research, monitoring, and intervention reports should be made public and published by the responsible government entity.

Article 25

Maintenance and monitoring. Maintenance and monitoring are fundamental to the conservation of heritage sites. Maintenance is the timely removal of potential problems that could cause damage or deterioration and also ensures it is kept clean and orderly. A maintenance program should be established and implemented at every heritage site.

Site monitoring is fundamental to understanding the processes of deterioration, as well as to identifying potential problems. Problems that cannot be dealt with through maintenance should be monitored regularly, documented, and collated. Monitoring data should be analyzed and become the basis for carrying out further conservation measures. Management should include costs associated with maintenance and monitoring in the site's annual budget.

Article 26

Stabilization measures. Stabilization and strengthening measures are direct interventions to prevent further deterioration or damage. Measures such as grouting, repointing or structural reinforcement are undertaken to a structure or its components when prevention has not been effective in solving the problem. These measures must be based on results of assessment and eliminate structural problems while not adversely affecting the site's physical fabric.

Article 27

Minor and major restoration. Minor restoration most frequently involves rectifying components that are deformed, displaced or collapsed, repairing damaged elements, and removing additions that have been assessed as inappropriate. Detailed documentation records should be kept of elements that are removed or added and those that have been added should be distinguishable from original fabric.

Major restoration is an intervention involving the most impact to original fabric. It includes returning a structure to a stable condition and also repair or replacement of damaged and key missing components. The decision to repair traditional wooden architecture through complete disassembly and reassembly should be taken with caution. All problems revealed in the course of disassembly and reassembly should be rectified. Restoration should, as far as possible, preserve the structures, components, and vestiges and traces of periods judged to have value. There needs to be ample evidence to justify restoration.

If the protection of associated contents cannot be assured during restoration, they may be temporarily dismantled and removed and reinstated after restoration. Heritage sites that have been damaged during a natural or human-made disaster may only be restored, provided sufficient evidence is available, once the disaster has past.

Minor and major restoration may also be categorized as repair of a building.

Article 28

Protective structures. Protective structures are used to ensure the preservation of a site and the protection of people. This is a preventive measure to address natural and human causes of deterioration to a site. Protective structures, such as shelters for archaeological sites, may be helpful in preventing or reducing the need for direct intervention. Buildings used for security or other equipment or the storage of artifacts may also be considered as protective structures. Construction or adaptation of such facilities needs to be undertaken according to the master plan and approved implementation plan. They should have minimal impact on the site and its setting.

Article 29

Relocation. Moving a site to a new location is a rare intervention, subject to strict controls and special approval. The decision to relocate a site must be based on substantial justification; this type of intervention is not permitted merely to facilitate tourism or sight-seeing. Relocation of a site must be deliberated on by a panel of experts and then approved in accordance with the law before implementation. The historic condition and the process of relocation should be thoroughly recorded and archived.

Article 30

Treatment of the setting. This is a comprehensive measure to protect a site, reveal its historic condition, and ensure its appropriate use. This mainly involves modification, removal or purchase of structures that adversely affect the landscape in the protected area, removal of hazardous accumulated debris, restrictions on activities that may harm the site, and prevention of environmental pollution. Modern landscaping should avoid any damage and visual intrusions and respect the historic features of the site and its setting through measures such as the use of indigenous vegetation.

Article 31

Architectural painting. Conservation of architectural painting on wooden structures may require minor or major restoration based on scientific analysis and assessment of the period, iconography, style, original material, techniques, rarity, and causes of deterioration together with an assessment of significance and condition.

The objective of conservation of architectural painting is to preserve as much of the original as possible, using appropriate stabilization and strengthening measures. Priority should be given to preserving historic decorative painting; however, where re-painting is deemed necessary after assessment, the original design must be respected and original techniques and materials used as far as possible. Each stage of the work must be documented in detail and samples of decorative painting of particular significance that cannot be conserved in situ should be archived after conservation treatment.

Article 32

Wall paintings. Measures for effective conservation of wall paintings in grottoes, temples, and tombs requires thorough research, analysis and testing of treatment methods prior to implementation. Preventive measures should always take priority. Strengthening and stabilization treatments may be required but must be the result of clear understanding of the causes of deterioration. Restoration is not an appropriate intervention for wall paintings as it destroys their authenticity. Removal and relocation of wall paintings should only be considered if conservation in their original setting is not possible.

Article 33

Painted statuary. Priority should be given to ensuring structural stability and protection of statuary. Measures used to conserve statuary must be proven effective through research, analysis and trials. Care should be taken to preserve decoration from different periods, thus avoiding privileging presentation of one particular period and losing information from other periods.

Article 34

Stone carvings. Conservation of stone carvings, sculpture, inscriptions, stele, and petroglyphs should focus on physical protection and safeguarding. Any protection or conservation measure or material in direct contact with the surface of the artefact must be proven effective without adverse effect as demonstrated through research, analysis and in situ trials prior to use.

Article 35

Archaeological sites and ruins. Archaeological sites, ruins and tombs threatened by development, changes to land usage, or environmental degradation should be given priority for excavation. Contingency plans for excavation and post-excavation conservation should be developed for planned or rescue excavations, including sites associated with major development projects of national importance. Materials and finds should be initially conserved at the excavation site itself to avoid or mitigate deterioration to artifacts caused by the change in environment. Excavated archaeological sites and tombs that do not lend themselves to interpretation should as far as possible be preserved through reburial with measures in place to deter human damage. A tomb or an archaeological site may only be relocated and conserved if assessment determines it cannot be preserved in situ.

Very large-scale archaeological sites of exceptional significance and influence should be preserved in their entirety. A variety of appropriate presentation and interpretation methods may be adopted, provided the protection of the site is ensured. Large-scale archaeological sites that have the resources, public support and lend themselves to visitation may be designated as national archaeological parks.

Article 36

Modern and contemporary sites and architecture. The conservation of modern and contemporary buildings and structures, industrial heritage and scientific and technological heritage should focus on the basic attributes of the original materials, design and function. Any stabilization measures should as far as possible not alter these attributes. Added components for strengthening a structure should be recognizable and reversible as far as possible, or at least not preclude further maintenance and repair.

Article 37

Commemorative site. Commemorative sites are places associated with important historic events or people. Their conservation should emphasize the protection of the features of the site and its setting that reflect these events or people.

Article 38

Cultural landscapes, heritage routes and canals. Conservation of cultural landscapes, heritage routes and canals should address the entirety of the site, while also conserving important, individual elements. Both the setting and natural landscape within the proximate area are important attributes. Conservation and restoration of the setting and natural landscape are integral to conservation of this category of heritage.

Article 39

Historically and culturally famous cities, towns and villages. In addition to conservation of their various components, consideration must be given to the protection of the historic landscape of this category of heritage. Conservation should preserve the urban design and the size, density, height, color and materials of the buildings, as well as safeguard and sustain the vitality of cultural traditions. Consideration also needs to be given to protecting visual catchments, the surrounding natural setting and environment, and the historic siting of cities, towns and villages that reveal the intentions of the original design.

Chapter 5 Appropriate use

Article 40

Appropriate use. Appropriate use can be an important means of conserving a heritage site. Use should take into consideration the values, attributes, state of preservation and setting, as well as the possibility of the site being used for research, presentation, continuation of original function or adaptation for an appropriate modern use. Use of a site should both be sustainable and promote community well-being. Overuse must be avoided.

Article 41

Research use. The use of heritage sites for research should be encouraged. Heritage sites comprise the physical evidence of history and the development of culture and as such are a resource for research. Research into a heritage site is an important means of actualizing its values.

Article 42

Presentation and interpretation. The values of a heritage site should be presented and interpreted in an authentic, integrated, and accurate manner and be based on comprehensive, in-depth research. Inaccurate interpretation of a site's history and culture must be avoided. Presentation and interpretation should meet the needs of various audiences and employ methods that are easily understandable.

The location of a site's interpretation and visitor facilities should be determined by the master plan and relevant implementation plan, and meet the requirements for conservation, interpretation of values, visitor safety, and minimal impact on the setting. Service facilities should be located away from the site. Exhibition and visitor facilities, infrastructure and signage should be consistent in design and placement.

Article 43

Reconstruction. Reconstruction in situ for purposes of presentation and interpretation is not advocated. It should not be undertaken on archaeological sites. Encouragement should be given to presenting and interpreting these sites by means of drawings, photos and sketches, and models, and the use of modern technology such as virtual reality presentations based on accurate archaeological and documentary evidence.

Article 44

Retaining historic function. Sites that retain their historic function, particularly those where the traditional way of life has become an integral part of the site's values should be encouraged to continue that function.

Article 45

Adaptive reuse. Adaptation of a heritage site for modern use must respect the values of the site and its attributes and ensure its protection without negatively impacting those values. Use of the site must not exceed its capacity. Facilities added to a site for the purpose of use must be reversible.

Chapter 6 Additional Principles

Article 46

New categories of heritage. When considering conserving new categories of heritage the adoption of applicable conservation methodologies in the China Principles is encouraged.

Article 47

Approval and amendments. These Principles were drafted and adopted by ICOMOS China and approved for public announcement by the State Administration of Cultural Heritage. ICOMOS China shall be responsible for the interpretation of these Principles and attachments. When amendments are made, the same procedures should be followed.

农业遗产

全球重要农业遗产系统（GIAHS）[①]（节选）

（联合国粮农组织，2017年1月1日）

全球重要农业遗产系统遴选标准

1. 粮食和生计保障

提名的农业系统有助于当地社区的粮食和/或生计保障。这包括各种各样的农业类型，如自给自足和半自给农业，在这种农业系统里当地社区之间进行供应和交换，有助于农村经济。

2. 农业生物多样性

农业生物多样性，按照联合国粮农组织的定义[②]，是指直接或间接用于粮食和农业的各种动物、植物和微生物，包括作物、牲畜、林业和渔业。该系统应拥有具全球重要性的生物多样性以及粮食和农业遗传资源（例如，地方性、家养、稀有、濒危的作物和动物物种）。

3. 地方和传统知识系统

该系统应保持当地宝贵的传统知识和实践，独创的适应性技术，和对支撑农业、林业和/或渔业活动的生物群、土地、水等自然资源的管理系统。

4. 文化、价值体系和社会组织[③]

文化认同和地方意识根植于并且属于特定的农业遗产。与资源管理和粮食生产相关的社会组织、价值体系和文化习俗可以确保保护和促进公平使用和获取自然资源。这种社会组织[④]和习俗可以采取习惯法和惯例以及仪式、宗教和/或精神体验的形式。

5. 景观和海景特征

全球重要农业遗产系统应该代表随着时间的推移，通过人类和环境之间的相互作用而发展起来的景观或海景，并且看起来已经稳定下来或者演化得非常缓慢。它们的形式、形状和链接，其特点是长期的历史持续性，并与产生它们的当地社会经济制度有着紧密联系。它们的稳定，或是缓慢的演化，是特定地区或区域的食物生产、环境和文化融合的证据。它们可能具有复杂的土地利用系统的形式，例如土地

---

① 译者：曹新。

② FAO（联合国粮农组织）对"农业生物多样性"定义如下：直接或间接用于食物和农业，包括作物、牲畜、林业和渔业的动物、植物和微生物的多样性、变异性。它包括用于食物、饲料、纤维、燃料和药品的遗传资源（品种、种类）和物种的多样性。它还包括支持生产的非收获物种的多样性（土壤微生物、捕食者、授粉者），以及支持农业生态系统（农业、畜牧、森林和水生物）的更广泛环境中的物种的多样性，以及农业生态系统的多样性。

③ 社会组织是指在农业系统组织和动态保护中发挥关键作用的个人、家庭、团体或社区。

④ 地方社会组织可以在平衡环境和社会经济目标、增强复原力和复制农业系统运作的所有关键要素和过程方面发挥关键作用。

利用的嵌合、水和海岸管理系统等。

可持续性行动计划

提名地必须随提名制定一项动态保护的行动计划。列入行动计划的项目建议是对威胁和挑战的分析，以及对政策、战略、行动和成果的详细描述，这些政策、战略、行动和成果已经在遗产地范围内得到实施和/或将由各利益相关方实施，通过下列补充信息来促进全球重要农业遗产系统的动态保护。

- 确定、分析威胁和挑战，包括社会经济压力和环境变化对该系统存在的连续性、可持续性和生存能力产生的影响；
- 计划的政策、战略和行动是什么？它们将如何应对所描述的威胁；
- 这些政策、战略和行动将如何有助于动态保护提名的全球重要农业遗产系统；
- 包括当地社区在内的多个利益相关方如何参与并支持在地方、国家和国际各层级执行"行动计划"；
- 政策、战略和行动如何在地方、国家和/或国际层面来筹集资金和/或调动资源；
- 如何监督和评估行动计划的进展情况和实施效果。

Globally Important Agricultural Heritage Systems (GIAHS)[①] (excerpts)

FAO, 1 January 2017

Criteria for Selection of GIAHS

1. Food and Livelihood Security

The proposed agricultural system contributes to food and/or livelihood security of local communities. This includes a wide variety of agricultural types such as self-sufficient and semi-subsistence agriculture where provisioning and exchanges take place among local communities, which contributes to rural economy.

2. Agro-biodiversity

Agricultural biodiversity, as defined by FAO[②] as the variety of animals, plants and micro-organisms that are used directly or indirectly for food and agriculture, including crops, livestock, forestry and fisheries. The system should be endowed with globally significant biodiversity and genetic resources for food and agriculture (e.g. endemic, domesticated, rare, endangered species of crops and animals).

3. Local and Traditional Knowledge systems

The system should maintain local and invaluable traditional knowledge and practices, ingenious adaptive technology and management systems of natural resources, including biota, land, water which have supported agricultural, forestry and/or fishery activities.

4. Cultures, Value systems and Social Organisations[③]

Cultural identity and sense of place are embedded in and belong to specific agricultural sites. Social organizations, value systems and cultural practices associated with resource management and food production may ensure conservation

---

[①] from: Food and Agriculture Organization of United Nations, www.fao.org.

[②] FAO defines agro-biodiversity as follows: The variety and variability of animals, plants and micro-organisms that are used directly or indirectly for food and agriculture, including crops, livestock, forestry and fisheries. It comprises the diversity of genetic resources (varieties, breeds) and species used for food, fodder, fibre, fuel and pharmaceuticals. It also includes the diversity of non-harvested species that support production (soil micro-organisms, predators, pollinators), and those in the wider environment that support agro-ecosystems (agricultural, pastoral, forest and aquatic) as well as the diversity of the agro-ecosystems.

[③] Social organization is defined as individuals, families, groups or communities that play a key role on the agricultural systems' organization and dynamic conservation.

of and promote equity in the use and access to natural resources. Such social organizations[①] and practices may take the form of customary laws and practices as well as ceremonial, religious and/or spiritual experiences.

5. Landscapes and Seascapes Features

GIAHS sites should represent landscapes or seascapes that have been developed over time through the interaction between humans and the environment, and appear to have stabilized or to evolve very slowly. Their form, shape and interlinkages are characterized by long historical persistence and a strong connection with the local socio-economic systems that produced them. Their stability, or slow evolution, is the evidence of integration of food production, the environment and culture in a given area or region. They may have the form of complex land use systems, such as land use mosaics, water and coastal management systems.

Action Plan for Sustainability of the System

An Action Plan for a dynamic conservation of the proposed GIAHS site must be developed with the proposal. The recommended items to be included in the Action Plan would be an analysis of threats and challenges and detailed descriptions of the policies, strategies, actions and outcomes which are already under implementation and/or will be implemented in the area by various relevant stakeholders to promote dynamic conservation of GIAHS with the following supplementary information:

• Identify and analyze threats and challenges, including socio-economic pressures and environmental changes to the continuity of the existence, sustainability and viability of the system;

• What are the proposed policies, strategies and actions and how will they respond to the threats as described;

• How these policies, strategies and actions will contribute to the dynamic conservation of the proposed GIAHS site;

• How multi-stakeholders are involved, including local communities, and support the implementation of the Action Plan at local, national and international levels;

• How policies, strategies and actions can be used to leverage funding and/or mobilize resources at the local, national and/or international level;

• How monitoring and evaluation of the progress and the effect of the implementation of the Action Plan will be undertaken.

---

① Local social organizations may play a critical role in balancing environmental and socio-economic objectives, creating enhancing resilience and reproducing all elements and processes critical to the functioning of the agricultural systems.

自然遗产

关于特别是作为水禽栖息地的国际重要湿地公约[①]（湿地公约）

（1971年2月2日在伊朗拉姆萨尔通过，经1982年12月3日和1987年5月28日修订，联合国教科文组织1994年版）

各缔约国，

确认人与其环境相互依存；

考虑到湿地的基本生态功能是作为水文状况的调节者，是某种独特植物区系和动物区系，特别是水禽赖以存活的生境；

深信湿地是具有重大经济、文化、科学和娱乐价值的一种资源，一旦丧失则不可弥补；

希望制止目前和今后对湿地的蚕食，乃至丧失；

确认水禽在季节性迁徙时可能会超越国界，因此，应视为一种国际资源；

确信具有远见的国家政策与协调一致的国际行动相结合，可以确保湿地及其动植物区系得到保护；

兹议定条款如下：

第1条

1. 为本公约之目的，湿地系指天然或人造、永久或暂时之死水或流水、淡水、微咸或咸水沼泽地、泥炭地或水域，包括低潮时水深不超过六米的海水区。

2. 为本公约之目的，水禽系指从生态学角度看以湿地为生存条件的鸟类。

第2条

1. 每个缔约国应指定其领土内适当湿地，列入《具有国际意义的湿地目录》（下称《目录》），该《目录》由根据第8条设立的办事处保管。每块湿地的边界应在地图上精确标明和划定，可包括与湿地毗邻的河岸和海岸地区，以及位于湿地内的岛屿或低潮时水深超过6米的海洋水体，特别是具有水禽生境意义的地区岛屿或水体。

2. 选择列入《目录》的湿地，应根据它们在生态学、植物学、动物学、湖沼学或水文学方面的国际意义来考虑。首先应列入一年四季均对水禽具有国际意义的湿地。

3. 将湿地列入《目录》，并不损害其所属缔约国的专有主权。

4. 每个缔约国在按照第9条规定签署本公约或交存其批准书或加入书时，应至少指定一块湿地列入《目录》。

5. 任何缔约国均有权将其领土内的其他湿地增列入《目录》，扩大已列入《目录》的湿地的边界，或者出于紧急的国家利益的考虑，取消列入《目录》的湿地或缩小其边界，并应尽快将这类变动通知负责

[①] UNESCO湿地公约最新文本，引自RAMSAR官网www.ramsar.org。编者根据现行通用的翻译对文本标题进行了修改。

第 8 条规定的常务办事处的组织或政府。

6. 每个缔约国在指定列入《目录》的湿地和就列入《目录》的其领土内的湿地行使修改条文的权利时，应考虑其对保护、管理和合理使用迁徙水禽所负的国际责任。

第 3 条

1. 各缔约国应制订和执行规划，以促进对列入《目录》的湿地的保护，并尽可能地合理使用其领土内的湿地。

2. 每个缔约国应作出安排，以便尽早获悉，由于技术发展、污染或其他人为干扰，列入《目录》的其领土内的湿地的生态特性已经发生变化，正在变化，或有可能发生变化。有关这类变化的情况应立即通知负责第 8 条规定的常务办事处的组织或政府。

第 4 条

1. 每个缔约国应在湿地（不论是否已列入《目录》）建立自然保护区，以促进对湿地和水禽的保护，并采取充分措施予以看管。

2. 当某一缔约国出于紧急的国家利益的考虑而取消列入《目录》的湿地或缩小其边界时，应尽可能弥补湿地资源的任何损失，特别应建立新的自然保护区，以供水禽生存，并在同一地区或其他地区保护原来生境的适当部分。

3. 各缔约国应鼓励就湿地及其动植物区系开展研究，交换资料和出版物。

4. 各缔约国应努力通过管理增加合适的湿地上的水禽数目。

5. 各缔约国应加强培训能胜任湿地研究、管理和看管的人员。

第 5 条

缔约国应就履行《公约》规定的义务，特别是在湿地扩及一个以上缔约国的领土或一条水系为数缔约国所共有的情况下，相互协商。

同时，各缔约国应努力协调和支持目前和将来就保护湿地及其动植物所制订的政策和条例。

第 6 条

1. 设立缔约国会议，以检查和促进这项公约的实施。第 8 条第 1 段所提及的常务办事处至少每三年召开一次缔约国会议之例会，除非会议另有决定。在至少有三分之一的缔约国提出书面要求的情况下，也可以召开特别会议。缔约国会议的每次例会均应确定举行下一次例会的时间及地点。

2. 缔约国会议具有下列职权：

（a）讨论本公约的执行情况；

（b）讨论《目录》的增补和修改；

（c）审议根据第 3 条第 2 段提供的关于《目录》中所列湿地生态特性变化的资料；

（d）就保护、管理和合理使用湿地及其动植物问题，向缔约国提出一般性建议或具体建议；

（e）要求有关国际机构就涉及湿地的国际问题提出报告和提供统计资料；

（f）通过其他建议或决议，来促进本公约的执行。

3. 各缔约国应保证从事湿地管理的各级负责人了解并考虑此类会议关于保护、管理和合理使用湿地及其动植物的建议。

4. 缔约国会议为每次会议制定议事规则。

5. 缔约国会议应制定本公约的财务条例，并定期对条例进行审议。缔约国会议应在其每次例会上以出席会议并参加表决之缔约国的三分之二多数通过下一财务期的预算。

6. 各缔约国应根据出席缔约国会议例会并参加表决之所有缔约国一致通过的会费额度向预算纳款。

第 7 条

1. 参加上述会议的各缔约国代表应包括在科学、行政或其他有关方面知识渊博、经验丰富的湿地或水禽专家。

2. 出席会议的每一缔约国有一票表决权；建议、决议和决定由出席会议及参加投票的缔约国的简单多数通过，除非本公约另作其他规定。

第 8 条

1. 国际自然及自然资源保护联盟执行本公约规定的常务办事处职责，直至全体缔约国的三分之二多数指定另一个组织或政府时止。

2. 常务办事处职责如下：

（a）协助召集和组织第 6 条规定的会议；

（b）保管《具有国际意义的湿地目录》，并接收各缔约国根据第 2 条第 5 段就列入《目录》的湿地的增补、扩大、取消或缩小所提供的资料；

（c）接收各缔约国根据第 3 条第 2 段就列入《目录》的湿地的生态特性变化所提供的资料；

（d）把对《目录》的任何修改或《目录》中所列湿地的特性变化通知所有缔约国，并为在下届会议上讨论这些事项作出安排；

（e）把会议就《目录》修改或《目录》中所列湿地的特性变化提出的建议通知有关缔约国。

第 9 条

1. 本公约无限期开放签字。

2. 联合国任何会员国、任何专门机构或国际原子能机构的会员国或国际法院规约任何当事国得依下列方式之一成为本公约缔约国：

（a）对于批准不附保留之签署；

（b）待批准之签署，继后批准；

（c）加入。

3. 向联合国教科文组织总干事（下称"保存人"）交存一份批准书或加入书；批准或加入即为生效。

第 10 条

1. 本公约在七个国家按第 9 条第 2 段方式成为本公约缔约国起四个月后生效。

2. 本公约嗣后对每个缔约国应自该国对于批准不附保留之签署或交存批准书或加入书之日起四个月后生效。

第 10 bis 条

1. 根据本条，缔约国可就《公约》修订问题召集会议，对《公约》进行修订。

2. 任何缔约国均可提出修订建议。

3. 所建议的任何修正案的文本及修订理由须通过根据《公约》行使常设主席团（下称"主席团"）职责的组织或政府，并由主席团随即转告所有缔约国。缔约国对文本的任何意见要在自主席团把修正案通知缔约国之日起三个月内通知主席团。主席团须于意见提交的最后一天之后立即把截至该日所收到的全部意见转告各缔约国。

4. 主席团将根据三分之一缔约国的书面要求召集缔约国会议，审议根据第 3 段提出的修正案。主席团将就会议的时间与地点同各缔约国进行协商。

5. 修正案须经与会缔约国投票表决以三分之二的多数通过。

6. 被通过的修正案将于三分之二缔约国向保管者交存接受书之日后第四个月的第一天起对接受修正

案的缔约国生效。对在三分之二缔约国交存接受书之日后交存接受书的任何缔约国，修正案将于该国交存接受书之日后第四个月第一天开始生效。

第 11 条

1. 本公约将无限期有效。

2. 任何缔约国可在本公约对该国生效之日起五年后书面通知保存人退出本公约。退约应于保存人接到通知之日起四个月后生效。

第 12 条

1. 保存人应尽快将下述事项通知所有业已签署或加入本公约的国家：

（a）《公约》之签署；

（b）本公约批准书之交存；

（c）本公约加入书之交存；

（d）本公约生效日期；

（e）退约通知。

2. 本公约生效之后，保存人应根据《联合国宪章》第 102 条在联合国秘书处予以登记。

下列签署人经正式授权签署本公约，以昭信守。

一九七一年二月二日订于拉姆萨尔，原本以英文本、法文本、德文本和俄文本各式一份。所有文本具有同等效力。文本均交保存人，保存人则将正式副本分送所有缔约国。

Convention on Wetlands of International Importance especially as Waterfowl Habitat [1]

Ramsar, Iran, 2.2.1971
as amended by the Protocol of 3.12.1982
and the Amendments of 28.5.1987
Paris, 13 July 1994

The Contracting Parties,

RECOGNIZING the interdependence of Man and his environment;

CONSIDERING the fundamental ecological functions of wetlands as regulators of water regimes and as habitats supporting a characteristic flora and fauna, especially waterfowl;

BEING CONVINCED that wetlands constitute a resource of great economic, cultural, scientific, and recreational value, the loss of which would be irreparable;

DESIRING to stem the progressive encroachment on and loss of wetlands now and in the future;

RECOGNIZING that waterfowl in their seasonal migrations may transcend frontiers and so should be regarded as an international resource;

BEING CONFIDENT that the conservation of wetlands and their flora and fauna can be ensured by combining far-sighted national policies with co-ordinated international action;

Have agreed as follows:

Article 1

1. For the purpose of this Convention wetlands are areas of marsh, fen, peatland or water, whether natural or artificial, permanent or temporary, with water that is static or flowing, fresh, brackish or salt, including areas of marine water the depth of which at low tide does not exceed six metres.

2. For the purpose of this Convention waterfowl are birds ecologically dependent on wetlands.

Article 2

1. Each Contracting Party shall designate suitable wetlands within its territory for inclusion in a List of Wetlands of International Importance, hereinafter referred to as "the List" which is maintained by the bureau established under Article 8. The boundaries of each wetland shall be precisely described and also delimited on a map and they may incorporate riparian and coastal zones adjacent to the wetlands, and islands or bodies of marine

---

[1] UNESCO RAMSAR Current Text. from: www. ramsar. org.

water deeper than six metres at low tide lying within the wetlands, especially where these have importance as waterfowl habitat.

2. Wetlands should be selected for the List on account of their international significance in terms of ecology, botany, zoology, limnology or hydrology. In the first instance wetlands of international importance to waterfowl at any season should be included.

3. The inclusion of a wetland in the List does not prejudice the exclusive sovereign rights of the Contracting Party in whose territory the wetland is situated.

4. Each Contracting Party shall designate at least one wetland to be included in the List when signing this Convention or when depositing its instrument of ratification or accession, as provided in Article 9.

5. Any Contracting Party shall have the right to add to the List further wetlands situated within its territory, to extend the boundaries of those wetlands already included by it in the List, or, because of its urgent national interests, to delete or restrict the boundaries of wetlands already included by it in the List and shall, at the earliest possible time, inform the organization or government responsible for the continuing bureau duties specified in Article 8 of any such changes.

6. Each Contracting Party shall consider its international responsibilities for the conservation, management and wise use of migratory stocks of waterfowl, both when designating entries for the List and when exercising its right to change entries in the List relating to wetlands within its territory.

Article 3

1. The Contracting Parties shall formulate and implement their planning so as to promote the conservation of the wetlands included in the List, and as far as possible the wise use of wetlands in their territory.

2. Each Contracting Party shall arrange to be informed at the earliest possible time if the ecological character of any wetland in its territory and included in the List has changed, is changing or is likely to change as the result of technological developments, pollution or other human interference. Information on such changes shall be passed without delay to the organization or government responsible for the continuing bureau duties specified in Article 8.

Article 4

1. Each Contracting Party shall promote the conservation of wetlands and waterfowl by establishing nature reserves on wetlands, whether they are included in the List or not, and provide adequately for their wardening.

2. Where a Contracting Party in its urgent national interest, deletes or restricts the boundaries of a wetland included in the List, it should as far as possible compensate for any loss of wetland resources, and in particular it should create additional nature reserves for waterfowl and for the protection, either in the same area or elsewhere, of an adequate portion of the original habitat.

3. The Contracting Parties shall encourage research and the exchange of data and publications regarding wetlands and their flora and fauna.

4. The Contracting Parties shall endeavour through management to increase waterfowl populations on appropriate wetlands.

5. The Contracting Parties shall promote the training of personnel competent in the fields of wetland research, management and gardening.

Article 5

The Contracting Parties shall consult with each other about implementing obligations arising from the

Convention especially in the case of a wetland extending over the territories of more than one Contracting Party or where a water system is shared by Contracting Parties. They shall at the same time endeavour to coordinate and support present and future policies and regulations concerning the conservation of wetlands and their flora and fauna.

Article 6

1. There shall be established a Conference of the Contracting Parties to review and promote the implementation of this Convention. The Bureau referred to in Article 8, paragraph 1, shall convene ordinary meetings of the Conference of the Contracting Parties at intervals of not more than three years, unless the Conference decides otherwise, and extraordinary meetings at the written requests of at least one third of the Contracting Parties. Each ordinary meeting of the Conference of the Contracting Parties shall determine the time and venue of the next ordinary meeting.

2. The Conference of the Contracting Parties shall be competent:

a) to discuss the implementation of this Convention;

b) to discuss additions to and changes in the List;

c) to consider information regarding changes in the ecological character of wetlands included in the List provided in accordance with paragraph 2 of Article 3;

d) to make general or specific recommendations to the Contracting Parties regarding the conservation, management and wise use of wetlands and their flora and fauna;

e) to request relevant international bodies to prepare reports and statistics on matters which are essentially international in character affecting wetlands;

f) to adopt other recommendations, or resolutions, to promote the functioning of this Convention.

3. The Contracting Parties shall ensure that those responsible at all levels for wetlands management shall be informed of, and take into consideration, recommendations of such Conferences concerning the conservation, management and wise use of wetlands and their flora and fauna.

4. The Conference of the Contracting Parties shall adopt rules of procedure for each of its meetings.

5. The Conference of the Contracting Parties shall establish and keep under review the financial regulations of this Convention. At each of its ordinary meetings, it shall adopt the budget for the next financial period by a two-third majority of Contracting Parties present and voting.

6. Each Contracting Party shall contribute to the budget according to a scale of contributions adopted by unanimity of the Contracting Parties present and voting at a meeting of the ordinary Conference of the Contracting Parties.

Article 7

1. The representatives of the Contracting Parties at such Conferences should include persons who are experts on wetlands or waterfowl by reason of knowledge and experience gained in scientific, administrative or other appropriate capacities.

2. Each of the Contracting Parties represented at a Conference shall have one vote, recommendations, resolutions and decisions being adopted by a simple majority of the Contracting Parties present and voting, unless otherwise provided for in this Convention.

Article 8

1. The International Union for Conservation of Nature and Natural Resources shall perform the continuing

bureau duties under this Convention until such time as another organization or government is appointed by a majority of two-thirds of all Contracting Parties.

2. The continuing bureau duties shall be, *inter alia*:

a) to assist in the convening and organizing of Conferences specified in Article 6;

b) to maintain the List of Wetlands of International Importance and to be informed by the Contracting Parties of any additions, extensions, deletions or restrictions concerning wetlands included in the List provided in accordance with paragraph 5 of Article 2;

c) to be informed by the Contracting Parties of any changes in the ecological character of wetlands included in the List provided in accordance with paragraph 2 of Article 3;

d) to forward notification of any alterations to the List, or changes in character of wetlands included therein, to all Contracting Parties and to arrange for these matters to be discussed at the next Conference;

e) to make known to the Contracting Party concerned, the recommendations of the Conferences in respect of such alterations to the List or of changes in the character of wetlands included therein.

Article 9

1. This Convention shall remain open for signature indefinitely.

2. Any member of the United Nations or of one of the Specialized Agencies or of the International Atomic Energy Agency or Party to the Statute of the International Court of Justice may become a Party to this Convention by:

a) signature without reservation as to ratification;

b) signature subject to ratification followed by ratification;

c) accession.

3. Ratification or accession shall be affected by the deposit of an instrument of ratification or accession with the Director-General of the United Nations Educational, Scientific and Cultural Organization (hereinafter referred to as "the Depositary").

Article 10

1. This Convention shall enter into force four months after seven States have become Parties to this Convention in accordance with paragraph 2 of Article 9.

2. Thereafter this Convention shall enter into force for each Contracting Party four months after the day of its signature without reservation as to ratification, or its deposit of an instrument of ratification or accession.

Article 10 bis

1. This Convention may be amended at a meeting of the Contracting Parties convened for that purpose in accordance with this article.

2. Proposals for amendment may be made by any Contracting Party.

3. The text of any proposed amendment and the reasons for it shall be communicated to the organization or government performing the continuing bureau duties under the Convention (hereinafter referred to as "the Bureau") and shall promptly be communicated by the Bureau to all Contracting Parties. Any comments on the text by the Contracting Parties shall be communicated to the Bureau within three months of the date on which the amendments were communicated to the Contracting Parties by the Bureau. The Bureau shall, immediately after the last day for submission of comments, communicate to the Contracting Parties all comments submitted by that day.

4. A meeting of Contracting Parties to consider an amendment communicated in accordance with paragraph 3 shall be convened by the Bureau upon the written request of one third of the Contracting Parties. The Bureau shall consult the Parties concerning the time and venue of the meeting.

5. Amendments shall be adopted by a two-thirds majority of the Contracting Parties present and voting.

6. An amendment adopted shall enter into force for the Contracting Parties which have accepted it on the first day of the fourth month following the date on which two thirds of the Contracting Parties have deposited an instrument of acceptance with the Depositary. For each Contracting Party which deposits an instrument of acceptance after the date on which two thirds of the Contracting Parties have deposited an instrument of acceptance, the amendment shall enter into force on the first day of the fourth month following the date of the deposit of its instrument of acceptance.

Article 11

1. This Convention shall continue in force for an indefinite period.

2. Any Contracting Party may denounce this Convention after a period of five years from the date on which it entered into force for that party by giving written notice thereof to the Depositary. Denunciation shall take effect four months after the day on which notice thereof is received by the Depositary.

Article 12

1. The Depositary shall inform all States that have signed and acceded to this Convention as soon as possible of :

a) signatures to the Convention;

b) deposits of instruments of ratification of this Convention;

c) deposits of instruments of accession to this Convention;

d) the date of entry into force of this Convention;

e) notifications of denunciation of this Convention.

2. When this Convention has entered into force, the Depositary shall have it registered with the Secretariat of the United Nations in accordance with Article 102 of the Charter.

IN WITNESS WHEREOF, the undersigned, being duly authorized to that effect, have signed this Convention.

DONE at Ramsar this 2nd day of February 1971, in a single original in the English, French, German and Russian languages, all texts being equally authentic[*] which shall be deposited with the Depositary which shall send true copies thereof to all Contracting Parties.

---

* *Pursuant to the Final Act of the Conference to conclude the Protocol, the Depositary provided the second Conference of the Contracting Parties with official versions of the Convention in the Arabic, Chinese and Spanish languages, prepared in consultation with interested Governments and with the assistance of the Bureau.*

国际重要湿地标准[1]

RAMSAR

A 组标准：区域内包含代表性的、稀有的或独一无二的湿地类型

标准 1：如果一块湿地包含有一个在适当的生物地理区内代表性的、稀有的或独一无二的自然或近自然的湿地类型，那么就应该认为其具有国际重要性。

B 组标准：湿地具有在生物多样性保护方面的国际重要性

基于物种和生态群落的标准

标准 2：如果一块湿地支持着脆弱的、濒危的、极度濒危的物种或者受威胁的生态群落，那么就应该认为其具有国际重要性。

标准 3：如果一块湿地支持着对于维持一个特定生物地理区的生物多样性具有重要意义的植物和／或动物种群，那么就应该认为其具有国际重要性。

标准 4：如果一块湿地支持着某些植物和／或动物物种生命周期的一个重要阶段，或者为它们处在不利生存条件下时提供庇护场所，那么就应该认为其具有国际重要性。

基于水禽的特定标准

标准 5：如果一块湿地规律性地支持着 20,000 只或更多的水禽的生存，那么就应该认为其具有国际重要性。

标准 6：如果一块湿地规律性地支持着一个水禽物种或亚种种群的 1% 的个体生存，那么就应该认为其具有国际重要性。

基于鱼类的特定标准

标准 7：如果一块湿地支持着很大比例的本土鱼类的亚种、种或科，生活史阶段，种间相互作用，或者代表湿地效益或价值的种群，从而有利于全球生物多样性，那么就应该认为其具有国际重要性。

标准 8：如果一块湿地是某些鱼类依赖的重要食物来源、产卵场、保育场和／或迁徙途径（无论这些鱼是生活在这块湿地里或是别处），那么就应该认为其具有国际重要性。

基于其他类群的特定标准

标准 9：如果一块湿地规律性地支持着一个非鸟类湿地动物物种或亚种种群的 1% 的个体生存，那么就应该认为其具有国际重要性。

---

[1] 译者：曹新。根据湿地公约RAMSAR官网文件The Ramsar Sites Criteria译。

The Ramsar Sites Criteria[1]
(The Nine Criteria for Identifying Wetlands of International Importance)

Group A of the Criteria. Sites containing representative, rare or unique wetland types

Criterion 1: A wetland should be considered internationally important if it contains a representative, rare, or unique example of a natural or near-natural wetland type found within the appropriate biogeographic region.

Group B of the Criteria. Sites of international importance for conserving biological diversity

Criteria based on species and ecological communities

Criterion 2: A wetland should be considered internationally important if it supports vulnerable, endangered, or critically endangered species or threatened ecological communities.

Criterion 3: A wetland should be considered internationally important if it supports populations of plant and/or animal species important for maintaining the biological diversity of a particular biogeographic region.

Criterion 4: A wetland should be considered internationally important if it supports plant and/or animal species at a critical stage in their life cycles, or provides refuge during adverse conditions.

Specific criteria based on waterbirds

Criterion 5: A wetland should be considered internationally important if it regularly supports 20,000 or more water birds.

Criterion 6: A wetland should be considered internationally important if it regularly supports 1% of the individuals in a population of one species or subspecies of waterbird.

Specific criteria based on fish

Criterion 7: A wetland should be considered internationally important if it supports a significant proportion of indigenous fish subspecies, species or families, life-history stages, species interactions and/or populations that are representative of wetland benefits and/or values and thereby contributes to global biological diversity.

Criterion 8: A wetland should be considered internationally important if it is an important source of food for fishes, spawning ground, nursery and/or migration path on which fish stocks, either within the wetland or elsewhere, depend.

Specific criteria based on other taxa

Criterion 9: A wetland should be considered internationally important if it regularly supports 1% of the individuals in a population of one species or subspecies of wetland-dependent non-avian animal species.

---

[1] from: www.ramsar.org.

联合国人类环境会议宣言[①]

（联合国人类环境会议1972年6月16日在斯德哥尔摩通过）

一、联合国人类环境会议宣言

联合国人类环境会议，

已于一九七二年六月五日至十六日在斯德哥尔摩开会，

鉴于需要有共同的展望，共同的原则，以激发和指引全世界的人民，来养护和改善人类环境，

兹宣布：

1. 人是环境的产物，也是环境的塑造者，环境予人以身体上的需要，也予人以智慧、道德、社会和精神滋长的机会。人类在这个地球上的悠久曲折的进化中，已经达到一个阶段，由于科学和技术的突飞猛进，他已经具有用无数的方法，以空前的规模，来改变环境的能力。人的环境，包括天然的和人为的两方面，对于他的福利以及对于享受基本人权——甚至生活本身的权利——都是必要的。

2. 保护和改善人类环境，是关系到世界各国人民福利和全世界经济发展的一个重要问题，是世界各国人民的迫切愿望，是各国政府应尽的责任。

3. 人类总得不断地总结经验，不断地发现、发明、创造和前进。在我们这个时代，人类改变环境的能力，如果妥善地加以运用，可为所有的人民带来发展的福利和改善生活素质的机会。如果错误地或者轻率地加以运用，这同一能力也能对人类和人类环境造成无可衡量的损害。我们处处可以看到地球上许多地区人为败害的愈来愈多的迹象：水、空气、土壤和生物的污染已到危险的程度；生物层的生态平衡，已受到重大的、不应有的扰乱；无法补充的资源已被毁坏和枯竭；在人为的环境中，特别是在工作和生活环境中，已经出现了有害于人的身体、精神和社会健康的重大缺陷。

4. 在发展中国家，多数的环境问题，是发展不足造成的。千千万万的人继续过着远在人类适当生活所需起码水平以下的生活，没有适当的食物和衣服，住处和教育，健康和卫生。因此，发展中国家必须致力于发展，顾及到它们的优先事项，也顾到保护并改善环境的必要。为了同一个目的，工业化国家应该作出努力，来缩短它们自己和发展中国家之间的差距。在工业化国家，环境问题多半是因为工业化和技术发展而产生的。

5. 人口的自然增长，对环境的维护，不断引起问题，因此应该斟酌情形，采取适当的方针和措施，来正视这些问题。世间一切事物中，人是最宝贵的。人民推动社会进步，创造社会财富，发展科学技术，并通过他们的辛勤劳动，不断地改造人类环境。随着社会的进步和生产、科学、技术的发展，人类改善环境的能力也是与日俱增。

[①] 引自：联合国人类环境会议报告书，斯德哥尔摩，1972年6月5日至16日。UN Document: A/CONF.48/14/Rev.1。

6. 我们在历史上已经到达一个阶段，使我们在全世界计划我们的行动，必须更加谨慎地顾到对于环境的后果。由于无知或漠不关心，我们对于我们的生命和幸福所依靠的地球环境，能够造成巨大的、无法挽救的损害。反过来，如果我们具有更充足的知识，采取更聪明的行动，便能为我们自己和我们的后代，在更符合人类需要和希望的环境里，创造更美满的生活。人类有提高环境素质和创造美好生活的广阔前景。现在所需要的，是热诚而平静的心境，全心全力而井井有条的工作。为了在自然界里获得自由，人类必须运用知识，同自然合作，建立更良好的环境。为今代和后世维护和改善人类环境，已经成为人类的迫切目标，这个目标应该连同和平及全世界经济和社会发展的既定基本目标，一并和谐实现。

7. 要达到这个环境目标，公民和社区以及每一阶层的企业和机关，都必须负起责任，公平地、各尽其份地作出共同努力。各行各业的个人，以及许多部门的组织，凭着他们的价值标准和它们的行动总和，将塑造未来的世界环境。地方和中央政府将各在其管辖范围内，对大规模的环境政策和行动，肩负最重大的担子。还需要国际合作，来筹集资源，支持发展中国家履行它们这方面的责任。有一类为数日增的环境问题，由于其区域性或全球性的范围，或由于其对共同国际领域的影响，需要在共同利益的前提下，由各国广泛合作，由各国际组织采取行动。会议呼吁各国政府和人民，为维护和改善人类环境，造福全体人民，造福后代，而共同努力。

二. 原则

声明下列共同信念：

原则一

人人都有在过着尊严和幸福生活的优良环境里享受自由、平等和适当生活条件的基本权利，同时也有为今代和后世保护和改善环境的神圣责任。在这方面，凡是促进或延续种族隔离、种族分隔、歧视、殖民及其他形式的压迫和外国统治的政策，应受谴责，必须予以肃清。

原则二

地球上的自然资源，包括空气、水、土地和动植物，尤其是自然生态系统的代表样品，必须为今代和后世的利益，酌量情形，通过仔细的设计或管理，加以保护。

原则三

地球生产重生性的重要资源的能力必须保持，可能时并予以恢复或增进。

原则四

人类对于保护和妥善管理现因种种不利因素而岌岌可危的野生物遗产及其生活地域，负有特别的责任。因此，大自然的养护、包括野生物在内，必须在经济发展设计中给予重要的地位。

原则五

地球上的非重生性资源，必须小心使用，以防将来有用完的危险，并保证全人类共享使用这种资源的利益。

原则六

含毒物质或其他物质和热的排出，其数量或浓度超过环境所能将其化为无害的能力时，必须加以阻止，以确保生态系统不致受严重的或无法补救的损害。对于各国人民进行的反污染的正当斗争，应该予以支持。

原则七

各国应采取一切可能的步骤，防止势将危害人类健康、损害生物资源和海洋生物、损坏环境优良条件或妨碍海洋其他正当用途的各种物质污染海洋。

原则八

经济和社会发展,是人类谋求良好的生活和工作环境及在地球上创造必要条件、以改善生活素质的必要工具。

原则九

发展落后情况和自然灾害所造成的环境缺陷,引起了严重的问题,补救的办法,最好是向发展中国家大量提供财政和技术协助,以补充这些国家的国内努力,而加速推进发展工作,并及时提供可能需要的协助。

原则十

就发展中国家而言,初级商品和原料价格的稳定与充分的收益,是环境管理的必要条件,因为经济因素以及生态程序都必须予以顾及。

原则十一

一切国家的环境政策,都应增进发展中国家现在和将来的发展潜能,而不应对它有不利的影响,也不妨碍全体人类获致更优良的生活条件,因此各国和各国际组织都应该采取适当步骤,就如何处理因实施环境措施而可能引起的国家和国际经济后果的问题达成协议。

原则十二

应提供资源,以保护和改善环境,唯须顾及发展中国家的情况和特殊需要,和这些国家因在其发展设计内加入环境保护办法而可能引起的任何费用,以及于它们请求时为此目的提供额外国际技术和财政协助的需要。

原则十三

为了对资源作更合理的管理,借以改善环境,各国于从事发展设计时,应该采用一种统筹协调的方法,务使发展工作,与保护和改善环境以谋人民福利的需要,互相融洽。

原则十四

合理的设计是一种必要的工具,用以调和发展的需要与保护和改善环境的需要之间的任何冲突。

原则十五

对于人类集居地和城市化必须加以设计,以免对环境发生不利影响,并为所有人民取得最大的社会、经济和环境利益。在这方面,凡是以殖民统治及种族统治为宗旨的种种计划,必须一律放弃。

原则十六

凡因人口增长速率或人口过分集中而势将对环境产生不利影响的区域,或因人口密度过低而可能阻止人类环境的改善和妨碍发展的区域,都应适用有关政府认为适当的、无损于基本人权的人口政策。

原则十七

必须指定适当的国家机关,负责设计、管理或控制国家环境资源,以提高环境素质。

原则十八

科学及技术,作为其对经济和社会发展的一项贡献,必须用以鉴定、避免和控制环境危险及解决环境问题,并谋人类的共同福利。

原则十九

为年轻人和成年人举办的、充分顾及穷苦人民的、有关环境问题的教育,是一项根本措施,借以扩大个人、企业和社区的开明舆论和负责行为的基础,俾对环境,顾到它对人类的充分含义,加以保护和改善。同样重要的是,新闻媒介必须避免助长环境的恶化;相反地,它们应该作教育性的报导,强调必须保护和改善环境,使人可在每一方面发展。

原则二十

所有国家，尤其是发展中国家，必须参酌涉及一个国家或许多国家的环境问题，提倡科学研究和发展。在这方面，对于最新科学资料的自由流通和经验的交换，必须予以支持和援助，以利环境问题的解决；环境技术必须按照足以鼓励广泛传播而对发展中国家不构成经济负担的条件，提供给发展中国家。

原则二十一

依照联合国宪章和国际法原则，各国具有按照其环境政策开发其资源的主权权利，同时亦负有责任，确保在它管辖或控制范围内的活动，不致对其他国家的环境或其本国管辖范围以外地区的环境引起损害。

原则二十二

各国应互相合作，进一步发展关于一国管辖或控制范围以内的活动对其管辖范围以外地区所引起的污染及其他环境损害的受害人的责任与赔偿问题的国际法。

原则二十三

在不妨害国际社会可能同意的一般准则，亦不妨害各国所须确定的标准的情形下，务须一律考虑每一个国家的现行价值制度，以及在什么程度内可以适用在最进步国家行之有效但对发展中国家则未必适合而且社会代价过高的标准。

原则二十四

关于保护和改善环境的国际问题，应由所有各国，不论大小，以平等地位本着合作精神来处理。通过多边或双边安排或其他适当办法的合作，是对各种领域内进行活动所引起的不良环境影响，加以有效控制预防、减少或消除的必要条件，唯须妥善顾及所有国家的主权和利益。

原则二十五

各国应确保各国际组织在环境的保护和改善方面，发挥协调、有效和有力的作用。

原则二十六

不能让人类及其环境遭受核武器及其他一切大规模毁灭性武器的影响。各国必须努力，在有关的国际机关内，就此种武器的消除和全部销毁，迅速达成协议。

Declaration of the United Nations Conference on the Human Environment [1]

Adopted by the United Nations Conference on the Human Environment, Stockholm, 16 June 1972

The United Nations Conference on the Human Environment,
Having met at Stockholm from 5 to 16 June 1972,
Having considered the need for a common outlook and for common principles to inspire and guide the peoples of the world in the preservation and enhancement of the human environment,

I.

Proclaims that:

1. Man is both creature and moulder of his environment, which gives him physical sustenance and affords him the opportunity for intellectual, moral, social and spiritual growth. In the long and tortuous evolution of the human race on this planet a stage has been reached when, through the rapid acceleration of science and technology, man has acquired the power to transform his environment in countless ways and on an unprecedented scale. Both aspects of man's environment, the natural and the man-made, are essential to his well-being and to the enjoyment of basic human rights—even the right to life itself.

2. The protection and improvement of the human environment is a major issue which affects the well-being of peoples and economic development throughout the world; it is the urgent desire of the peoples of the whole world and the duty of all Governments.

3. Man has constantly to sum up experience and go on discovering, inventing, creating and advancing. In our time, man's capability to transform his surroundings, if used wisely, can bring to all peoples the benefits of development and the opportunity to enhance the quality of life. Wrongly or heedlessly applied, the same power can do incalculable harm to human beings and the human environment. We see around us growing evidence of man-made harm in many regions of the earth: dangerous levels of pollution in water, air, earth and living beings; major and undesirable disturbances to the ecological balance of the biosphere; destruction and depletion of irreplaceable resources; and gross deficiencies, harmful to the physical, mental and social health of man, in the man-made environment, particularly in the living and working environment.

4. In the developing countries most of the environmental problems are caused by under-development.

---

[1] Report of the United Nations Conference on the Human Environment, Stockholm, 5-16 June 1972. UN Document: A/CONF.48/14/Rev.1.

Millions continue to have far below the minimum levels required for a decent human existence, deprived of adequate food and clothing, shelter and education, health and sanitation. Therefore, the developing countries must direct their efforts to development, bearing in mind their priorities and the need to safeguard and improve the environment. For the same purpose, the industrialized countries should make efforts to reduce the gap themselves and the developing countries. In the industrialized countries, environmental problems are generally related to industrialization and technological development.

5. The natural growth of population continuously presents problems for the preservation of the environment, and adequate policies and measures should be adopted, as appropriate, to face these problems. Of all things in the world, people are the most precious. It is the people that propel social progress, create social wealth, develop science and technology and, through their hard work, continuously transform the human environment. Along with social progress and the advance of production, science and technology, the capability of man to improve the environment increases with each passing day.

6. A point has been reached in history when we must shape our actions throughout the world with a more prudent care for their environmental consequences. Through ignorance or indifference we can do massive and irreversible harm to the earthly environment on which our life and well-being depend. Conversely, through fuller knowledge and wiser action, we can achieve for ourselves and our posterity a better life in an environment more in keeping with human needs and hopes. There are broad vistas for the enhancement of environmental quality and the creation of a good life. What is needed is an enthusiastic but calm state of mind and intense but orderly work. For the purpose of attaining freedom in the world of nature, man must use knowledge to build, in collaboration with nature, a better environment. To defend and improve the human environment for present and future generations has become an imperative goal for mankind—a goal to be pursued together with, and in harmony with, the established and fundamental goals of peace and of worldwide economic and social development.

7. To achieve this environmental goal will demand the acceptance of responsibility by citizens and communities and by enterprises and institutions at every level, all sharing equitably in common efforts. Individuals in all walks of life as well as organizations in many fields, by their values and the sum of their actions, will shape the world environment of the future. Local and national governments will bear the greatest burden for large-scale environmental policy and action within their jurisdictions. International co-operation is also needed in order to raise resources to support the developing countries in carrying out their responsibilities in this field. A growing class of environmental problems, because they are regional or global in extent or because they affect the common international realm, will require extensive co-operation among nations and action by international organizations in the common interest. The Conference calls upon Governments and peoples to exert common efforts for the preservation and improvement of the human environment, for the benefit of all the people and for their posterity.

II. Principles

States the common conviction that:

Principle 1

Man has the fundamental right to freedom, equality and adequate conditions of life, in an environment of a quality that permits a life of dignity and well-being, and he bears a solemn responsibility to protect and improve the environment for present and future generations. In this respect, policies promoting or perpetuating *apartheid*, racial segregation, discrimination, colonial and other forms of oppression and foreign domination stand condemned and must be eliminated.

Principle 2

The natural resources of the earth, including the air, water, land, flora and fauna and especially representative samples of natural ecosystems, must be safeguarded for the benefit of present and future generations through careful planning or management, as appropriate.

Principle 3

The capacity of the earth to produce vital renewable resources must be maintained and, wherever practicable, restored or improved.

Principle 4

Man has a special responsibility to safeguard and wisely manage the heritage of wildlife and its habitat, which are now gravely imperiled by a combination of adverse factors. Nature conservation, including wildlife, must therefore receive importance in planning for economic development.

Principle 5

The non-renewable resources of the earth must be employed in such a way as to guard against the danger of their future exhaustion and to ensure that benefits from such employment are shared by all mankind.

Principle 6

The discharge of toxic substances or of other substances and the release of heat, in such quantities or concentrations as to exceed the capacity of the environment to render them harmless, must be halted in order to ensure that serious or irreversible damage is not inflicted upon ecosystems. The just struggle of the peoples of all countries against pollution should be supported.

Principle 7

States shall take all possible steps to prevent pollution of the seas by substances that are liable to create hazards to human health, to harm living resources and marine life, to damage amenities or to interfere with other legitimate uses of the sea.

Principle 8

Economic and social development is essential for ensuring a favourable living and working environment for man and for creating conditions on earth that are necessary for the improvement of the quality of life.

Principle 9

Environmental deficiencies generated by the conditions of under-development and natural disasters pose grave problems and can best be remedied by accelerated development through the transfer of substantial quantities of financial and technological assistance as a supplement to the domestic effort of the developing countries and such timely assistance as may be required.

Principle 10

For the developing countries, stability of prices and adequate earnings for primary commodities and raw materials are essential to environmental management since economic factors as well as ecological processes must be taken into account.

Principle 11

The environmental policies of all States should enhance and not adversely affect the present or future development potential of developing countries, nor should they hamper the attainment of better living conditions for all, and appropriate steps should be taken by States and international organizations with a view to reaching agreement on meeting the possible national and international economic consequences resulting from the application of environmental measures.

Principle 12

Resources should be made available to preserve and improve the environment, taking into account the circumstances and particular requirements of developing countries and any costs which may emanate from their incorporating environmental safeguards into their development planning and the need for making available to them, upon their request, additional international technical and financial assistance for this purpose.

Principle 13

In order to achieve a more rational management of resources and thus to improve the environment, States should adopt an integrated and co-ordinated approach to their development planning so as to ensure that development is compatible with the need to protect and improve environment for the benefit of their population.

Principle 14

Rational planning constitutes an essential tool for reconciling any conflict between the needs of development and the need to protect and improve the environment.

Principle 15

Planning must be applied to human settlements and urbanization with a view to avoiding adverse effects on the environment and obtaining maximum social economic and environmental benefits for all. In this respect projects which are designed for colonialist and racist domination must be abandoned.

Principle 16

Demographic policies which are without prejudice to basic human rights and which are deemed appropriate by Governments concerned should be applied in those regions where the rate of population growth or excessive population concentrations are likely to have adverse effects on the environment of the human environment and impede development.

Principle 17

Appropriate national institutions must be entrusted with the task of planning, managing or controlling the environmental resources of States with a view to enhancing environmental quality.

Principle 18

Science and technology, as part of their contribution to economic and social development, must be applied to the identification, avoidance and control of environmental risks and the solution of environmental problems and for the common good of mankind.

Principle 19

Education in environmental matters, for the younger generation as well as adults, giving due consideration to the underprivileged, is essential in order to broaden the basis for an enlightened opinion and responsible conduct by individuals, enterprises and communities in protecting and improving the environment in its full human dimension. It is also essential that mass media of communications avoid contributing to the deterioration of the environment, but, on the contrary, disseminate information of an educational nature on the need to protect and improve the environment in order to enable man to develop in every respect.

Principle 20

Scientific research and development in the context of environmental problems, both national and multinational, must be promoted in all countries, especially the developing countries. In this connexion, the free flow of up-to-date scientific information and transfer of experience must be supported and assisted, to facilitate the solution of environmental problems; environmental technologies should be made available to developing countries on terms which would encourage their wide dissemination without constituting an economic burden on the developing countries.

Principle 21

States have, in accordance with the Charter of the United Nations and the principles of international law, the sovereign right to exploit their own resources pursuant to their own environmental policies, and the responsibility to ensure that activities within their jurisdiction or control do not cause damage to the environment of other States or of areas beyond the limits of national jurisdiction.

Principle 22

States shall co-operate to develop further the international law regarding liability and compensation for the victims of pollution and other environmental damage caused by activities within the jurisdiction or control of such States to areas beyond their jurisdiction.

Principle 23

Without prejudice to such criteria as may be agreed upon by the international community, or to standards which will have to be determined nationally, it will be essential in all cases to consider the system of values prevailing in each country, and the extent of the applicability of standards which are valid for the most advanced countries but which may be inappropriate and of unwarranted social cost for the developing countries.

Principle 24

International matters concerning the protection and improvement of the environment should be handled in a co-operative spirit by all countries, big and small, on an equal footing. Co-operation through multilateral or bilateral arrangements or other appropriate means is essential to effectively control, prevent, reduce and eliminate adverse environmental effects resulting from activities conducted in all spheres, in such a way that due account is taken of the sovereignty and interests of all States.

Principle 25

States shall ensure that international organizations play a co-ordinated, efficient and dynamic role for the protection and improvement of the environment.

Principle 26

Man and his environment must be spared the effects of nuclear weapons and all other means of mass destruction. States must strive to reach prompt agreement, in the relevant international organs, on the elimination and complete destruction of such weapons.

世界自然宪章[1]

(联合国第三十七届大会 1982 年 10 月 28 日通过)

大会,

重申联合国的基本宗旨,特别是维持国际和平与安全、发展各国间友好关系和进行国际合作以解决经济、社会、文化、技术、知识或人道方面的国际问题等宗旨,

认识到:

(a) 人类是自然的一部分,生命有赖于自然系统的功能维持不坠,以保证能源和养料的供应,

(b) 文明起源于自然,自然塑造了人类的文化,一切艺术和科学成就都受到自然的影响,人类与大自然和谐相处,才有最好的机会发挥创造力和得到休息与娱乐,

深信:

(a) 每种生命形式都是独特的,无论对人类的价值如何,都应得到尊重,为了给予其他有机体这样的承认,人类必须受行为道德准则的约束,

(b) 人类的行为或行为的后果,能够改变自然,耗尽自然资源;因此,人类必须充分认识到迫切需要维持大自然的稳定和素质,以及养护自然资源,

确信:

(a) 从大自然得到持久益处有赖于维持基本的生态过程和生命维持系统,也有赖于生命形式的多种多样,而人类过度开发或破坏生境会危害上述现象,

(b) 如果由于过度消耗和滥用自然资源以及各国和各国人民间未能建立起适当的经济秩序而使自然系统退化,文明的经济、社会、政治结构就会崩溃,

(c) 争夺稀有的资源会造成冲突,而养护大自然和自然资源则有助于伸张正义和维持和平,但只有在人类学会和平相处、摒弃战争和军备以后才能实现,

重申人类必须学会如何维持和增进他们利用自然资源的能力,同时保证能够保存各种物种和生态系统以造福今世和后代,

坚信有必要在国家和国际、个人和集体、公共和私人各级上采取适当措施,以保护大自然和促进这个领域内的国际合作,

为此目的,兹通过本《世界自然宪章》,宣布下列养护原则,指导和判断人类一切影响自然的行为。

一、一般原则

1. 应尊重大自然,不得损害大自然的基本过程。
2. 地球上的遗传活力不得加以损害;不论野生或家养,各种生命形式都必须至少维持其足以生存繁

---

[1] 引自:联合国大会第37/7号决议。

衍的数量，为此目的应该保障必要的生境。

3. 各项养护原则适用于地球上一切地区，包括陆地和海洋；独特地区、所有各种类生态系统的典型地带、罕见或有灭绝危险物种的生境，应受特别保护。

4. 对人类所利用的生态系统和有机体以及陆地、海洋和大气资源，应设法使其达到并维持最适宜的持续生产率，但不得危及与其共存的其他生态系统或物种的完整性。

5. 应保护大自然，使其免于因战争或其他敌对活动而退化。

二. 功能

6. 在决策过程中应认识到，只有确保自然系统适当发挥功能，并遵守本《宪章》载列的各项原则，才能够满足人类的需要。

7. 在规划和进行社会经济发展活动时，应适当考虑到养护自然是这些活动的一个组成部分。

8. 在制定经济发展、人口增长和提高生活水平的长期计划时，应适当考虑到自然系统须确有使有关人口的生存和居住的长期能力，同时认识到这种能力可以通过科学和技术加以提高。

9. 应计划地分配地球上各地区作何用途，并应适当考虑到有关地区的实质限制、生物生殖率和多样性以及自然美。

10. 自然资源不得浪费，应符合本《宪章》载列的原则，按照下列规则有节制地加以使用：

（a）生物资源的利用，不得超过其天然再生能力；

（b）应采取措施保持土壤的长期肥力和有机分解作用，并防止侵蚀和一切其他形式的退化，以维持或提高土壤的生产率；

（c）使用时并不消耗的资源，包括水资源，应将其回收利用或再循环；

（d）使用时会消耗的不可再生资源，应考虑到这些资源是否丰富、是否有可能合理地加以加工用于消费、其开发与自然系统的发挥功能是否相容等因素而有节制地开发。

11. 应控制那些可能影响大自然的活动，并应采用能尽量减轻对大自然构成重大危险或其他不利影响的现有最优良技术，特别是：

（a）应避免那些可能对大自然造成不可挽回的损害的活动；

（b）在进行可能对大自然构成重大危险的活动之前应先彻底调查；这种活动的倡议者必须证明预期的益处超过大自然可能受到的损害；如果不能完全了解可能造成的不利影响，活动即不得进行；

（c）在进行可能干扰大自然的活动之前应先估计后果，事先尽早研究发展项目对环境的影响；如确定要进行这些活动，则应周密计划之后再进行，以便最大限度地减低可能造成的不利影响；

（d）农、牧、林、渔业的活动应配合各自地区的自然特征和限制因素；

（e）因人类活动而退化的地区应予恢复，用于能配合其自然潜力并符合受损害居民福利的用途。

12. 应避免向自然系统排放污染物：

（a）如不得不排放污染物，应使用最佳的可行方法，于产生污染物的原地加以处理；

（b）应采取特殊预防措施，防止排放放射性或有毒废料。

13. 旨在预防、控制或限制自然灾害、虫害和病害的措施，应针对这些灾害的成因，并应避免对大自然产生有害的副作用。

三. 实施

14. 本《宪章》载列的各项原则应列入每个国家的以及国际一级的法律中，并予实行。

15. 有关大自然的知识应以一切可能手段广为传播，特别是应进行生态教育，使其成为普通教育的一个组成部分。

16. 所有规划工作都应将拟订养护大自然的战略、建立生态系统的清单、评估拟议的政策和活动对大自然的影响等列为基本要素；所有这些要素都应以适当方式及时公告周知，以便得到有效的咨商和参与。

17. 应提供必要的资金、计划和行政结构以实现养护大自然的目的。

18. 应经常努力进行科学研究以增进有关大自然的知识，并不受任何限制地广为传播这种知识。

19. 应密切监测自然过程、生态系统和物种的状况，以便尽早察觉退化或受威胁情况，保证及时干预，并便利对养护政策和方法的评价。

20. 应避免进行损及大自然的军事活动。

21. 各国和有此能力的其他公共机构、国际组织、个人、团体和公司都应：

（a）通过共同活动和其他有关活动，包括交换情报和协商，合作进行养护大自然的工作；

（b）制定可能对大自然有不利影响的产品和制作程序的标准，以及议定评估这种影响的方法；

（c）实施有关的养护大自然和保护环境的国际法律规定；

（d）确保在其管辖或控制下的活动不损害别国境内或国家管辖范围以外地区的自然系统；

（e）保护和养护位于国家管辖范围以外地区的大自然。

22. 在充分顾到各国对其自然资源主权的情形下，每个国家均应通过本国主管机构并与其他国家合作，执行《宪章》的各项规定。

23. 人人都应当有机会按照本国法律个别地或集体地参加拟订与其环境直接有关的决定；遇到此种环境受损或退化时，应有办法诉请补救。

24. 人人有义务按照本《宪章》的规定行事；人人都应个别地或集体地采取行动，或通过参与政治生活，尽力保证达到本《宪章》的目标和要求。

World Charter for Nature

Adopted by the 37th United Nations General Assembly, 28 October 1982

The General Assembly,

Reaffirming the fundamental purposes of the United Nations, in particular the maintenance of international peace and security, the development of friendly relations among nations and the achievement of international co-operation in solving international problems of an economic, social, cultural, technical, intellectual or humanitarian character,

Aware that:

(a) Mankind is a part of nature and life depends on the uninterrupted functioning of natural systems which ensure the supply of energy and nutrients,

(b) Civilization is rooted in nature, which has shaped human culture and influenced all artistic and scientific achievement, and living in harmony with nature gives man the best opportunities for the development of his creativity, and for rest and recreation,

Convinced that:

(a) Every form of life is unique, warranting respect regardless of its worth to man, and, to accord other organisms such recognition, man must be guided by a moral code of action,

(b) Man can alter nature and exhaust natural resources by his action or its consequences and, therefore, must fully recognize the urgency of maintaining the stability and quality of nature and of conserving natural resources,

Persuaded that:

(a) Lasting benefits from nature depend upon the maintenance of essential ecological processes and life support systems, and upon the diversity of life forms, which are jeopardized through excessive exploitation and habitat destruction by man,

(b) The degradation of natural systems owing to excessive consumption and misuse of natural resources, as well as to failure to establish an appropriate economic order among peoples and among States, leads to the breakdown of the economic, social and political framework of civilization,

(c) Competition for scarce resources creates conflicts, whereas the conservation of nature and natural resources contributes to justice and the maintenance of peace and cannot be achieved until mankind learns to live in peace and to forsake war and armaments,

Reaffirming that man must acquire the knowledge to maintain and enhance his ability to use natural resources in a manner which ensures the preservation of the species and ecosystems for the benefit of present and future generations,

---

① UN Resolution No. : A/RES/37/7.

Firmly convinced of the need for appropriate measures, at the national and international, individual and collective, and private and public levels, to protect nature and promote international co-operation in this field,

Adopts, to these ends, the present World Charter for Nature, which proclaims the following principles of conservation by which all human conduct affecting nature is to be guided and judged.

I. GENERAL PRINCIPLES

1. Nature shall be respected, and its essential processes shall not be impaired.

2. The genetic viability on the earth shall not be compromised; the population levels of all life forms, wild and domesticated, must be at least sufficient for their survival, and to this end necessary habitats shall be safeguarded.

3. All areas of the earth, both land and sea, shall be subject to these principles of conservation; special protection shall be given to unique areas, to representative samples of all the different types of ecosystems and to the habitats of rare or endangered species.

4. Ecosystems and organisms, as well as the land, marine and atmospheric resources that are utilized by man, shall be managed to achieve and maintain optimum sustainable productivity, but not in such a way as to endanger the integrity of those other ecosystems or species with which they coexist.

5. Nature shall be secured against degradation caused by warfare or other hostile activities.

II. FUNCTIONS

6. In the decision-making process it shall be recognized that man's needs can be met only by ensuring the proper functioning of natural systems and by respecting the principles set forth in the present Charter.

7. In the planning and implementation of social and economic development activities, due account shall be taken of the fact that the conservation of nature is an integral part of those activities.

8. In formulating long-term plans for economic development, population growth and the improvement of standards of living, due account shall be taken of the long-term capacity of natural systems to ensure the subsistence and settlement of the populations concerned, recognizing that this capacity may be enhanced through science and technology.

9. The allocation of areas of the earth to various uses shall be planned, and due account shall be taken of the physical constraints, the biological productivity and diversity and the natural beauty of the areas concerned.

10. Natural resources shall not be wasted, but used with a restraint appropriate to the principles set forth in the present Charter, in accordance with the following rules:

(a) Living resources shall not be utilized in excess of their natural capacity for regeneration;

(b) The productivity of soils shall be maintained or enhanced through measures which safeguard their long-term fertility and the process of organic decomposition, and prevent erosion and all other forms of degradation;

(c) Resources, including water, which are not consumed as they are used shall be reused or recycled;

(d) Non-renewable resources which are consumed as they are used shall be exploited with restraint, taking into account their abundance, the rational possibilities of converting them for consumption, and the compatibility of their exploitation with the functioning of natural systems.

11. Activities which might have an impact on nature shall be controlled, and the best available technologies that minimize significant risks to nature or other adverse effects shall be used; in particular:

(a) Activities which are likely to cause irreversible damage to nature shall be avoided;

(b) Activities which are likely to pose a significant risk to nature shall be preceded by an exhaustive examination; their proponents shall demonstrate that expected benefits outweigh potential damage to nature, and where potential adverse effects are not fully understood, the activities should not proceed;

(c) Activities which may disturb nature shall be preceded by assessment of their consequences, and environmental impact studies of development projects shall be conducted sufficiently in advance, and if they are to be undertaken, such activities shall be planned and carried out so as to minimize potential adverse effects;

(d) Agriculture, grazing, forestry and fisheries practices shall be adapted to the natural characteristics and constraints of given areas;

(e) Areas degraded by human activities shall be rehabilitated for purposes in accord with their natural potential and compatible with the well-being of affected populations.

12. Discharge of pollutants into natural systems shall be avoided and:

(a) Where this is not feasible, such pollutants shall be treated at the source, using the best practicable means available;

(b) Special precautions shall be taken to prevent discharge of radioactive or toxic wastes.

13. Measures intended to prevent, control or limit natural disasters, infestations and diseases shall be specifically directed to the causes of these scourges and shall avoid adverse side-effects on nature.

III. IMPLEMENTATION

14. The principles set forth in the present Charter shall be reflected in the law and practice of each State, as well as at the international level.

15. Knowledge of nature shall be broadly disseminated by all possible means, particularly by ecological education as an integral part of general education.

16. All planning shall include, among its essential elements, the formulation of strategies for the conservation of nature, the establishment of inventories of ecosystems and assessments of the effects on nature of proposed policies and activities; all of these elements shall be disclosed to the public by appropriate means in time to permit effective consultation and participation.

17. Funds, programmes and administrative structures necessary to achieve the objective of the conservation of nature shall be provided.

18. Constant efforts shall be made to increase knowledge of nature by scientific research and to disseminate such knowledge unimpeded by restrictions of any kind.

19. The status of natural processes, ecosystems and species shall be closely monitored to enable early detection of degradation or threat, ensure timely intervention and facilitate the evaluation of conservation policies and methods.

20. Military activities damaging to nature shall be avoided.

21. States and, to the extent they are able, other public authorities, international organizations, individuals, groups and corporations shall:

(a) Co-operate in the task of conserving nature through common activities and other relevant actions, including information exchange and consultations;

(b) Establish standards for products and manufacturing processes that may have adverse effects on nature, as well as agreed methodologies for assessing these effects;

(c) Implement the applicable international legal provisions for the conservation of nature and the protection of the environment;

(d) Ensure that activities within their jurisdictions or control do not cause damage to the natural systems located within other States or in the areas beyond the limits of national jurisdiction;

(e) Safeguard and conserve nature in areas beyond national jurisdiction.

22. Taking fully into account the sovereignty of States over their natural resources, each State shall give effect to the provisions of the present Charter through its competent organs and in co-operation with other States.

23. All persons, in accordance with their national legislation, shall have the opportunity to participate, individually or with others, in the formulation of decisions of direct concern to their environment, and shall have access to means of redress when their environment has suffered damage or degradation.

24. Each person has a duty to act in accordance with the provisions of the present Charter; acting individually, in association with others or through participation in the political process, each person shall strive to ensure that the objectives and requirements of the present Charter are met.

关于环境与发展的里约热内卢宣言[①]

（联合国环境与发展会议 1992 年 6 月 14 日在里约热内卢通过）

联合国环境与发展会议，

于 1992 年 6 月 3 日至 14 日在里约热内卢举行了会议，

重申 1972 年 6 月 16 日在斯德哥尔摩通过的《联合国人类环境会议的宣言》，并力求在其基础之上再提高一步；

怀着在各国、在社会各关键部门和在人民之间创造新的合作水平，从而建立一种新的、公平的全球伙伴关系的目标；

致力于达成既尊重所有各方的利益又能保护全球环境与发展体系的完整性的国际协定；

认识到我们地球的整体相互依存性质；

兹宣告：

原则 1

普受关注的可持续发展问题的中心是人。人有权顺应自然，过健康而有生产能力的生活。

原则 2

根据《联合国宪章》和国际法原则，各国拥有按照本国的环境与发展政策开发本国自然资源的主权权利，并负有确保在其管辖范围内或在其控制下的活动不致损害其他国家或在各国管辖范围以外地区的环境的责任。

原则 3

发展权利必须实现，以便能公平地满足今世后代在发展与环境方面的需要。

原则 4

为了实现可持续的发展，环境保护工作应是发展进程的一个整体构成部分，不能脱离这一进程予以孤立考虑。

原则 5

为了缩小世界上大多数人生活水平上的差距，更好地满足他们的需求，所有国家和所有人民都应在根除贫穷这项基本任务之上进行合作，这是实现可持续发展的绝对必要的条件。

原则 6

发展中国家、尤其是最不发达国家和在环境方面最易受伤害的发展中国家的特殊情况和需要应受到特别优先考虑。环境与发展领域的国际行动也应当着眼于所有国家的利益和需要。

原则 7

各国应本着全球伙伴精神，为保存、保护和恢复地球生态系统的健康和完整进行合作。鉴于导致全

[①] 引自：联合国环境与发展会议的报告，里约热内卢，1992年6月3至14日。UN Document: A/CONF.151/26/Rev.1(Vol.1)。

球环境退化的各种不同因素，各国负有共同的但是有差别的责任。发达国家承认，鉴于它们的社会给全球环境带来的压力，以及它们所掌握的技术和财力资源，它们在追求可持续发展的国际努力中负有责任。

原则 8

为了实现可持续的发展，使所有人民都享有较高的生活素质，各国应当减少和消除不能持续的生产和消费型态，并推行适当的人口政策。

原则 9

各国应当合作加强内部能力建设，以实现可持续的发展，做法是通过交流科技知识来提高科学认识，并增强各种技术包括新技术和革新性技术的开发、修改利用、传播和转让。

原则 10

环境问题最好是在所有关心环境的市民的参与下，在恰当的级别上加以处理。在国家一级，每一个人都应能适当取用公共当局所持有的关于环境的资料，包括关于在其社区内的危险物质和活动的资料，并应有机会参与各项决策进程。各国应通过广泛提供资料来便利及鼓励公众的认识和参与。应规定人人都能有效地使用司法和行政程序，包括补偿和补救程序。

原则 11

各国应制定有效的环境立法。环境标准、管理目标和优先次序应反映它们所适用的环境与发展情况。一些国家所实施的标准对别的国家特别是发展中国家来说可能是不适当的，也许会使它们承担不必要的经济和社会代价。

原则 12

为了更好地处理环境退化问题，各国应该合作促进一个起支持作用的、开放的国际经济制度，使所有国家实现经济增长和可持续的发展为环境目的而采取的贸易政策措施不应成为国际贸易中的一种任意或无理歧视的手段或成为变相的限制。应该避免在进口国家管辖范围以外单方面采取对付环境挑战的行动。解决跨越国界或全球性环境问题的环境措施应尽可能以国际共识为基础。

原则 13

各国应制定关于污染和其他环境损害的责任以及赔偿受害者的国内法。各国还应迅速并且更坚决地进行合作，进一步制定关于在其管辖或控制范围内的活动对在其管辖外的地区造成的环境损害的不利影响的责任和赔偿的国际法。

原则 14

各国应进行有效合作，劝阻或防止任何造成环境严重退化或证实有害人类健康的活动及物质迁移和转让他国。

原则 15

为了保护环境，各国应按照本国的能力，广泛采用防备措施。遇有严重或不可逆转损害的威胁时，不得以缺乏科学的充分可靠性为理由，延迟采取符合成本效益的措施防止环境退化。

原则 16

考虑到污染者原则上应承担污染费用的观点，国家当局应该努力促使内部吸收环境成本费用，并利用各种经济手段，要适当地照顾到公众利益，又不要使国际贸易和投资失常。

原则 17

凡是可能对环境产生重大不利影响的拟议活动，均应进行环境影响评价，环境影响评价是一种国家手段，须由主管国家当局作决定。

原则 18

各国应将可能对他国环境产生突发的有害影响的任何自然灾害或其他紧急情况立即通知这些国家。

国际社会应尽一切努力帮助受灾国家。

原则 19

各国应就可能具有重大不利的跨国界环境影响的活动向可能受影响的国家预先和及时地发出通知和提供有关资料，并应在早期阶段诚意地同这些国家进行磋商。

原则 20

妇女在环境管理和发展方面具有重大作用。因此，她们的充分参加对实现可持续发展至关重要。

原则 21

应调动世界青年的创造力、理想和勇气，培养全球伙伴精神，以期实现可持续发展，保证人人有一个更好的将来。

原则 22

由于土著人民及其社区和其他当地社区的知识和传统习惯，他们在环境管理和发展方面具有重大作用。各国应承认和适当维护他们的特性、文化和利益，并使他们能有效地参加实现可持续的发展。

原则 23

受压迫、遭统治和被占领的人民，其环境和自然资源应予保护。

原则 24

战争本来就会破坏可持续发展。因此各国应遵守国际法关于在武装冲突期间保护环境的规定，并于必要时合作促进其进一步发展。

原则 25

和平、发展和保护环境是互相依存、不可分割的。

原则 26

各国应按照《联合国宪章》用适当方法和平地解决其一切环境争端。

原则 27

所有国家和人民均应诚意地本着伙伴精神，合作实现本宣言所体现的各项原则，合作推动可持续发展方面的国际法的进一步发展。

Rio Declaration on Environment and Development [1]

Adopted by the United Nations Conference on Environment and Development, Rio de Janeiro, 14 June 1992

The United Nations Conference on Environment and Development,

Having met at Rio de Janeiro from 3 to 14 June 1992,

Reaffirming the Declaration of the United Nations Conference on the Human Environment, adopted at Stockholm on 16 June 1972 [2], and seeking to build upon it,

With the goal of establishing a new and equitable global partnership through the creation of new levels of cooperation among States, key sectors of societies and people,

Working towards international agreements which respect the interests of all and protect the integrity of the global environmental and developmental system,

Recognizing the integral and interdependent nature of the Earth, our home,

Proclaims that:

Principle 1

Human beings are at the centre of concerns for sustainable development. They are entitled to a healthy and productive life in harmony with nature.

Principle 2

States have, in accordance with the Charter of the United Nations and the principles of international law, the sovereign right to exploit their own resources pursuant to their own environmental and developmental policies, and the responsibility to ensure that activities within their jurisdiction or control do not cause damage to the environment of other States or of areas beyond the limits of national jurisdiction.

Principle 3

The right to development must be fulfilled so as to equitably meet developmental and environmental needs of present and future generations.

Principle 4

In order to achieve sustainable development, environmental protection shall constitute an integral part of the

---

[1] Report of the United Nations Conference on Environment and Development, Rio de Janeiro, 3-14 June 1992. UN Document: A/CONF.151/26/Rev.1(Vol.1).

[2] Report of the United Nations Conference on the Human Environment, Stockholm, 5-16 June 1972 (United Nations publication, Sales No. E.73.II.A.14 and corrigendum), chap. I.

development process and cannot be considered in isolation from it.

Principle 5

All States and all people shall cooperate in the essential task of eradicating poverty as an indispensable requirement for sustainable development, in order to decrease the disparities in standards of living and better meet the needs of the majority of the people of the world.

Principle 6

The special situation and needs of developing countries, particularly the least developed and those most environmentally vulnerable, shall be given special priority. International actions in the field of environment and development should also address the interests and needs of all countries.

Principle 7

States shall cooperate in a spirit of global partnership to conserve, protect and restore the health and integrity of the Earth's ecosystem. In view of the different contributions to global environmental degradation, States have common but differentiated responsibilities. The developed countries acknowledge the responsibility that they bear in the international pursuit of sustainable development in view of the pressures their societies place on the global environment and of the technologies and financial resources they command.

Principle 8

To achieve sustainable development and a higher quality of life for all people, States should reduce and eliminate unsustainable patterns of production and consumption and promote appropriate demographic policies.

Principle 9

States should cooperate to strengthen endogenous capacity-building for sustainable development by improving scientific understanding through exchanges of scientific and technological knowledge, and by enhancing the development, adaptation, diffusion and transfer of technologies, including new and innovative technologies.

Principle 10

Environmental issues are best handled with the participation of all concerned citizens, at the relevant level. At the national level, each individual shall have appropriate access to information concerning the environment that is held by public authorities, including information on hazardous materials and activities in their communities, and the opportunity to participate in decision-making processes. States shall facilitate and encourage public awareness and participation by making information widely available. Effective access to judicial and administrative proceedings, including redress and remedy, shall be provided.

Principle 11

States shall enact effective environmental legislation. Environmental standards, management objectives and priorities should reflect the environmental and developmental context to which they apply. Standards applied by some countries may be inappropriate and of unwarranted economic and social cost to other countries, in particular developing countries.

Principle 12

States should cooperate to promote a supportive and open international economic system that would lead to economic growth and sustainable development in all countries, to better address the problems of environmental degradation. Trade policy measures for environmental purposes should not constitute a means of arbitrary or unjustifiable discrimination or a disguised restriction on international trade. Unilateral actions to deal with environmental challenges outside the jurisdiction of the importing country should be avoided. Environmental measures addressing transboundary or global environmental problems should, as far as possible, be based on an international consensus.

Principle 13

States shall develop national law regarding liability and compensation for the victims of pollution and other environmental damage. States shall also cooperate in an expeditious and more determined manner to develop further international law regarding liability and compensation for adverse effects of environmental damage caused by activities within their jurisdiction or control to areas beyond their jurisdiction.

Principle 14

States should effectively cooperate to discourage or prevent the relocation and transfer to other States of any activities and substances that cause severe environmental degradation or are found to be harmful to human health.

Principle 15

In order to protect the environment, the precautionary approach shall be widely applied by States according to their capabilities. Where there are threats of serious or irreversible damage, lack of full scientific certainty shall not be used as a reason for postponing cost-effective measures to prevent environmental degradation.

Principle 16

National authorities should endeavour to promote the internalization of environmental costs and the use of economic instruments, taking into account the approach that the polluter should, in principle, bear the cost of pollution, with due regard to the public interest and without distorting international trade and investment.

Principle 17

Environmental impact assessment; as a national instrument, shall be undertaken for proposed activities that are likely to have a significant adverse impact on the environment and are subject to a decision of a competent national authority.

Principle 18

States shall immediately notify other States of any natural disasters or other emergencies that are likely to produce sudden harmful effects on the environment of those States. Every effort shall be made by the international community to help States so afflicted.

Principle 19

States shall provide prior and timely notification and relevant information to potentially affected States on activities that may have a significant adverse transboundary environmental effect and shall consult with those States at an early stage and in good faith.

Principle 20

Women have a vital role in environmental management and development. Their full participation is therefore essential to achieve sustainable development.

Principle 21

The creativity, ideals and courage of the youth of the world should be mobilized to forge a global partnership in order to achieve sustainable development and ensure a better future for all.

Principle 22

Indigenous people and their communities and other local communities have a vital role in environmental management and development because of their knowledge and traditional practices. States should recognize and duly support their identity, culture and interests and enable their effective participation in the achievement of sustainable development.

Principle 23

The environment and natural resources of people under oppression, domination and occupation shall be protected.

Principle 24

Warfare is inherently destructive of sustainable development. States shall therefore respect international law providing protection for environment in times of armed conflict and cooperate in its further development, as necessary.

Principle 25

Peace, development and environmental protection are interdependent and indivisible.

Principle 26

States shall resolve all their environmental disputes peacefully and by appropriate means in accordance with the Charter of the United Nations.

Principle 27

States and people shall cooperate in good faith and in a spirit of partnership in the fulfilment of the principles embodied in this Declaration and in the further development of international law in the field of sustainable development.

生物多样性公约[①]

(联合国环境与发展会议 1992 年 6 月 5 日在里约热内卢通过)

序 言

缔约国,

意识到生物多样性的内在价值,和生物多样性及其组成部分的生态、遗传、社会、经济、科学、教育、文化、娱乐和美学价值;

还意识到生物多样性对进化和保持生物圈的生命维持系统的重要性;

确认生物多样性的保护是全人类的共同关切事项;

重申各国对它自己的生物资源拥有主权权利;

也重申各国有责任保护它自己的生物多样性并以可持久的方式使用它自己的生物资源;

关切一些人类活动正在导致生物多样性的严重减少;

意识到普遍缺乏关于生物多样性的资料和知识,亟需开发科学、技术和机构能力,从而提供基本理解,据以策划与执行适当措施;

注意到预测、预防和从根源上消除导致生物多样性严重减少或丧失的原因,至为重要;

并注意到生物多样性遭受严重减少或损失的威胁时,不应以缺乏充分的科学定论为理由,而推迟采取旨在避免或尽量减轻此种威胁的措施;

注意到保护生物多样性的基本要求,是就地保护生态系统和自然生境,维持恢复物种在其自然环境中有生存力的群体;

并注意到移地措施,最好在原产国内实行,也可发挥重要作用;

认识到许多体现传统生活方式的土著和地方社区同生物资源有着密切和传统的依存关系,应公平分享从利用与保护生物资源及持久使用其组成部分有关的传统知识、创新和作法而产生的惠益;

并认识到妇女在保护和持久使用生物多样性中发挥的极其重要作用,并确认妇女必须充分参与保护生物多样性的各级政策的制订和执行;

强调为了生物多样性的保护及其组成部分的持久使用,促进国家、政府间组织和非政府部门之间的国际、区域和全球性合作的重要性和必要性;

承认提供新的和额外的资金和适当取得有关的技术,可对全世界处理生物多样性丧失问题的能力产生重大影响;

进一步承认有必要订立特别规定,以满足发展中国家的需要,包括提供新的和额外的资金和适当取得有关的技术;

[①] 引自:联合国文件UN FILE Ch_XXVII_8。

注意到最不发达国家和小岛屿国家这方面的特殊情况;

承认有必要大量投资以保护生物多样性,而且这些投资可望产生广泛的环境、经济和社会惠益;

认识到经济和社会发展以及根除贫困是发展中国家第一和压倒一切的优先事务;

意识到保护和持久使用生物多样性对满足世界日益增加的人口的粮食、健康和其他需求至为重要,而为此目的取得和分享遗传资源和遗传技术是必不可少的;

注重到保护和持久使用生物多样性终必增强国家间的友好关系,并有助于实现人类和平;

期望加强和补充现有保护生物多样性和持久使用其组成部分的各项国际安排;并

决心为今世后代的利益,保护和持久使用生物多样性,

兹协议如下:

第1条 目标

本公约的目标是按照本公约有关条款从事保护生物多样性、持久使用其组成部分以及公平合理分享由利用遗传资源而产生的惠益;实现手段包括遗传资源的适当取得及有关技术的适当转让,但需顾及对这些资源和技术的一切权利,以及提供适当资金。

第2条 用语

为本公约的目的:

"生物多样性"是指所有来源的形形色色生物体,这些来源除其他外包括陆地、海洋和其他水生生态系统及其所构成的生态综合体;这包括物种内部、物种之间和生态系统的多样性。

"生物资源"是指对人类具有实际或潜在用途或价值的遗传资源、生物体或其部分、生物群体、或生态系统中任何其他生物组成部分。

"生物技术"是指使用生物系统、生物体或其衍生物的任何技术应用,以制作或改变产品或过程以供特定用途。

"遗传资源的原产国"是指拥有处于原产境地的遗传资源的国家。

"提供遗传资源的国家"是指供应遗传资源的国家,此种遗传资源可能是取自原地来源,包括野生物种和驯化物种的群体,或取自移地保护来源,不论是否原产于该国。

"驯化或培殖物种"是指人类为满足自身需要而影响了其演化进程的物种。

"生态系统"是指植物、动物和微生物群落和它们的无生命环境作为一个生态单位交互作用形成的一个动态复合体。

"移地保护"是指将生物多样性的组成部分移到它们的自然环境之外进行保护。

"遗传材料"是指来自植物、动物、微生物或其他来源的任何含有遗传功能单位的材料。

"遗传资源"是指具有实际或潜在价值的遗传材料。

"生境"是指生物体或生物群体自然分布的地方或地点。

"原地条件"是指遗传资源生存于生态系统和自然生境之内的条件;对于驯化或培殖的物种而言,其环境是指它们在其中发展出其明显特性的环境。

"就地保护"是指保护生态系统和自然生境以及维持和恢复物种在其自然环境中有生存力的群体;对于驯化和培殖物种而言,其环境是指它们在其中发展出其明显特性的环境。

"保护区"是指一个划定地理界限、为达到特定保护目标而指定或实行管制和管理的地区。

"区域经济一体化组织"是指由某一区域的一些主权国家组成的组织,其成员国已将处理本公约范围内的事务的权力付托它并已按照其内部程序获得正式授权,可以签署、批准、接受、核准或加入本公约。

"持久使用"是指使用生物多样性组成部分的方式和速度不会导致生物多样性的长期衰落,从而保持其满足今世后代的需要和期望的潜力。

"技术"包括生物技术。

第3条 原则

依照联合国宪章和国际法原则,各国具有按照其环境政策开发其资源的主权权利,同时亦负有责任,确保在它管辖或控制范围内的活动,不致对其他国家的环境或国家管辖范围以外地区的环境造成损害。

第4条 管辖范围

以不妨碍其他国家权利为限,除非本公约另有明文规定,本公约规定应按下列情形对每一缔约国适用:

(a) 生物多样性组成部分位于该国管辖范围的地区内;

(b) 在该国管辖或控制下开展的过程和活动,不论其影响发生在何处,此种过程和活动可位于该国管辖区内也可在国家管辖区外。

第5条 合作

每一缔约国应尽可能并酌情直接与其他缔约国或酌情通过有关国际组织为保护和持久使用生物多样性在国家管辖范围以外地区并就共同关心的其他事项进行合作。

第6条 保护和持久使用方面的一般措施

每一缔约国应按照其特殊情况和能力:

(a) 为保护和持久使用生物多样性制定国家战略、计划或方案,或为此目的变通其现有战略、计划或方案;这些战略、计划或方案除其他外应体现本公约内载明与该缔约国有关的措施;

(b) 尽可能并酌情将生物多样性的保护和持久使用订入有关的部门或跨部门计划、方案和政策内。

第7条 查明与监测

每一缔约国应尽可能并酌情,特别是为了第8条至第10条的目的:

(a) 查明对保护和持久使用生物多样性至关重要的生物多样性组成部分,要顾及附件一所载指示性种类清单;

(b) 通过抽样调查和其他技术,监测依照以上(a)项查明的生物多样性组成部分,要特别注意那些需要采取紧急保护措施以及那些具有最大持久使用潜力的组成部分;

(c) 查明对保护和持久使用生物多样性产生或可能产生重大不利影响的过程和活动种类,并通过抽样调查和其他技术,监测其影响;

(d) 以各种方式维持并整理依照以上(a)(b)和(c)项从事查明和监测活动所获得的数据。

第8条 就地保护

每一缔约国应尽可能并酌情:

(a) 建立保护区系统或需要采取特殊措施以保护生物多样性的地区;

(b) 于必要时,制定准则据以选定、建立和管理保护区或需要采取特殊措施以保护生物多样性的地区;

(c) 管制或管理保护区内外对保护生物多样性至关重要的生物资源,以确保这些资源得到保护和持久使用;

(d) 促进保护生态系统、自然生境和维护自然环境中有生存力的物种群体;

(e) 在保护区域的邻接地区促进无害环境的持久发展以谋增进这些地区的保护;

(f) 除其他外,通过制定和实施各项计划或其他管理战略,重建和恢复已退化的生态系统,促进受威胁物种的复原;

(g) 制定或采取办法以酌情管制、管理或控制由生物技术改变的活生物体在使用和释放时可能产生的危险,即可能对环境产生不利影响,从而影响到生物多样性的保护和持久使用,也要考虑到对人类健康的危险;

(h) 防止引进、控制或消除那些威胁到生态系统、生境或物种的外来物种;

(i) 设法提供现时的使用与生物多样性的保护及其组成部分的持久使用彼此相辅相成所需的条件;

(j) 依照国家立法,尊重、保存和维持土著和地方社区体现传统生活方式而与生物多样性的保护和持久使用相关的知识、创新和做法并促进其广泛应用,由此等知识、创新和做法的拥有者认可和参与其事并鼓励公平地分享因利用此等知识、创新和做法而获得的惠益;

(k) 制定或维持必要立法和/或其他规范性规章,以保护受威胁物种和群体;

(l) 在依照第7条确定某些过程或活动类别已对生物多样性造成重大不利影响时,对有关过程和活动类别进行管制或管理;

(m) 进行合作,就以上(a)至(l)项所概括的就地保护措施特别向发展中国家提供财务和其他支助。

第9条 移地保护

每一缔约国应尽可能并酌情,主要为辅助就地保护措施起见:

(a) 最好在生物多样性组成部分的原产国采取措施移地保护这些组成部分;

(b) 最好在遗传资源原产国建立和维持移地保护及研究植物、动物和微生物的设施;

(c) 采取措施以恢复和复兴受威胁物种并在适当情况下将这些物种重新引进其自然生境中;

(d) 对于为移地保护目的在自然生境中收集生物资源实施管制和管理,以免威胁到生态系统和当地的物种群体,除非根据以上(c)项必须采取临时性特别移地措施;

(e) 进行合作,为以上(a)至(d)项所概括的移地保护措施以及在发展中国家建立和维持移地保护设施提供财务和其他援助。

第10条 生物多样性组成部分的持久使用

每一缔约国应尽可能并酌情:

(a) 在国家决策过程中考虑到生物资源的保护和持久使用;

(b) 采取关于使用生物资源的措施,以避免或尽量减少对生物多样性的不利影响;

(c) 保障及鼓励那些按照传统文化惯例而且符合保护或持久使用要求的生物资源习惯使用方式;

(d) 在生物多样性已减少的退化地区支助地方居民规划和实施补救行动;

(e) 鼓励其政府当局和私营部门合作制定生物资源持久使用的方法。

第11条 鼓励措施

每一缔约国应尽可能并酌情采取对保护和持久使用生物多样性组成部分起鼓励作用的经济和社会措施。

第12条 研究和培训

缔约国考虑到发展中国家的特殊需要,应:

(a) 在查明、保护和持久使用生物多样性及其组成部分的措施方面建立和维持科技教育和培训方案,并为此种教育和培训提供支助以满足发展中国家的特殊需要;

(b) 特别在发展中国家,除其他外,按照缔约国会议根据科学、技术和工艺咨询事务附属机构的建议作出的决定,促进和鼓励有助于保护和持久使用生物多样性的研究;

(c) 按照第16、18和20条的规定,提倡利用生物多样性科研进展,制定生物资源的保护和持久使用方法,并在这方面进行合作。

第13条 公众教育和认识

缔约国应:

(a) 促进和鼓励对保护生物多样性的重要性及所需要的措施的理解,并通过大众传播工具进行宣传和将这些题目列入教育课程;

(b) 酌情与其他国家和国际组织合作制定关于保护和持久使用生物多样性的教育和公众认识方案。

第14条 影响评估和尽量减少不利影响

1. 每一缔约国应尽可能并酌情:

(a) 采取适当程序,要求就其可能对生物多样性产生严重不利影响的拟议项目进行环境影响评估,以期避免或尽量减轻这种影响，并酌情允许公众参加此种程序；

（b）采取适当安排，以确保其可能对生物多样性产生严重不利影响的方案和政策的环境后果得到适当考虑。

（c）在互惠基础上，就其管辖或控制范围内对其他国家或国家管辖范围以外地区生物多样性可能产生严重不利影响的活动促进通报、信息交流和磋商，其办法是为此鼓励酌情订立双边、区域或多边安排；

（d）如遇其管辖或控制下起源的危险即将或严重危及或损害其他国家管辖的地区内或国家管辖地区范围以外的生物多样性的情况，应立即将此种危险或损害通知可能受影响的国家，并采取行动预防或尽量减轻这种危险或损害；

（e）促进做出国家紧急应变安排，以处理大自然或其他原因引起即将严重危及生物多样性的活动或事件，鼓励旨在补充这种国家努力的国际合作，并酌情在有关国家或区域经济一体化组织同意的情况下制订联合应急计划。

2. 缔约国会议应根据所作的研究，审查生物多样性所受损害的责任和补救问题，包括恢复和赔偿，除非这种责任纯属内部事务。

第15条　遗传资源的取得

1. 确认各国对其自然资源拥有的主权权利，因而可否取得遗传资源的决定权属于国家政府，并依照国家法律行使。

2. 每一缔约国应致力创造条件，便利其他缔约国取得遗传资源用于无害环境的用途，不对这种取得施加违背本公约目标的限制。

3. 为本公约的目的，本条以及第16和第19条所指缔约国提供的遗传资源仅限于这种资源原产国的缔约国或按照本公约取得该资源的缔约国所提供的遗传资源。

4. 取得经批准后，应按照共同商定的条件并遵照本条的规定进行。

5. 遗传资源的取得须经提供这种资源的缔约国事先知情同意，除非该缔约国另有决定。

6. 每一缔约国使用其他缔约国提供的遗传资源从事开发和进行科学研究时，应力求这些缔约国充分参与，并于可能时在这些缔约国境内进行。

7. 每一缔约国应按照第16和19条，并于必要时利用第20和21条设立的财务机制，酌情采取立法、行政或政策性措施，以期与提供遗传资源的缔约国公平分享研究和开发此种资源的成果以及商业和其他方面利用此种资源所获的利益。这种分享应按照共同商定的条件。

第16条　技术的取得和转让

1. 每一缔约国认识到技术包括生物技术，且缔约国之间技术的取得和转让均为实现本公约目标必不可少的要素，因此承诺遵照本条规定向其他缔约国提供和／或便利其取得并向其转让有关生物多样性保护和持久使用的技术或利用遗传资源而不对环境造成重大损害的技术。

2. 以上第1款所指技术的取得和向发展中国家转让，应按公平和最有利条件提供或给予便利，包括共同商定时，按减让和优惠条件提供或给予便利，并于必要时按照第20和21条设立的财务机制。此种技术属于专利和其他知识产权的范围时，这种取得和转让所根据的条件应承认且符合知识产权的充分有效保护。本款的应用应符合以下第3、4和5款的规定。

3. 每一缔约国应酌情采取立法、行政或政策措施，以期根据共同商定的条件向提供遗传资源的缔约国，特别是其中的发展中国家，提供利用这些遗传资源的技术和转让此种技术，其中包括受到专利和其他知识产权保护的技术，必要时通过第20条和第21条的规定，遵照国际法，以符合以下第4和5款规定的方式进行。

4. 每一缔约国应酌情采取立法、行政或政策措施，以期私营部门为第1款所指技术的取得、共同开发和转让提供便利，以惠益于发展中国家的政府机构和私营部门，并在这方面遵守以上第1、2和3款规定的义务。

5.缔约国认识到专利和其他知识产权可能影响到本公约的实施，因而应在这方面遵照国家立法和国际法进行合作，以确保此种权利有助于而不违反本公约的目标。

第17条　信息交流

1.缔约国应便利有关生物多样性保护和持久使用的一切公众可得信息的交流，要顾到发展中国家的特殊需要。

2.此种信息交流应包括交流技术、科学和社会经济研究成果，以及培训和调查方案的信息、专门知识、当地和传统知识本身及连同第16条第1款中所指的技术。可行时也应包括信息的归还。

第18条　技术和科学合作

1.缔约国应促进生物多样性保护和持久使用领域的国际科技合作，必要时可通过适当的国际机构和国家机构来开展这种合作。

2.每一缔约国应促进与其他缔约国尤其是发展中国家的科技合作，以执行本公约，办法之中包括制定和执行国家政策。促进此种合作时应特别注意通过人力资源开发和机构建设以发展和加强国家能力。

3.缔约国会议应在第一次会议上确定如何设立交换所机制以促进并便利科技合作。

4.缔约因为实现本公约的目标，应按照国家立法和政策，鼓励并制定各种合作方法以开发和使用各种技术，包括当地技术和传统技术在内。为此目的，缔约国还应促进关于人员培训和专家交流的合作。

5.缔约国应经共同协议促进设立联合研究方案和联合企业，以开发与本公约目标有关的技术。

第19条　生物技术的处理及其惠益的分配

1.每一缔约国应酌情采取立法、行政和政策措施，让提供遗传资源用于生物技术研究的缔约国，特别是其中的发展中国家，切实参与此种研究活动；可行时，研究活动宜在这些缔约国中进行。

2.每一缔约国应采取一切可行措施，以赞助和促进那些提供遗传资源的缔约国，特别是其中的发展中国家，在公平的基础上优先取得基于其提供资源的生物技术所产生成果和惠益。此种取得应按共同商定的条件进行。

3.缔约国应考虑是否需要一项议定书，规定适当程序，特别包括事先知情协议，适用于可能对生物多样性的保护和持久使用产生不利影响的由生物技术改变的任何活生物体的安全转让、处理和使用，并考虑该议定书的形式。

4.每一个缔约国应直接或要求其管辖下提供以上第3款所指生物体的任何自然人和法人，将该缔约国在处理这种生物体方面规定的使用和安全条例的任何现有资料以及有关该生物体可能产生的不利影响的任何现有资料，提供给将要引进这些生物体的缔约国。

第20条　资金

1.每一缔约国承诺依其能力为那些旨在根据其国家计划、优先事项和方案实现本公约目标的活动提供财政支助和鼓励。

2.发达国家缔约国应提供新的额外的资金，以使发展中国家缔约国能支付它们因执行那些履行本公约义务的措施而承负的议定的全部增加费用，并使它们能享到本公约条款产生的惠益；上项费用将由个别发展中国家同第21条所指的体制机构商定，但须遵循缔约国会议所制订的政策、战略、方案重点、合格标准和增加费用指示性清单。其他缔约国，包括那些处于向市场经济过渡进程的国家，得自愿承负发达国家缔约国的义务。为本条的目的，缔约国会议应在其第一次会议上确定一份发达国家缔约国和其他自愿承负发达国家缔约国义务的缔约国名单。缔约国会议应定期审查这份名单并于必要时加以修改。另将鼓励其他国家和来源以自愿方式作出捐款。履行这些承诺时，应考虑到资金提供必须充分、可预测和及时，且名单内缴款缔约国之间共同承担义务也极为重要。

3.发达国家缔约国也可通过双边、区域和其他多边渠道提供与执行本公约有关的资金，而发展中国家缔约国则可利用该资金。

4. 发展中国家缔约国有效地履行其根据公约作出的承诺的程度将取决于发达国家缔约国有效地履行其根据公约就财政资源和技术转让作出的承诺，并将充分顾及经济和社会发展以及消除贫困是发展中国家缔约国的首要优先事项这一事实。

5. 各缔约国在其就筹资和技术转让采取行动时应充分考虑到最不发达国家的具体需要和特殊情况。

6. 缔约国还应考虑到发展中国家缔约国、特别是小岛屿国家中由于对生物多样性的依赖、生物多样性的分布和地点而产生的特殊情况。

7. 发展中国家——包括环境方面最脆弱、例如境内有干旱和半干旱地带、沿海和山岳地区的国家的特殊情况也应予以考虑。

第 21 条　财务机制

1. 为本公约的目的，应有一机制在赠与或减让条件的基础上向发展中国家缔约国提供资金，本条中说明其主要内容。该机制应为本公约目的而在缔约国会议权力下履行职责，遵循会议的指导并向其负责。该机制的业务应由缔约国会议第一次会议或将决定采用的一个体制机构开展。为本公约的目的，缔约国会议应确定有关此项资源获取和利用的政策、战略、方案重点和资格标准。捐款额应按照缔约国会议定期决定所需的资金数额，考虑到第 20 条所指资金流动量充分、及时且可以预计的需要和列入第 20 条第 2 款所指名单的缴款缔约国分担负担的重要性。发达国家缔约国和其他国家及来源也可提供自愿捐款。该机制应在民主和透明的管理体制内开展业务。

2. 依据本公约目标，缔约国会议应在其第一次会议上确定政策、战略和方案重点，以及详细的资格标准和准则，用于资金的获取和利用，包括对此种利用的定期监测和评价。缔约国会议应在同受托负责财务机制运行的体制机构协商后，就实行以上第 1 款的安排作出决定。

3. 缔约国会议应在本公约生效后不迟于两年内，其后在定期基础上，审查依照本条规定设立的财务机制的功效，包括以上第 2 款所指的标准和准则。根据这种审查，会议应于必要时采取适当行动，以增进该机制的功效。

4. 缔约国应审议如何加强现有的金融机构，以便为生物多样性的保护和持久使用提供资金。

第 22 条　与其他国际公约的关系

1. 本公约的规定不得影响任何缔约国在任何现有国际协定下的权利和义务，除非行使这些权利和义务将严重破坏或威胁生物多样性。

2. 缔约国在海洋环境方面实施本公约不得抵触各国在海洋法下的权利和义务。

第 23 条　缔约国会议

1. 特此设立缔约国会议。缔约国会议第一次会议应由联合国环境规划署执行主任于本公约生效后一年内召开。其后，缔约国会议的常会应依照第一次会议所规定的时间定期举行。

2. 缔约国会议可于其认为必要的其他时间举行非常会议；如经任何缔约国书面请求，由秘书处将该项请求转致各缔约国后六个月内至少有三分之一缔约国表示支持时，亦可举行非常会议。

3. 缔约国会议应以协商一致方式商定和通过它本身的和它可能设立的任何附属机构的议事规则和关于秘书处经费的财务细则。缔约国会议应在每次常会通过到下届常会为止的财政期间的预算。

4. 缔约国会议应不断审查本公约的实施情形，为此应：

（a）就按照第 26 条规定递送的资料规定递送格式及间隔时间，并审议此种资料以及任何附属机构提交的报告；

（b）审查按照第 25 条提供的关于生物多样性的科学、技术和工艺咨询意见；

（c）视需要按照第 28 条审议并通过议定书；

（d）视需要按照第 29 和第 30 条审议并通过对本公约及其附件的修正；

（e）审议对任何议定书及其任何附件的修正，如做出修正决定，则建议有关议定书缔约国予以通过；
（f）视需要按照第 30 条审议并通过本公约的增补附件；
（g）视实施本公约的需要，设立附属机构，特别是提供科技咨询意见的机构；
（h）通过秘书处，与处理本公约所涉事项的各公约的执行机构进行接触，以期与它们建立适当的合作形式；
（i）参酌实施本公约取得的经验，审议并采取为实现本公约的目的可能需要的任何其他行动。

5. 联合国、其各专门机构和国际原子能机构以及任何非本公约缔约国的国家，均可派观察员出席缔约国会议。任何其他组织或机构，无论是政府性质或非政府性质，只要在与保护和持久使用生物多样性有关领域具有资格，并通知秘书处愿意以观察员身份出席缔约国会议，都可被接纳参加会议，除非有至少三分之一的出席缔约国表示反对。观察员的接纳与参加应遵照缔约国会议通过的议事规则处理。

第 24 条　秘书处

1. 特此设立秘书处，其职责如下：
（a）为第 23 条规定的缔约国会议作出安排并提供服务；
（b）执行任何议定书可能指派给它的职责；
（c）编制关于它根据本公约执行职责情况的报告，并提交缔约国会议；
（d）与其他有关国际机构取得协调，特别是订出各种必要的行政和合同安排，以便有效地执行其职责；
（e）执行缔约国会议可能规定的其他职责。

2. 缔约国会议应在其第一次常会上从那些已经表示愿意执行本公约规定的秘书处职责的现有合格国际组织之中指定某一组织为秘书处。

第 25 条　科学、技术和工艺咨询事务附属机构

1. 特此设立一个提供科学、技术和工艺咨询意见的附属机构，以向缔约国会议、并酌情向它的其他附属机构及时提供有关执行本公约的咨询意见。该机构应开放供所有缔约国参加，并应为多学科性。它应由有关专门知识领域内卓有专长的政府代表组成。它应定期向缔约国会议报告其各个方面的工作。

2. 这个机构应在缔约国会议的权力下，按照会议所订的准则并应其要求：
（a）提供关于生物多样性状况的科学和技术评估意见；
（b）编制有关按照本公约条款所采取各类措施的功效的科学和技术评估报告；
（c）查明有关保护和持久使用生物多样性的创新的、有效的和当代最先进的技术和专门技能，并就促进此类技术的开发和／或转让的途径和方法提供咨询意见；
（d）就有关保护和持久使用生物多样性的科学方案以及研究和开发方面的国际合作提供咨询意见；
（e）回答缔约国会议及其附属机构可能向其提出的有关科学、技术、工艺和方法的问题。

3. 这个机构的职责、权限、组织和业务可由缔约国会议进一步订立。

第 26 条　报告

每一缔约国应按缔约国会议决定的间隔时间，向缔约国会议提交关于该国为执行本公约条款已采取的措施以及这些措施在实现本公约目标方面的功效的报告。

第 27 条　争端的解决

1. 缔约国之间在就公约的解释或适用方面发生争端时，有关的缔约国应通过谈判方式寻求解决。

2. 如果有关缔约国无法以谈判方式达成协议，它们可以联合要求第三方进行斡旋或要求第三方出面调停。

3. 在批准、接受、核准或加入本公约时或其后的任何时候，一个国家或区域经济一体化组织可书面向保管者声明，对按照以上第 1 或第 2 款未能解决的争端，它接受下列一种或两种争端解决办法作为强制性办法：

（a）按照附件二第 1 部分规定的程序进行仲裁；

（b）将争端提交国际法院。

4. 如果争端各方尚未按照以上第 3 款规定接受同一或任何程序，则这项争端应按照附件二第 2 部分规定提交调解，除非缔约国另有协议。

5. 本项规定应适用于任何议定书，除非该议定书另有规定。

第 28 条 议定书的通过

1. 缔约国应合作拟订并通过本公约的议定书。

2. 议定书应由本公约缔约国会议举行会议通过。

3. 任何拟议议定书的案文应由秘书处至少在举行上述会议以前六个月递交各缔约国。

第 29 条 公约或议定书的修正

1. 任何缔约国均可就本公约提出修正案。议定书的任何缔约国可就该议定书提出修正案。

2. 本公约的修正案应由缔约国会议举行会议通过。对任何议定书的修正案应在该议定书缔约国的会议上通过。就本公约或任何议定书提出的修正案，除非该议定书另有规定，应由秘书处至少在举行拟议通过该修正案的会议以前六个月递交公约或有关议定书缔约国。秘书处也应将拟议的修正案递交本公约的签署国供其参考。

3. 缔约国应尽力以协商一致方式就本公约或任何议定书的任何拟议修正案达成协议，如果尽了一切努力仍无法以协商一致方式达成协议，则作为最后办法，应以出席并参加表决的有关文书的缔约国三分之二多数票通过修正案；通过的修正应由保管者送交所有缔约国批准、接受或核准。

4. 对修正案的批准、接受或核准，应以书面通知保管者。依照以上第 3 款通过的修正案，应于至少三分之二公约缔约国或三分之二有关议定书缔约国交存批准、接受或核准书之后第九十天在接受修正案的各缔约国之间生效，除非议定书内另有规定。其后，任何其他缔约国交存其对修正的批准、接受或核准书第九十天之后，修正即对它生效。

5. 为本条的目的，"出席并参加表决的缔约国"是指在场投赞成票或反对票的缔约国。

第 30 条 附件的通过和修正

1. 本公约或任何议定书的附件应成为本公约或该议定书的一个构成部分；除非另有明确规定，凡提及本公约或其议定书时，亦包括其任何附件在内。这种附件应以程序、科学、技术和行政事项为限。

2. 任何议定书就其附件可能另有规定者除外，本公约的增补附件或任何议定书的附件的提出、通过和生效，应适用下列程序：

（a）本公约或任何议定书的附件应依照第 29 条规定的程序提出和通过。

（b）任何缔约国如果不能接受本公约的某一增补附件或它作为缔约国的任何议定书的某一附件，应于保管者就其通过发出通知之日起一年内将此情况书面通知保管者。保管者应于接到任何此种通知后立即通知所有缔约国。一缔约国可于任何时间撤销以前的反对声明，有关附件即按以下（c）项规定对它生效。

（c）在保管者就附件通过发出通知之日起满一年后，该附件应对未曾依照以上（b）项发出通知的本公约或任何有关议定书的所有缔约国生效。

3. 本公约附件或任何议定书附件的修正案的提出、通过和生效，应遵照本公约附件或议定书附件的提出、通过和生效所适用的同一程序。

4. 如一个增补附件或对某一附件的修正案涉及对本公约或对任何议定书的修正，则该增补附件或修正案须于本公约或有关议定书的修正生效以后方能生效。

第 31 条 表决权

1. 除以下第 2 款之规定外，本公约或任何议定书的每一缔约国应有一票表决权。

2. 区域经济一体化组织对属于其权限的事项行使表决权时，其票数相当于其作为本公约或有关议定书缔约国的成员国数目。如果这些组织的成员国行使其表决权,则该组织就不应行使其表决权,反之亦然。

第 32 条　本公约与其议定书之间的关系

1. 一国或一区域经济一体化组织不得成为议定书缔约国,除非已是或同时成为本公约缔约国。

2. 任何议定书下的决定,只应由该议定书缔约国作出。尚未批准、接受或核准一项议定书的公约缔约国,得以观察员身份参加该议定书缔约国的任何会议。

第 33 条　签署

本公约应从 1992 年 6 月 5 日至 14 日在里约热内卢并从 1992 年 6 月 15 日至 1993 年 6 月 4 日在纽约联合国总部开放供各国和各区域经济一体化组织签署。

第 34 条　批准、接受或核准

1. 本公约和任何议定书须由各国和各区域经济一体化组织批准、接受或核准。批准、接受或核准书应交存保管者。

2. 以上第 1 款所指的任何组织如成为本公约或任何议定书的缔约组织而该组织没有任何成员国是缔约国,则该缔约组织应受公约或议定书规定的一切义务的约束。如这种组织的一个或多个成员国是本公约或有关议定书的缔约国,则该组织及其成员国应就履行其公约或议定书义务的各自责任作出决定。在这种情况下,该组织和成员国不应同时有权行使本公约或有关议定书规定的权利。

3. 以上第 1 款所指组织应在其批准、接受或核准书中声明其对本公约或有关议定书所涉事项的权限。这些组织也应将其权限的任何有关变化通知保管者。

第 35 条　加入

1. 本公约及任何议定书应自公约或有关议定书签署截止日期起开放供各国和各区域经济一体化组织加入。加入书应交存保管者。

2. 以上第 1 款所指组织应在其加入书中声明其对本公约或有关议定书所涉事项的权限。这些组织也应将其权限的任何有关变化通知保管者。

第 34 条第 2 款的规定应适用于加入本公约或任何议定书的区域经济一体化组织。

第 36 条　生效

1. 本公约应于第三十份批准、接受、核准或加入书交存之日以后第九十天生效。

2. 任何议定书应于该议定书订明份数的批准、接受、核准或加入书交存之日以后第九十天生效。

3. 对于在第三十份批准、接受、核准或加入书交存后批准、接受、核准本公约或加入本公约的每一缔约国,本公约应于该缔约国的批准、接受、核准或加入书交存之日以后第九十天生效。

4. 任何议定书,除非其中另有规定,对于在该议定书依照以上第 2 款规定生效后批准、接受、核准该议定书或加入该议定书的缔约国,应于该缔约国的批准、接受、核准或加入书交存之日以后第九十天生效,或于本公约对该缔约国生效之日生效,以两者中较后日期为准。

5. 为以上第 1 和第 2 款的目的,区域经济一体化组织交存的任何文书不得在该组织成员国所交存文书以外另行计算。

第 37 条　保留

不得对本公约作出任何保留。

第 38 条　退出

1. 一缔约国于本公约对其生效之日起两年之后的任何时间向保管者提出书面通知,可退出本公约。

2. 这种退出应在保管者接到退出通知之日起一年后生效,或在退出通知中指明的一个较后日期生效。

3. 任何缔约国一旦退出本公约,即应被视为也已退出它加入的任何议定书。

第 39 条　临时财务安排

在本公约生效之后至缔约国会议第一次会议期间,或至缔约国会议决定根据第 21 条指定某一体制机构为止，联合国开发计划署、联合国环境规划署和国际复兴开发银行合办的全球环境贷款设施若已按照第 21 条的要求充分改组，则应暂时为第 21 条所指的体制机构。

第 40 条 秘书处临时安排
在本公约生效之后至缔约国会议第一次会议期间，联合国环境规划署执行主任提供的秘书处应暂时为第 24 条第 2 款所指的秘书处。

第 41 条 保管者
联合国秘书长应负起本公约及任何议定书的保管者的职责。

第 42 条 作准文本
本公约原本应交存于联合国秘书长，其阿拉伯文、中文、英文、法文、俄文和西班牙文本均为作准文本。

为此，下列签名代表，经正式授权，在本公约上签字，以昭信守。

公元一千九百九十二年六月五日订于里约热内卢。

Convention on Biological Diversity

Adopted by the United Nations Conference on Environment and Development, Rio de Janeiro, 5 June 1992

Preamble

The Contracting Parties,

Conscious of the intrinsic value of biological diversity and of the ecological, genetic, social, economic, scientific, educational, cultural, recreational and aesthetic values of biological diversity and its components,

Conscious also of the importance of biological diversity for evolution and for maintaining life sustaining systems of the biosphere,

Affirming **that the conservation** of biological diversity is a common concern of humankind,

Reaffirming that States have sovereign rights over their own biological resources,

Reaffirming also that States are responsible for conserving their biological diversity and for using their biological resources in a sustainable manner,

Concerned that biological diversity is being significantly reduced by certain human activities,

Aware of the general lack of information and knowledge regarding biological diversity and of the urgent need to develop scientific, technical and institutional capacities to provide the basic understanding upon which to plan and implement appropriate measures,

Noting that it is vital to anticipate, prevent and attack the causes of significant reduction or loss of biological diversity at source,

Noting also that where there is a threat of significant reduction or loss of biological diversity, lack of full scientific certainty should not be used as a reason for postponing measures to avoid or minimize such a threat,

Noting further that the fundamental requirement for the conservation of biological diversity is the *in-situ* conservation of ecosystems and natural habitats and the maintenance and recovery of viable populations of species in their natural surroundings,

Noting further that *ex-situ* measures, preferably in the country of origin, also have an important role to play,

Recognizing the close and traditional dependence of many indigenous and local communities embodying traditional lifestyles on biological resources, and the desirability of sharing equitably benefits arising from the use of traditional knowledge, innovations and practices relevant to the conservation of biological diversity and the sustainable use of its components,

Recognizing also the vital role that women play in the conservation and sustainable use of biological diversity and affirming the need for the full participation of women at all levels of policy-making and implementation for biological diversity conservation,

---

① UN FILE Ch_XXVII_8.

Stressing the importance of, and the need to promote, international, regional and global cooperation among States and intergovernmental organizations and the non-governmental sector for the conservation of biological diversity and the sustainable use of its components,

Acknowledging that the provision of new and additional financial resources and appropriate access to relevant technologies can be expected to make a substantial difference in the world's ability to address the loss of biological diversity,

Acknowledging further that special provision is required to meet the needs of developing countries, including the provision of new and additional financial resources and appropriate access to relevant technologies,

Noting in this regard the special conditions of the least developed countries and small island States,

Acknowledging that substantial investments are required to conserve biological diversity and that there is the expectation of a broad range of environmental, economic and social benefits from those investments,

Recognizing that economic and social development and poverty eradication are the first and overriding priorities of developing countries,

Aware that conservation and sustainable use of biological diversity is of critical importance for meeting the food, health and other needs of the growing world population, for which purpose access to and sharing of both genetic resources and technologies are essential,

Noting that, ultimately, the conservation and sustainable use of biological diversity will strengthen friendly relations among States and contribute to peace for humankind,

Desiring to enhance and complement existing international arrangements for the conservation of biological diversity and sustainable use of its components, and

Determined to conserve and sustainably use biological diversity for the benefit of present and future generations.

Have agreed as follows:

Article 1   Objectives

The objectives of this Convention, to be pursued in accordance with its relevant provisions, are the conservation of biological diversity, the sustainable use of its components and the fair and equitable sharing of the benefits arising out of the utilization of genetic resources including by appropriate access to genetic resources and by appropriate transfer of relevant technologies, taking into account all rights over those resources and to technologies, and by appropriate funding.

Article 2   Use of Terms

For the purposes of this Convention:

"*Biological diversity*" means the variability among living organisms from all sources including, inter alia, terrestrial, marine and other aquatic ecosystems and the ecological complexes of which they are part; this includes diversity within species, between species and of ecosystems.

"*Biological resources* include genetic resources, organisms or parts thereof, populations, or any other biotic component of ecosystems with actual or potential use or value for humanity.

"*Biotechnology*" means any technological application that uses biological systems, living organisms, or derivatives thereof, to make or modify products or processes for specific use.

"*Country of origin of genetic resources*" means the country which possesses those genetic resources in *in-situ* conditions.

"*Country providing genetic resources*" means the country supplying genetic resources collected from *in-situ* sources, including populations of both wild and domesticated species, or taken from *ex-situ* sources, which may or may not have originated in that country.

"*Domesticated or cultivated species*" means species in which the evolutionary process has been influenced by humans to meet their needs.

"*Ecosystem*" means a dynamic complex of plant, animal and micro-organism communities and their non-living environment interacting as a functional unit.

"*Ex-situ conservation*" means the conservation of components of biological diversity outside their natural habitats.

"*Genetic material*" means any material of plant, animal, microbial or other origin containing functional units of heredity.

"*Genetic resources*" means genetic material of actual or potential value.

"*Habitat*" means the place or type of site where an organism or population naturally occurs.

"*In-situ conditions*" means conditions where genetic resources exist within ecosystems and natural habitats, and in the case of domesticated or cultivated species, in the surroundings where they have developed their distinctive properties.

"*In-situ conservation*" means the conservation of ecosystems and natural habitats and the maintenance and recovery of viable populations of species in their natural surroundings and, in the case of domesticated or cultivated species, in the surroundings where they have developed their distinctive properties.

"*Protected area*" means a geographically defined area which is designated or regulated and managed to achieve specific conservation objectives.

"*Regional economic integration organization*" means an organization constituted by sovereign States of a given region, to which its member States have transferred competence in respect of matters governed by this Convention and which has been duly authorized, in accordance with its internal procedures, to sign, ratify, accept, approve or accede to it.

"*Sustainable use*" means the use of components of biological diversity in a way and at a rate that does not lead to the long-term decline of biological diversity, thereby maintaining its potential to meet the needs and aspirations of present and future generations.

"*Technology*" includes biotechnology.

Article 3 Principle

States have, in accordance with the Charter of the United Nations and the principles of international law, the sovereign right to exploit their own resources pursuant to their own environmental policies, and the responsibility to ensure that activities within their jurisdiction or control do not cause damage to the environment of other States or of areas beyond the limits of national jurisdiction.

Article 4 Jurisdictional Scope

Subject to the rights of other States, and except as otherwise expressly provided in this Convention, the provisions of this Convention apply, in relation to each Contracting Party:

(a) In the case of components of biological diversity, in areas within the limits of its national jurisdiction; and

(b) In the case of processes and activities, regardless of where their effects occur, carried out under its jurisdiction or control, within the area of its national jurisdiction or beyond the limits of national jurisdiction.

Article 5 Cooperation

Each Contracting Party shall, as far as possible and as appropriate, cooperate with other Contracting Parties, directly or, where appropriate, through competent international organizations, in respect of areas beyond national jurisdiction and on other matters of mutual interest, for the conservation and sustainable use of biological diversity.

Article 6　General Measures for Conservation and Sustainable Use

Each Contracting Party shall, in accordance with its particular conditions and capabilities:

(a) Develop national strategies, plans or programmes for the conservation and sustainable use of biological diversity or adapt for this purpose existing strategies, plans or programmes which shall reflect, *inter alia*, the measures set out in this Convention relevant to the Contracting Party concerned and

(b) Integrate as far as possible and as appropriate, the conservation and sustainable use of biological diversity into relevant sectoral or cross-sectorial plans, programmes and policies.

Article 7　Identification and Monitoring

Each Contracting Party shall, as far as possible and as appropriate, in particular for the purposes of Articles 8 to 10:

(a) Identify components of biological diversity important for its conservation and sustainable use having regard to the indicative list of categories set down in Annex I ;

(b) Monitor, through sampling and other techniques, the components of biological diversity identified pursuant to subparagraph (a) above, paying particular attention to those requiring urgent conservation measures and those which offer the greatest potential for sustainable use;

(c) Identify processes and categories of activities which have or are likely to have significant adverse impacts on the conservation and sustainable use of biological diversity, and monitor their effects through sampling and other techniques; and

(d) Maintain and organize, by any mechanism data, derived from identification and monitoring activities pursuant to subparagraphs (a), (b) and (c) above.

Article 8　In-situ Conservation

Each Contracting Party shall, as far as possible and as appropriate:

(a) Establish a system of protected areas or areas where special measures need to be taken to conserve biological diversity;

(b) Develop, where necessary, guidelines for the selection, establishment and management of protected areas or areas where special measures need to be taken to conserve biological diversity;

(c) Regulate or manage biological resources important for the conservation of biological diversity whether within or outside protected areas, with a view to ensuring their conservation and sustainable use;

(d) Promote the protection of ecosystems, natural habitats and the maintenance of viable populations of species in natural surroundings;

(e) Promote environmentally sound and sustainable development in areas adjacent to protected areas with a view to furthering protection of these areas;

(f) Rehabilitate and restore degraded ecosystems and promote the recovery of threatened species, *inter alia*, through the development and implementation of plans or other management strategies;

(g) Establish or maintain means to regulate, manage or control the risks associated with the use and release of living modified organisms resulting from biotechnology which are likely to have adverse environmental impacts that could affect the conservation and sustainable use of biological diversity, taking also into account the risks to human health;

(h) Prevent the introduction of control or eradicate those alien species which threaten ecosystems, habitats or species;

(i) Endeavour to provide the conditions needed for compatibility between present uses and the conservation of biological diversity and the sustainable use of its components;

(j) Subject to its national legislation, respect, preserve and maintain knowledge, innovations and practices of indigenous and local communities embodying traditional lifestyles relevant for the conservation and sustainable use of biological diversity and promote their wider application with the approval and involvement of the holders of such knowledge, innovations and practices and encourage the equitable sharing of the benefits arising from the utilization of such knowledge, innovations and practices;

(k) Develop or maintain necessary legislation and/or other regulatory provisions for the protection of threatened species and populations;

(l) Where a significant adverse effect on biological diversity has been determined pursuant to Article 7, regulate or manage the relevant processes and categories of activities; and

(m) Cooperate in providing financial and other support for *in-situ* conservation outlined in subparagraphs (a) to (I) above, particularly to developing countries.

Article 9 Ex-situ Conservation

Each Contracting Party shall, as far as possible and as appropriate, and predominantly for the purpose of complementing *in-situ* measures:

(a) Adopt measures for the *ex-situ* conservation of components of biological diversity, preferably in the country of origin of such components;

(b) Establish and maintain facilities for *ex-situ* conservation of and research on plants, animals and micro-organisms, preferably in the country of origin of genetic resources;

(c) Adopt measures for the recovery and rehabilitation of threatened species and for their reintroduction into their natural habitats under appropriate conditions;

(d) Regulate and manage collection of biological resources from natural habitats for *ex-situ* conservation purposes so as not to threaten ecosystems and *in-situ* populations of species, except where special temporary *ex-situ* measures are required under subparagraph (c) above; and

(e) Cooperate in providing financial and other support for *ex-situ* conservation outlined in subparagraphs (a) to (d) above and in the establishment and maintenance of *ex-situ* conservation facilities in developing countries.

Article 10 Sustainable Use of Components of Biological Diversity

Each Contracting Party shall, as far as possible and as appropriate:

(a) Integrate consideration of the conservation and sustainable use of biological resources into national decision-making;

(b) Adopt measures relating to the use of biological resources to avoid or minimize adverse impacts on biological diversity;

(c) Protect and encourage customary use of biological resources in accordance with traditional cultural practices that are compatible with conservation or sustainable use requirements;

(d) Support local populations to develop and implement remedial action in degraded areas where biological diversity has been reduced; and

(e) Encourage cooperation between its governmental authorities and its private sector in developing methods for sustainable use of biological resources.

Article 11　Incentive Measures

Each Contracting Party shall, as far as possible and as appropriate, adopt economically and socially sound measures that act as incentives for the conservation and sustainable use of components of biological diversity.

Article 12　Research and Training

The Contracting Parties, taking into account the special needs of developing countries, shall:

(a) Establish and maintain programmes for scientific and technical education and training in measures for the identification, conservation and sustainable use of biological diversity and its components and provide support for such education and training for the specific needs of developing countries;

(b) Promote and encourage research which contributes to the conservation and sustainable use of biological diversity, particularly in developing countries, *inter alia*, in accordance with decisions of the Conference of the Parties taken in consequence of recommendations of the Subsidiary Body on Scientific, Technical and Technological Advice; and

(c) In keeping with the provisions of Articles 16, 18 and 20, promote and cooperate in the use of scientific advances in biological diversity research in developing methods for conservation and sustainable use of biological resources.

Article 13　Public Education and Awareness

The Contracting Parties shall:

(a) Promote and encourage understanding of the importance of and the measures required for, the conservation of biological diversity, as well as its propagation through media, and the inclusion of these topics in educational programmes; and

(b) Cooperate, as appropriate, with other States and international organizations in developing educational and public awareness programmes, with respect to conservation and sustainable use of biological diversity.

Article 14　Impact Assessment and Minimizing Adverse Impacts

1. Each Contracting Party, as far as possible and as appropriate shall:

(a) Introduce appropriate procedures requiring environmental impact assessment of its proposed projects that are likely to have significant adverse effects on biological diversity with a view to avoiding or minimizing such effects and, where appropriate, allow for public participation in such procedures;

(b) Introduce appropriate arrangements to ensure that the environmental consequences of its programmes and policies that are likely to have significant adverse impacts on biological diversity are duly taken into account;

(c) Promote, on the basis of reciprocity, notification, exchange of information and consultation on activities under their jurisdiction or control which are likely to significantly affect adversely the biological diversity of other States or areas beyond the limits of national jurisdiction, by encouraging the conclusion of bilateral, regional or multilateral arrangements, as appropriate;

(d) In the case of imminent or grave danger or damage, originating under its jurisdiction or control, to biological diversity within the area under jurisdiction of other States or in areas beyond the limits of national jurisdiction, notify immediately the potentially affected States of such danger or damage, as well as initiate action to prevent or minimize such danger or damage; and

(e) Promote national arrangements for emergency responses to activities or events, whether caused naturally or otherwise which present a grave and imminent danger to biological diversity and encourage international cooperation to supplement such national efforts and, where appropriate and agreed by the States or regional economic integration organizations concerned, to establish joint contingency plans.

2. The Conference of the Parties shall examine, on the basis of studies to be carried out, the issue of liability and redress, including restoration and compensation, for damage to biological diversity, except where such liability is a purely internal matter.

Article 15 Access to Genetic Resources

1. Recognizing the sovereign rights of States over their natural resources, the authority to determine access to genetic resources rests with the national governments and is subject to national legislation.

2. Each Contracting Party shall endeavor to create renditions to facilitate access to genetic resources for environmentally sound uses by other Contracting Parties and not to impose restrictions that run counter to the objectives of this Convention.

3. For the purpose of this Convention, the genetic resources being provided by a Contracting Party, as referred to in this Article and Articles 16 and 19, are only those that are provided by Contracting Parties that are countries of origin of such resources or by the Parties that have acquired the genetic resources in accordance with this Convention.

4. Access, where granted, shall be on mutually agreed terms and subject to the provisions of this Article.

5. Access to genetic resources shall be subject to prior informed consent of the Contracting Party providing such resources, unless otherwise determined by that Party.

6. Each Contracting Party shall endeavor to develop and carry out scientific research based on genetic resources provided by other Contracting Parties with the full participation of, and where possible in such Contracting Parties.

7. Each Contracting Party shall take legislative, administrative or policy measures, as appropriate, and in accordance with Articles 16 and 19 and, where necessary, through the financial mechanism established by Articles 20 and 21 with the aim of sharing in a fair and equitable way the results of research and development and the benefits arising from the commercial and other utilization of genetic resources with the Contracting Party providing such resources. Such sharing shall be upon mutually agreed terms.

Article 16 Access to and Transfer of Technology

1. Each Contracting Party, recognizing that technology includes biotechnology, and that both access to and transfer of technology among Contracting Parties are essential elements for the attainment of the objectives of this Convention, undertakes subject to the provisions of this Article to provide and/or facilitate access for and transfer to other Contracting Parties of technologies that are relevant to the conservation and sustainable use of biological diversity or make use of genetic resources and do not cause significant damage to the environment.

2. Access to and transfer of technology referred to in paragraph 1 above to developing countries shall be provided and/or facilitated under fair and most favourable terms, including on concessional and preferential terms where mutually agreed, and, where necessary, in accordance with the financial mechanism established by Articles 20 and 21. In the case of technology subject to patents and other intellectual property rights, such access and transfer shall be provided on terms which recognize and are consistent with the adequate and effective protection of intellectual property rights. The application of this paragraph shall be consistent with paragraphs 3, 4 and 5 below.

3. Each Contracting Party shall take legislative, administrative or policy measures, as appropriate, with the aim that Contracting Parties, in particular those that are developing countries, which provide genetic resources are provided access to and transfer of technology which makes use of those resources, on mutually agreed terms, including technology protected by patents and other intellectual property rights, where necessary, through the provisions of Articles 20 and 21 and in accordance with international law and consistent with paragraphs 4

and 5 below.

4. Each Contracting Party shall take legislative, administrative or policy measures, as appropriate with the aim that the private sector facilitates access to, joint development and transfer of technology referred to in paragraph 1 above for the benefit of both governmental institutions and the private sector of developing countries and in this regard shall abide by the obligations included in paragraphs 1, 2 and 3 above.

5. The Contracting Parties, recognizing that patents and other intellectual property rights may have an influence on the implementation of this Convention, shall cooperate in this regard subject to national legislation and international law in order to ensure that such rights are supportive of and do not run counter to its objectives.

Article 17   Exchange of Information

1. The Contracting Parties shall facilitate the exchange of information, from all publicly available sources, relevant to the conservation and sustainable use of biological diversity, taking into account the special needs of developing countries.

2. Such exchange of information shall include exchange of results of technical, scientific and socio-economic research, as well as information on training and surveying programmes, specialized knowledge, indigenous and traditional knowledge as such and in combination with the technologies referred to in Article 16, paragraph 1. It shall also, where feasible, include repatriation of information.

Article 18   Technical and Scientific Cooperation

1. The Contracting Parties shall promote international technical and scientific cooperation in the field of conservation and sustainable use of biological diversity, where necessary, through the appropriate international and national institutions.

2. Each Contracting Party shall promote technical and scientific cooperation with other Contracting Parties, in particular developing countries, in implementing this Convention, *inter alia*, through the development and implementation of national policies. In promoting such cooperation, special attention should be given to the development and strengthening of national capabilities, by means of human resources development and institution building.

3. The Conference of the Parties, at its first meeting, shall determine how to establish a clearing-house mechanism to promote and facilitate technical and scientific cooperation.

4. The Contracting Parties shall, in accordance with national legislation and policies, encourage and develop methods of cooperation for the development and use of technologies, including indigenous and traditional technologies, in pursuance of the objectives of this Convention. For this purpose, the Contracting Parties shall also promote cooperation in the training of personnel and exchange of experts.

5. The Contracting Parties shall, subject to mutual agreement, promote the establishment of joint research programmes and joint ventures for the development of technologies relevant to the objectives of this Convention.

Article 19   Handling of Biotechnology and Distribution of its Benefits

1. Each Contracting Party shall take legislative, administrative or policy measures, as appropriate, to provide for the effective participation in biotechnological research activities by those Contracting Parties, especially developing countries, which provide the genetic resources for such research, and where feasible in such Contracting Parties.

2. Each Contracting Party shall take all practicable measures to promote and advance priority access on a fair and equitable basis by Contracting Parties, especially developing countries, to the results and benefits arising from biotechnologies based upon genetic resources provided by those Contracting Parties. Such access shall be on

mutually agreed terms.

3. The Parties shall consider the need for and modalities of a protocol setting out appropriate procedures, including, in particular, advance informed agreement, in the field of the safe transfer, handling and use of any living modified organism resulting from biotechnology that may have adverse effect on the conservation and sustainable use of biological diversity.

4. Each Contracting Party shall, directly or by requiring any natural or legal person under its jurisdiction providing the organisms referred to in paragraph 3 above, provide any available information about the use and safety regulations required by that Contracting Party in handling such organisms, as well as any available information on the potential adverse impact of the specific organisms concerned to the Contracting Party into which those organisms are to be introduced.

Article 20   Financial Resources

1. Each Contracting Party undertakes to provide, in accordance with its capabilities, financial support and incentives in respect of those national activities which are intended to achieve the objectives of this Convention, in accordance with its national plans, priorities and programmes.

2. The developed country Parties shall provide new and additional financial resources to enable developing country Parties to meet the agreed full incremental costs to them of implementing measures which fulfil the obligations of this Convention and to benefit from its provisions and which costs are agreed between a developing country Party and the institutional structure referred to in Article 21, in accordance with policy, strategy, programme priorities and eligibility criteria and an indicative list of incremental costs established by the Conference of the Parties. Other Parties, including countries undergoing the process of transition to a market economy, may voluntarily assume the obligations of the developed country Parties. For the purpose of this Article, the Conference of the Parties, shall at its first meeting establish a list of developed country Parties and other Parties which voluntarily assume the obligations of the developed country Parties. The Conference of the Parties shall periodically review and if necessary, amend the list. Contributions from other countries and sources on a voluntary basis would also be encouraged. The implementation of these commitments shall take into account the need for adequacy, predictability and timely flow of funds and the importance of burden-sharing among the contributing Parties included in the list.

3. The developed country Parties may also provide, and developing country Parties avail themselves of, financial resources related to the implementation of this Convention through bilateral, regional and other multilateral channels.

4. The extent to which developing country Parties will effectively implement their commitments under this Convention will depend on the effective implementation by developed country Parties of their commitments under this Convention related to financial resources and transfer of technology and will take fully into account the fact that economic and social development and eradication of poverty are the first and overriding priorities of the developing country Parties.

5. The Parties shall take full account of the specific needs and special situation of least developed countries in their actions with regard to funding and transfer of technology.

6. The Contracting Parties shall also take into consideration the special conditions resulting from the dependence on, distribution and location of, biological diversity within developing country Parties, in particular small island States.

7. Consideration shall also be given to the special situation of developing countries, including those that are

most environmentally vulnerable, such as those with arid and semi-arid zones, coastal and mountainous areas.

Article 21　Financial Mechanism

1. There shall be a mechanism for the provision of financial resources to developing country Parties for purposes of this Convention on a grant or concessional basis the essential elements of which are described in this Article. The mechanism shall function under the authority and guidance of, and be accountable to, the Conference of the Parties for purposes of this Convention. The operations of the mechanism shall be carried out by such institutional structure as may be decided upon by the Conference of the Parties at its first meeting. For purposes of this Convention, the Conference of the Parties shall determine the policy, strategy, programme priorities and eligibility criteria relating to the access to and utilization of such resources. The contributions shall be such as to take into account the need for predictability, adequacy and timely flow of funds referred to in Article 20 in accordance with the amount of resources needed to be decided periodically by the Conference of the Parties and the importance of burden-sharing among the contributing Parties included in the list referred to in Article 20, paragraph 2. Voluntary contributions may also be made by the developed country Parties and by other countries and sources. The mechanism shall operate within a democratic and transparent system of governance.

2. Pursuant to the objectives of this Convention, the Conference of the Parties shall at its first meeting determine the policy, strategy and programme priorities, as well as detailed criteria and guidelines for eligibility for access to and utilization of the financial resources including monitoring and evaluation on a regular basis of such utilization. The Conference of the Parties shall decide on the arrangements to give effect to paragraph 1 above after consultation with the institutional structure entrusted with the operation of the financial mechanism.

3. The Conference of the Parties shall review the effectiveness of the mechanism established under this Article, including the criteria and guidelines referred to in paragraph 2 above, not less than two years after the entry into force of this Convention and thereafter on a regular basis. Based on such review, it shall take appropriate action to improve the effectiveness of the mechanism if necessary.

4. The Contracting Parties shall consider strengthening existing financial institutions to provide financial resources for the conservation and sustainable use of biological diversity.

Article 22　Relationship with Other International Conventions

1. The provisions of this Convention shall not affect the rights and obligations of any Contracting Party deriving from any existing international agreement, except where the exercise of those rights and obligations would cause a serious damage or threat to biological diversity.

2. Contracting Parties shall implement this Convention with respect to the marine environment consistently with the rights and obligations of States under the law of the sea.

Article 23　Conference of the Parties

1. A Conference of the Parties is hereby established. The first meeting of the conference of the Parties shall be convened by the Executive Director of the United Nations Environment Programme not later than one year after the entry into force of this Convention. Thereafter, ordinary meetings of the Conference of the Parties shall be held at regular intervals to be determined by the Conference at its first meeting.

2. Extraordinary meetings of the Conference of the Parties shall be held at such other times as may be deemed necessary by the Conference, or at the written request of any Party, provided that, within six months of the request being communicated to them by the Secretariat, it is supported by at least one third of the Parties.

3. The Conference of the Parties shall by consensus agree upon and adopt rules of procedure for itself and for any subsidiary body it may establish, as well as financial rules governing the funding of The Secretariat. At each

ordinary meeting, it shall adopt a budget for the financial period until the next ordinary meeting.

4. The Conference of the Parties shall keep under review the implementation of this Convention, and, for this purpose, shall:

(a) Establish the form and the intervals for transmitting the information to be submitted in accordance with Article 26 and consider such information as well as reports submitted by any subsidiary body;

(b) Review scientific, technical and technological advice on biological diversity provided in accordance with Article 25;

(c) Consider and adopt, as required, protocols in accordance with Article 28;

(d) Consider and adopt, as required, in accordance with Articles 29 and 30, amendments to this Convention and its annexes;

(e) Consider amendments to any protocol, as well as to any annexes thereto, and, if so decided, recommend their adoption to the parties to the protocol concerned;

(f) Consider and adopt, as required, in accordance with Article 30, additional annexes to this Convention;

(g) Establish such subsidiary bodies, particularly to provide scientific and technical advice, as are deemed necessary for the implementation of this Convention;

(h) Contact, through the Secretariat, the executive bodies of conventions dealing with matters covered by this Convention with a view to establishing appropriate forms of cooperation with them; and

(i) Consider and undertake any additional action that may be required for the achievement of the purposes of this Convention in the light of experience gained in its operation.

5. The United Nations, its specialized agencies and the International Atomic Energy Agency, as well as any State not Party to this Convention, may be represented as observers at meetings of the Conference of the Parties. Any other body or agency, whether governmental or nongovernmental, qualified in fields relating to conservation and sustainable use of biological diversity, which has informed the Secretariat of its wish to be represented as an observer at a meeting of the Conference of the Parties, may be admitted unless at least one third of the Parties present object. The admission and participation of observers shall be subject to the rules of procedure adopted by the Conference of the Parties.

Article 24 Secretariat

1. A secretariat is hereby established. Its functions shall be:

(a) To arrange for and service meetings of the Conference of the Parties provided for in Article 23;

(b) To perform the functions assigned to it by any protocol;

(c) To prepare reports on the execution of its functions under this Convention and present them to the Conference of the Parties;

(d) To coordinate with other relevant international bodies and, in particular to enter into such administrative and contractual arrangements as may be required for the effective discharge of its functions; and

(e) To perform such other functions as may be determined by the Conference of the Parties.

2. At its first ordinary meeting, the Conference of the Parties shall designate the secretariat from amongst those existing competent international organizations which have signified their willingness to carry out the secretariat functions under this Convention.

Article 25 Subsidiary Body on Scientific, Technical and Technological Advice

1. A subsidiary body for the provision of scientific, technical and technological advice is hereby established to provide the Conference of the Parties and, as appropriate, its other subsidiary bodies with timely advice relating

to the implementation of this Convention. This body shall be open to participation by all Parties and shall be multidisciplinary. It shall comprise government representatives competent in the relevant field of expertise. It shall report regularly to the Conference of the Parties on all aspects of its work.

2. Under the authority of and in accordance with guidelines laid down by the Conference of the Parties, and upon its request, this body shall:

(a) Provide scientific and technical assessments of the status of biological diversity;

(b) Prepare scientific and technical assessments of the effects of types of measures taken in accordance with the provisions of this Convention;

(c) Identify innovative, efficient and state-of-the-art technologies and know-how relating to the conservation and sustainable use of biological diversity and advise on the ways and means of promoting development and/or transferring such technologies;

(d) Provide advice on scientific programmes and international cooperation in research and development related to conservation and sustainable use of biological diversity; and

(e) Respond to scientific, technical, technological and methodological questions that the Conference of the Parties and its subsidiary bodies may put to the body.

3. The functions, terms of reference, organization and operation of this body may be further elaborated by the Conference of the Parties.

Article 26　Reports

Each Contracting Party shall, at intervals to be determined by the Conference of the Parties, present to the Conference of the Parties, reports on measures which it has taken for the implementation of the provisions of this Convention and their effectiveness in meeting the objectives of this Convention.

Article 27　Settlement of Disputes

1. In the event of a dispute between Contracting Parties concerning the interpretation or application of this Convention, the parties concerned shall seek solution by negotiation.

2. If the parties concerned cannot reach agreement by negotiation, they may jointly seek the good offices of, or request mediation by, a third party.

3. When ratifying, accepting, approving or acceding to this Convention, or at any time thereafter, a State or regional economic integration organization may declare in writing to the Depositary that for a dispute not resolved in accordance with paragraph 1 or paragraph 2 above, it accepts one or both of the following means of dispute settlement as compulsory:

(a) Arbitration in accordance with the procedure laid down in Part 1 of Annex Ⅱ;

(b) Submission of the dispute to the International Court of Justice.

4. If the parties to the dispute have not, in accordance with paragraph 3 above, accepted the same or any procedure, the dispute shall be submitted to conciliation in accordance with Part 2 of Annex Ⅱ unless the parties otherwise agree.

5. The provisions of this Article shall apply with respect to any protocol except as otherwise provided in the protocol concerned.

Article 28　Adoption of Protocols

1. The Contracting Parties shall cooperate in the formulation and adoption of protocols to this Convention.

2. Protocols shall be adopted at a meeting of the Conference of the Parties.

3. The text of any proposed protocol shall be communicated to the Contracting Parties by the Secretariat at

least six months before such a meeting.

Article 29   Amendment of the Convention or Protocols

1. Amendments to this Convention may be proposed by any Contracting Party. Amendments to any protocol may be proposed by any Party to that protocol.

2. Amendments to this Convention shall be adopted at a meeting of the Conference of the Parties. Amendments to any protocol shall be adopted at a meeting of the Parties to the Protocol in question. The text of any proposed amendment to this Convention or to any protocol, except as may otherwise be provided in such protocol, shall be communicated to the Parties to the instrument in question by the secretariat at least six months before the meeting at which it is proposed for adoption. The secretariat shall also communicate proposed amendments to the signatories to this Convention for information.

3. The Parties shall make every effort to reach agreement on any proposed amendment to this Convention or to any protocol by consensus. If all efforts at consensus have been exhausted, and no agreement reached, the amendment shall as a last resort be adopted by a two-third majority vote of the Parties to the instrument in question present and voting at the meeting and shall be submitted by the Depositary to all Parties for ratification, acceptance or approval.

4. Ratification, acceptance or approval of amendments shall be notified to the Depositary in writing. Amendments adopted in accordance with paragraph 3 above shall enter into force among Parties having accepted them on the ninetieth day after the deposit of instruments of ratification, acceptance or approval by at least two thirds of the Contracting Parties to this Convention or of the Parties to the protocol concerned, except as may otherwise be provided in such protocol. Thereafter the amendments shall enter into force for any other Party on the ninetieth day after that Party deposits its instrument of ratification, acceptance or approval of the amendments.

5. For the purposes of this Article, "Parties present and voting" means Parties present and casting an affirmative or negative vote.

Article 30   Adoption and Amendment of Annexes

1. The annexes to this Convention or to any protocol shall form an integral part of the Convention or of such protocol, as the case may be and, unless expressly provided otherwise, a reference to this Convention or its protocols constitutes at the same time a reference to any annexes thereto. Such annexes shall be restricted to procedural, scientific, technical and administrative matters.

2. Except as may be otherwise provided in any protocol with respect to its annexes, the following procedure shall apply to the proposal, adoption and entry into force of additional annexes to this Convention or of annexes to any protocol:

(a) Annexes to this Convention or to any protocol shall be proposed and adopted according to the procedure laid down in Article 29;

(b) Any Party that is unable to approve an additional annex to this Convention or an annex to any protocol to which it is Party shall so notify the Depositary, in writing, within one year from the date of the communication of the adoption by the Depositary. The Depositary shall without delay notify all Parties of any such notification received A Party may at any time withdraw a previous declaration of objection and the annexes shall thereupon enter into force for that Party subject to subparagraph (c) below:

(c) On the expiry of one year from the date of the communication of the adoption by the Depositary, the annex shall enter into force for all Parties to this Convention or to any protocol concerned which have not submitted a notification in accordance with the provisions of subparagraph (b) above.

3. The proposal, adoption and entry into force of amendments to annexes to this Convention or to any protocol shall be subject to the same procedure as for the proposal, adoption and entry into force of annexes to the Convention or annexes to any protocol.

4. If an additional annex or an amendment to an annex is related to an amendment to this Convention or to any protocol, the additional annex or amendment shall not enter into force until such time as the amendment to the Convention or to the protocol concerned enters into force.

Article 31   Right to Vote

1. Except as provided for in paragraph 2 below, each Contracting Party to this Convention or to any protocol shall have one vote.

2. Regional economic integration organizations, in matters within their competence, shall exercise their right to vote with a number of votes equal to the number of their member States which are Contracting Parties to this Convention or the relevant protocol. Such organizations shall not exercise their right to vote if their member States exercise theirs, and vice versa.

Article 32   Relationship between this Convention and Its Protocols

1. A State or a regional economic integration organization may not become a Party to a protocol unless it is, or becomes at the same time, a Contracting Party to this Convention.

2. Decisions under any protocol shall be taken only by the Parties to the protocol concerned. Any Contracting Party that has not ratified, accepted or approved a protocol may participate as an observer in any meeting of the parties to that protocol.

Article 33   Signature

This Convention shall be open for signature at Rio de Janeiro by all States and any regional economic integration organization from 5 June 1992 until 14 June 1992, and at the United Nations Headquarters in New York from 15 June 1992 to 4 June 1993.

Article 34   Ratification, Acceptance or Approval

1. This Convention and any protocol shall be subject to ratification, acceptance or approval by States and by regional economic integration organizations. Instruments of ratification, acceptance or approval shall be deposited with the Depositary.

2. Any organization referred to in paragraph 1 above which becomes a Contracting Party to this Convention or any protocol without any of its member States being a Contracting Party shall be bound by all the obligations under the Convention or the protocol, as the case may be. In the case of such organizations, one or more of whose member States is a Contracting Party to this Convention or relevant protocol, the organization and its member States shall decide on their respective responsibilities for the performance of their obligations under the Convention or protocol, as the case may be. In such cases, the organization and the member States shall not be entitled to exercise rights under the Convention or relevant protocol concurrently.

3. In their instruments of ratification, acceptance or approval, the organizations referred to in paragraph 1 above shall declare the extent of their competence with respect to the matters governed by the Convention or the relevant protocol. These organizations shall also inform the Depositary of any relevant modification in the extent of their competence.

Article 35   Accession

1. This Convention and any protocol shall be open for accession by States and by regional economic integration organizations from the date on which the Convention or the protocol concerned is closed for signature.

The instruments of accession shall be deposited with the Depositary.

2. In their instruments of accession, the organizations referred to in paragraph 1 above shall declare the extent of their competence with respect to the matters governed by the Convention or the relevant protocol. These organizations shall also inform the Depositary of any relevant modification in the extent of their competence.

3. The provisions of Article 34, paragraph 2, shall apply to regional economic integration organizations which accede to this Convention or any protocol.

Article 36   Entry into Force

1. This Convention shall enter into force on the ninetieth day after the date of deposit of the thirtieth instrument of ratification, acceptance, approval or accession.

2. Any protocol shall enter into force on the ninetieth day after the date of deposit of the number of instruments of ratification, acceptance, approval or accession, specified in that protocol, has been deposited.

3. For each Contracting Party which ratifies, accepts or approves this Convention or accedes thereto after the deposit of the thirtieth instrument of ratification, acceptance, approval or accession, it shall enter into force on the ninetieth day after the date of deposit by such Contracting Party of its instrument of ratification, acceptance, approval or accession.

4. Any protocol, except as otherwise provided in such protocol, shall enter into force for a Contracting Party that ratifies, accepts or approves that protocol or accedes thereto after its entry into force pursuant to paragraph 2 above, on the ninetieth day after the date on which that Contracting Party deposits its instrument of ratification, acceptance, approval or accession, or on the date on which this Convention enters into force for that Contracting Party, whichever shall be the later.

5. For the purposes of paragraphs 1 and 2 above, any instrument deposited by a regional economic integration organization shall not be counted as additional to those deposited by member States of such organization.

Article 37   Reservations

No reservations may be made to this Convention.

Article 38   Withdrawals

1. At any time after two years from the date on which this Convention has entered into force for a Contracting Party, that Contracting Party may withdraw from the Convention by giving written notification to the Depositary.

2. Any such withdrawal shall take place upon expiry of one year after the date of its receipt by the Depositary, or on such later date as may be specified in the notification of the withdrawal.

3. Any Contracting Party which withdraws from this Convention shall be considered as also having withdrawn from any protocol to which it is party.

Article 39   Financial Interim Arrangements

Provided that it has been fully restructured in accordance with the requirements of Article 21, the Global Environment Facility of the United Nations Development Programme, the United Nations Environment Programme and the International Bank for Reconstruction and Development shall be the institutional structure referred to in Article 21 on an interim basis, for the period between the entry into force of this Convention and the first meeting of the Conference of the Parties or until the Conference of the Parties decides which institutional structure will be designated in accordance with Article 21.

Article 40   Secretariat Interim Arrangements

The secretariat to be provided by the Executive Director of the united Nations Environment Programme shall be the secretariat referred to in Article 24, paragraph 2, on an interim basis for the period between the entry into force of this Convention and the first meeting of the Conference of the Parties.

Article 41　Depositary

The Secretary-General of the United Nations shall assume the functions of Depositary of this Convention and any protocols.

Article 42　Authentic Texts

The original of this Convention, of which the Arabic, Chinese, English, French, Russian and Spanish texts are equally authentic, shall be deposited with the Secretary-General of the United Nations.

IN WITNESS WHEREOF the undersigned, being duly authorized to that effect, have signed this Convention.

Done at Rio de Janeiro on this fifth day of June, one thousand nine hundred and ninety-two.

联合国气候变化框架公约[①]

(联合国气候变化框架公约委员会1992年5月9日在纽约通过)

本公约各缔约方,

承认地球气候的变化及其不利影响是人类共同关心的问题;

感到忧虑的是,人类活动已大幅增加大气中温室气体的浓度,这种增加增强了自然温室效应,平均而言将引起地球表面和大气进一步增温,并可能对自然生态系统和人类产生不利影响;

注意到历史上和目前全球温室气体排放的最大部分源自发达国家;发展中国家的人均排放仍相对较低;发展中国家在全球排放中所占的份额将会增加,以满足其社会和发展需要;

意识到陆地和海洋生态系统中温室气体汇和库的作用和重要性;

注意到在气候变化的预测中,特别是在其时间、幅度和区域格局方面,有许多不确定性;

承认气候变化的全球性要求所有国家根据其共同但有区别的责任和各自的能力及其社会和经济条件,尽可能开展最广泛的合作,并参与有效和适当的国际应对行动;

回顾1972年6月16日于斯德哥尔摩通过的《联合国人类环境会议宣言》的有关规定;

又回顾各国根据《联合国宪章》和国际法原则,拥有主权权利按自己的环境和发展政策开发自己的资源,也有责任确保在其管辖或控制范围内的活动不对其他国家的环境或国家管辖范围以外地区的环境造成损害;

重申在应付气候变化的国际合作中的国家主权原则;

认识到各国应当制定有效的立法;各种环境方面的标准、管理目标和优先顺序应当反映其所适用的环境和发展方面情况;并且有些国家所实行的标准对其他国家特别是发展中国家可能是不恰当的,并可能会使之承担不应有的经济和社会代价;

回顾联合国大会关于联合国环境与发展会议的1989年12月22日第44/228号决议的规定,以及关于为人类当代和后代保护全球气候的1988年12月6日第43/53号、1989年12月22日第44/207号、1990年12月21日第45/212号和1991年12月19日第46/169号决议;

又回顾联合国大会关于海平面上升对岛屿和沿海地区特别是低洼沿海地区可能产生的不利影响的1989年12月22日第44/206号决议各项规定,以及联合国大会关于防治沙漠化行动计划实施情况的1989年12月19日第44/172号决议的有关规定;

并回顾1985年《保护臭氧层维也纳公约》和于1990年6月29日调整和修正的1987年《关于消耗臭氧层物质的蒙特利尔议定书》;

注意到1990年11月7日通过的第二次世界气候大会部长宣言;

意识到许多国家就气候变化所进行的有价值的分析工作,以及世界气象组织、联合国环境规划署和联合国系统的其他机关、组织和机构及其他国际和政府间机构对交换科学研究成果和协调研究工作所作

[①] 引自:联合国大会第237/18号决议。

的重要贡献；

认识到了解和应付气候变化所需的步骤只有基于有关的科学、技术和经济方面的考虑，并根据这些领域的新发现不断加以重新评价，才能在环境、社会和经济方面最为有效；

认识到应付气候变化的各种行动本身在经济上就能够是合理的，而且还能有助于解决其他环境问题；

又认识到发达国家有必要根据明确的优先顺序，立即灵活地采取行动，以作为形成考虑到所有温室气体并适当考虑它们对增强温室效应的相对作用的全球、国家和可能议定的区域性综合应对战略的第一步；

并认识到地势低洼国家和其他小岛屿国家、拥有低洼沿海地区、干旱和半干旱地区或易受水灾、旱灾和沙漠化影响地区的国家以及具有脆弱的山区生态系统的发展中国家特别容易受到气候变化的不利影响；

认识到其经济特别依赖于矿物燃料的生产、使用和出口的国家特别是发展中国家由于为了限制温室气体排放而采取的行动所面临的特殊困难；

申明应当以统筹兼顾的方式把应付气候变化的行动与社会和经济发展协调起来，以免后者受到不利影响，同时充分考虑到发展中国家实现持续经济增长和消除贫困的正当的优先需要；

认识到所有国家特别是发展中国家需要得到实现可持续的社会和经济发展所需的资源；发展中国家为了迈向这一目标，其能源消耗将需要增加，虽然考虑到有可能包括通过在具有经济和社会效益的条件下应用新技术来提高能源效率和一般地控制温室气体排放；

决心为当代和后代保护气候系统；

兹协议如下：

第一条 定义

为本公约的目的：

1. "气候变化的不利影响"指气候变化所造成的自然环境或生物区系的变化，这些变化对自然的和管理下的生态系统的组成、复原力或生产力、或对社会经济系统的运作、或对人类的健康和福利产生重大的有害影响。

2. "气候变化"指除在类似时期内所观测的气候的自然变异之外，由于直接或间接的人类活动改变了地球大气的组成而造成的气候变化。

3. "气候系统"指大气圈、水圈、生物圈和地圈的整体及其相互作用。

4. "排放"指温室气体和/或其前体在一个特定地区和时期内向大气的释放。

5. "温室气体"指大气中那些吸收和重新放出红外辐射的自然的和人为的气态成分。

6. "区域经济一体化组织"指一个特定区域的主权国家组成的组织，有权处理本公约或其议定书所规定的事项，并经按其内部程序获得正式授权签署、批准、接受、核准或加入有关文书。

7. "库"指气候系统内存储温室气体或其前体的一个或多个组成部分。

8. "汇"指从大气中清除温室气体、气溶胶或温室气体前体的任何过程、活动或机制。

9. "源"指向大气排放温室气体、气溶胶或温室气体前体的任何过程或活动。

第二条 目标

本公约以及缔约方会议可能通过的任何相关法律文书的最终目标是：根据本公约的各项有关规定，将大气中温室气体的浓度稳定在防止气候系统受到危险的人为干扰的水平上。这一水平应当在足以使生态系统能够自然地适应气候变化、确保粮食生产免受威胁并使经济发展能够可持续地进行的时间范围内实现。

第三条 原则

各缔约方在为实现本公约的目标和履行其各项规定而采取行动时，除其他外，应以下列作为指导：

1. 各缔约方应当在公平的基础上，并根据它们共同但有区别的责任和各自的能力，为人类当代和后代的利益保护气候系统。因此，发达国家缔约方应当率先对付气候变化及其不利影响。

2. 应当充分考虑到发展中国家缔约方尤其是特别易受气候变化不利影响的那些发展中国家缔约方的具体需要和特殊情况，也应当充分考虑到那些按本公约必须承担不成比例或不正常负担的缔约方特别是发展中国家缔约方的具体需要和特殊情况。

3. 各缔约方应当采取预防措施，预测、防止或尽量减少引起气候变化的原因，并缓解其不利影响。当存在造成严重或不可逆转的损害的威胁时，不应当以科学上没有完全的确定性为理由推迟采取这类措施，同时考虑到应付气候变化的政策和措施应当讲求成本效益，确保以尽可能最低的费用获得全球效益。为此，这种政策和措施应当考虑到不同的社会经济情况，并且应当具有全面性，包括所有有关的温室气体源、汇和库及适应措施，并涵盖所有经济部门。应付气候变化的努力可由有关的缔约方合作进行。

4. 各缔约方有权并且应当促进可持续的发展。保护气候系统免遭人为变化的政策和措施应当适合每个缔约方的具体情况，并应当结合到国家的发展计划中去，同时考虑到经济发展对于采取措施应付气候变化是至关重要的。

5. 各缔约方应当合作促进有利的和开放的国际经济体系，这种体系将促成所有缔约方特别是发展中国家缔约方的可持续经济增长和发展，从而使它们有能力更好地应付气候变化的问题。为对付气候变化而采取的措施，包括单方面措施，不应当成为国际贸易上的任意或无理的歧视手段或者隐蔽的限制。

第四条 承诺

1. 所有缔约方，考虑到它们共同但有区别的责任，以及各自具体的国家和区域发展优先顺序、目标和情况，应：

（a）用待由缔约方会议议定的可行方法编制、定期更新、公布并按照第十二条向缔约方会议提供关于《蒙特利尔议定书》未予管制的所有温室气体的各种源的人为排放和各种汇的清除的国家清单；

（b）制订、执行、公布和经常地更新国家的以及在适当情况下区域的计划，其中包含从《蒙特利尔议定书》未予管制的所有温室气体的源的人为排放和汇的清除来着手减缓气候变化的措施，以及便利充分地适应气候变化的措施；

（c）在所有有关部门，包括能源、运输、工业、农业、林业和废物管理部门，促进和合作发展、应用和传播（包括转让）各种用来控制、减少或防止《蒙特利尔议定书》未予管制的温室气体的人为排放的技术、做法和过程；

（d）促进可持续地管理，并促进和合作酌情维护和加强《蒙特利尔议定书》未予管制的所有温室气体的汇和库，包括生物质、森林和海洋以及其他陆地、沿海和海洋生态系统；

（e）合作为适应气候变化的影响做好准备；拟订和详细制定关于沿海地区的管理、水资源和农业以及关于受到旱灾和沙漠化及洪水影响的地区特别是非洲的这种地区的保护和恢复的适当的综合性计划；

（f）在它们有关的社会、经济和环境政策及行动中，在可行的范围内将气候变化考虑进去，并采用由本国拟订和确定的适当办法，例如进行影响评估，以期尽量减少它们为了减缓或适应气候变化而进行的项目或采取的措施对经济、公共健康和环境质量产生的不利影响；

（g）促进和合作进行关于气候系统的科学、技术、工艺、社会经济和其他研究、系统观测及开发数据档案，目的是增进对气候变化的起因、影响、规模和发生时间以及各种应对战略所带来的经济和社会后果的认识，和减少或消除在这些方面尚存的不确定性；

（h）促进和合作进行关于气候系统和气候变化以及关于各种应对战略所带来的经济和社会后果的科学、技术、工艺、社会经济和法律方面的有关信息的充分、公开和迅速的交流；

（i）促进和合作进行与气候变化有关的教育、培训和提高公众意识的工作，并鼓励人们对这个过程最广泛参与，包括鼓励各种非政府组织的参与；

（j）依照第十二条向缔约方会议提供有关履行的信息。

2. 附件一所列的发达国家缔约方和其他缔约方具体承诺如下所规定：

（a）每一个此类缔约方应制定国家政策和采取相应的措施，通过限制其人为的温室气体排放以及保护和增强其温室气体库和汇，减缓气候变化。这些政策和措施将表明，发达国家是在带头依循本公约的目标，改变人为排放的长期趋势，同时认识到至本十年末使二氧化碳和《蒙特利尔议定书》未予管制的其他温室气体的人为排放回复到较早的水平，将会有助于这种改变，并考虑到这些缔约方的起点和做法、经济结构和资源基础方面的差别、维持强有力和可持续经济增长的需要、可以采用的技术以及其他个别情况，又考虑到每一个此类缔约方都有必要对为了实现该目标而作的全球努力作出公平和适当的贡献。这些缔约方可以同其他缔约方共同执行这些政策和措施，也可以协助其他缔约方为实现本公约的目标特别是本项的目标作出贡献。

（b）为了推动朝这一目标取得进展，每一个此类缔约方应依照第十二条，在本公约对其生效后六个月内，并在其后定期地就其上述（a）项所述的政策和措施，以及就其由此预测在（a）项所述期间内《蒙特利尔议定书》未予管制的温室气体的源的人为排放和汇的清除，提供详细信息，目的在个别地或共同地使二氧化碳和《蒙特利尔议定书》未予管制的其他温室气体的人为排放回复到1990年的水平。按照第七条，这些信息将由缔约方会议在其第一届会议上以及在其后定期地加以审评。

（c）为了上述（b）项的目的而计算各种温室气体源的排放和汇的清除时，应该参考可以得到的最佳科学知识，包括关于各种汇的有效容量和每一种温室气体在引起气候变化方面的作用的知识。缔约方会议应在其第一届会议上考虑和议定进行这些计算的方法，并在其后经常地加以审评。

（d）缔约方会议应在其第一届会议上审评上述（a）项和（b）项是否充足。进行审评时应参照可以得到的关于气候变化及其影响的最佳科学信息和评估，以及有关的工艺、社会和经济信息。在审评的基础上，缔约方会议应采取适当的行动，其中可以包括通过对上述（a）项和（b）项承诺的修正。缔约方会议第一届会议还应就上述（a）项所述共同执行的标准作出决定。对（a）项和（b）项的第二次审评应不迟于1998年12月31日进行，其后按由缔约方会议确定的定期间隔进行，直至本公约的目标达到为止。

（e）每一个此类缔约方应：

（一）酌情同其他此类缔约方协调为了实现本公约的目标而开发的有关经济和行政手段；和

（二）确定并定期审评其本身有哪些政策和做法鼓励了导致《蒙特利尔议定书》未予管制的温室气体的人为排放水平因而更高的活动。

（f）缔约方会议应至迟在1998年12月31日之前审评可以得到的信息，以便经有关缔约方同意，作出适当修正附件一和二内名单的决定。

（g）不在附件一之列的任何缔约方，可以在其批准、接受、核准或加入的文书中，或在其后任何时间，通知保存人其有意接受上述（a）项和（b）项的约束。保存人应将任何此类通知通报其他签署方和缔约方。

3. 附件二所列的发达国家缔约方和其他发达缔约方应提供新的和额外的资金，以支付经议定的发展中国家缔约方为履行第十二条第1款规定的义务而招致的全部费用。它们还应提供发展中国家缔约方所需要的资金，包括用于技术转让的资金，以支付经议定的为执行本条第1款所述并经发展中国家缔约方同第十一条所述那个或那些国际实体依该条议定的措施的全部增加费用。这些承诺的履行应考虑到资金流量应充足和可以预测的必要性，以及发达国家缔约方间适当分摊负担的重要性。

4. 附件二所列的发达国家缔约方和其他发达缔约方还应帮助特别易受气候变化不利影响的发展中国家缔约方支付适应这些不利影响的费用。

5. 附件二所列的发达国家缔约方和其他发达缔约方应采取一切实际可行的步骤，酌情促进、便利和资助向其他缔约方特别是发展中国家缔约方转让或使它们有机会得到无害环境的技术和专有技术，以使它们能够履行本公约的各项规定。在此过程中，发达国家缔约方应支持开发和增强发展中国家缔约方的自生能力和技术。有能力这样做的其他缔约方和组织也可协助便利这类技术的转让。

6. 对于附件一所列正在朝市场经济过渡的缔约方，在履行其在上述第 2 款下的承诺时，包括在《蒙特利尔议定书》未予管制的温室气体人为排放的可资参照的历史水平方面，应由缔约方会议允许它们有一定程度的灵活性，以增强这些缔约方应付气候变化的能力。

7. 发展中国家缔约方能在多大程度上有效履行其在本公约下的承诺，将取决于发达国家缔约方对其在本公约下所承担的有关资金和技术转让的承诺的有效履行，并将充分考虑到经济和社会发展及消除贫困是发展中国家缔约方的首要和压倒一切的优先事项。

8. 在履行本条各项承诺时，各缔约方应充分考虑按照本公约需要采取哪些行动，包括与提供资金、保险和技术转让有关的行动，以满足发展中国家缔约方由于气候变化的不利影响和/或执行应对措施所造成的影响，特别是对下列各类国家的影响，而产生的具体需要和关注：

（a）小岛屿国家；
（b）有低洼沿海地区的国家；
（c）有干旱和半干旱地区、森林地区和容易发生森林退化的地区的国家；
（d）有易遭自然灾害地区的国家；
（e）有容易发生旱灾和沙漠化的地区的国家；
（f）有城市大气严重污染的地区的国家；
（g）有脆弱生态系统包括山区生态系统的国家；
（h）其经济高度依赖于矿物燃料和相关的能源密集产品的生产、加工和出口所带来的收入，和/或高度依赖于这种燃料和产品的消费的国家；和
（i）内陆国和过境国。

此外，缔约方会议可酌情就本款采取行动。

9. 各缔约方在采取有关提供资金和技术转让的行动时，应充分考虑到最不发达国家的具体需要和特殊情况。

10. 各缔约方应按照第十条，在履行本公约各项承诺时，考虑到其经济容易受到执行应付气候变化的措施所造成的不利影响之害的缔约方，特别是发展中国家缔约方的情况。这尤其适用于其经济高度依赖于矿物燃料和相关的能源密集产品的生产、加工、出口所带来的收入，和/或高度依赖于这种燃料和产品的消费，和/或高度依赖于矿物燃料的使用，而改用其他燃料又非常困难的那些缔约方。

第五条 研究和系统观测

在履行第四条第 1 款（g）项下的承诺时，各缔约方应：

（a）支持并酌情进一步制订旨在确定、进行、评估和资助研究、数据收集和系统观测的国际和政府间计划和站网或组织，同时考虑到有必要尽量减少工作重复；

（b）支持旨在加强尤其是发展中国家的系统观测及国家科学和技术研究能力的国际和政府间努力，并促进获取和交换从国家管辖范围以外地区取得的数据及其分析；和

（c）考虑发展中国家的特殊关注和需要，并开展合作提高它们参与上述（a）项和（b）项中所述努力的自生能力。

第六条 教育、培训和公众意识

在履行第四条第 1 款（i）项下的承诺时，各缔约方应：

（a）在国家一级并酌情在次区域和区域一级，根据国家法律和规定，并在各自的能力范围内，促进和便利：

（一）拟订和实施有关气候变化及其影响的教育及提高公众意识的计划；
（二）公众获取有关气候变化及其影响的信息；
（三）公众参与应付气候变化及其影响和拟订适当的对策；和

（四）培训科学、技术和管理人员。

（b）在国际一级，酌情利用现有的机构，在下列领域进行合作并促进：

（一）编写和交换有关气候变化及其影响的教育及提高公众意识的材料；和

（二）拟订和实施教育和培训计划，包括加强国内机构和交流或借调人员来特别是为发展中国家培训这方面的专家。

第七条 缔约方会议

1. 兹设立缔约方会议。

2. 缔约方会议作为本公约的最高机构，应定期审评本公约和缔约方会议可能通过的任何相关法律文书的履行情况，并应在其职权范围内作出为促进本公约的有效履行所必要的决定。为此目的，缔约方会议应：

（a）根据本公约的目标，在履行本公约过程中取得的经验和科学与技术知识的发展，定期审评本公约规定的缔约方义务和机构安排；

（b）促进和便利就各缔约方为应付气候变化及其影响而采取的措施进行信息交流，同时考虑到各缔约方不同的情况、责任和能力以及各自在本公约下的承诺；

（c）应两个或更多的缔约方的要求，便利将这些缔约方为应付气候变化及其影响而采取的措施加以协调，同时考虑到各缔约方不同的情况、责任和能力以及各自在本公约下的承诺；

（d）依照本公约的目标和规定，促进和指导发展和定期改进由缔约方会议议定的，除其他外，用来编制各种温室气体源的排放和各种汇的清除的清单，和评估为限制这些气体的排放及增进其清除而采取的各种措施的有效性的可比方法；

（e）根据依本公约规定获得的所有信息，评估各缔约方履行公约的情况和依照公约所采取措施的总体影响，特别是环境、经济和社会影响及其累计影响，以及当前在实现本公约的目标方面取得的进展；

（f）审议并通过关于本公约履行情况的定期报告，并确保予以发表；

（g）就任何事项作出为履行本公约所必需的建议；

（h）按照第四条第3、第4和第5款及第十一条，设法动员资金；

（i）设立其认为履行公约所必需的附属机构；

（j）审评其附属机构提出的报告，并向它们提供指导；

（k）以协商一致方式议定并通过缔约方会议和任何附属机构的议事规则和财务规则；

（l）酌情寻求和利用各主管国际组织和政府间及非政府机构提供的服务、合作和信息；和

（m）行使实现本公约目标所需的其他职能以及依本公约所赋予的所有其他职能。

3. 缔约方会议应在其第一届会议上通过其本身的议事规则以及本公约所设立的附属机构的议事规则，其中应包括关于本公约所述各种决策程序未予规定的事项的决策程序。这类程序可包括通过具体决定所需的特定多数。

4. 缔约方会议第一届会议应由第二十一条所述的临时秘书处召集，并应不迟于本公约生效日期后一年举行。其后，除缔约方会议另有决定外，缔约方会议的常会应年年举行。

5. 缔约方会议特别会议应在缔约方会议认为必要的其他时间举行，或应任何缔约方的书面要求而举行，但须在秘书处将该要求转达给各缔约方后六个月内得到至少三分之一缔约方的支持。

6. 联合国及其专门机构和国际原子能机构，以及它们的非为本公约缔约方的会员国或观察员，均可作为观察员出席缔约方会议的各届会议。任何在本公约所涉事项上具备资格的团体或机构，不管其为国家或国际的、政府或非政府的，经通知秘书处其愿意作为观察员出席缔约方会议的某届会议，均可予以接纳，除非出席的缔约方至少三分之一反对。观察员的接纳和参加应遵循缔约方会议通过的议事规则。

第八条 秘书处

1. 兹设立秘书处。
2. 秘书处的职能应为：

（a）安排缔约方会议及依本公约设立的附属机构的各届会议，并向它们提供所需的服务；

（b）汇编和转递向其提交的报告；

（c）便利应要求时协助各缔约方特别是发展中国家缔约方汇编和转递依本公约规定所需的信息；

（d）编制关于其活动的报告，并提交给缔约方会议；

（e）确保与其他有关国际机构的秘书处的必要协调；

（f）在缔约方会议的全面指导下订立为有效履行其职能而可能需要的行政和合同安排；和

（g）行使本公约及其任何议定书所规定的其他秘书处职能和缔约方会议可能决定的其他职能。

3. 缔约方会议应在其第一届会议上指定一个常设秘书处，并为其行使职能作出安排。

第九条 附属科技咨询机构

1. 兹设立附属科学和技术咨询机构，就与公约有关的科学和技术事项，向缔约方会议并酌情向缔约方会议的其他附属机构及时提供信息和咨询。该机构应开放供所有缔约方参加，并应具有多学科性。该机构应由在有关专门领域胜任的政府代表组成。该机构应定期就其工作的一切方面向缔约方会议报告。

2. 在缔约方会议指导下和依靠现有主管国际机构，该机构应：

（a）就有关气候变化及其影响的最新科学知识提出评估；

（b）就履行公约所采取措施的影响进行科学评估；

（c）确定创新的、有效率的和最新的技术与专有技术，并就促进这类技术的发展和／或转让的途径与方法提供咨询；

（d）就有关气候变化的科学计划和研究与发展的国际合作，以及就支持发展中国家建立自生能力的途径与方法提供咨询；和

（e）答复缔约方会议及其附属机构可能向其提出的科学、技术和方法问题。

3. 该机构的职能和职权范围可由缔约方会议进一步制定。

第十条 附属履行机构

1. 兹设立附属履行机构，以协助缔约方会议评估和审评本公约的有效履行。该机构应开放供所有缔约方参加，并由为气候变化问题专家的政府代表组成。该机构应定期就其工作的一切方面向缔约方会议报告。

2. 在缔约方会议的指导下，该机构应：

（a）考虑依第十二条第 1 款提供的信息，参照有关气候变化的最新科学评估，对各缔约方所采取步骤的总体合计影响作出评估；

（b）考虑依第十二条第 2 款提供的信息，以协助缔约方会议进行第四条第 2 款（d）项所要求的审评；和

（c）酌情协助缔约方会议拟订和执行其决定。

第十一条 资金机制

1. 兹确定一个在赠予或转让基础上提供资金，包括用于技术转让的资金的机制。该机制应在缔约方会议的指导下行使职能并向其负责，并应由缔约方会议决定该机制与本公约有关的政策、计划优先顺序和资格标准。该机制的经营应委托一个或多个现有的国际实体负责。

2. 该资金机制应在一个透明的管理制度下公平和均衡地代表所有缔约方。

3. 缔约方会议和受托管资金机制的那个或那些实体应议定实施上述各款的安排，其中应包括：

（a）确保所资助的应付气候变化的项目符合缔约方会议所制定的政策、计划优先顺序和资格标准的办法；

（b）根据这些政策、计划优先顺序和资格标准重新考虑某项供资决定的办法；

（c）依循上述第1款所述的负责要求，由那个或那些实体定期向缔约方会议提供关于其供资业务的报告；

（d）以可预测和可认定的方式确定履行本公约所必需的和可以得到的资金数额，以及定期审评此一数额所应依据的条件。

4. 缔约方会议应在其第一届会议上作出履行上述规定的安排，同时审评并考虑到第二十一条第3款所述的临时安排，并应决定这些临时安排是否应予维持。在其后四年内，缔约方会议应对资金机制进行审评，并采取适当的措施。

5. 发达国家缔约方还可通过双边、区域性和其他多边渠道提供并由发展中国家缔约方获取与履行本公约有关的资金。

第十二条 提供有关履行的信息

1. 按照第四条第1款，每一缔约方应通过秘书处向缔约方会议提供含有下列内容的信息：

（a）在其能力允许的范围内，用缔约方会议所将推行和议定的可比方法编成的关于《蒙特利尔议定书》未予管制的所有温室气体的各种源的人为排放和各种汇的清除的国家清单；

（b）关于该缔约方为履行公约而采取或设想的步骤的一般性描述；和

（c）该缔约方认为与实现本公约的目标有关并且适合列入其所提供信息的任何其他信息，在可行情况下，包括与计算全球排放趋势有关的资料。

2. 附件一所列每一发达国家缔约方和每一其他缔约方应在其所提供的信息中列入下列各类信息：

（a）关于该缔约方为履行其第四条第2款（a）项和（b）项下承诺所采取政策和措施的详细描述；和

（b）关于本款（a）项所述政策和措施在第四条第2款（a）项所述期间对温室气体各种源的排放和各种汇的清除所产生影响的具体估计。

3. 此外，附件二所列每一发达国家缔约方和每一其他发达缔约方应列入按照第四条第3、第4和第5款所采取措施的详情。

4. 发展中国家缔约方可在自愿基础上提出需要资助的项目，包括为执行这些项目所需要的具体技术、材料、设备、工艺或做法，在可能情况下并附上对所有增加的费用、温室气体排放的减少量及其清除的增加量的估计，以及对其所带来效益的估计。

5. 附件一所列每一发达国家缔约方和每一其他缔约方应在公约对该缔约方生效后六个月内第一次提供信息。未列入该附件的每一缔约方应在公约对该缔约方生效后或按照第四条第3款获得资金后三年内第一次提供信息。最不发达国家缔约方可自行决定何时第一次提供信息。其后所有缔约方提供信息的频度应由缔约方会议考虑到本款所规定的差别时间表予以确定。

6. 各缔约方按照本条提供的信息应由秘书处尽速转交给缔约方会议和任何有关的附属机构。如有必要，提供信息的程序可由缔约方会议进一步考虑。

7. 缔约方会议从第一届会议起，应安排向有此要求的发展中国家缔约方提供技术和资金支持，以汇编和提供本条所规定的信息，和确定与第四条规定的所拟议的项目和应对措施相联系的技术和资金需要。这些支持可酌情由其他缔约方、主管国际组织和秘书处提供。

8. 任何一组缔约方遵照缔约方会议制定的指导方针并经事先通知缔约方会议，可以联合提供信息来履行其在本条下的义务，但这样提供的信息须包括关于其中每一缔约方履行其在本公约下的各自义务的信息。

9. 秘书处收到的经缔约方按照缔约方会议制订的标准指明为机密的信息，在提供给任何参与信息的提供和审评的机构之前，应由秘书处加以汇总，以保护其机密性。

10. 在不违反上述第9款，并且不妨碍任何缔约方在任何时候公开其所提供信息的能力的情况下，秘书处应将缔约方按照本条提供的信息在其提交给缔约方会议的同时予以公开。

第十三条 解决与履行有关的问题

缔约方会议应在其第一届会议上考虑设立一个解决与公约履行有关的问题的多边协商程序，供缔约方有此要求时予以利用。

第十四条 争端的解决

1. 任何两个或两个以上缔约方之间就本公约的解释或适用发生争端时，有关的缔约方应寻求通过谈判或它们自己选择的任何其他和平方式解决该争端。

2. 非为区域经济一体化组织的缔约方在批准、接受、核准或加入本公约时，或在其后任何时候，可在交给保存人的一份文书中声明，关于本公约的解释或适用方面的任何争端，承认对于接受同样义务的任何缔约方，下列义务为当然而具有强制性的，无须另订特别协议：

（a）将争端提交国际法院，和／或

（b）按照将由缔约方会议尽早通过的、载于仲裁附件中的程序进行仲裁。作为区域经济一体化组织的缔约方可就依上述（b）项中所述程序进行仲裁发表类似声明。

3. 根据上述第2款所作的声明，在其所载有效期期满前，或在书面撤回通知交存于保存人后的三个月内，应一直有效。

4. 除非争端各当事方另有协议，新作声明、作出撤回通知或声明有效期满丝毫不得影响国际法院或仲裁庭正在进行的审理。

5. 在不影响上述第2款运作的情况下，如果一缔约方通知另一缔约方它们之间存在争端，过了十二个月后，有关的缔约方尚未能通过上述第1款所述方法解决争端，经争端的任何当事方要求，应将争端提交调解。

6. 经争端一当事方要求，应设立调解委员会。调解委员会应由每一当事方委派的数目相同的成员组成。主席由每一当事方委派的成员共同推选。调解委员会应作出建议性裁决。各当事方应善意考虑之。

7. 有关调解的补充程序应由缔约方会议尽早以调解附件的形式予以通过。

8. 本条各项规定应适用于缔约方会议可能通过的任何相关法律文书，除非该文书另有规定。

第十五条 公约的修正

1. 任何缔约方均可对本公约提出修正。

2. 对本公约的修正应在缔约方会议的一届常会上通过。对本公约提出的任何修正案文应由秘书处在拟议通过该修正的会议之前至少六个月送交各缔约方。秘书处还应将提出的修正送交本公约各签署方，并送交保存人以供参考。

3. 各缔约方应尽一切努力以协商一致方式就对本公约提出的任何修正达成协议。如为谋求协商一致已尽了一切努力，仍未达成协议，作为最后的方式，该修正应以出席会议并参加表决的缔约方四分之三多数票通过。通过的修正应由秘书处送交保存人，再由保存人转送所有缔约方供其接受。

4. 对修正的接受文书应交存于保存人。按照上述第3款通过的修正，应于保存人收到本公约至少四分之三缔约方的接受文书之日后第九十天起对接受该修正的缔约方生效。

5. 对于任何其他缔约方，修正应在该缔约方向保存人交存接受该修正的文书之日后第九十天起对其生效。

6. 为本条的目的，"出席并参加表决的缔约方"是指出席并投赞成票或反对票的缔约方。

第十六条 公约附件的通过和修正

1. 本公约的附件应构成本公约的组成部分，除另有明文规定外，凡提到本公约时即同时提到其任何附件。在不妨害第十四条第2款（b）项和第7款规定的情况下，这些附件应限于清单、表格和任何其他属于科学、技术、程序或行政性质的说明性资料。

2. 本公约的附件应按照第十五条第 2、第 3 和第 4 款中规定的程序提出和通过。

3. 按照上述第 2 款通过的附件,应于保存人向公约的所有缔约方发出关于通过该附件的通知之日起六个月后对所有缔约方生效,但在此期间以书面形式通知保存人不接受该附件的缔约方除外。对于撤回其不接受的通知的缔约方,该附件应自保存人收到撤回通知之日后第九十天起对其生效。

4. 对公约附件的修正的提出、通过和生效,应依照上述第 2 和第 3 款对公约附件的提出、通过和生效规定的同一程序进行。

5. 如果附件或对附件的修正的通过涉及对本公约的修正,则该附件或对附件的修正应待对公约的修正生效之后方可生效。

第十七条 议定书

1. 缔约方会议可在任何一届常会上通过本公约的议定书。
2. 任何拟议的议定书案文应由秘书处在举行该届会议至少六个月之前送交各缔约方。
3. 任何议定书的生效条件应由该文书加以规定。
4. 只有本公约的缔约方才可成为议定书的缔约方。
5. 任何议定书下的决定只应由该议定书的缔约方作出。

第十八条 表决权

1. 除下述第 2 款所规定外,本公约每一缔约方应有一票表决权。
2. 区域经济一体化组织在其权限内的事项上应行使票数与其作为本公约缔约方的成员国数目相同的表决权。如果一个此类组织的任一成员国行使自己的表决权,则该组织不得行使表决权,反之亦然。

第十九条 保存人

联合国秘书长应为本公约及按照第十七条通过的议定书的保存人。

第二十条 签署

本公约应于联合国环境与发展会议期间在里约热内卢,其后自 1992 年 6 月 20 日至 1993 年 6 月 19 日在纽约联合国总部,开放供联合国会员国或任何联合国专门机构的成员国或《国际法院规约》的当事国和各区域经济一体化组织签署。

第二十一条 临时安排

1. 在缔约方会议第一届会议结束前,第八条所述的秘书处职能将在临时基础上由联合国大会 1990 年 12 月 21 日第 45/212 号决议所设立的秘书处行使。

2. 上述第 1 款所述的临时秘书处首长将与政府间气候变化专门委员会密切合作,以确保该委员会能够对提供客观科学和技术咨询的要求作出反应。也可以咨询其他有关的科学机构。

3. 在临时基础上,联合国开发计划署、联合国环境规划署和国际复兴开发银行的"全球环境融资"应为受托经营第十一条所述资金机制的国际实体。在这方面,"全球环境融资"应予适当改革,并使其成员具有普遍性,以使其能满足第十一条的要求。

第二十二条 批准、接受、核准或加入

1. 本公约须经各国和各区域经济一体化组织批准、接受、核准或加入。公约应自签署截止日之次日起开放供加入。批准、接受、核准或加入的文书应交存于保存人。

2. 任何成为本公约缔约方而其成员国均非缔约方的区域经济一体化组织应受本公约一切义务的约束。如果此类组织的一个或多个成员国为本公约的缔约方,该组织及其成员国应决定各自在履行公约义务方面的责任。在此种情况下,该组织及其成员国无权同时行使本公约规定的权利。

3. 区域经济一体化组织应在其批准、接受、核准或加入的文书中声明其在本公约所规定事项上的权限。此类组织还应将其权限范围的任何重大变更通知保存人,再由保存人通知各缔约方。

第二十三条 生效

1. 本公约应自第五十份批准、接受、核准或加入的文书交存之日后第九十天起生效。

2. 对于在第五十份批准、接受、核准或加入的文书交存之后批准、接受、核准或加入本公约的每一国家或区域经济一体化组织，本公约应自该国或该区域经济一体化组织交存其批准、接受、核准或加入的文书之日后第九十天起生效。

3. 为上述第1和第2款的目的，区域经济一体化组织所交存的任何文书不应被视为该组织成员国所交存文书之外的额外文书。

第二十四条 保留

对本公约不得作任何保留。

第二十五条 退约

1. 自本公约对一缔约方生效之日起三年后，该缔约方可随时向保存人发出书面通知退出本公约。

2. 任何退出应自保存人收到退出通知之日起一年期满时生效，或在退出通知中所述明的更后日期生效。

3. 退出本公约的任何缔约方，应被视为亦退出其作为缔约方的任何议定书。

第二十六条 作准文本

本公约正本应交存于联合国秘书长，其阿拉伯文、中文、英文、法文、俄文和西班牙文文本同为作准。

下列签署人，经正式授权，在本公约上签字，以昭信守。

一九九二年五月九日订于纽约。

United Nations Framework Convention on Climate Change[①]

Adopted by the UN Intergovernmental Negotiating Committee for a Framework Convention on Climate Change, New York, 9 May 1992

The Parties to this convention,

Acknowledging that change in the Earth's climate and its adverse effects are a common concern of humankind,

Concerned that human activities have been substantially increasing the atmospheric concentrations of greenhouse gases, that these increases enhance the natural greenhouse effect, and that this will result on average in an additional warming of the Earth's surface and atmosphere and may adversely affect natural ecosystems and humankind,

Noting that the largest share of historical and current global emissions of greenhouse gases has originated in developed countries, that per capita emissions in developing countries are still relatively low and that the share of global emissions originating in developing countries will grow to meet their social and development needs,

Aware of the role and importance in terrestrial and marine ecosystems of sinks and reservoirs of greenhouse gases,

Noting that there are many uncertainties in predictions of climate change, particularly with regard to the timing, magnitude and regional patterns thereof,

Acknowledging that the global nature of climate change calls for the widest possible cooperation by all countries and their participation in an effective and appropriate international response, in accordance with their common but differentiated responsibilities and respective capabilities and their social and economic conditions,

Recalling the pertinent provisions of the Declaration of the United Nations conference on the Human Environment, adopted at Stockholm on 16 June 1972,

Recalling also that States have, in accordance with the charter of the United Nations and the principles of international law, the sovereign right to exploit their own resources pursuant to their own environmental and developmental policies, and the responsibility to ensure that activities within their jurisdiction or control do not cause damage to the environment of other States or of areas beyond the limits of national jurisdiction,

Reaffirming the principle of sovereignty of States in international cooperation to address climate change,

Recognizing that States should enact effective environmental that environmental legislation, that

---

① Report of the Intergovernmental Negotiating Committee for a Framework Convention on Climate Change on the Work of the 2nd Part of its 5th Session, Held at New York from 30 April to 9 May 1992. UN Document: A/AC. 237/18(PART Ⅱ)/ADD. 1.

environmental standards, management objectives and priorities should reflect the environmental and developmental context to which they apply, and that standards applied by some countries may be inappropriate and of unwarranted economic and social cost to other countries, in particular developing countries,

Recalling the provisions of General Assembly resolution 44/228 of 22 December 1989 on the United Nations Conference on Environment and Development, and resolutions 43/53 of 6 December 1988, 44/207 of 22 December 1989, 45/212 of 21 December 1990 and 46/169 of 19 December 1991 on protection of global climate for present and future generations of mankind,

Recalling also the provisions of General Assembly resolution 44/206 of 22 December 1989 on the possible effects of sea-level rise on islands and coastal areas, particularly low-lying coastal areas and the pertinent provisions of General Assembly resolution 44/172 of 19 December 1989 on the implementation of the Plan of Action to Combat desertification,

Recalling further the Vienna Convention for the Protection of the Ozone Layer, 1985, and the Montreal Protocol on Substances that Deplete the Ozone Layer, 1987, as adjusted and amended on 29 June 1990,

Noting the Ministerial Declaration of the Second World Climate Conference adopted on 7 November 1990,

Conscious of the valuable analytical work being conducted by many states on climate change and of the important contributions of the World Meteorological Organization, the united Nations Environment Programme and other organs, organizations and bodies of the United Nations system, as well as other international and intergovernmental bodies, to the exchange of results of scientific research and the coordination of research,

Recognizing that steps required to understand and address climate change will be environmentally, socially and economically most effective if they are based on relevant scientific, technical and economic considerations and continually re-evaluated in the light of new findings in these areas,

Recognizing that various actions to address climate change can be justified economically in their own right and can also help in solving other environmental problems,

Recognizing also the need for developed countries to take immediate action in a flexible manner on the basis of clear priorities, as a first step towards comprehensive response strategies at the global, national and where greed, regional levels that take into account all greenhouse gases, with due consideration of their relative contributions to the enhancement of the greenhouse effect,

Recognizing further that low-lying and other small island countries, countries with low-lying coastal, arid and semi-arid areas or areas liable to floods, drought and desertification, and developing countries with fragile mountainous ecosystems are particularly vulnerable to the adverse effects of climate change,

Recognizing the special difficulties of those countries, especially developing countries, whose economies are particularly dependent on fossil fuel production, use and exportation, as a consequence of action taken on limiting greenhouse gas emissions,

Affirming that responses to climate change should be coordinated with social and economic development in an integrated manner with a view to avoiding adverse impacts on the latter, taking into full account the legitimate priority needs of developing countries for the achievement of sustained economic growth and the eradication of poverty,

Recognizing that all countries, especially developing countries, need access to resources required to achieve sustainable social and economic development and that, in order for developing countries to progress towards that goal, their energy consumption will need to grow taking into account the possibilities for achieving greater energy efficiency and for controlling greenhouse gas emissions in general, including through the application of new technologies on terms which make such an application economically and socially beneficial,

Determined to protect the climate system for present and future generations,

Have agreed as follows:

ARTICLE 1 DEFINITIONS[①]

For the purposes of this convention:

1. "Adverse effects of climate change" means changes in the physical environment or biota resulting from climate change which have significant deleterious effects on the composition, resilience or productivity of natural and managed ecosystems or on the operation of socio-economic systems or on human health and welfare.

2. "Climate change" means a change of climate which is attributed directly or indirectly to human activity that alters the composition of the global atmosphere and which is in addition to natural climate variability observed over comparable time periods.

3. "Climate system" means the totality of the atmosphere, hydrosphere, biosphere and geosphere and their interactions.

4. Emissions means the release of greenhouse gases and/or their precursors into the atmosphere over a specified area and period of time.

5. "Greenhouse gases" means those gaseous constituents of the atmosphere, both natural and anthropogenic, that absorb and re-emit infrared radiation.

6. "Regional economic integration organization" means an organization by constituted sovereign States of a given region which has competence in respect of matters governed by this convention or its protocols and has been duly authorized, in accordance with its internal procedures, to sign, ratify, accept, approve or accede to the instruments concerned.

7. "Reservoir" means a component or components of the climate system where a greenhouse gas or a precursor of a greenhouse gas is stored.

8. "Sink" means any process, activity or mechanism which removes a greenhouse gas, an aerosol or a precursor of a greenhouse gas from the atmosphere.

9. "Source" means any process or activity which releases a greenhouse gas, an aerosol or a precursor of a greenhouse gas into the atmosphere.

ARTICLE 2 OBJECTIVE

The ultimate objective of this Convention and any related legal instruments that the Conference of the Parties may adopt is to achieve, in accordance with the relevant provisions of the Convention, stabilization of greenhouse gas concentrations in the atmosphere at a level that would prevent dangerous anthropogenic interference with the climate system. Such a level should be achieved within a time-frame sufficient to allow ecosystems to adapt naturally to climate change, to ensure that food production is not threatened and to enable economic development to proceed in a sustainable manner.

ARTICLE 3 PRINCIPLES

In their actions to achieve the objective of the Convention and to implement its provisions, the Parties shall be guided, <u>inter alia</u>, by the following:

1. The Parties should protect the climate system for the benefit of present and future generations of humankind, on the basis of equity and in accordance with their common but differentiated responsibilities and

---

① Titles of articles are included solely to assist the reader.

respective capabilities. Accordingly, the developed country parties should take the lead in combating climate change and the adverse effects thereof.

2. The specific needs and special circumstances of developing country Parties, especially those that are particularly vulnerable to the adverse effects of climate change, and of those Parties, especially developing country Parties, that would have to bear a disproportionate or abnormal burden under the Convention, should be given full consideration.

3. The Parties should take precautionary measures to anticipate, prevent or minimize the causes of climate change and mitigate its adverse effects. Where there are threats of serious or irreversible damage, lack of full scientific certainty should not be used as a reason for postponing such measures, taking into account that policies and measures to deal with climate change should be cost-effective so as to ensure global benefits at the lowest possible cost. To achieve this, such policies and measures should take into account different socio-economic contexts, be comprehensive, cover all relevant sources, sinks and reservoirs of greenhouse gases and adaptation, and comprise all economic sectors. Efforts to address climate change may be carried out cooperatively by interested Parties.

4. The Parties have a right to, and should, promote sustainable development. Policies and measures to protect the climate system against human-induced change should be appropriate for the specific conditions of each party and should be integrated with national development programmes, taking into account that economic development is essential for adopting measures to address climate change.

5. The Parties should cooperate to promote a supportive and open international economic system that would lead to sustainable economic growth and development in all Parties, particularly developing country Parties, thus enabling them better to address the problems of climate change. Measures taken to combat climate change, including unilateral ones, should not constitute a means of arbitrary or unjustifiable discrimination or a disguised restriction on international trade.

ARTICLE 4 COMMITMENTS

1. All parties, taking into account their common but differentiated responsibilities and their specific national and regional development priorities, objectives and circumstances, shall:

(a) Develop, periodically update, publish and make available to the Conference of the Parties, in accordance with Article 12, national inventories of anthropogenic emissions by sources and removals by sinks of all greenhouse gases not controlled by the Montreal protocol, using comparable methodologies to be agreed upon by the Conference of the parties;

(b) Formulate, implement, publish and regularly update national and, where appropriate, regional programmes containing measures to mitigate climate change by addressing anthropogenic emissions by sources and removals by sinks of all greenhouse gases not controlled by the Montreal Protocol, and measures to facilitate adequate adaptation to climate change;

(c) Promote and cooperate in the development, application and diffusion, including transfer of technologies, practices and processes that control, reduce or prevent anthropogenic emissions of greenhouse gases not controlled by the Montreal Protocol in all relevant sectors, including the energy, transport, industry, agriculture, forestry and waste management sectors;

(d) Promote sustainable management, and promote and cooperate in the conservation and enhancement, as appropriate, of sinks and reservoirs of all greenhouse gases not controlled by the Montreal Protocol, including biomass, forests and oceans as well as other terrestrial, coastal and marine ecosystems;

(e) Cooperate in preparing for adaptation to the impacts of climate change; develop and elaborate appropriate and integrated plans for coastal zone management, water resources and agriculture, and for the protection and rehabilitation of areas, particularly in Africa, affected by drought and desertification, as well as floods;

(f) Take climate change considerations into account, to the extent feasible, in their relevant social, economic and environmental policies and actions, and employ appropriate methods, for example impact assessments, formulated and determined nationally, with a view to minimizing adverse effects on the economy, on public health and on the quality of the environment, of projects or measures undertaken by them to mitigate or adapt to climate change;

(g) Promote and cooperate in scientific, technological, technical, socio-economic and other research, systematic observation and development of data archives related to the climate system and intended to further the understanding and to reduce or eliminate the remaining uncertainties regarding the causes, effects, magnitude and timing of climate change and the economic and social consequences of various response strategies;

(h) Promote and cooperate in the full, open and prompt exchange of relevant scientific, technological, technical, socio-economic and legal information related to the climate system and climate change, and to the economic and social consequences of various response strategies.

(i) Promote and cooperate in education, training and public awareness related to climate change and encourage the widest participation in this process, including that of non-governmental organizations; and

(j) Communicate to the Conference of the Parties information related to implementation, in accordance with Article 12.

2. The developed country Parties and other Parties included in Annex Ⅰ commit themselves specifically as provided for in the following:

(a) Each of these Parties shall adopt national[①] policies and take corresponding measures on the mitigation of climate change, by limiting its anthropogenic emissions of greenhouse gases and protecting and enhancing its greenhouse gas sinks and reservoirs. These policies and measures will demonstrate that developed countries are taking the lead in modifying longer-term trends in anthropogenic emissions consistent with the objective of the Convention, recognizing that the return by the end of the present decade to earlier levels of anthropogenic emissions of carbon dioxide and other greenhouse gases not controlled by the Montreal Protocol would contribute to such modification, and taking into account the differences in these parties starting points and approaches, economic structures and resource bases, the need to maintain strong and sustainable economic growth, available technologies and other individual circumstances, as well as the need for equitable and appropriate contributions by each of these Parties to the global effort regarding that objective. These Parties may implement such policies and measures jointly with other Parties and may assist other Parties in contributing to the achievement of the objective of the Convention and, in particular, that of this subparagraph;

(b) In order to promote progress to this end, each of these Parties shall communicate, within six months of the entry into force of the Convention for it and periodically thereafter, and in accordance with Article 12, detailed information on its policies and measures referred to in subparagraph (a) above, as well as on its resulting projected anthropogenic emissions by sources and removals by sinks of greenhouse gases not controlled by the Montreal Protocol for the period referred to in subparagraph (a), with the aim of returning individually or jointly to their 1990 levels these anthropogenic emissions of carbon dioxide and other greenhouse gases not controlled by the

---

① This includes policies and measures adopted by regional economic integration organizations.

Montreal Protocol. This information will be reviewed by the Conference of the Parties, at its first session and periodically thereafter, in accordance with Article 7;

(c) Calculations of emissions by sources and removals by sinks of greenhouse gases for the purposes of subparagraph (b) above should take into account the best available scientific knowledge, including of the effective capacity of sinks and the respective contributions of such gases to climate change. The Conference of the Parties shall consider and agree on methodologies for these calculations at its first session and review them regularly thereafter;

(d) The Conference of the Parties shall, at its first session, review the adequacy of subparagraphs (a) and (b) above. Such review shall be carried out in the light of the best available scientific information and assessment on climate change and its impacts, as well as relevant technical, social and economic information. Based on this review, the Conference of the Parties take appropriate action, which may include the adoption of amendments to the commitments in subparagraphs (a) and (b) above. The Conference of the Parties, at its first session, shall also regarding take decisions regarding criteria for joint implementation as indicated in subparagraph (a) above. A second review of subparagraphs (a) and (b) shall take place not later than determined 31 December 1998, and thereafter at regular intervals by the Conference of the Parties, until the objective of the Convention is met;

(e) Each of these Parties shall:

(i) Coordinate as appropriate with other such Parties, relevant economic and administrative instruments developed to achieve the objective of the Convention; and

(ii) Identify and periodically review its own policies and practices which encourage activities that lead to greater levels of anthropogenic emissions of greenhouse gases not controlled by the Montreal Protocol than would otherwise occur;

(f) The Conference of the Parties shall review, not later than 31 December 1998, available information with a view to taking decisions regarding such amendments to the lists in Annexes Ⅰ and Ⅱ as may be appropriate, with the approval of the Party concerned;

(g) Any Party not included in Annex Ⅰ may, in its instrument of ratification acceptance, approval or accession, or at any time thereafter, notify the Depositary that it intends to be bound by subparagraphs (a) and (b) above. The Depositary shall inform the other signatories and Parties of any such notification.

3. The developed country Parties and other developed Parties included in Annex Ⅱ shall provide new and additional financial resources to meet the agreed full costs incurred by developing country Parties in complying with their obligations under Article 12, paragraph 1. They shall also provide such financial resources, including for the transfer of technology, needed by the developing country parties to meet the agreed full incremental costs of implementing measures that are covered by paragraph 1 of this Article and that are agreed between a developing country Party and the international entity or entities referred to in Article 11, in accordance with that Article. The implementation of these commitments shall take into account the need for adequacy and predictability in the flow of funds and the importance of appropriate burden sharing among the developed country Parties.

4. The developed country Parties and other developed Parties included in Annex Ⅱ shall also assist the developing country parties that are particularly vulnerable to the adverse effects of climate change in meeting costs of adaptation to those adverse effects.

5. The developed country Parties and other developed Parties included in Annex II shall take all practicable steps to promote, facilitate and finance, as appropriate, the transfer of, or access to, environmentally sound technologies and know-how to other Parties, particularly developing country Parties, to enable them to implement

the provisions of the Convention. In this process, the developed country Parties shall support the development and enhancement of endogenous capacities and technologies of developing country Parties. Other Parties and organizations in a position to do so may also assist in facilitating the transfer of such technologies.

6. In the implementation of their commitments under paragraph 2 above, a certain degree of flexibility shall be allowed by the Conference of the Parties to the Parties included in Annex I undergoing the process of transition to a market economy, in order to enhance the ability of these Parties to address climate change, including with regard to the historical level of anthropogenic emissions of greenhouse gases not controlled by the Montreal Protocol chosen as a reference.

7. The extent to which developing country Parties will effectively implement their commitments under the Convention will depend on the effective implementation by developed country Parties of their commitments under the Convention related to financial resources and transfer of technology and will take fully into account that economic and social development and poverty eradication are the first and overriding priorities of the developing country Parties.

8. In the implementation of the commitments in this Article, the Parties shall give full consideration to what actions are necessary under the Convention, including actions related to funding, insurance and the transfer of technology, to meet the specific needs and concerns of developing country Parties arising from the adverse effects of climate change and/or the impact of the implementation of response measures, especially on:

(a) Small island countries;

(b) Countries with low-lying coastal areas;

(c) Countries with arid and semi-arid areas, forested areas and areas liable to forest decay;

(d) Countries with areas prone to natural disasters;

(e) Countries with areas liable to drought and desertification;

(f) Countries with areas of high urban atmospheric pollution;

(g) Countries with areas with fragile ecosystems, including mountainous ecosystems;

(h) Countries whose economies are highly dependent on income generated from the production, processing and export, and/or on consumption of fossil fuels and associated energy-intensive products; and

(i) Land-locked and transit countries.

Further, the Conference of the Parties may take actions, as appropriate, with respect to this paragraph.

9. The Parties shall take full account of the specific needs and special situations of the least developed countries in their actions with regard to finding and transfer of technology.

10. The Parties shall, in accordance with Article 10, take into consideration in the implementation of the commitments of the Convention the situation of Parties, particularly developing country Parties, with economies that are vulnerable to the adverse effects of the implementation of measures to respond to climate change. This applies notably to Parties with economies that are highly dependent on income generated from the production, processing and export, and/or consumption of fossil fuels and associated energy-intensive products and/or the use of fossil fuels for which such Parties have serious difficulties in switching to alternatives.

ARTICLE 5 RESEARCH AND OBSERVATION

In carrying out their commitment under Article 4 paragraph 1 (g) the Parties shall:

(a) Support and further develop, as appropriate international and intergovernmental programmes and networks or organizations aimed at defining, conducting, assessing and financing research, data collection and systematic observation, taking into account the need to minimize duplication of efforts;

(b) Support international and intergovernmental efforts to strengthen systematic observation and national scientific and technical research capacities and capabilities, particularly in developing countries, and to promote access to, and the exchange of, data and analyses thereof obtained from areas beyond national jurisdiction; and

(c) Take into account the particular concerns and needs of developing countries and cooperate in improving their endogenous capacities and capabilities to participate in the efforts referred to in subparagraphs (a) and (b) above.

ARTICLE 6 EDUCATION, TRAINING AND PUBLIC AWARENESS

In carrying out their commitments under Article 4, paragraph 1 (i), the Parties shall:

(a) Promote and facilitate at the national and, as appropriate, subregional and regional levels, and in accordance with national laws and regulations, and within their respective capacities:

> (i) the development and implementation of educational and public awareness programmes on climate change and its effects;
>
> (ii) public access to information on climate change and its effects;
>
> (iii) public participation in addressing climate change and its effects and developing adequate responses; and
>
> (iv) training of scientific, technical and managerial personnel.

(b) Cooperate in and promote, at the international level, and, where appropriate, using existing bodies:

> (i) the development and exchange of educational and public awareness material on climate change and its effects; and
>
> (ii) the development and implementation of education and training programmes, including the strengthening of national institutions and the exchange or secondment of personnel to train experts in this field, in particular for developing countries.

ARTICLE 7 CONFERENCE OF THE PARTIES

1. A Conference of the Parties is hereby established.

2. The Conference of the Parties, as the supreme body of this Convention, shall keep under regular review the implementation of the Convention and any related legal instruments that the Conference of the Parties may adopt, and shall make, within its mandate, the decisions necessary to promote the effective implementation of the Convention. To this end, it shall:

(a) Periodically examine the obligations of the Parties and the institutional arrangements under the Convention, in the light of the objective of the convention, the experience gained in its implementation and the evolution of scientific and technological knowledge;

(b) Promote and facilitate the exchange of information on measures adopted by the Parties to address climate change and its effects, taking into account the differing circumstances, responsibilities and capabilities of the Parties and their respective commitments under the Convention;

(c) Facilitate, at the request of two or more Parties, the coordination of measures adopted by them to address climate change and its effects, taking into account the differing circumstances, responsibilities and capabilities of the Parties and their respective commitments under the Convention;

(d) Promote and guide, in accordance with the objective and provisions of the Convention, the development and periodic refinement of comparable methodologies, to be agreed on by the Conference of the Parties, inter alia, for preparing inventories of greenhouse gas emissions by sources and removals by sinks, and for evaluating the effectiveness of measures to limit the emissions and enhance the removals of these gases;

(e) Assess, on the basis of all information made available to it in accordance with the provisions of the Convention, the implementation of the Convention by the Parties, the overall effects of the measures taken pursuant to the Convention, in particular environmental, economic and social effects as well as their cumulative impacts and the extent to which progress towards the objective of the Convention is being achieved;

(f) Consider and adopt regular reports on the implementation of the Convention and ensure their publication;

(g) Make recommendations on any matters necessary for the implementation of the Convention;

(h) Seek to mobilize financial resources in accordance with Article 4, paragraphs 3, 4 and 5, and Article 11;

(i) Establish such subsidiary bodies as are deemed necessary for the implementation of the Convention;

(j) Review reports submitted by its subsidiary bodies and provide guidance to them;

(k) Agree upon and adopt, by consensus, rules of procedure and financial rules for itself and for any subsidiary bodies;

(l) Seek and utilize, where appropriate, the services and cooperation of, and information provided by, competent international organizations and intergovernmental and non-governmental bodies; and

(m) Exercise such other functions as are required for the achievement of the objective of the Convention as well as all other functions assigned to it under the Convention.

3. The Conference of the Parties shall, at its first session, adopt its own rules of procedure as well as those of the subsidiary bodies established by the Convention, which shall include decision-making procedures for matters not already covered by decision-making procedures stipulated in the Convention. Such procedures may include specified majorities required for the adoption of particular decisions.

4. The first session of the Conference of the Parties shall be convened by the interim secretariat referred to in Article 21 and shall take place not later than one year after the date of entry into force of the Convention. Thereafter, ordinary sessions of the Conference of the Parties shall be held every year unless otherwise decided by the Conference of the Parties.

5. Extraordinary sessions of the Conference of the Parties shall be held at such other times as may be deemed necessary by the Conference, or at the written request of any Party, provided that within six months of the request being communicated to the Parties by the secretariat, it is supported by at least one-third of the Parties.

6. The United Nations, its specialized agencies and the International Atomic Energy Agency, as well as any State member thereof or observers thereto not Party to the Convention, may be represented at sessions of the Conference of the Parties as observers. Any body or agency, whether national or international, governmental or non-governmental, which is qualified in matters covered by the Convention, and which has informed the secretariat of its wish to be represented at a session of the Conference of the Parties as an observer, may be so admitted unless at least one-third of the Parties present object. The admission and participation of observers shall be subject to the rules of procedure adopted by the Conference of the Parties.

ARTICLE 8   SECRETARIAT

1. A secretariat is hereby established.

2. The functions of the secretariat shall be:

(a) To make arrangements for sessions of the Conference of the Parties and its subsidiary bodies established under the Convention and to provide them with services as required;

(b) To compile and transmit reports submitted to it;

(c) To facilitate assistance to the Parties, particularly developing country Parties, on request, in the compilation and communication of information required in accordance with the provisions of the Convention;

(d) To prepare reports on its activities and present them to the Conference of the Parties;

(e) To ensure the necessary coordination with the secretariats of other relevant international bodies;

(f) To enter, under the overall guidance of the Conference of the Parties, into such administrative and contractual arrangements as may be required for the effective discharge of its functions; and

(g) To perform the other secretariat functions specified in the Convention and in any of its protocols and such other functions as may be determined by the Conference of the Parties.

3. The Conference of the Parties, at its first session, shall designate a permanent secretariat and make arrangements for its functioning.

ARTICLE 9 SUBSIDIARY BODY FOR SCIENTIFIC AND TECHNOLOGICAL ADVICE

1. A subsidiary body for scientific and technological advice is hereby established to provide the Conference of the Parties and, as appropriate, its other subsidiary bodies with timely information and advice on scientific and technological matters relating to the Convention. This body shall be open to participation by all Parties and shall be multidisciplinary. It shall comprise government representatives competent in the relevant field of expertise. It shall report regularly to the Conference of the Parties on all aspects of its work.

2. Under the guidance of the Conference of the Parties, and drawing upon existing competent international bodies, this body shall:

(a) Provide assessments of the state of scientific knowledge relating to climate change and its effects;

(b) Prepare scientific assessments on the effects of measures taken in the implementation of the Convention;

(c) Identify innovative, efficient and state-of-the-art technologies and know-how and advise on the ways and means of promoting development and/or transferring such technologies;

(d) Provide advice on scientific programmes, international cooperation in research and development related to climate change, as well as on ways and means of supporting endogenous capacity-building in developing countries; and

(e) Respond to scientific, technological and methodological questions that the Conference of the Parties and its subsidiary bodies may put to the body.

3. The functions and terms of reference of this body may be further elaborated by the Conference of the Parties.

ARTICLE 10 SUBSIDIARY BODY FOR IMPLEMENTATION

1. A subsidiary body for implementation is hereby established to assist the Conference of the Parties in the assessment and review of the effective implementation of the Convention. This body shall be open to participation by all Parties and comprise government representatives who are experts on matters related to climate change. It shall report regularly to the Conference of the Parties on all aspects of its work.

2. Under the guidance of the Conference of the Parties, this body shall;

(a) Consider the information communicated in accordance with Article 12, paragraph 1, to assess the overall aggregated effect of the steps taken by the Parties in the light of the latest scientific assessments concerning climate change;

(b) Consider the information communicated in accordance with Article 12 paragraph 2, in order to assist the Conference of the Parties in carrying out the reviews required by Article 4, paragraph 2 (d); and

(c) Assist the Conference of the Parties, as appropriate, in the preparation and implementation of its decisions.

ARTICLE 11 FINANCIAL MECHANISM

1. A mechanism for the provision of financial resources on a grant or concessional basis, including for

the transfer of technology, is hereby defined. It shall function under the guidance of and be accountable to the Conference of the Parties, which shall decide on its policies, programme priorities and eligibility criteria related to this convention. Its operation shall be entrusted to one or more existing international entities.

2. The financial mechanism shall have an equitable and balanced representation of all Parties within a transparent system of governance.

3. The Conference of the Parties and the entity or entities entrusted with the operation of the financial mechanism shall agree upon arrangements to give effect to the above paragraphs, which shall include the following:

(a) Modalities to ensure that the funded projects to address climate change are in conformity with the policies, programme priorities and eligibility criteria established by the Conference of the Parties;

(b) Modalities by which a particular funding decision may be reconsidered in light of these policies, programme priorities and eligibility criteria;

(c) Provision by the entity or entities of regular reports to the Conference of the Parties on its funding operations, which is consistent with the requirement for accountability set out in paragraph 1 above; and

(d) Determination in a predictable and identifiable manner of the amount of funding necessary and available for the implementation of this Convention and the conditions under which that amount shall be periodically reviewed.

4. The Conference of the Parties shall make arrangements to implement the above-mentioned provisions at its first session, reviewing and taking into account the interim arrangements referred to in Article 21, paragraph 3, and shall decide whether these interim arrangements shall be maintained, within four years thereafter, the Conference of the Parties shall review the financial mechanism and take appropriate measures.

5. The developed country Parties may also provide and developing country Parties avail themselves of, financial resources related to the implementation of the Convention through bilateral, regional and other multilateral channels.

ARTICLE 12   COMMUNICATION OF INFORMATION RELATED TO IMPLEMENTATION

1. In accordance with Article 4, paragraph 1, each Party shall communicate to the Conference of the Parties, through the secretariat, the following elements of information:

(a) A national inventory of anthropogenic emissions by sources and removals by sinks of all greenhouse gases not controlled by the Montreal Protocol, to the extent its capacities permit, using comparable methodologies to be promoted and agreed upon by the Conference of the Parties;

(b) A general description of steps taken or envisaged by the Party to implement the Convention; and

(c) Any other information that the Party considers relevant to the achievement of the objective of the Convention and suitable for inclusion in its communication, including, if feasible, material relevant for calculations of global emission trends.

2. Each developed country Party and each other Party included in Annex I shall incorporate in its communication the following elements of information:

(a) A detailed description of the policies and measures that it has adopted to implement its commitment under Article 4, paragraphs 2 (a) and 2 (b); and

(b) A specific estimate of the effects that the policies and measures referred to in subparagraph (a) immediately above will have on anthropogenic emissions by its sources and removals by its sinks of greenhouse gases during the period referred to in Article 4, paragraph 2 (a).

3. In addition, each developed country Party and each other developed Party included in Annex II shall incorporate details of measures taken in accordance with Article 4, paragraphs 3, 4 and 5.

4. Developing country Parties may, on a voluntary basis, propose projects for financing, including specific technologies, materials, equipment, techniques or practices that would be needed to implement such projects, along with, if possible, an estimate of all incremental costs, of the reductions of emissions and increments of removals of greenhouse gases, as well as an estimate of the consequent benefits.

5. Each developed country Party and each other Party included in Annex I shall make its initial communication within six months of the entry into force of the Convention for that Party. Each Party not so listed shall make its initial communication within three years of the entry into force of the Convention for that Party, or of the availability of financial resources in accordance with Article 4, paragraph 3. Parties that are least developed countries may make their initial communication at their discretion. The frequency of subsequent communications by all Parties shall be determined by the Conference of the Parties, taking into account the differentiated timetable set by this paragraph.

6. Information communicated by Parties under this Article shall be transmitted by the secretariat as soon as possible to the Conference of the Parties and to any subsidiary bodies concerned. If necessary, the procedures for the communication of information may be further considered by the Conference of the Parties.

7. From its first session the Conference of the Parties shall arrange for the provision to developing country Parties of technical and financial support, on request in compiling and communicating information under this Article, as well as in identifying the technical and financial needs associated with proposed projects and response measures under Article 4. Such support may be provided by other Parties, by competent international organizations and by the secretariat, as appropriate.

8. Any group of Parties may, subject to guidelines adopted by the Conference of the Parties, and to prior notification to the Conference of the Parties, make a joint communication in fulfilment of their obligations under this Article, provided that such a communication includes information on the fulfilment by each of these Parties of its individual obligations under the convention.

9. Information received by the secretariat that is designated by a Party as confidential, in accordance with criteria to be established by the Conference of the Parties, shall be aggregated by the secretariat to protect its confidentiality before being made available to any of the bodies involved in the communication and review of information.

10. Subject to paragraph 9 above, and without prejudice to the ability of any Party to make public its communication at any time, the secretariat shall make communications by Parties under this Article publicly available at the time they are submitted to the Conference of the Parties.

ARTICLE 13　RESOLUTION OF QUESTIONS REGARDING IMPLEMENTATION

The Conference of the Parties shall, at its first session, consider the establishment of a multilateral consultative process, available to Parties on their request, for the resolution of questions regarding the implementation of the Convention.

ARTICLE 14　SETTLEMENT OF DISPUTES

1. In the event of a dispute between any two or more Parties concerning the interpretation or application of the Convention, the Parties concerned shall seek a settlement of the dispute through negotiation or any other peaceful means of their own choice.

2. When ratifying, accepting, approving or acceding to the Convention, or at any time thereafter, a Party

which is not a regional economic integration organization may declare in a written instrument submitted to the Depositary that, in respect of any dispute concerning the interpretation or application of the Convention, it recognizes as compulsory ipso facto and without special agreement, in relation to any Party accepting the same obligation:

(a) Submission of the dispute to the International Court of Justice, and/or

(b) Arbitration in accordance with procedures to be adopted by the Conference of the Parties as soon as practicable, in an annex on arbitration.

A Party which is a regional economic integration organization may make a declaration with like effect in relation to arbitration in accordance with the procedures referred to in subparagraph (b) above.

3. A declaration made under paragraph 2 above shall remain in force until it expires in accordance with its terms or until three months after written notice of its revocation has been deposited with the Depositary.

4. A new declaration, a notice of revocation or the expiry of a declaration shall not in any way affect proceedings pending before the International Court of Justice or the arbitral tribunal, unless the parties to the dispute otherwise agree.

5. Subject to the operation of paragraph 2 above, if after twelve months following notification by one Party to another that a dispute exists between them, the Parties concerned have not been able to settle their dispute through the means mentioned in paragraph 1 above, the dispute shall be submitted, at the request of any of the parties to the dispute, to conciliation.

6. A conciliation commission shall be created upon the request of one of the parties to the dispute. The commission shall be composed of an equal number of members appointed by each party concerned and a chairman chosen jointly by the members appointed by each party. The commission shall render a recommendatory award, which the parties shall consider in food faith.

7. Additional procedures relating to conciliation shall be adopted by the Conference of the Parties, as soon as practicable, in an annex on conciliation.

8. The provisions of this Article shall apply to any related legal instrument which the Conference of the Parties may adopt, unless the instrument provides otherwise.

ARTICLE 15　AMENDMENT TO THE CONVENTION

1. Any Party may propose amendments to the convention.

2. Amendments to the Convention shall be adopted at an ordinary session of the Conference of the Parties. The text of any proposed amendment to the Convention shall be communicated to the Parties by the secretariat at least six months before the meeting at which it is proposed for adoption. The secretariat shall also communicate proposed amendments to the signatories to the convention and, for information, to the Depositary.

3. The Parties shall make every effort to reach agreement on any proposed amendment to the Convention by consensus. If all efforts at consensus have been exhausted, and no agreement reached, the amendment shall as a last resort be adopted by a three-fourths majority vote of the Parties present and voting at the meeting. The adopted amendment shall be communicated by the secretariat to the Depositary, who shall circulate it to all Parties for their acceptance.

4. Instruments of acceptance in respect of an amendment shall be deposited with the Depositary. An amendment adopted in accordance with paragraph 3 above shall enter into force for those Parties having accepted it on the ninetieth day after the date of receipt by the Depositary of an instrument of acceptance by at least three-fourths of the Parties to the Convention.

5. The amendment shall enter into force for any other Party on the ninetieth day after the date on which that Party deposits with the Depositary its instrument of acceptance of the said amendment.

6. For the purposes of this article, "Parties present and voting" means Parties present and casting an affirmative or negative vote.

ARTICLE 16　ADOPTION AND AMENDMENT OF ANNEXES TO THE CONVENTION

1. Annexes to the convention shall form an integral part thereof unless otherwise expressly provided, a reference to the Convention constitutes at the same time a reference to any annexes thereto. Without prejudice to the provisions of Article 14, paragraphs 2 (b) and 7, such annexes shall be restricted to lists, forms and any other material of a descriptive nature that is of a scientific, technical, procedural or administrative character.

2. Annexes to the Convention shall be proposed and adopted in accordance with the procedure set forth in Article 15, paragraphs 2, 3, and 4.

3. An annex that has been adopted in accordance with paragraph 2 above shall enter into force for all Parties to the Convention six months after the date of the communication by the Depositary to such Parties of the adoption of the annex, except for those Parties that have notified the Depositary, in writing, within that period of their non-acceptance of the annex. The annex shall enter into force for Parties which withdraw their notification of non-acceptance on the ninetieth day after the date on which withdrawal of such notification has been received by the Depositary.

4. The proposal, adoption and entry into force of amendments to annexes to the Convention shall be subject to the same procedure as that for the proposal, adoption and entry into force of annexes to the Convention in accordance with paragraphs 2 and 3 above.

5. If the adoption of an annex or an amendment to an annex involves an amendment to the convention, that annex or amendment to an annex shall not enter into force until such time as the amendment to the Convention enters into force.

ARTICLE 17　PROTOCOLS

1. The Conference of the Parties may, at any ordinary session, adopt protocols to the Convention.

2. The text of any proposed protocol shall be communicated to the Parties by the secretariat at least six months before such a session.

3. The requirements for the entry into force of any protocol shall be established by that instrument.

4. Only Parties to the Convention may be Parties to a protocol.

5. Decisions under any protocol shall be taken only by the Parties to the protocol concerned.

ARTICLE 18　RIGHT TO VOTE

1. Each Party to the Convention shall have one vote, except as provided for in paragraph 2 below.

2. Regional economic integration organizations, in matters within their competence, shall exercise their right to vote with a number of votes equal to the number of their member States that are Parties to the Convention. Such an organization shall not exercise its right to vote if any of its member States exercises its right, and vice versa.

ARTICLE 19　DEPOSITARY

The Secretary-General of the United Nations shall be the Depositary of the Convention and of protocols adopted in accordance with Article 17.

ARTICLE 20　SIGNATURE

This Convention shall be open for signature by States members of the United Nations or of any of its specialized agencies or that are Parties to the Statute of the International Court of and by regional economic integration organizations at Rio de Janeiro, during the United Nations Conference on Environment and Development, and thereafter at United Nations Headquarters in New York from 20 June 1992 to 19 June 1993.

ARTICLE 21 INTERIM ARRANGEMENTS

1. The secretariat functions referred to in Article 8 will be carried out on an interim basis by the secretariat established by the General Assembly of the United Nations in its resolution 45/212 of 21 December 1990, until the completion of the first session of the Conference of the Parties.

2. The head of the interim secretariat referred to in paragraph 1 above will cooperate closely with the Intergovernmental Panel on Climate Change to ensure that the Panel can respond to the need for objective scientific and technical advice. Other relevant scientific bodies could also be consulted.

3. The Global Environment Facility of the United Nations Development Programme, the United Nations Environment Programme and the International Bank for Reconstruction and Development shall be the international entity entrusted with the operation of the financial mechanism referred to in Article 11 on an interim basis. In this connection, the Global Environment Facility should be appropriately restructured, and its membership made universal to enable it to fulfil the requirements of Article 11.

ARTICLE 22 RATIFICATION, ACCEPTANCE, APPROVAL OR ACCESSION

1. The Convention shall be subject to ratification, acceptance, approval or accession by States and by regional economic integration organizations. It shall be open for accession from the day after the date on which the Convention is closed for signature. Instruments of ratification, acceptance, approval or accession shall be deposited with the Depositary.

2. Any regional economic integration organization which becomes a Party to the Convention without any of its member States being a Party shall be bound by all the obligations under the Convention. In the case of such organizations, one or more of whose member States is a Party to the Convention, the organization and its member States shall decide on their respective responsibilities for the performance of their obligations under the Convention. In such cases, the organization and the member States shall not be entitled to exercise rights under the Convention concurrently.

3. In their instruments of ratification, acceptance, approval or accession, regional economic integration organizations shall declare the extent of their competence with respect to the matters governed by the Convention. These organizations shall also inform the Depositary, who shall in turn inform the Parties, of any substantial modification in the extent of their competence.

ARTICLE 23 ENTRY INTO FORCE

1. The Convention shall enter into force on the ninetieth day after the date of deposit of the fiftieth instrument of ratification, acceptance, approval or accession.

2. For each State or regional economic integration organization that ratifies, accepts or approves the Convention or accedes thereto after the deposit of the fiftieth instrument of ratification, acceptance, approval or accession, the Convention shall enter into force on the ninetieth day after the day of deposit by such State or regional economic integration organization of its instrument of ratification, acceptance, approval or accession.

3. For the purposes of paragraphs 1 and 2 above, any instrument deposited by a regional economic integration organization shall not be counted as additional to those deposited by States members of the organization.

ARTICLE 24 RESERVATIONS

No reservations may be made to the Convention.

ARTICLE 25　WITHDRAWAL

1. At any time after three years from the date on which the Convention has entered into force for a Party, that Party may withdraw from the Convention by giving written notification to the Depositary.

2. Any such withdrawal shall take effect upon expiry of one year from the date of receipt by the Depositary of the notification of withdrawal, or on such later date as may be specified in the notification of withdrawal.

3. Any Party that withdraws from the Convention shall be considered as also having withdrawn from any protocol to which it is a Party.

ARTICLE 26　AUTHENTIC TEXTS

The original of this Convention, of which the Arabic, Chinese, English, French, Russian and Spanish texts are equally authentic, shall be deposited with the Secretary-General of the United Nations.

IN WITNESS WHEREOF the undersigned, being duly authorized to that effect, have signed this Convention.
DONE at New York this ninth day of May one thousand nine hundred and ninety-two.

//www.unccd.int。
联合国关于在发生严重干旱和/或荒漠化的国家特别是在非洲防治荒漠化的公约（防治荒漠化公约）[①]

（联合国防治荒漠化公约委员会 1994 年 6 月 17 日在巴黎通过）

本《公约》各缔约方，

申明在防治荒漠化和缓解干旱影响时，受影响或受威胁地区的人类是受关注的中心；

意识到国际社会，包括各国和各国际组织，迫切关注荒漠化和干旱的有害影响；

了解到干旱、半干旱和亚湿润干旱地区合计占地球陆地面积的很大一部分，而且是地球上很大一部分人口的居住地和生计来源；

承认荒漠化和干旱是全球范围问题，影响到世界所有区域，需要国际社会联合行动，防治荒漠化和/或缓解干旱影响；

注意到严重干旱和/或荒漠化高度集中在发展中国家，尤其是最不发达国家，并注意到这些现象在非洲造成了特别悲惨的后果；

还注意到荒漠化的成因是各种自然、生物、政治、社会、文化和经济因素的复杂相互作用；

考虑到贸易及国际经济关系的有关方面对受影响国家充分防治荒漠化的能力造成的影响；

意识到可持续的经济增长、社会发展和消灭贫困是受影响的发展中国家、尤其是非洲国家的优先任务，对可持续能力目标的实现至关重要；

铭记荒漠化和干旱经由与贫困、健康和营养不良、缺乏粮食保障、以及由移民、流离失所者和人口动态所引起的重大社会问题的相互关系而影响到可持续发展；

赞赏以往各国和各国际组织在防治荒漠化和缓解干旱影响方面，特别是在实施 1977 年联合国荒漠化问题会议制订的《联合国防治荒漠化行动计划》方面所作出的努力和所取得的经验的重大意义；

认识到尽管过去已做出了努力，但防治荒漠化和缓解干旱影响方面的进展未达预期效果，需要在可持续发展的框架内在所有各级推行新的更有效的方法；

确认联合国环境与发展会议通过的各项决定，特别是《21 世纪议程》及其第 12 章的正确性和适切性，它们为防治荒漠化奠定了基础；

为此重申发达国家在《21 世纪议程》第 33 章第 13 段的承诺；

回顾大会第 47/188 号决议，尤其是其中给予非洲的优先地位，并回顾有关荒漠化和干旱的所有其他联合国决议、决定和方案，以及非洲国家和其他区域国家的有关宣言；

[①] 引自：联合国防治荒漠化公约网站，www.unccd.int。

重申《里约环境与发展宣言》，其中原则 2 申明，按照《联合国宪章》和国际法原则，各国拥有按照本国的环境与发展政策开发本国自然资源的主权权利，并负有确保在其管辖范围内或在其控制下的活动不致损害其他国家或在各国管辖范围以外地区的环境的责任；

承认各国政府在防治荒漠化和缓解干旱影响方面发挥关键作用，这方面的进展取决于行动方案在受影响地区的当地实施工作；

还承认国际合作和伙伴关系在防治荒漠化和缓解干旱影响工作中的重要性和必要性；

进一步承认向受影响发展中国家特别是非洲这类国家提供有效手段十分重要，即除其他手段外，实质性资金资源，包括新的和额外资金和获得技术的机会，否则它们难以充分履行根据本《公约》所作的承诺；

关注荒漠化和干旱对亚洲中部受影响国家和外高加索所造成的影响；

强调许多受荒漠化和/或干旱影响区域特别是发展中国家农村地区的妇女所发挥的重要作用，以及在所有各级确保男女充分参与防治荒漠化和缓解干旱影响方案的重要性；

强调非政府组织和其他主要群体在防治荒漠化和缓解干旱影响方案中的特殊作用；

铭记荒漠化与国际和国家社会面临的其他全球范围环境问题之间的关系；

还铭记防治荒漠化有助于实现《联合国气候变化框架公约》《生物多样性公约》以及其他有关环境公约的目标；

相信防治荒漠化和缓解干旱影响战略只有基于完善可靠的系统观测和严密精确的科学知识并不断加以重新评价才能最为有效；

确认迫切需要提高国际合作效力并改善协调，以便推动国家计划和优先事项的执行；

决心为今世后代的利益采取适当行动，防治荒漠化和缓解干旱影响。

兹协议如下：

第一部分　导言

第1条　用语

为本《公约》之目的：

（a）"荒漠化"是指包括气候变异和人类活动在内的种种因素造成的干旱、半干旱和亚湿润干旱地区的土地退化；

（b）"防治荒漠化"包括干旱、半干旱和亚湿润干旱地区为可持续发展而进行的土地综合开发的部分活动，目的是：

（一）防止和/或减少土地退化；

（二）恢复部分退化的土地；及

（三）垦复已荒漠化的土地；

（c）"干旱"是指降水量大大低于正常记录水平时发生的自然现象，引起严重水文失衡，对土地资源生产系统造成有害影响；

（d）"缓解干旱影响"是指与预测干旱有关并旨在防治荒漠化方面减轻社会和自然系统易受干旱影响的活动；

（e）"土地"是指具有陆地生物生产力的系统，由土壤、植被、其他生物区系和在该系统中发挥作用的生态及水文过程组成；

（f）"土地退化"是指由于使用土地或由于一种营力或数种营力结合致使干旱、半干旱和亚湿润干旱地区雨浇地、水浇地或草原、牧场、森林和林地的生物或经济生产力和复杂性下降或丧失，其中包括：

（一）风蚀和水蚀致使土壤物质流失；

（二）土壤的物理、化学和生物特性或经济特性退化；及

（三）自然植被长期丧失；

（g）"干旱、半干旱和亚湿润干旱地区"是指年降水量与潜在蒸发散之比在 0.05 至 0.65 之间的地区，但不包括极区和副极区；

（h）"受影响地区"是指受荒漠化影响或威胁的干旱、半干旱和/或亚湿润干旱地区；

（i）"受影响国家"是指其全部或部分土地为受影响地区的国家；

（j）"区域经济一体化组织"是指由一个区域主权国家构成的组织，它对本《公约》所涉事项拥有管辖权并按其内部程序被正式授权签署、批准、接受、核准或加入本《公约》；

（k）"发达国家缔约方"是指发达国家缔约方和由发达国家组成的区域经济一体化组织。

第 2 条 目标

1. 本《公约》的目标是在发生严重干旱和/或荒漠化的国家，特别是在非洲防治荒漠化和缓解干旱影响，为此要在所有各级采取有效措施，辅之以在符合《21 世纪议程》的综合办法框架内建立的国际合作和伙伴关系安排，以期协助受影响地区实现可持续发展。

2. 实现这项目标将包括一项长期的综合战略，同时在受影响地区重点提高土地生产力，恢复、保护并以可持续的方式管理土地和水资源，从而改善特别是社区一级的生活条件。

第 3 条 原则

为实现本《公约》的目标和履行本《公约》各项规定，缔约方除其他外应以下列为指导：

（a）缔约方应当确保群众和地方社区参与关于防治荒漠化和/或缓解干旱影响的方案的设计和实施决策，并在较高各级为便利国家和地方两级采取行动创造一种扶持环境；

（b）缔约方应当本着国际团结和伙伴关系的精神，改善分区域、区域以及国际的合作和协调，并更好地将资金、人力、组织和技术资源集中用于需要的地方；

（c）缔约方应当本着伙伴关系的精神在政府所有各级、社区、非政府组织和土地所有者之间发展合作，更好地认识受影响地区土地资源和稀缺的水资源的性质和价值，并争取以可持续的方式利用这些资源；及

（d）缔约方应当充分考虑到受影响发展中国家缔约方、特别是其中最不发达国家的特殊需要和处境。

第二部分 总则

第 4 条 一般义务

1. 缔约方应通过现有的或预期的双边和多边安排，或酌情以两者相结合的方式，单独或共同履行本《公约》规定的义务，同时强调需要在所有各级协调努力，制订连贯一致的长期战略。

2. 为实现本《公约》的目标，缔约方应：

（a）采取综合办法，处理荒漠化和干旱过程中的自然、生物和社会经济因素；

（b）在有关的国际和区域机构内适当注意受影响发展中国家缔约方在国际贸易、市场安排和债务方面的情况，为促进可持续发展创立扶持性国际经济环境；

（c）把消灭贫困战略纳入防治荒漠化和缓解干旱影响的工作；

（d）促进受影响缔约方之间在与荒漠化和干旱有关的环境保护、土地和水资源养护领域的合作；

（e）加强分区域、区域和国际合作；

（f）在有关政府间组织内开展合作；

（g）适当时确定机构体制，要注意避免重复；并

（h）促进利用现有双边和多边资金机制和安排，为受影响发展中国家缔约方防治荒漠化和缓解干旱影响筹集和输送实质性资金资源。

3. 受影响发展中国家缔约方在执行《公约》中有资格获得援助。

第5条 受影响国家缔约方的义务

除根据第4条应承担的义务之外，受影响国家缔约方承诺：

（a）适当优先注意防治荒漠化和缓解干旱影响，按其情况和能力拨出适足的资源；

（b）在可持续发展计划和/或政策框架内制订防治荒漠化和缓解干旱影响的战略和优先顺序；

（c）处理造成荒漠化的根本原因，并特别注意助长荒漠化过程的社会经济因素；

（d）在防治荒漠化和缓解干旱影响的工作中，在非政府组织的支持下，提高当地群众尤其是妇女和青年的认识，并为他们的参与提供便利；以及

（e）于适当时加强相关的现有法律，如若没有这种法律，则颁布新的法律，和制定长期政策和行动方案，以提供一种扶持性环境。

第6条 发达国家缔约方的义务

除了按照第4条规定的一般义务外，发达国家缔约方承诺：

（a）在同意的基础上单独或共同地积极支持受影响发展中国家缔约方、特别是非洲国家缔约方、以及最不发达国家为防治荒漠化和缓解干旱影响所作的努力；

（b）提供实质性资金资源和其他形式的支助，以援助受影响发展中国家缔约方、特别是非洲国家缔约方有效地制订和执行防治荒漠化和缓解干旱影响的长期计划和战略；

（c）根据第20条第2款（b）项促进筹集新的和额外资金；

（d）鼓励从私营部门和其他非政府来源筹集资金；以及

（e）促进和便利受影响国家缔约方、特别是受影响发展中国家缔约方获得适用技术、知识和诀窍。

第7条 非洲的优先地位

鉴于非洲区域存在的特殊情况，缔约方在履行本《公约》时，应优先考虑受影响非洲国家缔约方，同时也不忽视其他区域受影响发展中国家缔约方。

第8条 与其他公约的关系

1. 缔约方应鼓励协调遵照本《公约》开展的活动，如果它们是其他有关国际协定的缔约方，则亦应协调遵照其他有关国际协定，特别是《联合国气候变化框架公约》和《生物多样性公约》开展的活动，以便争取按每一协定开展的活动都能产生最大成效，同时避免工作重复。缔约方应鼓励执行联合方案，特别是在研究、培训、系统观察和信息收集与交流领域，争取使这些活动有助于实现有关协定的目标。

2. 本《公约》的规定不应影响任何缔约方在本《公约》对它生效前参加的双边、区域或国际协定对它产生的权利和义务。

第三部分 行动方案、科学和技术合作以及支持措施

第1节 行动方案

第9条 基本方法

1. 为履行第5条规定的义务，受影响发展中国家缔约方和在区域执行附件框架内，或以书面通知常设秘书处打算制定国家行动方案的任何其他受影响国家缔约方应尽可能利用现有的、相关的、成功的计划和方案，并在其基础上，酌情制订、公布和实施国家行动方案，并制订、公布和实施分区域和区域行动方案，将它们作为防治荒漠化、缓解干旱影响战略的中心内容。这些方案应借鉴实地行动经验教训和研究成果在不间断的参与中加以更新。国家行动方案的制订应与制订国家可持续发展政策的其他努力密切配合。

2. 发达国家缔约方在按照第6条提供不同形式的援助时，应在同意基础上直接或通过有关多边组织

或两者优先支持受影响发展中国家缔约方特别是非洲国家缔约方、分区域或区域行动方案。

3. 缔约方应鼓励联合国系统的各机构、基金和方案以及有能力参与合作的其他有关政府间组织、学术机构、科学界和非政府组织根据其职权范围和能力，支持行动方案的拟订、实施及其后续工作。

第 10 条　国家行动方案

1. 国家行动方案的目的是查明造成荒漠化的因素，并提出防治荒漠化、缓解干旱影响所必需的实际措施。

2. 国家行动方案应当明确指出政府、地方社区和土地使用者各自的作用，同时确定可得到的和需要的资源。国家行动方案除其他外应：

（a）纳入防治荒漠化和缓解干旱影响的长期战略，强调贯彻实施并与国家可持续发展政策相结合；

（b）允许根据情况变化作出修改，并应在地方一级具有足够的灵活性，以适应不同的社会经济、生物及自然地理条件；

（c）特别注意为尚未退化或仅轻微退化的土地实行预防措施；

（d）提高国家气候、气象和水文能力以及增强提供干旱早期预警的手段；

（e）促进政策和加强机构框架，本着伙伴精神在捐助界、各级政府、当地群众和社区团体之间发展合作和协调，同时方便当地群众取得适当的信息和技术；

（f）设法在地方、国家和区域各级让非政府组织和当地男女群众，特别是资源的使用者，包括农民和牧民及他们的代表组织，有效参与国家行动方案的政策规划、决策、实施和审查；以及

（g）规定定期审查方案的实施情况并提出进展报告。

3. 国家行动方案，除其他外，可包括下列某些或所有旨在对付和缓解干旱影响的措施：

（a）酌情建立和/或加强早期预警系统，包括地方和国家设施及分区域和区域两级的联合系统，以及援助环境导致的流离失所者的机制；

（b）加强考虑到季节和年度气候预测的防旱抗旱工作，包括地方、国家、分区域和区域各级的干旱应急计划；

（c）酌情建立和/或加强粮食安全系统包括储存和销售设施，尤其是在农村地区；

（d）制订可以为易发生干旱地区创收的另谋生计项目；以及

（e）为农作物和牲畜制订可持续的灌溉方案。

4. 考虑到各个受影响国家缔约方有其具体的情况和要求，国家行动方案，除其他外，酌情包括下列某些或所有涉及在受影响地区防治荒漠化和缓解干旱影响、涉及其人口的优先领域措施：提倡另谋生计并改善国家经济环境，以争取加强消灭贫困方案，加强粮食保障；人口动态；以可持续方式管理自然资源；实行可持续的农业方式；开发和高效率地使用各种能源；体制和法律框架；加强评估和系统观察能力包括水文和气象服务以及能力建设、教育和公众意识。

第 11 条　分区域和区域行动方案

受影响国家缔约方应按照有关的区域执行附件酌情进行协商和合作，拟订分区域和/或区域行动方案，以协调、补充和提高国家方案的效率。第 10 条的规定经修改后应适用于分区域和区域方案。这种合作可包括关于对跨边界自然资源实行可持续管理、开展科学技术合作和加强有关机构的议定联合方案。

第 12 条　国际合作

受影响国家缔约方应协同其他缔约方和国际社会合力确保促进一个有利于实施《公约》的扶持性国际环境。这种合作也应包括技术转让、科学研究和发展、信息收集和传播以及资金资源等领域。

第 13 条　拟订和实施行动方案方面的支持

1. 根据第 9 条支持行动方案的措施除其他外包括：

（a）资金合作，为行动方案提供可预测性，以便能作出必要的长期规划；

（b）制订和利用能在地方一级更好地提供支持的合作机制，包括通过非政府组织的行动，以便促进有关成功试点方案活动的推广；

（c）按照为地方社区一级参与行动提出的试验性可推广的办法，提高项目设计、供资和实施的灵活性；以及

（d）酌情提高合作和支助方案效率的行政和预算程序。

2. 在向受影响发展中国家缔约方提供这种支持时，应优先重视非洲国家缔约方和最不发达国家缔约方。

第 14 条 拟订和执行行动方案方面的协调

1. 缔约方在拟订和执行行动方案方面应直接和通过有关政府间组织开展密切合作。

2. 缔约方应制订运作机制特别是在国家一级和实地方面，确保在发达国家缔约方、发展中国家缔约方、有关政府间组织和非政府组织之间尽可能全面协调，以避免重复，协调各种干预和做法，并最大限度地发挥援助的作用。在受影响发展中国家缔约方，要优先开展有关国际合作的协调活动，争取最有效利用资源，确保援助切合具体情况并促进实施本《公约》规定的国家行动方案和优先事项。

第 15 条 区域执行附件

列入行动方案的要点应有所选择，应适合受影响国家缔约方或区域的社会经济、地理和气候特点及其发展水平。各区域执行附件规定各具体分区域和区域拟订行动方案的准则及其确切重点和内容。

第 2 节 科学和技术合作

第 16 条 信息收集、分析和交流

缔约方同意根据各自能力综合和协调有关长、短期数据及信息的收集、分析和交流工作，确保有系统地观察受影响地区土地退化情况，更好地了解和评价干旱和荒漠化的过程和影响。除其他外，这将可以用适合所有各级用户，包括尤其是以当地群众能够实际应用的形式，对不利的气候变异时期提供早期预警和先期规划。为此，它们应酌情：

（a）促进和加强全球机构和设施网络，在所有各级进行信息收集、分析、交流以及系统观察，这种网络除了其他外应：

（一）争取使用彼此兼容的标准和系统；

（二）覆盖包括偏远地区在内的有关数据和台站；

（三）使用和推广有关土地退化的现代数据收集、传递和评价技术；以及

（四）将国家、分区域和区域数据和信息中心同全球信息来源更密切地连接起来；

（b）确保信息收集、分析和交流能满足地方社区和决策者的需要，以便能解决具体问题，这些活动应吸收地方社区参与；

（c）支持和进一步制订旨在界定、进行、评价和资助数据和信息的收集、分析和交流的双边和多边方案和项目，除其他外，包括汇编若干套自然、生物、社会和经济综合指标；

（d）充分利用有关政府间和非政府组织的专门知识，尤其要在不同区域的特定群体间传播有关信息和经验；

（e）充分注重收集、分析和交流社会经济数据并将其与自然和生物数据相结合；

（f）交流并充分、公开、及时提供有关防治荒漠化和缓解干旱影响的所有可以公开取得的信息；以及

（g）在符合各自国家立法和/或政策的前提下就当地和传统知识交流信息，确保充分保护这种知识，并且平等地以相互议定的条件向有关当地群众适当回报由此产生的利益。

第 17 条 研究与发展

1. 缔约方承诺根据自己的能力通过适当的国家、分区域、区域和国际机构促进防治荒漠化和缓解干

旱影响领域内的技术和科学合作。为此，它们应支持研究活动，这些研究活动：

（a）有助于增进对导致荒漠化和干旱的过程的认识，增进对自然及人为因素的影响及其区别的认识，以期防治荒漠化和缓解干旱影响，提高生产力，可持续地使用和管理资源；

（b）与明确的目标共鸣、针对当地群众的具体需要，据以查明和实施能改善受影响地区人民生活水平的办法；

（c）保护、综合、增进和验证传统的和当地的知识、诀窍和做法，在符合各自国家立法和/或政策的前提下确保拥有这种知识的人能以平等、相互商定的条件从这些知识的商业利用或从这些知识所带来的技术发展直接获益；

（d）在受影响发展中国家缔约方特别是非洲国家缔约方发展和加强国家、分区域和区域研究能力，包括当地技能的开发，尤其是在研究基础薄弱的国家加强适当的能力，特别重视多学科和参与式社会经济研究；

（e）考虑到相关的贫困、环境因素造成的移民与荒漠化之间的关系；

（f）促进开展国家、分区域、区域和国际研究组织在公营和私营部门的联合研究方案，以便通过当地群众和社区的有效参与为可持续的发展开发更优良的、不昂贵的和易于获得的技术；并

（g）增加受影响地区的水资源，除其他外通过人工降雨。

2. 行动方案中应列出反映不同地方条件的特定区域和分区域研究优先次序。缔约方会议应根据科学技术委员会的建议，定期审查研究优先次序。

第18条 技术的转让、获取、改造和开发

1. 缔约方承诺相互商定并依照各自的国家立法和/或政策促进、资助和/或便利资助、转让、获取、改造和开发有关防治荒漠化和/或缓解干旱影响的无害环境、经济上可行、社会上可以接受的技术，以此为受影响地区实现可持续发展作出贡献。这类合作应酌情以双边或多边方式开展，充分利用政府间组织和非政府组织的专门知识。缔约方尤应：

（a）充分利用有关的现有国家、分区域、区域和国际信息系统和交流中心，传播与下列各项有关的信息：可获得的技术、其来源、其环境风险，以及获得这些技术的大致条件；

（b）便利特别是受影响发展中国家缔约方以有利条件，包括相互议定的减让和优惠条件在顾及需保护知识产权的前提下获取最宜实际用来解决当地群众特殊需要的技术，要特别注意这类技术的社会、文化、经济和环境影响；

（c）通过资金援助或其他适当途径，便利受影响国家缔约方之间开展技术合作；

（d）尤其要把与受影响发展中国家缔约方开展的技术合作推广到促进另谋生计部门，相关情况下包括合资经营；以及

（e）采取措施，创造有利于发展、转让、获取、改造适用技术、知识、诀窍和做法的国内市场条件，提出财政鼓励或其他鼓励办法，包括确保充分和有效保护知识产权的措施。

2. 缔约方应根据各自能力并在符合各自国家立法和/或政策的前提下保护、促进和利用特别是有关的传统和当地技术、知识、诀窍和做法，为此，缔约方承诺：

（a）请当地群众参加将这种技术、知识、诀窍和做法及其潜在用途登记造册，并酌情与有关政府间组织和非政府组织合作传播这方面的信息；

（b）确保这种技术、知识、诀窍和做法受到充分保护，并确保当地群众能平等地和以相互商定的条件从这些知识或源自这些知识的任何技术发展的任何商业利用中直接获得利益；

（c）鼓励和积极支持改进和推广这种技术、知识、诀窍和做法或据以发展的新技术；并

（d）酌情便利改造这种技术、知识、诀窍和做法，以利广泛使用，并酌情将之与现代技术相结合。

第3节 支持措施
第19条 能力建设、教育和公众意识

1. 缔约方确认,能力建设——即所谓机构建设、培训和有关本地和本国能力的发展——对防治荒漠化和缓解干旱影响各种努力具有重要意义。缔约方应酌情以下列方式促进能力的建设:

(a) 鼓励所有各级的、尤其是地方一级的当地人民、特别是妇女和青年的充分参与,与非政府组织和地方组织合作;

(b) 增强国家一级在荒漠化和干旱领域的训练和研究能力;

(c) 建立和/或加强支助和推广服务,更有效地传播有关工艺方法和技术,培训实地工作人员和农村组织成员,采取群众参与的方法,以保护和可持续地使用自然资源;

(d) 尽可能地促进在技术合作方案中利用和传播当地人民的知识、诀窍和做法;

(e) 按照现代社会经济情况,在必要时改造有关的无害环境技术以及农牧业中的传统方法;

(f) 提供适当的培训和技术,利用替代能源,尤其是可再生能源,以期特别是减少燃料方面对木柴的依赖;

(g) 相互协议进行合作,加强受影响发展中国家缔约方按照第16条在收集、分析和交流信息领域制订和实施方案的能力;

(h) 以创新的方式促进另谋生计,包括新技能的培训;

(i) 培训决策者、管理人员和负责收集和分析数据的人员,以便传播和使用干旱状况早期预警信息和粮食生产;

(j) 提高现有国家机构和法律框架的运作效能,必要时建立新的机构和框架,同时加强战略规划和管理;以及

(k) 通过互访方案,长期的学习研究交流,增进受影响国家缔约方的能力建设。

2. 受影响发展中国家缔约方应酌情在其他缔约方和胜任的政府间和非政府组织的合作下,从跨学科的角度审查地方和国家现有的能力和设施,以及予以加强的可能性。

3. 缔约方应彼此并与胜任的政府间组织以及非政府组织开展合作,在受影响缔约方和适当时在未受影响国家缔约方推行和支持公众意识和教育方案,促进对荒漠化和干旱的原因和影响以及实现本《公约》目标的重要性的认识。为此,它们应:

(a) 组织对公众的宣传运动;

(b) 长期促进公众能得到有关的信息并让公众广泛参与教育和宣传活动;

(c) 鼓励建立有助于公众意识的协会;

(d) 制订和交流教育和公众意识材料,这类材料在可能的情况下应用当地语文编制,互派和调派专家训练受影响发展中国家缔约方的人员,使他们能够推行有关的教育和宣传方案,充分利用胜任的国际机构备有的有关教育材料;

(e) 评价受影响地区的教育需要,制订适当的学校课程,必要时,扩大教育和成人识字方案,并在查明、保护以及可持续使用和管理受影响地区资源方面,为所有人特别是女童和妇女创造更多的机会;并

(f) 制订跨学科参与式方案,把对荒漠化和干旱的意识纳入教育系统,并使之融入非正式教育方案、成人教育方案、远距离和实用教育方案。

4. 缔约方会议应为防治荒漠化和缓解干旱影响设立和/或加强区域教育和培训中心网络。这些网络应由为此目的设立或指定的机构加以协调,负责培训科学、技术和管理人员,同时应酌情加强受影响国家缔约方负责教育和培训的机构,以协调各项方案并组织经验交流。这些网络应与有关政府间和非政府组织密切合作,以避免工作重复。

第20条 资金资源

1. 鉴于为实现《公约》目标筹资至为重要,缔约方应视其能力尽力确保防治荒漠化和缓解干旱影响的方案得到充分的资金资源。

2. 在这方面，发达国家缔约方，在不忽视其他区域的受影响发展中国家缔约方的前提下，根据第 7 条规定对非洲给予优先，同时承诺：

（a）筹集实质性资金资源，包括赠款和减让贷款，以便支持执行防治荒漠化和缓解干旱影响的方案；

（b）促进筹集充分、及时和可预测的资金资源，其中包括根据《建立全球环境融资文件》的有关规定，为与全球环境融资的四个中心领域有关的涉及荒漠化的那些活动的议定增加费用，从全球环境融资中筹集新的和额外的资金；

（c）通过国际合作，便利技术知识和诀窍的转让；以及

（d）与受影响发展中国家缔约方合作，寻求筹集和输送资源的新办法和鼓励措施，包括各种基金、非政府组织和其他私营部门实体的资金，特别是债务交换和其他创新办法，通过减少特别是非洲受影响发展中国家缔约方的外债负担来增加融资。

3. 受影响发展中国家缔约方，按其能力，承诺为执行其国家行动方案筹集充分资金资源。

4. 缔约方在筹集资金资源时应充分利用，并继续在质量方面改善所有本国、双边和多边资金来源和机制，利用财团、联合方案和并行筹资，并应争取吸引私营部门资金来源和机制，包括非政府组织的资金和机制的参与。为此目的，缔约方应充分利用根据第 14 条制订的运作机制。

5. 为筹集受影响发展中国家缔约方防治荒漠化和缓解干旱影响所需的资金资源，缔约方应：

（a）理顺和加强管理为防治荒漠化和缓解干旱影响已拨出的资源，更切实际、更有效地利用它们，对其成败进行评估，消除妨碍其有效利用的阻力和必要时根据本《公约》采取的综合长期办法重新确定方案的方向；

（b）在多边资金机构、设施和基金包括区域开发银行和基金的理事会中，应优先支持受影响发展中国家缔约方特别是非洲此类国家促进执行《公约》的活动，尤其是在它们根据区域执行附件进行的行动方案方面；并

（c）审查能加强区域和分区域合作的途径，支持在国家一级进行的努力。

6. 鼓励其他缔约方向受影响发展中国家缔约方自愿提供与荒漠化有关的知识、诀窍和技术和/或资金资源。

7. 发达国家缔约方按《公约》规定履行义务，特别是有关资金资源和技术转让的义务，将能大大地帮助受影响发展中国家缔约方、特别是其中非洲国家充分履行它们按照《公约》所承担的义务。在履行其义务时，发达国家缔约方应充分考虑到经济和社会发展、消灭贫困是受影响发展中国家缔约方、特别是非洲此类国家的最优先事项。

第 21 条　资金机制

1. 缔约方会议应促进拥有资金机制并应鼓励这种机制尽量为受影响发展中国家缔约方，特别是非洲此类国家，执行《公约》获得资金。为此目的，缔约方会议应考虑除其他外采取各种办法和政策：

（a）便利在国家、分区域、区域和全球一级为根据《公约》有关规定进行的活动提供必要资金；

（b）促进符合第 20 条的多种来源的融资办法、机制和安排及其评估；

（c）定期向感兴趣的缔约方和有关政府间和非政府间组织提供有关资金来源和融资形式的信息，以促进它们之间的协调；

（d）酌情便利建立各种机制，如国家防治荒漠化基金，包括非政府组织参与的基金，迅速和有效地向受影响发展中国家缔约方地方一级输送资金资源；以及

（e）加强分区域和区域一级，特别是在非洲的现有基金和资金机制，以便更有效地支持执行《公约》。

2. 缔约方会议也应鼓励通过联合国系统内的各种机制和多边金融机构支持发展中国家缔约方为履行《公约》规定的义务在国家、分区域和区域一级进行的活动。

3. 受影响国家缔约方应利用，在需要时建立和/或加强即将并入国家发展方案的国家协调机制，以便

保证有效使用所有可获得的资金资源。这些国家在筹集资金、拟订以及执行各项方案和保证各团体在地方一级获得资金等方面，也应利用参与，包括非政府组织、当地团体和私营部门的介入。这些行动可通过提供援助者改进协调和拟订灵活方案得以加强。

4. 为了增加现有资金机制的效力和效率，兹建立一项全球机制以促进向受影响发展中国家缔约方以赠款、减让和／或以其他条件筹集和输送实质性资金资源的行动，包括技术转让。全球机制在缔约方会议授权和指导下进行工作，并对其负责。

5. 缔约方会议应在其第一次常会上确定一个容纳全球机制的组织。缔约方会议和它所确定的组织应就全球机制的方式取得协议，保证该机制除其他外：

（a）查明和拟订现有可用以执行《公约》的有关双边和多边合作方案的清单；

（b）根据要求，向缔约方提供有关筹资和资金援助来源的创新方法以及关于在国家一级改进合作活动之协调的意见；

（c）向感兴趣的缔约方和有关政府间和非政府组织提供关于现有资金来源和融资形式的信息，以促进它们之间的协调；并

（d）从缔约方会议第二届常会开始，提出其活动的报告。

6. 缔约方会议应在其第一届会议上同所确定容纳全球机制的组织为该机制的行政业务作出适当安排，在可能范围内使用现有预算和人力资源。

7. 缔约方会议应在其第三届常会上，考虑到第 7 条的规定，审查按照第 4 款向其负责的全球机制的政策、运作方式和活动。根据该项审查，缔约方会议应考虑和采取适当行动。

第四部分　机构

第 22 条　缔约方会议

1. 兹设立缔约方会议。

2. 缔约方会议是本《公约》的最高机构。缔约方会议应在其职权范围内作出必要的决定，促进本《公约》的有效实施。缔约方会议特别应：

（a）根据科技知识的发展，参照国家、分区域、区域和国际各级取得的经验，定期审查本《公约》的实施和机构安排的运作情况；

（b）促进和便利交换关于各缔约方所采取措施的信息、决定以何种形式、按何种时间程序转送根据第 26 条提供的信息和审查有关报告并就这些报告提出建议；

（c）设立实施本《公约》所需的附属机构；

（d）审查其附属机构提交的报告并给它们以指导；

（e）商定并以协商一致的方式通过缔约方会议及其任何附属机构的议事规则和财务细则；

（f）根据第 30 和第 31 条通过本《公约》的修正案；

（g）为其活动包括其附属机构的活动核定方案和预算，并为其筹资作出必要安排；

（h）酌情谋求胜任的国家机构、国际机构、政府间机构和非政府机构的合作，并利用它们提供的服务和信息；

（i）促进和加强同其他有关公约的关系，同时避免工作重复；并

（j）行使实现本《公约》目标所需的其他职能。

3. 缔约方会议应在第一届会议上以协商一致通过其议事规则，其中应包括本《公约》所规定的决策程序未包括的事项的决策程序。这种程序可包括通过某些决定所需要的特定多数票。

4. 缔约方会议第一届会议应由根据第 35 条所述临时秘书处召集，并应至迟于本《公约》生效之日起一年内举行。除非缔约方会议另有决定，第二、第三和第四届常会应每一年举行一次，此后应每两年举行一次常会。

5. 经缔约方会议常会决定或任何缔约方提出书面请求，缔约方会议特别会议可在其他时间举行，但须在常设秘书处将请求通知各缔约方起三个月之内得到至少三分之一缔约方的支持。

6. 在每届常会上，缔约方会议应选出一个主席团。主席团的结构和职能应在议事规则中确定。任命主席团成员时应适当顾及需要确保公平地域分配及受影响缔约方特别是非洲国家有足够的代表。

7. 联合国、其专门机构以及其中不属本《公约》缔约方的任何成员国或观察员可派代表以观察员身份出席缔约方会议各届会议。任何机关或机构，无论是国家的或国际的、政府的或非政府的，只要有资格处理本《公约》所涉事项，并已通知常设秘书处希望派代表以观察员身份出席缔约方会议的某届会议，均可予以接纳，除非出席会议的缔约方至少有三分之一表示反对。观察员的接纳和参加应遵循缔约方会议通过的议事规则。

8. 第一届缔约方会议可要求具有有关专长的国家组织和国际组织提供与第16条（g）款、第17条第1款（c）项和第18条第2款（b）项有关的信息。

第23条 常设秘书处

1. 兹设立常设秘书处。

2. 常设秘书处的职能是：

（a）为根据本《公约》设立的缔约方会议及其附属机构的会议作出安排并向它们提供所需要的服务；

（b）汇编和转送向其提交的报告；

（c）便利应请求向受影响发展中国家缔约方特别是非洲国家提供援助，帮助它们汇编和提交本《公约》要求的信息；

（d）同其他有关国际机构和《公约》的秘书处协调活动；

（e）以在缔约方会议的指导下，订立有效履行职能所需要的行政和合同安排；

（f）编写秘书处根据本《公约》履行其职能的情况报告，提交缔约方会议；

（g）履行缔约方会议决定的任何其他秘书处职能。

3. 缔约方会议应在第一届会议上选定常设秘书处并为其业务作好安排。

第24条 科学和技术委员会

1. 兹设立科学和技术委员会，作为缔约方会议的附属机构，向会议提供与防治荒漠化和缓解干旱影响有关的科技事务的信息和意见。委员会的会议应是多学科的，向所有缔约方开放，与缔约方会议常会同时举行。科学和技术委员会应由专门领域胜任的政府代表组成。缔约方会议第一届会议应决定该委员会的职权范围。

2. 缔约方会议应建立和保持一份具有有关领域专长和经验的独立专家名册。顾及多学科方式和广泛地域代表性，以各缔约方书面递交的提名为准。

3. 缔约方会议在需要时可任命特设工作组，经由委员会针对与防治荒漠化和缓解干旱影响有关之科技领域现状的具体问题，提供信息和意见。在考虑到多学科方式和广泛地域代表的情况下，这些工作组由其姓名见于名册的个人组成。这些专家应具有科学背景和实地经验，由缔约方会议根据委员会建议予以任命。缔约方会议应决定这些工作组的职权范围和工作方式。

第25条 机构和组织网络

1. 科学和技术委员会应在缔约方会议监督下，规定调查和评价现有网络和愿意联成网络的各类机构和组织。这种网络应当支持《公约》的执行。

2. 科学和技术委员会根据第1款所述调查和评价结果向缔约方会议建议如何便利和加强地方、国家和其他各级各单位之间的联网，以便确保第16和19条确定的专题需要能得到处理。

3. 缔约方会议参照这些建议，应当：

（a）确定最适宜联网的国家、分区域、区域和国际单位，就业务程序和时间范围向它们提出建议；

（b）确定最适宜在各级便利和加强这种联网的单位。

第五部分　程序

第 26 条　提交信息

1. 每一缔约方应通过常设秘书处向缔约方会议提交它为实施本《公约》所采取措施的报告，供缔约方会议常会审议。缔约方会议应确定这种报告的提交时间和格式。

2. 受影响国家缔约方应说明根据本《公约》第 5 条制订的战略及关于其实施情况的任何有关信息。

3. 根据第 9 至第 15 条实施行动方案的受影响国家缔约方应详细说明方案及其实施情况。

4. 任何一组受影响国家缔约方可提出联合呈文，说明在行动方案的范围内在分区域和／或区域一级采取的措施。

5. 发达国家缔约方应报告为协助拟订和实施行动方案而采取的措施，包括关于它们根据本《公约》已提供或正在提供的资金资源的信息。

6. 根据第 1 至 4 款提交的信息应由常设秘书处尽快转交缔约方会议及任何有关的附属机构。

7. 缔约方会议得便利应请求向受影响发展中国家缔约方、特别是非洲国家提供技术和资金支持，帮助它们按本条编辑和提交信息，认明与拟议行动方案有关的技术和资金需要。

第 27 条　解决执行问题的措施

缔约方会议应审议并通过解决在执行本《公约》时可能出现的问题的程序和机构机制。

第 28 条　争端的解决

1. 缔约方应通过谈判或自行选择的其他和平手段，解决相互之间关于本《公约》的解释或适用方面的任何争端。

2. 缔约方如果不是区域经济一体化组织，可在批准、接受、核准或加入本《公约》时或在其后任何时间向保存人提出一项文书，就本《公约》的解释或适用方面的任何争端作出声明，承认对于接受同样义务的任何缔约方而言，下列两者或其中之一为强制解决争端手段：

（a）按缔约方会议在实际可行的情况下尽快通过的一项附件中通过的程序进行仲裁；

（b）将争端提交国际法院审理。

3. 缔约方如果是区域经济一体化组织，可按照第 2 款（a）项所述程序就仲裁问题作出具有类似效果的声明。

4. 根据第 2 款作出的声明，其有效期至按其规定的时间或将书面撤销通知交存保存人三个月之后结束。

5. 除非争端当事方另有协议，否则声明有效期的结束、通知撤销或提出新的声明一律不影响仲裁庭或国际法院未决的诉讼。

6. 如果争端当事方未接受第 2 款规定的同一或任何程序，又如果一方通知另一方双方存在争端之后十二个月内未能解决争端，应按照争端任一当事方的请求，根据缔约方会议在实际可行的情况下尽快通过的一项附件中所列程序，将争端交付调解。

第 29 条　附件的地位

1. 各附件是本《公约》的组成部分，除非另有明文规定，否则提及本《公约》即同时提及其附件。

2. 各缔约方应以符合按本《公约》条款所享权利和所负义务的方式解释各附件的规定。

第 30 条　《公约》的修正

1. 任何缔约方均可对本《公约》提出修正。

2. 对本《公约》的修正应在缔约方会议的常会上通过。任何修正草案的案文均应由常设秘书处在提议通过修正案的会议召开前至少六个月交送各缔约方。常设秘书处还应将修正草案通报本《公约》签署方。

3. 缔约方应尽力通过协商一致的方式就任何修正草案达成协议。如已穷尽一切争取协商一致的努力仍未能达成协议，则作为最后手段，将修正案交由出席会议并参加表决的缔约方三分之二多数通过。通过的修正案应由常设秘书处交保存人，保存人应将其发交所有缔约方批准、接受、核准或加入。

4. 对修正案的批准书、接受书、核准书或加入书应交存于保存人。按第3款通过的修正案应于保存人收到在修正案通过时为缔约方的本《公约》至少三分之二缔约方的批准书、接受书、核准书或加入书之日起第九十天对接受修正的缔约方生效。

5. 对于任何其他缔约方，修正案应于缔约方向保存人交存对该修正案的批准书、接受书、核准书或加入书之日起第九十天生效。

6. 为本条和第31条的目的，"出席并参加表决的缔约方"是指出席并投赞成票或反对票的缔约方。

第31条　附件的通过和修正

1. 本《公约》的任何附加附件及对任一附件的任何修正均应按照第30条规定的修正程序提出和通过。但在通过附加区域执行附件或对任何区域执行附件的修正时，该条所规定的多数票应包括有关区域出席并参加表决的缔约方的三分之二多数票。附件的通过或修正均应由保存人通报所有缔约方。

2. 按照第1款通过的附件，附加区域执行附件除外，或附件的修正，对任何区域执行附件的修正除外，应于保存人将该附件或修正通过一事通报所有缔约方之日六个月之后起对所有缔约方生效，但在这段时间内书面通知保存人不接受该附件或修正的缔约方除外。对于撤回不接受通知的缔约方，有关附件或修正应于保存人收到这种撤回通知之日起第九十天生效。

3. 根据第1款通过的任何附加区域执行附件或区域执行附件的修正应于保存人通报该附件或修正通过一事之日后六个月对本《公约》所有缔约方生效，但以下不在其列：

（a）任何缔约方在六个月内以书面形式将其不接受该附加区域执行附件或区域执行附件的修正通知保存人，在这种情况该附件或修正对撤回不接受通知书的缔约方，在保存人收到上述通知后九十天起生效；以及

（b）对根据第34条第4款就附加区域执行附件或对区域执行附件的修正作出声明的任何缔约方，此种附件或修正应在该缔约方向交存人交存其有关该附件或修正的批准书、接受书、核准书或加入书后九十天起生效。

4. 如果附件或附件的修正涉及对本《公约》的修正，则在《公约》修正生效之前，该附件或附件的修正不得生效。

第32条　表决权

1. 除第2款规定的情况外，《公约》每一缔约方均有一票表决权。

2. 区域经济一体化组织应就其职权范围内的事项行使表决权，其票数相等于其参加本《公约》的成员国数目。如其任何成员国行使表决权，该组织即不得行使表决权，反之亦然。

第六部分　最后条款

第33条　签署

本《公约》应于1994年10月14日至15日在巴黎开放供联合国会员国或联合国任何专门机构的成员国或《国际法院规约》的当事国以及区域经济一体化组织签署。此后，本《公约》应在纽约联合国总部继续开放供签署，至1995年10月13日为止。

第34条　批准、接受、核准和加入

1. 本《公约》须经各国和各区域经济一体化组织批准、接受、核准或加入。它应于签署截止之日的次日起开放加入。批准、接受、核准或加入文书应交存于保存人。

2. 凡成为本《公约》缔约方而其任何成员国均非本《公约》缔约方的区域经济一体化组织应受本《公约》一切义务的约束。如这种组织的一个或多个成员国亦为本《公约》缔约方，该组织及其成员国应决定它们各自在履行《公约》义务方面的责任。在这种情况下，该组织及其成员国无权同时行使本《公约》赋予的权利。

3. 区域经济一体化组织在其批准、接受、核准或加入文书中应宣布它们对《公约》适用事项的权限范围。它们也应当将权限范围的任何重大改变迅速通知保存人，再由保存人告知各缔约方。

4. 在其批准、接受、核准或加入文书中，任何缔约方可宣布，对它而言，任何附加区域执行附件或对任何区域执行附件的任何修正仅在该缔约方交存批准、接受或核准文书时生效。

第35条 临时安排

第23条所述秘书处职能暂由联合国大会1992年12月22日第47/188号决议设立的秘书处执行，直至缔约方会议第一届会议结束时为止。

第36条 生效

1. 本《公约》应于第五十份批准、接受、核准或加入文书交存之后第九十天生效。

2. 对于在第五十份批准、接受、核准或加入文书交存之日后批准、接受、核准或加入本《公约》的国家或区域经济一体化组织，本《公约》应于该国或区域经济一体化组织交存批准、接受、核准或加入书之日后第九十天生效。

3. 为第1款和第2款的目的，由区域经济一体化组织交存的任何文书不应视为该组织成员国交存的文书以外的额外文书。

第37条 保留

对本《公约》不得提出任何保留。

第38条 退约

1. 缔约方在本《公约》对其生效之日起三年后，可随时书面通知保存人退出本《公约》。

2. 这种退出应于保存人收到退出通知之日起一年后或在退出通知说明的较后日期生效。

第39条 保存人

联合国秘书长为本《公约》保存人。

第40条 正式文本

本《公约》正本应交存于联合国秘书长，其阿拉伯文、中文、英文、法文、俄文和西班牙文本具有同等效力。

下列签署人，经正式授权，在本《公约》上签字，以资证明。

一九九四年六月十七日订于巴黎。

United Nations Convention to Combat Desertification in those Countries Experiencing Serious Drought and/or Desertification, Particularly in Africa[1]

Adopted by the UN Intergovernmental Negotiating Committee for the International Convention to Combat Desertification, Paris, 17 June 1994

The Parties to this Convention,

Affirming that human beings in affected or threatened areas are at the centre of concerns to combat desertification and mitigate the effects of drought,

Reflecting the urgent concern of the international community, including States and international organizations, about the adverse impacts of desertification and drought,

Aware that arid, semi-arid and dry sub-humid areas together account for a significant proportion of the Earth's land area and are the habitat and source of livelihood for a large segment of its population,

Acknowledging that desertification and drought are problems of global dimension in that they affect all regions of the world and that joint action of the international community is needed to combat desertification and/or mitigate the effects of drought,

Noting the high concentration of developing countries, notably the least developed countries, among those experiencing serious drought and/or desertification, and the particularly tragic consequences of these phenomena in Africa,

Noting also that desertification is caused by complex interactions among physical, biological, political, social, cultural and economic factors,

Considering the impact of trade and relevant aspects of international economic relations on the ability of affected countries to combat desertification adequately,

Conscious that sustainable economic growth, social development and poverty eradication are priorities of affected developing countries, particularly in Africa, and are essential to meeting sustainability objectives,

Mindful that desertification and drought affect sustainable development through their interrelationships with important social problems such as poverty, poor health and nutrition, lack of food security, and those arising from

---

[1] from: United Nations Convention to Combat Desertification, www. unccd. int.

migration, displacement of persons and demographic dynamics,

Appreciating the significance of the past efforts and experience of States and international organizations in combating desertification and mitigating the effects of drought, particularly in implementing the Plan of Action to Combat Desertification which was adopted at the United Nations Conference on Desertification in 1977,

Realizing that, despite efforts in the past, progress in combating desertification and mitigating the effects of drought has not met expectations and that a new and more effective approach is needed at all levels within the framework of sustainable development,

Recognizing the validity and relevance of decisions adopted at the United Nations Conference on Environment and Development, particularly of Agenda 21 and its chapter 12, which provide a basis for combating desertification,

Reaffirming in this light the commitments of developed countries as contained in paragraph 13 of chapter 33 of Agenda 21,

Recalling General Assembly resolution 47/188, particularly the priority in it prescribed for Africa, and all other relevant United Nations resolutions, decisions and programmes on desertification and drought, as well as relevant declarations by African countries and those from other regions,

Reaffirming the Rio Declaration on Environment and Development which states, in its Principle 2, that States have, in accordance with the Charter of the United Nations and the principles of international law, the sovereign right to exploit their own resources pursuant to their own environmental and developmental policies, and the responsibility to ensure that activities within their jurisdiction or control do not cause damage to the environment of other States or of areas beyond the limits of national jurisdiction,

Recognizing that national Governments play a critical role in combating desertification and mitigating the effects of drought and that progress in that respect depends on local implementation of action programmes in affected areas,

Recognizing also the importance and necessity of international cooperation and partnership in combating desertification and mitigating the effects of drought,

Recognizing further the importance of the provision to affected developing countries, particularly in Africa, of effective means, <u>inter alia</u> substantial financial resources, including new and additional funding, and access to technology, without which it will be difficult for them to implement fully their commitments under this Convention,

Expressing concern over the impact of desertification and drought on affected countries in Central Asia and the Transcaucasus,

Stressing the important role played by women in regions affected by desertification and/or drought, particularly in rural areas of developing countries, and the importance of ensuring the full participation of both men and women at all levels in programmes to combat desertification and mitigate the effects of drought,

Emphasizing the special role of non-governmental organizations and other major groups in programmes to combat desertification and mitigate the effects of drought,

Bearing in mind the relationship between desertification and other environmental problems of global dimension facing the international and national communities,

Bearing also in mind the contribution that combating desertification can make to achieving the objectives of the United Nations Framework Convention on Climate Change, the Convention on Biological Diversity and other related environmental conventions,

Believing that strategies to combat desertification and mitigate the effects of drought will be most effective if they are based on sound systematic observation and rigorous scientific knowledge and if they are continuously re evaluated,

Recognizing the urgent need to improve the effectiveness and coordination of international cooperation to facilitate the implementation of national plans and priorities,

Determined to take appropriate action in combating desertification and mitigating the effects of drought for the benefit of present and future generations,

Have agreed as follows:

PART I INTRODUCTION

Article 1 Use of terms

For the purposes of this Convention:

(a) "desertification" means land degradation in arid, semi-arid and dry sub-humid areas resulting from various factors, including climatic variations and human activities;

(b) "combating desertification" includes activities which are part of the integrated development of land in arid, semi-arid and dry sub-humid areas for sustainable development which are aimed at:

   (i) prevention and/or reduction of land degradation;

   (ii) rehabilitation of partly degraded land; and

   (iii) reclamation of desertified land;

(c) "drought" means the naturally occurring phenomenon that exists when precipitation has been significantly below normal recorded levels, causing serious hydrological imbalances that adversely affect land resource production systems;

(d) "mitigating the effects of drought" means activities related to the prediction of drought and intended to reduce the vulnerability of society and natural systems to drought as it relates to combating desertification;

(e) "land" means the terrestrial bio-productive system that comprises soil, vegetation, other biota, and the ecological and hydrological processes that operate within the system;

(f) "land degradation" means reduction or loss, in arid, semi-arid and dry sub-humid areas, of the biological or economic productivity and complexity of rainfed cropland, irrigated cropland, or range, pasture, forest and woodlands resulting from land uses or from a process or combination of processes, including processes arising from human activities and habitation patterns, such as:

   (i) soil erosion caused by wind and/or water;

   (ii) deterioration of the physical, chemical and biological or economic properties of soil; and

   (iii) long-term loss of natural vegetation;

(g) "arid, semi-arid and dry sub-humid areas" means areas, other than polar and sub-polar regions, in which the ratio of annual precipitation to potential evapotranspiration falls within the range from 0.05 to 0.65;

(h) "affected areas" means arid, semi-arid and/or dry sub-humid areas affected or threatened by desertification;

(i) "affected countries" means countries whose lands include, in whole or in part, affected areas;

(j) "regional economic integration organization" means an organization constituted by sovereign States of a given region which has competence in respect of matters governed by this Convention and has been duly authorized, in accordance with its internal procedures, to sign, ratify, accept, approve or accede to this Convention;

(k) "developed country Parties" means developed country Parties and regional economic integration organizations constituted by developed countries.

Article 2 Objective

1. The objective of this Convention is to combat desertification and mitigate the effects of drought in countries experiencing serious drought and/or desertification, particularly in Africa, through effective action at all levels, supported by international cooperation and partnership arrangements, in the framework of an integrated approach which is consistent with Agenda 21, with a view to contributing to the achievement of sustainable development in affected areas.

2. Achieving this objective will involve long-term integrated strategies that focus simultaneously, in affected areas, on improved productivity of land, and the rehabilitation, conservation and sustainable management of land and water resources, leading to improved living conditions, in particular at the community level.

Article 3 Principles

In order to achieve the objective of this Convention and to implement its provisions, the Parties shall be guided, inter alia, by the following:

(a) the Parties should ensure that decisions on the design and implementation of programmes to combat desertification and/or mitigate the effects of drought are taken with the participation of populations and local communities and that an enabling environment is created at higher levels to facilitate action at national and local levels;

(b) the Parties should, in a spirit of international solidarity and partnership, improve cooperation and coordination at subregional, regional and international levels, and better focus financial, human, organizational and technical resources where they are needed;

(c) the Parties should develop, in a spirit of partnership, cooperation among all levels of government, communities, non-governmental organizations and landholders to establish a better understanding of the nature and value of land and scarce water resources in affected areas and to work towards their sustainable use; and

(d) the Parties should take into full consideration the special needs and circumstances of affected developing country Parties, particularly the least developed among them.

PART II GENERAL PROVISIONS

Article 4 General obligations

1. The Parties shall implement their obligations under this Convention, individually or jointly, either through existing or prospective bilateral and multilateral arrangements or a combination thereof, as appropriate, emphasizing the need to coordinate efforts and develop a coherent long-term strategy at all levels.

2. In pursuing the objective of this Convention, the Parties shall:

(a) adopt an integrated approach addressing the physical, biological and socio-economic aspects of the processes of desertification and drought;

(b) give due attention, within the relevant international and regional bodies, to the situation of affected developing country Parties with regard to international trade, marketing arrangements and debt with a view to establishing an enabling international economic environment conducive to the promotion of sustainable development;

(c) integrate strategies for poverty eradication into efforts to combat desertification and mitigate the effects of drought;

(d) promote cooperation among affected country Parties in the fields of environmental protection and the conservation of land and water resources, as they relate to desertification and drought;

(e) strengthen subregional, regional and international cooperation;

(f) cooperate within relevant intergovernmental organizations;

(g) determine institutional mechanisms, if appropriate, keeping in mind the need to avoid duplication; and

(h) promote the use of existing bilateral and multilateral financial mechanisms and arrangements that mobilize and channel substantial financial resources to affected developing country Parties in combating desertification and mitigating the effects of drought.

3. Affected developing country Parties are eligible for assistance in the implementation of the Convention.

Article 5 Obligations of affected country Parties

In addition to their obligations pursuant to article 4, affected country Parties undertake to:

(a) give due priority to combating desertification and mitigating the effects of drought, and allocate adequate resources in accordance with their circumstances and capabilities;

(b) establish strategies and priorities, within the framework of sustainable development plans and/or policies, to combat desertification and mitigate the effects of drought;

(c) address the underlying causes of desertification and pay special attention to the socio-economic factors contributing to desertification processes;

(d) promote awareness and facilitate the participation of local populations, particularly women and youth, with the support of non-governmental organizations, in efforts to combat desertification and mitigate the effects of drought; and

(e) provide an enabling environment by strengthening, as appropriate, relevant existing legislation and, where they do not exist, enacting new laws and establishing long-term policies and action programmes.

Article 6 Obligations of developed country Parties

In addition to their general obligations pursuant to article 4, developed country Parties undertake to:

(a) actively support, as agreed, individually or jointly, the efforts of affected developing country Parties, particularly those in Africa, and the least developed countries, to combat desertification and mitigate the effects of drought;

(b) provide substantial financial resources and other forms of support to assist affected developing country Parties, particularly those in Africa, effectively to develop and implement their own long-term plans and strategies to combat desertification and mitigate the effects of drought;

(c) promote the mobilization of new and additional funding pursuant to article 20, paragraph 2 (b);

(d) encourage the mobilization of funding from the private sector and other non-governmental sources; and

(e) promote and facilitate access by affected country Parties, particularly affected developing country Parties, to appropriate technology, knowledge and know-how.

Article 7 Priority for Africa

In implementing this Convention, the Parties shall give priority to affected African country Parties, in the light of the particular situation prevailing in that region, while not neglecting affected developing country Parties in other regions.

Article 8   Relationship with other conventions

1. The Parties shall encourage the coordination of activities carried out under this Convention and, if they are Parties to them, under other relevant international agreements, particularly the United Nations Framework Convention on Climate Change and the Convention on Biological Diversity, in order to derive maximum benefit from activities under each agreement while avoiding duplication of effort. The Parties shall encourage the conduct of joint programmes, particularly in the fields of research, training, systematic observation and information collection and exchange, to the extent that such activities may contribute to achieving the objectives of the agreements concerned.

2. The provisions of this Convention shall not affect the rights and obligations of any Party deriving from a bilateral, regional or international agreement into which it has entered prior to the entry into force of this Convention for it.

PART III   ACTION PROGRAMMES, SCIENTIFIC AND TECHNICAL COOPERATION AND SUPPORTING MEASURES

Section 1: Action programmes
Article 9   Basic approach

1. In carrying out their obligations pursuant to article 5, affected developing country Parties and any other affected country Party in the framework of its regional implementation annex or, otherwise, that has notified the Permanent Secretariat in writing of its intention to prepare a national action programme, shall, as appropriate, prepare, make public and implement national action programmes, utilizing and building, to the extent possible, on existing relevant successful plans and programmes, and subregional and regional action programmes, as the central element of the strategy to combat desertification and mitigate the effects of drought. Such programmes shall be updated through a continuing participatory process on the basis of lessons from field action, as well as the results of research. The preparation of national action programmes shall be closely interlinked with other efforts to formulate national policies for sustainable development.

2. In the provision by developed country Parties of different forms of assistance under the terms of article 6, priority shall be given to supporting, as agreed, national, subregional and regional action programmes of affected developing country Parties, particularly those in Africa, either directly or through relevant multilateral organizations or both.

3. The Parties shall encourage organs, funds and programmes of the United Nations system and other relevant intergovernmental organizations, academic institutions, the scientific community and non-governmental organizations in a position to cooperate, in accordance with their mandates and capabilities, to support the elaboration, implementation and follow-up of action programmes.

Article 10   National action programmes

1. The purpose of national action programmes is to identify the factors contributing to desertification and practical measures necessary to combat desertification and mitigate the effects of drought.

2. National action programmes shall specify the respective roles of government, local communities and land users and the resources available and needed. They shall, inter alia:

(a) incorporate long-term strategies to combat desertification and mitigate the effects of drought, emphasize implementation and be integrated with national policies for sustainable development;

(b) allow for modifications to be made in response to changing circumstances and be sufficiently flexible at the local level to cope with different socio-economic, biological and geo-physical conditions;

(c) give particular attention to the implementation of preventive measures for lands that are not yet degraded or which are only slightly degraded;

(d) enhance national climatological, meteorological and hydrological capabilities and the means to provide for drought early warning;

(e) promote policies and strengthen institutional frameworks which develop cooperation and coordination, in a spirit of partnership, between the donor community, governments at all levels, local populations and community groups, and facilitate access by local populations to appropriate information and technology;

(f) provide for effective participation at the local, national and regional levels of non-governmental organizations and local populations, both women and men, particularly resource users, including farmers and pastoralists and their representative organizations, in policy planning, decision-making, and implementation and review of national action programmes; and

(g) require regular review of, and progress reports on, their implementation.

3. National action programmes may include, inter alia, some or all of the following measures to prepare for and mitigate the effects of drought:

(a) establishment and/or strengthening, as appropriate, of early warning systems, including local and national facilities and joint systems at the subregional and regional levels, and mechanisms for assisting environmentally displaced persons;

(b) strengthening of drought preparedness and management, including drought contingency plans at the local, national, subregional and regional levels, which take into consideration seasonal to interannual climate predictions;

(c) establishment and/or strengthening, as appropriate, of food security systems, including storage and marketing facilities, particularly in rural areas;

(d) establishment of alternative livelihood projects that could provide incomes in drought prone areas; and

(e) development of sustainable irrigation programmes for both crops and livestock.

4. Taking into account the circumstances and requirements specific to each affected country Party, national action programmes include, as appropriate, inter alia, measures in some or all of the following priority fields as they relate to combating desertification and mitigating the effects of drought in affected areas and to their populations; promotion of alternative livelihoods and improvement of national economic environments with a view to strengthening programmes aimed at the eradication of poverty and at ensuring food security; demographic dynamics; sustainable management of natural resources; sustainable agricultural practices; development and efficient use of various energy sources; institutional and legal frameworks; strengthening of capabilities for assessment and systematic observation, including hydrological and meteorological services, and capacity building, education and public awareness.

Article 11 Subregional and regional action programmes

Affected country Parties shall consult and cooperate to prepare, as appropriate, in accordance with relevant regional implementation annexes, subregional and/or regional action programmes to harmonize, complement and increase the efficiency of national programmes. The provisions of article 10 shall apply mutatis mutandis to subregional and regional programmes. Such cooperation may include agreed joint programmes for the sustainable management of transboundary natural resources, scientific and technical cooperation, and strengthening of relevant institutions.

Article 12 International cooperation

Affected country Parties, in collaboration with other Parties and the international community, should cooperate to ensure the promotion of an enabling international environment in the implementation of the Convention. Such cooperation should also cover fields of technology transfer as well as scientific research and development, information collection and dissemination and financial resources.

Article 13 Support for the elaboration and implementation of action programmes

1. Measures to support action programmes pursuant to article 9 include, <u>inter alia</u>:

(a) financial cooperation to provide predictability for action programmes, allowing for necessary long-term planning;

(b) elaboration and use of cooperation mechanisms which better enable support at the local level, including action through non-governmental organizations, in order to promote the replicability of successful pilot programme activities where relevant;

(c) increased flexibility in project design, funding and implementation in keeping with the experimental, iterative approach indicated for participatory action at the local community level; and

(d) as appropriate, administrative and budgetary procedures that increase the efficiency of cooperation and of support programmes.

2. In providing such support to affected developing country Parties, priority shall be given to African country Parties and to least developed country Parties.

Article 14 Coordination in the elaboration and implementation of action programmes

1. The Parties shall work closely together, directly and through relevant intergovernmental organizations, in the elaboration and implementation of action programmes.

2. The Parties shall develop operational mechanisms, particularly at the national and field levels, to ensure the fullest possible coordination among developed country Parties, developing country Parties and relevant intergovernmental and non-governmental organizations, in order to avoid duplication, harmonize interventions and approaches, and maximize the impact of assistance. In affected developing country Parties, priority will be given to coordinating activities related to international cooperation in order to maximize the efficient use of resources, to ensure responsive assistance, and to facilitate the implementation of national action programmes and priorities under this Convention.

Article 15 Regional implementation annexes

Elements for incorporation in action programmes shall be selected and adapted to the socio-economic, geographical and climatic factors applicable to affected country Parties or regions, as well as to their level of development. Guidelines for the preparation of action programmes and their exact focus and content for particular subregions and regions are set out in the regional implementation annexes.

Section 2: Scientific and technical cooperation

Article 16 Information collection, analysis and exchange

The Parties agree, according to their respective capabilities, to integrate and coordinate the collection, analysis and exchange of relevant short term and long-term data and information to ensure systematic observation of land degradation in affected areas and to understand better and assess the processes and effects of drought and desertification. This would help accomplish, <u>inter alia</u>, early warning and advance planning for periods of adverse climatic variation in a form suited for practical application by users at all levels, including especially local populations. To this end, they shall, as appropriate:

(a) facilitate and strengthen the functioning of the global network of institutions and facilities for the collection, analysis and exchange of information, as well as for systematic observation at all levels, which shall, inter alia:

(i) aim to use compatible standards and systems;

(ii) encompass relevant data and stations, including in remote areas;

(iii) use and disseminate modern technology for data collection, transmission and assessment on land degradation; and

(iv) link national, subregional and regional data and information centres more closely with global information sources;

(b) ensure that the collection, analysis and exchange of information address the needs of local communities and those of decision makers, with a view to resolving specific problems, and that local communities are involved in these activities;

(c) support and further develop bilateral and multilateral programmes and projects aimed at defining, conducting, assessing and financing the collection, analysis and exchange of data and information, including, inter alia, integrated sets of physical, biological, social and economic indicators;

(d) make full use of the expertise of competent intergovernmental and non-governmental organizations, particularly to disseminate relevant information and experiences among target groups in different regions;

(e) give full weight to the collection, analysis and exchange of socio-economic data, and their integration with physical and biological data;

(f) exchange and make fully, openly and promptly available information from all publicly available sources relevant to combating desertification and mitigating the effects of drought; and

(g) subject to their respective national legislation and/or policies, exchange information on local and traditional knowledge, ensuring adequate protection for it and providing appropriate return from the benefits derived from it, on an equitable basis and on mutually agreed terms, to the local populations concerned.

Article 17 Research and development

1. The Parties undertake, according to their respective capabilities, to promote technical and scientific cooperation in the fields of combating desertification and mitigating the effects of drought through appropriate national, subregional, regional and international institutions. To this end, they shall support research activities that:

(a) contribute to increased knowledge of the processes leading to desertification and drought and the impact of, and distinction between, causal factors, both natural and human, with a view to combating desertification and mitigating the effects of drought, and achieving improved productivity as well as sustainable use and management of resources;

(b) respond to well-defined objectives, address the specific needs of local populations and lead to the identification and implementation of solutions that improve the living standards of people in affected areas;

(c) protect, integrate, enhance and validate traditional and local knowledge, know-how and practices, ensuring, subject to their respective national legislation and/or policies, that the owners of that knowledge will directly benefit on an equitable basis and on mutually agreed terms from any commercial utilization of it or from any technological development derived from that knowledge;

(d) develop and strengthen national, subregional and regional research capabilities in affected developing country Parties, particularly in Africa, including the development of local skills and the strengthening of appropriate capacities, especially in countries with a weak research base, giving particular attention to multidisciplinary and participative socio-economic research;

(e) take into account, where relevant, the relationship between poverty, migration caused by environmental factors, and desertification;

(f) promote the conduct of joint research programmes between national, subregional, regional and international research organizations, in both the public and private sectors, for the development of improved, affordable and accessible technologies for sustainable development through effective participation of local populations and communities; and

(g) enhance the availability of water resources in affected areas, by means of, inter alia, cloud-seeding.

2. Research priorities for particular regions and subregions, reflecting different local conditions, should be included in action programmes. The Conference of the Parties shall review research priorities periodically on the advice of the Committee on Science and Technology.

Article 18 Transfer, acquisition, adaptation and development of technology

1. The Parties undertake, as mutually agreed and in accordance with their respective national legislation and/or policies, to promote, finance and/or facilitate the financing of the transfer, acquisition, adaptation and development of environmentally sound, economically viable and socially acceptable technologies relevant to combating desertification and/or mitigating the effects of drought, with a view to contributing to the achievement of sustainable development in affected areas. Such cooperation shall be conducted bilaterally or multilaterally, as appropriate, making full use of the expertise of intergovernmental and non-governmental organizations. The Parties shall, in particular:

(a) fully utilize relevant existing national, subregional, regional and international information systems and clearing-houses for the dissemination of information on available technologies, their sources, their environmental risks and the broad terms under which they may be acquired;

(b) facilitate access, in particular by affected developing country Parties, on favourable terms, including on concessional and preferential terms, as mutually agreed, taking into account the need to protect intellectual property rights, to technologies most suitable to practical application for specific needs of local populations, paying special attention to the social, cultural, economic and environmental impact of such technology;

(c) facilitate technology cooperation among affected country Parties through financial assistance or other appropriate means;

(d) extend technology cooperation with affected developing country Parties, including, where relevant, joint ventures, especially to sectors which foster alternative livelihoods; and

(e) take appropriate measures to create domestic market conditions and incentives, fiscal or otherwise, conducive to the development, transfer, acquisition and adaptation of suitable technology, knowledge, know-how and practices, including measures to ensure adequate and effective protection of intellectual property rights.

2. The Parties shall, according to their respective capabilities, and subject to their respective national legislation and/or policies, protect, promote and use in particular relevant traditional and local technology, knowledge, knowhow and practices and, to that end, they undertake to:

(a) make inventories of such technology, knowledge, know-how and practices and their potential uses with the participation of local populations, and disseminate such information, where appropriate, in cooperation with relevant intergovernmental and non-governmental organizations;

(b) ensure that such technology, knowledge, know-how and practices are adequately protected and that local populations benefit directly, on an equitable basis and as mutually agreed, from any commercial utilization of them or from any technological development derived therefrom;

(c) encourage and actively support the improvement and dissemination of such technology, knowledge, know-how and practices or of the development of new technology based on them; and

(d) facilitate, as appropriate, the adaptation of such technology, knowledge, know-how and practices to wide use and integrate them with modern technology, as appropriate.

Section 3: Supporting measures

Article 19 Capacity-building, education and public awareness

1. The Parties recognize the significance of capacity-building — that is to say, institution-building, training and development of relevant local and national capacities — in efforts to combat desertification and mitigate the effects of drought. They shall promote, as appropriate, capacity-building:

(a) through the full participation at all levels of local people, particularly at the local level, especially women and youth, with the cooperation of non-governmental and local organizations;

(b) by strengthening training and research capacity at the national level in the field of desertification and drought;

(c) by establishing and/or strengthening support and extension services to disseminate relevant technology methods and techniques more effectively, and by training field agents and members of rural organizations in participatory approaches for the conservation and sustainable use of natural resources;

(d) by fostering the use and dissemination of the knowledge, know-how and practices of local people in technical cooperation programmes, wherever possible;

(e) by adapting, where necessary, relevant environmentally sound technology and traditional methods of agriculture and pastoralism to modern socio-economic conditions;

(f) by providing appropriate training and technology in the use of alternative energy sources, particularly renewable energy resources, aimed particularly at reducing dependence on wood for fuel;

(g) through cooperation, as mutually agreed, to strengthen the capacity of affected developing country Parties to develop and implement programmes in the field of collection, analysis and exchange of information pursuant to article 16;

(h) through innovative ways of promoting alternative livelihoods, including training in new skills;

(i) by training of decision makers, managers, and personnel who are responsible for the collection and analysis of data for the dissemination and use of early warning information on drought conditions and for food production;

(j) through more effective operation of existing national institutions and legal frameworks and, where necessary, creation of new ones, along with strengthening of strategic planning and management; and

(k) by means of exchange visitor programmes to enhance capacity-building in affected country Parties through a long-term, interactive process of learning and study.

2. Affected developing country Parties shall conduct, in cooperation with other Parties and competent intergovernmental and non-governmental organizations, as appropriate, an interdisciplinary review of available capacity and facilities at the local and national levels, and the potential for strengthening them.

3. The Parties shall cooperate with each other and through competent intergovernmental organizations, as well as with non-governmental organizations, in undertaking and supporting public awareness and educational

programmes in both affected and, where relevant, unaffected country Parties to promote understanding of the causes and effects of desertification and drought and of the importance of meeting the objective of this Convention. To that end, they shall:

(a) organize awareness campaigns for the general public;

(b) promote, on a permanent basis, access by the public to relevant information, and wide public participation in education and awareness activities;

(c) encourage the establishment of associations that contribute to public awareness;

(d) develop and exchange educational and public awareness material, where possible in local languages, exchange and second experts to train personnel of affected developing country Parties in carrying out relevant education and awareness programmes, and fully utilize relevant educational material available in competent international bodies;

(e) assess educational needs in affected areas, elaborate appropriate school curricula and expand, as needed, educational and adult literacy programmes and opportunities for all, in particular for girls and women, on the identification, conservation and sustainable use and management of the natural resources of affected areas; and

(f) develop interdisciplinary participatory programmes integrating desertification and drought awareness into educational systems and in non-formal, adult, distance and practical educational programmes.

4. The Conference of the Parties shall establish and/or strengthen networks of regional education and training centres to combat desertification and mitigate the effects of drought. These networks shall be coordinated by an institution created or designated for that purpose, in order to train scientific, technical and management personnel and to strengthen existing institutions responsible for education and training in affected country Parties, where appropriate, with a view to harmonizing programmes and to organizing exchanges of experience among them. These networks shall cooperate closely with relevant intergovernmental and non-governmental organizations to avoid duplication of effort.

Article 20 Financial resources

1. Given the central importance of financing to the achievement of the objective of the Convention, the Parties, taking into account their capabilities, shall make every effort to ensure that adequate financial resources are available for programmes to combat desertification and mitigate the effects of drought.

2. In this connection, developed country Parties, while giving priority to affected African country Parties without neglecting affected developing country Parties in other regions, in accordance with article 7, undertake to:

(a) mobilize substantial financial resources, including grants and concessional loans, in order to support the implementation of programmes to combat desertification and mitigate the effects of drought;

(b) promote the mobilization of adequate, timely and predictable financial resources, including new and additional funding from the Global Environment Facility of the agreed incremental costs of those activities concerning desertification that relate to its four focal areas, in conformity with the relevant provisions of the Instrument establishing the Global Environment Facility;

(c) facilitate through international cooperation the transfer of technology, knowledge and know-how; and

(d) explore, in cooperation with affected developing country Parties, innovative methods and incentives for mobilizing and channeling resources, including those of foundations, non-governmental organizations and other private sector entities, particularly debt swaps and other innovative means which increase financing by reducing the external debt burden of affected developing country Parties, particularly those in Africa.

3. Affected developing country Parties, taking into account their capabilities, undertake to mobilize adequate

financial resources for the implementation of their national action programmes.

4. In mobilizing financial resources, the Parties shall seek full use and continued qualitative improvement of all national, bilateral and multilateral funding sources and mechanisms, using consortia, joint programmes and parallel financing, and shall seek to involve private sector funding sources and mechanisms, including those of non-governmental organizations. To this end, the Parties shall fully utilize the operational mechanisms developed pursuant to article 14.

5. In order to mobilize the financial resources necessary for affected developing country Parties to combat desertification and mitigate the effects of drought, the Parties shall:

(a) rationalize and strengthen the management of resources already allocated for combating desertification and mitigating the effects of drought by using them more effectively and efficiently, assessing their successes and shortcomings, removing hindrances to their effective use and, where necessary, reorienting programmes in light of the integrated long-term approach adopted pursuant to this Convention;

(b) give due priority and attention within the governing bodies of multilateral financial institutions, facilities and funds, including regional development banks and funds, to supporting affected developing country Parties, particularly those in Africa, in activities which advance implementation of the Convention, notably action programmes they undertake in the framework of regional implementation annexes; and

(c) examine ways in which regional and subregional cooperation can be strengthened to support efforts undertaken at the national level.

6. Other Parties are encouraged to provide, on a voluntary basis, knowledge, know-how and techniques related to desertification and/or financial resources to affected developing country Parties.

7. The full implementation by affected developing country Parties, particularly those in Africa, of their obligations under the Convention will be greatly assisted by the fulfilment by developed country Parties of their obligations under the Convention, including in particular those regarding financial resources and transfer of technology. In fulfilling their obligations, developed country Parties should take fully into account that economic and social development and poverty eradication are the first priorities of affected developing country Parties, particularly those in Africa.

Article 21 Financial mechanisms

1. The Conference of the Parties shall promote the availability of financial mechanisms and shall encourage such mechanisms to seek to maximize the availability of funding for affected developing country Parties, particularly those in Africa, to implement the Convention. To this end, the Conference of the Parties shall consider for adoption inter alia approaches and policies that:

(a) facilitate the provision of necessary funding at the national, subregional, regional and global levels for activities pursuant to relevant provisions of the Convention;

(b) promote multiple-source funding approaches, mechanisms and arrangements and their assessment, consistent with article 20;

(c) provide on a regular basis, to interested Parties and relevant intergovernmental and non-governmental organizations, information on available sources of funds and on funding patterns in order to facilitate coordination among them;

(d) facilitate the establishment, as appropriate, of mechanisms, such as national desertification funds, including those involving the participation of non-governmental organizations, to channel financial resources rapidly and efficiently to the local level in affected developing country Parties; and

(e) strengthen existing funds and financial mechanisms at the subregional and regional levels, particularly in Africa, to support more effectively the implementation of the Convention.

2. The Conference of the Parties shall also encourage the provision, through various mechanisms within the United Nations system and through multilateral financial institutions, of support at the national, subregional and regional levels to activities that enable developing country Parties to meet their obligations under the Convention.

3. Affected developing country Parties shall utilize, and where necessary, establish and/or strengthen, national coordinating mechanisms, integrated in national development programmes, that would ensure the efficient use of all available financial resources. They shall also utilize participatory processes involving non-governmental organizations, local groups and the private sector, in raising funds, in elaborating as well as implementing programmes and in assuring access to funding by groups at the local level. These actions can be enhanced by improved coordination and flexible programming on the part of those providing assistance.

4. In order to increase the effectiveness and efficiency of existing financial mechanisms, a Global Mechanism to promote actions leading to the mobilization and channeling of substantial financial resources, including for the transfer of technology, on a grant basis, and/or on concessional or other terms, to affected developing country Parties, is hereby established. This Global Mechanism shall function under the authority and guidance of the Conference of the Parties and be accountable to it.

5. The Conference of the Parties shall identify, at its first ordinary session, an organization to house the Global Mechanism. The Conference of the Parties and the organization it has identified shall agree upon modalities for this Global Mechanism to ensure <u>inter alia</u> that such Mechanism:

(a) identifies and draws up an inventory of relevant bilateral and multilateral cooperation programmes that are available to implement the Convention;

(b) provides advice, on request, to Parties on innovative methods of financing and sources of financial assistance and on improving the coordination of cooperation activities at the national level;

(c) provides interested Parties and relevant intergovernmental and non-governmental organizations with information on available sources of funds and on funding patterns in order to facilitate coordination among them; and

(d) reports to the conference of the Parties, beginning at its second ordinary session, on its activities.

6. The Conference of the Parties shall, at its first session, make appropriate arrangements with the organization it has identified to house the Global Mechanism for the administrative operations of such Mechanism, drawing to the extent possible on existing budgetary and human resources.

7. The Conference of the Parties shall, at its third ordinary session, review the policies, operational modalities and activities of the Global Mechanism accountable to it pursuant to paragraph 4, taking into account the provisions of article 7. On the basis of this review, it shall consider and take appropriate action.

PART IV INSTITUTIONS

Article 22 Conference of the Parties

1. A Conference of the Parties is hereby established.

2. The Conference of the Parties is the supreme body of the Convention. It shall make, within its mandate, the decisions necessary to promote its effective implementation. In particular, it shall:

(a) regularly review the implementation of the Convention and the functioning of its institutional arrangements in the light of the experience gained at the national, subregional, regional and international levels and on the basis of the evolution of scientific and technological knowledge;

(b) promote and facilitate the exchange of information on measures adopted by the Parties, and determine the form and timetable for transmitting the information to be submitted pursuant to article 26, review the reports and make recommendations on them;

(c) establish such subsidiary bodies as are deemed necessary for the implementation of the Convention;

(d) review reports submitted by its subsidiary bodies and provide guidance to them;

(e) agree upon and adopt, by consensus, rules of procedure and financial rules for itself and any subsidiary bodies;

(f) adopt amendments to the Convention pursuant to articles 30 and 31;

(g) approve a programme and budget for its activities, including those of its subsidiary bodies, and undertake necessary arrangements for their financing;

(h) as appropriate, seek the cooperation of, and utilize the services of and information provided by, competent bodies or agencies, whether national or international, intergovernmental or non-governmental;

(i) promote and strengthen the relationship with other relevant conventions while avoiding duplication of effort; and

(j) exercise such other functions as may be necessary for the achievement of the objective of the Convention.

3. The Conference of the Parties shall, at its first session, adopt its own rules of procedure, by consensus, which shall include decision-making procedures for matters not already covered by decision-making procedures stipulated in the Convention. Such procedures may include specified majorities required for the adoption of particular decisions.

4. The first session of the conference of the Parties shall be convened by the interim secretariat referred to in article 35 and shall take place not later than one year after the date of entry into force of the Convention. Unless otherwise decided by the Conference of the Parties, the second, third and fourth ordinary sessions shall be held yearly, and thereafter, ordinary sessions shall be held every two years.

5. Extraordinary sessions of the Conference of the Parties shall be held at such other times as may be decided either by the Conference of the Parties in ordinary session or at the written request of any Party, provided that, within three months of the request being communicated to the Parties by the Permanent Secretariat, it is supported by at least one third of the Parties.

6. At each ordinary session, the Conference of the Parties shall elect a Bureau. The structure and functions of the Bureau shall be determined in the rules of procedure. In appointing the Bureau, due regard shall be paid to the need to ensure equitable geographical distribution and adequate representation of affected country Parties, particularly those in Africa.

7. The United Nations, its specialized agencies and any State member thereof or observers thereto not Party to the Convention, may be represented at sessions of the Conference of the Parties as observers. Any body or agency, whether national or international, governmental or non-governmental, which is qualified in matters covered by the Convention, and which has informed the Permanent Secretariat of its wish to be represented at a session of the Conference of the Parties as an observer, may be so admitted unless at least one third of the Parties present object. The admission and participation of observers shall be subject to the rules of procedure adopted by the Conference of the Parties.

8. The Conference of the Parties may request competent national and international organizations which have relevant expertise to provide it with information relevant to article 16, paragraph (g), article 17, paragraph 1 (c)

and article 18, paragraph 2 (b).

Article 23 Permanent Secretariat

1. A Permanent Secretariat is hereby established.

2. The functions of the Permanent Secretariat shall be:

(a) to make arrangements for sessions of the Conference of the Parties and its subsidiary bodies established under the Convention and to provide them with services as required;

(b) to compile and transmit reports submitted to it;

(c) to facilitate assistance to affected developing country Parties, on request, particularly those in Africa, in the compilation and communication of information required under the Convention;

(d) to coordinate its activities with the secretariats of other relevant international bodies and conventions;

(e) to enter, under the guidance of the Conference of the Parties, into such administrative and contractual arrangements as may be required for the effective discharge of its functions;

(f) to prepare reports on the execution of its functions under this Convention and present them to the Conference of the Parties; and

(g) to perform such other secretariat functions as may be determined by the Conference of the Parties.

3. The Conference of the Parties, at its first session, shall designate a Permanent Secretariat and make arrangements for its functioning.

Article 24 Committee on Science and Technology

1. A Committee on Science and Technology is hereby established as a subsidiary body of the Conference of the Parties to provide it with information and advice on scientific and technological matters relating to combating desertification and mitigating the effects of drought. The Committee shall meet in conjunction with the ordinary sessions of the Conference of the Parties and shall be multidisciplinary and open to the participation of all Parties. It shall be composed of government representatives competent in the relevant fields of expertise. The Conference of the Parties shall decide, at its first session, on the terms of reference of the Committee.

2. The Conference of the Parties shall establish and maintain a roster of independent experts with expertise and experience in the relevant fields. The roster shall be based on nominations received in writing from the Parties, taking into account the need for a multidisciplinary approach and broad geographical representation.

3. The Conference of the Parties may, as necessary, appoint ad hoc panels to provide it, through the Committee, with information and advice on specific issues regarding the state of the art in fields of science and technology relevant to combating desertification and mitigating the effects of drought. These panels shall be composed of experts whose names are taken from the roster, taking into account the need for a multidisciplinary approach and broad geographical representation. These experts shall have scientific backgrounds and field experience and shall be appointed by the Conference of the Parties on the recommendation of the Committee. The Conference of the Parties shall decide on the terms of reference and the modalities of work of these panels.

Article 25 Networking of institutions, agencies and bodies

1. The Committee on Science and Technology shall, under the supervision of the Conference of the Parties, make provision for the undertaking of a survey and evaluation of the relevant existing networks, institutions, agencies and bodies willing to become units of a network. Such a network shall support the implementation of the Convention.

2. On the basis of the results of the survey and evaluation referred to in paragraph 1, the Committee on Science and Technology shall make recommendations to the Conference of the Parties on ways and means to

facilitate and strengthen networking of the units at the local, national and other levels, with a view to ensuring that the thematic needs set out in articles 16 to 19 are addressed.

3. Taking into account these recommendations, the Conference of the Parties shall:

(a) identify those national, subregional, regional and international units that are most appropriate for networking, and recommend operational procedures, and a time-frame, for them; and

(b) identify the units best suited to facilitating and strengthening such networking at all levels.

PART V PROCEDURES

Article 26 Communication of information

1. Each Party shall communicate to the Conference of the Parties for consideration at its ordinary sessions, through the Permanent Secretariat, reports on the measures which it has taken for the implementation of the Convention. The Conference of the Parties shall determine the timetable for submission and the format of such reports.

2. Affected country Parties shall provide a description of the strategies established pursuant to article 5 and of any relevant information on their implementation.

3. Affected country Parties which implement action programmes pursuant to articles 9 to 15 shall provide a detailed description of the programmes and of their implementation.

4. Any group of affected country Parties may make a joint communication on measures taken at the subregional and/or regional levels in the framework of action programmes.

5. Developed country Parties shall report on measures taken to assist in the preparation and implementation of action programmes, including information on the financial resources they have provided, or are providing, under the Convention.

6. Information communicated pursuant to paragraphs 1 to 4 shall be transmitted by the Permanent Secretariat as soon as possible to the Conference of the Parties and to any relevant subsidiary body.

7. The Conference of the Parties shall facilitate the provision to affected developing countries, particularly those in Africa, on request, of technical and financial support in compiling and communicating information in accordance with this article, as well as identifying the technical and financial needs associated with action programmes.

Article 27 Measures to resolve questions on implementation

The Conference of the Parties shall consider and adopt procedures and institutional mechanisms for the resolution of questions that may arise with regard to the implementation of the Convention.

Article 28 Settlement of disputes

1. Parties shall settle any dispute between them concerning the interpretation or application of the Convention through negotiation or other peaceful means of their own choice.

2. When ratifying, accepting, approving, or acceding to the Convention, or at any time thereafter, a Party which is not a regional economic integration organization may declare in a written instrument submitted to the Depositary that, in respect of any dispute concerning the interpretation or application of the Convention, it recognizes one or both of the following means of dispute settlement as compulsory in relation to any Party accepting the same obligation:

(a) arbitration in accordance with procedures adopted by the Conference of the Parties in an annex as soon as practicable;

(b) submission of the dispute to the International Court of Justice.

3. A Party which is a regional economic integration organization may make a declaration with like effect in relation to arbitration in accordance with the procedure referred to in paragraph 2 (a).

4. A declaration made pursuant to paragraph 2 shall remain in force until it expires in accordance with its terms or until three months after written notice of its revocation has been deposited with the Depositary.

5. The expiry of a declaration, a notice of revocation or a new declaration shall not in any way affect proceedings pending before an arbitral tribunal or the International Court of Justice unless the Parties to the dispute otherwise agree.

6. If the Parties to a dispute have not accepted the same or any procedure pursuant to paragraph 2 and if they have not been able to settle their dispute within twelve months following notification by one Party to another that a dispute exists between them, the dispute shall be submitted to conciliation at the request of any Party to the dispute, in accordance with procedures adopted by the Conference of the Parties in an annex as soon as practicable.

Article 29 Status of annexes

1. Annexes form an integral part of the Convention and, unless expressly provided otherwise, a reference to the Convention also constitutes a reference to its annexes.

2. The Parties shall interpret the provisions of the annexes in a manner that is in conformity with their rights and obligations under the articles of this Convention.

Article 30 Amendments to the Convention

1. Any Party may propose amendments to the Convention.

2. Amendments to the Convention shall be adopted at an ordinary session of the Conference of the Parties. The text of any proposed amendment shall be communicated to the Parties by the Permanent Secretariat at least six months before the meeting at which it is proposed for adoption. The Permanent Secretariat shall also communicate proposed amendments to the signatories to the Convention.

3. The Parties shall make every effort to reach agreement on any proposed amendment to the Convention by consensus. If all efforts at consensus have been exhausted and no agreement reached, the amendment shall, as a last resort, be adopted by a two-thirds majority vote of the Parties present and voting at the meeting. The adopted amendment shall be communicated by the Permanent Secretariat to the Depositary, who shall circulate it to all Parties for their ratification, acceptance, approval or accession.

4. Instruments of ratification, acceptance, approval or accession in respect of an amendment shall be deposited with the Depositary. An amendment adopted pursuant to paragraph 3 shall enter into force for those Parties having accepted it on the ninetieth day after the date of receipt by the Depositary of an instrument of ratification, acceptance, approval or accession by at least two thirds of the Parties to the Convention which were Parties at the time of the adoption of the amendment.

5. The amendment shall enter into force for any other Party on the ninetieth day after the date on which that Party deposits with the Depositary its instrument of ratification, acceptance or approval of, or accession to the said amendment.

6. For the purposes of this article and article 31, "Parties present and voting" means Parties present and casting an affirmative or negative vote.

Article 31 Adoption and amendment of annexes

1. Any additional annex to the Convention and any amendment to an annex shall be proposed and adopted in

accordance with the procedure for amendment of the Convention set forth in article 30, provided that, in adopting an additional regional implementation annex or amendment to any regional implementation annex, the majority provided for in that article shall include a two-thirds majority vote of the Parties of the region concerned present and voting. The adoption or amendment of an annex shall be communicated by the Depositary to all Parties.

2. An annex, other than an additional regional implementation annex, or an amendment to an annex, other than an amendment to any regional implementation annex, that has been adopted in accordance with paragraph 1, shall enter into force for all Parties to the Convention six months after the date of communication by the Depositary to such Parties of the adoption of such annex or amendment, except for those Parties that have notified the Depositary in writing within that period of their non-acceptance of such annex or amendment. Such annex or amendment shall enter into force for Parties which withdraw their notification of non-acceptance on the ninetieth day after the date on which withdrawal of such notification has been received by the Depositary.

3. An additional regional implementation annex or amendment to any regional implementation annex that has been adopted in accordance with paragraph 1, shall enter into force for all Parties to the Convention six months after the date of the communication by the Depositary to such Parties of the adoption of such annex or amendment, except with respect to:

(a) any Party that has notified the Depositary in writing, within such six month period, of its non-acceptance of that additional regional implementation annex or of the amendment to the regional implementation annex, in which case such annex or amendment shall enter into force for Parties which withdraw their notification of non-acceptance on the ninetieth day after the date on which withdrawal of such notification has been received by the Depositary; and

(b) any Party that has made a declaration with respect to additional regional implementation annexes or amendments to regional implementation annexes in accordance with article 34, paragraph 4, in which case any such annex or amendment shall enter into force for such a Party on the ninetieth day after the date of deposit with the Depositary of its instrument of ratification, acceptance, approval or accession with respect to such annex or amendment.

4. If the adoption of an annex or an amendment to an annex involves an amendment to the Convention, that annex or amendment to an annex shall not enter into force until such time as the amendment to the Convention enters into force.

Article 32　Right to vote

1. Except as provided for in paragraph 2, each Party to the Convention shall have one vote.

2. Regional economic integration organizations, in matters within their competence, shall exercise their right to vote with a number of votes equal to the number of their member States that are Parties to the Convention. Such an organization shall not exercise its right to vote if any of its member States exercises its right, and vice versa.

PART Ⅵ　FINAL PROVISIONS

Article 33　Signature

This Convention shall be opened for signature at Paris, on 14-15 October 1994, by States Members of the United Nations or any of its specialized agencies or that are Parties to the Statute of the International Court of Justice and by regional economic integration organizations. It shall remain open for signature, thereafter, at the United Nations Headquarters in New York until 13 October 1995.

Article 34　Ratification, acceptance, approval and accession

1. The Convention shall be subject to ratification, acceptance, approval or accession by States and by regional economic integration organizations. It shall be open for accession from the day after the date on which the Convention is closed for signature. Instruments of ratification, acceptance, approval or accession shall be deposited with the Depositary.

2. Any regional economic integration organization which becomes a Party to the Convention without any of its member States being a Party to the Convention shall be bound by all the obligations under the Convention. Where one or more member States of such an organization are also Party to the Convention, the organization and its member States shall decide on their respective responsibilities for the performance of their obligations under the Convention. In such cases, the organization and the member States shall not be entitled to exercise rights under the Convention concurrently.

3. In their instruments of ratification, acceptance, approval or accession, regional economic integration organizations shall declare the extent of their competence with respect to the matters governed by the Convention. They shall also promptly inform the Depositary, who shall in turn inform the Parties, of any substantial modification in the extent of their competence.

4. In its instrument of ratification, acceptance, approval or accession, any Party may declare that, with respect to it, any additional regional implementation annex or any amendment to any regional implementation annex shall enter into force only upon the deposit of its instrument of ratification, acceptance, approval or accession with respect thereto.

Article 35　Interim arrangements

The secretariat functions referred to in article 23 will be carried out on an interim basis by the secretariat established by the General Assembly of the United Nations in its resolution 47/188 of 22 December 1992, until the completion of the first session of the Conference of the Parties.

Article 36　Entry into force

1. The Convention shall enter into force on the ninetieth day after the date of deposit of the fiftieth instrument of ratification, acceptance, approval or accession.

2. For each State or regional economic integration organization ratifying, accepting, approving or acceding to the Convention after the deposit of the fiftieth instrument of ratification, acceptance, approval or accession, the Convention shall enter into force on the ninetieth day after the date of deposit by such State or regional economic integration organization of its instrument of ratification, acceptance, approval or accession.

3. For the purposes of paragraphs 1 and 2, any instrument deposited by a regional economic integration organization shall not be counted as additional to those deposited by States members of the organization.

Article 37　Reservations

No reservations may be made to this Convention.

Article 38　Withdrawal

1. At any time after three years from the date on which the Convention has entered into force for a Party, that Party may withdraw from the Convention by giving written notification to the Depositary.

2. Any such withdrawal shall take effect upon expiry of one year from the date of receipt by the Depositary of the notification of withdrawal, or on such later date as may be specified in the notification of withdrawal.

Article 39　Depositary

The Secretary-General of the United Nations shall be the Depositary of the Convention.

Article 40　Authentic texts

The original of the present Convention, of which the Arabic, Chinese, English, French, Russian and Spanish texts are equally authentic, shall be deposited with the Secretary-General of the United Nations.

IN WITNESS WHEREOF the undersigned, being duly authorized to that effect, have signed the present Convention.

DONE AT Paris, this 17th day of June one thousand nine hundred and ninety-four.

世界生物圈保护区网络章程框架[1]

(联合国教科文组织第二十八届大会1995年11月通过)

序 言

在联合国教科文组织人与生物圈(MAB)计划下发起的,申报MAB计划国际协调理事会批准建立的生物圈保护区,旨在展示和促进一种人与生物圈之间的平衡关系。这些生物圈保护区组成一个由各国自愿参加的世界网络,但每个生物圈保护区仍仅属于其所在国家的主权范围,因此只受该国国家立法的制约。

现制定的《世界生物圈保护区网络章程框架》以下简称"章程框架",目的在于增强各个生物圈保护区的作用,加强地区和国际一级的共同认识、交流与合作。

本"章程框架"旨在促进人们广泛认可生物圈保护区,并鼓励和宣传这项工作中的突出典型。应将规定的除名程序视为这一基本积极方针的一个例外,只有在完全尊重有关国家的文化和社会经济状况的情况下经过认真审查,并与有关国家政府磋商之后方可予以采用。

本"章程框架"制定了认定、支持和宣传生物圈保护区的程序,同时考虑到不同国家和地方的实际情况不尽相同,鼓励各国根据其国家具体情况制定和实施国家生物圈保护区标准。

第1条 定 义

生物圈保护区是根据本"章程框架",纳入教科文组织人与生物圈(MAB)计划并在国际上得到公认的陆地和沿海/海洋生态系统或兼而有之的地区。

第2条 世界生物圈保护区网络

1. 生物圈保护区组成一个世界范围的网络,称为"世界生物圈保护区网络"(以下简称网络)。

2. 网络是用以保护生物多样性和持续利用其资源的一种手段,以此为实施《生物多样性公约》和其他有关公约的目标作出贡献。

3. 各个生物圈保护区依然属于其所在国家的主权管辖范围,各国在本"章程框架"下根据其国家法律采取必要的措施。

第3条 功 能

生物圈保护区具有以下三种功能,应努力成为探索和示范地区范围有关保护和持续发展之方法的最佳场所:

• 保护功能——致力于自然景观、生态系统、物种和遗传变异的保护;

• 发展功能——促进具有社会文化和生态持续性的经济与人类发展;

• 后勤支持功能——支持与地方、地区、国家和全球性保护和持续发展问题有关的示范项目、环境教育与培训、研究和监测。

---

[1] 引自:北京大学世界遗产研究中心编.世界遗产相关文件选编[M].北京:北京大学出版社,2004.

第4条 标准

建立生物圈保护区，必须符合以下一般标准：

1. 该地区应包含具有代表性的主要生物地理区域的各种生态系统，其中包括因人类介入而逐渐产生的变化。
2. 该地区应对保护生物多样性具有重大意义。
3. 该地区应具有探索和示范地区持续发展途径的可能性。
4. 该地区应具有按照第3条规定发挥生物圈保护区三大功能的适宜面积。
5. 该地区应包括实现这三大功能的必要区域，即：

- 根据生物圈保护区的保护目标，专用于长期保护而合法设立的一个或数个核心区，该区域应具有符合保护目标足够大的面积；
- 环绕或紧邻一个或数个核心区，具有明确边界的一个或数个缓冲带，在此地带只能进行符合保护目标的活动；
- 一个边缘过渡区，在该地区推行和发展可持续资源管理的方法。

6. 应组织安排适当的机构，尤其是行政当局、当地社区和民间机构涉入并参与制定和实施生物圈保护区的多项功能。
7. 此外，应做出下述几方面的规定：

- 人类在缓冲带或其他区域开展资源利用活动的管理机制；
- 生物圈保护区所在地区的管理政策或计划；
- 实施此项政策或计划的指定当局或机构；
- 研究、监测、教育和培训计划。

第5条 认定程序

1. 生物圈保护区由人与生物圈计划国际协调理事会（ICC）根据下列程序认定网络成员：

- 各国在根据第4条所确定之标准对可能的地点进行审议之后，通过本国的人与生物圈计划国家委员会，于适当时候将其提名连同有关证明材料一并提交秘书处；
- 秘书处核实提名内容及其证明文件，如提名材料不全，秘书处则请提名国提供所缺材料；
- 提名将由生物圈保护区咨询委员会审议后向国际协调理事会提出建议；
- 人与生物圈计划国际协调理事会对认定纳入网络的提名做出决定；
- 教科文组织总干事将国际协调理事会的决定通知有关国家。

2. 鼓励各国审查和改进任何现有生物圈保护区的合格性，并提出适当的扩展建议，以使其能够在网络范围内充分发挥作用。扩展建议的提交程序与上述认定新的生物圈保护区所用程序相同。
3. 在本"章程框架"通过之前已被认定的生物圈保护区，应视为已是网络的组成部分。因此本"章程框架"之规定亦适用于它们。

第6条 宣传

1. 有关国家和当局应对申报加入生物圈保护区网络之事宜给予适当宣传，包括制作纪念徽章和散发宣传材料。
2. 对网络范围内的生物圈保护区及其目标应给予恰当和不断的宣传。

第7条 参加网络

1. 各国参加或促进全球、地区和亚地区一级网络的合作活动，包括科研与监测活动。
2. 有关当局应在考虑知识产权的情况下，提供研究成果、有关出版物和其他资料，以确保网络的正常运转和充分利用信息交流的益处。
3. 各国和有关当局应与网络其他生物圈保护区进行合作，促进环境教育与培训以及人力资源的开发。

第8条　地区和专题性分网络

各国应鼓励建立并合作管理地区和／或专题性生物圈保护区分网络，促进这些分网络范围内的信息交流、包括开展电子信息交流。

第9条　定期评估

1. 每隔十年，应根据有关当局依照第4条的标准编写并由该国国家委员会提交秘书处的报告，对各生物圈保护区的状况进行定期评估。

2. 该报告将由生物圈保护区咨询委员会审议后向国际协调理事会提出建议。

3. 国际协调理事会将审议有关国家提交的定期报告。

4. 如国际协调理事会认为该生物圈保护区的状况或管理情况是令人满意的，或者自认定或上次评估以来已有所改善，国际协调理事会将对此做出正式确认。

5. 如国际协调理事会认为该生物圈保护区不再符合第4条之标准，将建议有关国家在考虑到其国家文化和社会经济状况的情况下，采取措施以确保其符合第4条之规定，国际协调理事会向秘书处说明其应采取的行动，以协助有关国家执行该措施。

6. 如国际协调理事会认为该生物圈保护区在相当一段时期内仍不符合第4条之标准，则该生物圈保护区将不再作为网络的组成部分。

7. 教科文组织总干事将国际协调理事会的决定通知有关国家。

8. 如某一国家希望将其管辖下的一个生物圈保护区从网络上除名，它应通知秘书处。该通知应作为通报转交国际协调理事会，自此该生物圈保护区亦不再作为网络的组成部分。

第10条　秘书处

1. 教科文组织应行使网络秘书处之职责，负责网络的工作运转与宣传。秘书处应促进各个生物圈保护区之间以及专家间的相互交流与合作。教科文组织还应建立和保持一个在世界范围内均能查询的生物圈保护区信息系统，以便与其他有关活动联系起来。

2. 为加强各个生物圈保护区和网络与分网络的工作运转，教科文组织应通过双边和多边途径寻求财政资助。

3. 秘书处应对组成网络之生物圈保护区的名录及其保护目标和细则定期予以更新、出版和发行。

The Statutory Framework of the World Network of Biosphere Reserves[1]

Adopted by the UNESCO General Conference at its 28th Session, November 1995

Introduction

Within UNESCO's Man and the Biosphere (MAB) programme, biosphere reserves are established to promote and demonstrate a balanced relationship between humans and the biosphere. Biosphere reserves are designated by the International Co-ordinating Council of the MAB Programme, at the request of the State concerned. Biosphere reserves, each of which remains under the sole sovereignty of the State where it is situated and thereby submitted to State legislation only, form a World Network in which participation by the States is voluntary.

The present Statutory Framework of the World Network of Biosphere Reserves has been formulated with the objectives of enhancing the effectiveness of individual biosphere reserves and strengthening common understanding, communication and co-operation at regional and international levels.

This Statutory Framework is intended to contribute to the widespread recognition of biosphere reserves and to encourage and promote good working examples. The delisting procedure foreseen should be considered as an exception to this basically positive approach, and should be applied only after careful examination, paying due respect to the cultural and socio-economic situation of the country, and after consulting the government concerned.

The text provides for the designation, support and promotion of biosphere reserves, while taking account of the diversity of national and local situations. States are encouraged to elaborate and implement national criteria for biosphere reserves which take into account the special conditions of the State concerned.

Article 1 Definition

Biosphere reserves are areas of terrestrial and coastal/marine ecosystems or a combination thereof, which are internationally recognized within the framework of UNESCO's programme on Man and the Biosphere (MAB), in accordance with the present Statutory Framework.

Article 2 World Network of Biosphere Reserves

1. Biosphere reserves form a worldwide network, known as the World Network of Biosphere Reserves, hereafter called the Network.

2. The Network constitutes a tool for the conservation of biological diversity and the sustainable use of its components, thus contributing to the objectives of the Convention on Biological Diversity and other pertinent

---

[1] UNESCO, 1996. *Biosphere Reserves: the Seville Strategy and the Statutory Framework of the World Network*. UNESCO, Paris.

conventions and instruments.

3. Individual biosphere reserves remain under the sovereign jurisdiction of the States where they are situated. Under the present Statutory Framework, States take the measures which they deem necessary according to their national legislation.

Article 3   Functions

In combining the three functions below, biosphere reserves should strive to be sites of excellence to explore and demonstrate approaches to conservation and sustainable development on a regional scale:

(a) conservation-contribute to the conservation of landscapes, ecosystems, species and genetic variation;

(b) development-foster economic and human development which is socio-culturally and ecologically sustainable;

(c) logistic support-support for demonstration projects, environmental education and training, research and monitoring related to local, regional, national and global issues of conservation and sustainable development.

Article 4   Criteria

General criteria for an area to be qualified for designation as a biosphere reserve:

1. It should encompass a mosaic of ecological systems representative of major bio-geographic regions, including a gradation of human interventions.

2. It should be of significance for biological diversity conservation.

3. It should provide an opportunity to explore and demonstrate approaches to sustainable development on a regional scale.

4. It should have an appropriate size to serve the three functions of biosphere reserves, as set out in Article 3.

5. It should include these functions, through appropriate zonation, recognizing:

(a) a legally constituted core area or areas devoted to long-term protection, according to the conservation objectives of the biosphere reserve, and of sufficient size to meet these objectives;

(b) a buffer zone or zones clearly identified and surrounding or contiguous to the core area or areas, where only activities compatible with the conservation objectives can take place;

(c) an outer transition area where sustainable resource management practices are promoted and developed.

6. Organizational arrangements should be provided for the involvement and participation of a suitable range of *inter alia* public authorities, local communities and private interests in the design and carrying out the functions of a biosphere reserve.

7. In addition, provisions should be made for:

(a) mechanisms to manage human use and activities in the buffer zone or zones;

(b) a management policy or plan for the area as a biosphere reserve;

(c) a designated authority or mechanism to implement this policy or plan;

(d) programmes for research, monitoring, education and training.

Article 5   Designation procedure

1. Biosphere reserves are designated for inclusion in the Network by the International Co-ordinating Council (ICC) of the MAB programme in accordance with the following procedure:

(a) States, through National MAB Committees where appropriate, forward nominations with supporting documentation to the secretariat after having reviewed potential sites, taking into account the criteria as defined in Article 4;

(b) the secretariat verifies the content and supporting documentation: in the case of incomplete nomination, the secretariat requests the missing information from the nominating State;

(c) nominations will be considered by the Advisory Committee for Biosphere Reserves for recommendation to ICC;

(d) ICC of the MAB programme takes a decision on nominations for designation.

The Director-General of UNESCO notifies the State concerned of the decision of ICC.

2. States are encouraged to examine and improve the adequacy of any existing biosphere reserve, and to propose extension as appropriate, to enable it to function fully within the Network. Proposals for extension follow the same procedure as described above for new designations.

3. Biosphere reserves which have been designated before the adoption of the present Statutory Framework are considered to be already part of the Network. The provisions of the Statutory Framework therefore apply to them.

Article 6　Publicity

1. The designation of an area as a biosphere reserve should be given appropriate publicity by the State and authorities concerned, including commemorative plaques and dissemination of information material.

2. Biosphere reserves within the Network, as well as the objectives, should be given appropriate and continuing promotion.

Article 7　Participation in the Network

1. States participate in or facilitate co-operative activities of the Network, including scientific research and monitoring, at the global, regional and subregional levels.

2. The appropriate authorities should make available the results of research, associated publications and other data, taking into account intellectual property rights, in order to ensure the proper functioning of the Network and maximize the benefits from information exchanges.

3. States and appropriate authorities should promote environmental education and training, as well as the development of human resources, in co-operation with other biosphere reserves in the Network.

Article 8　Regional and thematic subnetworks

States should encourage the constitution and co-operative operation of regional and/or thematic subnetworks of biosphere reserves, and promote development of information exchanges, including electronic information, within the framework of these subnetworks.

Article 9　Periodic review

1. The status of each biosphere reserve should be subject to a periodic review every ten years, based on a report prepared by the concerned authority, on the basis of the criteria of Article 4, and forwarded to the secretariat by the State concerned.

2. The report will be considered by the Advisory Committee for Biosphere Reserves for recommendation to ICC.

3. ICC will examine the periodic reports from States concerned.

4. If ICC considers that the status or management of the biosphere reserve is satisfactory, or has improved since designation or the last review, this will be formally recognized by ICC.

5. If ICC considers that the biosphere reserve no longer satisfies the criteria contained in Article 4, it may recommend that the State concerned take measures to ensure conformity with the provisions of Article 4, taking into account the cultural and socio-economic context of the State concerned. ICC indicates to the secretariat actions that it should take to assist the State concerned in the implementation of such measures.

6. Should ICC find that the biosphere reserve in question still does not satisfy the criteria contained in Article 4, within a reasonable period, the area will no longer be referred to as a biosphere reserve which is part of the

Network.

7. The Director-General of UNESCO notifies the State concerned of the decision of ICC.

8. Should a State wish to remove a biosphere reserve under its jurisdiction from the Network, it notifies the secretariat. This notification shall be transmitted to ICC for information. The area will then no longer be referred to as a biosphere reserve which is part of the Network.

Article 10　Secretariat

1. UNESCO shall act as the secretariat of the Network and be responsible for its functioning and promotion. The secretariat shall facilitate communication and interaction among individual biosphere reserves and among experts. UNESCO shall also develop and maintain a worldwide accessible information system on biosphere reserves, to be linked to other relevant initiatives.

2. In order to reinforce individual biosphere reserves and the functioning of the Network and subnetworks, UNESCO shall seek financial support from bilateral and multilateral sources.

3. The list of biosphere reserves forming part of the Network, their objectives and descriptive details, shall be updated, published and distributed by the secretariat periodically.

可持续发展问题世界首脑会议执行计划
（节选）[①]

（可持续发展问题世界首脑会议2002年9月4日在南非约翰内斯堡通过）

四．保护和管理经济和社会发展的自然资源基础

24. 人类活动对生态系统品质影响日益增加，生态系为人类福祉和经济活动提供必要的资源和服务。持续和综合管理自然资源的基础对可持续发展至关紧要。在这方面，为了尽早扭转自然资源损害的目前趋势，必须执行将国家以及酌情在区域一级通过的目标包括在内的战略，以保护生态系统和统一管理土地、水和生物质资源，同时加强区域、国家和地方的能力，其中包括在各级采取的行动如下。

* * *

25. 发起一项行动方案，提供财政和技术援助，以实现关于安全饮水的千年发展目标。在这方面，我们同意在至迟2015年使无法得到或负担不起安全饮用水的人口降低一半的《联合国千年宣言》目标，并使无法得到较好卫生设施的人口降低一半。

这将包括在各级采取行动，以便：

（a）在各级调动国际、国内资金，转让技术，促进最佳做法并支持能力建设，用于发展水和环境卫生基础设施和服务，确保这些基础设施和服务满足穷人的需要，并照顾到性别；

（b）便利获得公开信息和在各级的参与，包括妇女的参与，支持与水资源管理和项目实施有关的政策和决策；

（c）促进政府在其他利害攸关者的支持下优先采取行动，国家一级和酌情在区域一级对水进行管理及进行能力建设，并促进和提供新的和额外财政资源，以执行《21世纪议程》第18章；

（d）采用负担得起的环境卫生技术以及工业和国内废水处理技术，以及减少地下水污染的影响，并在国家一级制定监测制度和有效的法律框架，以加紧防治水污染，减少卫生危害和保护生态系统；

（e）采用预防和保护措施，促进可持续的水利用，并处理水短缺问题。

26. 支持发展中国家到2005年年底前制定出水资源综合管理和提高用水效率的规划，需在各级采取行动，以便：

（a）制定和执行关于河流流域、水域和地下水综合管理的国家和区域战略、规划和方案，以及采取措施提高水基础设施的效率，减少流失，增加水的回收；

（b）使用包括管制、监测、自愿措施、市场工具和信息工具、土地使用管理和回收供水服务成本等整套政策工具，但回收供水服务成本的目标不应成为穷人获得安全用水的障碍，并采用综合水域管理办法；

[①] 节选自：可持续发展问题世界首脑会议的报告，南非约翰内斯堡，2002年8月26日至9月4日。UN Document: A/CONF.199/20。

（c）提高水资源使用效率，提倡优先注意满足人的基本需要，并均衡处理养护或恢复特别是脆弱环境中生态品质的需要，同人类家庭、工农业，包括保护饮用水质量的需要，促进各种用途的水的分配；

（d）制定方案，减少与水有关的极端事件的影响；

（e）通过提供技术和财政支助以及能力建设，将非常规水资源技术和能力建设以及养护技术传播给面临缺水或遭受干旱和荒漠化的发展中国家和地区；

（f）通过技术援助以及技术性和财政援助和其他方式，支持高能效、可持续和高成本效益的海水淡化、水回收和从发展中国家岸边的雾回收用过的水；

（g）在政府提供的稳定和透明的国家管理框架内，便利建立优先照顾穷人需要的公私伙伴关系及其他形式的伙伴关系，同时尊重当地情况，吸纳一切相关的利益有关者参加，并监测效益和改进公共机构和私人公司的问责制。

27. 支持发展中国家和转型期经济国家监测和评估水资源的数量和质量的工作，包括通过建立和（或）进一步发展国家监测网和水资源数据库并制定有关的国家指标。

28. 通过合作进行联合观测和研究，改善水资源管理和科学地了解水的周期，并为此目的鼓励并提倡知识分享，进行能力建设，相互商定特别向发展中国家和转型期经济国家转让技术，包括遥感和卫星技术。

29. 促进与水问题有关的各种国际和政府间机构及过程在联合国系统之内和联合国与国际金融机构之间的有效协调，并吸收其他国际机构和民间社会的意见，在知情后作出政府间决策，还应进行更密切的协调，就《国际淡水年（2003年）》之前和之后的活动，详细制定和支助各项建议并开展活动。

* * *

30. 大洋、各种海洋、岛屿和沿岸地区是地球生态系统的完整和必要的组成部分，是全球粮食安全、可持续经济繁荣和许多国家经济体，尤其是发展中国家的幸福的关键。保证海洋的可持续发展需要有关机构包括在全球和区域两级进行有效协调和合作，并在各级采取行动，以便：

（a）请各国批准或加入和执行1982年《联合国海洋法公约》[①]，该《公约》为海洋活动提供了总的法律框架；

（b）促进执行《21世纪议程》第17章，该章规定了实现大洋、沿岸区和各种海洋可持续发展的行动纲领包括下列方案领域：沿海区、包括专属经济区的综合管理和可持续发展；海洋环境保护；可持续地善用和保护公海的海洋生物资源；处理海洋环境管理方面的重大不确定因素和气候变化；加强国际，包括区域的合作和协调；小岛屿的可持续发展；

（c）在联合国系统内建立有效的、透明的和经常性的机构间海洋和沿岸问题协调机制；

（d）鼓励在2010年年底前推行生态系统办法，注意到《在海洋生态系统负责任渔业雷克雅未克宣言》[②]和《生物多样性公约》缔约国会议的第5/6号决定[③]；

（e）促进在国家一级综合、多学科及多部门沿岸及海洋鼓励和协助沿海国制订关于综合沿岸管理的海洋政策及机制；

（f）加强有关区域组织和方案、环境规划署区域环境方案、区域渔业管理组织和其他区域科学卫生和发展组织之间的区域合作和协调；

（g）协助发展中国家在区域和分区域两级协调政策及方案，以养护和可持续管理渔业资源，并执行综合沿岸地区管理计划，包括通过促进可持续沿岸及小规模捕鱼活动，并酌情建立相关基础设施；

---

① 《联合国第三届海洋法会议的正式记录》，第十七卷（联合国出版物，出售品编号E.84.V.3），文件A/CONF.62/122。
② 见粮农组织文件C200/INF/25，附录一。
③ 见UNEP/CBD/COP/5/23，附件三。

（h）注意到联合国大会第 54/33 号决议建立的不限参加者名额的非正式协商进程为便利大会每年审查海洋事务的发展情况而进行的工作，以及大会第五十七届会议上即将根据上述决议的规定对于该进程的效果和作用进行审查。

31. 为实现可持续渔业，应在各级采取以下行动：

（a）维持种群数量或使之恢复到可以生产最佳可持续产出的水平，以期为枯竭的种群紧急实现这些目标，在可能情况下不迟于 2015 年实现；

（b）批准或加入和有效执行有关的联合国渔业协定或安排，并酌情执行有关区域渔业协定和安排，尤其是《执行 1982 年 12 月 10 日联合国海洋法公约有关养护和管理跨界鱼类种群和高度洄游鱼类种群的规定的协定》① 以及 1993 年《促进公海渔船遵守国际养护和管理措施的协定》②；

（c）执行 1995 年《负责任渔业行动守则》③，并考虑到第 5 款、以及联合国粮食及农业组织有关国际行动计划和技术准则所述发展中国家的特殊需要；

（d）紧急制定和实施国家行动计划，并酌情实施区域行动计划，实施粮农组织国际行动计划，特别是在 2005 年年底前实施《管理捕捞能力国际行动计划》④ 和 2004 年年底前实施《预防、阻止和消除非法、未报告和无管制的捕捞活动国际行动计划》⑤。建立有效监测、报告和强制执行以及控制渔船包括由船旗国进行的机制，以进一步实行《预防、阻止和消除非法、未报告和无管制的捕捞活动国际行动计划》；

（e）鼓励有关区域渔业管理组织和安排，在审议分配跨界鱼类种群和高度洄游鱼类种群的渔业资源问题时充分考虑到沿海国的权利、义务和利益以及发展中国家的特别需求，顾及《联合国海洋法公约》的规定以及《执行 1982 年 12 月 10 日联合国海洋法公约有关在公海和专属经济区内养护和管理跨界鱼类种群和高度洄游鱼类种群的规定的协定》；

（f）消除补贴导致非法、未报告和无管制的捕捞和能力过剩，完成世界贸易组织（世贸组织）所致力的澄清和改善渔业补贴纪律的工作，并考虑到这一部门对发展中国家的重要性；

（g）加强捐助者的合作和国际金融机构、双边机构和其他相关利益有关者之间的伙伴关系，使发展中国家，尤其是最不发达国家和小岛屿发展中国家和经济转型期国家发展本国、本区域和分区域的能力，促进渔业基础设施的综合管理和可持续利用；

（h）支助水产养殖，包括小规模水产养殖的可持续发展，考虑到它对粮食安全和经济发展越来越重要。

32. 按照《21 世纪议程》第 17 章，促进养护和管理海洋，办法是在各级采取行动，并充分考虑到有关国际文书，以便：

（a）维持重要、脆弱的海洋和沿海地区，包括国际管辖以外地区的生产力和生物多样性；

（b）通过紧急调动资金、技术援助和尤其是在发展中国家开发人力和建设机构能力等，实施根据《关于养护和可持续利用海洋和沿海生物多样性的雅加达任务规定》⑥ 制定的工作方案；

（c）制定和便利使用多种办法和工具，包括生态系统办法，消除破坏性的捕鱼做法，在 2010 年年底前根据国际法和科学情报（包括代表参加的网络）建立海洋保护区，以及建立保护育苗场和期间的时间/地区包围圈，恰当的沿岸土地使用，分水规划并将海洋和沿岸地区管理纳入关键部门；

（d）制订国家、区域和国际方案，以阻止海洋生物多样性包括珊瑚礁和湿地的消失；

---

① 见《国际渔业文书》（联合国出版物，出售品编号 E.98.V.II），第一节，又见/CONF.164/137。
② 同上。
③ 同上，第三节。
④ 罗马，粮农组织，1999 年。
⑤ 同上，2001 年。
⑥ 见 A/51/312，附件二，决定 2/10。

（e）实施《拉姆萨尔公约》[①]，包括与《生物多样性公约》[②]和《国际珊瑚礁倡议》要求执行的行动方案有关的联合工作方案，加强联合管理计划和沿海区湿地生态系统，包括珊瑚礁、红树林、海草床和感潮淤泥地的国际网络。

33. 提前执行《保护海洋环境免受陆上活动影响全球行动纲领》[③]和《保护海洋环境免受陆上活动影响蒙特利尔宣言》[④]，在2002至2006年期间特别侧重注意城市废水、生境的改变和破坏，及养分，在各级采取行动，以：

（a）促进伙伴关系、科学研究和传播技术知识；调动国内、区域和国际资源；提倡人力和机构能力建设，特别注意发展中国家的需要；

（b）加强发展中国家在下列方面的能力：制订本国和区域方案和机制，将《全球行动纲领》的目标纳入主流，并管理海洋污染的风险和影响；

（c）拟订区域行动纲领并改进海岸和和海洋资源可持续发展战略计划的联系，特别注意环境加速变化和遭受发展压力的领域；

（d）尽一切努力，在2006年下一次全球行动纲领会议举行之前取得实质性的进展，保护海洋环境不受陆上活动的影响。

34. 为加强海洋安全和保护海洋环境不受污染，在各级采取行动，以便：

（a）请批准、加入和执行国际海事组织（海事组织）有关下列方面的各项公约、议定书和其他有关文书：提高海洋安全和保护海洋环境免受船只包括使用有毒防污油漆造成的海洋污染和环境破坏，并促请国际海事组织（海事组织）考虑实施更大力的机制以确保船旗国执行海事组织的文书；

（b）加速制订各种措施，以处理压载水中的外来物种入侵的问题。敦促海事组织订定其将于2003年通过的《船只压载水和沈积物的控制和管理国际公约》草案。

35. 回顾国际原子能机构大会GC（44）/RES/17号决议第8段，并考虑到放射性废物可能对环境和人类健康造成非常严重的影响，鼓励各国政府在考虑到其本国国情，作出努力审查并进一步改进关于安全问题的各种措施和国际议定的条例，同时强调必须设立有效的涉及下列方面的赔偿责任机制：辐射性材料、辐射性废物和用过的核燃料的国际海上运输和其他跨边界移动，其中特别包括依照有关国际文书事先通知和协商的安排。

36. 改进对海洋和沿岸生态系统的科学认识和评估，作为健全决策的根本依据，通过各级的行动，以便：

（a）在全球和区域两级增加科技合作，包括适当转让海洋科学和海洋技术和养护以及管理海洋生物和非生物资源的技术，扩大海洋观测能力，及时预测和评估海洋环境状况；

（b）在2004年在联合国建立一个经常过程，在现有区域评估的基础上，就海洋环境、包括社会经济方面的状况作出全球报告和评估；

（c）建立海洋科学、信息和管理能力，除其他外，对于可能有害沿海和海洋环境及其生物和非生物资源的项目或活动，提倡使用环境影响评估和环境评价和报告技术；

（d）加强联合国教科文组织政府间海洋学委员会、粮农组织和其他有关国际、区域和分区域组织下列的能力：在海洋科学以及海洋及其资源的可持续管理方面建立国家和地方能力。

* * *

37. 在21世纪，为了使世界更加安全，必须采取综合、对付多种危害和广泛包含的方法来处理脆弱性、

---

① 《关于特别是作为水禽栖息地的国际重要湿地拉姆萨尔公约》（《联合国条约汇编》，第996卷，第14583号）。

② 见联合国环境规划署，《生物多样性公约》（环境法和机构方案活动中心），1992年6月。

③ A/51/116，附件二。

④ 见/E/CN.17/2002/PC.2/15。

风险评估和灾害管理的问题，包括预防、减轻、事先准备、应付和复原。必须在各级采取行动，以便：

（a）加强国际减少灾害战略的作用，鼓励国际社会向其信托基金提供必要的财政资源；

（b）支助制定有效的区域、分区域和国家战略并为灾害管理提供机构性科学和技术支助；

（c）改进地面的监测和增加使用卫星数据，传播技术和科学知识，并向易受侵害的国家提供援助，以加强国家的机构能力和促进国际联合观测和研究；

（d）除其他外，促进湿地和集水区的保护和复原，改进土地使用计划，更广泛应用改进的技术和方法来评估气候变化对湿地可能造成的不利影响，斟酌情况协助特别受这方面侵害的国家，以减低易受侵害的国家遭受水灾和干旱的危险；

（e）改进评估气候变化的影响的技术和方法，并鼓励政府间气候变化问题小组继续评估这种不利的影响；

（f）鼓励传播和使用传统的和本地的知识，减轻自然灾害的影响，促进地方当局制订社区灾害管理计划，包括举行训练活动和提高大众的意识；

（g）斟酌情况，依照议定的有关准则支助非政府组织、科技界和其他伙伴目前在自然灾害管理方面作出的自愿贡献；

（h）发展和加强灾害管理的、符合国际减少灾害战略的早期警报系统和信息网络；

（i）发展和加强各级收集和传播科技信息的能力，包括改进预测极端气候、特别是关于厄尔尼诺／拉尼娜现象的早期警报系统，向机构、包括国际厄尔尼诺现象研究中心提供专门应付这些气候的援助；

（j）在对环境有不利影响的重大技术灾害和其他灾害后，提倡在预防、减轻、救济和灾后复原中进行合作，以便提高受灾害国家应对这一局面的能力。

* * *

38. 全球气候变化及其所产生的不利影响是人类共同关心的问题。我们仍然深为关切所有国家，特别是发展中国家，其中包括最不发达国家和小岛屿发展中国家，日益面临气候改变的不良影响，并认识到在这方面，贫穷、土地退化、获取饮水和粮食和人类健康仍然是全球最关注的问题。《联合国气候变化框架公约》[①]是关于气候改变这项全球关注问题的关键文书，我们重申我们决心实现该公约的最终目标：将大气温室气体浓度稳定下来，使人类对气候系统进行的干扰不到达危险的程度，必须根据我们不同的责任和各自的能力，在一定的时限内实现这一目标，以便生态系统能够自然地适应气候变化，确保粮食生产不受到威胁、经济发展能够持续进行。回顾《联合国千年宣言》，各国元首和政府首脑在宣言中决心竭尽全力确保《联合国气候变化框架公约》的《京都议定书》[②]生效，最好在 2002 年联合国环境与发展会议十周年之前生效，而且开始按规定减少温室气体的排放，已批准《京都议定书》的国家大力敦促尚未这样做的国家及时批准该文书。需要在各级采取行动，以便：

（a）履行《联合国气候变化框架公约》下的一切承诺和义务；

（b）合作致力达成《公约》的各项目标；

（c）按照在《公约》，包括《马拉克什协定》[③]下所作的承诺，向发展中国家和经济转型期国家提供技术和财政援助；

（d）为交换科学数据和资料，除了别的以外通过持续支助政府间气候变化问题小组，建立和加强科学和技术能力，尤其是在发展中国家；

（e）开发和转让技术解决办法；

---

① A/AC.237/18（Part II）/Add.1 和 Corr.1，附件。
② FCCC/CP/1997/7/Add.1，决定 1/CP.3，附件。
③ FCCC/CP/2001/13 和 Add.1 至 4。

（f）发展和散播关键发展部门，特别是能源方面的创新技术，和这方面的投资，包括通过私营部门的参与、面向市场的办法、和有利的公共政策和国际合作；

（g）促进系统地观察地球的大气层、陆地和海洋，方法是改善观测站，扩大利用卫星，适当归纳这些观察结果，以产生可传播供各国，尤其是发展中国家使用的高质量数据；

（h）除了别的以外在与相关的国际组织，特别是各专门机构协作下，同《公约》合作，扩大实施国家、区域和国际战略，以监测地球的大气层、陆地和海洋，包括斟酌情况，实施全球综合观察战略；

（i）支持各项评估气候变化后果的倡议，例如北极理事会倡议，包括评估对地方和土著社区的环境、经济和社会影响。

39. 铭记着里奥各项原则，特别包括下列原则：鉴于各国在造成全球环境退化方面的作用不同，而负有共同但有区别的责任，加强在国际、区域和国家各级的合作，减少空气污染，包括越境空气污染、酸沉积作用和臭氧枯竭并在各级采取行动，以便：

（a）加强发展中国家和经济转型期国家测量、减少和评估空气污染影响的能力，包括对健康的影响，并为这些活动提供财政和技术支助；

（b）确保在2003/2005年之前充分补充资金，促进执行《关于消耗臭氧层物质的蒙特利尔议定书》；

（c）进一步支持《保护臭氧层维也纳公约》和《蒙特利尔议定书》所建立的关于保护臭氧层的有效机制，包括其遵守机制；

（d）铭记臭氧枯竭和气候变化的科学和技术方面是相互有关的，在2010年之前，加强向发展中国家提供负担得起、容易得到、成本效益高、安全和无害环境的物质，以取代消耗臭氧层物质，协助这些国家遵守《蒙特利尔议定书》规定的分阶段淘汰计划；

（e）采取措施对付非法贩运消耗臭氧层的物质。

* * *

40. 农业在满足不断增加的全球人口的需求方面发挥至关重要的作用，而且与消除贫穷密切相关，尤其是在发展中国家。必须提高妇女在农村发展、农业、营养和粮食安全等的所有层面和所有方面上的作用。可持续农业和农村发展，对于以环境上可持续的方式在扩大粮食生产和加强粮食安全及食品无害方面采取综合办法是至关重要的。这需要所有各级采取行动：

（a）实现《千年宣言》的目标，至迟在2015年将世界遭受饥馑的人口减少一半，并使他们及其家人达到足以维持安康的生活水平，包括足够的食物，办法包括促进粮食安全和与饥馑作斗争，并结合采取解决贫穷问题的措施，同时符合世界粮食问题首脑会议的结果，且各缔约国应履行《经济、社会、文化权利国际盟约》[①]第11条规定的义务；

（b）根据可持续利用可再生资源和对社会经济和环境潜力的综合评估，制定和执行综合土地管理和用水计划，并加强政府、地方当局和社区监测和管理土地和水资源数量和质量的能力；

（c）扩大了解如何能可持续地使用、保护和管理水资源，提高淡水、沿海及海洋环境的长期可持续性；

（d）促进以可持续的方式加强土地生产力和在农业、林业、湿地、手工渔业和养殖业有效利用水资源的各项方案，尤其是通过基于土著和当地社区的办法；

（e）通过提供适当的技术和财政援助以支持发展中国家保护绿洲不致发生淤塞、土地退化和盐渍度增高等情况；

（f）扩大妇女在同可持续农业和粮食安全有关的所有方面和所有层面上的参与；

（g）整合关于土地使用办法的现有信息系统，办法是加强国家研究和推广服务以及农民组织，以便在有关国际组织的协助下，促进农民之间就诸如无害环境的低成本技术等方面的良好做法进行交流；

[①] 见大会第2200A（XXI）号决议，附件。

（h）酌情颁布各种措施，保护土著资源管理制度，并支持所有相关的利益有关者，不论男女，对农村规划和地方施政的贡献；

（i）通过各项政策，执行各种法律，确保界定明确、可实施的使用土地和水资源的权利，并促进土地保有权的法律保证，同时承认存在不同的国家法律和（或）获得土地和土地保有权制度，并向进行土地保有权制度改革的发展中国家以及经济转型期国家提供技术和财政援助以期提高可持续生计；

（j）扭转公共部门为可持续农业提供的经费不断下降的趋势，提供适当的技术和财政援助，和促进私营部门进行投资和支持发展中国家和经济转型期国家加强农业研究和自然资源管理的能力和向农牧界散播研究成果；

（k）采用面向市场的各种奖励措施，使农业企业和农民能监测和管理水资源的使用和水质，尤其是通过诸如小型灌溉系统、废水回收和再使用等办法；

（l）加强进入现有市场的机会，并开发增值农产品的新市场；

（m）在污染问题严重的发达国家和经济转型期国家，配合适当的技术协助，扩大重新开发褐土地；

（n）加强国际合作打击非法种植麻醉药品作物，考虑到它们产生的消极的社会、经济和环境影响；

（o）促进无害环境的、效果好而且效率高的土壤肥力改善办法和对农业害虫的控制；

（p）加强和改善现有各项提高可持续农产品和粮食安全的倡议间的协调；

（q）请尚未批准《粮农植物遗传资源国际公约》^①的国家批准该公约；

（r）促进传统和土著农业系统的保护，可持续利用和管理，并加强土著的农业生产模式。

* * *

41. 加强执行《联合国关于在发生严重干旱和/或荒漠化的国家特别是在非洲防治荒漠化的公约》，处理荒漠化和土地退化的原因以期保持和恢复土地，和处理因土地退化造成的贫穷现象。这需要在所有各级上采取行动，以便：

（a）调动充足的和可预计的财政资源，转让技术和在各级进行能力建设；

（b）制定国家行动方案，确保在国际社会的支持下，包括通过将项目的权力下放到地方一级，及时和有效地执行公约及其相关的项目；

（c）在根据《联合国气候变化框架公约》、《生物多样性公约》和《防治荒漠化公约》的规定拟定和执行各项计划和战略中，鼓励这几项公约继续探索和提高协同作用，同时，适当考虑到这几项公约各自的任务规定；

（d）采取综合措施，通过相关的政策和方案，防治荒漠化和减轻干旱的影响，例如通过土地、水和森林的管理、农业、农村发展、预警系统、环境、能源、自然资源、保健和教育以及消除贫穷和可持续发展战略等；

（e）提供当地承受得了的获得信息的办法，加强与荒漠化和干旱有关的监测和预警；

（f）呼吁全球环境基金第二届大会就全球环境基金理事会关于指定土地退化（荒漠化和毁林）为全球环境基金重点领域，以此作为全球环境基金支持成功执行《防治荒漠化公约》的一种手段的建议采取行动；并因而考虑使全球环境基金成为该《公约》的一个财政机制，其中考虑到《公约》缔约国会议的特权和决定，同时确认全球环境基金和《公约》全球机制在为拟订和执行各项行动方案提供和调动资源方面的补充作用；

（g）改善草原资源的可持续性，办法是加强管理和执法，并由国际社会向发展中国家提供财政和技术支助。

* * *

42. 山脉生态系统支持特定的生计，并包括重要的流域资源、生物多样性和独特的动植物群。其中许

---

① 《粮农组织大会的报告，第三十三届会议，罗马，2001年11月2日至13日》（C 2001/REP），附录D。

多十分脆弱，易遭受气候变化的不利影响，需要得到特定的保护。需要在各级采取行动，以便：

（a）制订和促进各种方案、政策和办法，综合可持续山脉发展的环境、经济和社会组成部分，并加强国际合作使它对消除贫穷方案产生积极影响，特别是在发展中国家里；

（b）执行各项方案，酌情处理毁林、土地流失、土地退化、生物多样性减少、水流中断以及冰川缩退等问题；

（c）酌情制订和执行各项对性别问题敏感的政策和方案，包括公共和私人投资的政策和方案，协助消除山地社区面临的不公平现象；

（d）执行各项方案，促进多样化和传统的山地经济、可持续生计和小规模生产体系，包括能更好地进入国内和国际市场、通信和运输规划，同时考虑到山脉的特殊敏感性；

（e）促进山地社区全面参与和参加影响到它们的决策，并将土著人的知识、遗产和价值观念纳入所有发展倡议中；

（f）为应用研究和能力建设调动国内和国际支助，为发展中国家和经济转型期国家有效执行山脉生态系统的可持续发展提供财政和技术援助，并通过具体的计划、项目和方案，解决在山地生活的人的贫穷问题，对所有利益有关者提供充分的支持，同时考虑到2002年国际山岳年的精神。

* * *

43. 促进可持续的旅游发展，包括非消费型生态旅游，其中考虑到2002年国际生态旅游年、2002联合国文化遗产年、2002年世界生态旅游首脑会议及其《魁北克宣言》和世界旅游组织通过的《全球旅游业道德守则》的精神，以增加旅游资源对旅游区人民的收益，同时保持旅游区文化与环境的完整性和加强生态敏感区和自然遗产的保护工作。促进可持续的旅游发展和能力建设，以帮助加强农村和当地社区的工作，这包括在各级采取以下行动：

（a）在各级加强国际合作、外国直接投资和与公营和私营部门的伙伴关系；

（b）制订包括教育和培训方案在内的各种方案，鼓励人们参与生态旅游、让土著和当地社区能从生态旅游中获得发展和收益并增强利益相关者在旅游发展和遗产保护中的合作，以改进环境、自然资源和文化遗产的保护工作；

（c）向发展中国家和转型期经济国家提供技术援助，支持可持续旅游业发展、投资和旅游意识的方案，改进国内旅游工作和促进企业家精神的发展；

（d）在世界旅游组织和其他有关组织的支持下，协助旅游区管理旅游景点的游览工作，以获得最大效益，同时确保游览对旅游景点的传统、文化和环境产生最小的消极影响和危害；

（e）促进经济活动的多样化，包括由新兴的当地企业，特别是中小企业通过市场准入、获得商业信息和参与开展经济活动。

* * *

44. 生物多样性在整个可持续发展和消除贫穷中发挥着关键作用，它对地球、人类福祉、人民生计和文化完整性也是必不可少的。不过，由于人类的活动，生物多样性目前正以前所未有的速度消失；只有根据《生物多样性公约》第15条的规定，让当地人民，特别是遗传资源原产国从生物多样性的保护和可持续利用中受益，才能扭转这种趋势。该《公约》是生物多样性的保护和可持续利用以及公正和公平分享遗传资源的使用收益的重要文书。更有效率和一致地执行《公约》的三项目标和在2010年底前大幅度降低目前生物多样性损失的速率，需要向发展中国家提供新的和额外的财务和技术资源，并需要在各级采取行动，以便：

（a）把《公约》的目标纳入全球、区域和国家的部门和跨部门方案和政策，特别是纳入国家经济部门和国际金融机构的方案和政策；

（b）作为与不同生态系统、部门和主题领域相关的一个交叉问题，根据《公约》促进目前可持续利用生物多样性的工作，包括可持续的旅游业；

（c）除其他外，通过编写关于共同责任和关注问题的联合计划和方案，其中适当考虑各自的任务，促进该《公约》和其他多边环境协议之间发挥有效的增效作用；

（d）执行《公约》及其各项规定，包括通过国家、区域和全球的行动纲领，特别是国家生物多样性的战略和行动计划，对其工作方案和决定积极采取后续行动，并加强它们与可持续发展和消除贫穷等有关跨学科战略、方案和政策的结合，包括促进以社区为基础的可持续利用生物多样性的主动行动；

（e）以及《公约》的目前工作所述，促进生态系统方式的广泛实施和进一步发展；

（f）在生态多样性，包括生态系统和世界遗产旧址的保护和可持续利用以及濒于灭绝物种的保护方面，促进具体的国际支助和伙伴关系，特别是通过适当渠道向发展中国家和转型期经济国家提供财政资源和技术；

（g）有效保护和可持续利用生物多样性，促进和支持生物多样性必不可少的热点地区和其他地区的主动行动并促进国家和区域生态网络和走廊的发展；

（h）向发展中国家提供财政和技术支助，包括能力建设，以便加强以土著人和社区为基础的生物多样性保护工作；

（i）加强国家、区域和国际控制侵入性外来物种的工作，这是生物多样性损失的重要原因之一，并鼓励各级编写关于侵入性外来物种的有效工作方案；

（j）承认当地和土著社区拥有传统知识、革新和惯例的权利，但须经国家立法批准，征得这些知识、革新和惯例的拥有者同意并在他们的参与下，制定和实施经双方商定的利用这些知识、革新和惯例的收益分享机制；

（k）鼓励和让所有利益相关者协助实现《公约》的目标，特别是确认青年、妇女和土著及当地社区在可持续地保护和利用生物多样性中的特定作用；

（l）促进土著和当地社区有效参与关于利用其传统知识的决定和决策工作；

（m）鼓励各方向发展中国家和转型期经济国家提供技术和财政支助，帮助它们根据本国优先事项和立法，除其他外酌情编写和实施国家的特有制度和传统制度，以保护和可持续利用生物多样性；

（n）促进《关于取用遗传资源和公平及公正分享其利用资源的收益的波恩准则》的广泛执行并继续这方面的工作，作为一种投入，协助公约缔约国编写和起草关于取用资源和分享收益的立法、行政或政策的措施以及经双方商定的取用资源和分享收益的合同和其他安排；

（o）在《生物多样性公约》的框架内，考虑到波恩准则，经谈判成立一个国际制度，以促进和保障使用遗传资源所产生的利益得到公平及公正的分享；

（p）鼓励各国圆满完成在世界知识产权组织知识产权与遗产资源、传统知识和民俗政府间委员会主持下和关于《公约》第 8 条（j）款和有关规定的不限成员名额特设工作组发起的一些现有的进程；

（q）根据《公约》第 15 条和第 19 条，促进各国采取具体措施，包括交换专家、培训人力资源和发展面向研究的机构能力等加强关于生物技术和生物安全性的科学和技术合作，取用以遗传资源为基础的生物技术成果和收益；

（r）正如《多哈部长级宣言》[①]所述，为了加强增效作用和相互支持，在不事先确定结果的情况下促进各国就该《公约》和国际贸易与知识产权协定的关系进行讨论；

（s）促进全球生物分类学倡议工作方案的执行工作；

（t）请还没有批准《生物多样性公约卡塔赫纳生物技术安全议定书和其他生物多样性协定》[②]的国家尽

---

① 见 A/C.2/56/7，附件。
② http://www.biodiv.org/biosafety/protocol.asp。

快这样做,并请已经批准这些协定的国家促进它们在国家、区域和国际三级的有效实施并从技术上和财政上在这方面支持发展中国家和转型期经济国家。

* * *

45. 森林和树木覆盖将近三分之一的地球表面。对自然林和人造林、木材产品和非木材产品进行可持续森林管理是实现可持续发展所必不可少的,也是消除贫穷、大大减少伐林、遏止丧失森林多样性和减少土地和资源退化、提高粮食安全以及取用安全饮水和负担得起的能源的关键手段,这突出说明自然林木和人造林木的诸多益处,并有助于促进地球和人类的福祉。在国家和全球两级实现可持续森林管理,包括通过有关政府与利益相关者,包括民营部门、土著和当地社区及非政府组织,形成伙伴关系,是可持续发展的一项基本目标,将需要在所有各级采取行动:

(a) 提高对可持续森林管理的政治承诺,以之作为国际政治议程上的一项优先事项,同时通过综合办法充分顾及森林部门和其他部门之间的联系;

(b) 在森林问题合作伙伴关系的协助下,支助联合国森林问题论坛,以之作为在国家、区域和全球促进和协调可持续森林管理执行工作的关键性政府间机制,从而促进森林多样性的养护和可持续利用;

(c) 在国际社会的支助下,立即对国内森林法的强制执行和森林产品、包括森林生物资源的非法国际贸易采取行动,并就这些领域内国家法规的强制执行提供人力和体制两方面的能力建设;

(d) 在国家和国际两级立即采取行动,宣传和促进可以实现可持续砍伐木材的方法,促进提供财政资源及转让并开发无害环境技术,从而纠正不可持续的砍伐木材习惯;

(e) 制订和执行各种倡议,以解决世界上目前深受贫穷和森林砍伐率偏高之苦的地区和国际合作将得到受害政府欢迎的地区的需要;

(f) 建立并加强伙伴关系及国际合作,以促进提供更多资金,转让无害环境技术、贸易、能力建设、森林法的执法和各级施政、以及土地和资源综合管理,以便实施可持续森林管理,包括政府间森林问题小组(森林小组)/森林问题论坛(森林论坛)关于采取行动的提案;

(g) 由各国和森林问题合作伙伴关系加速执行森林小组/森林论坛的行动建议,并加紧努力,向联合国森林问题论坛提出报告,以便为2005年的进度评估作出贡献;

(h) 承认并支助当地及基于社区的森林管理制度,确保它们充分、有效地参与可持续森林管理;

(i) 同论坛、伙伴关系成员及其他与森林有关的进程和公约密切协作,并让所有利益相关者参与,实施《生物多样性公约》关于所有类型森林生物多样性的、面向行动的扩大工作方案。

* * *

46. 采矿、矿物和金属业对许多国家的经济和社会发展十分重要。矿物对现代生活是必需品。为了提高采矿、矿物和金属业对可持续发展的贡献,在所有各级需要采取下列行动:

(a) 支持着手研究采矿、矿物和金属业对环境、经济、健康和社会方面在其整个生命周期中所产生的影响及惠益,包括对工人健康与安全的影响,以及利用伙伴关系,在各有关政府、非政府组织矿业公司和工人和其他利益相关者之间,促进国家和国际上的现有活动,以提高可持续采矿和矿物业的透明度和问责制;

(b) 加强当地和土著社区及妇女等利益相关者的参与,遵照国家法规并考虑到重大的跨界影响,在采矿的整个生命周期,包括为复原而关闭矿场之后,在矿物、金属和采矿发展方面积极发挥作用;

(c) 向发展中国家和经济转型国家提供资金、技术和能力建设支助,用于采矿和矿物加工,包括小型采矿、并在可能与适当时,提高增值加工提供最新科学技术信息,和回收与恢复已经退化的场地,从而促进可持续的采矿做法。

Plan of Implementation of the World Summit on Sustainable Development (excerpts)[①]

Adopted by UN at the World Summit on Sustainable Development, Johannesburg, South Africa, 4 September 2002

IV. Protecting and managing the natural resource base of economic and social development

24. Human activities are having an increasing impact on the integrity of ecosystems that provide essential resources and services for human well-being and economic activities. Managing the natural resources base in a sustainable and integrated manner is essential for sustainable development. In this regard, to reverse the current trend in natural resource degradation as soon as possible, it is necessary to implement strategies which should include targets adopted at the national and, where appropriate, regional levels to protect ecosystems and to achieve integrated management of land, water and living resources, while strengthening regional, national and local capacities. This would include actions at all levels as set out below.

25. Launch a programme of actions, with financial and technical assistance, to achieve the Millennium development goal on safe drinking water. In this respect, we agree to halve, by the year 2015, the proportion of people who are unable to reach or to afford safe drinking water, as outlined in the Millennium Declaration, and the proportion of people without access to basic sanitation, which would include actions at all levels to:

(a) Mobilize international and domestic financial resources at all levels, transfer technology, promote best practice and support capacity-building for water and sanitation infrastructure and services development, ensuring that such infrastructure and services meet the needs of the poor and are gender-sensitive;

(b) Facilitate access to public information and participation, including by women, at all levels in support of policy and decision-making related to water resources management and project implementation;

(c) Promote priority action by Governments, with the support of all stakeholders, in water management and capacity-building at the national level and, where appropriate, at the regional level, and promote and provide new and additional financial resources and innovative technologies to implement chapter 18 of Agenda 21;

(d) Intensify water pollution prevention to reduce health hazards and protect ecosystems by introducing technologies for affordable sanitation and industrial and domestic wastewater treatment, by mitigating the effects of groundwater contamination and by establishing, at the national level, monitoring systems and effective legal

---

① Report of the World Summit on Sustainable Development, Johannesburg, South Africa, 26 August-4 September 2002. UN Document: A/CONF.199/20.

frameworks;

(e) Adopt prevention and protection measures to promote sustainable water use and to address water shortages.

26. Develop integrated water resources management and water efficiency plans by 2005, with support to developing countries, through actions at all levels to:

(a) Develop and implement national/regional strategies, plans and programmes with regard to integrated river basin, watershed and groundwater management and introduce measures to improve the efficiency of water infrastructure to reduce losses and increase recycling of water;

(b) Employ the full range of policy instruments, including regulation, monitoring, voluntary measures, market and information-based tools, land-use management and cost recovery of water services, without cost recovery objectives becoming a barrier to access to safe water by poor people, and adopt an integrated water basin approach;

(c) Improve the efficient use of water resources and promote their allocation among competing uses in a way that gives priority to the satisfaction of basic human needs and balances the requirement of preserving or restoring ecosystems and their functions, in particular in fragile environments, with human domestic, industrial and agriculture needs, including safeguarding drinking water quality;

(d) Develop programmes for mitigating the effects of extreme water-related events;

(e) Support the diffusion of technology and capacity-building for non-conventional water resources and conservation technologies, to developing countries and regions facing water scarcity conditions or subject to drought and desertification, through technical and financial support and capacity-building;

(f) Support, where appropriate, efforts and programmes for energy-efficient, sustainable and cost-effective desalination of seawater, water recycling and water harvesting from coastal fogs in developing countries, through such measures as technological, technical and financial assistance and other modalities;

(g) Facilitate the establishment of public-private partnerships and other forms of partnership that give priority to the needs of the poor, within stable and transparent national regulatory frameworks provided by Governments, while respecting local conditions, involving all concerned stakeholders, and monitoring the performance and improving accountability of public institutions and private companies.

27. Support developing countries and countries with economies in transition in their efforts to monitor and assess the quantity and quality of water resources, including through the establishment and/or further development of national monitoring networks and water resources databases and the development of relevant national indicators.

28. Improve water resource management and scientific understanding of the water cycle through cooperation in joint observation and research, and for this purpose encourage and promote knowledge-sharing and provide capacity-building and the transfer of technology, as mutually agreed, including remote-sensing and satellite technologies, particularly to developing countries and countries with economies in transition.

29. Promote effective coordination among the various international and intergovernmental bodies and processes working on water-related issues, both within the United Nations system and between the United Nations and international financial institutions, drawing on the contributions of other international institutions and civil society to inform intergovernmental decision-making; closer coordination should also be promoted to elaborate and support proposals and undertake activities related to the International Year of Freshwater, 2003 and beyond.

* * *

30. Oceans, seas, islands and coastal areas form an integrated and essential component of the Earth's ecosystem and are critical for global food security and for sustaining economic prosperity and the well-being of many national economies, particularly in developing countries. Ensuring the sustainable development of the oceans requires effective coordination and cooperation, including at the global and regional levels, between relevant bodies, and actions at all levels to:

(a) Invite States to ratify or accede to and implement the United Nations Convention on the Law of the Sea of 1982[①], which provides the overall legal framework for ocean activities;

(b) Promote the implementation of chapter 17 of Agenda 21, which provides the programme of action for achieving the sustainable development of oceans, coastal areas and seas through its programme areas of integrated management and sustainable development of coastal areas, including exclusive economic zones; marine environmental protection; sustainable use and conservation of marine living resources; addressing critical uncertainties for the management of the marine environment and climate change; strengthening international, including regional, cooperation and coordination; and sustainable development of small islands;

(c) Establish an effective, transparent and regular inter-agency coordination mechanism on ocean and coastal issues within the United Nations system;

(d) Encourage the application by 2010 of the ecosystem approach, noting the Reykjavik Declaration on Responsible Fisheries in the Marine Ecosystem[②] and decision V/6 of the Conference of Parties to the Convention on Biological Diversity[③];

(e) Promote integrated, multidisciplinary and multisectoral coastal and ocean management at the national level and encourage and assist coastal States in developing ocean policies and mechanisms on integrated coastal management;

(f) Strengthen regional cooperation and coordination between the relevant regional organizations and programmes, the regional seas programmes of the United Nations Environment Programme, regional fisheries management organizations and other regional science, health and development organizations;

(g) Assist developing countries in coordinating policies and programmes at the regional and subregional levels aimed at the conservation and sustainable management of fishery resources and implement integrated coastal area management plans, including through the promotion of sustainable coastal and small-scale fishing activities and, where appropriate, the development of related infrastructure;

(h) Take note of the work of the open-ended informal consultative process established by the United Nations General Assembly in its resolution 54/33 in order to facilitate the annual review by the Assembly of developments in ocean affairs and the upcoming review of its effectiveness and utility to be held at its fifty-seventh session under the terms of the above-mentioned resolution.

31. To achieve sustainable fisheries, the following actions are required at all levels:

(a) Maintain or restore stocks to levels that can produce the maximum sustainable yield with the aim of achieving these goals for depleted stocks on an urgent basis and where possible not later than 2015;

---

① Official Records of the Third United Nations Conference on the Law of the Sea, vol. XVII (United Nations publication, Sales No. E.84.V.3), document A/CONF.62/122.

② See Food and Agriculture Organization of the United Nations document C200/INF/25, appendix I.

③ See UNEP/CBD/COP/5/23, annex III.

(b) Ratify or accede to and effectively implement the relevant United Nations and, where appropriate, associated regional fisheries agreements or arrangements, noting in particular the Agreement for the Implementation of the Provisions of the United Nations Convention on the Law of the Sea of 10 December 1982 relating to the Conservation and Management of Straddling Fish Stocks and Highly Migratory Fish Stocks[1] and the 1993 Agreement to Promote Compliance with International Conservation and Management Measures by Fishing Vessels on the High Seas[2];

(c) Implement the 1995 Code of Conduct for Responsible Fisheries[3], taking note of the special requirements of developing countries as noted in its article 5, and the relevant international plans of action and technical guidelines of the Food and Agriculture Organization of the United Nations;

(d) Urgently develop and implement national and, where appropriate, regional plans of action, to put into effect the international plans of action of the Food and Agriculture Organization of the United Nations, in particular the international Plan of Action for the Management of Fishing Capacity[4] by 2005 and the International Plan of Action to Prevent, Deter and Eliminate illegal, Unreported and Unregulated Fishing[5] by 2004. Establish effective monitoring, reporting and enforcement, and control of fishing vessels, including by flag States, to further the international Plan of Action to Prevent, Deter and Eliminate illegal, Unreported and Unregulated Fishing;

(e) Encourage relevant regional fisheries management organizations and arrangements to give due consideration to the rights, duties and interests of coastal States and the special requirements of developing States when addressing the issue of the allocation of share of fishery resources for straddling stocks and highly migratory fish stocks, mindful of the provisions of the United Nations Convention on the Law of the Sea and the Agreement for the Implementation of the Provisions of the United Nations Convention on the Law of the Sea of 10 December 1982 relating to the Conservation and Management of Straddling Fish Stocks and Highly Migratory Fish Stocks, on the high seas and within exclusive economic zones;

(f) Eliminate subsidies that contribute to illegal, unreported and unregulated fishing and to over-capacity, while completing the efforts undertaken at the World Trade Organization to clarify and improve its disciplines on fisheries subsidies, taking into account the importance of this sector to developing countries;

(g) Strengthen donor coordination and partnerships between international financial institutions, bilateral agencies and other relevant stakeholders to enable developing countries, in particular the least developed countries and small island developing States and countries with economies in transition, to develop their national, regional and subregional capacities for infrastructure and integrated management and the sustainable use of fisheries;

(h) Support the sustainable development of aquaculture, including small-scale aquaculture, given its growing importance for food security and economic development.

32. In accordance with chapter 17 of Agenda 21, promote the conservation and management of the oceans through actions at all levels, giving due regard to the relevant international instruments to:

(a) Maintain the productivity and biodiversity of important and vulnerable marine and coastal areas, including in areas within and beyond national jurisdiction;

(b) Implement the work programme arising from the Jakarta Mandate on the Conservation and Sustainable

---

[1] See International Fisheries Instruments (United Nations publication, Sales No. E.98.V.11), sect. I; see also A/CONF.164/37.
[2] Ibid.
[3] Ibid., sect. III.
[4] Rome, Food and Agriculture Organization of the United Nations, 1999.
[5] Ibid., 2001.

Use of Marine and Coastal Biological Diversity of the Convention on Biological Diversity①, including through the urgent mobilization of financial resources and technological assistance and the development of human and institutional capacity, particularly in developing countries;

(c) Develop and facilitate the use of diverse approaches and tools, including the ecosystem approach, the elimination of destructive fishing practices, the establishment of marine protected areas consistent with international law and based on scientific information, including representative networks by 2012 and time/area closures for the protection of nursery grounds and periods, proper coastal land use and watershed planning and the integration of marine and coastal areas management into key sectors;

(d) Develop national, regional and international programmes for halting the loss of marine biodiversity, including in coral reefs and wetlands;

(e) Implement the Ramsar Convention②, including its joint work programme with the Convention on Biological Diversity③, and the programme of action called for by the International Coral Reef Initiative to strengthen joint management plans and international networking for wetland ecosystems in coastal zones, including coral reefs, mangroves, seaweed beds and tidal mud flats.

33. Advance implementation of the Global Programme of Action for the Protection of the Marine Environment from Land-based Activities④ and the Montreal Declaration on the Protection of the Marine Environment from Land-based Activities⑤, with particular emphasis during the period from 2002 to 2006 on municipal wastewater, the physical alteration and destruction of habitats, and nutrients, by actions at all levels to:

(a) Facilitate partnerships, scientific research and diffusion of technical knowledge; mobilize domestic, regional and international resources; and promote human and institutional capacity-building, paying particular attention to the needs of developing countries;

(b) Strengthen the capacity of developing countries in the development of their national and regional programmes and mechanisms to mainstream the objectives of the Global Programme of Action and to manage the risks and impacts of ocean pollution;

(c) Elaborate regional programmes of action and improve the links with strategic plans for the sustainable development of coastal and marine resources, noting in particular areas that are subject to accelerated environmental changes and development pressures;

(d) Make every effort to achieve substantial progress by the next Global Programme of Action conference in 2006 to protect the marine environment from land-based activities.

34. Enhance maritime safety and protection of the marine environment from pollution by actions at all levels to:

(a) Invite States to ratify or accede to and implement the conventions and protocols and other relevant instruments of the International Maritime Organization relating to the enhancement of maritime safety and protection of the marine environment from marine pollution and environmental damage caused by ships, including the use of toxic anti-fouling paints, and urge the International Maritime Organization (IMO) to consider stronger mechanisms to secure the implementation of IMO instruments by flag States;

---

① See A/51/312, annex II, decision II/10.
② Ramsar Convention on Wetlands of International Importance Especially as Waterfowl Habitat (United Nations, Treaty Series, vol. 996, No. 14583).
③ See United Nations Environment Programme, Convention on Biological Diversity (Environmental Law and Institution Programme Activity Centre), June 1992.
④ A/51/116, annex II.
⑤ See E/CN.17/2002/PC.2/15.

(b) Accelerate the development of measures to address invasive alien species in ballast water. Urge the International Maritime Organization to finalize its draft International Convention on the Control and Management of Ships' Ballast Water and Sediments.

35. Governments, taking into account their national circumstances, are encouraged, recalling paragraph 8 of resolution GC (44)/RES/17 of the General Conference of the International Atomic Energy Agency, and taking into account the very serious potential for environment and human health impacts of radioactive wastes, to make efforts to examine and further improve measures and internationally agreed regulations regarding safety, while stressing the importance of having effective liability mechanisms in place, relevant to international maritime transportation and other transboundary movement of radioactive material, radioactive waste and spent fuel, including, inter alia, arrangements for prior notification and consultations done in accordance with relevant international instruments.

36. Improve the scientific understanding and assessment of marine and coastal ecosystems as a fundamental basis for sound decision-making, through actions at all levels to:

(a) Increase scientific and technical collaboration, including integrated assessment at the global and regional levels, including the appropriate transfer of marine science and marine technologies and techniques for the conservation and management of living and non-living marine resources and expanding ocean-observing capabilities for the timely prediction and assessment of the state of marine environment;

(b) Establish by 2004 a regular process under the United Nations for global reporting and assessment of the state of the marine environment, including socio-economic aspects, both current and foreseeable, building on existing regional assessments;

(c) Build capacity in marine science, information and management, through inter alia, promoting the use of environmental impact assessments and environmental evaluation and reporting techniques, for projects or activities that are potentially harmful to the coastal and marine environments and their living and non-living resources;

(d) Strengthen the ability of the Intergovernmental Oceanographic Commission of the United Nations Educational, Scientific and Cultural Organization, the Food and Agriculture Organization of the United Nations and other relevant international and regional and subregional organizations to build national and local capacity in marine science and the sustainable management of oceans and their resources.

* * *

37. An integrated, multi-hazard, inclusive approach to address vulnerability, risk assessment and disaster management, including prevention, mitigation, preparedness, response and recovery, is an essential element of a safer world in the twenty-first century. Actions are required at all levels to:

(a) Strengthen the role of the International Strategy for Disaster Reduction and encourage the international community to provide the necessary financial resources to its Trust Fund;

(b) Support the establishment of effective regional, subregional and national strategies and scientific and technical institutional support for disaster management;

(c) Strengthen the institutional capacities of countries and promote international joint observation and research, through improved surface-based monitoring and increased use of satellite data, dissemination of technical and scientific knowledge, and the provision of assistance to vulnerable countries;

(d) Reduce the risks of flooding and drought in vulnerable countries by, inter alia, promoting wetland and watershed protection and restoration, improved land-use planning, improving and applying more widely techniques and methodologies for assessing the potential adverse effects of climate change on wetlands and, as appropriate, assisting countries that are particularly vulnerable to those effects;

(e) Improve techniques and methodologies for assessing the effects of climate change, and encourage the continuing assessment of those adverse effects by the Intergovernmental Panel on Climate Change;

(f) Encourage the dissemination and use of traditional and indigenous knowledge to mitigate the impact of disasters and promote community-based disaster management planning by local authorities, including through training activities and raising public awareness;

(g) Support the ongoing voluntary contribution of, as appropriate, non-governmental organizations, the scientific community and other partners in the management of natural disasters according to agreed, relevant guidelines;

(h) Develop and strengthen early warning systems and information networks in disaster management, consistent with the International Strategy for Disaster Reduction;

(i) Develop and strengthen capacity at all levels to collect and disseminate scientific and technical information, including the improvement of early warning systems for predicting extreme weather events, especially El Niño/La Nina, through the provision of assistance to institutions devoted to addressing such events, including the International Centre for the Study of the El Niño phenomenon;

(j) Promote cooperation for the prevention and mitigation of, preparedness for, response to and recovery from major technological and other disasters with an adverse impact on the environment in order to enhance the capabilities of affected countries to cope with such situations.

* * *

38. Change in the Earth's climate and its adverse effects are a common concern of humankind. We remain deeply concerned that all countries, particularly developing countries, including the least developed countries and small island developing States, face increased risks of negative impacts of climate change and recognize that, in this context, the problems of poverty, land degradation, access to water and food and human health remain at the centre of global attention. The United Nations Framework Convention on Climate Change① is the key instrument for addressing climate change, a global concern, and we reaffirm our commitment to achieving its ultimate objective of stabilization of greenhouse gas concentrations in the atmosphere at a level that would prevent dangerous anthropogenic interference with the climate system, within a time frame sufficient to allow ecosystems to adapt naturally to climate change, to ensure that food production is not threatened and to enable economic development to proceed in a sustainable manner, in accordance with our common but differentiated responsibilities and respective capabilities. Recalling the United Nations Millennium Declaration, in which heads of State and Government resolved to make every effort to ensure the entry into force of the Kyoto Protocol to the United Nations Framework Convention on Climate Change②, preferably by the tenth anniversary of the United Nations Conference on Environment and Development in 2002, and to embark on the required reduction of emissions of greenhouse gases, States that have ratified the Kyoto Protocol strongly urge States that have not already done so to ratify it in a timely manner. Actions at all levels are required to:

(a) Meet all the commitments and obligations under the United Nations Framework Convention on Climate Change;

(b) Work cooperatively towards achieving the objectives of the Convention;

(c) Provide technical and financial assistance and capacity-building to developing countries and countries

---

① A/AC.237/18 (Part II)/Add.1 and Corr.1, annex I.

② FCCC/CP/1997/7/Add.1, decision 1/CP.3, annex.

with economies in transition in accordance with commitments under the Convention, including the Marrakesh Accords[①];

(d) Build and enhance scientific and technological capabilities, inter alia, through continuing support to the Intergovernmental Panel on Climate Change for the exchange of scientific data and information especially in developing countries;

(e) Develop and transfer technological solutions;

(f) Develop and disseminate innovative technologies in regard to key sectors of development, particularly energy, and of investment in this regard, including through private sector involvement, market-oriented approaches, and supportive public policies and international cooperation;

(g) Promote the systematic observation of the Earth's atmosphere, land and oceans by improving monitoring stations, increasing the use of satellites and appropriate integration of these observations to produce high-quality data that could be disseminated for the use of all countries, in particular developing countries;

(h) Enhance the implementation of national, regional and international strategies to monitor the Earth's atmosphere, land and oceans, including, as appropriate, strategies for integrated global observations, inter alia, with the cooperation of relevant international organizations, especially the specialized agencies, in cooperation with the Convention;

(i) Support initiatives to assess the consequences of climate change, such as the Arctic Council initiative, including the environmental, economic and social impacts on local and indigenous communities.

39. Enhance cooperation at the international, regional and national levels to reduce air pollution, including transboundary air pollution, acid deposition and ozone depletion, bearing in mind the Rio principles, including, inter alia, the principle that, in view of the different contributions to global environmental degradation, States have common but differentiated responsibilities, with actions at all levels to:

(a) Strengthen capacities of developing countries and countries with economies in transition to measure, reduce and assess the impacts of air pollution, including health impacts, and provide financial and technical support for these activities;

(b) Facilitate implementation of the Montreal Protocol on Substances that Deplete the Ozone Layer by ensuring adequate replenishment of its fund by 2003/2005;

(c) Further support the effective regime for the protection of the ozone layer established in the Vienna Convention for the Protection of the Ozone Layer and the Montreal Protocol, including its compliance mechanism;

(d) Improve access by developing countries to affordable, accessible, cost-effective, safe and environmentally sound alternatives to ozone-depleting substances by 2010, and assist them in complying with the phase-out schedule under the Montreal Protocol, bearing in mind that ozone depletion and climate change are scientifically and technically interrelated;

(e) Take measures to address illegal traffic in ozone-depleting substances.

* * *

40. Agriculture plays a crucial role in addressing the needs of a growing global population and is inextricably linked to poverty eradication, especially in developing countries. Enhancing the role of women at all levels and in all aspects of rural development, agriculture, nutrition and food security is imperative. Sustainable agriculture and rural development are essential to the implementation of an integrated approach to increasing food production and

---

① FCCC/CP/2001/13 and Add.1-4.

enhancing food security and food safety in an environmentally sustainable way. This would include actions at all levels to:

(a) Achieve the Millennium Declaration target to halve by the year 2015 the proportion of the world's people who suffer from hunger and realize the right to a standard of living adequate for the health and well-being of themselves and their families, including food, including by promoting food security and fighting hunger in combination with measures which address poverty, consistent with the outcome of the World Food Summit and, for States Parties, with their obligations under article 11 of the International Covenant on Economic, Social and Cultural Rights[①];

(b) Develop and implement integrated land management and water-use plans that are based on sustainable use of renewable resources and on integrated assessments of socio-economic and environmental potentials and strengthen the capacity of Governments, local authorities and communities to monitor and manage the quantity and quality of land and water resources;

(c) Increase understanding of the sustainable use, protection and management of water resources to advance long-term sustainability of freshwater, coastal and marine environments;

(d) Promote programmes to enhance in a sustainable manner the productivity of land and the efficient use of water resources in agriculture, forestry, wetlands, artisanal fisheries and aquaculture, especially through indigenous and local community-based approaches;

(e) Support the efforts of developing countries to protect oases from silt, land degradation and increasing salinity by providing appropriate technical and financial assistance;

(f) Enhance the participation of women in all aspects and at all levels relating to sustainable agriculture and food security;

(g) Integrate existing information systems on land-use practices by strengthening national research and extension services and farmer organizations to trigger farmer-to-farmer exchange on good practices, such as those related to environmentally sound, low-cost technologies, with the assistance of relevant international organizations;

(h) Enact, as appropriate, measures that protect indigenous resource management systems and support the contribution of all appropriate stakeholders, men and women alike, in rural planning and development;

(i) Adopt policies and implement laws that guarantee well defined and enforceable land and water use rights and promote legal security of tenure, recognizing the existence of different national laws and/or systems of land access and tenure, and provide technical and financial assistance to developing countries as well as countries with economies in transition that are undertaking land tenure reform in order to enhance sustainable livelihoods;

(j) Reverse the declining trend in public sector finance for sustainable agriculture, provide appropriate technical and financial assistance, and promote private sector investment and support efforts in developing countries and countries with economies in transition to strengthen agricultural research and natural resource management capacity and dissemination of research results to the farming communities;

(k) Employ market-based incentives for agricultural enterprises and farmers to monitor and manage water use and quality, inter alia, by applying such methods as small-scale irrigation and wastewater recycling and reuse;

(l) Enhance access to existing markets and develop new markets for value-added agricultural products;

(m) Increase brown-field redevelopment in developed countries and countries with economies in transition,

---

① See General Assembly resolution 2200 A (XXI), annex.

with appropriate technical assistance where contamination is a serious problem;

(n) Enhance international cooperation to combat the illicit cultivation of narcotic plants, taking into account their negative social, economic and environmental impacts;

(o) Promote programmes for the environmentally sound, effective and efficient use of soil fertility improvement practices and agricultural pest control;

(p) Strengthen and improve coordination of existing initiatives to enhance sustainable agricultural production and food security;

(q) Invite countries that have not done so to ratify the International Treaty on Plant Genetic Resources for Food and Agriculture[①];

(r) Promote the conservation, and sustainable use and management of traditional and indigenous agricultural systems and strengthen indigenous models of agricultural production.

* * *

41. Strengthen the implementation of the United Nations Convention to Combat Desertification in Those Countries Experiencing Serious Drought and/or Desertification, particularly in Africa, to address causes of desertification and land degradation in order to maintain and restore land, and to address poverty resulting from land degradation. This would include actions at all levels to:

(a) Mobilize adequate and predictable financial resources, transfer of technologies and capacity-building at all levels;

(b) Formulate national action programmes to ensure timely and effective implementation of the Convention and its related projects, with the support of the international community, including through decentralized projects at the local level;

(c) Encourage the United Nations Framework Convention on Climate Change, the Convention on Biological Diversity and the Convention to Combat Desertification to continue exploring and enhancing synergies, with due regard to their respective mandates, in the elaboration and implementation of plans and strategies under the respective Conventions;

(d) Integrate measures to prevent and combat desertification as well as to mitigate the effects of drought through relevant policies and programmes, such as land, water and forest management, agriculture, rural development, early warning systems, environment, energy, natural resources, health and education, and poverty eradication and sustainable development strategies;

(e) Provide affordable local access to information to improve monitoring and early warning related to desertification and drought;

(f) Call on the Second Assembly of the Global Environment Facility (GEF) to take action on the recommendations of the GEF Council concerning the designation of land degradation (desertification and deforestation) as a focal area of GEF as a means of GEF support for the successful implementation of the Convention to Combat Desertification; and consequently, consider making GEF a financial mechanism of the Convention, taking into account the prerogatives and decisions of the Conference of the Parties to the Convention, while recognizing the complementary roles of GEF and the Global Mechanism of the Convention in providing and mobilizing resources for the elaboration and implementation of action programmes;

---

① Report of the Conference of the Food and Agriculture Organization of the United Nations, Thirty-first Session, Rome, 2-13 November 2001 (C2001/REP), appendix D.

(g) Improve the sustainability of grassland resources through strengthening management and law enforcement and providing financial and technical support by the international community to developing countries.

* * *

42. Mountain ecosystems support particular livelihoods and include significant watershed resources, biological diversity and unique flora and fauna. Many are particularly fragile and vulnerable to the adverse effects of climate change and need specific protection. Actions at all levels are required to:

(a) Develop and promote programmes, policies and approaches that integrate environmental, economic and social components of sustainable mountain development and strengthen international cooperation for its positive impacts on poverty eradication programmes, especially in developing countries;

(b) Implement programmes to address, where appropriate, deforestation, erosion, land degradation, loss of biodiversity, disruption of water flows and retreat of glaciers;

(c) Develop and implement, where appropriate, gender-sensitive policies and programmes, including public and private investments that help eliminate inequities facing mountain communities;

(d) Implement programmes to promote diversification and traditional mountain economies, sustainable livelihoods and small-scale production systems, including specific training programmes and better access to national and international markets, communications and transport planning, taking into account the particular sensitivity of mountains;

(e) Promote full participation and involvement of mountain communities in decisions that affect them and integrate indigenous knowledge, heritage and values in all development initiatives;

(f) Mobilize national and international support for applied research and capacity-building, provide financial and technical assistance for the effective implementation of the sustainable development of mountain ecosystems in developing countries and countries with economies in transition, and address the poverty among people living in mountains through concrete plans, projects and programmes, with sufficient support from all stakeholders, taking into account the spirit of the International Year of Mountains, 2002.

* * *

43. Promote sustainable tourism development, including non-consumptive and eco-tourism, taking into account the spirit of the International Year of Eco-tourism 2002, the United Nations Year for Cultural Heritage in 2002, the World Eco-tourism Summit 2002 and its Quebec Declaration, and the Global Code of Ethics for Tourism as adopted by the World Tourism Organization in order to increase the benefits from tourism resources for the population in host communities while maintaining the cultural and environmental integrity of the host communities and enhancing the protection of ecologically sensitive areas and natural heritages. Promote sustainable tourism development and capacity-building in order to contribute to the strengthening of rural and local communities. This would include actions at all levels to:

(a) Enhance international cooperation, foreign direct investment and partnerships with both private and public sectors, at all levels;

(b) Develop programmes, including education and training programmes, that encourage people to participate in eco-tourism, enable indigenous and local communities to develop and benefit from eco-tourism, and enhance stakeholder cooperation in tourism development and heritage preservation, in order to improve the protection of the environment, natural resources and cultural heritage;

(c) Provide technical assistance to developing countries and countries with economies in transition to support sustainable tourism business development and investment and tourism awareness programmes, to improve domestic tourism, and to stimulate entrepreneurial development;

(d) Assist host communities in managing visits to their tourism attractions for their maximum benefit, while ensuring the least negative impacts on and risks for their traditions, culture and environment, with the support of the World Tourism Organization and other relevant organizations;

(e) Promote the diversification of economic activities, including through the facilitation of access to markets and commercial information, and participation of emerging local enterprises, especially small and medium-sized enterprises.

* * *

44. Biodiversity, which plays a critical role in overall sustainable development and poverty eradication, is essential to our planet, human well-being and to the livelihood and cultural integrity of people. However, biodiversity is currently being lost at unprecedented rates due to human activities; this trend can only be reversed if the local people benefit from the conservation and sustainable use of biological diversity, in particular in countries of origin of genetic resources, in accordance with article 15 of the Convention on Biological Diversity. The Convention is the key instrument for the conservation and sustainable use of biological diversity and the fair and equitable sharing of benefits arising from use of genetic resources. A more efficient and coherent implementation of the three objectives of the Convention and the achievement by 2010 of a significant reduction in the current rate of loss of biological diversity will require the provision of new and additional financial and technical resources to developing countries, and includes actions at all levels to:

(a) Integrate the objectives of the Convention into global, regional and national sectoral and cross-sectoral programmes and policies, in particular in the programmes and policies of the economic sectors of countries and international financial institutions;

(b) Promote the ongoing work under the Convention on the sustainable use on biological diversity, including on sustainable tourism, as a cross-cutting issue relevant to different ecosystems, sectors and thematic areas;

(c) Encourage effective synergies between the Convention and other multilateral environmental agreements, inter alia, through the development of joint plans and programmes, with due regard to their respective mandates, regarding common responsibilities and concerns;

(d) Implement the Convention and its provisions, including active follow-up of its work programmes and decisions through national, regional and global action programmes, in particular the national biodiversity strategies and action plans, and strengthen their integration into relevant cross-sectoral strategies, programmes and policies, including those related to sustainable development and poverty eradication, including initiatives which promote community-based sustainable use of biological diversity;

(e) Promote the wide implementation and further development of the ecosystem approach, as being elaborated in the ongoing work of the Convention;

(f) Promote concrete international support and partnership for the conservation and sustainable use of biodiversity, including in ecosystems, at World Heritage sites and for the protection of endangered species, in particular through the appropriate channelling of financial resources and technology to developing countries and countries with economies in transition;

(g) To effectively conserve and sustainably use biodiversity, promote and support initiatives for hot spot areas and other areas essential for biodiversity and promote the development of national and regional ecological networks and corridors;

(h) Provide financial and technical support to developing countries, including capacity-building, in order to enhance indigenous and community-based biodiversity conservation efforts;

(i) Strengthen national, regional and international efforts to control invasive alien species, which are one of the main causes of biodiversity loss, and encourage the development of effective work programme on invasive alien species at all levels;

(j) Subject to national legislation, recognize the rights of local and indigenous communities who are holders of traditional knowledge, innovations and practices, and, with the approval and involvement of the holders of such knowledge, innovations and practices, develop and implement benefit-sharing mechanisms on mutually agreed terms for the use of such knowledge, innovations and practices;

(k) Encourage and enable all stakeholders to contribute to the implementation of the objectives of the Convention and, in particular, recognize the specific role of youth, women and indigenous and local communities in conserving and using biodiversity in a sustainable way;

(l) Promote the effective participation of indigenous and local communities in decision and policy-making concerning the use of their traditional knowledge;

(m) Encourage technical and financial support to developing countries and countries with economies in transition in their efforts to develop and implement, as appropriate, inter alia, national sui generis systems and traditional systems according to national priorities and legislation, with a view to conserving and the sustainable use of biodiversity;

(n) Promote the wide implementation of and continued work on the Bonn Guidelines on Access to Genetic Resources and Fair and Equitable Sharing of Benefits arising out of their Utilization, as an input to assist the Parties when developing and drafting legislative, administrative or policy measures on access and benefit-sharing as well as contract and other arrangements under mutually agreed terms for access and benefit-sharing;

(o) Negotiate within the framework of the Convention on Biological Diversity, bearing in mind the Bonn Guidelines, an international regime to promote and safeguard the fair and equitable sharing of benefits arising out of the utilization of genetic resources;

(p) Encourage successful conclusion of existing processes under the auspices of the Intergovernmental Committee on Intellectual Property and Genetic Resources, Traditional Knowledge and Folklore of the World Intellectual Property Organization, and in the ad hoc open-ended working group on article 8 (j) and related provisions of the Convention;

(q) Promote practicable measures for access to the results and benefits arising from biotechnologies based upon genetic resources, in accordance with articles 15 and 19 of the Convention, including through enhanced scientific and technical cooperation on biotechnology and biosafety, including the exchange of experts, training human resources and developing research-oriented institutional capacities;

(r) With a view to enhancing synergy and mutual supportiveness, taking into account the decisions under the relevant agreements, promote the discussions, without prejudging their outcome, with regard to the relationships between the Convention and agreements related to international trade and intellectual property rights, as outlined in the Doha Ministerial Declaration[①];

(s) Promote the implementation of the programme of work of the Global Taxonomy Initiative;

(t) Invite all States that have not already done so to ratify the Convention, the Cartagena Protocol on

---

① See A/C.2/56/7, annex.

Biosafety to the Convention[①] and other biodiversity-related agreements, and invite those that have done so to promote their effective implementation at the national, regional and international levels and to support developing countries and countries with economies in transition technically and financially in this regard.

* * *

45. Forests and trees cover nearly one third of the Earth's surface. Sustainable forest management of both natural and planted forests and for timber and non-timber products is essential to achieving sustainable development as well as a critical means to eradicate poverty, significantly reduce deforestation, halt the loss of forest biodiversity and land and resource degradation and improve food security and access to safe drinking water and affordable energy; in addition, it highlights the multiple benefits of both natural and planted forests and trees and contributes to the well-being of the planet and humanity. The achievement of sustainable forest management, nationally and globally, including through partnerships among interested Governments and stakeholders, including the private sector, indigenous and local communities and non-governmental organizations, is an essential goal of sustainable development. This would include actions at all levels to:

(a) Enhance political commitment to achieve sustainable forest management by endorsing it as a priority on the international political agenda, taking full account of the linkages between the forest sector and other sectors through integrated approaches;

(b) Support the United Nations Forum on Forests, with the assistance of the Collaborative Partnership on Forests, as key intergovernmental mechanisms to facilitate and coordinate the implementation of sustainable forest management at the national, regional and global levels, thus contributing, inter alia, to the conservation and sustainable use of forest biodiversity;

(c) Take immediate action on domestic forest law enforcement and illegal international trade in forest products, including in forest biological resources, with the support of the international community, and provide human and institutional capacity-building related to the enforcement of national legislation in those areas;

(d) Take immediate action at the national and international levels to promote and facilitate the means to achieve sustainable timber harvesting and to facilitate the provision of financial resources and the transfer and development of environmentally sound technologies, and thereby address unsustainable timber-harvesting practices;

(e) Develop and implement initiatives to address the needs of those parts of the world that currently suffer from poverty and the highest rates of deforestation and where international cooperation would be welcomed by affected Governments;

(f) Create and strengthen partnerships and international cooperation to facilitate the provision of increased financial resources, the transfer of environmentally sound technologies, trade, capacity-building, forest law enforcement and governance at all levels and integrated land and resource management to implement sustainable forest management, including the proposals for action of the Intergovernmental Panel on Forests/Intergovernmental Forum on Forests;

(g) Accelerate implementation of the proposals for action of the Intergovernmental Panel on Forests/Intergovernmental Forum on Forests by countries and by the Collaborative Partnership on Forests and intensify efforts on reporting to the United Nations Forum on Forests to contribute to an assessment of progress in 2005;

(h) Recognize and support indigenous and community-based forest management systems to ensure their full

---

① Http://www.biodiv.org/biosafety/protocol.asp.

and effective participation in sustainable forest management;

(i) Implement the expanded action-oriented work programme of the Convention on Biological Diversity on all types of forest biological diversity, in close cooperation with the Forum, Partnership members and other forest-related processes and conventions, with the involvement of all relevant stakeholders.

* * *

46. Mining, minerals and metals are important to the economic and social development of many countries. Minerals are essential for modern living. Enhancing the contribution of mining, minerals and metals to sustainable development includes actions at all levels to:

(a) Support efforts to address the environmental, economic, health and social impacts and benefits of mining, minerals and metals throughout their life cycle, including workers' health and safety, and use a range of partnerships, furthering existing activities at the national and international levels among interested Governments, intergovernmental organizations, mining companies and workers and other stakeholders to promote transparency and accountability for sustainable mining and minerals development;

(b) Enhance the participation of stakeholders, including local and indigenous communities and women, to play an active role in minerals, metals and mining development throughout the life cycles of mining operations, including after closure for rehabilitation purposes, in accordance with national regulations and taking into account significant transboundary impacts;

(c) Foster sustainable mining practices through the provision of financial, technical and capacity-building support to developing countries and countries with economies in transition for the mining and processing of minerals, including small-scale mining, and, where possible and appropriate, improve value-added processing, upgrade scientific and technological information and reclaim and rehabilitate degraded sites.

教科文组织世界地质公园操作指南[①]（节选）

（联合国教科文组织第三十八届大会2015年11月17日在巴黎通过）

1. 导言

1990年代中期产生了地质公园的概念，它响应了保护和增加地球历史上具有地质意义地区的价值的需要。景观和地质构造是地球演变的重要见证，也是决定人类今后可持续发展的因素。从一开始，地质公园就采用了"自下而上"的办法，又称"社区主导型"办法，旨在确保为科学、教育和文化之目的，保护和增进此类地区的地质意义，此外还旨在将此类地区用作可持续的经济资产，例如通过发展负责任的旅游业。2004年，在教科文组织的支持下，欧洲地质公园网络的17个成员及8个中国地质公园共同创建了世界地质公园网络(GGN)，此后有100多家世界地质公园成为该网络的成员，该网络于2014年获得法律地位。

教科文组织世界地质公园必须在地质上具有国际意义。此类公园由地球科学相关学科的科学专家独立进行评估。教科文组织世界地质公园是具有生命力、正在发挥作用的景观，在那里，科学界和地方社区以互利互惠的方式参与进来。

各级教育是教科文组织世界地质公园概念的核心。从大学研究者到地方社区的群体，教科文组织世界地质公园鼓励人们从岩石、景观和正在进行的地质过程中了解地球的故事。教科文组织世界地质公园还增进了地质遗产与该区域自然和文化遗产的所有其他方面之间的联系，清楚地表明地质多样性不仅是所有生态系统的基础，也是人类与景观互动的基础。

通过更广泛地促进教科文组织的任务，推广地质科学和一般科学，同时贯通教育、文化和通信，教科文组织世界地质公园为实现教科文组织的各项目标做出了贡献。

2. 基本概念

2.1 教科文组织国际地球科学和地质公园计划范围内的教科文组织世界地质公园

作为教科文组织国际地球科学和地质公园计划(IGGP)的一部分，教科文组织世界地质公园鼓励拥有具有国际价值的地质遗产的各个地区彼此开展国际合作，在地方社区的支持下，采用自下而上的办法保护和增进这些地区的遗产，实现其可持续发展。通过国际地球科学和地质公园计划，这些地区可利用教科文组织更广泛的任务，向教科文组织申请指定为"教科文组织世界地质公园"，教科文组织是联合国唯一具有地球科学职权范围的组织。

2.2 教科文组织世界地质公园

教科文组织世界地质公园是单一、统一的地理区域，依照统一的保护、教育和可持续发展概念对那

[①] 引自：国际地球科学和地质公园计划章程。UNESCO Document Code: IGGP/2015/ST。

里具有国际地质意义的地点和景观进行管理。教科文组织世界地质公园是否具有国际地质意义，应由构成"教科文组织世界地质公园评估小组"的科学专家来确定，这些专家将根据对该区域的地质地点开展的、已经过同行审议并公布的研究，开展全球性的比较评估。利用与该区域自然和文化遗产的所有其他方面有关联的地质遗产，教科文组织世界地质公园提高了人们对我们居住的这个不断变化的星球上的社会面临的重大问题的认识和理解。

2.3 标识的使用

教科文组织世界地质公园有权使用为其制定的"关联标识"。使用该标识时应遵守2007年"关于使用教科文组织名称、简称、标识和因特网域名的指示"或任何后续的指示。

2.4 地域代表性

作为教科文组织的一部分，国际地球科学和地质公园计划致力于促进教科文组织世界地质公园具有均衡的全球地域代表性。

3. 教科文组织世界地质公园的标准

（i）教科文组织世界地质公园必须为单一、统一的地理区域，依照统一的保护、教育和可持续发展概念对那里具有国际地质意义的地点和景观进行管理。教科文组织世界地质公园必须具有明确界定的边界、具备足以发挥其职能的适当面积并拥有经科学专家独立核实具有国际意义的地质遗产。

（ii）教科文组织世界地质公园应利用与该区域自然和文化遗产的所有其他方面有关联的地质遗产，提高对我们居住的这个不断变化的星球上的社会面临的重大问题的认识，包括但不限于增加对以下方面的知识和了解：地质过程；地质灾害；气候变化；可持续利用地球自然资源的必要性；生命的进化以及土著人民权能的增强。

（iii）教科文组织世界地质公园应设立法律地位受国家立法承认的管理机构。管理机构应适当配备，以充分管理教科文组织世界地质公园的全部区域。

（iv）申请的区域与教科文组织指定的其他地点，例如世界遗产地或生物圈保护区出现重叠的，必须在申请中给出明确的理由，并提供证据，证明无论作为独立的品牌还是与其他名称共同存在，都能增加拥有教科文组织世界地质公园地位的价值。

（v）教科文组织世界地质公园应促使地方社区和土著人民作为关键的利益攸关方积极参与管理地质公园。必须与地方社区结成伙伴关系，共同拟定和实施共同管理计划，并在其中规定当地人民的社会和经济需要，保护他们生活在其中的景观，保护其文化特性。建议所有相关的地方和区域行为者以及管理当局派代表参与管理教科文组织世界地质公园。在规划和管理该区域时，除考虑到科学之外，还应结合地方和土著的知识、做法及管理系统。

（vi）鼓励各个教科文组织世界地质公园分享经验，交流意见，并在世界地质公园网络的范围内开展联合项目。世界地质公园网络实行强制会员制。

（vii）教科文组织世界地质公园必须尊重与保护地质遗产有关的地方和国家法律。在提交任何申请之前，必须合法地保护教科文组织世界地质公园内正在确定的地质遗产地点。与此同时，应利用教科文组织世界地质公园增进地方和国家对地质遗产的保护。管理机构不得直接参与出售地质物品，例如化石、矿物、抛光岩石以及通常在教科文组织世界地质公园的所谓岩石商店出售的那一类装饰用岩石（无论其来源如何），并应积极阻止整体上不可持续的地质材料贸易。允许可持续地从教科文组织世界地质公园范围内的自然可再生地点收集地质材料，用于科学和教育目的，但必须明确证明此举是负责任的行动，并且是最有效的遗产地可持续管理办法的组成部分。在特殊情况下，可允许交易此类系统中的地质材料，但前提是，应明确、公开地解释该交易，证明该交易是该世界地质公园与当地具体情况有关的最佳选择，并进行监督。此类当地具体情况应由教科文组织世界地质公园理事会逐案核准。

（viii）通过评估和重新验证清单核实这些标准。

4. 机构结构和职能

4.1 教科文组织世界地质公园理事会

理事会是新的教科文组织世界地质公园申请和重新验证方面的决策机构，负责就国际地球科学和地质公园计划的世界地质公园活动的战略规划和实施问题向总干事提出建议。理事会由十二名常任成员构成，常任成员拥有表决权，是教科文组织总干事根据世界地质公园网络和会员国的推荐而任命的个人。此外，教科文组织总干事、世界地质公园网络主席、国际地质科学联合会秘书长、国际自然保护联盟总干事或者他们的代表是理事会的当然成员，但没有表决权。应当从具有相关领域的丰富经验、拥有科学或专业资格的著名专家中选出理事会常任成员，同时考虑到公平地域分配和性别平等。常任成员应以个人身份任职，不代表各自的国家或任何其他所属实体。理事会成员必须以书面形式同意，在新的教科文组织世界地质公园申请或需要重新验证的世界地质公园方面，如果出现利益冲突，他们将回避。

4.2 教科文组织世界地质公园主席团

主席团由 5 名成员构成，即：教科文组织世界地质公园理事会的主席、副主席和报告员。教科文组织总干事和世界地质公园网络（GGN）主席或者他们的代表是主席团的当然成员，但没有表决权。

主席团的主要职责是与秘书处共同编写必要文件，以便教科文组织执行局根据理事会的决定，最终核可新的教科文组织世界地质公园提名。教科文组织世界地质公园主席团将与国际地球科学计划（IGCP）主席团举行联合协调会议。

4.3 教科文组织世界地质公园评估小组

在初次申请和重新验证期间，一个由信息顾问和评估员组成的独立小组将开展实地考察，对教科文组织世界地质公园进行评估。

每个新的教科文组织世界地质公园申请中的地质遗产是否具有国际意义，将由信息顾问依照具体和公开可用的科学标准进行评估。要求国际地质科学联合会协调这一职能，并确保每年及时提供所有关于准教科文组织世界地质公园的科学价值和国际意义的声明，以便评估员能在开展实地评估任务时获得这些声明。可酌情邀请其他组织参与。

教科文组织秘书处将会同世界地质公园网络确定和保持一份评估员名册，评估员负责对准教科文组织世界地质公园的新申请开展实地评估。评估员应拥有世界地质公园发展（地质遗产、保护、可持续发展、开发和促进旅游、环境问题）方面经证明的综合专业经验。评估员还将开展重新验证任务。

教科文组织世界地质公园评估员必须遵守理事会关于申请和重新验证任务的严格准则。评估员以个人身份履行职责，不代表各自的国家或任何其他所属实体。世界地质公园网络应确保评估员在新的教科文组织世界地质公园申请或需要重新验证的世界地质公园方面不存在利益冲突。评估员不寻求或接受来自政府或其他当局的指示，也不在本国执行任何任务。如果国家地质公园委员会寻求对一项评估或重新验证任务提出意见，则其中哪些意见或信息将纳入评估员的最终报告，将由评估员全权决定。评估员应及时向教科文组织提交报告。根据 1946 年《联合国特权和豁免公约》，评估员不具有"为联合国执行使命的专家"地位。

4.4 国家地质公园委员会

会员国应在发展本国的教科文组织世界地质公园中发挥积极作用。因此，而且只有在会员国愿意时，才建议设立国家地质公园委员会。这些"国家委员会"的名称可以不同，例如，可以命名为国家论坛、国家工作队或工作组。这些委员会可以由会员国负责地质公园事务的主管实体设立。这些委员会必须得到会员国的教科文组织全国委员会或者负责与教科文组织联系的相关政府机构的认可。在适用时，这些委员会还应联络现有关于国际地球科学计划的国家委员会。

国家地质公园委员会可能的均衡成员构成：
- 教科文组织全国委员会和／或负责与教科文组织联系的相关政府机构的代表；
- 国家地质组织或地质调查机构的代表；
- 国家环境／保护区组织的代表；
- 国家文化遗产机构的代表；
- 国家旅游组织的代表；
- 国际地球科学计划全国委员会的代表；
- 在某个会员国拥有教科文组织世界地质公园的情况下，由该地质公园派出的代表（在拥有多个教科文组织世界地质公园的国家，该人选可能轮换）；
- 根据具体国情，酌情增加不同的额外成员。

国家地质公园委员会可在国家层面开展以下工作：
- 协调国家对国际地球科学和地质公园计划范围内的教科文组织世界地质公园的贡献；
- 查明地质遗产并提高公众对其重要性的认识；
- 促进发展新的教科文组织世界地质公园，对申请、重新验证和扩展进行评估和核可；
- 自行决定是否对在会员国开展的任何评估或重新验证任务提出意见；
- 向所在会员国的教科文组织全国委员会或者负责与教科文组织联系的相关政府机构提交所有的教科文组织世界地质公园申请，申请将随后转交教科文组织；
- 确保某区域适当退出国际地球科学和地质公园计划范围内的教科文组织世界地质公园，前提是该区域愿意这样做，或者其未能通过重新验证程序；
- 促进各个教科文组织世界地质公园彼此开展国际合作；
- 在国家一级提供关于教科文组织世界地质公园世界和地区网络的信息；
- 在教科文组织世界地质公园启动并支持可持续发展战略和行动。

教科文组织世界地质公园操作指南提出了最佳做法。通过本国的国家地质公园委员会，会员国有权制定本国补充性的具体准则，以适应具体国情。

在评估和重新验证准教科文组织世界地质公园和现有的教科文组织世界地质公园的进程中，教科文组织秘书处可在所有阶段密切联络国家地质公园委员会以及会员国的教科文组织全国委员会或者负责与教科文组织联系的相关国家机构。

所有申请书和重新验证函都必须附有教科文组织全国委员会或负责与教科文组织联系的相关国家机构出具的支持函。

4.5 地区和世界地质公园网络

自制定该概念伊始，建立网络就已成为地质公园的核心原则之一。建立网络有力地推动了地质公园运动顺利开展，在促进交流经验、开展质量管理、形成联合倡议、制定项目和开展能力建设方面，发挥了宝贵的作用。教科文组织鼓励加强地区性的地质公园网络和世界地质公园网络。受各个地质公园网络开展的工作的鼓舞，教科文组织将继续为这些网络提供支持和协助，并协调关于教科文组织世界地质公园的能力建设活动，鼓励各个教科文组织世界地质公园彼此交流最佳做法。

Operational Guidelines for UNESCO Global Geoparks[①] (excerpts)

Adopted by the UNESCO General Conference at its 38th Session, Paris, 17 November 2015

1. INTRODUCTION

The Geopark concept arose in the mid-1990s as a response to the need to conserve and enhance the value of areas of geological significance in Earth history. Landscapes and geological formations are key witnesses to the evolution of our planet and determinants for our future sustainable development. From the outset, Geoparks adopted a "bottom-up" or community-led approach to ensure that an area's geological significance could be conserved and promoted for science, education and culture, in addition to being used as a sustainable economic asset such as through the development of responsible tourism. In 2004, with the support of UNESCO, 17 members of the European Geoparks Network and eight Chinese Geoparks came together to create the Global Geoparks Network (GGN) which, with then more than 100 Global Geoparks as members, acquired legal status in 2014.

A UNESCO Global Geopark must contain geology of international significance. It is independently evaluated by scientific professionals in the relevant discipline of Earth Science. UNESCO Global Geoparks are living, working landscapes where science and local communities engage in a mutually beneficial way.

Education at all levels is at the core of the UNESCO Global Geopark concept. From university researchers to local community groups, UNESCO Global Geoparks encourage awareness of the story of the planet as read in the rocks, landscape and ongoing geological processes. UNESCO Global Geoparks also promote the links between geological heritage and all other aspects of the area's natural and cultural heritage, clearly demonstrating that geodiversity is the foundation of all ecosystems and the basis of human interaction with the landscape.

UNESCO Global Geoparks contribute to achieving UNESCO's objectives by promoting geology and science in general through a wider contribution to UNESCO's mandate while cutting across education, culture and communication.

2. THE BASIC CONCEPTS

2.1 UNESCO Global Geoparks within UNESCO's International Geoscience and Geoparks Programme

UNESCO Global Geoparks, within UNESCO's International Geoscience and Geoparks Programme (IGGP), encourage international cooperation between areas with geological heritage of international value, through a

---

[①] Statutes of the International Geoscience and Geoparks Programme. UNESCO Document Code: IGGP/2015/ST.

bottom-up approach to conservation, local community support, promotion of heritage and sustainable development of the area. Through the IGGP, these areas apply to UNESCO as the only United Nations organization with a remit in the Earth Sciences to designate as a "UNESCO Global Geopark", which draws upon the broader mandate of the Organization.

2.2　UNESCO Global Geoparks

UNESCO Global Geoparks are single, unified geographical areas where sites and landscapes of international geological significance are managed with a holistic concept of protection, education and sustainable development. The international geological significance of a UNESCO Global Geopark is determined by scientific professionals, as part of a "UNESCO Global Geopark Evaluation Team", who make a globally comparative assessment based on the peer-reviewed, published research conducted on geological sites within the area. UNESCO Global Geoparks use geological heritage, in connection with all other aspects of that area's natural and cultural heritage, to enhance awareness and understanding of key issues facing society in the context of the dynamic planet we all live on.

2.3　Use of logos

UNESCO Global Geoparks will be entitled to use a "linked logo" to be developed for UNESCO Global Geoparks. This use will be governed under the 2007 "Directives concerning the use of the name, acronym, logo and Internet domain names of UNESCO" or by any subsequent directive.

2.4　Geographical representation

As part of UNESCO, the IGGP is committed to promote balanced global geographical representation for UNESCO Global Geoparks.

3. CRITERIA FOR UNESCO GLOBAL GEOPARKS

(i) UNESCO Global Geoparks must be single, unified geographical areas where sites and landscapes of international geological significance are managed with a holistic concept of protection, education, research and sustainable development. A UNESCO Global Geopark must have a clearly defined border, be of adequate size to fulfil its functions and contain geological heritage of international significance as independently verified by scientific professionals.

(ii) UNESCO Global Geoparks should use that heritage, in connection with all other aspects of that area's natural and cultural heritage, to promote awareness of key issues facing society in the context of the dynamic planet we all live on, including but not limited to increasing knowledge and understanding of: geoprocesses; geohazards; climate change; the need for the sustainable use of Earth's natural resources; the evolution of life and the empowerment of indigenous peoples.

(iii) UNESCO Global Geoparks should be areas with a management body having legal existence recognized under national legislation. The management bodies should be appropriately equipped to adequately address the area of the UNESCO Global Geopark in its entirety.

(iv) In the case where an applying area overlaps with another UNESCO designated site, such as a World Heritage Site or Biosphere Reserve, the request must be clearly justified and evidence must be provided for how UNESCO Global Geopark status will add value by being both independently branded and in synergy with the other designations.

(v) UNESCO Global Geoparks should actively involve local communities and indigenous peoples as key stakeholders in the Geopark. In partnership with local communities, a co-management plan needs to be drafted and implemented that provides for the social and economic needs of local populations, protects the landscape in which they live and conserves their cultural identity. It is recommended that all relevant local and regional actors and authorities be represented in the management of a UNESCO Global Geopark. Local and indigenous knowledge, practice and management systems should be included, alongside science, in the planning and management of the area.

(vi) UNESCO Global Geoparks are encouraged to share their experience and advice and to undertake joint projects within the GGN. Membership of GGN is obligatory.

(vii) A UNESCO Global Geopark must respect local and national laws relating to the protection of geological heritage. The defining geological heritage sites within a UNESCO Global Geopark must be legally protected in advance of any application. At the same time, a UNESCO Global Geopark should be used as leverage for promoting the protection of geological heritage locally and nationally. The management body must not participate directly in the sale of geological objects such as fossils, minerals, polished rocks and ornamental rocks of the type normally found in so-called "rock-shops" within the UNESCO Global Geopark (regardless of their origin) and should actively discourage unsustainable trade in geological materials as a whole. Where clearly justified as a responsible activity and as part of delivering the most effective and sustainable means of site management, it may permit sustainable collecting of geological materials for scientific and educational purposes from naturally renewable sites within the UNESCO Global Geopark. Trade of geological materials based on such a system may be tolerated in exceptional circumstances, provided it is clearly and publicly explained, justified and monitored as the best option for the Global Geopark in relation to local circumstances. Such circumstances will be subject to approval by the UNESCO Global Geoparks Council on a case by case basis.

(viii) These criteria are verified through checklists for evaluation and revalidation.

4. THE INSTITUTIONAL STRUCTURE AND FUNCTIONS

4.1 UNESCO Global Geoparks Council

The Council is the decision-making body for new UNESCO Global Geopark applications and re-validations, and it is responsible for advising the Director-General on the strategy planning and implementation of the Global Geoparks activity of the IGGP. The Council is composed of 12 ordinary members, with the right to vote, who are individuals appointed by the Director-General of UNESCO on recommendation of GGN and Member States. In addition, the Director-General of UNESCO, the President of GGN, the Secretary-General of IUGS, the Director-General of IUCN or their representatives shall be *ex officio* members of the Council without the right to vote. Ordinary Members appointed to the Council shall be high-profile experts chosen for their proven experience, scientific or professional qualification in relevant fields, taking into account an equitable geographical distribution and gender equality. Ordinary members will serve in their personal capacity, not as representatives of their respective States or any other affiliated entities. Council members will have to agree in writing that they will abstain in cases of conflict of interest regarding new UNESCO Global Geopark applications or those requiring revalidation.

4.2 UNESCO Global Geoparks Bureau

The Bureau will consist of five members: The Chairperson, the Vice-Chairperson and the Rapporteur of the Council of the UNESCO Global Geoparks. The Director-General of UNESCO and the President of the Global Geoparks Network (GGN) or their representatives shall be *ex officio* members of the Bureau without the right to vote.

Its main duty will be to prepare with the secretariat the necessary documentation for the Executive Board of UNESCO to provide a final endorsement of new UNESCO Global Geopark nominations based on decisions of the Council. The UNESCO Global Geoparks Bureau will hold joint coordination meetings with the Bureau of the International Geoscience Programme (IGCP).

4.3 UNESCO Global Geoparks Evaluation Team

UNESCO Global Geoparks will be evaluated – both during the initial application and during revalidation – by an independent team composed of desk-top advisors and evaluators carrying out field missions.

The international significance of the geological heritage of each new UNESCO Global Geopark application will be assessed by desk-top advisors following specific and publicly available scientific criteria. IUGS will be asked to coordinate this role and to ensure that all statements on the scientific value and international significance of the geological heritage of an aspiring UNESCO Global Geopark are available annually in time so that evaluators can access them ahead of the field evaluation mission. Other organizations may also be involved as appropriate.

The UNESCO Secretariat in conjunction with the GGN will establish and maintain a roster of evaluators who will undertake field evaluations of new applications for aspiring UNESCO Global Geoparks. These evaluators will have combined and proven professional experience relevant for Global Geopark development (geological heritage, conservation, sustainable development, tourism development and promotion, and environmental issues). These evaluators will also conduct revalidation missions.

Evaluators for UNESCO Global Geoparks must follow strict guidelines provided by the Council for new application and revalidation missions. These evaluators will serve in their personal capacity, not as representatives of their respective States or any other affiliated entities. GGN will be required to ensure that evaluators have no conflict of interest regarding new UNESCO Global Geopark applications or those requiring revalidation. Evaluators will not seek or accept instructions from governments or other authorities and will not conduct missions in their own country. If any National Geopark Committee seeks to observe an evaluation or revalidation mission, it will be fully up to the evaluators which observations and information provided they will include into their final reports. They are expected to submit their reports to UNESCO in a timely manner. Evaluators will not have the status of "experts on mission" pursuant to the Convention on the Privileges and Immunities of the United Nations of 1946.

4.4 National Geopark Committees

Member States should play an active role in the development of their UNESCO Global Geoparks. As such, and only if the Member State wishes to do so, the creation of a National Geopark Committee is recommended. These "National Committees" could be named differently, for example, National Forum, National Task Force or Task Group. These committees may be created by the competent entity in charge of Geoparks in that Member State. The committees must be recognized by that Member State's National Commission for UNESCO or the relevant government body in charge of relations with UNESCO. These committees should also liaise with existing national committees for the IGCP where applicable.

Possible balanced National Geopark Committee composition:
- Representative(s) of the National Commission for UNESCO and/or the relevant government body in charge of relations with UNESCO;
- Representative(s) of the national geological organization or survey;

- Representative(s) of the national environmental/protected area organization;
- Representative(s) of the national cultural heritage body;
- Representative(s) of the national tourism organization;
- Representative(s) of the national committee for IGCP;
- Representatives from UNESCO Global Geoparks, where they exist, in that Member State (possibly rotating in countries with many UNESCO Global Geoparks); and
- Different and additional members may be included as seen appropriate to fit the particular national context.

Its work at national level may consist of:
- Coordinating the national contribution to UNESCO Global Geoparks within the IGGP;
- Identifying the geological heritage and raising public awareness of its importance;
- Promoting the development of new UNESCO Global Geoparks, assessing and endorsing applications, revalidations and extensions;
- Observing any evaluation or revalidation mission in that Member State should they wish to;
- Presenting to that Member State's National Commission for UNESCO or the relevant government body in charge of relations with UNESCO all UNESCO Global Geopark applications, which will then be forwarded to UNESCO.
- Ensuring the proper withdrawal of the area as a UNESCO Global Geopark within the IGGP, should the area so wish or should they fail the revalidation process;
- Promoting international cooperation between UNESCO Global Geoparks;
- Providing information at the national level about the global and regional networks of UNESCO Global Geoparks;
- Initiating and supporting strategies and actions for sustainable development in and among UNESCO Global Geoparks.

These Operational Guidelines for UNESCO Global Geoparks represent best practice. Member States through their National Geopark Committees are entitled to formulate additional, more specific guidelines on a national basis to fit a particular national context.

The UNESCO Secretariat will liaise closely with National Geopark Committees and Member State's National Commission for UNESCO or the relevant government body in charge of relations with UNESCO at all stages during the evaluation and revalidation processes of aspiring and existing UNESCO Global Geoparks.

All applications and revalidations must be accompanied by a letter of support from the National Commission for UNESCO or the relevant government body in charge of relations with UNESCO.

4.5 Regional and Global Geopark networks

From the start of the development of the concept, networking has been one of the core principles of Geoparks. Networking strongly contributes to the success of the Geoparks movement and plays a valuable role in facilitating the sharing of experience, quality management, formation of joint initiatives and projects and capacity-building. UNESCO encourages the strengthening of regional Geopark networks and the GGN. UNESCO, inspired by the work of Geopark networks, will continue to offer its support and assistance to such networks, will coordinate capacity-building for UNESCO Global Geoparks and will encourage exchange of best practice between UNESCO Global Geoparks.

保护地管理分类应用指南[①](节选)

(世界自然保护联盟,2013)

保护地是一个明确界定的地理空间,通过法律或其他有效方式获得认可、得到承诺和进行管理,以实现对自然及其所拥有的生态系统服务和文化价值的长期保护。

第Ⅰa类 严格的自然保护地

第Ⅰa类保护地是指受到严格保护的区域,设立目的是为了保护生物多样性,亦可能涵盖地质和地貌保护。这些区域中,人类活动、资源利用和影响受到严格控制,以确保其保护价值不受影响。这些保护地在科学研究和监测中发挥着不可或缺的参照价值。

首要目标

• 保护具有区域、国家或全球重要意义的生态系统、物种(单一物种或物种集群)和/或地质多样性特征:这些属性的形成与人类活动无关或者关系不大,但可能会因为轻微的人为影响而发生退化或遭到破坏。

其他目标

• 尽可能在未经人类活动干扰的状态下,保护生态系统、物种和地质多样性特征;
• 获得用于科学研究、环境监测和教育的自然环境的实例,包括作为相对原始状态的本底,拒绝所有访问;
• 对科学研究和其他许可活动进行认真规划和执行,减少干扰;
• 保护与自然相关的文化和精神价值。

第Ⅰb类 荒野保护地

第Ⅰb类保护地通常是指大部分保留原貌,或仅有微小变动的区域,保存了其自然特征和影响,没有永久性或者明显的人类居住痕迹。保护和管理的目的是为了保持其自然原貌。

首要目标

• 保护自然区域的长期生态完整性,这些区域未受人类活动的明显影响,没有现代基础设施建设,且自然力量和过程占主导地位,从而使现代人和未来世代的人能够有机会体验这些荒野区域。

其他目标

• 为人们提供进入这些区域的可能性,其强度和方式将维护该区域的野生状态,供现代人和未来世代人的体验;

---

① 节选自:Nigel Dudley主编. 朱春全,欧阳志云等译. IUCN自然保护地管理分类应用指南[M]. 北京:中国林业出版社,2016. 因英文原文为Protected Area,故编者做了小的修改,根据英文原文将原译本的"自然保护地"全部改为"保护地"。

- 确保当地社区能够维持以自然为基础的传统生活方式和习惯，居住密度和自然资源的利用方式满足保护目标的要求；
- 保护当地土著或非土著人的文化和精神价值以及非物质权益，包括他们相对隔绝的生活状态，尊重他们的圣地及祖先等；
- 当这些活动无法在荒野保护地以外的区域开展的时候，允许开展环境影响较低，干扰程度最小的教育和科研活动；

第Ⅱ类　国家公园

第Ⅱ类保护地是指大面积的自然或接近自然的区域，设立的目的是为了保护大尺度的生态过程，以及相关的物种和生态系统特性。这些保护地提供了环境和文化兼容的精神享受、科研、教育、娱乐和参观的机会。

首要目标
- 保护自然生物多样性及作为其基础的生态结构和他们所支撑的环境过程，推动环境教育和游憩。

其他目标
- 通过对保护地管理，使地理区域、生物群落、基因资源以及未受影响的自然过程的典型实例尽可能在自然状态中长久生存；
- 维持可长久生存和具有健康生态功能的本地物种的种群和种群集合的足够密度，以保护长远的生态系统完整性和弹性；
- 为生境需求范围大的物种、区域性生态过程和迁徙路线的保护作出特别贡献；
- 对用该保护地开展精神、教育、文化和游憩为目的访客进行管理，避免对自然资源造成严重的生物和生态退化；
- 考虑土著居民和当地社区的需要，包括基本生活资源的使用，前提是不影响保护地的首要保护目标；
- 通过开展旅游对当地经济发展做出贡献。

第Ⅲ类　自然历史遗迹或地貌

第Ⅲ类保护地是指为保护某一特别自然历史遗迹所特设的区域，可能是地貌、海山、海底洞穴、也可能是一般洞穴甚至是古老的小树林这样依然存活的地质形态。这些区域一般面积较小，但通常具有较高的参观价值。

首要目标
- 保护特别杰出的自然特征和相关生物多样性及栖息地。

其他目标
- 对尚未经历重大变化的陆地景观和海洋景观中的生物多样性进行保护；
- 保护具有精神或文化价值，并具有生物多样性价值的特定自然地点；
- 保护当地的传统精神和文化价值。

第Ⅳ类　栖息地／物种管理区

第Ⅳ类保护地主要用来保护特定物种或栖息地，在管理工作中也体现这种优先性。第Ⅳ类保护地需要经常性的、积极的干预，以满足特定物种的需要或维持栖息地，但这并不是该类保护地必须满足的条件。

首要目标
- 维持、保护和恢复物种种群和栖息地。

其他目标
- 通过传统管理方式，保护植被格局或其他生物特征；
- 保护栖息地的碎片化区域，作为陆地景观或海洋景观保护策略的组成部分；
- 提高公众教育和关注的物种和栖息地的价值；
- 为城市居民提供定期获得接触自然的途径。

第 V 类　陆地景观 / 海洋景观

这类保护地是指人类和自然长期相互作用而产生鲜明特点的区域，具有重要的生态、生物、文化和风景价值。这种人与自然相互作用的完整性的保护，对于保护和长久维持该区域及其相伴相生的自然保护和其他价值都至关重要。

首要目标
- 保护和维持重要的的陆地景观 / 海洋景观和相关的自然保护价值，以及由传统管理方式通过与人互动产生的其他价值。

其他目标
- 通过对陆地景观或海洋景观以及相关的传统管理方式、社团、文化和其他精神价值进行保护，维持自然与文化之间的平衡互动；
- 通过维持与文化景观相关的物种，并 / 或在受到高度利用的景观内提供保护机会，为更大范围的保护做出贡献；
- 通过开展游憩和旅游，提供休闲放松和社会经济活动的机会；
- 提供自然产品和环境服务；
- 提供一个框架以支持社区积极参与管理具有重要价值的陆地或海洋景观及其所拥有的自然和文化遗产；
- 鼓励保护农业生物多样性和水产多样性；
- 成为可持续性的典范，其经验和教训得到广泛的借鉴。

第 VI 类　自然资源可持续利用保护地

这种保护地是指为了保护生态系统和栖息地、文化价值和传统自然资源管理系统的区域。这些保护地通常面积庞大，大部分地区处于自然状态，其中一部分处于可持续自然资源管理利用之中，且该区域的主要目标是保证自然资源的低水平非工业利用与自然保护相互兼容。

首要目标
- 保护自然生态系统，实现自然资源的可持续利用，实现保护和可持续利用的双赢目标。

其他目标
- 推动生态、经济和社会层面的自然资源可持续利用；
- 为当地社区带来社会和经济收益；
- 维系当地社区代代相传的生计方式，确保这些生计可持续发展；
- 各种社会和经济的自然保护方法与其他文化方式、信仰体系和世俗看法相结合；
- 为发展和维护人与自然间更为和谐的关系做出贡献；
- 为国家、地区和当地的发展做出贡献（当地指的是依赖受保护的自然资源生存的当地社区和 / 或当地居民）；
- 促进与保护和自然资源可持续利用相关的科研和环境监测；
- 加强合作，为人们提供更多收益——特别是对居住在邻近保护地的当地社区而言；
- 推动休闲活动或者适度的小型旅游活动。

Guidelines for Applying Protected Area Management Categories[①] (excerpts)

IUCN, 2013

The new IUCN definition of a protected area:

A protected area is: "**A clearly defined geographical space, recognized, dedicated and managed, through legal or other effective means, to achieve the long-term conservation of nature with associated ecosystem services and cultural values**".

Categories:

Category I a: Strict nature reserve

Category I a are strictly protected areas set aside to protect biodiversity and also possibly geological/geomorphological features, where human visitation, use and impacts are strictly controlled and limited to ensure protection of the conservation values. Such protected areas can serve as indispensable reference areas for scientific research and monitoring.

Primary objective

• To conserve regionally, nationally or globally outstanding ecosystems, species (occurrences or aggregations) and/or geodiversity features: these attributes will have been formed mostly or entirely by non-human forces and will be degraded or destroyed when subjected to all but very light human impact.

Other objectives

• To preserve ecosystems, species and geodiversity features in a state as undisturbed by recent human activity as possible;

• To secure examples of the natural environment for scientific studies, environmental monitoring and education, including baseline areas from which all avoidable access is excluded;

• To minimize disturbance through careful planning and implementation of research and other approved activities;

• To conserve cultural and spiritual values associated with nature.

[①] Dudley, N. (Editor) (2008). *Guidelines for Applying Protected Area Management Categories*. Gland, Switzerland: IUCN. x + 86pp. WITH Stolton, S., P. Shadie and N. Dudley (2013). *IUCN WCPA Best Practice Guidance on Recognising Protected Areas and Assigning Management Categories and Governance Types*, Best Practice Protected Area Guidelines Series No. 21, Gland, Switzerland: IUCN. xxpp.

Category Ib: Wilderness area

Category Ib protected areas are usually large unmodified or slightly modified areas, retaining their natural character and influence, without permanent or significant human habitation, which are protected and managed so as to preserve their natural condition.

Primary objective

- To protect the long-term ecological integrity of natural areas that are undisturbed by significant human activity, free of modern infrastructure and where natural forces and processes predominate, so that current and future generations have the opportunity to experience such areas.

Other objectives

- To provide for public access at levels and of a type which will maintain the wilderness qualities of the area for present and future generations;
- To enable indigenous communities to maintain their traditional wilderness-based lifestyle and customs, living at low density and using the available resources in ways compatible with the conservation objectives;
- To protect the relevant cultural and spiritual values and non-material benefits to indigenous or non-indigenous populations, such as solitude, respect for sacred sites, respect for ancestors etc.;
- To allow for low-impact minimally invasive educational and scientific research activities, when such activities cannot be conducted outside the wilderness area.

Category II : National park

Category II protected areas are large natural or near natural areas set aside to protect large-scale ecological processes, along with the complement of species and ecosystems characteristic of the area, which also provide a foundation for environmentally and culturally compatible spiritual, scientific, educational, recreational and visitor opportunities.

Primary objective

- To protect natural biodiversity along with its underlying ecological structure and supporting environmental processes, and to promote education and recreation.

Other objectives:

- To manage the area in order to perpetuate, in as natural a state as possible, representative examples of physiographic regions, biotic communities, genetic resources and unimpaired natural processes;
- To maintain viable and ecologically functional populations and assemblages of native species at densities sufficient to conserve ecosystem integrity and resilience in the long term;
- To contribute in particular to conservation of wide-ranging species, regional ecological processes and migration routes;
- To manage visitor use for inspirational, educational, cultural and recreational purposes at a level which will not cause significant biological or ecological degradation to the natural resources;
- To take into account the needs of indigenous people and local communities, including subsistence resource use, in so far as these will not adversely affect the primary management objective;
- To contribute to local economies through tourism.

Category Ⅲ: Natural monument or feature

Category Ⅲ protected areas are set aside to protect a specific natural monument, which can be a landform, sea mount, submarine cavern, geological feature such as a cave or even a living feature such as an ancient grove. They are generally quite small protected areas and often have high visitor value.

Primary objective

• To protect specific outstanding natural features and their associated biodiversity and habitats.

Other objectives

• To provide biodiversity protection in landscapes or seascapes that have otherwise undergone major changes;

• To protect specific natural sites with spiritual and/or cultural values where these also have biodiversity values;

• To conserve traditional spiritual and cultural values of the site.

Category Ⅳ: Habitat/species management area

Category Ⅳ protected areas aim to protect particular species or habitats and management reflects this priority. Many category Ⅳ protected areas will need regular, active interventions to address the requirements of particular species or to maintain habitats, but this is not a requirement of the category.

Primary objective

• To maintain, conserve and restore species and habitats.

Other objectives:

• To protect vegetation patterns or other biological features through traditional management approaches;

• To protect fragments of habitats as components of landscape or seascape-scale conservation strategies;

• To develop public education and appreciation of the species and/or habitats concerned;

• To provide a means by which the urban residents may obtain regular contact with nature.

Category Ⅴ: Protected landscape/seascape

A protected area where the interaction of people and nature over time has produced an area of distinct character with significant ecological, biological, cultural and scenic value: and where safeguarding the integrity of this interaction is vital to protecting and sustaining the area and its associated nature conservation and other values.

Primary objective

• To protect and sustain important landscapes/seascapes and the associated nature conservation and other values created by interactions with humans through traditional management practices.

Other objectives

• To maintain a balanced interaction of nature and culture through the protection of landscape and/or seascape and associated traditional management approaches, societies, cultures and spiritual values;

• To contribute to broad-scale conservation by maintaining species associated with cultural landscapes and/or by providing conservation opportunities in heavily used landscapes;

• To provide opportunities for enjoyment, well-being and socio-economic activity through recreation and

tourism;
- To provide natural products and environmental services;
- To provide a framework to underpin active involvement by the community in the management of valued landscapes or seascapes and the natural and cultural heritage that they contain;
- To encourage the conservation of agrobiodiversity and aquatic biodiversity;
- To act as models of sustainability so that lessons can be learnt for wider application.

Category VI: Protected area with sustainable use of natural resources

Category VI protected areas conserve ecosystems and habitats, together with associated cultural values and traditional natural resource management systems. They are generally large, with most of the area in a natural condition, where a proportion is under sustainable natural resource management and where low-level non-industrial use of natural resources compatible with nature conservation is seen as one of the main aims of the area.

Primary objective
- To protect natural ecosystems and use natural resources sustainably, when conservation and sustainable use can be mutually beneficial.

Other objectives
- To promote sustainable use of natural resources, considering ecological, economic and social dimensions;
- To promote social and economic benefits to local communities where relevant;
- To facilitate inter-generational security for local communities' livelihoods-therefore ensuring that such livelihoods are sustainable;
- To integrate other cultural approaches, belief systems and world-views within a range of social and economic approaches to nature conservation;
- To contribute to developing and/or maintaining a more balanced relationship between humans and the rest of nature;
- To contribute to sustainable development at national, regional and local level (in the last case mainly to local communities and/or indigenous peoples depending on the protected natural resources);
- To facilitate scientific research and environmental monitoring, mainly related to the conservation and sustainable use of natural resources;
- To collaborate in the delivery of benefits to people, mostly local communities, living in or near to the designated protected area;
- To facilitate recreation and appropriate small-scale tourism.

无形文化遗产

保护非物质文化遗产公约[①]

（联合国教科文组织第三十二届大会2003年10月17日在巴黎通过）

联合国教科文组织（以下简称教科文组织）大会于2003年9月29日至10月17日在巴黎举行的第32届会议，

参照现有的国际人权文书，尤其是1948年的《世界人权宣言》以及1966年的《经济、社会及文化权利国际公约》和《公民权利和政治权利国际公约》，

考虑到1989年的《保护民间创作建议书》、2001年的《教科文组织世界文化多样性宣言》和2002年第三次文化部长圆桌会议通过的《伊斯坦布尔宣言》强调非物质文化遗产的重要性，它是文化多样性的熔炉，又是可持续发展的保证，

考虑到非物质文化遗产与物质文化遗产和自然遗产之间的内在相互依存关系，承认全球化和社会转型进程在为各群体之间开展新的对话创造条件的同时，也与不容忍现象一样，使非物质文化遗产面临损坏、消失和破坏的严重威胁，在缺乏保护资源的情况下，这种威胁尤为严重，

意识到保护人类非物质文化遗产是普遍的意愿和共同关心的事项，

承认各社区，尤其是原住民、各群体，有时是个人，在非物质文化遗产的生产、保护、延续和再创造方面发挥着重要作用，从而为丰富文化多样性和人类的创造性做出贡献，

注意到教科文组织在制定保护文化遗产的准则性文件，尤其是1972年的《保护世界文化和自然遗产公约》方面所做的具有深远意义的工作，

还注意到迄今尚无有约束力的保护非物质文化遗产的多边文件，

考虑到国际上现有的关于文化遗产和自然遗产的协定、建议书和决议需要有非物质文化遗产方面的新规定有效地予以充实和补充，

考虑到必须提高人们，尤其是年轻一代对非物质文化遗产及其保护的重要意义的认识，

考虑到国际社会应当本着互助合作的精神与本公约缔约国一起为保护此类遗产做出贡献，

忆及教科文组织有关非物质文化遗产的各项计划，尤其是"宣布人类口头遗产和非物质遗产代表作"计划，

认为非物质文化遗产是密切人与人之间的关系以及他们之间进行交流和了解的要素，它的作用是不可估量的，

于2003年10月17日通过本公约。

第一章 总则

第一条 本公约的宗旨

本公约的宗旨如下：

[①] UNESCO Document Code: MISC/2003/CLT/CH/14 REV.1。

（一）保护非物质文化遗产；
（二）尊重有关社区、群体和个人的非物质文化遗产；
（三）在地方、国家和国际一级提高对非物质文化遗产及其相互欣赏的重要性的意识；
（四）开展国际合作及提供国际援助。

第二条 定义

在本公约中：

（一）"非物质文化遗产"，指被各社区、群体，有时是个人，视为其文化遗产组成部分的各种社会实践、观念表述、表现形式、知识、技能以及相关的工具、实物、手工艺品和文化场所。这种非物质文化遗产世代相传，在各社区和群体适应周围环境以及与自然和历史的互动中，被不断地再创造，为这些社区和群体提供认同感和持续感，从而增强对文化多样性和人类创造力的尊重。在本公约中，只考虑符合现有的国际人权文件，各社区、群体和个人之间相互尊重的需要和顺应可持续发展的非物质文化遗产。

（二）按上述第（一）项的定义，"非物质文化遗产"包括以下方面：

1. 口头传统和表现形式，包括作为非物质文化遗产媒介的语言；
2. 表演艺术；
3. 社会实践、仪式、节庆活动；
4. 有关自然界和宇宙的知识和实践；
5. 传统手工艺。

（三）"保护"指确保非物质文化遗产生命力的各种措施，包括这种遗产各个方面的确认、立档、研究、保存、保护、宣传、弘扬、传承（特别是通过正规和非正规教育）和振兴。

（四）"缔约国"指受本公约约束且本公约在它们之间也通用的国家。

（五）本公约经必要修改对根据第三十三条所述之条件成为其缔约方之领土也适用。在此意义上，"缔约国"亦指这些领土。

第三条 与其他国际文书的关系

本公约的任何条款均不得解释为：

（一）改变与任一非物质文化遗产直接相关的世界遗产根据1972年《保护世界文化和自然遗产公约》所享有的地位，或降低其受保护的程度；

（二）影响缔约国从其作为缔约方的任何有关知识产权或使用生物和生态资源的国际文书所获得的权利和所负有的义务。

第二章 公约的有关机关

第四条 缔约国大会

一、兹建立缔约国大会，下称"大会"。大会为本公约的最高权力机关。

二、大会每两年举行一次常会。如若它作出此类决定或政府间保护非物质文化遗产委员会或至少三分之一的缔约国提出要求，可举行特别会议。

三、大会应通过自己的议事规则。

第五条 政府间保护非物质文化遗产委员会

一、兹在教科文组织内设立政府间保护非物质文化遗产委员会，下称"委员会"。在本公约依照第三十四条的规定生效之后，委员会由参加大会之缔约国选出的18个缔约国的代表组成。

二、在本公约缔约国的数目达到50个之后，委员会委员国的数目将增至24个。

第六条　委员会委员国的选举和任期

一、委员会委员国的选举应符合公平的地理分配和轮换原则。

二、委员会委员国由本公约缔约国大会选出，任期四年。

三、但第一次选举当选的半数委员会委员国的任期为两年。这些国家在第一次选举后抽签指定。

四、大会每两年对半数委员会委员国进行换届。

五、大会还应选出填补空缺席位所需的委员会委员国。

六、委员会委员国不得连选连任两届。

七、委员会委员国应选派在非物质文化遗产各领域有造诣的人士为其代表。

第七条　委员会的职能

在不妨碍本公约赋予委员会的其他职权的情况下，其职能如下：

（一）宣传公约的目标，鼓励并监督其实施情况；

（二）就好的做法和保护非物质文化遗产的措施提出建议；

（三）按照第二十五条的规定，拟订利用基金资金的计划并提交大会批准；

（四）按照第二十五条的规定，努力寻求增加其资金的方式方法，并为此采取必要的措施；

（五）拟订实施公约的业务指南并提交大会批准；

（六）根据第二十九条的规定，审议缔约国的报告并将报告综述提交大会；

（七）根据委员会制定的、大会批准的客观遴选标准，审议缔约国提出的申请并就以下事项作出决定：

　　1. 列入第十六条、第十七条和第十八条述及的名录和提名；

　　2. 按照第二十二条的规定提供国际援助。

第八条　委员会的工作方法

一、委员会对大会负责。它向大会报告自己的所有活动和决定。

二、委员会以其委员的三分之二多数通过自己的议事规则。

三、委员会可设立其认为执行任务所需的临时特设咨询机构。

四、委员会可邀请在非物质文化遗产各领域确有专长的任何公营或私营机构以及任何自然人参加会议，就任何具体的问题向其请教。

第九条　咨询组织的认证

一、委员会应建议大会认证在非物质文化遗产领域确有专长的非政府组织具有向委员会提供咨询意见的能力。

二、委员会还应向大会就此认证的标准和方式提出建议。

第十条　秘书处

一、委员会由教科文组织秘书处协助。

二、秘书处起草大会和委员会文件及其会议的议程草案和确保其决定的执行。

第三章　在国家一级保护非物质文化遗产

第十一条　缔约国的作用

各缔约国应该：

（一）采取必要措施确保其领土上的非物质文化遗产受到保护；

（二）在第二条第（三）项提及的保护措施内，由各社区、群体和有关非政府组织参与，确认和确定其领土上的各种非物质文化遗产。

第十二条　清单

一、为了使其领土上的非物质文化遗产得到确认以便加以保护，各缔约国应根据自己的国情拟订一份或数份关于这类遗产的清单，并应定期加以更新。

二、各缔约国在按第二十九条的规定定期向委员会提交报告时，应提供有关这些清单情况。

第十三条　其他保护措施

为了确保其领土上的非物质文化遗产得到保护、弘扬和展示，各缔约国应努力做到：

（一）制定一项总的政策，使非物质文化遗产在社会中发挥应有的作用，并将这种遗产的保护纳入规划工作；

（二）指定或建立一个或数个主管保护其领土上的非物质文化遗产的机构；

（三）鼓励开展有效保护非物质文化遗产，特别是濒危非物质文化遗产的科学、技术和艺术研究以及方法研究；

（四）采取适当的法律、技术、行政和财政措施，以便：

　1. 促进建立或加强培训管理非物质文化遗产的机构以及通过为这种遗产提供活动和表现的场所和空间，促进这种遗产的传承；

　2. 确保对非物质文化遗产的享用，同时对享用这种遗产的特殊方面的习俗做法予以尊重；

　3. 建立非物质文化遗产文献机构并创造条件促进对它的利用。

第十四条　教育、宣传和能力培养

各缔约国应竭力采取种种必要的手段，以便：

（一）使非物质文化遗产在社会中得到确认、尊重和弘扬，主要通过：

　1. 向公众，尤其是向青年进行宣传和传播信息的教育计划；

　2. 有关社区和群体的具体的教育和培训计划；

　3. 保护非物质文化遗产，尤其是管理和科研方面的能力培养活动；

　4. 非正规的知识传播手段。

（二）不断向公众宣传对这种遗产造成的威胁以及根据本公约所开展的活动；

（三）促进保护表现非物质文化遗产所需的自然场所和纪念地点的教育。

第十五条　社区、群体和个人的参与

缔约国在开展保护非物质文化遗产活动时，应努力确保创造、延续和传承这种遗产的社区、群体，有时是个人的最大限度的参与，并吸收他们积极地参与有关的管理。

第四章　在国际一级保护非物质文化遗产

第十六条　人类非物质文化遗产代表作名录

一、为了扩大非物质文化遗产的影响，提高对其重要意义的认识和从尊重文化多样性的角度促进对话，委员会应该根据有关缔约国的提名编辑、更新和公布人类非物质文化遗产代表作名录。

二、委员会拟订有关编辑、更新和公布此代表作名录的标准并提交大会批准。

第十七条　急需保护的非物质文化遗产名录

一、为了采取适当的保护措施，委员会编辑、更新和公布急需保护的非物质文化遗产名录，并根据有关缔约国的要求将此类遗产列入该名录。

二、委员会拟订有关编辑、更新和公布此名录的标准并提交大会批准。

三、委员会在极其紧急的情况（其具体标准由大会根据委员会的建议加以批准）下，可与有关缔约国协商将有关的遗产列入第一款所提之名录。

第十八条　保护非物质文化遗产的计划、项目和活动

一、在缔约国提名的基础上，委员会根据其制定的、大会批准的标准，兼顾发展中国家的特殊需要，

定期遴选并宣传其认为最能体现本公约原则和目标的国家、分地区或地区保护非物质文化遗产的计划、项目和活动。

二、为此，委员会接受、审议和批准缔约国提交的关于要求国际援助拟订此类提名的申请。

三、委员会按照它确定的方式，配合这些计划、项目和活动的实施，随时推广有关经验。

第五章　国际合作与援助

第十九条　合作

一、在本公约中，国际合作主要是交流信息和经验，采取共同的行动，以及建立援助缔约国保护非物质文化遗产工作的机制。

二、在不违背国家法律规定及其习惯法和习俗的情况下，缔约国承认保护非物质文化遗产符合人类的整体利益，保证为此目的在双边、分地区、地区和国际各级开展合作。

第二十条　国际援助的目的

可为如下目的提供国际援助：

（一）保护列入《急需保护的非物质文化遗产名录》的遗产；

（二）按照第十一条和第十二条的精神编制清单；

（三）支持在国家、分地区和地区开展的保护非物质文化遗产的计划、项目和活动；

（四）委员会认为必要的其他一切目的。

第二十一条　国际援助的形式

第七条的业务指南和第二十四条所指的协定对委员会向缔约国提供援助作了规定，可采取的形式如下：

（一）对保护这种遗产的各个方面进行研究；

（二）提供专家和专业人员；

（三）培训各类所需人员；

（四）制订准则性措施或其他措施；

（五）基础设施的建立和营运；

（六）提供设备和技能；

（七）其他财政和技术援助形式，包括在必要时提供低息贷款和捐助。

第二十二条　国际援助的条件

一、委员会确定审议国际援助申请的程序和具体规定申请的内容，包括打算采取的措施、必需开展的工作及预计的费用。

二、如遇紧急情况，委员会应对有关援助申请优先审议。

三、委员会在作出决定之前，应进行其认为必要的研究和咨询。

第二十三条　国际援助的申请

一、各缔约国可向委员会递交国际援助的申请，保护在其领土上的非物质文化遗产。

二、此类申请亦可由两个或数个缔约国共同提出。

三、申请应包含第二十二条第一款规定的所有资料和所有必要的文件。

第二十四条　受援缔约国的任务

一、根据本公约的规定，国际援助应依据受援缔约国与委员会之间签署的协定来提供。

二、受援缔约国通常应在自己力所能及的范围内分担国际所援助的保护措施的费用。

三、受援缔约国应向委员会报告关于使用所提供的保护非物质文化遗产援助的情况。

第六章 非物质文化遗产基金

第二十五条 基金的性质和资金来源

一、兹建立一项"保护非物质文化遗产基金",下称"基金"。

二、根据教科文组织《财务条例》的规定,此项基金为信托基金。

三、基金的资金来源包括:

(一)缔约国的纳款;

(二)教科文组织大会为此所拨的资金;

(三)以下各方可能提供的捐款、赠款或遗赠:

    1. 其他国家;

    2. 联合国系统各组织和各署(特别是联合国开发计划署)以及其他国际组织;

    3. 公营或私营机构和个人。

(四)基金的资金所得的利息;

(五)为本基金募集的资金和开展活动之所得;

(六)委员会制定的基金条例所许可的所有其他资金。

四、委员会对资金的使用视大会的方针来决定。

五、委员会可接受用于某些项目的一般或特定目的的捐款及其他形式的援助,只要这些项目已获委员会的批准。

六、对基金的捐款不得附带任何与本公约所追求之目标不相符的政治、经济或其他条件。

第二十六条 缔约国对基金的纳款

一、在不妨碍任何自愿补充捐款的情况下,本公约缔约国至少每两年向基金纳一次款,其金额由大会根据适用于所有国家的统一的纳款额百分比加以确定。缔约国大会关于此问题的决定由出席会议并参加表决,但未作本条第二款中所述声明的缔约国的多数通过。在任何情况下,此纳款都不得超过缔约国对教科文组织正常预算纳款的百分之一。

二、但是,本公约第三十二条或第三十三条中所指的任何国家均可在交存批准书、接受书、核准书或加入书时声明不受本条第一款规定的约束。

三、已作本条第二款所述声明的本公约缔约国应努力通知联合国教科文组织总干事收回所作声明。但是,收回声明之举不得影响该国在紧接着的下一届大会开幕之日前应缴的纳款。

四、为使委员会能够有效地规划其工作,已作本条第二款所述声明的本公约缔约国至少应每两年定期纳一次款,纳款额应尽可能接近它们按本条第一款规定应交的数额。

五、凡拖欠当年和前一日历年的义务纳款或自愿捐款的本公约缔约国不能当选为委员会委员,但此项规定不适用于第一次选举。已当选为委员会委员的缔约国的任期应在本公约第六条规定的选举之时终止。

第二十七条 基金的自愿补充捐款

除了第二十六条所规定的纳款,希望提供自愿捐款的缔约国应及时通知委员会以使其能对相应的活动作出规划。

第二十八条 国际筹资运动

缔约国应尽力支持在教科文组织领导下为该基金发起的国际筹资运动。

第七章 报告

第二十九条 缔约国的报告

缔约国应按照委员会确定的方式和周期向其报告它们为实施本公约而通过的法律、规章条例或采取的其他措施的情况。

第三十条 委员会的报告

一、委员会应在其开展的活动和第二十九条提及的缔约国报告的基础上，向每届大会提交报告。

二、该报告应提交教科文组织大会。

第八章 过渡条款

第三十一条 与宣布人类口头和非物质遗产代表作的关系

一、委员会应把在本公约生效前宣布为"人类口头和非物质遗产代表作"的遗产纳入人类非物质文化遗产代表作名录。

二、把这些遗产纳入人类非物质文化遗产代表作名录绝不是预设按第十六条第二款将确定的今后列入遗产的标准。

三、在本公约生效后，将不再宣布其他任何人类口头和非物质遗产代表作。

第九章 最后条款

第三十二条 批准、接受或核准

一、本公约须由教科文组织会员国根据各自的宪法程序予以批准、接受或核准。

二、批准书、接受书或核准书应交存教科文组织总干事。

第三十三条 加入

一、所有非教科文组织会员国的国家，经本组织大会邀请，均可加入本公约。

二、没有完全独立，但根据联合国大会第1514（XV）号决议被联合国承认为充分享有内部自治，并且有权处理本公约范围内的事宜，包括有权就这些事宜签署协议的地区也可加入本公约。

三、加入书应交存教科文组织总干事。

第三十四条 生效

本公约在第三十份批准书、接受书、核准书或加入书交存之日起的三个月后生效，但只涉及在该日或该日之前交存批准书、接受书、核准书或加入书的国家。对其他缔约国来说，本公约则在这些国家的批准书、接受书、核准书或加入书交存之日起的三个月之后生效。

第三十五条 联邦制或非统一立宪制

对实行联邦制或非统一立宪制的缔约国实行下述规定：

（一）在联邦或中央立法机构的法律管辖下实施本公约各项条款的国家的联邦或中央政府的义务与非联邦国家的缔约国的义务相同；

（二）在构成联邦，但按照联邦立宪制无须采取立法手段的各个州、成员国、省或行政区的法律管辖下实施本公约的各项条款时，联邦政府应将这些条款连同其建议一并通知各个州、成员国、省或行政区的主管当局。

第三十六条 退出

一、各缔约国均可宣布退出本公约。

二、退约应以书面退约书的形式通知教科文组织总干事。

三、退约在接到退约书十二个月之后生效。在退约生效日之前不得影响退约国承担的财政义务。

第三十七条　保管人的职责

教科文组织总干事作为本公约的保管人,应将第三十二条和第三十三条规定交存的所有批准书、接受书、核准书或加入书和第三十六条规定的退约书的情况通告本组织各会员国、第三十三条提到的非本组织会员国的国家和联合国。

第三十八条　修订

一、任何缔约国均可书面通知总干事,对本公约提出修订建议。总干事应将此通知转发给所有缔约国。如在通知发出之日起六个月之内,至少有一半的缔约国回复赞成此要求,总干事应将此建议提交下一届大会讨论,决定是否通过。

二、对本公约的修订须经出席并参加表决的缔约国三分之二多数票通过。

三、对本公约的修订一旦通过,应提交缔约国批准、接受、核准或加入。

四、对于那些已批准、接受、核准或加入修订的缔约国来说,本公约的修订在三分之二的缔约国交存本条第三款所提及的文书之日起三个月之后生效。此后,对任何批准、接受、核准或加入修订的缔约国来说,在其交存批准书、接受书、核准书或加入书之日起三个月之后,本公约的修订即生效。

五、第三款和第四款所确定的程序对有关委员会委员国数目的第五条的修订不适用。此类修订一经通过即生效。

六、在修订依照本条第四款的规定生效之后成为本公约缔约国的国家如无表示异议,应:

(一)被视为修订的本公约的缔约方;

(二)但在与不受这些修订约束的任何缔约国的关系中,仍被视为未经修订之公约的缔约方。

第三十九条　有效文本

本公约用英文、阿拉伯文、中文、西班牙文、法文和俄文拟定,六种文本具有同等效力。

第四十条　登记

根据《联合国宪章》第一百零二条的规定,本公约应按教科文组织总干事的要求交联合国秘书处登记。

Convention for the Safeguarding of the Intangible Cultural Heritage[①]

Adopted by the UNESCO General Conference at its 32nd Session, Paris, 17 October 2003

The General Conference of the United Nations Educational, Scientific and Cultural Organization hereinafter referred to as UNESCO, meeting in Paris, from 29 September to 17 October 2003, at its 32nd session,

Referring to existing international human rights instruments, in particular to the Universal Declaration on Human Rights of 1948, the International Covenant on Economic, Social and Cultural Rights of 1966, and the International Covenant on Civil and Political Rights of 1966,

Considering the importance of the intangible cultural heritage as a mainspring of cultural diversity and a guarantee of sustainable development, as underscored in the UNESCO Recommendation on the Safeguarding of Traditional Culture and Folklore of 1989, in the UNESCO Universal Declaration on Cultural Diversity of 2001, and in the Istanbul Declaration of 2002 adopted by the Third Round Table of Ministers of Culture,

Considering the deep-seated interdependence between the intangible cultural heritage and the tangible cultural and natural heritage,

Recognizing that the processes of globalization and social transformation, alongside the conditions they create for renewed dialogue among communities, also give rise, as does the phenomenon of intolerance, to grave threats of deterioration, disappearance and destruction of the intangible cultural heritage, in particular owing to a lack of resources for safeguarding such heritage,

Being aware of the universal will and the common concern to safeguard the intangible cultural heritage of humanity,

Recognizing that communities, in particular indigenous communities, groups and, in some cases, individuals, play an important role in the production, safeguarding, maintenance and recreation of the intangible cultural heritage, thus helping to enrich cultural diversity and human creativity,

Noting the far-reaching impact of the activities of UNESCO in establishing normative instruments for the protection of the cultural heritage, in particular the Convention for the Protection of the World Cultural and Natural Heritage of 1972,

Noting further that no binding multilateral instrument as yet exists for the safeguarding of the intangible cultural heritage,

Considering that existing international agreements, recommendations and resolutions concerning the cultural and natural heritage need to be effectively enriched and supplemented by means of new provisions relating to the

---

① UNESCO Document Code: MISC/2003/CLT/CH/14.

intangible cultural heritage,

Considering the need to build greater awareness, especially among the younger generations, of the importance of the intangible cultural heritage and of its safeguarding,

Considering that the international community should contribute, together with the States Parties to this Convention, to the safeguarding of such heritage in a spirit of cooperation and mutual assistance,

Recalling UNESCO's programmes relating to the intangible cultural heritage, in particular the Proclamation of Masterpieces of the Oral and Intangible Heritage of Humanity,

Considering the invaluable role of the intangible cultural heritage as a factor in bringing human beings closer together and ensuring exchange and understanding among them,

Adopts this Convention on this seventeenth day of October 2003.

I. General provisions

Article 1　Purposes of the Convention

The purposes of this Convention are:

(a) to safeguard the intangible cultural heritage;

(b) to ensure respect for the intangible cultural heritage of the communities, groups and individuals concerned;

(c) to raise awareness at the local, national and international levels of the importance of the intangible cultural heritage, and of ensuring mutual appreciation thereof;

(d) to provide for international cooperation and assistance.

Article 2　Definitions

For the purposes of this Convention,

1. The "intangible cultural heritage" means the practices, representations, expressions, knowledge, skills – as well as the instruments, objects, artefacts and cultural spaces associated therewith – that communities, groups and, in some cases, individuals recognize as part of their cultural heritage. This intangible cultural heritage, transmitted from generation to generation, is constantly recreated by communities and groups in response to their environment, their interaction with nature and their history, and provides them with a sense of identity and continuity, thus promoting respect for cultural diversity and human creativity. For the purposes of this Convention, consideration will be given solely to such intangible cultural heritage as is compatible with existing international human rights instruments, as well as with the requirements of mutual respect among communities, groups and individuals, and of sustainable development.

2. The "intangible cultural heritage", as defined in paragraph 1 above, is manifested inter alia in the following domains:

(a) oral traditions and expressions, including language as a vehicle of the intangible cultural heritage;

(b) performing arts;

(c) social practices, rituals and festive events;

(d) knowledge and practices concerning nature and the universe;

(e) traditional craftsmanship.

3. "Safeguarding" means measures aimed at ensuring the viability of the intangible cultural heritage, including the identification, documentation, research, preservation, protection, promotion, enhancement,

transmission, particularly through formal and non-formal education, as well as the revitalization of the various aspects of such heritage.

4. "States Parties" means States which are bound by this Convention and among which this Convention is in force.

5. This Convention applies mutatis mutandis to the territories referred to in Article 33 which become Parties to this Convention in accordance with the conditions set out in that Article. To that extent the expression "States Parties" also refers to such territories.

Article 3　Relationship to other international instruments

Nothing in this Convention may be interpreted as:

(a) altering the status or diminishing the level of protection under the 1972 Convention concerning the Protection of the World Cultural and Natural Heritage of World Heritage properties with which an item of the intangible cultural heritage is directly associated; or

(b) affecting the rights and obligations of States Parties deriving from any international instrument relating to intellectual property rights or to the use of biological and ecological resources to which they are parties.

II. Organs of the Convention

Article 4　General Assembly of the States Parties

1. A General Assembly of the States Parties is hereby established, hereinafter referred to as "the General Assembly". The General Assembly is the sovereign body of this Convention.

2. The General Assembly shall meet in ordinary session every two years. It may meet in extraordinary session if it so decides or at the request either of the Intergovernmental Committee for the Safeguarding of the Intangible Cultural Heritage or of at least one-third of the States Parties.

3. The General Assembly shall adopt its own Rules of Procedure.

Article 5　Intergovernmental Committee for the Safeguarding of the Intangible Cultural Heritage

1. An Intergovernmental Committee for the Safeguarding of the Intangible Cultural Heritage, hereinafter referred to as "the Committee", is hereby established within UNESCO. It shall be composed of representatives of 18 States Parties, elected by the States Parties meeting in General Assembly, once this Convention enters into force in accordance with Article 34.

2. The number of States Members of the Committee shall be increased to 24 once the number of the States Parties to the Convention reaches 50.

Article 6　Election and terms of office of States Members of the Committee

1. The election of States Members of the Committee shall obey the principles of equitable geographical representation and rotation.

2. States Members of the Committee shall be elected for a term of four years by States Parties to the Convention meeting in General Assembly.

3. However, the term of office of half of the States Members of the Committee elected at the first election is limited to two years. These States shall be chosen by lot at the first election.

4. Every two years, the General Assembly shall renew half of the States Members of the Committee.

5. It shall also elect as many States Members of the Committee as required to fill vacancies.

6. A State Member of the Committee may not be elected for two consecutive terms.

7. States Members of the Committee shall choose as their representative persons who are qualified in the various fields of the intangible cultural heritage.

Article 7 Functions of the Committee

Without prejudice to other prerogatives granted to it by this Convention, the functions of the Committee shall be to:

(a) promote the objectives of the Convention, and to encourage and monitor the implementation thereof;

(b) provide guidance on best practices and make recommendations on measures for the safeguarding of the intangible cultural heritage;

(c) prepare and submit to the General Assembly for approval a draft plan for the use of the resources of the Fund, in accordance with Article 25;

(d) seek means of increasing its resources, and to take the necessary measures to this end, in accordance with Article 25;

(e) prepare and submit to the General Assembly for approval operational directives for the implementation of this Convention;

(f) examine, in accordance with Article 29, the reports submitted by States Parties, and to summarize them for the General Assembly;

(g) examine requests submitted by States Parties, and to decide thereon, in accordance with objective selection criteria to be established by the Committee and approved by the General Assembly for:

(i) inscription on the lists and proposals mentioned under Articles 16, 17 and 18;

(ii) the granting of international assistance in accordance with Article 22.

Article 8 Working methods of the Committee

1. The Committee shall be answerable to the General Assembly. It shall report to it on all its activities and decisions.

2. The Committee shall adopt its own Rules of Procedure by a two-thirds majority of its Members.

3. The Committee may establish, on a temporary basis, whatever ad hoc consultative bodies it deems necessary to carry out its task.

4. The Committee may invite to its meetings any public or private bodies, as well as private persons, with recognized competence in the various fields of the intangible cultural heritage, in order to consult them on specific matters.

Article 9 Accreditation of advisory organizations

1. The Committee shall propose to the General Assembly the accreditation of non-governmental organizations with recognized competence in the field of the intangible cultural heritage to act in an advisory capacity to the Committee.

2. The Committee shall also propose to the General Assembly the criteria for and modalities of such accreditation.

Article 10 The Secretariat

1. The Committee shall be assisted by the UNESCO Secretariat.

2. The Secretariat shall prepare the documentation of the General Assembly and of the Committee, as well as the draft agenda of their meetings, and shall ensure the implementation of their decisions.

III. Safeguarding of the intangible cultural heritage at the national level

Article 11 Role of States Parties

Each State Party shall:

(a) take the necessary measures to ensure the safeguarding of the intangible cultural heritage present in its territory;

(b) among the safeguarding measures referred to in Article 2, paragraph 3, identify and define the various elements of the intangible cultural heritage present in its territory, with the participation of communities, groups and relevant non-governmental organizations.

Article 12 Inventories

1. To ensure identification with a view to safeguarding, each State Party shall draw up, in a manner geared to its own situation, one or more inventories of the intangible cultural heritage present in its territory. These inventories shall be regularly updated.

2. When each State Party periodically submits its report to the Committee, in accordance with Article 29, it shall provide relevant information on such inventories.

Article 13 Other measures for safeguarding

To ensure the safeguarding, development and promotion of the intangible cultural heritage present in its territory, each State Party shall endeavour to:

(a) adopt a general policy aimed at promoting the function of the intangible cultural heritage in society, and at integrating the safeguarding of such heritage into planning programmes;

(b) designate or establish one or more competent bodies for the safeguarding of the intangible cultural heritage present in its territory;

(c) foster scientific, technical and artistic studies, as well as research methodologies, with a view to effective safeguarding of the intangible cultural heritage, in particular the intangible cultural heritage in danger;

(d) adopt appropriate legal, technical, administrative and financial measures aimed at:

(i) fostering the creation or strengthening of institutions for training in the management of the intangible cultural heritage and the transmission of such heritage through forums and spaces intended for the performance or expression thereof;

(ii) ensuring access to the intangible cultural heritage while respecting customary practices governing access to specific aspects of such heritage;

(iii) establishing documentation institutions for the intangible cultural heritage and facilitating access to them.

Article 14 Education, awareness-raising and capacity-building

Each State Party shall endeavour, by all appropriate means, to:

(a) ensure recognition of, respect for, and enhancement of the intangible cultural heritage in society, in particular through:

(i) educational, awareness-raising and information programmes, aimed at the general public, in particular young people;

(ii) specific educational and training programmes within the communities and groups concerned;

(iii) capacity-building activities for the safeguarding of the intangible cultural heritage, in particular management and scientific research; and

  (iv) non-formal means of transmitting knowledge;

(b) keep the public informed of the dangers threatening such heritage, and of the activities carried out in pursuance of this Convention;

(c) promote education for the protection of natural spaces and places of memory whose existence is necessary for expressing the intangible cultural heritage.

Article 15   Participation of communities, groups and individuals

Within the framework of its safeguarding activities of the intangible cultural heritage, each State Party shall endeavour to ensure the widest possible participation of communities, groups and, where appropriate, individuals that create, maintain and transmit such heritage, and to involve them actively in its management.

Ⅳ. Safeguarding of the intangible cultural heritage at the international level

Article 16   Representative List of the Intangible Cultural Heritage of Humanity

1. In order to ensure better visibility of the intangible cultural heritage and awareness of its significance, and to encourage dialogue which respects cultural diversity, the Committee, upon the proposal of the States Parties concerned, shall establish, keep up to date and publish a Representative List of the Intangible Cultural Heritage of Humanity.

2. The Committee shall draw up and submit to the General Assembly for approval the criteria for the establishment, updating and publication of this Representative List.

Article 17   List of Intangible Cultural Heritage in Need of Urgent Safeguarding

1. With a view to taking appropriate safeguarding measures, the Committee shall establish, keep up to date and publish a List of Intangible Cultural Heritage in Need of Urgent Safeguarding, and shall inscribe such heritage on the List at the request of the State Party concerned.

2. The Committee shall draw up and submit to the General Assembly for approval the criteria for the establishment, updating and publication of this List.

3. In cases of extreme urgency–the objective criteria of which shall be approved by the General Assembly upon the proposal of the Committee–the Committee may inscribe an item of the heritage concerned on the List mentioned in paragraph 1, in consultation with the State Party concerned.

Article 18   Programmes, projects and activities for the safeguarding of the intangible cultural heritage

1. On the basis of proposals submitted by States Parties, and in accordance with criteria to be defined by the Committee and approved by the General Assembly, the Committee shall periodically select and promote national, sub regional and regional programmes, projects and activities for the safeguarding of the heritage which it considers best reflect the principles and objectives of this Convention, taking into account the special needs of developing countries.

2. To this end, it shall receive, examine and approve requests for international assistance from States Parties for the preparation of such proposals.

3. The Committee shall accompany the implementation of such projects, programmes and activities by disseminating best practices using means to be determined by it.

V. International cooperation and assistance

Article 19 Cooperation

1. For the purposes of this Convention, international cooperation includes, inter alia, the exchange of information and experience, joint initiatives, and the establishment of a mechanism of assistance to States Parties in their efforts to safeguard the intangible cultural heritage.

2. Without prejudice to the provisions of their national legislation and customary law and practices, the States Parties recognize that the safeguarding of intangible cultural heritage is of general interest to humanity, and to that end undertake to cooperate at the bilateral, sub regional, regional and international levels.

Article 20 Purposes of international assistance

International assistance may be granted for the following purposes:

(a) the safeguarding of the heritage inscribed on the List of Intangible Cultural Heritage in Need of Urgent Safeguarding;

(b) the preparation of inventories in the sense of Articles 11 and 12;

(c) support for programmes, projects and activities carried out at the national, sub regional and regional levels aimed at the safeguarding of the intangible cultural heritage;

(d) any other purpose the Committee may deem necessary.

Article 21 Forms of international assistance

The assistance granted by the Committee to a State Party shall be governed by the operational directives foreseen in Article 7 and by the agreement referred to in Article 24, and may take the following forms:

(a) studies concerning various aspects of safeguarding;

(b) the provision of experts and practitioners;

(c) the training of all necessary staff;

(d) the elaboration of standard-setting and other measures;

(e) the creation and operation of infrastructures;

(f) the supply of equipment and know-how;

(g) other forms of financial and technical assistance, including, where appropriate, the granting of low-interest loans and donations.

Article 22 Conditions governing international assistance

1. The Committee shall establish the procedure for examining requests for international assistance and shall specify what information shall be included in the requests, such as the measures envisaged and the interventions required, together with an assessment of their cost.

2. In emergencies, requests for assistance shall be examined by the Committee as a matter of priority.

3. In order to reach a decision, the Committee shall undertake such studies and consultations as it deems necessary.

Article 23 Requests for international assistance

1. Each State Party may submit to the Committee a request for international assistance for the safeguarding of the intangible cultural heritage present in its territory.

2. Such a request may also be jointly submitted by two or more States Parties.

3. The request shall include the information stipulated in Article 22, paragraph 1, together with the necessary

documentation.

Article 24　Role of beneficiary States Parties

1. In conformity with the provisions of this Convention, the international assistance granted shall be regulated by means of an agreement between the beneficiary State Party and the Committee.

2. As a general rule, the beneficiary State Party shall, within the limits of its resources, share the cost of the safeguarding measures for which international assistance is provided.

3. The beneficiary State Party shall submit to the Committee a report on the use made of the assistance provided for the safeguarding of the intangible cultural heritage.

VI. Intangible Cultural Heritage Fund

Article 25　Nature and resources of the Fund

1. A "Fund for the Safeguarding of the Intangible Cultural Heritage", hereinafter referred to as "the Fund", is hereby established.

2. The Fund shall consist of funds-in-trust established in accordance with the Financial Regulations of UNESCO.

3. The resources of the Fund shall consist of:

(a) contributions made by States Parties;

(b) funds appropriated for this purpose by the General Conference of UNESCO;

(c) contributions, gifts or bequests which may be made by:

   (i) other States;

   (ii) organizations and programmes of the United Nations system, particularly the United Nations Development Programme, as well as other international organizations;

   (iii) public or private bodies or individuals;

(d) any interest due on the resources of the Fund;

(e) funds raised through collections, and receipts from events organized for the benefit of the Fund;

(f) any other resources authorized by the Fund's regulations, to be drawn up by the Committee.

4. The use of resources by the Committee shall be decided on the basis of guidelines laid down by the General Assembly.

5. The Committee may accept contributions and other forms of assistance for general and specific purposes relating to specific projects, provided that those projects have been approved by the Committee.

6. No political, economic or other conditions which are incompatible with the objectives of this Convention may be attached to contributions made to the Fund.

Article 26　Contributions of States Parties to the Fund

1. Without prejudice to any supplementary voluntary contribution, the States Parties to this Convention undertake to pay into the Fund, at least every two years, a contribution, the amount of which, in the form of a uniform percentage applicable to all States, shall be determined by the General Assembly. This decision of the General Assembly shall be taken by a majority of the States Parties present and voting which have not made the declaration referred to in paragraph 2 of this Article. In no case shall the contribution of the State Party exceed 1% of its contribution to the regular budget of UNESCO.

2. However, each State referred to in Article 32 or in Article 33 of this Convention may declare, at the time

of the deposit of its instruments of ratification, acceptance, approval or accession, that it shall not be bound by the provisions of paragraph 1 of this Article.

3. A State Party to this Convention which has made the declaration referred to in paragraph 2 of this Article shall endeavour to withdraw the said declaration by notifying the Director-General of UNESCO. However, the withdrawal of the declaration shall not take effect in regard to the contribution due by the State until the date on which the subsequent session of the General Assembly opens.

4. In order to enable the Committee to plan its operations effectively, the contributions of States Parties to this Convention which have made the declaration referred to in paragraph 2 of this Article shall be paid on a regular basis, at least every two years, and should be as close as possible to the contributions they would have owed if they had been bound by the provisions of paragraph 1 of this Article.

5. Any State Party to this Convention which is in arrears with the payment of its compulsory or voluntary contribution for the current year and the calendar year immediately preceding it shall not be eligible as a Member of the Committee; this provision shall not apply to the first election. The term of office of any such State which is already a Member of the Committee shall come to an end at the time of the elections provided for in Article 6 of this Convention.

Article 27　Voluntary supplementary contributions to the Fund

States Parties wishing to provide voluntary contributions in addition to those foreseen under Article 26 shall inform the Committee, as soon as possible, so as to enable it to plan its operations accordingly.

Article 28　International fund-raising campaigns

The States Parties shall, insofar as is possible, lend their support to international fund-raising campaigns organized for the benefit of the Fund under the auspices of UNESCO.

Ⅶ. Reports

Article 29　Reports by the States Parties

The States Parties shall submit to the Committee, observing the forms and periodicity to be defined by the Committee, reports on the legislative, regulatory and other measures taken for the implementation of this Convention.

Article 30　Reports by the Committee

1. On the basis of its activities and the reports by States Parties referred to in Article 29, the Committee shall submit a report to the General Assembly at each of its sessions.

2. The report shall be brought to the attention of the General Conference of UNESCO.

Ⅷ. Transitional clause

Article 31　Relationship to the Proclamation of Masterpieces of the Oral and Intangible Heritage of Humanity

1. The Committee shall incorporate in the Representative List of the Intangible Cultural Heritage of Humanity the items proclaimed "Masterpieces of the Oral and Intangible Heritage of Humanity" before the entry into force of this Convention.

2. The incorporation of these items in the Representative List of the Intangible Cultural Heritage of Humanity shall in no way prejudge the criteria for future inscriptions decided upon in accordance with Article 16, paragraph 2.

3. No further Proclamation will be made after the entry into force of this Convention.

IX. Final clauses

Article 32　Ratification, acceptance or approval

1. This Convention shall be subject to ratification, acceptance or approval by States Members of UNESCO in accordance with their respective constitutional procedures.

2. The instruments of ratification, acceptance or approval shall be deposited with the Director-General of UNESCO.

Article 33　Accession

1. This Convention shall be open to accession by all States not Members of UNESCO that are invited by the General Conference of UNESCO to accede to it.

2. This Convention shall also be open to accession by territories which enjoy full internal self-government recognized as such by the United Nations, but have not attained full independence in accordance with General Assembly resolution 1514 (XV), and which have competence over the matters governed by this Convention, including the competence to enter into treaties in respect of such matters.

3. The instrument of accession shall be deposited with the Director-General of UNESCO.

Article 34　Entry into force

This Convention shall enter into force three months after the date of the deposit of the thirtieth instrument of ratification, acceptance, approval or accession, but only with respect to those States that have deposited their respective instruments of ratification, acceptance, approval, or accession on or before that date. It shall enter into force with respect to any other State Party three months after the deposit of its instrument of ratification, acceptance, approval or accession.

Article 35　Federal or non-unitary constitutional systems

The following provisions shall apply to States Parties which have a federal or non-unitary constitutional system:

(a) with regard to the provisions of this Convention, the implementation of which comes under the legal jurisdiction of the federal or central legislative power, the obligations of the federal or central government shall be the same as for those States Parties which are not federal States;

(b) with regard to the provisions of this Convention, the implementation of which comes under the jurisdiction of individual constituent States, countries, provinces or cantons which are not obliged by the constitutional system of the federation to take legislative measures, the federal government shall inform the competent authorities of such States, countries, provinces or cantons of the said provisions, with its recommendation for their adoption.

Article 36　Denunciation

1. Each State Party may denounce this Convention.

2. The denunciation shall be notified by an instrument in writing, deposited with the Director-General of UNESCO.

3. The denunciation shall take effect twelve months after the receipt of the instrument of denunciation. It shall in no way affect the financial obligations of the denouncing State Party until the date on which the withdrawal takes effect.

Article 37　Depositary functions

The Director-General of UNESCO, as the Depositary of this Convention, shall inform the States Members of the Organization, the States not Members of the Organization referred to in Article 33, as well as the United Nations, of the deposit of all the instruments of ratification, acceptance, approval or accession provided for in Articles 32 and 33, and of the denunciations provided for in Article 36.

Article 38 Amendments

1. A State Party may, by written communication addressed to the Director-General, propose amendments to this Convention. The Director-General shall circulate such communication to all States Parties. If, within six months from the date of the circulation of the communication, not less than one half of the States Parties reply favourably to the request, the Director-General shall present such proposal to the next session of the General Assembly for discussion and possible adoption.

2. Amendments shall be adopted by a two-thirds majority of States Parties present and voting.

3. Once adopted, amendments to this Convention shall be submitted for ratification, acceptance, approval or accession to the States Parties.

4. Amendments shall enter into force, but solely with respect to the States Parties that have ratified, accepted, approved or acceded to them, three months after the deposit of the instruments referred to in paragraph 3 of this Article by two-thirds of the States Parties. Thereafter, for each State Party that ratifies, accepts, approves or accedes to an amendment, the said amendment shall enter into force three months after the date of deposit by that State Party of its instrument of ratification, acceptance, approval or accession.

5. The procedure set out in paragraphs 3 and 4 shall not apply to amendments to Article 5 concerning the number of States Members of the Committee. These amendments shall enter into force at the time they are adopted.

6. A State which becomes a Party to this Convention after the entry into force of amendments in conformity with paragraph 4 of this Article shall, failing an expression of different intention, be considered:

(a) as a Party to this Convention as so amended; and

(b) as a Party to the unamended Convention in relation to any State Party not bound by the amendments.

Article 39 Authoritative texts

This Convention has been drawn up in Arabic, Chinese, English, French, Russian and Spanish, the six texts being equally authoritative.

Article 40 Registration

In conformity with Article 102 of the Charter of the United Nations, this Convention shall be registered with the Secretariat of the United Nations at the request of the Director-General of UNESCO.

保护和促进文化表现形式多样性公约[①]

（联合国教科文组织第三十三届大会2005年10月20日在巴黎通过）

联合国教科文组织大会于2005年10月3日至21日在巴黎举行第三十三届会议，

确认文化多样性是人类的一项基本特性；

认识到文化多样性是人类的共同遗产，应当为了全人类的利益对其加以珍爱和维护；

意识到文化多样性创造了一个多姿多彩的世界，它使人类有了更多的选择，得以提高自己的能力和形成价值观，并因此成为各社区、各民族和各国可持续发展的一股主要推动力；

忆及在民主、宽容、社会公正以及各民族和各文化间相互尊重的环境中繁荣发展起来的文化多样性对于地方、国家和国际层面的和平与安全是不可或缺的；

颂扬文化多样性对充分实现《世界人权宣言》和其他公认的文书主张的人权和基本自由所具有的重要意义；

强调需要把文化作为一个战略要素纳入国家和国际发展政策，以及国际发展合作之中，同时也要考虑特别强调消除贫困的《联合国千年宣言》（2000年）；

考虑到文化在不同时间和空间具有多样形式，这种多样性体现为人类各民族和各社会文化特征和文化表现形式的独特性和多元性；

承认作为非物质和物质财富来源的传统知识的重要性，特别是原住民知识体系的重要性，其对可持续发展的积极贡献，及其得到充分保护和促进的需要；

认识到需要采取措施保护文化表现形式连同其内容的多样性，特别是当文化表现形式有可能遭到灭绝或受到严重损害时；

强调文化对社会凝聚力的重要性，尤其是对提高妇女的社会地位、发挥其社会作用所具有的潜在影响力；

意识到文化多样性通过思想的自由交流得到加强，通过文化间的不断交流和互动得到滋养；

重申思想、表达和信息自由以及媒体多样性使各种文化表现形式得以在社会中繁荣发展；

认识到文化表现形式，包括传统文化表现形式的多样性，是个人和各民族能够表达并同他人分享自己的思想和价值观的重要因素；

忆及语言多样性是文化多样性的基本要素之一，并重申教育在保护和促进文化表现形式中发挥着重要作用；

考虑到文化活力的重要性，包括对少数民族和原住民人群中的个体的重要性，这种重要的活力体现为创造、传播、销售及获取其传统文化表现形式的自由，以有益于他们自身的发展；

强调文化互动和文化创造力对滋养和革新文化表现形式所发挥的关键作用，它们也会增强那些为社会整体进步而参与文化发展的人们所发挥的作用；

[①] UNESCO Document Code: CLT.2005/CONVENTION DIVERSITE-CULT REV.2。

认识到知识产权对支持文化创造的参与者具有重要意义；

确信传递着文化特征、价值观和意义的文化活动、产品与服务具有经济和文化双重性质，故不应视为仅具商业价值；

注意到信息和传播技术飞速发展所推动的全球化进程为加强各种文化互动创造了前所未有的条件，但同时也对文化多样性构成挑战，尤其是可能在富国与穷国之间造成种种失衡；

意识到联合国教科文组织肩负的特殊使命，即确保对文化多样性的尊重以及建议签订有助于推动通过语言和图像进行自由思想交流的各种国际协定；

根据联合国教科文组织通过的有关文化多样性和行使文化权利的各种国际文书的条款，特别是2001年通过的《世界文化多样性宣言》；

于2005年10月20日通过本公约。

第一章　目标与指导原则

第1条　目标

本公约的目标是：

一、保护和促进文化表现形式的多样性；

二、以互利的方式为各种文化的繁荣发展和自由互动创造条件；

三、鼓励不同文化间的对话，以保证世界上的文化交流更广泛和均衡，促进不同文化间的相互尊重与和平文化建设；

四、加强文化间性，本着在各民族间架设桥梁的精神开展文化互动；

五、促进地方、国家和国际层面对文化表现形式多样性的尊重，并提高对其价值的认识；

六、确认文化与发展之间的联系对所有国家，特别是对发展中国家的重要性，并支持为确保承认这种联系的真正价值而在国内和国际采取行动；

七、承认文化活动、产品与服务具有传递文化特征、价值观和意义的特殊性；

八、重申各国拥有在其领土上维持、采取和实施他们认为合适的保护和促进文化表现形式多样性的政策和措施的主权；

九、本着伙伴精神，加强国际合作与团结，特别是要提高发展中国家保护和促进文化表现形式多样性的能力。

第2条　指导原则

一、尊重人权和基本自由原则

只有确保人权，以及表达、信息和交流等基本自由，并确保个人可以选择文化表现形式，才能保护和促进文化多样性。任何人都不得援引本公约的规定侵犯《世界人权宣言》规定的或受到国际法保障的人权和基本自由或限制其适用范围。

二、主权原则

根据《联合国宪章》和国际法原则，各国拥有在其境内采取保护和促进文化表现形式多样性措施和政策的主权。

三、所有文化同等尊严和尊重原则

保护与促进文化表现形式多样性的前提是承认所有文化，包括少数民族和原住民的文化在内，具有同等尊严，并应受到同等尊重。

四、国际团结与合作原则

国际合作与团结的目的应当是使各个国家，尤其是发展中国家都有能力在地方、国家和国际层面上创建和加强其文化表现手段，包括其新兴的或成熟的文化产业。

五、经济和文化发展互补原则

文化是发展的主要推动力之一，所以文化的发展与经济的发展同样重要，且所有个人和民族都有权参与两者的发展并从中获益。

六、可持续发展原则

文化多样性是个人和社会的一种财富。保护、促进和维护文化多样性是当代人及其后代的可持续发展的一项基本要求。

七、平等享有原则

平等享有全世界丰富多样的文化表现形式，所有文化享有各种表现形式和传播手段，是增进文化多样性和促进相互理解的要素。

八、开放和平衡原则

在采取措施维护文化表现形式多样性时，各国应寻求以适当的方式促进向世界其他文化开放，并确保这些措施符合本公约的目标。

第二章 适用范围

第3条 公约的适用范围

本公约适用于缔约方采取的有关保护和促进文化表现形式多样性的政策和措施。

第三章 定义

第4条 定义

在本公约中，应作如下理解：

一、文化多样性

"文化多样性"指各群体和社会借以表现其文化的多种不同形式。这些表现形式在他们内部及其间传承。

文化多样性不仅体现在人类文化遗产通过丰富多彩的文化表现形式来表达、弘扬和传承的多种方式，也体现在借助各种方式和技术进行的艺术创造、生产、传播、销售和消费的多种方式。

二、文化内容

"文化内容"指源于文化特征或表现文化特征的象征意义、艺术特色和文化价值。

三、文化表现形式

"文化表现形式"指个人、群体和社会创造的具有文化内容的表现形式。

四、文化活动、产品与服务

"文化活动、产品与服务"是指从其具有的特殊属性、用途或目的考虑时，体现或传达文化表现形式的活动、产品与服务，无论他们是否具有商业价值。文化活动可能以自身为目的，也可能是为文化产品与服务的生产提供帮助。

五、文化产业

"文化产业"指生产和销售上述第（四）项所述的文化产品或服务的产业。

六、文化政策和措施

"文化政策和措施"指地方、国家、区域或国际层面上针对文化本身或为了对个人、群体或社会的文化表现形式产生直接影响的各项政策和措施，包括与创作、生产、传播、销售和享有文化活动、产品与服务相关的政策和措施。

七、保护

名词"保护"意指为保存、卫护和加强文化表现形式多样性而采取措施。

动词"保护"意指采取这类措施。

八、文化间性

"文化间性"指不同文化的存在与平等互动，以及通过对话和相互尊重产生共同文化表现形式的可能性。

第四章 缔约方的权利和义务

第 5 条 权利和义务的一般规则

一、缔约方根据《联合国宪章》、国际法原则及国际公认的人权文书，重申拥有为实现本公约的宗旨而制定和实施其文化政策、采取措施以保护和促进文化表现形式多样性及加强国际合作的主权。

二、当缔约方在其境内实施政策和采取措施以保护和促进文化表现形式的多样性时，这些政策和措施应与本公约的规定相符。

第 6 条 缔约方在本国的权利

一、各缔约方可在第四条第（6）项所定义的文化政策和措施范围内，根据自身的特殊情况和需求，在其境内采取措施保护和促进文化表现形式的多样性。

二、这类措施可包括：

（1）为了保护和促进文化表现形式的多样性所采取的管理性措施；

（2）以适当方式在本国境内为创作、生产、传播和享有本国的文化活动、产品与服务提供机会的有关措施，包括其语言使用方面的规定；

（3）为国内独立的文化产业和非正规产业部门活动能有效获取生产、传播和销售文化活动、产品与服务的手段采取的措施；

（4）提供公共财政资助的措施；

（5）鼓励非营利组织以及公共和私人机构、艺术家及其他文化专业人员发展和促进思想、文化表现形式、文化活动、产品与服务的自由交流和流通，以及在这些活动中激励创新精神和积极进取精神的措施；

（6）建立并适当支持公共机构的措施；

（7）培育并支持参与文化表现形式创作活动的艺术家和其他人员的措施；

（8）旨在加强媒体多样性的措施，包括运用公共广播服务。

第 7 条 促进文化表现形式的措施

一、缔约方应努力在其境内创造环境，鼓励个人和社会群体：

（1）创作、生产、传播、销售和获取他们自己的文化表现形式，同时对妇女及不同社会群体，包括少数民族和原住民的特殊情况和需求给予应有的重视；

（2）获取本国境内及世界其他国家的各种不同的文化表现形式。

二、缔约方还应努力承认艺术家、参与创作活动的其他人员、文化界以及支持他们工作的有关组织的重要贡献，以及他们在培育文化表现形式多样性方面的核心作用。

第 8 条 保护文化表现形式的措施

一、在不影响第五条和第六条规定的前提下，缔约一方可以确定其领土上哪些文化表现形式属于面临消亡危险、受到严重威胁、或是需要紧急保护的特殊情况。

二、缔约方可通过与本公约的规定相符的方式，采取一切恰当的措施保护处于第一款所述情况下的文化表现形式。

三、缔约方应向下文第二十三条所述的政府间委员会报告为应对这类紧急情况所采取的所有措施，该委员会则可以对此提出合适的建议。

第 9 条　信息共享和透明度

缔约方应：

（1）在向联合国教科文组织四年一度的报告中，提供其在本国境内和国际层面为保护和促进文化表现形式多样性所采取的措施的适当信息；

（2）指定一处联络点，负责共享有关本公约的信息；

（3）共享和交流有关保护和促进文化表现形式多样性的信息。

第 10 条　教育和公众认知

缔约方应：

（1）鼓励和提高对保护和促进文化表现形式多样性重要意义的理解，尤其是通过教育和提高公众认知的计划；

（2）为实现本条的宗旨与其他缔约方和相关国际组织及地区组织开展合作；

（3）通过制定文化产业方面的教育、培训和交流计划，致力于鼓励创作和提高生产能力，但所采取的措施不能对传统生产形式产生负面影响。

第 11 条　公民社会的参与

缔约方承认公民社会在保护和促进文化表现形式多样性方面的重要作用。缔约方应鼓励公民社会积极参与其为实现本公约各项目标所作的努力。

第 12 条　促进国际合作

缔约方应致力于加强双边、区域和国际合作，创造有利于促进文化表现形式多样性的条件，同时特别考虑第八条和第十七条所述情况，以便着重：

（1）促进缔约方之间开展文化政策和措施的对话；

（2）通过开展专业和国际文化交流及有关成功经验的交流，增强公共文化部门战略管理能力；

（3）加强与公民社会、非政府组织和私人部门及其内部的伙伴关系，以鼓励和促进文化表现形式的多样性；

（4）提倡应用新技术，鼓励发展伙伴关系以加强信息共享和文化理解，促进文化表现形式的多样性；

（5）鼓励缔结共同生产和共同销售的协定。

第 13 条　将文化纳入可持续发展

缔约方应致力于将文化纳入其各级发展政策，创造有利于可持续发展的条件，并在此框架内完善与保护和促进文化表现形式多样性相关的各个环节。

第 14 条　为发展而合作

缔约方应致力于支持为促进可持续发展和减轻贫困而开展合作，尤其要关注发展中国家的特殊需要，主要通过以下途径来推动形成富有活力的文化部门：

（一）通过以下方式加强发展中国家的文化产业：

1. 建立和加强发展中国家文化生产和销售能力；

2. 推动其文化活动、产品与服务更多地进入全球市场和国际销售网络；

3. 促使形成有活力的地方市场和区域市场；

4. 尽可能在发达国家采取适当措施，为发展中国家的文化活动、产品与服务进入这些国家提供方便；

5. 尽可能支持发展中国家艺术家的创作，促进他们的流动；

6. 鼓励发达国家与发展中国家之间开展适当的协作，特别是在音乐和电影领域。

（二）通过在发展中国家开展信息、经验和专业知识交流以及人力资源培训，加强公共和私人部门的能力建设，尤其是在战略管理能力、政策制定和实施、文化表现形式的促进和推广、中小企业和微型企业的发展、技术的应用及技能开发与转让等方面。

（三）通过采取适当的鼓励措施来推动技术和专门知识的转让，尤其是在文化产业和文化企业领域。

（四）通过以下方式提供财政支持：
  1. 根据第十八条的规定设立文化多样性国际基金；
  2. 提供官方发展援助，必要时包括提供技术援助，以激励和支持创作；
  3. 提供其他形式的财政援助，比如提供低息贷款、赠款以及其他资金机制。

第 15 条　协作安排

缔约方应鼓励在公共、私人部门和非营利组织之间及其内部发展伙伴关系，以便与发展中国家合作，增强他们在保护和促进文化表现形式多样性方面的能力。这类新型伙伴关系应根据发展中国家的实际需求，注重基础设施建设、人力资源开发和政策制定，以及文化活动、产品与服务的交流。

第 16 条　对发展中国家的优惠待遇

发达国家应通过适当的机构和法律框架，为发展中国家的艺术家和其他文化专业人员及从业人员，以及那里的文化产品和文化服务提供优惠待遇，促进与这些国家的文化交流。

第 17 条　在文化表现形式受到严重威胁情况下的国际合作

在第八条所述情况下，缔约方应开展合作，相互提供援助，特别要援助发展中国家。

第 18 条　文化多样性国际基金

一、兹建立"文化多样性国际基金"（以下简称"基金"）。

二、根据教科文组织《财务条例》，此项基金为信托基金。

三、基金的资金来源为：

（1）缔约方的自愿捐款；

（2）教科文组织大会为此划拨的资金；

（3）其他国家、联合国系统组织和计划署、其他地区和国际组织、公共和私人部门以及个人的捐款、赠款和遗赠；

（4）基金产生的利息；

（5）为基金组织募捐或其他活动的收入；

（6）基金条例许可的所有其他资金来源。

四、政府间委员会应根据下文第 22 条所述的缔约方大会确定的指导方针决定基金资金的使用。

五、对已获政府间委员会批准的具体项目，政府间委员会可以接受为实现这些项目的整体目标或具体目标而提供的捐款及其他形式的援助。

六、捐赠不得附带任何与本公约目标不相符的政治、经济或其他条件。

七、缔约方应努力定期为实施本公约提供自愿捐款。

第 19 条　信息交流、分析和传播

一、缔约方同意，就有关文化表现形式多样性以及对其保护和促进方面的成功经验的数据收集和统计，开展信息交流和共享专业知识。

二、教科文组织应利用秘书处现有的机制，促进各种相关的信息、统计数据和成功经验的收集、分析和传播。

三、教科文组织还应建立一个关于文化表现形式领域内各类部门和政府组织、私人及非营利组织的数据库，并更新其内容。

四、为了便于收集数据，教科文组织应特别重视申请援助的缔约方的能力建设和专业知识积累。

五、本条涉及的信息收集应作为第 9 条规定的信息收集的补充。

第五章 与其他法律文书的关系

第 20 条 与其他条约的关系：相互支持，互为补充和不隶属

一、缔约方承认，他们应善意履行其在本公约及其为缔约方的其他所有条约中的义务。因此，在本公约不隶属于其他条约的情况下，

（1）缔约方应促使本公约与其为缔约方的其他条约相互支持；

（2）缔约方解释和实施其为缔约方的其他条约或承担其他国际义务时应考虑到本公约的相关规定。

二、本公约的任何规定不得解释为变更缔约方在其为缔约方的其他条约中的权利和义务。

第 21 条 国际磋商与协调

缔约方承诺在其他国际场合倡导本公约的宗旨和原则。为此，缔约方在需要时应进行相互磋商，并牢记这些目标与原则。

第六章 公约的机构

第 22 条 缔约方大会

一、应设立一个缔约方大会。缔约方大会应为本公约的全会和最高权力机构。

二、缔约方大会每两年举行一次例会，尽可能与联合国教科文组织大会同期举行。缔约方大会作出决定，或政府间委员会收到至少三分之一缔约方的请求，缔约方大会可召开特别会议。

三、缔约方大会应通过自己的议事规则。

四、缔约方大会的职能应主要包括以下方面：

（1）选举政府间委员会的成员；

（2）接受并审议由政府间委员会转交的本公约缔约方的报告；

（3）核准政府间委员会根据缔约方大会的要求拟订的操作指南；

（4）采取其认为有必要的其他措施来推进本公约的目标。

第 23 条 政府间委员会

一、应在联合国教科文组织内设立"保护与促进文化表现形式多样性政府间委员会"（以下简称"政府间委员会"）。在本公约根据其第 29 条规定生效后，政府间委员会由缔约方大会选出的 18 个本公约缔约国的代表组成，任期四年。

二、政府间委员会每年举行一次会议。

三、政府间委员会根据缔约方大会的授权和在其指导下运作并向其负责。

四、一旦公约缔约方数目达到 50 个，政府间委员会的成员应增至 24 名。

五、政府间委员会成员的选举应遵循公平的地理代表性以及轮换的原则。

六、在不影响本公约赋予它的其他职责的前提下，政府间委员会的职责如下：

（1）促进本公约目标，鼓励并监督公约的实施；

（2）应缔约方大会要求，起草并提交缔约方大会核准履行和实施公约条款的操作指南；

（3）向缔约方大会转交公约缔约方的报告，并随附评论及报告内容概要；

（4）根据公约的有关规定，特别是第 8 条规定，对本公约缔约方提请关注的情况提出适当的建议；

（5）建立磋商程序和其他机制，以在其他国际场合倡导本公约的目标和原则；

（6）执行缔约方大会可能要求的其他任务。

七、政府间委员会根据其议事规则，可随时邀请公共或私人组织或个人参加就具体问题进行的磋商会议。

八、政府间委员会应制定并提交缔约方大会核准自己的议事规则。

第 24 条　联合国教科文组织秘书处

一、联合国教科文组织秘书处应为本公约的有关机构提供协助。

二、秘书处编制缔约方大会和政府间委员会的文件及其会议的议程，协助实施会议的决定，并报告缔约方大会决定的实施情况。

第七章　最后条款

第 25 条　争端的解决

一、本公约缔约方之间关于公约的解释或实施产生的争端，应通过谈判寻求解决。

二、如果有关各方不能通过谈判达成一致，可共同寻求第三方斡旋或要求第三方调停。

三、如果没有进行斡旋或调停，或者协商、斡旋或调停均未能解决争端，一方可根据本公约附件所列的程序要求调解。相关各方应善意考虑调解委员会为解决争端提出的建议。

四、任何缔约方均可在批准、接受、核准或加入本公约时，声明不承认上述调解程序。任何发表这一声明的缔约方，可随时通知教科文组织总干事，宣布撤回该声明。

第 26 条　会员国批准、接受、核准或加入

一、联合国教科文组织会员国依据各自的宪法程序批准、接受、核准或加入本公约。

二、批准书、接受书、核准书或加入书应交联合国教科文组织总干事保存。

第 27 条　加入

一、所有非联合国教科文组织会员国，但为联合国或其任何一个专门机构成员的国家，经联合国教科文组织大会邀请，均可加入本公约。

二、没有完全独立，但根据联合国大会第 1514（XV）号决议被联合国承认为充分享有内部自治，并且有权处理本公约范围内的事宜，包括有权就这些事宜签署协议的地区也可加入本公约。

三、对区域经济一体化组织适用如下规定：

（1）任何一个区域经济一体化组织均可加入本公约，除以下各项规定外，这类组织应以与缔约国相同的方式，完全受本公约规定的约束；

（2）如果这类组织的一个或数个成员国也是本公约的缔约国，该组织与这一或这些成员国应确定在履行本公约规定的义务上各自承担的责任。责任的分担应在完成第（三）项规定的书面通知程序后生效；该组织与成员国无权同时行使本公约规定的权利。此外，经济一体化组织在其权限范围内，行使与其参加本公约的成员国数目相同的表决权。如果其任何一个成员国行使其表决权，此类组织则不应行使表决权，反之亦然。

（3）同意按照第（2）项规定分担责任的区域经济一体化组织及其一个或数个成员国，应按以下方式将所建议的责任分担通知各缔约方：

①该组织在加入书内，应具体声明对本公约管辖事项责任的分担；

②在各自承担的责任变更时，该经济一体化组织应将拟议的责任变更通知保管人，保管人应将此变更通报各缔约方。

（4）已成为本公约缔约国的区域经济一体化组织的成员国在其没有明确声明或通知保管人将管辖权转给该组织的所有领域应被推断为仍然享有管辖权。

（5）"区域经济一体化组织"，系指由作为联合国或其任何一个专门机构成员国的主权国家组成的组织，这些国家已将其在本公约所辖领域的权限转移给该组织，并且该组织已按其内部程序获得适当授权成为本公约的缔约方。

四、加入书应交存联合国教科文组织总干事处。

第 28 条 联络点

在成为本公约缔约方时，每一缔约方应指定第 9 条所述的联络点。

第 29 条 生效

一、本公约在第三十份批准书、接受书、核准书或加入书交存之日起的三个月后生效，但只针对在该日或该日之前交存批准书、接受书、核准书或加入书的国家或区域经济一体化组织。对其他缔约方，本公约则在其批准书、接受书、核准书或加入书交存之日起的三个月之后生效。

二、就本条而言，一个区域经济一体化组织交存的任何文书不得在该组织成员国已交存文书之外另行计算。

第 30 条 联邦制或非单一立宪制

鉴于国际协定对无论采取何种立宪制度的缔约方具有同等约束力，对实行联邦制或非单一立宪制的缔约方实行下述规定：

（1）对于在联邦或中央立法机构的法律管辖下实施的本公约各项条款，联邦或中央政府的义务与非联邦国家的缔约方的义务相同；

（2）对于在构成联邦，但按照联邦立宪制无须采取立法手段的单位，如州、县以及省或行政区的法律管辖下实施的本公约各项条款，联邦政府须将这些条款连同其关于采用这些条款的建议一并通知各个州、县以及省或行政区等单位的主管当局。

第 31 条 退约

一、本公约各缔约方均可宣布退出本公约。

二、退约决定须以书面形式通知，有关文件交存联合国教科文组织总干事处。

三、退约在收到退约书 12 个月后开始生效。退约国在退约生效之前的财政义务不受任何影响。

第 32 条 保管职责

联合国教科文组织总干事作为本公约的保管人，应将第 26 条和第 27 条规定的所有批准书、接受书、核准书或加入书和第 31 条规定的退约书的交存情况通告本组织各会员国、第 27 条提到的非会员国和区域经济一体化组织以及联合国。

第 33 条 修正

一、本公约缔约方可通过给总干事的书面函件，提出对本公约的修正。总干事应将此类函件周知全体缔约方。如果通知发出的六个月内对上述要求做出积极反应的成员国不少于半数，总干事则可将公约修正建议提交下一届缔约方大会进行讨论或通过。

二、对公约的修正须经出席并参加表决的缔约方三分之二多数票通过。

三、对本公约的修正一旦获得通过，须交各缔约方批准、接受、核准或加入。

四、对于批准、接受、核准或加入修正案的缔约方来说，本公约修正案在三分之二的缔约方递交本条第三款所提及的文件之日起三个月后生效。此后，对任何批准、接受、核准或加入该公约修正案的缔约方来说，在其递交批准书、接受书、核准书或加入书之日起三个月之后，本公约修正案生效。

五、第三款及第四款所述程序不适用第 23 条所述政府间委员会成员国数目的修改。该类修改一经通过即生效。

六、在公约修正案按本条第四款生效之后加入本公约的那些第 27 条所指的国家或区域经济一体化组织，如未表示异议，则应：

（1）被视为经修正的本公约的缔约方；

（2）但在与不受修正案约束的任何缔约方的关系中，仍被视为未经修正的公约的缔约方。

第 34 条　有效文本

本公约用阿拉伯文、中文、英文、法文、俄文和西班牙文制定，六种文本具有同等效力。

第 35 条　登记

根据《联合国宪章》第 102 条的规定，本公约将应联合国教科文组织总干事的要求交联合国秘书处登记。

Convention on the Protection and Promotion of the Diversity of Cultural Expressions[1]

Adopted by the UNESCO General Conference at its 33rd Session, Paris, 20 October 2005

The General Conference of the United Nations Educational, Scientific and Cultural Organization, meeting in Paris from 3 to 21 October 2005 at its 33rd session,

Affirming that cultural diversity is a defining characteristic of humanity,

Conscious that cultural diversity forms a common heritage of humanity and should be cherished and preserved for the benefit of all,

Being aware that cultural diversity creates a rich and varied world, which increases the range of choices and nurtures human capacities and values, and therefore is a mainspring for sustainable development for communities, peoples and nations,

Recalling that cultural diversity, flourishing within a framework of democracy, tolerance, social justice and mutual respect between peoples and cultures, is indispensable for peace and security at the local, national and international levels,

Celebrating the importance of cultural diversity for the full realization of human rights and fundamental freedoms proclaimed in the Universal Declaration of Human Rights and other universally recognized instruments,

Emphasizing the need to incorporate culture as a strategic element in national and international development policies, as well as in international development cooperation, taking into account also the United Nations Millennium Declaration (2000) with its special emphasis on poverty eradication,

Taking into account that culture takes diverse forms across time and space and that this diversity is embodied in the uniqueness and plurality of the identities and cultural expressions of the peoples and societies making up humanity,

Recognizing the importance of traditional knowledge as a source of intangible and material wealth, and in particular the knowledge systems of indigenous peoples, and its positive contribution to sustainable development, as well as the need for its adequate protection and promotion,

Recognizing the need to take measures to protect the diversity of cultural expressions, including their contents, especially in situations where cultural expressions may be threatened by the possibility of extinction or serious impairment,

Emphasizing the importance of culture for social cohesion in general, and in particular its potential for the enhancement of the status and role of women in society,

---

[1] UNESCO Document Code: CLT.2005/CONVENTION DIVERSITE-CULT REV.2.

Being aware that cultural diversity is strengthened by the free flow of ideas, and that it is nurtured by constant exchanges and interaction between cultures,

Reaffirming that freedom of thought, expression and information, as well as diversity of the media, enable cultural expressions to flourish within societies,

Recognizing that the diversity of cultural expressions, including traditional cultural expressions, is an important factor that allows individuals and peoples to express and to share with others their ideas and values,

Recalling that linguistic diversity is a fundamental element of cultural diversity, and *reaffirming* the fundamental role that education plays in the protection and promotion of cultural expressions,

Taking into account the importance of the vitality of cultures, including for persons belonging to minorities and indigenous peoples, as manifested in their freedom to create, disseminate and distribute their traditional cultural expressions and to have access thereto, so as to benefit them for their own development,

Emphasizing the vital role of cultural interaction and creativity, which nurture and renew cultural expressions and enhance the role played by those involved in the development of culture for the progress of society at large,

Recognizing the importance of intellectual property rights in sustaining those involved in cultural creativity,

Being convinced that cultural activities, goods and services have both an economic and a cultural nature, because they convey identities, values and meanings, and must therefore not be treated as solely having commercial value,

Noting that while the processes of globalization, which have been facilitated by the rapid development of information and communication technologies, afford unprecedented conditions for enhanced interaction between cultures, they also represent a challenge for cultural diversity, namely in view of risks of imbalances between rich and poor countries,

Being aware of UNESCO's specific mandate to ensure respect for the diversity of cultures and to recommend such international agreements as may be necessary to promote the free flow of ideas by word and image,

Referring to the provisions of the international instruments adopted by UNESCO relating to cultural diversity and the exercise of cultural rights, and in particular the Universal Declaration on Cultural Diversity of 2001,

Adopts this Convention on 20 October 2005.

Ⅰ. Objectives and guiding principles

Article 1 OBJECTIVES

The objectives of this Convention are:

(a) to protect and promote the diversity of cultural expressions;

(b) to create the conditions for cultures to flourish and to freely interact in a mutually beneficial manner;

(c) to encourage dialogue among cultures with a view to ensuring wider and balanced cultural exchanges in the world in favour of intercultural respect and a culture of peace;

(d) to foster interculturality in order to develop cultural interaction in the spirit of building bridges among peoples;

(e) to promote respect for the diversity of cultural expressions and raise awareness of its value at the local, national and international levels;

(f) to reaffirm the importance of the link between culture and development for all countries, particularly for developing countries, and to support actions undertaken nationally and internationally to secure recognition of the true value of this link;

(g) to give recognition to the distinctive nature of cultural activities, goods and services as vehicles of identity, values and meaning;

(h) to reaffirm the sovereign rights of States to maintain, adopt and implement policies and measures that they deem appropriate for the protection and promotion of the diversity of cultural expressions on their territory;

(i) to strengthen international cooperation and solidarity in a spirit of partnership with a view, in particular, to enhancing the capacities of developing countries in order to protect and promote the diversity of cultural expressions.

Article 2　GUIDING PRINCIPLES

1. Principle of respect for human rights and fundamental freedoms

Cultural diversity can be protected and promoted only if human rights and fundamental freedoms, such as freedom of expression, information and communication, as well as the ability of individuals to choose cultural expressions, are guaranteed. No one may invoke the provisions of this Convention in order to infringe human rights and fundamental freedoms as enshrined in the Universal Declaration of Human Rights or guaranteed by international law, or to limit the scope thereof.

2. Principle of sovereignty

States have, in accordance with the Charter of the United Nations and the principles of international law, the sovereign right to adopt measures and policies to protect and promote the diversity of cultural expressions within their territory.

3. Principle of equal dignity of and respect for all cultures

The protection and promotion of the diversity of cultural expressions presuppose the recognition of equal dignity of and respect for all cultures, including the cultures of persons belonging to minorities and indigenous peoples.

4. Principle of international solidarity and cooperation

International cooperation and solidarity should be aimed at enabling countries, especially developing countries, to create and strengthen their means of cultural expression, including their cultural industries, whether nascent or established, at the local, national and international levels.

5. Principle of the complementarity of economic and cultural aspects of development

Since culture is one of the mainsprings of development, the cultural aspects of development are as important as its economic aspects, which individuals and peoples have the fundamental right to participate in and enjoy.

6. Principle of sustainable development

Cultural diversity is a rich asset for individuals and societies. The protection, promotion and maintenance of cultural diversity are an essential requirement for sustainable development for the benefit of present and future generations.

7. Principle of equitable access

Equitable access to a rich and diversified range of cultural expressions from all over the world and access of cultures to the means of expressions and dissemination constitute important elements for enhancing cultural diversity and encouraging mutual understanding.

8. Principle of openness and balance

When States adopt measures to support the diversity of cultural expressions, they should seek to promote, in an appropriate manner, openness to other cultures of the world and to ensure that these measures are geared to the objectives pursued under the present Convention.

II. Scope of application

Article 3   SCOPE OF APPLICATION

This Convention shall apply to the policies and measures adopted by the Parties related to the protection and promotion of the diversity of cultural expressions.

III. Definitions

Article 4   DEFINITIONS

For the purposes of this Convention, it is understood that:

1. Cultural diversity

"Cultural diversity" refers to the manifold ways in which the cultures of groups and societies find expression. These expressions are passed on within and among groups and societies.

Cultural diversity is made manifest not only through the varied ways in which the cultural heritage of humanity is expressed, augmented and transmitted through the variety of cultural expressions, but also through diverse modes of artistic creation, production, dissemination, distribution and enjoyment, whatever the means and technologies used.

2. Cultural content

"Cultural content" refers to the symbolic meaning, artistic dimension and cultural values that originate from or express cultural identities.

3. Cultural expressions

"Cultural expressions" are those expressions that result from the creativity of individuals, groups and societies, and that have cultural content.

4. Cultural activities, goods and services

"Cultural activities, goods and services" refers to those activities, goods and services, which at the time they are considered as a specific attribute, use or purpose, embody or convey cultural expressions, irrespective of the commercial value they may have. Cultural activities may be an end in themselves, or they may contribute to the production of cultural goods and services.

5. Cultural industries

"Cultural industries" refers to industries producing and distributing cultural goods or services as defined in paragraph 4 above.

6. Cultural policies and measures

"Cultural policies and measures" refers to those policies and measures relating to culture, whether at the local, national, regional or international level that are either focused on culture as such or are designed to have a direct effect on cultural expressions of individuals, groups or societies, including on the creation, production, dissemination, distribution of and access to cultural activities, goods and services.

7. Protection

"Protection" means the adoption of measures aimed at the preservation, safeguarding and enhancement of the diversity of cultural expressions.

"Protect" means to adopt such measures.

8. Interculturality

"Interculturality" refers to the existence and equitable interaction of diverse cultures and the possibility of generating shared cultural expressions through dialogue and mutual respect.

IV. Rights and obligations of Parties

Article 5   GENERAL RULE REGARDING RIGHTS AND OBLIGATIONS

1. The Parties, in conformity with the Charter of the United Nations, the principles of international law and universally recognized human rights instruments, reaffirm their sovereign right to formulate and implement their cultural policies and to adopt measures to protect and promote the diversity of cultural expressions and to strengthen international cooperation to achieve the purposes of this Convention.

2. When a Party implements policies and takes measures to protect and promote the diversity of cultural expressions within its territory, its policies and measures shall be consistent with the provisions of this Convention.

Article 6   RIGHTS OF PARTIES AT THE NATIONAL LEVEL

1. Within the framework of its cultural policies and measures as defined in Article 4.6 and taking into account its own particular circumstances and needs, each Party may adopt measures aimed at protecting and promoting the diversity of cultural expressions within its territory.

2. Such measures may include the following:

(a) regulatory measures aimed at protecting and promoting diversity of cultural expressions;

(b) measures that, in an appropriate manner, provide opportunities for domestic cultural activities, goods and services among all those available within the national territory for the creation, production, dissemination, distribution and enjoyment of such domestic cultural activities, goods and services, including provisions relating to the language used for such activities, goods and services;

(c) measures aimed at providing domestic independent cultural industries and activities in the informal sector effective access to the means of production, dissemination and distribution of cultural activities, goods and services;

(d) measures aimed at providing public financial assistance;

(e) measures aimed at encouraging non-profit organizations, as well as public and private institutions and artists and other cultural professionals, to develop and promote the free exchange and circulation of ideas, cultural expressions and cultural activities, goods and services, and to stimulate both the creative and entrepreneurial spirit in their activities;

(f) measures aimed at establishing and supporting public institutions, as appropriate;

(g) measures aimed at nurturing and supporting artists and others involved in the creation of cultural expressions;

(h) measures aimed at enhancing diversity of the media, including through public service broadcasting.

Article 7   MEASURES TO PROMOTE CULTURAL EXPRESSIONS

1. Parties shall endeavour to create in their territory an environment which encourages individuals and social groups:

(a) to create, produce, disseminate, distribute and have access to their own cultural expressions, paying due attention to the special circumstances and needs of women as well as various social groups, including persons belonging to minorities and indigenous peoples;

(b) to have access to diverse cultural expressions from within their territory as well as from other countries of the world.

2. Parties shall also endeavour to recognize the important contribution of artists, others involved in the creative process, cultural communities, and organizations that support their work, and their central role in nurturing the diversity of cultural expressions.

Article 8　MEASURES TO PROTECT CULTURAL EXPRESSIONS

1. Without prejudice to the provisions of Articles 5 and 6, a Party may determine the existence of special situations where cultural expressions on its territory are at risk of extinction, under serious threat, or otherwise in need of urgent safeguarding.

2. Parties may take all appropriate measures to protect and preserve cultural expressions in situations referred to in paragraph 1 in a manner consistent with the provisions of this Convention.

3. Parties shall report to the Intergovernmental Committee referred to in Article 23 all measures taken to meet the exigencies of the situation, and the Committee may make appropriate recommendations.

Article 9　INFORMATION SHARING AND TRANSPARENCY

Parties shall:

(a) provide appropriate information in their reports to UNESCO every four years on measures taken to protect and promote the diversity of cultural expressions within their territory and at the international level;

(b) designate a point of contact responsible for information sharing in relation to this Convention;

(c) share and exchange information relating to the protection and promotion of the diversity of cultural expressions.

Article 10　EDUCATION AND PUBLIC AWARENESS

Parties shall:

(a) encourage and promote understanding of the importance of the protection and promotion of the diversity of cultural expressions, inter alia, through educational and greater public awareness programmes;

(b) cooperate with other Parties and international and regional organizations in achieving the purpose of this article;

(c) endeavour to encourage creativity and strengthen production capacities by setting up educational, training and exchange programmes in the field of cultural industries. These measures should be implemented in a manner which does not have a negative impact on traditional forms of production.

Article 11　PARTICIPATION OF CIVIL SOCIETY

Parties acknowledge the fundamental role of civil society in protecting and promoting the diversity of cultural expressions. Parties shall encourage the active participation of civil society in their efforts to achieve the objectives of this Convention.

Article 12　PROMOTION OF INTERNATIONAL COOPERATION

Parties shall endeavour to strengthen their bilateral, regional and international cooperation for the creation of conditions conducive to the promotion of the diversity of cultural expressions, taking particular account of the situations referred to in Articles 8 and 17, notably in order to:

(a) facilitate dialogue among Parties on cultural policy;

(b) enhance public sector strategic and management capacities in cultural public sector institutions, through professional and international cultural exchanges and sharing of best practices;

(c) reinforce partnerships with and among civil society, non-governmental organizations and the private sector in fostering and promoting the diversity of cultural expressions;

(d) promote the use of new technologies, encourage partnerships to enhance information sharing and cultural understanding, and foster the diversity of cultural expressions;

(e) encourage the conclusion of co-production and co-distribution agreements.

Article 13 INTEGRATION OF CULTURE IN SUSTAINABLE DEVELOPMENT

Parties shall endeavour to integrate culture in their development policies at all levels for the creation of conditions conducive to sustainable development and, within this framework, foster aspects relating to the protection and promotion of the diversity of cultural expressions.

Article 14 COOPERATION FOR DEVELOPMENT

Parties shall endeavour to support cooperation for sustainable development and poverty reduction, especially in relation to the specific needs of developing countries, in order to foster the emergence of a dynamic cultural sector by, inter alia, the following means:

(a) the strengthening of the cultural industries in developing countries through:

(i) creating and strengthening cultural production and distribution capacities in developing countries;

(ii) facilitating wider access to the global market and international distribution networks for their cultural activities, goods and services;

(iii) enabling the emergence of viable local and regional markets;

(iv) adopting, where possible, appropriate measures in developed countries with a view to facilitating access to their territory for the cultural activities, goods and services of developing countries;

(v) providing support for creative work and facilitating the mobility, to the extent possible, of artists from the developing world;

(vi) encouraging appropriate collaboration between developed and developing countries in the areas, *inter alia*, of music and film;

(b) capacity-building through the exchange of information, experience and expertise, as well as the training of human resources in developing countries, in the public and private sector relating to, *inter alia*, strategic and management capacities, policy development and implementation, promotion and distribution of cultural expressions, small-, medium- and micro-enterprise development, the use of technology, and skills development and transfer;

(c) technology transfer through the introduction of appropriate incentive measures for the transfer of technology and know-how, especially in the areas of cultural industries and enterprises;

(d) financial support through:

(i) the establishment of an International Fund for Cultural Diversity as provided in Article 18;

(ii) the provision of official development assistance, as appropriate, including technical assistance, to stimulate and support creativity;

(iii) other forms of financial assistance such as low interest loans, grants and other funding mechanisms.

Article 15 COLLABORATIVE ARRANGEMENTS

Parties shall encourage the development of partnerships, between and within the public and private sectors and non-profit organizations, in order to cooperate with developing countries in the enhancement of their capacities in the protection and promotion of the diversity of cultural expressions. These innovative partnerships shall, according to the practical needs of developing countries, emphasize the further development of infrastructure, human resources and policies, as well as the exchange of cultural activities, goods and services.

Article 16 PREFERENTIAL TREATMENT FOR DEVELOPING COUNTRIES

Developed countries shall facilitate cultural exchanges with developing countries by granting, through the appropriate institutional and legal frameworks, preferential treatment to artists and other cultural professionals and practitioners, as well as cultural goods and services from developing countries.

Article 17 INTERNATIONAL COOPERATION IN SITUATIONS OF SERIOUS THREAT TO CULTURAL EXPRESSIONS

Parties shall cooperate in providing assistance to each other, and, in particular to developing countries, in situations referred to under Article 8.

Article 18 INTERNATIONAL FUND FOR CULTURAL DIVERSITY

1. An International Fund for Cultural Diversity, hereinafter referred to as "the Fund", is hereby established.

2. The Fund shall consist of funds-in-trust established in accordance with the Financial Regulations of UNESCO.

3. The resources of the Fund shall consist of:

(a) voluntary contributions made by Parties;

(b) funds appropriated for this purpose by the General Conference of UNESCO;

(c) contributions, gifts or bequests by other States; organizations and programmes of the United Nations system, other regional or international organizations; and public or private bodies or individuals;

(d) any interest due on resources of the Fund;

(e) funds raised through collections and receipts from events organized for the benefit of the Fund;

(f) any other resources authorized by the Fund's regulations.

4. The use of resources of the Fund shall be decided by the Intergovernmental Committee on the basis of guidelines determined by the Conference of Parties referred to in Article 22.

5. The Intergovernmental Committee may accept contributions and other forms of assistance for general and specific purposes relating to specific projects, provided that those projects have been approved by it.

6. No political, economic or other conditions that are incompatible with the objectives of this Convention may be attached to contributions made to the Fund.

7. Parties shall endeavour to provide voluntary contributions on a regular basis towards the implementation of this Convention.

Article 19 EXCHANGE, ANALYSIS AND DISSEMINATION OF INFORMATION

1. Parties agree to exchange information and share expertise concerning data collection and statistics on the diversity of cultural expressions as well as on best practices for its protection and promotion.

2. UNESCO shall facilitate, through the use of existing mechanisms within the Secretariat, the collection, analysis and dissemination of all relevant information, statistics and best practices.

3. UNESCO shall also establish and update a data bank on different sectors and governmental, private and non- profit organizations involved in the area of cultural expressions.

4. To facilitate the collection of data, UNESCO shall pay particular attention to capacity-building and the strengthening of expertise for Parties that submit a request for such assistance.

5. The collection of information identified in this Article shall complement the information collected under the provisions of Article 9.

V. Relationship to other instruments

Article 20　RELATIONSHIP TO OTHER TREATIES: MUTUAL SUPPORTIVENESS, COMPLEMENTARITY AND NON-SUBORDINATION

1. Parties recognize that they shall perform in good faith their obligations under this Convention and all other treaties to which they are parties. Accordingly, without subordinating this Convention to any other treaty,

(a) they shall foster mutual supportiveness between this Convention and the other treaties to which they are parties; and

(b) when interpreting and applying the other treaties to which they are parties or when entering into other international obligations, Parties shall take into account the relevant provisions of this Convention.

2. Nothing in this Convention shall be interpreted as modifying rights and obligations of the Parties under any other treaties to which they are parties.

Article 21　INTERNATIONAL CONSULTATION AND COORDINATION

Parties undertake to promote the objectives and principles of this Convention in other international forums. For this purpose, Parties shall consult each other, as appropriate, bearing in mind these objectives and principles.

VI. Organs of the Convention

Article 22　CONFERENCE OF PARTIES

1. A Conference of Parties shall be established. The Conference of Parties shall be the plenary and supreme body of this Convention.

2. The Conference of Parties shall meet in ordinary session every two years, as far as possible, in conjunction with the General Conference of UNESCO. It may meet in extraordinary session if it so decides or if the Intergovernmental Committee receives a request to that effect from at least one-third of the Parties.

3. The Conference of Parties shall adopt its own rules of procedure.

4. The functions of the Conference of Parties shall be, *inter alia*:

(a) to elect the Members of the Intergovernmental Committee;

(b) to receive and examine reports of the Parties to this Convention transmitted by the Intergovernmental Committee;

(c) to approve the operational guidelines prepared upon its request by the Intergovernmental Committee;

(d) to take whatever other measures it may consider necessary to further the objectives of this Convention.

Article 23　INTERGOVERNMENTAL COMMITTEE

1. An Intergovernmental Committee for the Protection and Promotion of the Diversity of Cultural Expressions, hereinafter referred to as "the Intergovernmental Committee", shall be established within UNESCO. It shall be composed of representatives of 18 States Parties to the Convention, elected for a term of four years by the Conference of Parties upon entry into force of this Convention pursuant to Article 29.

2. The Intergovernmental Committee shall meet annually.

3. The Intergovernmental Committee shall function under the authority and guidance of and be accountable to the Conference of Parties.

4. The Members of the Intergovernmental Committee shall be increased to 24 once the number of Parties to the Convention reaches 50.

5. The election of Members of the Intergovernmental Committee shall be based on the principles of equitable geographical representation as well as rotation.

6. Without prejudice to the other responsibilities conferred upon it by this Convention, the functions of the Intergovernmental Committee shall be:

(a) to promote the objectives of this Convention and to encourage and monitor the implementation thereof;

(b) to prepare and submit for approval by the Conference of Parties, upon its request, the operational guidelines for the implementation and application of the provisions of the Convention;

(c) to transmit to the Conference of Parties reports from Parties to the Convention, together with its comments and a summary of their contents;

(d) to make appropriate recommendations to be taken in situations brought to its attention by Parties to the Convention in accordance with relevant provisions of the Convention, in particular Article 8;

(e) to establish procedures and other mechanisms for consultation aimed at promoting the objectives and principles of this Convention in other international forums;

(f) to perform any other tasks as may be requested by the Conference of Parties.

7. The Intergovernmental Committee, in accordance with its Rules of Procedure, may invite at any time public or private organizations or individuals to participate in its meetings for consultation on specific issues.

8. The Intergovernmental Committee shall prepare and submit to the Conference of Parties, for approval, its own Rules of Procedure.

Article 24　UNESCO SECRETARIAT

The organs of the Convention shall be assisted by the UNESCO Secretariat.

The Secretariat shall prepare the documentation of the Conference of Parties and the Intergovernmental Committee as well as the agenda of their meetings and shall assist in and report on the implementation of their decisions.

Ⅶ. Final clauses

Article 25　SETTLEMENT OF DISPUTES

1. In the event of a dispute between Parties to this Convention concerning the interpretation or the application of the Convention, the Parties shall seek a solution by negotiation.

2. If the Parties concerned cannot reach agreement by negotiation, they may jointly seek the good offices of, or request mediation by, a third party.

3. If good offices or mediation are not undertaken or if there is no settlement by negotiation, good offices or mediation, a Party may have recourse to conciliation in accordance with the procedure laid down in the Annex of this Convention. The Parties shall consider in good faith the proposal made by the Conciliation Commission for the resolution of the dispute.

4. Each Party may, at the time of ratification, acceptance, approval or accession, declare that it does not recognize the conciliation procedure provided for above. Any Party having made such a declaration may, at any time, withdraw this declaration by notification to the Director-General of UNESCO.

Article 26　RATIFICATION, ACCEPTANCE, APPROVAL OR ACCESSION BY MEMBER STATES

1. This Convention shall be subject to ratification, acceptance, approval or accession by Member States of

UNESCO in accordance with their respective constitutional procedures.

2. The instruments of ratification, acceptance, approval or accession shall be deposited with the Director-General of UNESCO.

Article 27　ACCESSION

1. This Convention shall be open to accession by all States not Members of UNESCO but members of the United Nations, or of any of its specialized agencies, that are invited by the General Conference of UNESCO to accede to it.

2. This Convention shall also be open to accession by territories which enjoy full internal self-government recognized as such by the United Nations, but which have not attained full independence in accordance with General Assembly resolution 1514 (XV), and which have competence over the matters governed by this Convention, including the competence to enter into treaties in respect of such matters.

3. The following provisions apply to regional economic integration organizations:

(a) This Convention shall also be open to accession by any regional economic integration organization, which shall, except as provided below, be fully bound by the provisions of the Convention in the same manner as States Parties;

(b) In the event that one or more Member States of such an organization is also Party to this Convention, the organization and such Member State or States shall decide on their responsibility for the performance of their obligations under this Convention. Such distribution of responsibility shall take effect following completion of the notification procedure described in subparagraph (c). The organization and the Member States shall not be entitled to exercise rights under this Convention concurrently. In addition, regional economic integration organizations, in matters within their competence, shall exercise their rights to vote with a number of votes equal to the number of their Member States that are Parties to this Convention. Such an organization shall not exercise its right to vote if any of its Member States exercises its right, and vice-versa;

(c) A regional economic integration organization and its Member State or States which have agreed on a distribution of responsibilities as provided in subparagraph (b) shall inform the Parties of any such proposed distribution of responsibilities in the following manner:

(i) in their instrument of accession, such organization shall declare with specificity, the distribution of their responsibilities with respect to matters governed by the Convention;

(ii) in the event of any later modification of their respective responsibilities, the regional economic integration organization shall inform the depositary of any such proposed modification of their respective responsibilities; the depositary shall in turn inform the Parties of such modification;

(d) Member States of a regional economic integration organization which become Parties to this Convention shall be presumed to retain competence over all matters in respect of which transfers of competence to the organization have not been specifically declared or informed to the depositary;

(e) "Regional economic integration organization" means an organization constituted by sovereign States, members of the United Nations or of any of its specialized agencies, to which those States have transferred competence in respect of matters governed by this Convention and which has been duly authorized, in accordance with its internal procedures, to become a Party to it.

4. The instrument of accession shall be deposited with the Director-General of UNESCO.

Article 28　POINT OF CONTACT

Upon becoming Parties to this Convention, each Party shall designate a point of contact as referred to in

Article 9.

Article 29　ENTRY INTO FORCE

1. This Convention shall enter into force three months after the date of deposit of the thirtieth instrument of ratification, acceptance, approval or accession, but only with respect to those States or regional economic integration organizations that have deposited their respective instruments of ratification, acceptance, approval, or accession on or before that date. It shall enter into force with respect to any other Party three months after the deposit of its instrument of ratification, acceptance, approval or accession.

2. For the purposes of this Article, any instrument deposited by a regional economic integration organization shall not be counted as additional to those deposited by Member States of the organization.

Article 30　FEDERAL OR NON-UNITARY CONSTITUTIONAL SYSTEMS

Recognizing that international agreements are equally binding on Parties regardless of their constitutional systems, the following provisions shall apply to Parties which have a federal or non-unitary constitutional system:

(a) with regard to the provisions of this Convention, the implementation of which comes under the legal jurisdiction of the federal or central legislative power, the obligations of the federal or central government shall be the same as for those Parties which are not federal States;

(b) with regard to the provisions of the Convention, the implementation of which comes under the jurisdiction of individual constituent units such as States, counties, provinces, or cantons which are not obliged by the constitutional system of the federation to take legislative measures, the federal government shall inform, as necessary, the competent authorities of constituent units such as States, counties, provinces or cantons of the said provisions, with its recommendation for their adoption.

Article 31　DENUNCIATION

1. Any Party to this Convention may denounce this Convention.

2. The denunciation shall be notified by an instrument in writing deposited with the Director-General of UNESCO.

3. The denunciation shall take effect 12 months after the receipt of the instrument of denunciation. It shall in no way affect the financial obligations of the Party denouncing the Convention until the date on which the withdrawal takes effect.

Article 32　DEPOSITARY FUNCTIONS

The Director-General of UNESCO, as the depositary of this Convention, shall inform the Member States of the Organization, the States not members of the Organization and regional economic integration organizations referred to in Article 27, as well as the United Nations, of the deposit of all the instruments of ratification, acceptance, approval or accession provided for in Articles 26 and 27, and of the denunciations provided for in Article 31.

Article 33　AMENDMENTS

1. A Party to this Convention may, by written communication addressed to the Director-General, propose amendments to this Convention. The Director-General shall circulate such communication to all Parties. If, within six months from the date of dispatch of the communication, no less than one half of the Parties reply favourably to the request, the Director-General shall present such proposal to the next session of the Conference of Parties for discussion and possible adoption.

2. Amendments shall be adopted by a two-thirds majority of Parties present and voting.

3. Once adopted, amendments to this Convention shall be submitted to the Parties for ratification, acceptance, approval or accession.

4. For Parties which have ratified, accepted, approved or acceded to them, amendments to this Convention shall enter into force three months after the deposit of the instruments referred to in paragraph 3 of this Article by two-thirds of the Parties. Thereafter, for each Party that ratifies, accepts, approves or accedes to an amendment, the said amendment shall enter into force three months after the date of deposit by that Party of its instrument of ratification, acceptance, approval or accession.

5. The procedure set out in paragraphs 3 and 4 shall not apply to amendments to Article 23 concerning the number of Members of the Intergovernmental Committee. These amendments shall enter into force at the time they are adopted.

6. A State or a regional economic integration organization referred to in Article 27 which becomes a Party to this Convention after the entry into force of amendments in conformity with paragraph 4 of this Article shall, failing an expression of different intention, be considered to be:

(a) Party to this Convention as so amended; and

(b) a Party to the unamended Convention in relation to any Party not bound by the amendments.

Article 34　AUTHORITATIVE TEXTS

This Convention has been drawn up in Arabic, Chinese, English, French, Russian and Spanish, all six texts being equally authoritative.

Article 35　REGISTRATION

In conformity with Article 102 of the Charter of the United Nations, this Convention shall be registered with the Secretariat of the United Nations at the request of the Director-General of UNESCO.

文献遗产

关于保存和获取包括数字遗产在内的文献遗产的建议书[①]

(联合国教科文组织第三十八届大会2015年11月17日在巴黎通过)

序言

联合国教科文组织大会于2015年11月3日至18日在巴黎举行的第三十八届会议,

考虑到长期以来以各种模拟和数字形式生产和保存的文献跨越时空,构成知识创造和表达的主要手段,影响着人类文明及进步的各个方面,

还考虑到文献遗产记录了人类思想与活动的演变和语言、文化、民族及其对世界认识的发展,

强调文献遗产对于促进知识共享以利于增进了解和对话、促进和平及对自由、民主、人权和人的尊严的尊重所具有的重要意义,

注意到文献遗产的发展有助于实现跨文化教育、个人充实和科技进步,因此是发展的关键资源,

同时考虑到文献遗产的保存和长久获取是言论、表达和信息自由等基本人权的基础,

还考虑到文献遗产的普遍获取必须既尊重权利持有人的合法权益,也尊重保存和获取文献遗产的公共利益,

认识到以文献遗产形式存在的历史和文化内容可能不便于获取,

还认识到随着时间的推移,大量文献遗产已经因为自然或人为灾害而消失,或者因为技术的快速变革而逐渐变得不可获取,强调立法缺失阻碍记忆机构应对文献遗产不可逆转的损失和枯竭问题,

忆及教科文组织针对这一挑战于1992年设立世界记忆计划,以增强对世界文献遗产的认识和保护,实现文献遗产的普遍和长久获取,

考虑到技术迅速发展,以及建立保存数字遗产物品,包括多媒体作品、互动超媒体、在线对话、来自复杂系统的动态数据对象、移动内容以及未来出现的新格式等复杂数字遗产的模式和流程所构成的挑战,

还考虑到附录中所列出的国际准则性文书和其他相关条约和声明,

铭记各国、社区和个人需要采取适当措施,保护、保存、获取、提高文献遗产的价值,

在大会第三十七届会议上决定应就这一问题向会员国提出一份建议书,

兹于2015年11月17日通过本《建议书》:

定义

在本《建议书》中,"文件"指包括模拟或数字信息内容及其载体的物品。该物品可保存,而且通常

[①] UNESCO Document Code: CL/4155。

是可移动的。其内容可以包括能够复制或转移的符号或代码（例如文本）、图像（静止或活动）和声音。载体可具有重要的审美、文化或技术特性。内容与载体之间的关系既可能是附带的，也可能是不可分割的。

"文献遗产"包含那些对某个社群、文化、国家或全人类具有重大和持久价值，且其老化或丧失会构成严重损失的单一文件或组合文件。这种遗产的重要意义只有随着时间的推移才可能逐步显现。世界文献遗产具有全球性重要意义，人人都负有责任，应当为全人类保护和保存好文献遗产，并应适当尊重和认可文化习俗和习惯。文献遗产始终都应当能够让所有人都毫无阻碍地获取和使用。文献遗产为了解社会、政治、社群以及个人历史提供手段，为善治和可持续发展提供支撑。每个国家的文献遗产都是其记忆和身份的反映，因而有助于确立其在国际社会中的地位。

"记忆机构"可包括但不限于档案馆、图书馆、博物馆和其他教育、文化和研究机构。

1. 文献遗产的确认

1.1 鼓励会员国，在国际上确立和界定的与其领土内文献遗产相关的标准指导下，支持其记忆机构通过研究和协商制定遴选、收集和保存方面的政策。这些文献、全宗档案和藏品的管理方式应确保其长久得到保存并可获取，并指定查询方式，其中包括编目和元数据。

1.2 各记忆机构应与民间社会协调，制定文献遗产的选择、购置和取消选择的政策、机制及标准，不仅要考虑主要文件，还要考虑其背景资料，包括社交媒体。选择标准必须是非歧视的、清晰界定的。与知识领域、艺术表现形式和历史时代相关的选择还必须保持平衡和中立。由于数字文件固有的临时性，在数字文献创建之时或之前可能就需要就其保存问题作出决定。

1.3 鼓励会员国找出那些面临潜在或迫在眉睫的存亡风险的文献遗产，并提请能够采取适当保护措施的主管机构注意。会员国应支持并加强其相关记忆机构，并在可行和适当的情况下鼓励学术研究界和私人所有者为了公众利益爱护自己的文献遗产。同样，公共和私营机构也应确保其自己创建的文献得到专业保护。

1.4 会员国应鼓励确认并向国家、地区或国际性的世界记忆名录申报重要的文献遗产，将其作为提高认识的一种手段。

1.5 请会员国酌情制定培训和能力建设计划，确保文献遗产的确认、保存和获取。

2. 文献遗产的保存

2.1 文献遗产的保存包含各种预防性和补救性的技巧、处理方法、程序和技术，目的是保存文献及其包含的信息。

2.2 保存是一个持续的过程，需要对模拟和数字物品进行管理，可通过学术研究、技术和科学加以促进。模拟载体如为原始真本、手工艺品或承载信息的物品，拥有持续价值，即应予以保留。数字文献宜在创建或购置之前即采取行动和干预措施，以便优化管理、降低成本并妥善管控相关风险。还应当鼓励各国政府、记忆机构和私营部门之间相互合作。

2.3 采取保存措施应以完整性、原真性和可靠性为指导原则。具体措施和行动应遵循记忆机构制定或支持的国际立法及建议、准则、最佳做法和标准。世界记忆计划应当提供一个推广标准和分享最佳做法的平台。

2.4 作为保护工作的一项关键内容，鼓励会员国制定提高认识和能力建设的措施与政策，包括倡导研究以及开展文献遗产专业人员培训，并为此提供设施。内容应涵盖策展最佳做法、现有技术与新技术、法医技能以及相关学术研究、科技和工程学领域的核心技能，从而提高人们对于在不断变化的环境中及时采取保存措施之紧迫性的认识。

2.5 对获取文献遗产的任何内容进行可能合理的限制，不应妨碍或限制记忆机构采取保存措施的能力。请会员国在实施本建议书并更新其相关的国内立法时考虑到这一问题。

2.6 鼓励在其记忆机构中保留有源于他国或与他国相关的收藏品的会员国与有关方面分享此类遗产的数字计划及副本。

2.7 会员国应鼓励记忆机构之间在最佳做法和保存标准方面保持一致，包括在文献的受损和失窃等风险的管理以及投资于适宜的技术基础设施等方面保持一致。这可能需要进行全国范围的协调并使各个记忆机构根据其现在的作用、优势与职责分担任务。

2.8 鼓励会员国支持记忆机构参与制定国际保存标准。还请会员国鼓励记忆机构与相关专业协会建立联系，增进并共享技术知识，促进不断完善国际标准。

2.9 请会员国支持开发数字化保存领域的学术课程，并在国家、地区和国际层面开展网络联系活动，以便更加切实有效地实施世界记忆计划，促进教科文组织会员国之间在最佳做法模式的基础上进行经验交流等。

3. 文献遗产的获取

3.1 鼓励会员国为记忆机构提供妥善的立法框架，确保它们在文献遗产的保存和提供获取机会问题上享有必要的独立性，从而保持公众对资料选择范围以及保存方式的信任。提供获取机会是在保存方面投入公共支出的明显证据和理由。

3.2 敦请会员国增强记忆机构的权能，使其能够利用国际最佳做法标准，提供准确和最新的编目和检索工具、公平的人对人原始文献获取服务、为研究所必需的互联网和基于网络的出版物与门户网站、电子和数字化内容，促进并便利最具包容性地获取和使用文献遗产。还鼓励会员国支持记忆机构采用支持可共同操作的公认标准，参与制定获取和使用方面的国际标准。应当尽可能使内容做到安排合理、可以机读、可以互联。

3.3 随着信息通信技术的进步和记忆机构及其合作伙伴全球网络的发展，提供文献遗产的路径也在激增。会员国应鼓励并支持制定外联计划，包括展览、巡回演示、广播电视节目、出版物、消费者产品、在线流媒体、社交媒体、讲座、教育计划、专场活动以及下载内容数字化。

3.4 获取文献遗产的计划可通过公共—私营部门等形式的伙伴关系得到促进。若此类安排是负责任的和公平的，请会员国对此予以鼓励。

3.5 若出于保护隐私、人身安全、安保、保密或其他合理原因需要对文献遗产的获取予以限制，则此类限制应有明确界定、表述和期限的限定。此类限制应以适用的国家法律或条例为依据，包括针对这类决定的上诉机制。

3.6 若更新或制定新的法律影响到文献遗产的获取，会员国应考虑最大程度地便利文献遗产获取的必要性，同时又要尊重权利持有人的合法权益。鼓励会员国将这种公众获取扩展至拥有共同历史文献遗产的国家。

3.7 请会员国酌情通过外联活动和世界记忆计划出版物的方式，提高本国文献遗产的知名度和可获取性，世界记忆计划现在的一项核心内容就是为改善获取而对内容数字化的工作进行投资。会员国应支持和促进公共领域的获取，并尽可能地鼓励使用公众授权和开放获取解决方案。

4. 政策措施

4.1 促请会员国将其文献遗产视为珍贵资产，并将这一观点落实在国家立法、发展政策和议程的制定工作中。会员国还应认识到需要在保存不同类型的模拟格式原始资料和数字基础设施与技能上进行新的长期投资，并为记忆机构提供充足的资金。

4.2 与此同时，鼓励会员国在本国遗产政策范围内，不囿于基础设施的具体问题，全面地看待记忆机构的需求，鼓励与其他实体通过建立共用设施、流程及服务，发展适宜的伙伴关系并分担费用。

4.3 拥有珍贵藏品的私营和地方机构及个人需要公共部门的鼓励和支持，并在全国性目录里具有足够的知名度。

4.4 会员国应通过鼓励开发有关文献遗产及其在公众领域存在的教育和研究的新形式和新工具，改进文献遗产的获取。

4.5 鼓励会员国通过立法和政策，用参与的方式建立稳定、有利的环境，激励赞助者、基金会及其他外部各方支持记忆机构并与它们一道投资于公益性文献遗产的保存、获取和利用。

4.6 鼓励会员国定期审查版权法和法定交存制度，及其限制和例外规定，确保其在保存和获取各种形式的文献遗产方面具有充分的效力。会员国加强和统一立法，协调政策，也会提高有效性。

4.7 如文献遗产保存和获取需要使用不在版权例外范围的软件或其他专有技术，则请会员国协助在非盈利的基础上获取专有代码、密钥以及解锁的技术版本。

4.8 为了最大限度地促进数据交流，会员国应鼓励开发和利用国际公认的开放源码软件和标准化的界面管理数字文献遗产，并寻求与软件和硬件开发者合作，从专有技术系统提取数据和内容。同样，会员国的记忆机构也应在编目方法和标准方面力求实现国际标准化和互换性。

4.9 请会员国支持并制定影响文献遗产的政策和倡议，包括监测列入世界记忆名录的文献遗产的状况。

4.10 鼓励会员国促进世界记忆计划和其他遗产计划之间的协同合作，以保障各方行动协调一致。

5. 国家和国际合作

5.1 鉴于有必要加强国家和国际合作与交流，特别是汇聚人力和物力帮助开展文献遗产的研究、保护和保存，会员国应支持研究数据、出版物和信息的交流；支持专业人员的培训及设备方面的交流。会员国应就特定专题，如编目、风险管理、濒危文献遗产的确认和现代研究等，举办会议、研究班及工作组会议。

5.2 会员国应鼓励与文献遗产保存和获取相关的国际和地区性专业协会、机构和组织开展合作，以便实施双边或多边研究项目并发布准则、政策以及最佳做法模式。

5.3 请会员国为国家之间交流与其自身的文化、共有历史或遗产相关的文献遗产副本，以及一直是另一国家保存工作之对象的其他经确认的文献遗产副本提供便利，在它们拥有共同的、交织在一起的历史时，或者在复原失散的原始文件的范围内，尤为如此。副本的交流将不对原始物品的所有权产生影响。

5.4 会员国应竭尽所能，采取一切适当措施保护本国文献遗产，使其免遭一切人为和自然危险，包括武装冲突所造成的风险。同样，对于无论是在某一会员国领土上还是在其他国家领土上的文献遗产，会员国均应避免采取可能损害它们、减损其价值或妨碍其传播和使用的行为。

5.5 鼓励会员国应另一会员国的要求，参与国际合作，用数字化或其他方式保护濒危文献遗产。

5.6 请会员国酌情设立"世界记忆"国家委员会和国家名录，通过其记忆机构加强与世界记忆计划的合作。

* * *

大会建议会员国适用保护和获取文献遗产的上述有关规定，根据各自的宪法规定，采取可能需要的任何立法措施、政策措施或其他步骤，在其各自领土内落实本建议书规定的原则、措施和规范。

大会建议会员国提请相关当局和机构注意本《建议书》。

大会建议会员国按大会确定的日期和方式，向大会报告其为落实本《建议书》所采取的措施。

Recommendation concerning the Preservation of, and Access to, Documentary Heritage Including in Digital Form

Adopted by the UNESCO General Conference at its 38th Session, Paris, 17 November 2015

PREAMBLE

The General Conference of the United Nations Educational, Scientific and Cultural Organization, meeting in Paris from 3 to 18 November 2015, at its 38th session,

Considering that documents produced and preserved over time, in all their analogue and digital forms through time and space, constitute the primary means of knowledge creation and expression, having an impact on all areas of humanity's civilization and its further progress,

Also considering that documentary heritage records the unfolding of human thought and events, the evolution of languages, cultures, peoples and their understanding of the world,

Underlining the importance of documentary heritage to promote the sharing of knowledge for greater understanding and dialogue, in order to promote peace and respect for freedom, democracy, human rights and dignity,

Noting that the evolution of documentary heritage enables intercultural education and personal enrichment, scientific and technological progress and is a crucial resource for development,

Considering at the same time that the preservation of, and long-term accessibility to documentary heritage underpins fundamental freedoms of opinion, expression and information as human rights,

Also considering that universal access to documentary heritage must respect both the legitimate interests of right holders and the public interest in its preservation and accessibility,

Recognizing that aspects of the history and culture which exist in the form of documentary heritage may not be conveniently accessible,

Recognizing also that over time considerable parts of documentary heritage have disappeared due to natural or human disasters or are becoming inaccessible through rapid technological change, and *underlining* that lack of legislation impedes memory institutions to counter irreversible loss and impoverishment of that heritage,

Recalling that, in response to this challenge, UNESCO established the Memory of the world Programme in

---

[1] UNESCO Document Code: CL/4155.

1992 to increase awareness and protection of the world's documentary heritage, and to provide for its universal and permanent accessibility,

Taking into account the rapid evolution of technology, and the challenge of establishing models and processes for preserving digital heritage objects including complex ones, such as multi-media works, interactive hypermedia online dialogues and dynamic data objects from complex systems, mobile content and future emerging formats,

Also taking into account the international standard-setting instruments and other relevant treaties and statements, as listed in the Appendix,

Bearing in mind the need for States, communities and individuals to take appropriate measures for the protection, preservation, accessibility and enhancement of the value of documentary heritage,

Having decided at its 37th session that this question should be the subject of a Recommendation to Member States, Adopts, on this seventeenth day of November 2015, the present Recommendation:

DEFINITIONS

For the purposes of this Recommendation, a **document** is an object comprising analogue or digital informational *content* and the *carrier* on which it resides. It is preservable and usually moveable. The content may comprise signs or codes (such as text), images (still or moving) and sounds, which can be copied or migrated. The carrier may have important aesthetic, cultural or technical qualities. The relationship between content and carrier may range from incidental to integral.

Documentary heritage comprises those single documents—or groups of documents—of significant and enduring value to a community, a culture, a country or to humanity generally, and whose deterioration or loss would be a harmful impoverishment. Significance of this heritage may become clear only with the passage of time. The world's documentary heritage is of global importance and responsibility to all, and should be fully preserved and protected for all, with due respect to and recognition of cultural mores and practicalities. It should be permanently accessible and re-usable by all without hindrance. It provides the means for understanding social, political, collective as well as personal history. It can help to underpin good governance and sustainable development. For each State, its documentary heritage reflects its memory and identity, and thus contributes to determine its place in the global community.

Memory institutions may include but are not limited to archives, libraries, museums and other educational, cultural and research organizations.

1. IDENTIFICATION OF DOCUMENTARY HERITAGE

1.1 Member States are encouraged to support their memory institutions in establishing selection, collection and preservation policies by research and consultation, guided by internationally established and defined standards regarding documentary heritage in their territories. The documents, fonds and collections should be managed in a way that ensures their preservation and accessibility over time, and assigns means of discovery, including cataloguing and metadata.

1.2 Policies, mechanisms and criteria for selecting, acquiring and de-selecting documentary heritage should be developed by memory institutions in coordination with civil society, taking into account not only key documents but also their contextual material, including social media. Selection criteria must be non-discriminatory and clearly defined. Selection must also be neutrally balanced with respect to knowledge fields, artistic expressions and historic eras. Because of their inherently temporary nature, decisions concerning the preservation of digital documents may need to be made at or before the time of creation.

1.3 Member States are encouraged to identify specific documentary heritage the survival of which is at potential or imminent risk, and draw it to the attention of competent bodies able to take appropriate preservation measures. They should support and strengthen their relevant memory institutions and, where practical and appropriate, encourage research communities and private owners to care for their own documentary heritage in the public interest. Similarly, public and private institutions should ensure professional care for the documents which they themselves create.

1.4 Member States should encourage the identification and nomination of significant documentary heritage to national, regional or international Memory of the World Registers as a means of raising awareness.

1.5 Member States are invited to develop training and capacity-building schemes as appropriate to ensure the identification, preservation and access to documentary heritage.

2. PRESERVATION OF DOCUMENTARY HERITAGE

2.1 Preservation of documentary heritage means encompassing techniques, treatments, procedures and technologies of any nature, preventive and remedial, aiming at the preservation of the documents and of the information contained therein.

2.2 Preservation is an ongoing process requiring the management of both analogue and digital objects and can be enhanced by scholarship, technology and science. Analogue carriers should be retained where they have continuing value as authentic originals, artefacts or information bearing objects. In the case of digital documents, action and intervention are desirable from before the point of creation and acquisition, in order to optimize further management, minimize costs and to properly manage the risks involved. Cooperation should be further encouraged among governments, memory institutions and the private sector.

2.3 In pursuing measures of preservation, integrity, authenticity and reliability should be the guiding principles. Concrete measures and actions should follow the international legislation and the recommendations, guidelines, best practices and standards developed or supported by memory institutions. The Memory of the World Programme should provide a platform to promote standards and share best practices.

2.4 Member States are encouraged to develop awareness-raising and capacity-building measures and policies as a key component of preservation, including promoting research as well as training for documentary heritage professionals and providing facilities for such. These should embrace curatorial best practices, current and emerging technologies, forensic skills and core competencies in relevant scholarship, science, technology and engineering, thereby raising awareness of the urgency of timely preservation action in a constantly changing environment.

2.5 The existence of possibly legitimate access restrictions on any part of the documentary heritage should not inhibit or limit the ability of memory institutions to take preservation action. Member States are invited to take this consideration into account while implementing this recommendation and through updating their relevant domestic legislation.

2.6 Member States that hold in their memory institutions collections originating in or of relevance to other States are encouraged to share digital programmes and copies of such heritage with the Parties concerned.

2.7 Member States should encourage consistency of best practice and preservation standards across memory institutions, including risk management, such as the degradation and theft of documents, and investment in appropriate technical infrastructure. This may include nationwide coordination and sharing of tasks among memory institutions, based on their existing roles, strengths and responsibilities.

2.8 Member States are encouraged to support memory institutions' participation in the development of international standards for preservation. Member States are further invited to encourage memory institutions to link with the appropriate professional associations to both enhance and share their technical knowledge, and contribute to the ongoing development of international standards.

2.9 Member States are invited to support the development of academic curricula for digital preservation, as well as networking activities at national, regional and international levels for more effective implementation of the Memory of the World Programme, and the promotion of exchanges of experiences among UNESCO Member States based on best practice models.

3. ACCESS TO DOCUMENTARY HERITAGE

3.1 Member States are encouraged to provide appropriate legislative frameworks for memory institutions and ensure their necessary independence in preserving and providing access to documentary heritage, so as to sustain public trust in the scope of material selected, and the way in which it is preserved. The provision of access is visible evidence and justification of public expenditure on preservation.

3.2 Member States are urged to promote and facilitate maximum inclusive access to, and use of, documentary heritage by empowering memory institutions to provide accurate and up-to-date catalogues and finding aids, equitable person-to person access services to the original documents, if necessary for research, internet and web-based publications and portals, electronic and digitized content, using international best practice standards. Member States are further encouraged to support memory institution in the development of international standards for access and use, using recognized standards that support interoperability. Whenever possible, content should be structured, machine-readable and linkable.

3.3 The avenues for providing access to documentary heritage are multiplying through the growth of information and communication technologies and the development of global networks among memory institutions and their partners. Member States should encourage and support the development of outreach programmes, including exhibitions, travelling presentations, radio and television programmes, publications, consumer products, online streaming, social media, lectures, educational programmes, special events and the digitization of content for downloading.

3.4 Programmes for access to documentary heritage may be facilitated by partnerships, including public-private ones. Member States are invited to encourage such arrangements if they are responsible and equitable.

3.5 Where restrictions to accessing documentary heritage are necessary to protect privacy, human safety, security, confidentiality or for other legitimate reasons, they should be clearly defined and stated and be of limited duration. They should be underpinned by appropriate national legislation or regulation by including an appeals mechanism against such decisions.

3.6 When updating or enacting new legislation which impacts on access to documentary heritage, Member

States should consider the need to maximize such access while respecting the legitimate interests of the rights-holders. Member States are encouraged to extend this public access to countries with which they have shared a historical documentary heritage.

3.7 Member States are invited to enhance the visibility and accessibility of their documentary heritage through the outreach activities and publications of the Memory of the World Programme as appropriate, with investment in digitization of content for access purposes now being one of its key components. Member States should support and promote public domain access, and wherever possible, encourage the use of public licensing and open access solutions.

4. POLICY MEASURES

4.1 Member States are urged to consider their documentary heritage as an invaluable asset and to apply this perspective in national legislation, development policies and agendas. They are further encouraged to recognize the long-term need for new investment in the preservation of different types of originals in analogue format, in digital infrastructure and skills, and to adequately endow memory institutions.

4.2 At the same time, in the context of their national heritage policies, Member States are encouraged to take a global view of the needs of memory institutions, beyond the practicalities of infrastructure, and encourage logical partnerships and cost sharing with other entities in setting up shared facilities, processes and services.

4.3 private and local institutions and individuals holding valuable collections need public encouragement and support as well as adequate visibility in national directories.

4.4 Member States should improve access to documentary heritage by encouraging the development of new forms and tools of education and research on documentary heritage and their presence in the public domain.

4.5 Through legislation and policy, Member States are encouraged to create in a participatory approach a stable, enabling environment that will give incentives to sponsors, foundations and other external parties to support memory institutions and, with them, to invest in the preservation, accessibility and use of documentary heritage in the public interest.

4.6 Member States are encouraged to periodically review copyright codes and legal deposit regimes to ensure they are fully effective, with limitations and exceptions, for preserving and accessing documentary heritage in all its forms. Effectiveness would also profit from the strengthening and harmonization of legislation and alignment of policies among Member States.

4.7 Where preserving and accessing documentary heritage requires the use of software or other proprietary technology not covered by copyright exceptions, Member States are invited to facilitate access to proprietary codes, keys and unlocked versions of technology on a non-profit basis.

4.8 In order to facilitate optimal exchange of data, Member States should encourage the development and use of internationally recognized open source software and standardized interfaces for managing digital documentary heritage, and seek the cooperation of software and hardware developers in extracting data and content from proprietary technologies. Likewise, their memory institutions should aim for international standardization and interchangeability of cataloguing methods and standards.

4.9 Member States are invited to support and develop policies and initiatives affecting documentary heritage, including monitoring the status of documentary heritage inscribed on the Memory of the World Registers.

4.10 Member States are encouraged to contribute building synergies between the Memory of the World

Programme and other heritage programmes in order to assure further coherence of actions.

5. NATIONAL AND INTERNATIONAL COOPERATION

5.1   In view of the need to intensify national and international cooperation and exchanges, in particular through the pooling of human and material resources to assist research and the protection and preservation of documentary heritage, Member States should support the exchange of research data, publications, and information; the training and exchange of specialist personnel and equipment. They should promote the organization of meetings, study courses and working groups on particular subjects, such as cataloguing, risk management, identification of endangered documentary heritage and modern research.

5.2   Member States should encourage cooperation with international and regional professional associations, institutions and organizations concerned with documentary heritage preservation and access, with a view to implementing bilateral or multilateral research projects and publishing guidelines, policies and best practice models.

5.3   Member States are invited to facilitate the exchange between countries of copies of documentary heritage that relate to their own culture, shared history or heritage, and of other identified documentary heritage, in particular due to their shared and entangled historical nature or in the framework of the reconstitution of dispersed original documents, as appropriate, which has been the object of preservation work in another country. The exchange of copies will have no implications on the ownership of originals.

5.4   To the best of their ability, Member States should take all appropriate measures to safeguard their documentary heritage against all human and natural dangers to which it is exposed, including the risks deriving from armed conflicts. Likewise, they should refrain from acts likely to damage documentary heritage or diminish its value or impede its dissemination or use, whether it is to be found on the territory of other States.

5.5   Member States are encouraged to engage in international cooperation to safeguard endangered documentary heritage through digitization or other means following a request made by another Member State.

5.6   Member States are invited to strengthen their cooperation with the Memory of the World Programme through their memory institutions by establishing national Memory of the world committees and registers, when deemed appropriate.

* * *

The General Conference recommends that Member States should apply the above provisions concerning the preservation of and access to documentary heritage by taking whatever legislative or policy measures or other steps that may be required, in conformity with the constitutional practice of each State, to give effect, within their respective territories to the principles, measures and norms set forth in this Recommendation.

The General Conference recommends that Member States bring this Recommendation to the attention of the appropriate authorities and bodies.

The General Conference recommends that Member States should report to it, by the dates and in a manner to be determined by it, on the action they have taken to give effect to this Recommendation.

联合国教科文组织世界记忆计划：
通用指南[①]（节选）

世界记忆计划指南审议组，2017年12月批准之文本

2.1 引言

2.1.1 世界记忆（MoW）是联合国教科文组织保护文献遗产的计划，意味着文献遗产对人类文明的发展、维护和进一步前行的核心作用。由于过去传承的许多遗产是脆弱和易逝的，所以，为后代保护现在和未来的文件是一个不小的挑战。这两者都取决于深思熟虑和持续不断的行动。

2.1.2 为了防止集体记忆不可逆转的损失，联合国教科文组织于1992[②]年设立了 MoW 计划，其目标是保护文献遗产，促进其获取和传播，并提高公众对其重要性和保护文献遗产必要性的认识。教科文组织制定各种标准措施以支持和指导该计划（MoW），最新一项文件是《关于保存和获取包括数字遗产在内的文献遗产的建议书》（2015年），以下称为《建议书》。

2.1.7 在最广泛的范围内，文献遗产记录了人类思想、创造力和事件的发展，语言、文化、民族的演变以及各民族对世界和宇宙的理解。它有助于跨文化教育和个人充实，以及科学和技术进步，它也是人类发展的重要资源。它支持见解、言论和信息的基本人权自由。这类遗产为未来提供了资源[③]。

2.3 目标

2.3.1 因此，世界记忆计划有三个密切相关的主要目标：

（a）以最适当的技术促进世界过去、现在和未来文献遗产的保存。这可以通过直接的实际援助，发布建议和信息，以及鼓励培训、促进政策制定等来实现，并通过将赞助者与及时和适当的项目链接起来，或以其他方式促进开发所有广泛可用的资源来实施。

（b）协助普遍获取文献遗产。这将包括鼓励保存文献遗产的机构酌情以模拟和/或数字形式尽可能广泛和公平地使公众能获取文献遗产。这包括出版物和产品，以及在网站上放置数字化拷贝和目录。当访问对托管人有影响时，这些影响应得到尊重。对档案可及性的立法和其他限制应予以承认。文化敏感性，包括本土社区对其材料和对文献获取的监管，将得到尊重。私有财产权应受到法律的保障。

（c）提高全世界对文献遗产的存在和重要性的认识。从而促进民族和文化之间的对话和相互理解。方法包括但不限于发展"世界记忆名录（MoW）"（见第六章）、媒体、宣传和信息出版物、展览、奖项、

[①] 译者：曹新。
[②] 联合国教科文组织执行委员会于1996年2月29日通过了该计划（MoW）的国际咨询委员会的章程(149 EX/13)。
[③] 完整的阐述见《关于保存和获取包括数字遗产在内的文献遗产的建议书》（2015）中的前言。

奖励、教育计划和 MoW 标志的使用。就保存和获取而言，它们本身不仅相辅相成，而且能提高认识，因为获取文献的需求促进了保存工作。

2.6 定义和说明

2.6.1 如《建议书》中所述，有三个关键术语：

2.6.2 文件是包含模拟或数字信息的内容及其载体。它是可保存的，通常是可移动的。内容可以包括符号或代码（如文本）、图像（静止或移动的）和声音，能够被复制或迁移。其载体可能具有重要的美学、文化或技术品质。内容和载体之间的关系可能是附带性的，也可以是整体性的。

2.6.3 文献遗产包括那些对一个社区、一种文化、一个国家或整个人类具有重要和持久价值的单一文献或文献组，其退化或消失是有害的，将造成资源的枯竭。只有随着时间的推移，这一遗产的意义才会变得清晰。世界文献遗产具有全球重要性，所有人对它都负有责任，因此，应当为所有人而充分保存和保护这些遗产，同时充分尊重和承认文化习俗和实践。它应该是所有人都永久可及，并能无妨碍地重复使用。它提供了理解社会、政治、集体和个人历史的途径。它有助于巩固良好的管理和可持续发展。对每个国家来说，其文献遗产反映了他们的记忆和身份，从而有助于确定每个国家在国际社会中的地位。

2.6.4 记忆机构可能包括但不限于档案馆、图书馆、博物馆和其他教育、文化和研究机构。

6.3 登录标准

6.3.2 以下标准适用于整个评估过程中的所有提名项目。

6.3.3 评估是比较的和相对的。没有绝对的文化意义的衡量标准。评估是相对的。参照选择标准，参照这些指南的要旨，参照过去的提名（不论登录的或拒绝的），根据文献遗产本身的价值对其进行评估，以确定是否登录遗产。

6.3.4 真实性和完整性。门槛检验是，文献遗产是否是它看上去的样子。**真实性**是指实际的、真实的或真正的、并没有原件损坏的品质。它的身份和出处是否得到可靠证实？副本、复制品、赝品、伪造文件或恶作剧可能出于好意被误认为是真品①。对于一份文献来说，**完整性**是指整体和完整的品质。文献遗产的一部分是否保存在别处，而未包含在本次提名中？它们是否都是同一年代，或者丢失的部分是否已被新的副本所替换？它是原作吗？如果不是，它是已知的最早一版？百分之多少的遗产保持原状？

6.3.5 基于所讨论的文献的性质，这可能是一个复杂的问题。一些文献，如视听媒体、数字文件和中世纪手稿，可能以多种不同的版本或标本存在，具有相同的或不同的古老、完整程度或保存状态。

6.3.6 世界意义：首要标准

6.3.6.1 国际咨询委员会（IAC）必须确信文献遗产具有世界意义。应参照以下一项或多项标准做出评估。并非所有的标准都必须适用于特定的提名项目，只应选择相关的标准。

6.3.6.2 历史意义。关于世界历史，文献遗产可以告诉我们什么？例如，它涉及以下哪些因素？
- 政治或经济发展，社会或精神运动
- 世界历史上的名人
- 具有改变世界意义的事件
- 与时间、事件或人物有关的特定场所
- 独特的现象
- 显著的传统习俗

---

① 当精心制作的恶作剧被清楚地提出来而不是声称是别的东西时，就可以评估它们的重要性。

- 国家或社区之间或之内演变的关系
- 生活和文化模式的改变
- 历史上的一个转折点，或者一个关键的创新
- 艺术、文学、科学、技术、体育或其他生活和文化领域的优秀范例

6.3.6.3 形式和风格。重要意义可能存在于文献遗产的物理属性。在这方面，有些文献可能看起来并不引人注目，例如手写稿件或打字记录，但也可能具有值得注意的文体特征或个人关联。其他形式的文献遗产可能表现出创新的品质、高水平的艺术性或其他显著的特征。例如：

- 文献遗产可能是某种特定类型的一个极佳范例
- 它可能具有突出的美学和工艺品质
- 它可能是一种新的或不寻常的载体
- 它可能是一种现在已经废弃的或被取代的文献类型的范例

6.3.6.4 社会、社区或精神意义。它可能是对于某一特定的现存社区确实重要的文献遗产。例如，一个社区可能强烈地依赖于一个敬爱的（甚至是憎恨的）领袖的遗产，或者依赖于与特定事变、事件或地点具有特定关联的文献证据。或者这个社区可能崇敬与精神领袖或圣人相关的文献遗产。而这种联系是如何表达的，应提供这些的信息。

6.3.7 世界意义：比较标准

6.3.7.1 IAC 需要关于文献遗产本身特征的进一步信息。

6.3.7.2 **独一无二或稀有珍品**。这份文献或收藏品可以被描述为独一无二的（唯一一个被创造出来的）还是稀有的（为数不多的幸存物之一）？这种特质可能需要详细阐述：收藏品、手稿或其他物品可能是独一无二的，但不一定罕见。可能有其他类似但不完全相同的收藏品或物品。

6.3.7.3 **状况**。一份文献本身的状况可能不是对其重要性的检验，但它与其登录资格相关。如果严重退化的文献其内容和特征已经损坏，已无法修复，则该文献可能不合格。相反，一份文献可能状况良好，但存放不良或不安全，因此可能会有风险。根据文献或收藏品的性质，提名表格中的描述需要足够详细，以便能够评估当前的风险和/或保护需求。它提供了一个基础，如果登录了文献遗产，就可以基于此对其持续的状况和安全进行监测。

6.3.8 重要性陈述

重要性陈述是在首要标准和比较标准下作出的总结，以及对真实性和完整性的检验。它应该继续解释：

- 为什么这份文献遗产对世界记忆很重要，以及为什么它的消失会使人类遗产变得枯竭。
- 它对一个民族国家或地区之外的生活和文化积极或消极的影响，是什么或已经是什么。

UNESCO Memory of the World Programme: General Guidelines (excerpts)

MoW Guidelines Review Group. Approved Text December 2017

2.1 Introduction

2.1.1 *Memory of the World (MoW)* is UNESCO's Programme for the protection of the documentary heritage, a metaphor for its central role for the development, maintenance and further progress of human civilisation. While much of the transmitted legacy of the past is fragile and fugitive, the protection of present and future documents for the generations to come is not a lesser challenge. Both depend on deliberate and ongoing action.

2.1.2 In order to help prevent the irrevocable loss of collective memory, UNESCO set up the MoW Programme in 1992[1] with the objectives of safeguarding the documentary heritage, facilitating access to it and disseminating it, and raising public awareness of its significance and the need to preserve it. The Programme is underpinned and guided by various UNESCO standard-setting instruments, most recently the *Recommendation concerning the preservation of, and access to, documentary heritage including in digital form* (2015), hereafter referred to as the Recommendation.

2.1.7 At its widest scope, the documentary heritage records the unfolding of human thought, creativity and events, the evolution of languages, cultures, peoples and their understanding of the world and the cosmos/universe. It enables intercultural education and personal enrichment, scientific and technological progress and is a crucial resource for human development. It underpins fundamental freedoms of opinion, expression and information as human rights. This legacy provides resources for the future[2].

2.3 Objectives

2.3.1 Accordingly, the MoW Programme has three main objectives that are closely interlinked:

(a) To facilitate preservation, by the most appropriate techniques, of the world's past, present and future documentary heritage. This may be done by direct practical assistance, by the dissemination of advice and information and the encouragement of training, policy development and implementation by linking sponsors

---

[1] Statutes of the Programme's International Advisory Committee were adopted by UNESCO's Executive Board on 29 February 1996 (149 EX/13).

[2] For a fuller statement see the preamble to the Recommendation concerning the preservation of, and access to, documentary heritage including in digital form (2015).

with timely and appropriate projects, or in other ways fostering the development of widely available resources in all its forms.

(b) To assist universal access to documentary heritage. This will include encouraging institutions holding documentary heritage to make it accessible as widely and equitably as possible, in analogue and/or digital form, as appropriate. This includes publications and products, and the placing of digitized copies and catalogues on websites. Where access has implications for custodians, these are respected. Legislative and other limitations on the accessibility of archives are recognised. Cultural sensitivities, including indigenous communities' custodianship of their materials, and their guardianship of access, will be honoured. Private property rights should be guaranteed in law.

(c) To increase awareness worldwide of the existence and significance of documentary heritage and thereby foster dialogue and mutual understanding between peoples and cultures. Means include, but are not limited to, developing the MoW registers (see Chapter 6), the media, promotional and informational publications, exhibitions, prizes, awards, education programmes and use of the MoW logo. Preservation and access, in and of themselves, not only complement each other, but also raise awareness, as demand for access stimulates preservation work.

2.6 Definitions and explanations

2.6.1 There are three key terms, as set out in the *Recommendation*:

2.6.2 A **document** is an object comprising analogue or digital informational *content* and the *carrier* on which it resides. It is preservable and usually moveable. The content may comprise signs or codes (such as text), images (still or moving) and sounds, which can be copied or migrated. The carrier may have important aesthetic, cultural or technical qualities. The relationship between content and carrier may range from incidental to integral.

2.6.3 **Documentary heritage** comprises those single documents – or groups of documents – of significant and enduring value to a community, a culture, a country or to humanity generally, and whose deterioration or loss would be a harmful impoverishment. Significance of this heritage may become clear only with the passage of time. The world's documentary heritage is of global importance and responsibility to all, and should be fully preserved and protected for all, with due respect to and recognition of cultural mores and practicalities. It should be permanently accessible and re-usable by all without hindrance. It provides the means for understanding social, political, and collective as well as personal history. It can help to underpin good governance and sustainable development. For each State, its documentary heritage reflects its memory and identity, and thus contributes to determining its place in the global community.

2.6.4 **Memory institutions** may include but are not limited to archives, libraries, museums and other educational, cultural and research organizations.

6.3 Criteria for inscription

6.3.2 The following criteria are applied to all nominations throughout the assessment process.

6.3.3 **Assessment is comparative and relative**. There is no absolute measure of cultural significance. Assessment is relative. Selection for inscription results from assessing the documentary heritage on its own merits against the selection criteria, against the general tenor of these Guidelines, and in the context of past nominations, whether included or rejected.

6.3.4 Authenticity and integrity. The threshold test is whether the documentary heritage is what it appears to be. **Authenticity** is the quality of being real, true or genuine and not corrupted from the original. Has its identity and provenance been reliably established? Copies, replicas, forgeries, bogus documents or hoaxes can, with the best of intentions, be mistaken for the genuine article[①]. For a document, **integrity** is the quality of being whole and complete. Is part of the documentary heritage being kept elsewhere and not included in this nomination? Is it all of the same age or have missing parts been replaced with newer copies? Is it an original—or if not, is it the earliest known generation? What percentage of the heritage remains in its original state?

6.3.5 This can be a complex matter, depending on the nature of the documents in question. Some documents —such as audiovisual media, digital files, and medieval manuscripts — may exist in variant versions or exemplars of the same or differing antiquity, integrity or state of preservation.

6.3.6 World significance: *Primary criteria*

6.3.6.1 The IAC must be satisfied that the documentary heritage is of world significance. Comments should be made in relation to one or more of the following criteria. *Not all the criteria will necessarily apply to a particular nomination – only those relevant should be chosen.*

6.3.6.2 **Historical significance.** What does the documentary heritage tell us in relation to the history of the world? For example, does it deal with:

- Political or economic developments, or social or spiritual movements
- Eminent personalities in world history
- Events of world-changing import
- Specific places relating to times, events or people
- Unique phenomena
- Noteworthy traditional customs
- Evolving relations between or among countries or communities
- Changes in patterns of life and culture
- A turning point in history, or a critical innovation
- An example of excellence in the arts, literature, science, technology, sport or other parts of life and culture

6.3.6.3 **Form and style.** Significance may lie in the physical nature of the documentary heritage. Some documents may seem unremarkable in this respect — for example, hand written manuscript or typescript paper records–but can, for example, have stylistic qualities or personal associations that deserve attention. Other forms of documentary heritage may display innovative qualities, high levels of artistry or other notable features. For example：

- The documentary heritage may be a particularly fine exemplar of its type
- It may have outstanding qualities of beauty and craftsmanship
- It may be a new or unusual type of carrier
- It may be an example of a type of document that is now obsolete or superseded

6.3.6.4 **Social, community or spiritual significance.** It may be that the documentary heritage attached to a specific existing community is demonstrably significant. For example, a community may be strongly attached to the heritage of a beloved (or even a hated) leader, or to the documentary evidence related to a specific incident, event or site with particular associations. Or it may revere the documentary heritage associated with a spiritual

---

① Deliberately crafted hoaxes, when clearly proposed as such rather than purporting to be something else, can be assessed for their significance.

leader or a saint. Information should be provided on how this attachment is expressed.

6.3.7 World significance: *Comparative criteria*

6.3.7.1 The IAC needs further information on the character of the documentary heritage itself.

6.3.7.2 **Uniqueness or rarity.** Can the document or the collection be described as unique (the only one of its kind ever created) or rare (one of a few survivors from a larger number)? This quality may need elaboration: a collection or manuscript or other item may be unique but not necessarily rare. There may be other collections or items which are similar but not identical.

6.3.7.3 **Condition.** The condition of a document may not, in itself, be a test of its significance but it is relevant to its eligibility for inscription. A severely degraded document may be ineligible if its content and character have been compromised beyond the possibility of restoration. Conversely, a document may be in good condition but be poorly or insecurely housed, and may therefore be at risk. Depending on the nature of the document or the collection, the description in the nomination form will need to be sufficiently detailed to allow an appreciation of current risk and/or conservation needs. It provides the baseline from which, if inscribed, their ongoing condition and security is monitored.

6.3.8 *Statement of Significance*

This statement is a summary of the points made under the primary and comparative criteria, and the test of authenticity and integrity. It should go on to explain:

- Why this documentary heritage is important to the memory of world and why its loss would impoverish the heritage of humanity
- What its impact — positive or negative — is or has been on life and culture beyond the boundaries of a nation state or region